CASES AND MATERIALS IN REVENUE LAW

AUSTRALIA
The Law Book Company Ltd.
Sydney : Melbourne : Brisbane

CANADA AND U.S.A.
The Carswell Company Ltd
Agincourt, Ontario

INDIA
N. M. Tripathi Private Ltd.
Bombay

ISRAEL
Steimatzky's Agency Ltd.
Jerusalem : Tel Aviv : Haifa

MALAYSIA : SINGAPORE : BRUNEI
Malayan Law Journal (Pte) Ltd.
Singapore

NEW ZEALAND
Sweet & Maxwell (N.Z.) Ltd.
Wellington

PAKISTAN
Pakistan Law House
Karachi

CASES AND MATERIALS
IN
REVENUE LAW

By

A. J. EASSON B.A., LL.M.

Solicitor, Lecturer in Law at the
University of Southampton

LONDON
SWEET & MAXWELL
1973

Published in 1973 by
Sweet & Maxwell Limited of
11 New Fetter Lane, London
and printed in Great Britain
by The Eastern Press Limited
of London and Reading

SBN Hardback 421 16770 X
      Paperback 421 16780 Y

PREFACE

In few areas of the law are the changes so regular and so substantial as in that of Revenue Law. The student (and for that matter the teacher and practising lawyer or accountant) is faced with an ever-increasing mass of complex rules, knowing that, if he should ever succeed in mastering them, they will immediately be amended, revised, repealed or replaced. To study whatever may be the current leading case may well be a frustrating exercise; it will almost inevitably be concerned with a minute loophole in some complex legislation. No sooner has the student unravelled the detail and appreciated the ingenuity of the taxpayer or his adviser than he learns that special legislation is to be introduced to prevent imitation. Why, then, a collection of cases and materials in Revenue Law?

In my opinion, before the student attempts to learn the details of an existing system of taxation, he must first understand the nature of the problems which the system (or, in effect, any system of taxation) attempts to solve and the basic philosophy upon which the preferred solution is founded. He must also be familiar with the manner in which the law plays its part in the attainment of the solution. No better way exists of appreciating the role of the law in the tax system than to study the leading cases over the past century, not for what was decided but for the manner in which the decision was reached. It is only necessary to remark that the two cases which are probably quoted in argument more than any others, *I.R.C.* v. *Duke of Westminster* and *L.C.C.* v. *Attorney-General*, were both concerned with points which no longer have any practical importance, yet the wider issues involved remain of great significance.

Decided cases may also often serve to show the purpose underlying otherwise obscure statutory provisions, illustrating sometimes the loophole and sometimes the snare. Many a complex section owes its creation to a previous decision in favour of the taxpayer and can be comprehended only in the light of the " abuse " which it was designed to counter. The nature of a particular problem, or the reason for a particular solution, may be discovered in one of the reports of a Royal Commission or a committee, or in a Government paper of one colour or another.

Revenue Law is the creature of the legislature and there can be no substitute for the actual text of the statutes. The student has a choice of excellent books which set out reliably the various rules and explain them as comprehensibly as the subject-matter permits. What I have attempted to provide is a collection of materials to illustrate the basic principles, the nature of the more important problems and the application of the law to their attempted solution. This book is directed primarily towards the university law student and those studying for professional examinations in law.

v

It is also hoped that it may assist the student of accountancy, commerce or economics to appreciate the role of the law in taxation and, perhaps, that the practitioner may find it a useful source of apposite quotations.

I owe many debts of gratitude. My thanks are due to many of my colleagues at Southampton for their help and encouragement, in particular to Gerald Dworkin and Malcolm Grant and to Robert Burgess, now in Edinburgh, without whose constant willingness to discuss difficulties and suggest improvements the task of compiling this book would have been far more onerous; to the charming and long-suffering ladies who deciphered my handwriting and typed the manuscript; and to the publishers who first encouraged me to undertake the task.

A. J. Easson

Faculty of Law,
University of Southampton,
December 1972.

CONTENTS

Preface . . . . *page* v

Acknowledgments xi

Table of Cases xiii

Table of Statutes xxv

PART I
PRINCIPLES OF REVENUE LAW

1. STATUTORY INTERPRETATION 3

2. TAX AVOIDANCE 26
   1. General Considerations 26
   2. Judicial Attitudes to Tax Avoidance 32
   3. Judicial Participation in Tax Avoidance 34
   4. Anti-avoidance Legislation 39

3. FACT AND LAW 46
   1. The Distinction Between Fact and Law 46
   2. The Findings of the Commissioners as to the Facts is Final 49
   3. Appeals from the Conclusions of the Commissioners . . 50

PART II
TAXES ON INCOME AND GAINS

4. " INCOME " 65
   1. The Concept of Income 65
   2. Income as a Tax Base: The Problem of Definition . . 70
   3. Capital and Income: The Importance of the Distinction . 75
   4. " Income " Means " Taxable Income " 81

5. THE SCHEDULES 85
   1. The " Source " Concept 85
   2. Interrelationship of the Schedules 87

6. INCOME FROM LAND 96
   1. Schedule A 96
   2. Schedule B 105

7. INTEREST, ANNUITIES AND OTHER ANNUAL PAYMENTS . . . 110

    1. The Charge to Tax 110
    2. Transfers of Income 121
    3. Deduction at Source 125

8. TRADE, PROFESSION OR VOCATION 128

    1. Case Law 128
    2. Definitions 129
    3. The Profit Motive 132
    4. The Badges of Trade 140

9. PROFITS 152

    1. Receipts 154
    2. Expenditure 168
    3. Valuation of Stock 191
    4. The Accounting Period 202
    5. Losses 209
    6. Capital Allowances 214

10. SCHEDULE D, CASE VI 219

    1. Annual Profits or Gains 219
    2. Capital and Income 221
    3. Sale of Asset or Performance of Services? . . 224

11. EMOLUMENTS OF EMPLOYMENT 229

    1. " Office " or " Employment " 229
    2. Emoluments 234
    3. Allowable Expenditure 267

12. INCOME FROM FOREIGN SOURCES 277

    1. Profits of a Foreign Trade 277
    2. Securities and Possessions 283
    3. Capital and Income 287
    4. The Remittance Basis 290
    5. Double Taxation 295

13. CAPITAL GAINS 306

    1. Capital Gains and the Tax Base 306
    2. Taxation of Capital Gains 311

PART III
TAXABLE PERSONS

14. THE INDIVIDUAL AND THE FAMILY 335

    1. Progressive Taxation 335
    2. The Structure of Personal Taxation 338

14. THE INDIVIDUAL AND THE FAMILY—*continued*.
    3. Total Income 339
    4. Reliefs and Allowances 344
    5. The Family Unit 351

15. ESTATES, TRUSTS AND PARTNERSHIPS 367
    1. The Income of Estates and Trusts 367
    2. The Income of the Settlor 380
    3. Partnerships 404

16. COMPANIES 413
    1. Theories of Corporate Taxation 413
    2. Related Companies 425
    3. Close Companies 426

17. DOMICILE AND RESIDENCE 432
    1. Residence of Individuals 433
    2. Ordinary Residence 442
    3. Domicile and Residence of Corporations 446

PART IV

ESTATE DUTY

18. INTRODUCTION: THE CHARGE TO DUTY 453
    1. Property of which the Deceased was Competent to Dispose 464
    2. Settled Property 467

19. CONTINUATION: THE CHARGE TO DUTY 468
    3. Gifts 468
    4. Other Charging Provisions 498

20. VALUATION 500
    1. Market Value 500
    2. Particular Types of Property 510

21. EXEMPTIONS AND RELIEFS 522
    1. Bona Fide Purchase 522
    2. Settled Property 528
    3. Gifts 533

Index 539

ACKNOWLEDGMENTS

I AM most grateful to all those who gave permission for the various materials to be published in this form and wish to record and express my thanks to

The Accountant.

Butterworth & Co. Ltd.

Canada Law Book Ltd.

Director of Publications, Her Majesty's Stationery Office.

Information Canada.

The Incorporated Council of Law Reporting for England and Wales.

The Law Society.

The Lawyers' Co-operative Publishing Co., Rochester, New York.

The Scottish Council of Law Reporting.

The University of Chicago Press.

TABLE OF CASES

[Figures in *italics* refer to the pages on which extracts from judgments appear.]

PAGE

Abbot *v.* Philbin [1961] A.C. 352 .... 214, 256, *257*
Absalom *v.* Talbot [1944] A.C. 204 196
Adams *v.* Musker (1930) 15 T.C. 413 .... 344, *347*
Adamson *v.* Att.-Gen. [1933] A.C. 257 8
Aikin *v.* MacDonald's Trustees (1894) 3 T.C. 306 .... *370*
Aked *v.* Shaw (1947) 28 T.C. 286 .... 380, *396*
Allchin *v.* Coulthard [1943] A.C. 607 .... *126*
American Thread Co. *v.* Joyce (1913) 6 T.C. 163 284
Anglo-Persian Oil Co. *v.* Dale [1932] 1 K.B. 124 .... 80, 156, 157, *172*
Apthorpe *v.* Peter Schoenhofen Brewing Co. Ltd. (1899) 4 T.C. 41 49
Archer-Shee *v.* Garland [1931] A.C. 212 .... 285, *289*
Aschrott, *Re* [1927] 1 Ch. 313 .... *509*
Asher *v.* London Film Productions Ltd. [1944] 1 K.B. 133 .... 116, *219*
Ashton Gas Co. *v.* Att.-Gen. [1900] A.C. 10 184
Associated Portland Cement Manufacturers *v.* Kerr [1946] 1 All E.R. 68 .... *173*, 246
Astor *v.* Perry [1935] A.C. 398 .... *15*, 83, 84, *385*
Att.-Gen. *v.* Black (1871) L.R. 6 Exch. 308 222
—— *v.* Boden [1912] 1 K.B. 539 .... 498, *522*
—— *v.* Clarkson [1900] 1 Q.B. 156 18
—— *v.* De Preville [1900] 1 Q.B. 223 497
—— *v.* Dobree [1900] 1 Q.B. 442 .... 525, *526*, 527
—— *v.* Gretton and Shrimpton [1945] 1 All E.R. 628 .... 453, *522*
—— *v.* Grey (Earl) [1900] A.C. 124 .... 471, *477*, 479
—— *v.* Jameson [1905] 2 I.R. 218 513
—— *v.* Johnson [1903] 1 K.B. 617 .... 470, *471*, 477, 491, 493, 522
—— *v.* Kitchin [1941] 2 All E.R. 735 522
—— *v.* L.C.C. *See* L.C.C. *v.* Att.-Gen.
—— *v.* Oldham [1940] 2 K.B. 485 495
—— *v.* Penrhyn (1900) 83 L.T. 103 .... *531*
—— *v.* Quixley (1929) 98 L.J.K.B. 652 .... *466*
—— *v.* Sandwich (Earl) [1922] 2 K.B. 500 .... 453, 522, *525*
—— *v.* Seccombe [1911] 2 K.B. 688 .... 477, *490*
—— *v.* Smith Marriott [1894] 2 Q.B. 595 522
—— *v.* Worrall [1895] 1 Q.B. 99 .... 471, 472, 477, 479, *491*
Att.-Gen. of Ceylon *v.* Mackie [1952] 2 All E.R. 775 .... *516*
Ayrshire Employers Mutual Association Ltd. *v.* I.R.C. (1944) 27 T.C. 344 .... *5*, 11
Ayrshire Pullman Motor Services *v.* I.R.C. (1929) 14 T.C. 754 .... *33*, 410

B.P. Australia Ltd. *v.* Commissioner of Taxation of the Commonwealth of Australia
    [1966] A.C. 224 171
B.P. Refinery (Kent) Ltd. *v.* Lower Medway Internal Drainage Board [1957] 1 Q.B. 84 .. 409
B.S.C. Footwear Ltd. *v.* Ridgway [1972] A.C. 544 .... 154, *191*, *196*, *201*
Back *v.* Daniels [1925] 1 K.B. 526 .... 106, 107
—— *v.* Whitlock [1932] 1 K.B. 747 433
Baden's Deed Trusts (No. 2), *Re* [1971] 3 W.L.R. 475 380
Baker *v.* Archer-Shee [1927] A.C. 844 .... *284*, 351
—— *v.* Cook (1937) 21 T.C. 337 151
Balgownie Land Trust *v.* I.R.C. (1929) 14 T.C. 648 150
Ball *v.* National and Grindlays Bank [1972] 3 W.L.R. 17 .... 116, 413
Barclays Bank *v.* I.R.C. [1961] A.C. 509 .... 16, 479, *517*
—— *v.* Naylor [1961] Ch. 7 .... 116, 253
Barr, Crombie & Co. *v.* I.R.C. (1945) 26 T.C. 406 .... 79, 150
Bartholomay Brewing Co. Ltd. *v.* Wyatt [1893] 2 Q.B. 499 283
Bateman (Baroness), *Re* [1925] 2 K.B. 429 .... 470, 522, *527*
Bates *v.* I.R.C. [1968] A.C. 483 .... *15*, 26, 40, *401*, 426
Bayard Brown *v.* Burt (1911) 5 T.C. 667 435
Beak *v.* Robson [1943] A.C. 352 .... 177, *245*

PAGE

Bean *v.* Doncaster Amalgamated Collieries Ltd. [1946] 1 All E.R. 642 .... *48*, 75
Becker *v.* Wright [1966] 1 W.L.R. 215 .... *82*, 385
Bendit (Julius) Ltd. *v.* I.R.C. (1945) 27 T.C. 44 166
Bennett *v.* Ogston (1930) 15 T.C. 374 .... *86*, 110
Bentleys, Stokes and Lowless *v.* Beeson [1952] W.N. 280 .... 181, *186*, 188
Berry (L. G.) Investments *v.* Attwooll [1964] 1 W.L.R. 693 104
Beswick *v.* Beswick [1968] A.C. 58 497
Bidwell *v.* Gardiner [1960] T.R. 13 .... 103, 179
Birmingham Corporation *v.* I.R.C. [1930] A.C. 307 127
Bishop *v.* Finsbury Securities [1966] 1 W.L.R. 1402 .... 136, 137, 139
Blakiston *v.* Cooper [1909] A.C. 104 .... 240, *241*, 242, 243
Blausten *v.* I.R.C. [1972] Ch. 256 393
Bloom *v.* Kinder [1958] T.R. 91 228
Bolam *v.* Barlow (1949) 31 T.C. 136 276
Bouch *v.* Sproule (1887) 12 App.Cas. 385 66
Bourne and Hollingsworth Ltd. *v.* Ogden (1929) 14 T.C. 349 169
Bowden *v.* Russell and Russell [1965] 1 W.L.R. 711 .... 183, *187*
Bracegirdle *v.* Oxley [1947] K.B. 349 47
Bradbury *v.* Arnold (1957) 37 T.C. 665 228
—— *v.* English Sewing Cotton Co. [1923] A.C. 744 .... *283*, 288
Brassard *v.* Smith [1925] A.C. 371 284
Bridges *v.* Hewitt [1957] 1 W.L.R. 674 248
Brigg, Neumann & Co. *v.* I.R.C. (1928) 12 T.C. 1191 198
Brighton College *v.* Marriott [1926] A.C. 192 .... *134*
Brister *v.* Brister [1970] 1 W.L.R. 664 348
British American Tobacco Co. Ltd. *v.* I.R.C. [1943] A.C. 335 518
British Commonwealth International Newsfilm Agency *v.* Mahany [1962] 1 W.L.R. 560 .. 117
British Insulated and Helsby Cables *v.* Atherton [1926] A.C. 205 .... 79, 156, 157, *169*,
                                                                      170, 172, 173, 177
British Launderers' Research Association *v.* Borough of Hendon Rating Authority [1949]
  1 K.B. 462 .... *46*
Briton Ferry Steel Co. *v.* Barry [1940] 1 K.B. 463 164
Brocklesby *v.* Merricks (1934) 18 T.C. 576 228
Brodie's Will Trustees *v.* I.R.C. (1933) 17 T.C. 432 .... 117, 290, *377*
Bromilow and Edwards Ltd. *v.* I.R.C. [1969] 1 W.L.R. 1180 .... 9, 44
Brown *v.* Att.-Gen. (1898) 79 L.T. 572 527
—— *v.* Bullock [1961] 1 W.L.R. 1095 .... 254, 268, 276
—— *v.* I.R.C. [1965] A.C. 244 367
—— *v.* National Provident Institution [1921] 2 A.C. 222 .... 5, *16*, *85*, 205
Buccleuch (Duke) *v.* I.R.C. [1967] 1 A.C. 506 .... 500, *501*
Bucks *v.* Bowers [1970] Ch. 431 .... 347, 406
Bulmer *v.* I.R.C. [1967] Ch. 145 384
Burdge *v.* Pyne [1969] 1 W.L.R. 364 .... 65, 132
Burmah Steamship Co. *v.* I.R.C. (1931) 16 T.C. 67 79
Burrell, Webber, Magness, Austin and Austin *v.* Davis [1958] T.R. 365 149
Bush, Beach & Gent Ltd. *v.* Road (1939) 22 T.C. 519 159
Butter *v.* Bennett [1963] Ch. 185 .... *263*

Calvert *v.* Wainwright [1947] K.B. 526 .... *242*
Cameron, *Re* [1967] Ch. 1 353
—— *v.* Prendergast [1940] A.C. 549 247
Camille and Henry Dreyfus Foundation Inc. *v.* I.R.C. [1958] A.C. 39 20
Campbell *v.* I.R.C. [1970] A.C. 77 .... 77, 116, *123*, 385
Canada Southern Railway Co. *v.* International Bridge Co. (1883) 8 App.Cas. 723 19
Canadian Eagle Oil Co. Ltd. *v.* R. [1946] A.C. 119 .... *10*, 44
Cannon Industries *v.* Edwards [1966] 1 W.L.R. 580 128
Cape Brandy Syndicate *v.* I.R.C. [1921] 2 K.B. 403 .... *10*, *18*, 21, 43, 84, *149*
Carlisle and Silloth Golf Club *v.* Smith [1913] 3 K.B. 75 135
Carson *v.* Cheyney's Executors [1959] A.C. 412 .... 87, 167
Carter *v.* Sharon [1936] 1 All E.R. 720 .... 293, 433
Cesena Sulphur Co. *v.* Nicholson (1876) 1 Ex.D. 428 .... 279, 448
Chadwick *v.* Pearl Life Insurance Co. [1905] 2 K.B. 507 117
Chamberlain *v.* I.R.C. (1943) 25 T.C. 317 .... 384, 390, 391
Chamney *v.* Lewis (1932) 17 T.C. 318 286
Chancery Lane Safe Deposit and Offices Co. *v.* I.R.C. [1966] A.C. 89 127
Chapman *v.* Chapman [1954] A.C. 429 35
Chick *v.* Commissioner of Stamp Duties [1958] A.C. 435 .... 482, *486*

PAGE

Christie *v.* Davies [1945] 1 All E.R. 870 107
Clayton *v.* Gothorp [1971] 1 W.L.R. 999 .... *237*
Cleary *v.* I.R.C. [1968] A.C. 766 .... *41*
Coates *v.* Holker Estates Co. [1961] T.R. 249 .... *105*
Cohan's Executors *v.* I.R.C. (1924) 131 L.T. 377 .... *150*
Cole, a Bankrupt, *Re* [1964] Ch. 175 473
Collins *v.* Fraser [1965] 1 W.L.R. 823 .... *107*, 163
Colquhoun *v.* Brooks (1889) 14 App.Cas. 493 .... 82, *277*, 280, 283, 447
Coltness Iron Co. *v.* Black (1881) 6 App.Cas. 315 .... *4*
Coman *v.* Governors of the Rotunda Hospital, Dublin [1921] 1 A.C. 1 134
Commissioners for General Purposes of Income Tax for the City of London *v.* Gibbs
    [1942] A.C. 402 .... 407, 409
Commissioner of Estate and Succession Duties (Barbados) *v.* Bowring [1962] A.C. 171 .. *466*
Commissioner of Internal Revenue *v.* Glenshaw Glass Co., 348 U.S. 426 (1955) 75
Commissioner of Stamp Duties *v.* Gale (1958) 101 C.L.R. 96 .... *497*
—— *v.* Owens (1953) 88 C.L.R. 67 .... *487*
—— *v.* Permanent Trustee Co. of New South Wales [1956] A.C. 512 .... 487, *488*
—— *v.* Perpetual Trustee Co. [1943] A.C. 425 .... *478*, 483, 484
Conn *v.* Robins Bros. [1966] T.R. 61 180
Cook *v.* Knott (1887) 2 T.C. 246 273
Cooke *v.* Haddock [1960] T.R. 133 .... *147*
Cooper *v.* Cadwalader (1904) 5 T.C. 101 .... 434, 440, 441, 448
—— *v.* Stubbs [1925] 2 K.B. 753 .... 53, 54, *61*, 128, 222, *223*, 224
Copeman *v.* Coleman [1939] 2 K.B. 484 383
—— *v.* Flood (William) & Sons [1941] 1 K.B. 202 .... 183, *190*, 413, 430
Corbett *v.* Duff [1941] 1 K.B. 730 239
Cordy *v.* Gordon (1925) 9 T.C. 304 248
Cornwell *v.* Barry [1955] T.R. 255 .... *374*
Coutts & Co. *v.* I.R.C. [1953] A.C. 267 .... 520, 521
Cowan *v.* Seymour [1920] 1 K.B. 500 248
Cowley (Earl) *v.* I.R.C. [1899] A.C. 198 .... *453*
Crabtree *v.* Hinchcliffe [1972] A.C. 707 .... 329, 508, 510, 516
Crossland *v.* Hawkins [1961] Ch. 537 .... *382*
Cunard's Trustees *v.* I.R.C.; McPheeters *v.* I.R.C. (1946) 174 L.T. 133 .... 117, *379*
Currie *v.* I.R.C. [1921] 2 K.B. 332 .... *50*, 55, 128, 131

Dale *v.* De Soissons [1950] W.N. 354 247
—— *v.* I.R.C. [1954] A.C. 11 .... *345*, 347, 367
D'Ambrumenil *v.* I.R.C. [1940] 1 K.B. 850 386
Davies *v.* Braithwaite [1931] 2 K.B. 628 .... 131, *230*, 277
—— *v.* Shell Company of China Ltd. (1951) 32 T.C. 133 154
Dealler *v.* Bruce (1934) 19 T.C. 1 348
De Beers Consolidated Mines Ltd. *v.* Howe [1906] A.C. 455 .... 50, *447*, 448, 449
De Vigier *v.* I.R.C. [1964] 1 W.L.R. 1073 .... 26, 40, 398, 401, 402, *404*
Dewar *v.* I.R.C. [1935] 2 K.B. 351 .... *340*, 372, 412
Dewhurst *v.* Hunter (1932) 146 L.T. 510 247
Dickenson *v.* Gross (1927) 137 L.T. 351 .... 33, *410*
Dickinson *v.* Abel [1969] 1 All E.R. 484 .... 85, 228
Donaldson's Executors *v.* I.R.C. (1927) 13 T.C. 461 379
Down *v.* Compston (1937) 21 T.C. 60 132
Doyle *v.* Davison [1962] T.R. 147 .... 265, 266
—— *v.* Mitchell Bros. Co., 247 U.S. 179 (1917) 68
Drummond *v.* Collins [1915] A.C. 1011 .... 110, *286*, 372
Dublin Corporation *v.* M'Adam (1887) 2 T.C. 387 .... 162, 165
Ducker *v.* Rees Roturbo Development Syndicate Ltd. [1928] A.C. 132 77
Duckering *v.* Gollan [1965] 1 W.L.R. 680 .... *205*
Duffy, *Re* [1949] Ch. 28 519
Dunn Trust Ltd. *v.* Williams (1950) 31 T.C. 477 .... 128, 129
Duple Motor Bodies *v.* Ostime. *See* Ostime *v.* Duple Motor Bodies.

Eames *v.* Stepnell Properties Ltd. [1967] 1 W.L.R. 593 129
Edwards *v.* Bairstow and Harrison [1956] A.C. 14 .... 47, *51*, 60, 128, 129, *145*, 189
—— *v.* Warmsley, Henshall & Co. [1968] 1 All E.R. 1089 189
Egyptian Delta Land and Investment Co. Ltd. *v.* Todd [1929] A.C. 1 .... *447*, 449, 450
Egyptian Hotels *v.* Mitchell. *See* Mitchell *v.* Egyptian Hotels.
Eisner *v.* Macomber, 252 U.S. 189 (1919) *68*

PAGE

Ellesmere (Earl) *v*. I.R.C. [1918] 2 K.B. 735 .... *500*, 504
Elson *v*. Johnston (James G.) [1965] T.R. 333 159
—— *v*. Prices Tailors [1963] 1 W.L.R. 287 206
Elwood *v*. Utitz [1966] N.I. 93 254
Emanuel (Lewis) & Son Ltd. *v*. White (1965) 42 T.C. 369 128
English, Scottish and Australian Bank *v*. I.R.C. [1932] A.C. 238 455
Erichsen *v*. Last (1881) 8 Q.B.D. 414 .... *152*
Ewing, In the Goods of (1881) 6 P.D. 19 283
Eyre, *Re* [1907] 1 K.B. 331 .... 519, 520

Fairrie *v*. Hall (1947) 177 L.T. 600 182
Fattorini (Thomas) (Lancashire) Ltd. *v*. I.R.C. [1942] A.C. 643 427
Fenston *v*. Johnstone (1940) 23 T.C. 29 410
Ferguson (Harry) (Motors) Ltd. *v*. I.R.C. [1951] N.I. 115 .... *79*, 155
Fergusson *v*. Noble (1919) 7 T.C. 176 .... *250*, 252, 261, 268
Findlay's Trustees *v*. I.R.C. (1937) 22 A.T.C. 437 511
Finsbury Securities *v*. Bishop. *See* Bishop *v*. Finsbury Securities.
Firestone Tyre and Rubber Co. *v*. Llewellin [1957] 1 W.L.R. 464 .... 277, 283
Fitzwilliam's (Earl) Agreement, *Re* [1950] Ch. 448 .... 453, 469, *470*, 526
Fleming *v*. Associated Newspapers [1972] Ch. 170 .... 9, 187
Fletcher *v*. Income Tax Commissioner [1972] A.C. 414 135
Foley (Lady) *v*. Fletcher (1858) 28 L.J.Ex. 100 .... 112, 117, 377
Forbes *v*. Scottish Provident Institution (1895) 3 T.C. 443 290
Fry, *Re* [1940] Ch. 312 467
—— *v*. I.R.C. [1959] Ch. 86 .... 16, *519*
—— *v*. Salisbury House Estates [1930] A.C. 432 .... 90, 93, 219
—— *v*. Shiel's Trustees (1915) 6 T.C. 583 .... *346*, 367
Fuge *v*. McClelland (1956) 36 T.C. 571 233

Gartside *v*. I.R.C. [1968] A.C. 553 467
Gasque *v*. I.R.C. [1940] 2 K.B. 80 446
Gaunt *v*. I.R.C. [1941] 1 K.B. 706 392
Gillies *v*. I.R.C. (1928) 14 T.C. 329 380
Glanely (Lord) *v*. Wightman [1933] A.C. 618 .... *92*
Glass *v*. I.R.C., 1915 S.C. 449 508
Glenboig Union Fireclay Co. *v*. I.R.C. (1921) 12 T.C. 427 .... 157, *159*
Glicksten (J.) & Son *v*. Green [1929] A.C. 381 .... 157, 161
Gloucester Railway Carriage and Wagon Co. Ltd. *v*. I.R.C. [1925] A.C. 469 128
Goerz Co. *v*. Bell [1904] 2 K.B. 136 449
Gold Coast Selection Trust *v*. Humphrey [1948] A.C. 459 161
Golden Horse Shoe (New) *v*. Thurgood [1934] 1 K.B. 548 .... *80*, 169
Graham *v*. Green [1925] 2 K.B. 37 .... 65, 130, *132*
Grainger *v*. Maxwell [1926] 1 K.B. 430 86
Grainger & Son *v*. Gough [1896] A.C. 325 .... *282*
Great Western Ry. Co. *v*. Bater [1922] 2 A.C. 1 .... 230, 231, 233, 238
Green *v*. Cravens Railway Carriage and Wagon Co. Ltd. (1951) 32 T.C. 359 80
Greenwood *v*. Smidth (F. L.) & Co. [1922] 1 A.C. 417 283
Gregory *v*. Helvering, 293 U.S. 465 (1935) 25
Gresham Life Assurance Society *v*. Bishop [1902] A.C. 287 .... 290, 292
—— *v*. Styles [1892] A.C. 309 .... *152*, 162, 165, 205
Griffiths *v*. Harrison (J. P.) (Watford) [1963] A.C. 1 .... 47, 128, *129*, 137
Grove *v*. Young Men's Christian Association (1903) 88 L.T. 696 134
Gulbenkian's Settlement Trusts (No. 2), *Re* [1970] Ch. 408 467

Haig's (Earl) Trustees *v*. I.R.C., 1939 S.C. 676 225
Haldane's Trustees *v*. Lord Advocate, 1954 S.C. 156 496
Hale *v*. Shea [1965] 1 W.L.R. 290 347
Hall, *Re* [1942] Ch. 140 .... 470, 530
Hall (J. P.) & Co. *v*. I.R.C. [1921] 3 K.B. 152 .... *205*
Hamilton-Russell's Executors *v*. I.R.C. (1943) 25 T.C. 200 .... *340*, 372, 375
Hanbury, *Re* (1939) 38 T.C. 588 .... *113*, 123, 342
Hancock *v*. General Reversionary and Investment Co. [1919] 1 K.B. 25 80
Harmsworth, *Re* [1967] Ch. 826 .... 469, 471, 522, *524*
Harrison *v*. Cronk (John) & Sons Ltd. [1937] A.C. 185 207
—— *v*. Willis Bros. [1966] Ch. 619 408

PAGE

Harrison (J. P.) (Watford) *v.* Griffiths. *See* Griffiths *v.* Harrison (J. P.) (Watford).
Harrods (Buenos Aires) *v.* Taylor-Gooby (1964) 41 T.C. 450 .... *184*
Hartland *v.* Diggines [1926] A.C. 289 260
Hawes *v.* Gardiner (1957) 37 T.C. 671 128
Hayes *v.* Duggan [1929] I.R. 406 130
Heaslip *v.* Hasemer (1927) 138 L.T. 207 .... *348*
Heather *v.* P.E. Consulting Group Ltd. [1972] 2 All E.R. 107 .... 80, 103, 154
Heaton *v.* Bell [1970] A.C. 728 .... *248, 256*, 258
Henley *v.* Murray [1950] W.N. 241 .... *246*
Henry *v.* Foster, Hunter *v.* Dewhurst. *See* Dewhurst *v.* Hunter.
Herbert *v.* McQuade [1902] 2 K.B. 631 .... 242, 243
Higgs *v.* Olivier [1952] Ch. 311 .... *154*
Hillerns and Fowler *v.* Murray (1932) 17 T.C. 77 .... 151, 410
Hinchcliffe *v.* Crabtree. *See* Crabtree *v.* Hinchcliffe.
Hinton *v.* Maden and Ireland [1959] 1 W.L.R. 875 .... *216*, 218
Hobbs *v.* Hussey [1942] 1 K.B. 491 224
Hochstrasser *v.* Mayes [1960] A.C. 376 .... *235, 239*, 245
Hodge's Policy, *Re* [1958] Ch. 239 .... *10*
Holt, *Re*, Holt *v.* I.R.C. [1953] 1 W.L.R. 1488 .... *510*, 516
Hommel, *Re* (1953) 1 D.L.R. (2d) 536 .... *492, 493*
Hood-Barrs *v.* I.R.C. (1946) 27 T.C. 385 .... *382, 383*
Hopwood *v.* Spencer (C. N.) [1964] T.R. 361 68
Horton *v.* Young [1972] Ch. 157 274
Housden *v.* Marshall [1959] 1 W.L.R. 1 225
Household *v.* Grimshaw [1953] 1 W.L.R. 710 .... 131, 232
Howard de Walden (Lord) *v.* Beck (1940) 23 T.C. 384 77
—— *v.* I.R.C. [1942] 1 K.B. 389 .... *34*
Howe (Earl) *v.* I.R.C. [1919] 2 K.B. 336 .... *112*, 113, 123, *341*, 344
Hudson *v.* Wrightson (1934) 26 T.C. 55 .... 149, 150
Hudson's Bay Company, The *v.* Stevens (1909) 5 T.C. 424 .... *150*
Humbles *v.* Brooks (1962) 40 T.C. 500 276
Hunter *v.* Dewhurst. *See* Dewhurst *v.* Hunter.

Inchiquin (Lord) *v.* I.R.C. (1948) 31 T.C. 125 434
Inchyra (Baron) *v.* Jennings [1966] Ch. 37 .... 283, 289, *379*
Incorporated Council of Law Reporting for England and Wales, *Re* Duty on the Estate
     of (1888) 22 Q.B.D. 279 .... *132*
Ingram & Son Ltd. *v.* Callaghan [1969] 1 W.L.R. 456 211
I.R.C. *v.* Alexander von Glehn & Co. Ltd. [1920] 2 K.B. 553 .... 182, 209
—— *v.* Allan (1925) **9 T.C. 234** 380
—— *v.* Anderstrom (1927) 13 T.C. 482 286
—— *v.* Ayrshire Employers Mutual Assurance Association Ltd. [1946] 1 All E.R. 637
                                                                       5, *11*, 15, 135
—— *v.* Barclay Curle & Co. Ltd. [1969] 1 W.L.R. 675 .... *218*
—— *v.* Bates. *See* Bates *v.* I.R.C.
—— *v.* Bibby (J.) & Sons (1945) 114 L.J.K.B. 353 .... 426, 518
—— *v.* Black [1940] 4 All E.R. 445 .... 111, *386*
—— *v.* Blackwell Minor's Trustees [1924] 2 K.B. 351 .... *376*, 380
—— *v.* Blott [1921] 2 A.C. 171 .... 69, 290, 340, 412, 427
—— *v.* Brander and Cruickshank [1971] 1 W.L.R. 212 .... 95, *232*, 248
—— *v.* Brebner [1967] 2 A.C. 18 .... *41*
—— *v.* British Salmson Aero Engines [1938] 2 K.B. 482 .... *78*, 154
—— *v.* Broadway Cottages Trust [1955] Ch. 20 .... 380, 396
—— *v.* Brown [1971] 1 W.L.R. 1495 41
—— *v.* Buchanan [1958] 1 Ch. 289 382
—— *v.* Carron Company (1968) 45 T.C. 18 .... *171*, 177, *185*
—— *v.* Castlemain (Lady) (1943) 112 L.J.K.B. 508 379
—— *v.* City of London (as Conservators of Epping Forest) [1953] 1 W.L.R. 652 .. *116*, 123
—— *v.* Clarke (F. A.) & Son Ltd. (1942) 29 T.C. 49 518
—— *v.* Clarkson-Webb [1933] 1 K.B. 507 384
—— *v.* Clay [1914] 3 K.B. 466 .... 500, *507*, 511
—— *v.* Cleary. *See* Cleary *v.* I.R.C.
—— *v.* Cock, Russell & Co. (1949) 65 T.L.R. 725 .... *195*
—— *v.* Combe (1932) 17 T.C. 405 434
—— *v.* Coutts & Co. [1964] A.C. 1393 .... 528, *529*
—— *v.* Crossman [1937] A.C. 26 .... *508*, 513

PAGE

I.R.C. *v.* De Vigier. *See* De Vigier *v.* I.R.C.
—— *v.* Dowdall O'Mahoney & Co. Ltd. [1952] A.C. 401 .... *13*
—— *v.* Eccentric Club Ltd. (1925) 12 T.C. 657 135
—— *v.* Fisher's Executors [1926] A.C. 395 .... *32*
—— *v.* Fraser (1942) 24 T.C. 498 .... *48, 55,* 128
—— *v.* Frere [1965] A.C. 402 .... *342*
—— *v.* Gibbs. *See* Commissioners for General Purposes of Income Tax for the City of London *v.* Gibbs.
—— *v.* Glenconner (Lord) [1941] 2 K.B. 339 387
—— *v.* Granite City Steamship Co. (1927) 13 T.C. 1 10
—— *v.* Gull (1937) 21 T.C. 374 20
—— *v.* Hamilton-Russell's Executors. *See* Hamilton-Russell's Executors v. I.R.C.
—— *v.* Hawley [1928] 1 K.B. 578 377
—— *v.* Helical Bar Ltd. [1971] Ch. 813 204
—— *v.* Henderson's Executors (1931) 16 T.C. 282 372
—— *v.* Hinchy [1960] A.C. 748 .... *13*
—— *v.* Hobhouse [1956] 1 W.L.R. 1393 386
—— *v.* Holmden [1968] A.C. 685 .... *454*
—— *v.* Jameson [1964] A.C. 1445 387
—— *v.* Kenmare (Countess). *See* Kenmare (Countess) *v.* I.R.C.
—— *v.* Kleinwort Benson Ltd. [1969] 2 Ch. 221 41
—— *v.* Land Securities Investment Trust [1969] 1 W.L.R. 604 .... 24, 119
—— *v.* Lebus' Executors [1946] 1 All E.R. 476 .... 340, 407, *411*
—— *v.* Lee. *See* Lee *v.* I.R.C.
—— *v.* Leiner (1964) 41 T.C. 589 .... *384*
—— *v.* Littlewoods Mail Order Stores [1963] A.C. 135 .... *23*
—— *v.* Livingston (1927) 11 T.C. 538 .... 146, 150
—— *v.* Longford (Countess) [1928] A.C. 252 .... *370*
—— *v.* Lysaght [1928] A.C. 234 .... *50, 54,* 433, 434, *441, 443,* 445
—— *v.* Mallaby-Deeley (1938) 55 T.L.R. 293 .... *25, 76, 118,* 385, 386
—— *v.* Maxse [1919] 1 K.B. 647 .... *131*
—— *v.* Miller (Lady) [1930] A.C. 222 .... 104, 378, 379
—— *v.* Morris (1967) 44 T.C. 685 244
—— *v.* National Book League [1957] Ch. 488 .... 77, *114,* 124, 125, 385
—— *v.* Nelson & Sons (1938) 22 T.C. 716 151
—— *v.* Newcastle Breweries Ltd. (1927) 12 T.C. 927 157
—— *v.* Nicholson [1953] 1 W.L.R. 809 386
—— *v.* Northfleet Coal and Ballast Co. (1927) 12 T.C. 1102 157
—— *v.* Old Bushmills Distillery Co. (1928) 12 T.C. 1148 151
—— *v.* Oswald [1945] A.C. 360 127
—— *v.* Parker [1966] A.C. 141 .... *40*
—— *v.* Pay (1955) 36 T.C. 109 .... *384*
—— *v.* Payne (1940) 110 L.J.K.B. 323 .... 383, 390
—— *v.* Priestley [1901] A.C. 208 .... 464, 519, *528,* 530
—— *v.* Prince-Smith (1943) 168 L.T. 406 383
—— *v.* Rainsford-Hannay (1941) 24 T.C. 273 390
—— *v.* Ramsay (1935) 154 L.T. 141 385
—— *v.* Ransom (William) & Son Ltd. [1918] 2 K.B. 709 164
—— *v.* Reid's Trustees [1949] A.C. 361 .... 287, 289
—— *v.* Reinhold [1953] T.R. 11 .... 53, *148*
—— *v.* Rennell [1964] A.C. 173 .... *8, 533*
—— *v.* Richards' Executors [1971] 1 W.L.R. 571 .... 190, 455
—— *v.* Ross and Coulter (Bladnoch Distillery Co. Ltd.) [1948] W.N. 114 .... *8*
—— *v.* St. Luke's Hostel Trustees (1930) 144 L.T. 50 385
—— *v.* Scott Adamson (1933) 17 T.C. 679 214
—— *v.* Tennant (1942) 24 T.C. 215 393
—— *v.* Toll Property Co. Ltd. (1952) 34 T.C. 13 151
—— *v.* Verdon Roe [1962] T.R. 379 386
—— *v.* Wachtel [1971] Ch. 573 396
—— *v.* Watts (1958) 38 T.C. 146 432
—— *v.* Wemyss (1924) 8 T.C. 551 .... 376, 379
—— *v.* Wesleyan and General Assurance Society [1948] W.N. 120 22
—— *v.* Westminster (Duke) [1936] A.C. 1 .... 22, *23,* 28, 236
—— *v.* Whitworth Park Coal Co. *See* Whitworth Park Coal Co. *v.* I.R.C.
—— *v.* Williamson Brothers (1950) 31 T.C. 370 .... *106,* 109
—— *v.* Wilson's Executors (1934) 18 T.C. 465 .... *103*
—— *v.* Wolfson [1949] W.N. 190 .... 7, 111, *388*

PAGE

I.R.C. *v*. Zorab (1926) 11 T.C. 289 436
Innes *v*. Harrison [1954] 1 W.L.R. 608 380
Iswera *v*. I.R.C. [1965] 1 W.L.R. 663 ....61, 129, 139
Iveagh *v*. I.R.C. [1954] Ch. 364 495

Jacgilden (Weston Hall) *v*. Castle [1971] Ch. 408 166
Jackson *v*. Laskers Home Furnishers [1957] 1 W.L.R. 69 .... 103, 179
Jackson's Trustees *v*. I.R.C. (1942) 25 T.C. 13 378
Jardine *v*. Gillespie (1906) 5 T.C. 263 273
Jarrold *v*. Boustead [1964] 1 W.L.R. 1357 .... 237, 244
Jay's the Jewellers *v*. I.R.C. [1947] 2 All E.R. 762 206
Jenkins *v*. I.R.C. [1944] 2 All E.R. 491 .... 387, 398, 399
Jenkinson *v*. Freedland (1961) 39 T.C. 636 .... 129, 150
Joffe *v*. Thain (1955) 36 T.C. 199 283
Johnson *v*. Jewitt (1961) 40 T.C. 231 .... *136*
Johnston *v*. Heath [1970] 1 W.L.R. 1567 .... 129, 148
Johnstone *v*. Chamberlain (1933) 17 T.C. 706 .... 350, 373
Jones *v*. I.R.C. [1920] 1 K.B. 711 .... *117*
—— *v*. Leeming [1930] A.C. 415 .... 52, 54, 128, 140, 143, *221*, 223, 224, 227, 306
—— *v*. South-West Lancashire Coal Owners' Association [1927] A.C. 827 283
Jones (M.) *v*. Jones (R. R.) [1971] 1 W.L.R. 840 519

Kauri Timber Co. Ltd. *v*. Commissioner of Taxes [1913] A.C. 771 68
Kelly *v*. Rogers [1935] 2 K.B. 446 369
Kelsall Parsons & Co. *v*. I.R.C. (1938) 21 T.C. 608 159
Kenmare (Countess) *v*. I.R.C. [1958] A.C. 267 390
Kettle's Gift, *Re* [1968] 1 W.L.R. 1459 455
Kilpatrick's Policies Trusts, *Re* [1966] Ch. 730 .... *454*
Kirkness *v*. John Hudson & Co. Ltd. [1955] A.C. 696 .... 6, *9*, *19*
Kneen *v*. Martin [1935] 1 K.B. 499 290
Koitaki Para Rubber Estates Ltd. *v*. Federal Commissioner of Taxation (1940) 64 C.L.R.
    15 449

L.C.C. *v*. Att.-Gen. [1901] A.C. 26 .... 65, 74, 86, *87*, 91, 92, 93, 103, 222
Laidler *v*. Perry [1966] A.C. 16 .... 237, *239*
Lamport & Holt Line *v*. Langwell [1958] 2 Lloyd's Rep. 53 161
Lang *v*. Webb (1912) 13 C.L.R. 503 488
Latilla *v*. I.R.C. [1943] A.C. 377 .... 28, *34*
Law Shipping Co. *v*. I.R.C. (1924) 12 T.C. 621 .... 68, 99, 100, *178*
Lawson *v*. Rolfe [1970] 1 Ch. 613 .... 289, 379
Leach *v*. Pogson (1962) 40 T.C. 585 149
Leader *v*. Counsell [1942] 1 K.B. 364 .... 223, 224
Lee *v*. I.R.C. [1943] 170 L.T. 151 380
Leek, decd., *Re* [1969] 1 Ch. 563 .... 467, 473
Leeming *v*. Jones. *See* Jones *v*. Leeming.
Leigh *v*. I.R.C. [1928] 1 K.B. 73 .... *339*
Leitch *v*. Emmott [1929] 2 K.B. 236 .... *352*
Lethbridge *v*. Att.-Gen. [1907] A.C. 19 522
Letts *v*. I.R.C. [1957] 1 W.L.R. 201 .... 469, 476
Leven and Melville (Earl), *Re* [1954] 1 W.L.R. 1228 469
Levene *v*. I.R.C. [1928] A.C. 217 .... 33, *49*, 433, 434, *438*, *444*
Lewin *v*. Aller [1954] 1 W.L.R. 1063 348
Lewis *v*. I.R.C. [1933] 2 K.B. 557 412
Lilley *v*. Harrison (1952) 33 T.C. 344 283
Lincolnshire Sugar Co. *v*. Smart [1937] A.C. 697 206
Lindus and Hortin *v*. I.R.C. (1933) 17 T.C. 442 379
Littlewoods Mail Order Stores *v*. I.R.C. *See* I.R.C. *v*. Littlewoods Mail Order Stores.
—— *v*. McGregor [1969] 1 W.L.R. 1241 24
Liverpool and London and Globe Insurance Co. *v*. Bennett [1913] A.C. 610 .... 95, 129
Lloyd *v*. Sulley (1884) 2 T.C. 37 .... *437*
Lochgelly Iron and Coal Co. Ltd. *v*. Crawford (1913) 6 T.C. 267 183
Loewenstein *v*. de Salis (1926) 10 T.C. 424 .... 434, 440
Lomax *v*. Dixon (Peter) & Son [1943] K.B. 671 110
—— *v*. Newton [1953] 1 W.L.R. 1128 .... *272*
Lombard, *Re* [1904] 2 I.R. 621 527

                                                                                    PAGE
London and Northern Estate Co. *v*. Harris [1939] 1 K.B. 335 104
Longsdon *v*. Minister of Pensions and National Insurance [1956] 2 W.L.R. 176 66
Lord Advocate *v*. Lyell, 1918 S.C. 125 522
Lothian Chemical Co. Ltd. *v*. Rogers (1926) 11 T.C. 508 .... *155*
Lowe *v*. J. W. Ashmore Ltd. [1971] Ch. 545 92
Lucy and Sunderland Ltd. *v*. Hunt [1962] 1 W.L.R. 7 .... *61*, 128, 129
Luke *v*. I.R.C. [1963] A.C. 557 .... 15, *16*, *265*, 268
Lupton *v*. F.A. & A.B. Ltd. [1972] A.C. 634 .... *137*
—— *v*. Potts [1969] 1 W.L.R. 1749 .... 270, *275*
Lurcott *v*. Wakely & Wheeler [1911] 1 K.B. 905 180
Lynall *v*. I.R.C. [1972] A.C. 680 .... 500, 508, 510, *512*
Lyons *v*. Cowcher (1926) 10 T.C. 438 220

McAndrew *v*. I.R.C. (1943) 25 T.C. 500 388
McClelland *v*. Commissioner of Taxation of the Commonwealth of Australia [1971] 1
    W.L.R. 191 150
McCrone *v*. I.R.C. (1967) 44 T.C. 142 404
M'Dougall *v*. Smith (1919) 7 T.C. 134 346
Macfarlane *v*. I.R.C. (1929) 14 T.C. 532 371
Machon *v*. McLoughlin (1926) 11 T.C. 83 248
Mackenzie, *Re* [1941] Ch. 69 .... 444, *445*
McKie *v*. Warner [1961] 1 W.L.R. 1230 265
McMillan *v*. Guest [1942] A.C. 561 .... *229*, 233
McPhail *v*. Doulton [1971] A.C. 424 380
Mallett *v*. Staveley Coal and Iron Co. [1928] 2 K.B. 405 157
Mangin *v*. I.R.C. [1971] A.C. 739 .... 39, *42*
Mann *v*. Nash [1932] 1 K.B. 752 .... *130*
Mapp *v*. Oram [1970] A.C. 362 .... *83*, 350
Marsden *v*. I.R.C. [1965] 1 W.L.R. 734 .... 253, 275
Marshall and Hood's Executors and Rogers *v*. Joly [1936] 1 All E.R. 851 151
Martin *v*. Lowry [1927] A.C. 312 .... 78, 111, *149*, 150, *152*, 202, 220, 225
Marx *v*. I.R.C. [1970] N.Z.L.R. 182 43
Mason *v*. Innes [1967] Ch. 1079 .... *166*
Massy (Lord) *v*. I.R.C. [1919] 2 K.B. 354n. 112
Mersey Docks and Harbour Board *v*. Lucas (1883) 8 App.Cas. 891 .... *133*, 134, 184, 185, 413
Michelham's Trustees *v*. I.R.C. (1930) 144 L.T. 163 .... 377, 378
Micklethwait, *Re* (1885) 11 Exch. 456 4
Miesegaes *v*. I.R.C. [1957] T.R. 231 .... *444*
Miles *v*. Morrow (1940) 23 T.C. 465 350
Miller (Lady) *v*. I.R.C. *See* I.R.C. *v*. Miller.
Miller's Agreement, *Re* [1947] Ch. 615 497
Milne's Executors *v*. I.R.C. [1956] T.R. 283 379
Milroy *v*. Lord (1862) 31 L.J.Ch. 798 .... 475, 476
Minister of Finance *v*. Smith [1927] A.C. 193 130
Minister of National Revenue *v*. Anaconda American Brass Ltd. [1956] A.C. 85 ...... *194*
Mitchell *v*. Egyptian Hotels [1915] A.C. 1022 .... 277, *280*, 449
—— *v*. Noble (B. W.) [1927] 1 K.B. 719 .... 157, *172*, 177
Mitchell and Edon *v*. Ross [1962] A.C. 814 .... 93, *233*, 234
Monthly Salaries Loan Co. Ltd. *v*. Furlong (1962) 44 T.C. 313 .... 201, 204
Moorhouse *v*. Dooland [1955] Ch. 284 .... 239, 240, 242
Morgan *v*. Tate & Lyle Ltd. [1955] A.C. 21 .... 181, *186*, 188
Morley *v*. Tattersall (1938) 108 L.J.K.B. 11 206
Morley's Estate, *Re* [1937] Ch. 491 377
Moss' Empires *v*. I.R.C. [1937] A.C. 785 .... *111*
Muir *v*. I.R.C. [1966] 1 W.L.R. 251 399
Munro *v*. Commissioner of Stamp Duties [1934] A.C. 61 .... 453, *486*, 487, 493
Murgatroyd *v*. Evans-Jackson [1967] 1 W.L.R. 423 .... *189*, 191
Murray *v*. I.R.C. (1926) 11 T.C. 133 371

N.A.L.G.O. *v*. Watkins (1934) 18 T.C. 499 135
Naval Colliery Co. *v*. I.R.C. (1928) 138 L.T. 593 209
Nelson *v*. Adamson [1941] 2 K.B. 12 285
New York Life Insurance Co. *v*. Public Trustee [1924] 2 Ch. 101 455
—— *v*. Styles (1889) 14 App.Cas. 381 .... *134*
New Zealand Shipping Co. Ltd. *v*. Thew (1922) 8 T.C. 208 449
Newbarns Syndicate *v*. Hay (1939) 22 T.C. 461 151

PAGE

Newsom *v*. Robertson [1953] Ch. 7 274
Newton *v*. Commissioner of Taxation of the Commonwealth of Australia [1958] A.C.
    450 .... *42, 44*
Nicoll *v*. Austin (1935) 19 T.C. 531 254
Nobes (B. W.) & Co. *v*. I.R.C. [1966] 1 W.L.R. 111 127
Noble (B. W.) Ltd. *v*. I.R.C. (1926) 12 T.C. 911 518
Nolder *v*. Walters (1930) 46 T.L.R. 397 .... 250, 253, *274*
Norman *v*. Evans [1965] 1 W.L.R. 348 224
—— *v*. Golder [1945] 114 L.J.K.B. 108 189

Oakes *v*. Commissioner of Stamp Duties of New South Wales [1954] A.C. 57 .. 479, *480*, 488
O'Callaghan *v*. Newstead (1940) 23 T.C. 535 348
Odeon Associated Theatres Ltd. *v*. Jones [1972] 2 W.L.R. 331 .... 68, 99, *100*, 154, 179
Ogilvie *v*. Kitton (1908) 5 T.C. 338 .... *279*, 282, 447
O'Grady *v*. Markham Main Colliery Ltd. (1932) 17 T.C. 93 .... *180*
O'Kane (J. and R.) & Co. *v*. I.R.C. (1922) 126 L.T. 707 .... 15, 410
Ormond Investment Company *v*. Betts [1928] A.C. 143 .... *17, 19*, 21
Ormonde (Marchioness) *v*. Brown (1932) 17 T.C. 333 385
Osler *v*. Hall & Co. [1933] 1 K.B. 720 405
Ostime *v*. Duple Motor Bodies [1961] 1 W.L.R. 739 .... 197, *199*
Ounsworth *v*. Vickers Ltd. [1915] 3 K.B. 267 170
Owen, *Re* [1949] W.N. 201 .... *473*
—— *v*. Burden [1972] 1 All E.R. 356 276
—— *v*. Pook [1970] A.C. 244 .... 250, *251*, 261, 268, *273*, 275
Oxford Motors Ltd. *v*. Minister of National Revenue (1959) 18 D.L.R. (2d) 712 .... *74*

Paddington Burial Board *v*. I.R.C. (1884) 13 Q.B.D. 9 133
Page *v*. Pogson (1954) 35 T.C. 545 .... 129, 149
Park, decd. (No. 2), *Re* [1972] Ch. 385 .... *537*
Parsons, *Re* [1943] Ch. 12 .... 464, 470, *530*
Partington *v*. Att.-Gen. (1869) L.R. 4 H.L. 100 9
Partridge *v*. Mallandaine (1886) 18 Q.B.D. 276 .... *131*
Patrick *v*. Broadstone Mills Ltd. [1954] 1 W.L.R. 158 194
Patuck *v*. Lloyd (1944) 171 L.T. 340 290
Payne, *Re* [1940] Ch. 576 495
Peate *v*. Commissioner of Taxation of the Commonwealth of Australia [1967] 1 A.C.
    308 43
Peirse-Duncombe Trust (Trustees) *v*. I.R.C. (1940) 23 T.C. 199 378
Penrose, *Re* [1933] Ch. 793 .... *465*
Perpetual Executors and Trustees Association of Australia Ltd. *v*. Commissioner of Taxes
    of the Commonwealth of Australia [1954] A.C. 114 498
Perrin *v*. Dickson [1930] 1 K.B. 107 .... 77, *377*
Peters' Executors *v*. I.R.C. [1941] 2 All E.R. 620 110
Petrotim Securities *v*. Ayres [1964] 1 W.L.R. 190 .... *136*, 161, 167
Phillips *v*. Whieldon Sanitary Potteries [1952] T.R. 113 180
Pickford *v*. Quirke (1927) 138 L.T. 500 .... *149*, 412
Pilkington *v*. Randall (1966) 42 T.C. 662 .... 57, 128, 129
Pook *v*. Owen. *See* Owen *v*. Pook.
Pool *v*. Royal Exchange Assurance [1921] 1 A.C. 65 368
Poplar Assessment Committee *v*. Roberts [1922] 2 A.C. 93 509
Potter *v*. Lord Advocate [1958] T.R. 55 .... *497*
Potts' Executors *v*. I.R.C. [1951] A.C. 443 .... 8, *23*, 26, 40, 397, *399*, 426
Prince *v*. Mapp [1970] 1 W.L.R. 261 190
Pritchard *v*. Arundale [1972] 1 Ch. 229 245
—— *v*. M. H. Builders (Wilmslow) [1969] 1 W.L.R. 409 .... 211, *425*
Pryce *v*. Monmouthshire Canal and Railway Companies (1879) 4 App.Cas. 197 6
Public Trustee *v*. I.R.C. [1960] A.C. 398 464

Rae *v*. Lazard Investment Co. Ltd. [1963] 1 W.L.R. 555 .... *288*
Raja Vyricherla Narayana Gajapatiraju *v*. Revenue Divisional Officer, Vizagapatam [1939]
    A.C. 302 508
Ralli Bros. Trustee Co. *v*. I.R.C. [1968] Ch. 215 .... *495*
Ralli's Settlements, *Re* [1965] Ch. 286 .... *35*
Rand *v*. Alberni Land Co. Ltd. (1920) 7 T.C. 629 59
Ransom *v*. Higgs [1972] 2 All E.R. 817 191

PAGE

Recknell v. I.R.C. [1952] 2 All E.R. 147 347
Regent Oil Co. v. Strick [1966] A.C. 295 .... 102, *169*, 217
Reid v. I.R.C. (1926) 10 T.C. 673 .... 440, *442*
Reid's Trustees v. I.R.C. (1929) 14 T.C. 512 .... *369*
Religious Tract and Book Society of Scotland v. Forbes (1896) 3 T.C. 415 .... 133, 134
Rendell v. Went [1964] 1 W.L.R. 650 .... 265, *266*, 268
Rennell v. I.R.C. *See* I.R.C. v. Rennell.
Richardson v. Lyon (1943) 25 T.C. 497 .... 253, 268
Riches v. Westminster Bank [1947] A.C. 390 .... *75*, 110
Ricketts v. Colquhoun [1926] A.C. 1 .... 253, *272*, 273
Ridge Securities v. I.R.C. [1964] 1 W.L.R. 479 .... 110, 136
Riley v. Coglan [1967] 1 W.L.R. 1300 245
Rogers v. Inland Revenue (1879) 1 T.C. 225 .... *436*, 439
Rose, *Re* [1952] Ch. 499 .... *473*
Roxburghe's (Duke) Executors v. I.R.C. (1936) 20 T.C. 711 .... 290, 295
Royal Insurance Co. v. Watson [1897] A.C. 1 172
Russell v. I.R.C. (1944) 171 L.T. 249 380
—— v. Scott [1948] A.C. 422 .... *4*
—— v. Town and Country Bank (1888) 13 App.Cas. 418 194
Rutledge v. I.R.C. (1929) 14 T.C. 490 .... *146*
Ryall v. Hoare [1923] 2 K.B. 447 .... 75, 76, 153, *219*, 224, 225, 227

Sainsbury v. I.R.C. [1970] Ch. 712 467
St. Andrew's Hospital, Northampton v. Shearsmith (1887) 19 Q.B.D. 624 134
St. Aubyn v. Att.-Gen. [1952] A.C. 15 .... 477, *479*, 481, 482, 483, 487, 489, 493, 499
Salmon v. Weight (1935) 153 L.T. 55 258
San Paulo (Brazilian) Ry. Co. v. Carter [1896] A.C. 31 .... *278*, 280
Sanderson v. I.R.C. [1956] A.C. 491 464
Saunders v. Pilcher [1949] 2 All E.R. 1097 169
Schioler v. Westminster Bank Ltd. [1970] 2 Q.B. 719 .... *293*
Scott v. Ricketts [1967] 1 W.L.R. 828 .... 86, *226*
Scottish Provident Institution v. Allan [1903] A.C. 129 290
Seale's Marriage Settlement, *Re* [1961] Ch. 574 .... 36, 37
Secretan v. Hart (1969) 45 T.C. 701 .... 320, *330*
Secretary of State for India v. Scoble [1903] A.C. 299 .... 77, 117, *119*, 377
Severn Fishery Board v. O'May [1919] 2 K.B. 484 222
Seymour v. Reed [1927] A.C. 554 .... *237*, 242
Shadbolt v. Salmon Estate (Kingbury) Ltd. (1943) 25 T.C. 52 161
Sharkey v. Wernher [1956] A.C. 58 .... 136, *161*, 166
Sherwin v. Barnes (1931) 16 T.C. 278 .... 220, 224, 225
Shop and Store Developments v. I.R.C. [1967] 1 A.C. 472 .... 8, 26
Short Brothers Ltd. v. I.R.C. (1927) 12 T.C. 955 157
Simpson v. Tate [1925] 2 K.B. 214 .... *275*, 276
Singer v. Williams [1921] A.C. 41 283
Skinner v. Berry Head Lands Ltd. [1970] 1 W.L.R. 1441 161
Smart v. Lincolnshire Sugar Co. *See* Lincolnshire Sugar Co. v. Smart.
Smidth (F. L.) & Co. v. Greenwood. *See* Greenwood v. Smidth (F. L.) & Co.
Smith v. Incorporated Council of Law Reporting for England and Wales [1914] 3 K.B.
    674 .... 80, *180*
Smith (John) & Son v. Moore [1921] 2 A.C. 13 .... 67, 75, 81, 157, 158, 169
Smith's Potato Estates v. Bolland [1948] A.C. 508 .... 184, *185*
Sneddon v. Lord Advocate [1954] A.C. 257 .... *494*, 495, 497
Snell v. Rosser, Thomas & Co. Ltd. [1968] 1 W.L.R. 295 129
Snook (James) & Co. v. Blasdale [1952] T.R. 233 181
Southern v. Aldwych Property Trust [1940] 2 K.B. 266 .... *104*
—— v. Borax Consolidated [1941] 1 K.B. 111 .... 177, 185
Southern (S.) v. A.B. [1933] 1 K.B. 713 130
Southern Railway of Peru v. Owen [1957] A.C. 334 .... 154, *206*
Sowrey v. Harbour Mooring Commissioners of King's Lynn (1887) 2 T.C. 201 133
Spens v. I.R.C. [1970] 1 W.L.R. 1173 341
Spiers & Son Ltd. v. Ogden (1932) 17 T.C. 117 128
Stainer's Executors v. Purchase [1952] A.C. 280 .... *87*
Stanley v. I.R.C. [1944] K.B. 255 .... *373*, 374
Stedeford v. Beloe [1932] A.C. 388 65
Stephenson v. Payne, Stone, Fraser & Co. [1968] 1 W.L.R. 858 .... 205, *207*
Stevens v. Tirard [1940] 1 K.B. 204 .... *350*

PAGE

Strathcona (Lord) v. Lord Advocate, 1929 S.C. 800 .... *493*
Stratton's Disclaimer, Re [1958] Ch. 42 .... *469*
Stratton's Independence v. Howbert, 231 U.S. 399 (1913) 68
Strick v. Regent Oil Co. See Regent Oil Co. v. Strick.
Strong & Co. v. Woodifield [1906] A.C. 448 .... 181, *184*
Sulley v. Att.-Gen. (1860) 5 H. & N. 711 278
Sun Insurance Office v. Clark [1912] A.C. 443 .... 196, 206
Sutherland, decd., Re [1963] A.C. 235 519
Swedish Central Railway Co. Ltd. v. Thompson [1925] A.C. 495 .... 277, *448*, 449, 450

Taw and Torridge Festival Society v. I.R.C. [1959] T.R. 291 .... 116, 124
Taylor, Re; Hume, Re (1958) 13 D.L.R. (2d) 470 .... 453, 477, 482, *492*
—— v. I.R.C. [1964] 1 All E.R. 488n. 386
Tennant v. Smith [1892] A.C. 150 .... 3, 165, *255*, 258, 379
Thomas v. Marshall [1953] A.C. 543 .... *381*
Thompson v. Bruce (1927) 11 T.C. 607 .... 347, 351
—— v. Swedish Central Railway Co. Ltd. See Swedish Central Railway Co. Ltd. v. Thompson.
—— v. Trust and Loan Company of Canada [1932] 1 K.B. 517 93
Thomson v. Gurneville Securities Ltd. [1972] A.C. 661 .... 50, 140
—— v. Moyse [1961] A.C. 967 290
Thyateira (Archbishop) v. Hubert (1942) 25 T.C. 249 242
Tilley v. Wales [1943] A.C. 386 247
Timpson's Executors v. Yerbury [1936] 1 K.B. 645 292
Tollemache (Lord) v. I.R.C. (1926) 11 T.C. 277 .... 373, *379*
Tomlinson v. Glyn's Executor and Trustee Co. [1970] Ch. 112 367
Townsend v. Grundy (1933) 18 T.C. 140 223
Turnbull v. Foster (1904) 6 T.C. 206 .... *436*

Union Corporation Ltd. v. I.R.C. [1953] A.C. 482 .... 446, 449
Unit Construction Co. v. Bullock [1960] A.C. 351 .... *449*
Usher's Wiltshire Brewery v. Bruce [1915] A.C. 433 .... 47, 79, 153, *168*, 181

Vallambrosa Rubber Co. v. Farmer (1910) 5 T.C. 529 .... 80, 170
Van den Berghs v. Clark [1935] A.C. 431 .... 80, *156*, 169
Vandervell v. I.R.C. [1967] 2 A.C. 291 .... 380, *394*
Vestey v. I.R.C. [1962] Ch. 861 .... 119, 385
Vestey's Executors v. I.R.C. [1949] 1 All E.R. 1108 .... *33*, *391*

Waddington v. O'Callaghan (1931) 16 T.C. 187 410
Wale, decd., Re [1956] 1 W.L.R. 1346 473
Waley-Cohen v. I.R.C. (1945) 26 T.C. 471 380
Walsh v. Randall (1940) 23 T.C. 55 293
Watson Bros. v. Hornby (1942) 24 T.C. 506 .... 163, 164
—— v. Lothian (1902) 4 T.C. 441 179
Weight v. Salmon. See Salmon v. Weight.
Weir's Settlement, Re [1971] Ch. 145 464
Weisberg's Executrices v. I.R.C. (1933) 17 T.C. 696 151
West v. Phillips (1958) 38 T.C. 203 84
Westcott v. Bryan [1969] Ch. 324 265
Westminster (Duke) v. I.R.C. See I.R.C. v. Westminster (Duke).
Weston's Settlements, Re [1969] Ch. 223 .... 26, *35*
Westward Television Ltd. v. Hart [1969] 1 Ch. 201 .... 205, *212*
Whimster & Co. v. I.R.C. (1926) 12 T.C. 813 .... *154*, 170, 200, 207
White v. Franklin [1965] 1 W.L.R. 492 .... *346*
Whitehead's Will Trusts, Re [1971] 1 W.L.R. 833 39
Whitney v. I.R.C. [1926] A.C. 37 .... 74, 82
Whitworth Park Coal Co. v. I.R.C. [1961] A.C. 311 .... *110*, 125
Whyte v. Clancy (1936) 20 T.C. 679 223
Wilcox v. Smith (1857) 4 Drew. 49 .... 9, 19
Wilkins v. Rogerson [1961] Ch. 133 .... 251, 258
Williams v. Doulton [1948] 1 All E.R. 603 350
—— v. Singer [1921] 1 A.C. 65 .... *367*

PAGE

Williamson *v*. Ough [1936] A.C. 384 .... 117, 379
Willingale *v*. Islington Green Investment Co. [1972] 1 All E.R. 199 426
Willis and Willis' Executors *v*. Harrison. *See* Harrison *v*. Willis Bros.
Wilson *v*. Mannooch (1937) 21 T.C. 178 .... 220, 224
Wisdom *v*. Chamberlain [1968] 1 W.L.R. 1230 .... 147, *148*
Withers *v*. Nethersole [1948] 1 All E.R. 400 225
—— *v*. Wynyard (1938) 21 T.C. 724 434
Wood Preservation Ltd. *v*. Prior [1969] 1 W.L.R. 1077 211
Woodhouse *v*. I.R.C. (1936) 20 T.C. 673 372
Wright *v*. Boyce [1958] 1 W.L.R. 832 240

Yarmouth *v*. France (1887) 19 Q.B.D. 647 .... 217, 218
Yates *v*. Starkey [1951] Ch. 465 .... *349*, 382
Young, *Re* (1875) 1 T.C. 57 .... *435*, 439
Young (J. H.) & Co. *v*. I.R.C. (1925) 12 T.C. 827 207

TABLE OF STATUTES

PAGE

1799 Income Tax Act (39 Geo. 3, c. 13)   89
1803 Income Tax Act (43 Geo. 3, c. 122)
           72, 74, 415
1806 Income Tax Act (46 Geo. 3, c. 65)   441
1842 Income Tax Act (5 & 6 Vict. c. 35)
           86, 121, 184, 210, 279,
           341, 344, 347, 352, 368
1853 Income Tax Act (16 & 17 Vict.
     c. 34) 86, 273, 286
1869 Valuation (Metropolis) Act (32 &
     33 Vict. c. 67) 90
1876 Customs and Inland Revenue Act
     (39 & 40 Vict. c. 16), s. 8 ... 256
1881 Customs and Inland Revenue Act
     (44 & 45 Vict. c. 12), s. 38 .. 468,
           469, 470, 473, 490, 537
1882 Customs and Inland Revenue Act
     (45 & 46 Vict. c. 41) 86
1885 Customs and Inland Revenue Act
     (48 & 49 Vict. c. 51), s. 11 .. 133
1888 Customs and Inland Revenue Act
     (51 & 52 Vict. c. 8), s. 24 88
1889 Customs and Inland Revenue Act
     (52 & 53 Vict. c. 7), s. 11 .. 469,
           470, 471, 473, 481,
           490, 526
1890 Partnership Act (53 & 54 Vict.
     c. 39), s. 2 412
1894 Finance Act (57 & 58 Vict. c. 30)
           453, 501
     s. 1 .... 453, 464, 466, 467, 500, 528
     s. 2 .... 453, 464, 466
         (1) (a) ... 464, 467, 498, 525, 528
           (b) 467, 477, 480, 481
           (c) .. 468, 469, 470, 471, 473,
           490, 493, 526
           (e) (f) (g) 498, 499
     s. 3 .... 470, 471, 498, 522, 524,
           525, 526, 527
     s. 4 496
     s. 5 .... 464, 528, 529, 530
     s. 7 (5) 465, 493, 494, 500, 502,
           503, 505–508, 511–513, 518
         (6) 519, 520, 521
     s. 8 464
     s. 16 528
1896 Finance Act (59 & 60 Vict. c. 28),
     s. 15 .... 464, 531
1910 Finance (1909–10) Act (10 Edw. 7
     & 1 Geo. 5, c. 8)—
     s. 59 .... 468, 469, 533, 536, 537
     s. 60 .... 500, 506
1911 Finance Act (1 & 2 Geo. 5, c. 48),
     s. 18 510
1914 Finance Act (4 & 5 Geo. 5, c. 10)—
     s. 9 352
     s. 14 528

PAGE

1915 Finance (No. 2) Act (5 & 6 Geo. 5,
     c. 89) 159
     s. 40 178
     s. 44 31
1916 Finance Act (6 & 7 Geo. 5, c. 24)—
     s. 45 18
     s. 47 178
1918 Income Tax Act (8 & 9 Geo. 5,
     c. 40) 111, 352
     s. 17 347
     s. 33 105
     s. 37 20
     s. 46 .... 439, 441
     s. 107 14
     s. 210 153
     s. 237 .... 146, 156
     Sched. A 5, 163
     Sched. D 221, 443
     Sched. E 230, 238, 246
1920 Finance Act (10 & 11 Geo. 5,
     c. 18), s. 21 349
1922 Finance Act (12 & 13 Geo. 5,
     c. 17)—
     s. 18 231
     s. 20 386
     s. 21 427
1923 Finance Act (13 & 14 Geo. 5,
     c. 14), s. 21 20
1924 Finance Act (14 & 15 Geo. 5,
     c. 21)—
     s. 26 17
     s. 32 20
1925 Settled Land Act (15 & 16 Geo. 5,
     c. 18), s. 64 34
     Trustee Act (15 & 16 Geo. 5,
     c. 19)—
     s. 31 373
     s. 41 35
     s. 57 34
     Finance Act (15 & 16 Geo. 5,
     c. 36), s. 21 20
1926 Finance Act (16 & 17 Geo. 5,
     c. 22) 203
     s. 23 20
1931 Finance Act (21 & 22 Geo. 5,
     c. 28), s. 40 533
     Finance (No. 2) Act (21 & 22 Geo.
     5, c. 49), s. 22 ...... 433, 445, 455
1933 Finance Act (23 & 24 Geo. 5,
     c. 19), s. 31 11
1936 Finance Act (26 Geo. 5 & 1 Edw.
     8, c. 34)—
     s. 18 .... 33, 34, 392
     s. 21 .... 349, 381, 383, 387
1938 Finance Act (1 & 2 Geo. 6, c. 46)—
     s. 38 .... 388, 391, 392
     s. 40 400
1939 Finance Act (2 & 3 Geo. 6, c. 41),
     s. 31 468

PAGE

1940 Finance Act (3 & 4 Geo. 6, c. 29)—
    s. 30 13
    s. 43 .... 480, 481
    s. 44 .... 468, 469, 471, 526
    s. 45 .... 468, 469, 470
    s. 55 .... 510, 517, 518, 522
    s. 56 480
    s. 58 517
    Finance (No. 2) Act (3 & 4 Geo. 6,
        c. 48), s. 17 519
1941 Finance Act (4 & 5 Geo. 6, c. 30),
    s. 10 .... 161, 164
1945 Income Tax Act (8 & 9 Geo. 6,
        c. 32)—
    s. 17 .... 6, 19
    s. 27 212
1946 Finance Act (9 & 10 Geo. 6, c. 64) 469
1947 Transport Act (10 & 11 Geo. 6,
        c. 49), ss. 29, 30 6
1948 Companies Act (11 & 12 Geo. 6,
        c. 38), s. 110 233
    Finance Act (11 & 12 Geo. 6, c. 49)
                            261, 262
    s. 31 161
1949 Lands Tribunal Act (12, 13 & 14
        Geo. 6, c. 42), s. 3 510
    Finance Act (12, 13 & 14 Geo. 6,
        c. 47)—
    s. 28 .... 36, 433, 455
    s. 33 .... 468, 533
1950 Finance Act (14 Geo. 6, c. 15),
    s. 46 .... 469, 471, 526
1951 Finance Act (14 & 15 Geo. 6,
        c. 43)—
    s. 33 533
    s. 34 .... 433, 455
1952 Income Tax Act (15 & 16 Geo. 6 &
        1 Eliz. 2, c. 10)—
    s. 25 .... 13, 14
    s. 47 408
    s. 64 .... 57, 59
    s. 123 114
    ss. 127, 128 .... 207, 213
    s. 132 294
    s. 137 ...... 95, 101, 187, 188, 189
    s. 144 409
    ss. 160–162 .... 16, 240, 262–265
    ss. 189, 190 294
    s. 212 .... 83, 84
    s. 237 .... 30, 56
    s. 241 30
    s. 341 .... 137, 213
    s. 342 213
    ss. 392–415 393
    s. 392 .... 82, 83, 393
    s. 397 .... 383, 384
    s. 403 383
    s. 405 .... 396, 398
    s. 408 .... 396, 398, 401–404
    s. 411 .... 397, 398, 402, 403
    s. 415 395
    s. 447 .... 114, 116
    s. 471 167
    s. 526 136
    Sched. 9 251
1954 Finance Act (2 & 3 Eliz. 2, c. 44),
    s. 32 528
1956 Finance Act (4 & 5 Eliz. 2, c. 54),
    Sched. 2 239

PAGE

1957 Finance Act (5 & 6 Eliz. 2, c. 49),
    s. 38 .... 493, 494, 495, 500
1958 Variation of Trusts Act (6 & 7
        Eliz. 2, c. 53) 35, 39, 461
    Finance Act (6 & 7 Eliz. 2, c. 56),
        ss. 20–22 393
1959 Finance Act (7 & 8 Eliz. 2, c. 58)—
    s. 34 .... 11, 468
    s. 35 .... 477, 487, 488
1960 Finance Act (8 & 9 Eliz. 2, c. 44)—
    s. 32 167
    ss. 37, 38 233
    s. 43 40
    s. 53 408
    s. 63 409
    s. 64 .... 468, 533
1961 Trusts (Scotland) Act (9 & 10 Eliz.
        2, c. 57) 461
1962 Finance Act (10 & 11 Eliz. 2,
        c. 44), s. 28 455
1963 Finance Act (11 & 12 Eliz. 2,
        c. 25), s. 53 ...... 468, 533, 537
1965 Finance Act (c. 25)—
    s. 19 330
    s. 20 .... 330, 432
    s. 22 .... 327, 330, 367
    s. 25 .... 36, 367
    s. 26 500
    s. 44 510
    s. 88 517
    Sched. 6 .... 331, 332
    Sched. 18 17
1966 Finance Act (c. 18), s. 41 464
1967 Finance Act (c. 54), Sched. 11 .. 17
1968 Capital Allowances Act (c. 3)—
    ss. 6, 12, 46 219
    s. 80 7
    Finance Act (c. 44), ss. 35–37 . 468, 533
1969 Finance Act (c. 32) 431, 453, 467,
                        477, 481, 498
    s. 30 464
    s. 36 465
    s. 37 498
    s. 38 465
    s. 40 496
    Sched. 17 .... 528, 530, 531
1970 Taxes Management Act (c. 9)—
    s. 9 404
    s. 31 46
    s. 34 408
    ss. 36–41 408
    s. 56 109
    s. 72 369
    ss. 92, 95 14
    s. 118 .... 46, 409
    Income and Corporation Taxes Act
        (c. 10)—
    s. 5 22
    s. 8 351
    s. 9 347
    s. 10 .... 83, 348, 358
    s. 11 350
    ss. 19–21 .... 112, 350
    s. 25 347
    s. 27 432
    s. 30 30
    s. 34 .... 177, 246
    s. 37 351

PAGE

1970 Income and Corporation Taxes
Act—cont.
s. 38 .... 352, 353
ss. 43–48 .... 351, 360
s. 49 .... 432, 433
s. 50 .... 434, 435
ss. 52–54 .... 79, 111, 113, 126, 127
s. 65 126
s. 67 .... 96, 277
ss. 71–77 99
ss. 80–82 .... 97, 98
ss. 83–85 98
s. 87 341
ss. 91–92 .... 105, 277
s. 93 .... 110, 277
s. 99 .... 433, 439
s. 108 .... 128, 192, 202
s. 109 .. 110, 114, 128, 152, 219, 277
s. 110 161
s. 111 .... 105, 106
s. 112 5
ss. 115–128 .... 204, 207
s. 115 213
s. 122 ...... 278, 290, 294, 432, 433
s. 129 .... 204, 446
s. 130 ...... 95, 101, 168, 180, 187
ss. 143, 144 .... 87, 167, 219
s. 152 .... 404, 409
s. 157 97
s. 159 294
ss. 168–180 .... 212, 213
s. 171 211
s. 174 212
ss. 177–178 247
s. 181 ...... 229, 230, 235, 277, 290
s. 183 234
s. 185 .... 255, 256, 260
ss. 187–188 ...... 233, 235, 237, 246,
247, 248
s. 189 258
s. 192 275
ss. 195–203 .... 255, 260, 261
s. 195 263
s. 196 .... 240, 263, 265
s. 197 265
ss. 208–231 253
s. 230 .... 117, 121
s. 232 413
s. 238 .... 413, 446
s. 243 .... 204, 413
. 247 446
s. 248 413
s. 250 413
ss. 252, 253 425
ss. 256, 257 425
ss. 258–264 425
s. 282 .... 29, 426
ss. 284–288 426
ss. 289–295 .... 323, 426
ss. 290, 293 428
ss. 296–300 323
s. 302 426
s. 303 .... 17, 426
ss. 345–347 .... 11, 135
s. 360 .... 114, 132
s. 379 219
s. 380 .... 79, 219

PAGE

1970 Income and Corporation Taxes
Act—cont.
s. 385 219
s. 389 167
ss. 403–404 30
s. 411 187
s. 418 290
ss. 426–433 372
ss. 434–459 .... 29, 40, 380, 393
s. 434 ...... 82, 114, 122, 343, 381,
385, 386
s. 437 ...... 349, 352, 358, 381,
383, 384
ss. 438, 439 387
s. 441 384
s. 444 .... 381, 383
s. 445 219
s. 446 .... 387, 391
s. 447 ...... 390, 395, 396, 399, 401
s. 451 ...... 23, 396, 399, 400, 401,
404, 426
s. 454 .... 381, 397, 401
s. 457 385
s. 458 .... 24, 390, 395
s. 459 381
ss. 460–477 .... 40, 323
s. 460 65
s. 466 40
ss. 478–481 .... 30, 34, 219, 286, 446
s. 482 446
s. 483 425
ss. 486–488 ...... 65, 131, 219
s. 488 97
s. 526 .... 129, 136, 156
s. 528 339
s. 530 345
Sched. 1 350
Sched. 3 98
Matrimonial Proceedings and Property Act (c. 45), s. 4 34
1971 Finance Act (c. 68)—
s. 15 358
s. 16 .... 351, 352, 360
s. 23 .... 351, 358
ss. 32–39 338
s. 32 335
s. 59 327
Sched. 4 351
Scheds. 6, 7 .... 246, 338
Sched. 12 500
1972 Finance Act (c. 41)—
s. 73 235
s. 75 .... 121, 126, 341
ss. 77–79 258
s. 81 97
ss. 84–111 .... 413, 423
s. 91 425
ss. 94, 95 .... 427, 429
s. 121 .... 468, 522
Sched. 12 258
Scheds. 16, 17 427

Australia
Commonwealth Income Tax and Social
Services Contribution Act
1936–1951, s. 260 .... 42, 44
Stamp Duties Act 1920–1949 (New
South Wales), s. 102 .... 481, 485,
486, 498

PAGE

PAGE

Barbados
Estate and Succession Act 1941, s. 3   466

New Zealand
Land and Income Tax Act 1954, s. 108 .   43

Ceylon
Estate Duty Ordinance 1938, s. 20   516

United States of America
Internal Revenue Code 1954
    s. 61 .... 75, 313

Netherlands
Law for the Promotion of the Correct
     Assessment of Direct Taxes
     (April 29, 1925)   31

    s. 1201   308
    s. 1221   309
    s. 1222   310

TABLE OF PARLIAMENTARY
PAPERS, REPORTS, ETC.

[Figures in *italics* refer to the pages on which extracts from reports appear.]

PAGE

1919 Report of the Committee on Financial Risks attaching to the
holding of Trading Stocks
(Cmd. 9924) 195
1920 Royal Commission on the Income
Tax—Report (Cmd. 615)—
§§ 86–91 .... *141*, 142, 307
§§ 101, 102 .... *254*
§§ 251, 252, 257–260 ...... *353–355*
§§ 290, 291, 296 .... *350, 351*
§ 459 .... *105*
1927 Report of the Committee on
National Debt and Taxation
(Cmd. 2800) 459
1936 Report of the Committee on
Codification of Income Tax
Law (Cmnd. 5131) 145, 434
1951 Report of the Committee on the
Taxation of Trading Profits
(Cmd. 8189)—
§§ 19–24 .... *203, 204*
§§ 25–28 .... *404, 405*
§§ 33, 34 .... *204*
§§ 69–72 .... *405–407*
§§ 79–81 .... *211, 212*
§§ 149–162 .... *181–184*, 191
§ 192 214
§§ 194–198 .... *215, 216*
§ 281 .... *195*
§§ 289, 290 .... *426*
§ 297 .... *426*
1953 Royal Commission on the Taxation
of Profits and Income—First
Report (Cmd. 8761)—
§ 8 .... *277*, 432
§§ 25, 26 .... *295*
1954 Report of the Committee on the
Taxation Treatment of Provisions for Retirement (Cmd.
9063) 351
§§ 477, 496, 497, 503 .... *120*
Royal Commission on the Taxation
of Profits and Income—Second
Report (Cmd. 9105)—
§§ 101–103 .... *335, 336*
§§ 113–121 .... *355–358*
§§ 122–126 .... *358, 359*
§ 132 .... *358*
§§ 212–214 .... *345*
Reservation by Mr. G. Woodcock and others.
§§ 23–25 .... *359, 360*

PAGE

1955 Royal Commission on the Taxation
of Profits and Income—Final
Report (Cmd. 9474)—
§§ 26, 28–34 .... *71–73*
§§ 44–57 .... *414–418*
§ 84 .... *306*
§§ 88–108 ...... 308, *313–319*, 322
§§ 109–117 .... *142–145*, 146
§ 127 182
§§ 129–140 .... *268–271*
§§ 144–150 .... *121, 122*, 385
§§ 208–211 .... *254, 255*
§ 213 .... *261*
§§ 224–227 .... *261, 262*
§ 245 248
§§ 279–282 .... *432, 433*, 442
§§ 289–292 .... *433, 434*, 442
§§ 322–325 216
§§ 448–454 .... *192–194*
§§ 470, 471 194
§§ 480–486 .... *209–211*
§ 544 .... *418*
§ 559 .... *429*
§ 776 204
§§ 826, 827 98
§ 851 97
§§ 865, 866 .... *97, 98*
§ 988 .... *126*
§§ 1015–1027 .... *27–32*, 40, 41
Memorandum of Dissent by Mr.
G. Woodcock and others.
§ 5 69
§§ 9–11 .... *73, 74*
§§ 34–70 .... *319–329*
§§ 45–48 307
§§ 90–95 .... *418–420*
§§ 181, 182 262
Reservation by Mr. W. F.
Crick.
§§ 2–4 420
1969 Law Commission Report, " The
Interpretation of Statutes "
(H.C. 256) 3
1970 White Paper, " Investment Incentives " (Cmnd. 4516)—
§ 1 214
1971 Green Paper, " Reform of Corporation Tax " (Cmnd. 4630)—
§§ 1–9 .... *420–422*
§§ 26, 27 .... *428, 429*
White Paper, " Reform of Personal
Direct Taxation " (Cmnd.
4653) 335
§§ 3–6, 12 .... *338, 339*

PAGE

1971 Law Commission Report, "Taxa-
        tion of Income and Gains
        derived from Land " (Cmnd.
        4654)—
        §§ 18–22 .... 98, 99
        §§ 31–33 .... 99, 100
        §§ 60–63 .... 96, 97
      Report of the Committee of Inquiry
        on Small Firms (Cmnd.
        4811) 456
        § 13.56 428
        § 13.57 430
        § 13.58 .... 416, 431
      Report of the Select Committee on
        Corporation Tax (H.C. 622) .. 423,
                                      431

1972 Green Paper, " Taxation of Capi-
        tal on Death: A possible
        Inheritance Tax in place of
        Estate Duty " (Cmnd. 4930) .. 453
        §§ 1–4 454
        §§ 12–14 455

PAGE

1972 Green Paper, " Taxation of Capi-
        tal on Death: A possible
        Inheritance Tax in place of
        Estate Duty "—cont.
        §§ 23–31 455–457
        § 23 503
        §§ 33–63 457–464
        §§ 35–37 503
      White Paper, " Industrial and Reg-
        ional Development " (Cmnd.
        4942) 214, 215

Canada
1966 Report of the Royal Commission
        on Taxation (Queen's Printer,
        Ottawa)—
        Vol. I 70, 71, 306, 307, 308,
                      323, 326, 336, 337, 355,
                      360–362, 414, 423, 424
        Vol. III 123, 260, 271, 272,
                         329, 362–366, 424
        Vol. IV 424, 425, 430

Part One

PRINCIPLES OF REVENUE LAW

Chapter 1

STATUTORY INTERPRETATION

Revenue law is wholly the creature of statute; that is to say, there is no common law of taxation, no principle of law which is applicable other than those principles which are found in the taxing Acts themselves according to their true meaning and effect. In any tax case it is consequently necessary for the court or Commissioners to determine the true meaning and effect of the particular statutory provision which is in question. How, then, is a provision in a taxing Act to be interpreted?

It is often stated that the general rules of statutory interpretation apply; but:

> " The basic principles of statutory interpretation are not to be found in any statute. They have developed from the decisions of the courts. The principles which have thus evolved are sometimes called 'rules,' but it would be more accurate to describe them as different approaches to interpretation, on which at different periods of our legal history greater or lesser emphasis has been placed." [1]

The approach of the courts to the interpretation of taxing Acts has been fairly consistent throughout the years [2] : but it is generally recognised that taxing Acts are a rather special type of statute, demanding a predictable, and hence strict, form of interpretation. Certain general principles, characteristic to this approach, may thus be formulated.

(A) A Tax Must be Expressly Imposed Upon the Subject by the Clear Words of the Statute

TENNANT v. SMITH

House of Lords [1892] A.C. 150; 61 L.J.P.C. 11; 66 L.T. 327; 56 J.P. 596; 8 T.L.R. 434; 3 T.C. 158 (also *post*, p. 255)

Lord Halsbury L.C.: My Lords, to put this case very simply, the question depends upon what is Mr. Tennant's income. This is an Income Tax Act, and what is intended to be taxed is income. And when I say " what is intended to be taxed," I mean what is the intention of the Act as expressed in its provisions, because in a taxing Act it is impossible, I believe, to assume any intention, any governing purpose in the Act, to do more than take such tax as the statute imposes. In various cases the principle of construction of a taxing Act has been referred to in various forms, but I believe they may be all reduced to this, that

---

[1] Law Commission Report, " The Interpretation of Statutes " (1969) H.C. 256, at p. 14, para. 22.
[2] The attitude of the courts to the problems of tax avoidance has tended to vary: see Chap. 2.

inasmuch as you have no right to assume that there is any governing object which a taxing Act is intended to attain other than that which it has expressed by making such and such objects the intended subject for taxation, you must see whether a tax is expressly imposed.

Cases, therefore under the taxing Acts always resolve themselves into a question whether or not the words of the Act have reached the alleged subject of taxation. Lord Wensleydale said, in *In re Micklethwait*,[3] " It is a well-established rule, that the subject is not to be taxed without clear words for that purpose; and also, that every Act of Parliament must be read according to the natural construction of its words. . . ."

COLTNESS IRON COMPANY v. BLACK

House of Lords (1881) 6 App.Cas. 315; 51 L.J.Q.B. 626; 45 L.T. 145; 46 J.P. 20; 29 W.R. 717; 1 T.C. 311

LORD BLACKBURN: . . . No tax can be imposed on the subject without words in an Act of Parliament clearly showing an intention to lay a burden on him. But when that intention is sufficiently shewn it is, I think, vain to speculate on what would be the fairest and most equitable mode of levying that tax. The object of those framing a taxing Act is to grant to Her Majesty a revenue; no doubt they would prefer, if it were possible, to raise that revenue equally from all, and, as that cannot be done, to raise it from those on whom the tax falls with as little trouble and annoyance and as equally as can be contrived; and when any enactments for the purpose can bear two interpretations, it is reasonable to put that construction on them which will produce these effects. But the object is to grant a revenue at all events, even though a possible nearer approximation to equality may be sacrificed in order more easily and certainly to raise that revenue, and I think the only safe rule is to look at the words of the enactments and see what is the intention expressed by those words. . . .

RUSSELL v. SCOTT

House of Lords [1948] A.C. 422; [1948] L.J.R. 1265; 64 T.L.R. 297; 92 S.J. 424; [1948] 2 All E.R. 1; 30 T.C. 394

LORD SIMONDS: . . . My Lords, there is a maxim of income tax law which, though it may sometimes be overstressed, yet ought not to be forgotten. It is that the subject is not to be taxed unless the words of the taxing statute unambiguously impose the tax upon him. It is necessary that this maxim should on occasion be reasserted and this is such an occasion. Here it is sought to tax the owner and occupier of land in respect of the profits made by him from the sale of sand on the footing that in effecting those sales he is carrying on a concern which is " of the like nature " to " ironworks, gasworks, salt springs or works, alum mines or works, waterworks, streams of water, canals, inland navigations, docks, drains or levels, fishings, rights of markets and fairs, tolls, railways and other ways, bridges, ferries." I need go no further into the history of this catalogue than to say that with some additions it goes back for nearly 150 years. During the whole of that time there can have been no more familiar feature of the landscape than pits of sand or gravel or clay and I cannot doubt that during that time and before it the owners of such pits have been accustomed in greater or less degree to exploit them not only for their own use but by profitable sales.

[3] (1855) 11 Exch. 456.

Yet it is suggested that the legislature, while expressly including in the catalogue such comparatively rare concerns as alum mines or works and salt springs or works, yet left to the precarious embrace of the expression " other concerns of the like nature " the commonplace operations which it is now sought to tax. Nor does the matter rest there. For the catalogue which I have recited follows immediately after rule 1, which deals with quarries of stone, slate, limestone, or chalk, and rule 2, which deals with mines of coal, tin, lead, copper, mundic, iron, and other mines. Here, surely, would be the appropriate setting in which, had the legislature so intended, pits of sand or gravel or clay should eo nomine have been placed or included by words of general description. I cannot bring myself to suppose that the legislature either overlooked what almost obtrudes itself on the eye of any observer, or, observing it, deliberately refrained either from mentioning it or from putting it in its proper place. I am brought back, then, to the maxim that I have mentioned. For it appears to me that here is a case in which the subject is entitled to say that the words of the section under which it is sought to tax him do not do so with the clarity which the subject-matter demands. . . .

Note
This case turned upon the meaning of rule 3 of No. III of Schedule A to the Income Tax Act 1918. See now I.C.T.A. 1970, s. 112 (1) (2).

AYRSHIRE EMPLOYERS MUTUAL INSURANCE ASSOCIATION LTD. v. I.R.C.

Court of Session (1944) 27 T.C. 344; 1944 S.C. 421; 1945 S.L.T. 102 (also *post*, p. 11)

THE LORD PRESIDENT (NORMAND): I seem in the end to be driven to that last refuge of judicial hesitation when confronted with a difficulty of interpretation, the doctrine that no tax can be imposed on the subject without words in an Act of Parliament clearly showing an intention to lay a burden on him. . . .

BROWN v. NATIONAL PROVIDENT INSTITUTION

House of Lords [1921] 2 A.C. 222; 90 L.J.K.B. 1009; 125 L.T. 417; 37 T.L.R. 804; 8 T.C. 80 (also *post*, pp. 16, 85, 205)

LORD SUMNER: . . . It is a most wholesome rule that in taxing the subject the Crown must show that clear powers to tax were given by the legislature. Applied to income tax, however, this is an ironical proposition. Most of the operative clauses are unintelligible to those who have to pay the taxes and in any case derive such clarity as they possess from the judges, who have interpreted them. After the puzzle has been solved no doubt the answer seems clear and the solution is arrived at as a matter of construction. The question is always what is the meaning of the words of the Statute? If they have none there is no need to invoke the proposition, that the meaning must be clear. . . .

(B) THE WORDS OF THE ACT MUST BE GIVEN THEIR NATURAL MEANING

The taxpayer is entitled to stand upon a literal construction of the statutory provision, even if the result produced is anomalous.

PRYCE v. MONMOUTHSHIRE CANAL AND RAILWAY COMPANIES

House of Lords (1879) 4 App.Cas. 197; 49 L.J.Q.B. 130; 40 L.T. 630; 43 J.P. 524; 27 W.R. 666

EARL CAIRNS L.C.: My Lords, the cases which have decided that taxing Acts are to be construed with strictness, and that no payment is to be exacted from the subject which is not clearly and unequivocally required by Act of Parliament to be made, probably meant little more than this, that, inasmuch as there was not any *à priori* liability in a subject to pay any particular tax, nor any antecedent relationship between the tax-payer and the taxing authority, no reasoning founded upon any supposed relationship of the tax-payer and the taxing authority, could be brought to bear upon the construction of the Act, and therefore the tax-payer had a right to stand upon a literal construction of the words used, whatever might be the consequence. . . .

KIRKNESS v. JOHN HUDSON & CO. LTD.

House of Lords [1955] A.C. 696; [1955] 2 W.L.R. 1135; 99 S.J. 368; [1955] 2 All E.R. 345; *sub nom. Hudson (John) & Co.* v. *Kirkness*, 36 T.C. 28 (also *post*, p. 19)

VISCOUNT SIMONDS: My Lords, this appeal raises questions of some difficulty in regard to the meaning and effect of section 17 of the Income Tax Act 1945. The material parts of that section are as follows: " (1) Subject to the provisions of this section, where, on or after the appointed day, any of the following events occurs in the case of any machinery or plant in respect of which an initial allow-ance or a deduction under Rule 6 of the Rules applicable to Cases I and II of Schedule D has been made or allowed for any year of assessment to a person carrying on a trade, that is to say, either—(*a*) the machinery or plant is sold, whether while still in use or not; or (*b*) the machinery or plant, whether still in use or not, ceases to belong to the person carrying on the trade by reason of the coming to an end of a foreign concession; or (*c*) the machinery or plant is destroyed; or (*d*) the machinery or plant is put out of use as being worn out or obsolete or otherwise useless or no longer required, and the event in question occurs before the trade is permanently discontinued, an allowance or charge (in this Part of this Act referred to as ' a balancing allowance ' or ' a balancing charge ') shall, in the circumstances mentioned in this section, be made to, or, as the case may be, on, that person for the year of assessment in his basis period for which that event occurs ": . . . . It will be observed that in subsection (1) (*a*) occur the words " is sold," and it is around these two plain English words that a controversy arose between the Crown and the respondents which occupied your Lordships for several days.

The relevant facts are simple and few. At all material times the business of the respondents was that of coal merchants and they owned a large number of wagons which they used for the transport of coal. These wagons were on January 1, 1948, under requisition by the Minister of Transport under the powers contained in regulation 53 of the Defence (General) Regulations 1939.

On January 1, 1948, the property in these wagons was vested in the British Transport Commission by virtue of section 29 of the Transport Act 1947.

. . . Pursuant to section 29 of the Act, the respondent company's wagons were duly vested in the Commission, and in due course the company received an amount of compensation determined in accordance with the provisions of section 30 and Schedule VI which was satisfied by the issue of an equivalent amount of British Transport Stock. This amount was substantially higher than the written down value of the wagons for the purposes of the income tax allowances in respect of wear and tear as appearing in the company's books. On these facts a balancing charge of £29,021 was made on the company in pursuance of section 17 of the Income Tax Act 1945.

. . . My Lords, in my opinion the company's wagons were not sold, and it would be a grave misuse of language to say that they were sold. To say of a man who has had his property taken from him against his will and been awarded compensation in the settlement of which he has had no voice, to say of such a man that he has sold his property appears to me to be as far from the truth as to say of a man who has been deprived of his property without compensation that he has given it away.

. . . It was urged upon your Lordships that, after all, the result in law of a sale is to transfer the ownership of property from A to B for a consideration in money or money's worth, and that this is just what the Transport Act does to the respondent company's wagons. But, my Lords, if I may say so without disrespect to the very able and helpful argument of the Attorney-General, I find it in this aspect dangerously near a logical fallacy. A dog is an animal that has four legs and a tail, but not every animal that has four legs and a tail is a dog. Nor is a statutory vesting of A's property in B and the award of compensation to A a sale, though its result may be the same as if A had sold that property to B. . . .

Note
The position is now governed by section 80 of the Capital Allowances Act 1968.

I.R.C. v. WOLFSON

House of Lords [1949] W.N. 190; 65 T.L.R. 260; 93 S.J. 355; [1949] 1 All E.R. 865; 31 T.C. 141 (also *post*, p. 388)

A settlor covenanted to make annual payments to his sisters equal to dividends which he might receive from certain shares held in a company which he controlled. The Crown contended that, as he controlled the company, he was in a position to determine whether or not any dividend should be paid and that he therefore, in effect, possessed a power of revocation. In such a case the income ought to be treated as his income, rather than that of his sisters, for income tax and surtax purposes.

Held, the terms of the Deed of Covenant were not such that the settlor had a power of revocation.

LORD SIMONDS: . . . It was urged that the construction that I favour leaves an easy loophole through which the evasive taxpayer may find escape. That may be so, but I will repeat what has been said before. It is not the function of a court of law to give to words a strained and unnatural meaning because only thus will a taxing section apply to a transaction which, had the legislature thought of it, would have been covered by appropriate words. It is the duty of the court to give to the words of this subsection their reasonable meaning and I must decline on any ground of policy to give to them a meaning which, with all respect to the dissentient Lord Justice, I regard as little short of extravagant. It cannot even be urged that, unless this meaning is given to the subsection, it can have no operation. On the contrary, given its natural meaning it will bring within the area of taxation a number of cases in which by a familiar device tax had formerly been avoided. . . . (Quoted from All England Reports.)

Notes
This approach may also be compared to that in the cases quoted under the heading "Form and Substance," *post*, p. 21.

As to the relevance of the argument that a strict construction leaves an easy loophole for evasion, see *Potts' Executors* v. *I.R.C. (infra)*, *cf.* Lord Guest in *Shop and Store Developments Ltd.* v. *I.R.C.* [1967] A.C. 472 at pp. 501–502, a stamp duty case in which a rather different approach is adopted.

POTTS' EXECUTORS v. I.R.C.

House of Lords [1951] A.C. 443; [1951] 1 T.L.R. 152; [1951] 1 All E.R. 76; 32 T.C. 211 (also *post*, pp. 23, 399)

LORD SIMONDS : . . . It was finally urged by learned counsel for the respondents that, if this appeal is allowed, an easy way of evading [4] tax will be open to the taxpayer. This is an argument which is of no weight whatever. The question is what is the fair meaning of words in a taxing Act. I have given my answer to it and move that this appeal be allowed and the matter be remitted accordingly.

RENNELL v. I.R.C.

Court of Appeal [1962] Ch. 329; [1961] 3 W.L.R. 1322; 105 S.J. 948; [1961] 3 All E.R 1028; affirmed by the House of Lords [1964] A.C. 173; [1963] 2 W.L.R. 745; 107 S.J. 232; [1963] 1 All E.R. 803 (also *post*, p. 533)

DONOVAN L.J.: . . . Nevertheless, in the end, one simply has to look at the words of the statute and construe them fairly and reasonably, and if such a construction yields anomalous results in particular cases, it is a common-place that they must be accepted, whether it be the Crown or the taxpayer who is thereby advantaged. . . .

(C) WHERE THE MEANING OF A STATUTORY PROVISION IS AMBIGUOUS, THE TAXPAYER MUST BE GIVEN THE BENEFIT OF THE DOUBT

This principle follows naturally from the principle that a tax must be expressly imposed upon the subject by clear words.

ADAMSON v. ATTORNEY-GENERAL

House of Lords [1933] A.C. 257; 102 L.J.K.B. 129; 49 T.L.R. 169; *sub nom. Att.-Gen* v. *Adamson* [1932] All E.R.Rep. 159; 148 L.T. 365

LORD WARRINGTON OF CLYFFE: . . . The section is one that imposes a tax upon the subject, and it is well settled that in such cases it is incumbent on the Crown to establish that its claim comes within the very words used, and if there is any doubt or ambiguity this defect—if it be in view of the Crown a defect—can only be remedied by legislation. . . .

I.R.C. v. ROSS AND COULTER (BLADNOCH DISTILLERY CO. LTD.)

House of Lords [1948] 1 All E.R. 616; [1948] W.N. 114; [1948] T.R. 77; *sub nom. Ross and Coulter* v. *I.R.C.*, 1948 S.C. 1; 1948 S.L.T. 303

LORD THANKERTON : . . . I cannot think that there can be much doubt as to the

---

[4] It is thought that Lord Simonds meant " avoiding " rather than " evading," see *post*, p. 26.

proper canons of construction of this taxing section. It is not a penal provision; counsel are apt to use the adjective " penal " in describing the harsh consequences of a taxing provision, but, if the meaning of the provision is reasonably clear, the courts have no jurisdiction to mitigate such harshness. On the other hand, if the provision is reasonably capable of two alternative meanings, the courts will prefer the meaning more favourable to the subject. If the provision is so wanting in clarity that no meaning is reasonably clear, the courts will be unable to regard it as of any effect. . . .

WILCOX v. SMITH

Court of Chancery (1857) 4 Drew. 49; 26 L.J.Ch. 596; 3 Jur.(N.S.) 604; 5 W.R. 667; 29 L.T.(O.S.) 235

SIR R. T. KINDERSLEY V.C.: The question is whether succession duty is payable? Now it is unquestionably a principle established in reference to Acts of Parliament of this kind imposing duties, that they must be construed strictly, and that, if the Act is ambiguous, the subject is entitled to the benefit of the doubt; but the principle is, not that the subject is to have that benefit if, upon any argument that the ingenuity of counsel can suggest, the Act does not appear perfectly accurate; but that if, after careful examination of all the clauses, a judicial mind shall entertain any reasonable doubt as to what the legislature intended, then the subject shall have the benefit of the doubt. . . .

Note
    A provision is not ambiguous simply because some other interpretation may be put upon it. If the court is satisfied that of two possible interpretations one is clearly the right one, the question of benefit of doubt does not arise—see the judgment of Megarry J. in *Bromilow and Edwards Ltd.* v. *I.R.C.* [1969] 1 W.L.R. 1180. Nor is a provision to be considered ambiguous merely because different judges have differed on the meaning of the words in dispute—see Viscount Simonds in *Kirkness* v. *John Hudson & Co. Ltd.* [1955] A.C. 696, 712 (*ante,* p. 6; *post,* p. 19) and Megarry J. in *Fleming* v. *Associated Newspapers Ltd.* [1972] Ch. 170.

(D) THERE IS NO EQUITY IN TAXATION

Unlike the previous principle, this proposition may operate either in favour of the taxpayer or against him.

PARTINGTON v. ATTORNEY-GENERAL

House of Lords (1869) L.R. 4 H.L. 100; 38 L.J.Ex. 205; 21 L.T. 370

LORD CAIRNS: . . . but I am bound to say that I myself have arrived, without hesitation, at the conclusion that the judgment ought to be affirmed.

I do so both upon form and also upon substance. I am not at all sure that, in a case of this kind—a fiscal case—form is not amply sufficient,[5] because, as I understand the principle of all fiscal legislation, it is this: If the person sought to be taxed comes within the letter of the law he must be taxed, however great the hardship may appear to the judicial mind to be. On the other hand, if the Crown, seeking to recover the tax, cannot bring the subject within the letter of the law, the subject is free, however apparently within the spirit of the law the case might otherwise appear to be. In other words, if there be admissible, in

---

[5] On the question of form and substance, see *post*, p. 21.

any statute, what is called an equitable construction, certainly such a construction is not admissible in a taxing statute, where you can simply adhere to the words of the statute. . . .

CAPE BRANDY SYNDICATE v. I.R.C.

King's Bench Division [1921] 1 K.B. 64; 90 L.J.K.B. 461; 125 L.T. 108; 37 T.L.R. 402; 65 S.J. 379; 12 T.C. 358 (also *post*, pp. 18, 149)

Rowlatt J.: . . . It is urged by Sir William Finlay that in a taxing Act clear words are necessary in order to tax the subject. Too wide and fanciful a construction is often sought to be given to that maxim, which does not mean that words are to be unduly restricted against the Crown, or that there is to be any discrimination against the Crown in those Acts. It simply means that in a taxing Act one has to look merely at what is clearly said. There is no room for any intendment. There is no equity about a tax. There is no presumption as to a tax. Nothing is to be read in, nothing is to be implied. One can only look fairly at the language used. . . .

Note
In the words of Lord Sands, " Equity and Income Tax are strangers "—*I.R.C.* v. *The Granite City Steamship Co. Ltd.* (1927) 13 T.C. 1, 16.

CANADIAN EAGLE OIL COMPANY LTD. v. THE KING

House of Lords [1946] A.C. 119; 114 L.J.K.B. 451; 173 L.T. 234; 61 T.L.R. 577; [1945] 2 All E.R. 499; 27 T.C. 205

The appellants claimed that where dividends on shares in a foreign company are paid to a shareholder resident in the United Kingdom, thus attracting income tax under Case V of Schedule D, relief from taxation should be given in so far as the income of the foreign company has already borne tax in the United Kingdom, *e.g.* on its trading profits here. The claim to relief was based upon an alleged necessity to avoid " double taxation."

Lord Russell of Killowen : . . . The theory that this species of double taxation gives rise to a claim to exemption from or repayment of tax must rest on some express enactment in the Income Tax Acts, or on some principle to be implied from those Acts, or to be found in the common law. Express provision there is none. . . .

Lord Thankerton : . . . It is clearly beyond the province of the courts either to correct hardship or afford justice by an implication which is not based on the language of the statute.

Re HODGE'S POLICY

Court of Appeal [1958] Ch. 239; [1957] 3 W.L.R. 958; 101 S.J. 920; [1957] 3 All E.R. 584; [1957] T.R. 281

A policy of life insurance had been effected by the deceased upon his own life and later assigned to his son more than twelve years before his death. The policy had been fully paid for more than forty years. Nevertheless, the proceeds of the policy were held to be liable to estate duty.

LORD EVERSHED M.R.: ... I associate myself entirely with all that I have read from that judgment.[6] There is no doubt about the facts of which the judge said that there was no doubt, and it is to me no less shocking than it was to him that in such a case duty should be exigible, as upon a passing on the death of the assured, on the sums payable under this policy.

Still, to be shocked is not to make a useful advance towards the solution of the problem presented to the court. If the language of the section imposes the duty, then it is the section and Parliament which have done the shocking thing, and it will likewise be for Parliament and the legislators of today, if they suffer a similar shock, to alter the law . . . . If the language used by Parliament is ambiguous or doubtful, it is no doubt legitimate to inquire, by reference to the surrounding circumstances, what was the mischief which Parliament was seeking to amend, and to get some assistance from the answer to that question in construing the section. . . .

ROMER L.J.: I agree. This claim for duty appears to me to be wholly devoid of any merit at all. . . .

Note
Largely as a result of this judicial criticism, a temporary extra-statutory concession was announced in 1958, since replaced by the Finance Act 1959, s. 34.

(E) WHERE THE MEANING OF THE STATUTE IS CLEARLY EXPRESSED, THE COURT WILL NOT HAVE REGARD TO ANY CONTRARY INTENTION OR BELIEF OF PARLIAMENT

It sometimes happens that the statute as worded does not carry out the known intention of the legislature, or that a piece of legislation was introduced in an erroneous belief as to the state of the existing law. Although the court is aware of the true intention of Parliament, the application of the principles (A) and (B) above requires the court to adhere firmly to the literal interpretation.

I.R.C. v. AYRSHIRE EMPLOYERS MUTUAL INSURANCE ASSOCIATION LTD.

House of Lords [1946] 1 All E.R. 637; 175 L.T. 22; 62 T.L.R. 317; *sub nom. Ayrshire Employers Mutual Insurance Association* v. *I.R.C.*, 27 T.C. 331 (*ante*, p. 5)

LORD MACMILLAN: ... My Lords, the respondent association was assessed to income tax on a sum of £13,492 for the year ended April 5, 1936. This sum represented the surplus arising from the association's transactions of mutual insurance with its members. The question of law for determination is formulated in the case stated by the Special Commissioners as follows:

Whether the surplus arising from transactions of insurance of the association with its members is assessable to income tax by virtue of section 31 (1) of the Finance Act 1933.[7] The Special Commissioners answered the question in the affirmative, but their decision was reversed by the First Division of the Court of

[6] Of Harman J. at first instance [1957] Ch. 339.
[7] See now I.C.T.A. 1970, s. 346.

Session on appeal. The Crown is now in turn the appellant in your Lordships' House.

The association was incorporated in 1898 as a company limited by guarantee. It has no share capital and its transactions are exclusively with its own members. Its purpose is to insure its members on the mutual principle against liability for injuries to their workmen. The constitution of the association is typical of mutual insurance companies and its familiar provisions are fully set out in the opinion of Lord Fleming. In a series of well known cases before the enactment of the Finance Act 1933, this House held that a mutual insurance company was not liable to be taxed in respect of a surplus arising from the excess of premiums contributed over claims met. The ground of these decisions was that such a surplus was not profit within the meaning of the Income Tax Acts, but merely represented the extent to which the contributions of those participating in the scheme had proved in experience to have been more than was necessary to meet their liabilities. The balance or surplus was the contributors' own money and returnable to them. Nothing had been earned and nobody had made a profit. Section 31 (1) of the Act of 1933 was passed after these decisions and no doubt in consequence of them.

Counsel for the appellants with engaging candour submitted that he ought to succeed because, although the subsection might not in terms fit the case, it was nevertheless manifest that Parliament must have intended to cover it; if it did not cover it, then he could not figure any case which it could cover and Parliament must be presumed to have intended to effect something. I can imagine what he would have said had the case been the converse one of a taxpayer pleading that although the words of the charging enactment covered his case, it was nevertheless manifest that Parliament could not have intended to tax him. With this deprecatory preface counsel endeavoured to attack the decision of the First Division.

The structure of section 31 (1) is quite simple. It assumes that a surplus arising from the transactions of an incorporated company with its members is not taxable as profits or gains. To render such a surplus taxable it enacts that the surplus, although in fact arising from transactions of the company with its members, shall be deemed to be something which it is not, namely a surplus arising from transactions of the company with non-members. The hypothesis is that a surplus arising on the transactions of a mutual insurance company with non-members is taxable as profits or gains of the company. But unfortunately for the Inland Revenue the hypothesis is wrong. It is not membership or non-membership which determines immunity from or liability to tax; it is the nature of the transactions. If the transactions are of the nature of mutual insurance, the resultant surplus is not taxable whether the transactions are with members or with non-members.

The argument for the Crown sought to make out that the expression " transactions with non-members " in the subsection meant transactions not of a mutual character and submitted that a mutual transaction with a non-member was a contradiction in terms. But this is a misconception. There is nothing to prevent a mutual insurance company entering into a contract of mutual insurance with a person who is not a member of the company. The argument will not fit the terms of the subsection. It is " those transactions," that is, mutual transactions with members, which are to be treated as if they were transactions, that is, mutual transactions, with non-members. But it is unnecessary to elaborate the point, for I find myself in complete agreement with the opinions expressed by the Lord President (Normand) and his brethren, which are as unanswerable as they are admirably lucid.

The legislature has plainly missed fire. Its failure is perhaps less regrettable than it might have been, for the subsection has not the meritorious object of preventing evasion of taxation, but the less laudable design of subjecting to tax as profit what the law has consistently and emphatically declared not to be profit. I should dismiss the appeal.

LORD SIMONDS: ... The case is an unusual one. The section under discussion, section 31 of the Finance Act 1933, is clearly a remedial section, if that is a proper description of a section intended to bring further subject-matter within the ambit of taxation. It is at least clear what is the gap that is intended to be filled and hardly less clear how it is intended to fill that gap. Yet I can come to no other conclusion than that the language of the section fails to achieve its apparent purpose and I must decline to insert words or phrases which might succeed where the draftsman failed.

I.R.C. v. DOWDALL O'MAHONEY & CO. LTD.

House of Lords [1952] A.C. 401; [1952] 1 T.L.R. 560; 96 S.J. 148; [1952] 1 All E.R. 531; 33 T.C. 259

An Irish company with branches in the United Kingdom paid Irish tax on the whole of its profits. It was assessed to United Kingdom excess profits tax on profits from its branches in the United Kingdom.

Held, although Parliament had, in enacting a particular provision, assumed that the foreign tax would be properly deductible as disbursements wholly or exclusively laid out for the purposes of trade (*post*, Chap. 9), this was not in law the case.[8]

LORD RADCLIFFE: ... What it comes to is this. Parliament has not made any enactment that requires or authorises the making of the allowances now claimed. It has not declared the law to be that such allowances are proper deductions. The most that can be said is that it is fairly certain that those who framed section 30 of the Finance Act 1940 believed that such allowances ought to be given or were in fact being given (which is not always quite the same thing in this field). But if that is all that can be said, it is, with all respect to the Court of Appeal, a misuse of words to say that the Law Courts ought to give effect to the " intention " of Parliament that overseas excess profits tax should be allowed. The beliefs or assumptions of those who frame Acts of Parliament cannot make the law. ...

I.R.C. v. HINCHY

House of Lords [1960] A.C. 748; [1960] 2 W.L.R. 448; 104 S.J. 188; [1960] 1 All E.R. 505; 38 T.C. 625

LORD REID: ... I do not propose to examine the other penalty provisions in the Act of 1952. It is no doubt true that every Act should be read as a whole, but that is, I think, because one assumes that in drafting one clause of a Bill the draftsman had in mind the language and substance of other clauses, and attributes to Parliament a comprehension of the whole Act. But where, as here, quite incongruous provisions are lumped together and it is impossible to suppose that anyone, draftsman or Parliament, ever considered one of these sections in light of another, I think that it would be just as misleading to base

---

[8] Thus a specific provision, *e.g.* in a double taxation convention, would be necessary in order to permit such a deduction.

conclusions on the different language of different sections as it is to base conclusions on the different language of sections in different Acts. As an example of incongruity I need only to refer to the admitted fact that the penalty in sections dealing expressly with fraud is less than the penalty under section 25 (if the appellants' construction of section 25 is right) for errors which may only be due to mistake.

I can now state what I understand to be the rival contentions as to the meaning of section 25 (3). The appellants contend that " treble the tax which he ought to be charged under this Act " means treble his whole liability to income tax for the year in question (less surtax and tax deducted at source, as I have already explained). It is not so easy to state the contrary contention briefly and accurately.

. . . Broadly, the contention is that it cannot have been intended that that which would have been chargeable in any event on the inaccurate return which was sent in should enter into the computation of the penalty, that the penalty must have been intended to have some relation to the offence, and that the tax which he ought to be charged must be the additional tax which he ought to be charged by reason of the discovery of the true state of affairs. Otherwise the penalty will often be grossly and extravagantly disproportionate to the offences. A man might be properly chargeable to £5,000 tax on his actual return and properly chargeable to £5,100 tax on the correct return. If the appellants are right the penalty would be £15,320: if the other view is right it would only be £320.

. . . Difficulties and extravagant results of this kind caused Diplock J. and the Court of Appeal to search for an interpretation which would yield a more just result. What we must look for is the intention of Parliament, and I also find it difficult to believe that Parliament ever really intended the consequences which flow from the appellants' contention. But we can only take the intention of Parliament from the words which they have used in the Act, and therefore the question is whether these words are capable of a more limited construction. If not, then we must apply them as they stand, however unreasonable or unjust the consequences, and however strongly we may suspect that this was not the real intention of Parliament.

. . . One is entitled and indeed bound to assume that Parliament intends to act reasonably, and therefore to prefer a reasonable interpretation of a statutory provision if there is any choice. But I regret that I am unable to agree that this case leaves me with any choice.

. . . The Act of 1952 is a consolidating Act, and one must presume that such an Act makes no substantial change in the previous law unless forced by the words of the Act to a contrary conclusion. Therefore, in interpreting a consolidating Act, it is proper to look at the earlier provisions which it consolidated.

. . . I find it impossible to hold that the words " not exceeding £20 and treble the tax which he ought to be charged under this Act " in section 107 (1) (a) of the Act of 1918 meant anything other than treble the whole tax which he ought to be charged for the relevant year. . . .

Note

Penalties are now governed by Part X, Taxes Management Act 1970. See in particular ss. 92 (2), 95 (2).

In the *Hinchy* case the Revenue subsequently announced that it was not intended to enforce the full amount of the penalty—see [1960] B.T.R. 1, 285. As a result of criticism, new provisions were introduced in the Finance Act 1960.

I.R.C. v. BATES

Court of Appeal [1965] 1 W.L.R. 1133; 109 S.J. 517; [1965] 3 All E.R. 64; 44 T.C. 225
(affirmed by House of Lords, *sub nom. Bates* v. *I.R.C.* [1968] A.C. 483; [1967] 2 W.L.R.
60; 111 S.J. 56; [1967] 1 All E.R. 84; 44 T.C. 252) (also *post*, p. 401)

Lord Denning M.R.: . . . Mr. Heyworth Talbot [Counsel for the taxpayers]
recognised that his contentions in this case rendered paragraphs meaningless or
ridiculous. If we gave them his interpretation, it would make nonsense of the
statute. But he exhorted us to take heart from the decision of the House of
Lords in *Inland Revenue Comrs.* v. *Ayrshire Employers Mutual Insurance
Association Ltd.*,[9] where the legislature "plainly missed fire." So here we
should give the words their literal interpretation heedless of what Parliament
intended. I cannot think this is right. It would reduce the interpretation of
statutes to a mere exercise in semantics. Whereas the object, as I have always
understood it, is to ascertain the intention of the legislature. This intention
must be discovered, of course, from the words which they have used. For the
words are the vehicle by which the meaning is conveyed. But the words must
be sensibly interpreted. We do not sit here to make nonsense of them. . . .

(F) Where the Meaning of the Statute is not Clear it Should, if
Possible, be Construed so as to Carry Out the Expressed or Presumed
Intention of Parliament

This proposition is in contrast to principle (E) above. If the words of the
statute are clear they must be adhered to; but if there is doubt as to the
meaning it is then legitimate to have regard to the intention of the legislature. This in turn appears to conflict with principles (A) and (C); but the
conflict is more apparent than real. If the particular provision can reasonably be read so as to mean what Parliament intended it to mean, then it will
be so read. It is only where it cannot be so read or where, having regard to
the intention of Parliament, ambiguity remains, that the taxpayer must be
given the benefit of the doubt.

ASTOR v. PERRY

House of Lords [1935] A.C. 398; 104 L.J.K.B. 423; 153 L.T. 1; 51 T.L.R. 325; 79 S.J. 231;
[1935] All E.R.Rep. 713; *sub nom. Perry* v. *Astor*, 19 T.C. 255

Lord Macmillan: . . . However anomalous an enactment may be, it must
be applied by the Courts according to its terms, unless these terms are susceptible,
according to the accepted canons of construction, of an interpretation which
avoids the anomalies.

. . . So far as the intention of an enactment may be gathered from its own
terms it is permissible to have regard to that intention in interpreting it, and
if more than one interpretation is possible that interpretation should be adopted
which is most consonant with and is best calculated to give effect to the intention
of the enactment as so ascertained. More especially, where two sections forming

9 [1946] 1 All E.R. 637; 27 T.C. 331; *ante*, p. 11.
    The approach of Lord Denning in this case may be seen as an example of a more
"liberal," or less strict, modern approach—see also *Luke* v. *I.R.C.* (*post*, pp. 16, 265).
This may be the case, particularly where there is an element of tax avoidance—see Chap. 2.

part of a single statutory code are found, when read literally, to conflict, a Court of construction may properly so read their terms as, if possible, to effect their reconciliation. . . .

LUKE v. I.R.C.

House of Lords [1963] A.C. 557; [1963] 2 W.L.R. 559; 107 S.J. 174; [1963] 1 All E.R. 655; 40 T.C. 630 (also *post*, p. 265)

LORD REID : . . . How, then, are we to resolve the difficulty? To apply the words literally is to defeat the obvious intention of the legislation and to produce a wholly unreasonable result. To achieve the obvious intention and produce a reasonable result we must do some violence to the words. This is not a new problem, though our standard of drafting is such that it rarely emerges. The general principle is well settled. It is only where the words are absolutely incapable of a construction which will accord with the apparent intention of the provision and will avoid a wholly unreasonable result, that the words of the enactment must prevail.

. . . If it is right that, in order to avoid imputing to Parliament an intention to produce an unreasonable result, we are entitled, and indeed bound, to discard the ordinary meaning of any provision and adopt some other possible meaning which will avoid that result, then what I am looking for in examining the obscure provision at the end of section 161 (1) is not its ordinary meaning (if it has one) but some possible meaning which will produce a reasonable result. I think that the interpretation which I have given is a possible interpretation and does produce a reasonable result, and therefore I adopt it.

. . . I cannot recollect ever having seen statutory provisions which lead to a more unreasonable result if read literally. I cannot believe that this can have been the intention either of Parliament or of the draftsman or of those who advise Parliament and instruct the draftsman. So the case for adopting a secondary meaning, if that is possible, is overwhelming. . . .

Note
   Cf. the remarks of Lord Reid in *Barclays Bank Ltd*. v. *I.R.C.* [1961] A.C. 509, 525, *post*, p. 517, and see *Fry* v. *I.R.C.* [1959] Ch. 86, *post*, p. 519.

BROWN v. NATIONAL PROVIDENT INSTITUTION

House of Lords (*ante*, p. 5; *post*, pp. 85, 205)

VISCOUNT CAVE : . . . It is no doubt true that if on the true construction of a statute, not excluding a taxing statute, a lacuna or defect appears, it is no part of the duty of the Court to supply the deficiency; but in choosing between two competing constructions, each of them possible, it is not irrelevant to consider that one of them is consistent with the obvious purpose of the Act while the other would render the statute capricious or abortive. . . .

(G) AMBIGUITY MAY BE RESOLVED BY SUBSEQUENT LEGISLATION

In certain circumstances it may be legitimate to consider a particular provision in the context of the statute which imposes it as a whole, and in the context of prior or subsequent taxing Acts, so that the provision is seen as a part of a wider scheme. A subsequent Act can amend an earlier one, in which case the Act *as amended* applies in future. It can even do so retrospectively. Alternatively, a subsequent Act may *declare* what is the meaning of an earlier provision, this having an effect akin to that of retrospective legislation. Neither course presents any special problem as regards interpretation. But a later statute may also be enacted on the basis that an existing provision has a particular meaning. In such a case, the later provision may be referred to as an aid to the interpretation of the earlier if there is an ambiguity in the earlier provision; but, as stated above, if the earlier provision is clear a subsequent enactment made under an erroneous belief cannot alter it.

ORMOND INVESTMENT COMPANY v. BETTS

House of Lords [1928] A.C. 143; 97 L.J.K.B. 342; 138 L.T. 600; [1928] All E.R.Rep. 709; 13 T.C. 400

It was held that section 26 of the Finance Act 1924 was founded on an erroneous assumption as to the effect of rule 1 of Case V of Schedule D in the Finance Act 1918. As the latter was unambiguous, the subsequent provision could not be referred to in interpreting the earlier.

LORD BUCKMASTER: . . . In the view that I have formed, the consideration of the question as to the effect of the subsequent statute does not become material, but the point has been dealt with by the Court of Appeal, and it is, therefore, not desirable that I should abstain from stating my opinion. I do not think that, in the circumstances of this case, the subsequent statute can properly be referred to for the purpose of interpreting the earlier. It is, of course, certain that Parliament can by statute declare the meaning of previous Acts. It would be competent for them to do so, even though their declaration offended the plain language of the earlier Act. It would be an unnecessary step to take, unless it were intended, contrary to the general principles of legislation, to make the explanatory Act retrospective, seeing that the subsequent statute could by independent enactment do what was desired.[10] It is also possible that where Acts are to be read together, as they are in this case, a provision in an earlier Act that was so ambiguous that it was open to two perfectly clear and plain constructions could, by a subsequent incorporated statute, be interpreted so as to make the second statute effectual, which is what the Courts would desire to do, and it is also possible that, where a statute has created a crime or imposed a penalty, a subsequent Act showing that that crime was intended to have a limited interpretation or the circumstances regarded as narrow in which the penalty attached, would be used for the purpose of giving effect to the well-known principle of construction to which I referred at an earlier stage.

. . . Now, there are several important distinctions between wills and codicils and successive Acts of Parliament.[11] In the first place, however long the will has preceded the codicil, they both operate from the same moment, and, by the ordinary rules of construction, are construed together. In an Act of Parliament this is not so. The first Act will operate from its fixed date, so that its inter-

---

[10] See, for example, Finance Act 1967, Sched. 11, para. 9, declaring the meaning of " with " in Finance Act 1965, Sched. 18, para. 6 (2) (*c*) and para. 6 (3)—now ss. 303 (5) (*c*) and 303 (6), I.C.T.A. 1970.
[11] Lord Buckmaster is dealing with arguments based on decisions concerning wills and codicils, which the appellants claimed to be analogous.

pretation becomes at once a matter of necessity, and great unfairness may ensue
if an interpretation which an Act of Parliament would fairly bear unaided by
subsequent statutes was inferentially changed by other words in a subsequent
Act. I find it difficult to assimilate the comparison between private individuals,
who are masters of their own estate, and the claims of beneficiaries under their
dispositions to the operations of a Legislature which apply equally to all His
Majesty's subjects.

. . . The case of *Cape Brandy Syndicate* v. *Inland Revenue Commissioners* [12]
follows in effect the case of *Attorney-General* v. *Clarkson*,[13] as is seen in the
following passage from the judgment of Lord Sterndale: " I think it is clearly
established in *Attorney-General* v. *Clarkson* that subsequent legislation on the
same subject may be looked to in order to see the proper construction to be put
upon an earlier Act where that earlier Act is ambiguous. I quite agree that
subsequent legislation, if it proceed upon an erroneous construction of previous
legislation, cannot alter that previous legislation; but if there be any ambiguity
in the earlier legislation then the subsequent legislation may fix the proper interpretation which is to be put upon the earlier." This is, in my opinion, an
accurate expression of the law, if by " any ambiguity " is meant a phrase fairly
and equally open to divers meanings, but in this case the difficulty is not due
to ambiguity but to the application of rules suitable for one purpose to another
for which they are wholly unfit. The only possible ambiguity is in considering
whether the words " as directed in Case I." are specially limited to the solitary
rule to which I have referred or to all rules applicable to Case I. This to my
mind is not ambiguous, and there is no need to have recourse to the later statute
for its interpretation.

But for the reasons I have given I think the appeal fails.

CAPE BRANDY SYNDICATE v. I.R.C.

King's Bench Division (*ante*, p. 10; *post*, p. 149)

ROWLATT J.: . . . Sir William Finlay drew my attention to a series of cases
which decided that an Act of Parliament does not alter the law by merely betray-
ing an erroneous opinion of it. But that principle does not cover this case. The
decisions cited by him were given in cases in which argumentatively and
indirectly it was suggested that Parliament thought the law to be different from
what it in fact was. Thus, where a statute enacted that a trader's shopbooks
should not be evidence above a year before action, it was held that that did not
make them evidence within the year, though Parliament thought that they were.
In the present case Parliament is saying that the two Acts—of 1915 and 1916—
are to be read together, and it provides that the tax shall be levied on businesses
of this character—that is, on post-war businesses.

I have come to the conclusion that section 45, subsection 2, of the Act of
1916 extends the scope of the Act of 1915. I must treat this exposition in the Act
of 1916 in the same way as if it had been given by a court binding upon me,
compelling me to construe the Act of 1915 in a way that I could not otherwise
have done. . . .

Note
    Rowlatt J.'s approach to the problem is quoted as an example of one type of approach.
It is not the only one, as is demonstrated by this rather complicated decision. In the Court
of Appeal ([1921] 2 K.B. 403), Lord Sterndale M.R. appears to agree with Rowlatt J., while
Scrutton L.J. and Younger L.J. arrive at a similar conclusion by a different route.

[12] [1921] 2 K.B. 403, C.A.   [13] [1900] 1 Q.B. 156.

KIRKNESS v. JOHN HUDSON & CO. LTD.

House of Lords (*ante*, p. 6)

VISCOUNT SIMONDS: . . . At an early stage in this opinion I indicated that I would have to refer to an argument founded on the provisions of later Acts. Two questions here arise: (1) whether it is legitimate to seek guidance from the later Acts in construing the earlier one, and (2) if it is, what light the later Acts throw upon the earlier one.

I must preface my consideration of these questions by a reference to the case of *Ormond Investment Co. Ltd.* v. *Betts*,[14] for at more than one point it is a direct authority upon the questions we have to decide. In the first place, I will quote a passage from Lord Buckmaster's speech.[15]

. . . In this case Lord Buckmaster was of opinion, as had been at least one of the members of the Court of Appeal, that the first contention of the Crown was right, and that the words of the earlier Act had the meaning they sought to put upon them. The other noble and learned Lords thought otherwise. It would have been easy then to say that, since judicial opinion differed as to the meaning of these words, there was such an ambiguity as to justify recourse to a later Act to resolve it. But the decision of this House was unanimously to the contrary. That means that each of one of us has the task of deciding what the relevant words mean. In coming to that decision he will necessarily give great weight to the opinion of others, but if at the end of the day he forms his own clear judgment and does not think that the words are " fairly and equally open to divers meanings " he is not entitled to say that there is an ambiguity. For him at least there is no ambiguity and on that basis he must decide the case.[16] So here, for me the meaning of section 17 of the Income Tax Act 1945, is clear beyond a peradventure, and I cannot look to later Acts for its meaning and effect.

. . . When an Act of Parliament becomes law, and its meaning is plain and unambiguous, a citizen is entitled to order his affairs accordingly, and to act upon the footing that the law is what it unambiguously is. He must be assumed to know that the law may be altered but, if so, he may be assumed to know also that it is contrary to the general principles of legislation in this country to alter the law retrospectively. He should know, too, that, if Parliament alters the existing law retrospectively, it does so by an amendment which is an express enactment, and above all he is surely entitled to be confident that it will not do so by force merely of an assumption or an allusion in a later Act. When the *Ormond* case was heard at first instance by Rowlatt J. he described an argument to the contrary as " a sinister and menacing proposition." So it is, and I hope that your Lordships will have none of it.

My Lords, it follows from what I have said that, even where two Acts are to be read together, it is not permissible to make what is clear in the earlier Act obscure and ambiguous by reference to something in the later Act. The contrary view would be in direct conflict with the decision of this House in the *Ormond* case. What, then, is meant, it may be asked, when it is said that the earlier and later Acts are to be read as one, and how is the decision in the *Ormond* case to be reconciled with what Lord Selborne said in *Canada Southern Railway Co.* v. *International Bridge Co.*? [17] My Lords, I think that the question is easily answered. In the first place, if the earlier Act contains such an ambiguity as I have described, then the proposition can be accepted in its widest sense and

---

[14] [1928] A.C. 143; *ante*, p. 17.
[15] This is substantially the passage quoted at p. 17, *ante*.
[16] See *Wilcox* v. *Smith*, *ante*, p. 9.
[17] (1883) 8 App.Cas. 723.

recourse can be had to the later to explain the earlier Act. But, secondly, if there is no ambiguity in the earlier Act, then the proposition must have a more limited meaning, and it will be the earlier Act to which recourse may be had to explain a provision of the later Act. It is upon the same principle that, where there has been a judicial interpretation of words in a statute, those words will be deemed to have the same meaning in a subsequent statute dealing with the same subject-matter. . . .

My Lords, I have looked at the later Acts to which the Attorney-General referred in order to satisfy myself that they do not contain a retrospective declaration as to the meaning of the earlier Act. They clearly do not, and I do not think that it has been contended that they do. At the highest it can be said that they may proceed upon an erroneous assumption that the word " sold " in section 17 (1) (a) of the Income Tax Act 1945 has a meaning which I hold it has not. . . . I return to the Act of 1945 and reaffirm that, according to the plain and unambiguous meaning of section 17 (1) (a), the respondent company did not sell its wagons to the British Transport Commission. . . .

CAMILLE AND HENRY DREYFUS FOUNDATION INC. v. I.R.C.

Court of Appeal [1954] Ch. 672; [1954] 3 W.L.R. 167; 98 S.J. 455; [1954] 2 All E.R. 466; 36 T.C. 126 (affirmed by House of Lords [1956] A.C. 39; [1955] 3 W.L.R. 451; [1955] 3 All E.R. 97)

The court was required to determine whether or not a corporation incorporated in the U.S.A. for charitable purposes was exempted from income tax on its United Kingdom royalties as a charity.

JENKINS L.J.: . . . At the request of the foundation the Special Commissioners stated a case for the opinion of the High Court on the following questions of law: " (a) whether the foundation, not being a body of persons established in the United Kingdom, is thereby precluded from exemption from tax under the provisions of section 37, Income Tax Act 1918; and (b) if the foundation is not so precluded, whether on the evidence set out in this case it is a body of persons established for charitable purposes only within the meaning of the said section 37."

. . . The consideration, which Lawrence J. regarded as constraining him to construe section 37 as he did,[18] was the legislative interpretation placed on section 37 by section 21 of the Finance Act 1923, which provided for the exemption of charities in the Irish Free State in respect of income tax for the year 1923–4, and by section 32 of the Finance Act 1924, and section 21 of the Finance Act 1925, which respectively provided for a like exemption for the years 1924–5 and 1925–6, 1926–7 and 1927–8, and finally by the Finance Act 1926, s. 23, and Part II of the Second Schedule to that Act which provided under paragraph 3 of the latter that " section 21 of the Finance Act, 1925, which grants an exemption for charities in the Irish Free State shall cease to have effect." To appreciate the force of this consideration it is necessary to read at length section 21 of the Finance Act 1923. [His Lordship read the section, and continued:]

It is clear that, for the purposes of this section and the subsequent legislation on the same topic, it was assumed that the exemption afforded by section 37 to bodies of persons or trusts established for charitable purposes only was limited to bodies of persons or trusts established in the United Kingdom, and that the secession of the Irish Free State from the United Kingdom would consequently

---

[18] By the decision of Wynn-Parry J. in *I.R.C.* v. *Gull* (1937) 21 T.C. 374.

have the effect of depriving bodies of persons or trusts established in the Irish Free State of the exemption in the absence of legislation continuing it in their favour.

We were referred to a number of authorities regarding the effect (if any) upon the construction of a given enactment of assumptions as to its meaning expressly or impliedly made in later legislation, not amounting to an amendment of the earlier enactment.

In *Ormond Investment Co. Ltd.* v. *Betts*,[19] Lord Buckmaster cited with approval the following passage from the judgment of Lord Sterndale M.R. in *Cape Brandy Syndicate* v. *Inland Revenue Commissioners* [20]:

. . . Having regard to the nature of the later enactments here in question, passed as they were to meet the peculiar situation created by the secession of the Irish Free State from the United Kingdom, and designed as they were to preserve, until such time as other arrangements were made, the exemption theretofore enjoyed by charitable institutions in that part of Ireland, I find it impossible to regard them as additions to or modifications of the income tax code which operated by way of necessary implication to restrict the application of the exemption provided for by section 37 (1) (*b*) to bodies and trusts established in the United Kingdom, if, apart from those enactments, the exemption was not upon its true construction so restricted. The framers of these enactments used language at least suggestive of a definite view that upon the true construction of section 37 the exemption would be lost by charities in the Irish Free State unless expressly preserved.

If a definite view to that effect is rightly to be imputed to the legislature, then I think the case would be within the principle stated by Lord Sterndale M.R. in the *Cape Brandy Syndicate* case [21] that " subsequent legislation, if it proceed upon an erroneous construction of previous legislation, cannot alter that previous legislation; but if there be any ambiguity in the earlier legislation then the subsequent legislation may fix the proper interpretation which is to be put upon the earlier." On the other hand, it is perhaps arguable that these enactments may have been the product of nothing more than a doubt as to how, in view of the secession of the Irish Free State from the United Kingdom, charitable institutions in that part of Ireland would stand as regards exemption from income tax, and were passed simply an ex abundanti cautela for the purpose of removing that doubt and preserving the status quo; and, if capable of being so explained, they could not be regarded as throwing any light on the construction of section 37. In my view, however, the former explanation is to be preferred to the latter, . . . Accordingly, I think that the enactments relating to Irish Free State charities, while not directly altering the construction or effect of section 37 of the Act of 1918, can properly be regarded as providing a legislative interpretation of section 37 to which recourse may legitimately be had for the purpose of resolving any ambiguity there may be in the construction of section 37 itself. . . .

(H) FORM AND SUBSTANCE

In applying the appropriate statutory provision to a given set of facts, the court will not go behind the form of the transaction or document concerned and have regard to the substance unless the form is a " mere sham."

[19] [1928] A.C. 143. *Ante*, p. 17.
[20] Quoted at p. 18, *ante*.
[21] [1921] 2 K.B. 403.

I.R.C. v. WESLEYAN AND GENERAL ASSURANCE SOCIETY

Court of Appeal [1946] 2 All E.R. 749; 62 T.L.R. 741; 176 L.T. 84; 90 S.J. 600; 30 T.C. 11

LORD GREENE M.R.: The appellants, the Wesleyan and General Assurance Society, appealed to the Special Commissioners against an assessment to income tax in respect of certain sums which had been paid by them to a policyholder, Charles Hart. The only question arising on this appeal is whether or not, on the true construction of the contractual documents executed between Hart and the society, and in view of the legal rights and obligations which these documents create, the sums so paid were payments of an annuity, or, as the society contends, merely loans. If the Crown is right, the payments attract income tax. If the society is right, income tax is not payable. The Special Commissioners decided, in favour of the society, that the payments were loans and not payments of an annuity. Macnaughten J. reversed that decision, and this appeal results.

It is, perhaps, convenient to call to mind some of the elementary principles which govern cases of this kind. The function of the court in dealing with contractual documents is to construe those documents according to the ordinary principles of construction, giving to the language used its normal, ordinary meaning save in so far as the context requires some different meaning to be attributed to it. Effect must be given to every word in the contract save in so far as the context otherwise requires. In considering tax matters a document is not to have placed on it a strained or forced construction in order to attract tax, nor is a strained or forced construction to be placed on it in order to avoid tax. The document must be construed in the ordinary way and the provisions of the relevant tax legislation then applied to it. If, on its true construction, it falls within a certain taxing category, then it is taxed. If, on its true construction, it falls outside the taxing category, then it escapes tax.

In dealing with income tax questions it frequently happens that there are two methods at least of achieving a particular financial result. If one of those methods is adopted, tax will be payable. If the other method is adopted, tax will not be payable. It is sufficient to refer to the common case where property is sold for a lump sum payable by instalments. If a piece of property is sold for £1,000 and the purchase price is to be paid in ten instalments of £100 each, no tax is payable. If, on the other hand, the property is sold in consideration of an annuity of £100 a year for ten years, tax is payable. The net result, from the financial point of view, is precisely the same in each case, but one method of achieving it attracts tax and the other method does not.

There have been cases in the past where what has been called " the substance of the transaction " has been thought to enable the court to construe a document in such a way as to attract tax. That doctrine was, I hope, finally exploded by the decision of the House of Lords in *Inland Revenue Comrs.* v. *Westminster (Duke)*.[22] The argument of the Crown in the present case, when really understood, appears to me to be an attempt to resurrect it. The doctrine means no more than that the language that the parties use is not necessarily to be adopted as conclusive proof of what the legal relationship is. That is, indeed, a common principle of construction. To take one example, where parties enter into a contract, though they describe it as a licence, but the contract, according to its true interpretation, creates the relationship of landlord and tenant, the parties can call it a licence as much as they like, but it will be a lease. There are other cases in the books in which the parties have described a particular document as a lease when the relationship created by it is that of licensor and

---

[22] [1936] A.C. 1; *post*, p. 23.

licensee. In those cases it is not a lease, but a licence. Similarly here, if the parties have entered into a contract, the legal result of which, on its true construction, is to create an annuity, the parties cannot avoid the legal consequences by referring to the payments as loans. . . .

LITTLEWOODS MAIL ORDER STORES LTD. v. I.R.C.

House of Lords [1963] A.C. 135; [1962] 2 W.L.R. 1228; 106 S.J. 351; [1962] 2 All E.R. 279; [1962] T.R. 107

LORD REID: My Lords, on Monday morning the Oddfellows Trustees held the freehold of a valuable property and Littlewoods held a lease of it with some 88 years to run at a rent of £23,444 which was much less than a rack-rent. On Saturday afternoon the freehold was held by a dummy company, Fork, owned by Littlewoods, the Oddfellows held a lease for 22 years and 10 days at a nominal rent, and Littlewoods held a sublease for 22 years at a rent of £42,450. The practical result was the same as if Oddfellows had simply sold the freehold to Littlewoods for 22 annual instalments of £42,450 secured on the property. But Littlewoods wished to minimise stamp duty so they and Oddfellows made no contract; they left it to their advisers to devise a method whereby Oddfellows would give up the freehold and become entitled to these annual payments. The result was a bizarre series of six deeds. But none of these deeds was a sham. Each had the effect which it purported to have, and if the parties chose to proceed in this way they were quite entitled to do so. There is no question of any of these deeds purporting to do something different from what the parties had agreed to do. So each must be stamped according to what it purported to do and in fact did.

POTTS' EXECUTORS v. I.R.C.

House of Lords (*ante*, p. 8; *post*, p. 399)

This case concerned what is now I.C.T.A. 1970, s. 451 (see *post*, p. 399). The question was whether sums paid by a company (whose shares he had settled) to discharge certain obligations of the settlor, in particular, payment of income tax owed by him, were paid directly or indirectly by way of loan to him. It was held that they were not.

LORD SIMONDS: . . . But this is not the way in which a taxing statute is to be read. I am not, in the construction of such a statute, entitled to say that, because the legal or business result is the same whether on the one hand I borrow money from the company and with it make certain payments, or on the other hand the company at my request makes certain payments on my implied promise to repay, therefore it is immaterial what words are in the statute if that result is attained. . . .

I.R.C. v. DUKE OF WESTMINSTER

House of Lords [1936] A.C. 1; 104 L.J.K.B. 383; 153 L.T. 223; 51 T.L.R. 467; 79 S.J. 362; [1935] All E.R.Rep. 259; *sub nom. Westminster (Duke)* v. *I.R.C.*, 19 T.C. 490

The Duke of Westminster executed a series of deeds in which he covenanted to pay certain of his employees weekly sums for a period of seven years or for the joint lives of the parties. The covenantees continued in their employment and continued to receive such sums as, together with the payments under the covenants, made up the amount of their wages before the deeds were executed.

The employees could have left their employment and still enforced the covenants; however, there was an " understanding " that an employee would not sue for full remuneration so long as he continued to receive the covenanted sums.

The Crown contended that the payments were, in reality, remuneration for services and could not be deducted from the Duke's total income for surtax purposes (the employees were not employed in any *business* by the Duke); the Duke contended that they were deductible as annual payments.[23]

LORD ATKIN: . . . It was not, I think, denied—at any rate it is incontrovertible—that the deeds were brought into existence as a device by which the respondent might avoid some of the burden of surtax. I do not use the word device in any sinister sense, for it has to be recognised that the subject, whether poor and humble or wealthy and noble, has the legal right so to dispose of his capital and income as to attract upon himself the least amount of tax. The only function of a Court of law is to determine the legal result of his dispositions so far as they affect tax. . . .

LORD TOMLIN: . . . Apart, however, from the question of contract with which I have dealt, it is said that in revenue cases there is a doctrine that the Court may ignore the legal position and regard what is called " the substance of the matter," and that here the substance of the matter is that the annuitant was serving the Duke for something equal to his former salary or wages, and that therefore, while he is so serving, the annuity must be treated as salary or wages. This supposed doctrine (upon which the Commissioners apparently acted) seems to rest for its support upon a misunderstanding of language used in some earlier cases. The sooner this misunderstanding is dispelled, and the supposed doctrine given its quietus, the better it will be for all concerned, for the doctrine seems to involve substituting " the incertain and crooked cord of discretion " for " the golden and streight metwand of the law." Every man is entitled if he can to order his affairs so as that the tax attaching under the appropriate Acts is less than it otherwise would be. If he succeeds in ordering them so as to secure this result, then, however unappreciative the Commissioners of Inland Revenue or his fellow taxpayers may be of his ingenuity, he cannot be compelled to pay an increased tax. This so-called doctrine of " the substance " seems to me to be nothing more than an attempt to make a man pay notwithstanding that he has so ordered his affairs that the amount of tax sought from him is not legally claimable.

. . . There may, of course, be cases where documents are not bona fide nor intended to be acted upon, but are only used as a cloak to conceal a different transaction. No such case is made or even suggested here. The deeds of covenant are admittedly bona fide and have been given their proper legal operation. They cannot be ignored or treated as operating in some different way because as a result less duty is payable than would have been the case if some other arrangement (called for the purpose of the appellants' argument " the substance ") had been made. . . .

Note

Recently, the courts appear to be more willing to go behind the machinery of a transaction and to have regard to its substance, *e.g. I.R.C.* v. *Land Securities Investment Trust* [1969] 1 W.L.R. 604 (H.L.) and *Littlewoods Mail Order Stores Ltd.* v. *McGregor* [1969]

[23] Annual payments of this nature are now treated as the income of the settlor: I.C.T.A. 1970, s. 458.

1 W.L.R. 1241 (C.A.). See R. S. Nock, " Form or Substance " [1969] B.T.R. 256; " Lifting the Veil " [1969] B.T.R. 323. See also *I.R.C.* v. *Mallaby-Deeley* [1938] 4 All E.R. 818 (*post*, pp. 76, 118).

The Estate Duty cases also reveal a tendency to place greater emphasis on the substance, rather than the form, of the transaction, see *post*, p. 453, notes 2 and 3, and the cases referred to therein.

The attitude in the *Westminster* case may be contrasted with that in a leading American case, *Gregory* v. *Helvering*, *infra*.

GREGORY v. HELVERING

Supreme Court of the United States (1935) 293 U.S. 465

MR. JUSTICE SUTHERLAND (delivering the opinion of the court): . . . In these circumstances, the facts speak for themselves and are susceptible of but one interpretation. The whole undertaking, though conducted according to the terms of subdivision (B), was in fact an elaborate and devious form of conveyance masquerading as a corporate reorganisation, and nothing else. The rule which excludes from consideration the motive of tax avoidance is not pertinent to the situation, because the transaction upon its face lies outside the plain intent of the statute. To hold otherwise would be to exalt artifice above reality and to deprive the statutory provision in question of all serious purpose.

Chapter 2

TAX AVOIDANCE

1. General Considerations

It is first necessary to draw the distinction between tax avoidance, which is lawful, and tax evasion, which is not.[1] The legality of tax avoidance is a direct consequence of the principles of interpretation of taxing statutes—that the taxpayer is entitled to rely upon the strict words of the statute. Whatever the morality of tax avoidance,[2] the legality of arranging one's affairs so as to minimise one's potential tax burden is undoubted. In consequence, it is scarcely necessary to attempt to define " tax avoidance " since, provided the taxpayer does not transgress the frontiers of legality, he is as entitled to minimise his tax as not to do so.

The term " avoidance " has, nevertheless, been employed in recent years in certain statutory provisions[3] and the motive of avoidance may also be relevant in other areas.[4] Tax avoidance has variously been described as " the art of dodging tax without actually breaking the law "[5] and " the lawfully carrying out of a transaction which was either entered into, or which took a particular form, for the purpose of minimising taxation."[6] It would seem that motive is an essential element in tax avoidance; a tax avoidance transaction is one which would not have been adopted if the tax-saving element had not been present.[7] But the intention to save tax does not of itself make a transaction into a tax avoidance transaction; not infrequently the legislature provides tax incentives to encourage particular transactions.[8] From the point of view of the Inland Revenue, tax avoidance is the *abuse* of the statutory provisions as opposed to their proper use, *i.e.* utilising the provisions for a purpose which was not intended or accepted by the Inland Revenue.

---

[1] Unfortunately, the courts have not always been too careful in drawing the distinction, sometimes saying " evasion " when " avoidance " is intended, *e.g. I.R.C.* v. *De Vigier* (1964) 42 T.C. 24, 35 and *post,* p. 404; *Potts' Executors* v. *I.R.C.* [1951] A.C. 443, 459 and *ante,* p. 8; *post,* p. 399; *Shop and Store Developments Ltd.* v. *I.R.C.* [1967] A.C. 472, 501–502; and see especially *Bates* v. *I.R.C.* [1968] A.C. 483, 503–504 and *ante,* p. 15, *post,* p. 401.

[2] And opinions differ on this, see *post,* pp. 32–34. See also P. F. Vineberg, " The Ethics of Tax Planning " [1969] B.T.R. 31 (a Canadian view) and A. A. Shenfield, " The Political Economy of Tax Avoidance " (1968) Institute of Economic Affairs, Occasional Paper No. 24.

[3] *Post,* p. 39.

[4] See, for example, *Re Weston's Settlements, post,* p. 35.

[5] G. S. A. Wheatcroft, " The Attitude of the Legislature and the Courts to Tax Avoidance " (1955) 18 M.L.R. 209.

[6] M. C. Flesch, " Tax Avoidance—the Attitude of the Courts and the Legislature " (1968) 21 *Current Legal Problems* 215.

[7] For an American view, see J. A. Young, " The role of Motive in evaluating tax-sheltered Investments " [1970] B.T.R. 156, 255. And see M. B. Angell, " Tax Evasion and Tax Avoidance," 38 *Columbia Law Review* 80.

[8] For example, certain forms of saving or investment in development areas.

FINAL REPORT OF THE ROYAL COMMISSION ON THE TAXATION OF PROFITS AND INCOME

1955 Cmd. 9474

CHAPTER 32

Tax Avoidance

General Considerations

1015. Avoidance of tax is a problem that faces every tax system and is likely to continue to do so when rates of tax are high and the burden of tax is seen to have a major influence upon the affairs of business and upon every aspect of social and personal life. Not all systems attempt to solve the problem in the same way, nor is there necessarily any large measure of agreement as to what is involved in the idea of tax avoidance. But until some certainty is reached upon this question of definition, the question as to what sort of steps should be taken to prevent or correct it remains an aimless one. We propose therefore to begin by discussing the meaning of tax avoidance in so far as the phrase is used to denote something which a tax system should be concerned to control.

1016. It is usual to draw a distinction between tax avoidance and tax evasion. The latter denotes all those activities which are responsible for a person not paying the tax that the existing law charges upon his income. *Ex hypothesi* he is in the wrong, though his wrongdoing may range from the making of a deliberately fraudulent return to a mere failure to make his return or to pay his tax at the proper time. By tax avoidance, on the other hand, is understood some act by which a person so arranges his affairs that he is liable to pay less tax than he would have paid but for the arrangement. Thus the situation which he brings about is one in which he is legally in the right, except so far as some special rule may be introduced that puts him in the wrong.

1017. The treatment of tax avoidance in the United Kingdom would present much less difficulty if it were possible to assert as a matter of general principle that a man owes a duty not to alter the disposition of his affairs so as to reduce his existing liability to tax or, alternatively, for the purpose or for the main purpose or partly for the purpose of bringing this result about. But there is no such general principle, and we are satisfied that it neither could nor ought to be introduced. First, it is too wide to be maintainable. Suppose that a man, influenced by the high rate of taxation on his marginal income, distributes some of his investments among adult members of his family to whom he had been in the habit of paying allowances out of his taxed income. Suppose that another man, similarly influenced, sells some of his income-yielding investments in order to put the proceeds into National Savings Certificates. Is either a case in which the man ought to be treated for tax purposes as if his income was still what it was before the transaction? Secondly, there is no true equity to support such a general principle. Taken at any one moment of time the affairs of different tax-payers are arranged in the most various forms and the extent to which they respectively incur a burden of tax may vary correspondingly. There is no reason to assume that the situation of any one tax-payer at that moment is the fairest possible as between himself and others differently situated: and if there is not, it seems wrong to propound any principle that would have the effect of fixing each tax-payer in his situation, without allowing him any chance of so altering his arrangements as to reduce his liability to assessment.

1018. In fact the prevailing doctrine in this country tends in the opposite direction. To quote from a speech made in the House of Lords in a surtax appeal: " Every man is entitled if he can to order his affairs so that the tax attaching under the appropriate Acts is less than it otherwise would be. If he succeeds in ordering them so as to secure this result, then, however unappreciative the Commissioners of Inland Revenue or his fellow tax-payers may be of his ingenuity, he cannot be compelled to pay an increased tax." [9] This principle, well known, must not be understood as going beyond what it says. It does mean that the taxing authorities and the courts of law, if appealed to, must take the law and the legal consequences of transactions as they find them and that they have no mandate to impute to a man an income that he does not legally possess merely because he has dispossessed himself of it in order to save tax. But it does not mean, on the other hand, that a man has any right violated or grievance inflicted if the statute law is so amended as to impute to him or to make it possible to impute to him for tax assessment an income larger than his legal one.[10] When these general principles are set against each other neither is seen to be of any assistance in identifying what are the special circumstances that justify such an imputation.

Individual incomes

1019. We propose to address ourselves first to the subject of tax avoidance in connection with the income of individuals. It seems to us that the kind of avoidance which the tax system should be protected against in this field can be defined with reasonable clarity if it is related to the final purpose of the system itself. That purpose is to assess each person upon his true income and to collect his share of tax accordingly. But, for the purpose of a progressive system, it is not enough to ascertain what income there is that is assessable; it is important to ascertain who is the real owner of each part of income. In some respects the legal system is inadequate to serve as a final determinant upon the question of real ownership if by real ownership we understand the effective control of the enjoyment and disposition of property. The complications introduced by the separate personality attributed to a corporation afford an obvious instance; for, but for the effect of special tax provisions, a man might transfer his land or business or investments to a corporation which he had formed and of which he owned virtually all the shares and yet maintain that the accruing income must be taxed as that of the corporation and had no connection with his own income for purposes of income tax or surtax. Again, our law of trusts or trustees makes it possible that a man can divest himself of income so that in law it belongs to another and yet retain the assurance that in practice it will be applied as he desires and for the satisfaction of purposes which he would otherwise have had to meet out of his own resources. These are only instances; but they have led us to conclude that the tax avoidance that should be struck at is to be found in those situations in which a man, without being in law the owner of income, yet has in substance the power to enjoy it or to control the disposition of it in his own interest. For it is in such situations that a man can be seen to be the effective owner of income, though he would not be liable, if legal forms alone were attended to, to pay his share of tax in respect of it. We do not go so far as to suggest that all such situations automatically involve an avoidance of tax that calls for intervention. They may be justified by good reasons of their own. But it seems fair to say that each such situation invites a careful scrutiny to see whether it has been brought about for any reason other than a desire to avoid the natural burden of tax.

[9] *I.R.C.* v. *Duke of Westminster* [1936] A.C. 1, 19. *Ante*, pp. 23–24.
[10] See *Latilla* v. *I.R.C.* [1943] A.C. 377, 381. *Post*, p. 34.

1020. If this conception is allowed to serve as a guiding principle, it assists to determine the kind of measures that the tax system should adopt to correct avoidance. The choice seems to lie between the enactment of some general provision which nullifies or controls the effect of transactions that violate the suggested principle, and the enactment of specific provisions which identify with precision the kind of transaction that is to be struck at and prescribe with corresponding precision the consequences that are to follow for the purposes of tax assessment.

1021. Hitherto United Kingdom legislation has followed in the main the second course. Over the period of the last 30 years there has been built up a very considerable structure of legislation dealing with particular forms of tax avoidance. It would be laborious, without being useful, to attempt to set down here any detailed account of these enactments, which are always complicated and often obscure. But it is possible to recognise three main categories distinguishable according to the kind of transaction or situation that is dealt with and we accordingly summarise below the purport of them. From this summary it is possible to see that they are all related with sufficient relevance to the main principle.

(1) By a series of sections, enacted between 1922 and 1938 [11] (to some of which we have already referred when discussing the alienation of income by covenant), the conditions have been laid down under which a man may effectively divest himself of income through the use of covenants, trusts or voluntary dispositions generally. Generally speaking, the divesting must not be for a period of less than 6 years and must not be revocable. In the case of settlements in favour of a child of the settlor, the income settled ranks as if it were still his income, so long as the child is an infant and unmarried, unless there is an irrevocable settlement of capital under which the income is accumulated and not paid out for the child's benefit. There are also provisions dealing with undistributed income under settlements in cases where the benefit of it could at any time accrue to the settlor or his wife; and in 1946 a special enactment was passed to secure that no disposition other than an out-and-out transfer of property with no interest in it retained should rank as an alienation of income for the purpose of the maker's surtax assessment if the income was (in effect) payable for the benefit of charities or for the benefit of the maker's own agents or employees.

(2) Between the years 1922 and 1939 a code of sections was built up in relation to devices for using the structure of the limited company to give a person the control or enjoyment of income without its formal ownership.[12] In the case of the investment company that is in a few hands the income from its investments is now treated as the income of its members and the Special Commissioners have full discretion to look beyond the legal ownership of shares in deciding who is to be treated as a member and to apportion the company's income for assessment purposes in accordance with this discretion. Moreover, income arising to such a company in liquidation can be treated, for surtax, as the income of its members. Apart from the special system for these private investment companies, there is a much wider set of provisions that cover all companies that are in a few hands, these companies being defined as those which are under the control of five persons or less and in which the public are not substantially interested. Both the word

---

[11] Now I.C.T.A. 1970, Pt. XVI, ss. 434–459.
[12] Now I.C.T.A. 1970, Pt. XI, Chap. III, ss. 282–303.

"control" and the word "person" are given very extensive statutory definitions in this context. For instance, a man's relatives or nominees count as the same person as himself. If such a company—it is convenient to refer to them as "close corporations"—withholds an unreasonably large proportion of its income from distribution among its members, the Special Commissioners have authority to direct that the whole of the company's income is to be treated as the income of its members and apportioned among them for the purpose of their surtax assessments. The test to be applied is whether a reasonable amount of the income has been distributed having regard to the company's business requirements, including requirements necessary or advisable for the maintenance and development of the business.

(3) In the Finance Acts of 1936 and 1938 provisions were introduced for countering the loss of revenue that arose from schemes by which persons resident in this country transferred investments or other property to a company or trust abroad, so that the income became income of a person resident abroad, while the equivalent of the income was returned to the transferor or a member of his family or a nominee of his by some method of payment that did not rank as income in his hands.[13] A scheme of this sort gave the recipient the substance of income without liability to surtax: whether he escaped income tax as well depended upon the nature of the property transferred. In either event such schemes were flagrant devices by which rich men were enabled to get out of their responsibilities. The form of legislation adopted in this case is to define not the type of transaction that is to be struck at but the situation itself. Broadly, the law says that where there has been a transfer of assets whereby income has become payable to persons not resident or domiciled in the United Kingdom and an individual ordinarily resident in the United Kingdom has "power to enjoy" the income, that income is to be deemed for tax purposes to be the income of the individual who has the power to enjoy it. The phrase "power to enjoy" is given by statute a very comprehensive significance. There is provision to the effect that the special legislation does not apply to a bona fide commercial transaction not designed for the purpose of tax avoidance or to any transfer which did not include such avoidance among its purposes.

1022. These are the three main categories of anti-avoidance legislation. But an account of them does not, on the other hand, give even a summary picture of the whole range of that legislation, which covers what may be regarded as merely precautionary provisions (such as section 237 of the Income Tax Act 1952,[14] which deals with the surtax assessment of an individual who has carried out sales of securities cum dividend, or section 241 of the same Act,[15] which permits disallowance for surtax assessment of interest on money borrowed to pay an assurance premium) as well as provisions in which the motive of the avoider is more directly in point.

1023. Here, then, is a detailed set of rules specially enacted by Parliament to counter particular devices and to deal with particular situations. There are not inconsiderable objections to such a method of handling a problem so comprehensive as tax avoidance. Since, as we have said, the pressure to find ways of lessening the personal burden of taxation is strong and continuous,

---

[13] Now I.C.T.A. 1970, Pt. XVII, Chap. III, ss. 478–481.
[14] Now I.C.T.A. 1970, s. 30.
[15] Now I.C.T.A. 1970, ss. 403, 404.

it is to be expected that new gaps will be found in the hedge as old ones are stopped up and that the code will contain an increasingly lengthy and complicated set of provisions as time goes on. Indeed, the mere attempt to deal with particular transactions with particular provisions is of some assistance to the avoider, because it defines for him the obstacle that he must be ingenious to get round. And to meet this the statutory provisions come to be expressed in language that is more and more vague and imprecise in the hope of covering some unforeseen situation. Even at this stage of development it is very difficult for anyone who does not belong to a small body of experts to say exactly what proceedings are within and what outside the scope of avoidance legislation. Much the same could be said about other branches of the tax code. But such obscurity remains a defect wherever encountered, not the less because the class of persons affected may not deserve sympathy: and we thought it desirable therefore to enquire whether it might be better to approach this whole subject in a different way by prescribing some simple definition that would serve to separate the transactions that were not to be allowed to have their ostensible legal effect, for tax purposes, from other transactions.

1024. For instance, in the E.P.D. legislation that accompanied the war of 1914–18 it was enacted that " A person shall not, for the purpose of avoiding payment of excess profits duty, enter into any fictitious or artificial transaction or carry out any fictitious or artificial operation." [16] The objection to a criterion based on phrases of this kind is that if a transaction really is fictitious it ought to be ignored, without the aid of special legislation; and a transaction is not well described as " artificial " if it has valid legal consequences, unless some standard can be set up to establish what is " natural " for the same purpose. Such standards are not readily discernible. We may compare a provision of this kind with the scheme that is now in force in Canada. Under this the Treasury Board (a Committee of the Cabinet) has power to decide that one of the main purposes of a transaction was " improper " avoidance or reduction of taxes (improper avoidance not necessarily connoting illegality) and to give directions to counteract the avoidance or reduction, subject to appeal to the Exchequer Court of Canada. On similar lines is another provision that disallows deductions in respect of a disbursement or expense in respect of a transaction or operation that if allowed would " unduly or artificially " reduce the income. Or, again, another kind of general regulation is to be found in Article 1 of the Netherlands Law (April 29, 1925), for the Promotion of the Correct Assessment of Direct Taxes, which runs as follows: " In the assessment of the direct State taxes, legal transactions are not taken into account if it must be assumed—by reason of the fact that they have not aimed at a material modification of the existing circumstances or by reason of other specific acts or circumstances—that they would not have been entered into but for the fact that liability for any of the said taxes, in the event of it having been applied or being likely to be applied, would be avoided either in whole or in part for the future."

1025. A survey of the tax systems of several other countries suggests to us that the usual course is to approach the problem on the lines of some general declaration of principle governing tax avoidance—though the principles are not necessarily easy to interpret for those who are not accustomed to the way that they are applied in practice—and to leave the application of the principle and the consequential tax adjustments to the decision of a special tribunal, subject in most cases to some appeal to a court of law. In some cases this course has avowedly been taken because of the impossibility of foreseeing all possible methods of avoidance, and it has been felt that if they are to be countered the

[16] Finance (No. 2) Act 1915, s. 44 (3).

only thing to do is, in effect, to hand over the individual and his tax assessment
to the discretion of a tribunal appointed for the purpose. The United Kingdom
seems to have been singular in trying to maintain a regular control of avoidance
by specific enactments that identify more or less precisely the cause of offence
and, in some, but not all, cases actually prescribe what is to be the consequential
adjustment.

1026. When we came to contrast the one system with the other the advantages and disadvantages could not easily be weighed in the abstract. The United
Kingdom system does preserve the conception that a person's liability to pay
taxes should be imposed in explicit terms and with the authority of Parliament.
It does make it possible that there should be some informed discussion and
criticism of specific proposals advanced by the Chancellor of the Exchequer
before they become law. We think that those are advantages of great importance; all the more so because, as we have tried to show, avoidance is not a
word of exact meaning or at any rate does not denote an activity which is in all
contexts obnoxious. The cost of the present system is represented in part by
additions to the tax code that are certainly prolix and sometimes obscure. If
it was also represented by any considerable measure of failure to control the
progress of avoidance, we think that it might be necessary to suggest a different
and more radical approach to the problem on the lines pursued in other
countries. But our general impression is that there has not been any failure of
this sort.

1027. The Board are not dissatisfied with the position that has now been
reached. They think it probable that the main heads of possible avoidance
have been covered by existing legislation, and they regard the control established
by that legislation as reasonably satisfactory. Other devices will no doubt appear
from time to time, just as there are some known of now as to which the
Board have not recommended intervention mainly because they are not of a
scale or significance to justify it. Such devices can best be dealt with by new
legislation directed to them, if they become important enough. We do not refer
to them in detail since there is no advantage in describing what we do not
positively recommend for action. But the Board's general conclusion is that
" future devices are more likely to be related to new taxes or new relieving provisions or to be capable of use only in narrow and specialised fields." They do
not think that the introduction of some general anti-avoidance provision is
desirable or necessary.

2. Judicial Attitudes to Tax Avoidance [17]

I.R.C. v. FISHER'S EXECUTORS

House of Lords [1926] A.C. 395; 95 L.J.K.B. 487; 134 L.T. 681; 42 T.L.R. 340; 10 T.C. 329

LORD SUMNER : . . . My Lords, the highest authorities have always recognised
that the subject is entitled so to arrange his affairs as not to attract taxes imposed
by the Crown, so far as he can do so within the law, and that he may legitimately claim the advantage of any express terms or of any omissions that he
can find in his favour in taxing Acts. In so doing he neither comes under
liability nor incurs blame. . . .

[17] For fuller consideration of this topic, see Wheatcroft, op. cit. note 5, ante; Flesch, op. cit.
note 6, ante; Farnsworth, Income Tax Case Law (1947), Chap. 6. The extracts from
judgments quoted in this section have been selected as examples of various, typical,
attitudes. Consider also the attitudes displayed in the " dividend-stripping " cases, post,
pp. 135–140.

LEVENE v. I.R.C.

House of Lords [1928] A.C. 217; 97 L.J.K.B. 377; 139 L.T. 1; 44 T.L.R. 374; 72 S.J. 270; [1928] All E.R.Rep. 746; 13 T.C. 486 (also *post*, pp. 49, 438, 444)

VISCOUNT SUMNER: . . . It is trite law that His Majesty's subjects are free, if they can, to make their own arrangements, so that their cases may fall outside the scope of the taxing Acts. They incur no legal penalties and, strictly speaking, no moral censure if, having considered the lines drawn by the Legislature for the imposition of taxes, they make it their business to walk outside them. . . .

Note
The facts of the case are contained in the extract quoted at *post*, p. 438.

AYRSHIRE PULLMAN MOTOR SERVICES v. I.R.C.[18]

Court of Session (1929) 14 T.C. 754

The case concerned a partnership agreement, whereby a Mr. Ritchie, who had hitherto been sole owner of a transport business, agreed to share the profits with his five children, to the great improvement of the position of the family as a whole in relation to the Inland Revenue.

Held, the agreement was not a fraud or sham and, from the date of the agreement, Mr. Ritchie was taxable only on his share of the partnership profits.

THE LORD PRESIDENT (CLYDE): . . . So far as my point of view is concerned, the agreement is neither better nor worse for that reason. No man in this country is under the smallest obligation, moral or other, so to arrange his legal relations to his business or to his property as to enable the Inland Revenue to put the largest possible shovel into his stores. The Inland Revenue is not slow— and quite rightly—to take every advantage which is open to it under the taxing statutes for the purpose of depleting the taxpayer's pocket. And the taxpayer is, in like manner, entitled to be astute to prevent, so far as he honestly can, the depletion of his means by the Revenue. . . .

LORD VESTEY'S EXECUTORS v. I.R.C.

House of Lords [1949] 1 All E.R. 1108; [1949] W.N. 233; 31 T.C. 1 (also *post*, p. 391)

LORD NORMAND: . . . Parliament in its attempts to keep pace with the ingenuity devoted to tax avoidance may fall short of its purpose. That is a misfortune for the taxpayers who do not try to avoid their share of the burden, and it is disappointing to the Inland Revenue. But the court will not stretch the terms of taxing Acts in order to improve on the efforts of Parliament and to stop gaps which are left open by the statutes. Tax avoidance is an evil, but it would be the beginning of much greater evils if the courts were to overstretch the language of the statute in order to subject to taxation people of whom they disapproved. . . .

Note
This case, and the two cases which follow, was concerned with section 18 of the Finance Act 1936 which attempted to prevent avoidance by a U.K. resident transferring property to a

[18] *Cf. Dickenson* v. *Gross* (1927) 11 T.C. 614, *post*, p. 410.

non-resident and, in return, deriving some enjoyment from that property abroad. The provisions, which have been reinforced from time to time as new " loopholes " become apparent, are now contained in I.C.T.A. 1970, ss. 478–481.

LATILLA v. I.R.C.

House of Lords [1943] A.C. 377; 112 L.J.K.B. 158; 168 L.T. 411; 59 T.L.R. 163; 87 S.J. 101; [1943] 1 All E.R. 265; 25 T.C. 107

VISCOUNT SIMON L.C.: My Lords, of recent years much ingenuity has been expended in certain quarters in attempting to devise methods of disposition of income by which those who were prepared to adopt them might enjoy the benefits of residence in this country while receiving the equivalent of such income without sharing in the appropriate burden of British taxation. Judicial dicta may be cited which point out that, however elaborate and artificial such methods may be, those who adopt them are " entitled " to do so. There is, of course, no doubt that they are within their legal rights, but that is no reason why their efforts, or those of the professional gentlemen who assist them in the matter, should be regarded as a commendable exercise of ingenuity or as a discharge of the duties of good citizenship. On the contrary, one result of such methods, if they succeed, is, of course, to increase pro tanto the load of tax on the shoulders of the great body of good citizens who do not desire, or do not know how, to adopt these manœuvres. Another consequence is that the legislature has made amendments to our income tax code which aim at nullifying the effectiveness of such schemes. The question in the present appeal is whether section 18 of the Finance Act 1936 has the result of checkmating the design of avoiding income tax and sur-tax which was the main purpose of certain highly artificial dispositions made in 1933. . . .

LORD HOWARD DE WALDEN v. I.R.C.

Court of Appeal [1942] 1 K.B. 389; 111 L.J.K.B. 273; [1942] 1 All E.R. 287; 25 T.C. 121

LORD GREENE M.R.: . . . The section is a penal one, and its consequences, whatever they may be, are intended to be an effective deterrent which will put a stop to practices which the legislature considers to be against the public interest. For years a battle of manœuvre has been waged between the legislature and those who are minded to throw the burden of taxation off their own shoulders on to those of their fellow subjects. In that battle the legislature has often been worsted by the skill, determination and resourcefulness of its opponents of whom the present appellant has not been the least successful. It would not shock us in the least to find that the legislature has determined to put an end to the struggle by imposing the severest of penalties. It scarcely lies in the mouth of the taxpayer who plays with fire to complain of burnt fingers. . . .

3. Judicial Participation in Tax Avoidance

Not only have the courts recognised the legality of tax avoidance and generally displayed an attitude of tolerance, if not of approval, but in certain instances, positive assistance has been given in minimising taxation. Thus judges, in exercise of their powers under section 64 of the Settled Land Act 1925, section 57 of the Trustee Act 1925, and what is now section 4 of the

Matrimonial Proceedings and Property Act 1970, have authorised the variation of settlements or dealing with trust property in such a way as to reduce tax or estate duty liability. More especially, the powers conferred by the Variation of Trusts Act 1958 have mostly been used for the purpose of reducing such liability.[19]

Re RALLI'S SETTLEMENTS

Court of Appeal [1965] Ch. 286; [1964] 3 W.L.R. 1240; 108 S.J. 857; [1964] 3 All E.R. 780; [1964] T.R. 317; 43 A.T.C. 377

RUSSELL L.J.: I wish at the outset to make this general observation. The question in every estate duty case is whether the Crown demonstrates that the circumstances fall within the ambit of a relevant charging provision. The fact that a settlement is drawn with a view to avoiding particular charging provisions is neither reprehensible, nor a proper ground for inclination to a conclusion that it ought to come within those or some other charging provisions. It is not right to label something a " device " and then strain to see that it fails. The question remains that which I have stated. These principles equally apply to cases in which ingenuity in avoiding a charge to estate duty is not confined to the framing of the original settlement, but extends to subsequent transactions. If by an adjustment or variation of beneficial interests a small group can avoid contributing, say, £100,000 to the Crown out of their own pockets, they are well entitled to do so. If any moral criticism could be levelled at them, then the consciences of the judges of the Chancery Division, in the exercise of their discretionary jurisdiction under the Variation of Trusts Act 1958, would be in a sorry state. . . .

Note
In this context, the remarks of Lord Morton of Henryton in *Chapman* v. *Chapman* [1954] A.C. 429, 468, when the powers under the Variation of Trusts Act 1958 did not exist, make most interesting reading.

Re WESTON'S SETTLEMENTS

Chancery Division [1969] 1 Ch. 223; [1968] 2 W.L.R. 1154; [1968] 1 All E.R. 720; [1968] T.R. 215; affirmed by the Court of Appeal [1969] 1 Ch. 234; [1968] 3 W.L.R. 786; 112 S.J. 641; [1968] 3 All E.R. 338; [1968] T.R. 295

STAMP J.: . . . The immediate purpose of this application is to produce a result under which the whole of the assets of the two English settlements will be removed from the jurisdiction of this court and from the clutches of the Commissioners of Inland Revenue and made subject to a Jersey settlement or settlements, such settlements being framed to produce or to reproduce the trusts of the two English settlements which they will respectively replace. As a result of the transaction, the English settlements will no longer comprise any property at all, and this result is to be achieved by a somewhat delicate operation, the immediate result of which, it is said, will avoid a liability or potential liability for a very large sum of capital gains tax. First, this court is asked, in exercise of its jurisdiction under section 41 of the Trustee Act 1925, to appoint two professional gentlemen of the highest reputation resident in Jersey to be trustees of

---

[19] See J. W. Harris, " Ten Years of Variation of Trusts " (1969) 33 *Conveyancer* (N.S.) 113, 183, especially pp. 191–194; G. R. Bretten, " Tax Avoidance and the Variation of Trusts Act " (1968) 32 *Conveyancer* (N.S.) 194.

the English settlements in place of the three existing individual trustees, two of whom are resident in England and the third of whom is the wife of Mr. Stanley Weston. The court is then asked to exercise its jurisdiction under the Variation of Trusts Act 1958 by approving, on behalf of Mr. Alan Clive Weston and the infant son of Mr. Robert Lawrence Weston, and all persons unborn or unascertained who may hereafter become beneficially interested under the settlements, a variation of both settlements by inserting in each of them a power for the two new Jersey trustees, after the expiration of three months, to discharge the trust property from the trusts of that English settlement and to subject it to the trusts of a new Jersey settlement containing, as I have indicated, almost precisely the same or precisely the same beneficial trusts as are at present contained in the two English settlements.

. . . I will assume, following the decisions to which I have referred,[20] that I have the necessary jurisdiction to take this course.

This, however, leaves open the serious question whether, on the facts of this case, the court ought, in the exercise of its jurisdiction, to countenance the proposals which are put before it. The benefits sought to be achieved by the orders that I am invited to make are, to all intents and purposes, entirely of a fiscal character. The fiscal advantages which are envisaged are, as I understand them, these: first of all, as to capital gains tax, under section 25 (1) of the Finance Act 1965, it is provided as follows:

> "In relation to settled property, the trustees of the settlement shall for the purposes of this Part of this Act be treated as being a single and continuing body of persons (distinct from the persons who may from time to time be the trustees), and that body shall be treated as being resident and ordinarily resident in the United Kingdom unless the general administration of the trusts is ordinarily carried on outside the United Kingdom and the trustees or a majority of them for the time being are not resident or not ordinarily resident in the United Kingdom: . . ."

What is anticipated is that after an appropriate period, which, as I have already mentioned, is three months, the trustees will be able to claim that within the meaning of the subsection which I have just read the general administration of the trusts is ordinarily carried on outside the United Kingdom, and unquestionably the trustees will then not be resident or ordinarily resident in the United Kingdom.

If the shares in the company, Stanley Weston Group Limited were sold today and in existing circumstances, a liability to capital gains tax amounting to no less than £163,000 would be attracted. If I approved the proposals which are put before me, the effect would be, so it is said, that if the shares were disposed of after the interval to which I have referred, the trustees will not be accountable for that sum. Furthermore, provided that the beneficiaries are, as I understand it, neither resident nor ordinarily resident in the United Kingdom during the year of assessment in which the shares are disposed of, none of them will be personally liable for capital gains tax.

Estate duty on the deaths of the two principal beneficiaries will also be avoided if the proposals are sanctioned, or so, at any rate, it is submitted. Under section 28 of the Finance Act 1949 exemption is conferred from estate duty in respect of property passing on death if the property is not situate in the United Kingdom and it is shown that the proper law regulating the devolution of property or the disposition under or by reason of which it passes is the law neither of England nor of Scotland, and one of the conditions following is satisfied. Among those conditions is the condition that the property passes

---

[20] In particular *Re Seale's Marriage Settlement* [1961] Ch. 574; [1961] 3 W.L.R. 262.

under or by reason of a disposition made by a person who, at the date at which the disposition took effect, was domiciled elsewhere than in some part of Great Britain. What is said is that once these transactions have been carried out, the proper law regulating the devolution of the property will be that of Jersey and that, provided the property is not brought back to the United Kingdom—there is no difficulty there, because a small company can be formed in Jersey for the purpose of holding the trusts' funds—the new settlements will have been made by a person who, at the date at which the disposition took effect, was domiciled elsewhere than in some part of Great Britain. What is said is that these new Jersey settlements will have been made by the existing tenants for life and the infant child of Robert Lawrence Weston, all of whom, it is said, are now domiciled outside the United Kingdom, and by the persons unascertained and unborn who are, one would think, at least not domiciled in the United Kingdom.

It is to be noted, in connection with the avoidance of estate duty, that by the effect of the contemplated transaction the large claims for duty which, it is thought, will ultimately be avoided on the respective deaths of the principal beneficiaries will be achieved in the case of Mr. Robert Lawrence Weston, now aged twenty-five, even if he at the end of a further twelve weeks in Jersey should come to the conclusion that that island is a less desirable place than the first two months led him to believe, and should change his declared intention of living out the rest of his life there and dying there, and should again return to the United Kingdom. Similarly, if Mr. Alan Clive Weston, when he is a little older, were to find that life as an employee in one of his father's hotels in Jersey was less satisfactory than a life, however penurious, in this country, and determined to come and live in this country, he would have the happy advantage that when, in the course of nature, he died, the fund—subject to the trusts of the voluntary settlement—would pass to his children unravaged by claims for duty.

This court is not the watch-dog of the Commissioners of Inland Revenue, and day after day variations of trusts are sanctioned which will, on the one hand, provide a tenant for life with capital instead of income, and, on the other, mitigate the burden of duty which would otherwise be payable on his death and would fall upon his children. But there must, in my judgment, be some limit to the devices which this court ought to countenance in order to defeat the fiscal intentions of the legislature. In my judgment, these proposals overstep that limit. The facts of this case are, in my view, wholly different from the facts with which Buckley J. had to deal in *Re Seale's Marriage Settlement*. There Buckley J. said this [21] : " The evidence establishes to my satisfaction that the husband and the wife intend to continue to live in Canada. . . ." As regards the present case I am by no means satisfied that any of the beneficiaries intend to continue to live in the Channel Islands. He went on: ". . . that their children who are living in Canada and have been brought up as Canadians are likely to continue to live in Canada. . . ." That, of course, does not apply in this case; none of the beneficiaries have any ties whatsoever with the island of Jersey. Buckley J. goes on: ". . . and that it will be for the general advantage of all the beneficiaries that the administrative difficulties and the difficulties of other kinds which result from the fact that it is an English settlement and the beneficiaries all reside in Canada should be brought to an end; . . ."

I am not satisfied that any administrative difficulties, or difficulties other than the fiscal difficulties with which all Her Majesty's subjects are confronted, exist in this case. In the present case the family have only just moved to Jersey, and I draw the inference from the facts that the purpose of this family exodus—or its principal purpose—is the avoidance of taxation. Of course, the family are

[21] [1961] Ch. 574 at p. 579; [1961] 3 All E.R. 136 at p. 139.

perfectly entitled to make their permanent home in Jersey for the purpose of avoiding taxation, and if this family had settled there I might well think it right to accede to the application, though I would remark in passing that there are certain difficulties in connection with the law of Jersey in relation to trusts which leave me in some doubt whether the courts of that island are so well adapted as the courts in this country to administer such trusts as are found in English settlements. But the family has not been in Jersey for more than a few months and I do not on the evidence accept that any member of it could possibly establish that he is now domiciled in Jersey.

To vest all the assets subject to a settlement in trustees outside the jurisdiction is, I think, a strong thing to do. To allow those assets to be made subject to a settlement over which the court has no control is a stronger thing. Where the beneficiaries have only been in that other country a few short months and one of the purposes of the transaction is to obtain an exemption from estate duty which the legislature has thought fit to grant in respect of foreign settlements, I am not persuaded that I ought, in the exercise of the discretion of the court, to countenance the proposals. The objection to so doing would be made apparent if, in fact, Mr. Robert Lawrence Weston did, so soon as the capital gains tax liability had been avoided by a disposal of the assets, in fact abandon his home in Jersey and return to this country. I am not persuaded that this application represents more than a cheap exercise in tax avoidance which I ought not to sanction, as distinct from a legitimate avoidance of liability to taxation. . . .

LORD DENNING M.R. [on appeal] : . . . Two propositions are clear : (i) In exercising its discretion, the function of the court is to protect those who cannot protect themselves. It must do what is truly for their benefit. (ii) It can give its consent to a scheme to avoid death duties or other taxes. Nearly every variation that has come before the court has tax avoidance for its principal object : and no one has ever suggested that this is undesirable or contrary to public policy.

But I think it necessary to add this third proposition : (iii) The court should not consider merely the financial benefit to the infants or unborn children, but also their educational and social benefit. There are many things in life more worth while than money. One of these things is to be brought up in this our England, which is still " the envy of less happier lands." [22] I do not believe it is for the benefit of children to be uprooted from England and transported to another country simply to avoid tax. It was very different with the children of the Seale family, which Buckley J. considered. That family had emigrated to Canada many years before, with no thought of tax avoidance, and had brought up the children there as Canadians. It was very proper that the trust should be transferred to Canada. But here the family had only been in Jersey three months when they presented this scheme to the court. The inference is irresistible : the underlying purpose was to go there in order to avoid tax. I do not think that this will be all to the good for the children. I should imagine that, even if they had stayed in this country, they would have had a very considerable fortune at their disposal, even after paying tax. The only thing that Jersey can do for them is to give them an even greater fortune. Many a child has been ruined by being given too much. The avoidance of tax may be lawful, but it is not yet a virtue. The Court of Chancery should not encourage or support it—it should not give its approval to it—if by so doing it would imperil the true welfare of the children, already born or yet to be born.

There is one thing more. I cannot help wondering how long these young people will stay in Jersey. It may be to their financial interest at present to make

[22] Shakespeare, *Richard II*, Act II, Scene I.

their home there permanently. But will they remain there once the capital gains are safely in hand, clear of tax? They may well change their minds and come back to enjoy their untaxed gains. Is such a prospect really for the benefit of the children? Are they to be wanderers over the face of the earth, moving from this country to that, according to where they can best avoid tax? I cannot believe that to be right. Children are like trees: they grow stronger with firm roots.

The long and short of it is, as the judge said,[23] that the exodus of this family to Jersey is done to avoid British taxation. Having made great wealth here, they want to quit without paying the taxes and duties which are imposed on those who stay. So be it. If it really be for the benefit of the children, let it be done. Let them go, taking their money with them. But, if it be not truly for their benefit, the court should not countenance it. It should not give the scheme its blessing. The judge refused his approval. So would I. I would dismiss this appeal.

HARMAN L.J.: This is an essay in tax avoidance naked and unashamed, and none the worse for that, says the applicant. Indeed the judge agreed that this court is not the watch-dog of the Inland Revenue, and it is well known that much and perhaps the main use which has been made of the [Variation of Trusts] Act [1958] has been to produce schemes of variation of English trusts which will have the effect of reducing the liabilities either on capital of the trusts or the income of the beneficiaries.

Nevertheless this scheme on its facts goes beyond any of which I have experience and obviously needs careful scrutiny by the court. The two settlements were only made in the year 1964, and it is not suggested that their terms have produced any difficulty or inconvenience or that they need any alteration. This therefore is not a scheme for variation of the trusts but for removing them bodily from the United Kingdom and setting them up elsewhere.

. . . In the circumstances the judge was entitled to consider whether the court " should think fit " to accede to the scheme. The judge professed himself unsatisfied, and I think he was entitled to take that view. It is true that he expressed some dislike of tax avoidance of this sort, and in that he may have been mistaken, but he was in my opinion well justified in not being satisfied that a transfer of the whole trust to Jersey is expedient. . . .

Note
    The attitude of Stamp J. suggests that the courts may sometimes recognise two classes of tax-avoidance—the respectable and the " device "; *cf.* Lord Wilberforce's dissenting view in *Mangin* v. *I.R.C.* (*post*, p. 42) where he asks: " Is there a distinction between ' proper ' tax avoidance and ' improper ' tax avoidance? By what sense is this distinction to be perceived? " [1971] 1 All E.R. 179 at p. 190. See also the note, by J. G. M., " Drawing the Line Somewhere " [1968] B.T.R. 198. N.B. *Re Whitehead's Will Trusts* [1971] 1 W.L.R. 833.

4. Anti-avoidance Legislation

A recurring theme in cases concerned with tax avoidance is the continuing struggle between the legislature on the one hand and the ingenious taxpayer and his advisers on the other. In introducing provisions designed to impose tax, the legislature will seek to ensure that such provisions are effective and to block all potential " loopholes." The various methods of doing so are

[23] Stamp J.

discussed by the Royal Commission on the Taxation of Profits and Income.[24] These methods may be considered under the following heads:

(A) Specific Provisions

Such provisions are the most common type. The charge to tax is imposed in certain circumstances or upon certain transactions, whether or not there was any motive of tax avoidance. A typical example of such legislation is contained in the Settlements provisions,[25] referred to in the Royal Commission Report.[26] Thus, the net may be cast so widely that perfectly " innocent " transactions may be caught.

(B) Specific Anti-avoidance Provisions

Such provisions are aimed at particular types of transaction when such transaction is entered into for the purpose of tax avoidance, but not otherwise. Most of the provisions contained in Part XVII of the Income and Corporation Taxes Act 1970 are of this type, in particular those provisions designed to cancel a tax advantage obtained from transactions in securities.[27] In construing such provisions, the Court must have regard to the *motive* of the taxpayer and must also determine what amounts to " tax avoidance " or a " tax advantage."

I.R.C. v. PARKER

House of Lords [1966] A.C. 141; [1966] 2 W.L.R. 486; 110 S.J. 91; [1966] 1 All E.R. 399; 43 T.C. 396

Lord Wilberforce: . . . For this purpose it is necessary to look carefully at the definition of tax advantage in section 43 (4) (g)[28] as

" a relief or increased relief from, or repayment or increased repayment of, income tax, or the avoidance or reduction of an assessment to income tax or the avoidance of a possible assessment thereto, whether the avoidance or reduction is effected by receipts accruing in such a way that the recipient does not pay or bear tax on them, or by a deduction in computing profits or gains."

Can these words fairly be applied to the debentures? In my opinion, they cannot. The paragraph, as I understand it, presupposes a situation in which an assessment to tax, or increased tax, either is made or may possibly be made, that the taxpayer is in a position to resist the assessment by saying that *the way in*

---

[24] 1955 Cmd. 9474, paras. 1020–1027. *Ante*, p. 29. Other valuable discussions of the possible methods appear in G. S. A. Wheatcroft, " The Attitude of the Legislature and the Courts to Tax Avoidance " (1955) 18 M.L.R. 209, and M. C. Flesch, " Tax Avoidance—the Attitude of the Courts and the Legislature " (1968) 21 *Current Legal Problems* 215.

[25] Now Chap. XVI of the I.C.T.A. 1970 (ss. 434–459).

[26] *Op. cit.*, para. 1021 (1). *Ante*, p. 29. See especially the cases concerning s. 451, *I.R.C.* v. *Bates* (*ante*, p. 15 and *post*, p. 401); *Potts' Executors* v. *I.R.C.* (*ante*, pp. 8, 23 and *post*. p. 399) and *De Vigier* v. *I.R.C.* (*post*, p. 404).

[27] I.C.T.A. 1970, ss. 460–477.

[28] Now I.C.T.A. 1970, s. 466 (1).

which he received what it is sought to tax prevents him from being taxed on it; and that the Revenue is in a position to reply that if he had received what it is sought to tax *in another way* he would have had to bear tax. In other words, there must be a contrast as regards the " receipts " between the actual case where these accrue in a non-taxable way with a possible accruer in a taxable way, and unless this contrast exists, the existence of the advantage is not established. . . .

CLEARY v. I.R.C.

House of Lords [1968] A.C. 766; [1967] 2 W.L.R. 1271; 111 S.J. 277; [1967] 2 All E.R. 48; [1967] T.R. 57; 44 T.C. 399

VISCOUNT DILHORNE: . . . That the appellant received £60,500 in such a way that she did not pay or bear tax on it, is not disputed. It could have been distributed to her by way of dividend and, if it had been, she would have been liable to tax. There is thus in this case the contrast to which Lord Wilberforce referred.[29] It is clear that in consequence of a transaction in securities she avoided a possible assessment to income tax, the possible assessment being that which would have been made if she had received the sum by way of dividend. She therefore obtained a tax advantage within the meaning of the section. . . .

I.R.C. v. BREBNER

House of Lords [1967] 2 A.C. 18; [1967] 2 W.L.R. 1001; 111 S.J. 216; [1967] 1 All E.R. 779; [1967] T.R. 21; 43 T.C. 705; 1967 S.C. 31; 1967 S.L.T. 113

LORD UPJOHN: . . . My Lords, I would only conclude my speech by saying, when the question of carrying out a genuine commercial transaction, as this was, is reviewed, the fact that there are two ways of carrying it out—one by paying the maximum amount of tax, the other by paying no, or much less, tax—it would be quite wrong, as a *necessary* consequence, to draw the inference that, in adopting the latter course, one of the main objects is, for the purposes of the section, avoidance of tax. No commercial man in his senses is going to carry out a commercial transaction except upon the footing of paying the smallest amount of tax that he can. The question whether in fact one of the main objects was to avoid tax is one for the Special Commissioners to decide upon a consideration of all the relevant evidence before them and the proper inferences to be drawn from that evidence. . . .

Note
For a similar view, see Cross J. in *I.R.C.* v. *Kleinwort Benson Ltd.* [1969] 2 Ch. 221 at pp. 237–238. See also *I.R.C.* v. *Brown* [1971] 1 W.L.R. 1495.

(C) GENERAL ANTI-AVOIDANCE PROVISIONS

This type of provision, which seeks to nullify the effect of tax avoidance transactions in general, was considered and rejected by the Royal Commission.[30] Such provisions have been considered by the Privy Council in appeals from Commonwealth countries and the decisions are most instructive.

[29] In the passage in *I.R.C.* v. *Parker* quoted above.
[30] 1955 Cmd. 9474, paras. 1024–1027. *Ante*, p. 31.

NEWTON v. COMMISSIONER OF TAXATION OF THE COMMONWEALTH OF AUSTRALIA

Privy Council [1958] A.C. 450; [1958] 3 W.L.R. 195; 102 S.J. 544; [1958] 2 All E.R. 759; *sub nom. Newton* v. *Federal Commissioner of Taxation,* 37 A.T.C. 245

LORD DENNING (delivering the judgment of their Lordships): In these days, when rates of tax are high, it is natural enough for a man to seek so to order his affairs that the tax attaching under the appropriate Acts is less than it otherwise would be. In England there is no general provision against it, but special provisions have been enacted so as to counter particular devices and to deal with particular situations. In Australia there is a general provision [31] which is said to cover " tax avoidance," and it comes now before their Lordships for the first time.

. . . In order to bring the arrangement within the section you must be able to predicate—by looking at the overt acts by which it was implemented—that it was implemented in that particular way so as to avoid tax. If you cannot so predicate, but have to acknowledge that the transactions are capable of explanation by reference to ordinary business or family dealing, without necessarily being labelled as a means to avoid tax, then the arrangement does not come within the section. . . .

Note
The arrangement in question involved an increase of capital by a company accompanied by a capital payment to shareholders out of undistributed profits. It was held to be an " arrangement " within the meaning of section 260 and to be " absolutely void " as against the Commissioner.

MANGIN v. I.R.C.

Privy Council [1971] A.C. 739; [1971] 2 W.L.R. 39; 114 S.J. 910; [1971] 1 All E.R. 179; [1970] T.R. 249; 49 A.T.C. 272

LORD DONOVAN (delivered the majority opinion): . . . The appellant, a farmer in New Zealand, desired to reduce his burden of income tax. After seeking the advice of his accountant and solicitor he created what is called a " paddock trust."

This involved his leasing in 1965 25 acres of his farm of 385 acres to trustees. These 25 acres were sown with wheat. The trustees were to hold the land for one year at a rent of £3 per acre and were to cultivate it. Under a separate trust deed any resulting income was to be held on trust for the appellant's wife and children.

The appellant himself, as the employee of the trustees, harvested and sold the ensuing wheat crop and accounted to the trustees for the proceeds. The trustees paid him for his labour and certain expenses which he had incurred. They then distributed the bulk of the net income so remaining in their hands to the appellant's wife, partly for herself and partly for the benefit of his children.

In 1966 a similar transaction took place in relation to another 24 acres which were ready to be sown with wheat. These were leased to the trustees at £4 an acre. The appellant again sowed and reaped the crop as employee of the trustees, and again sold it and accounted to the trustees for the proceeds. They reimbursed him as before for his labour and expenses. Once more the bulk of

[31] Australian Commonwealth Income Tax and Social Services Contribution Act 1936–1951, s. 260.

the net income so accruing to the trustees was distributed by them under the still existing trust deed for the benefit of the appellant's wife and children.

By these transactions part of what would have been the appellant's total income from his farm was hived off and became (via the trustees) the income of his wife and children. This meant that each of the beneficiaries could claim allowances and reduced rates of tax. Thus the appellant mitigated what would otherwise have been his burden of tax. The " spreading of the liability " led to less tax being paid on the profits of the whole 385 acres.

The respondent made amended assessments on the appellant for the years ending March 31, 1966 and 1967, with the object of restoring the appellant's income tax liability to what it would have been for these years but for these " paddock trusts." Against these amended assessments the appellant appealed to the Supreme Court in New Zealand and won. In the Court of Appeal, however, he lost; and now appeals to this Board.

The respondent justified the amended assessments in terms of section 108 of the Land and Income Tax Act 1954 (" the Act of 1954 "). This reads:

"Every contract, agreement, or arrangement made or entered into, whether before or after the commencement of this Act, shall be absolutely void in so far as, directly or indirectly, it has or purports to have the purpose or effect of in any way altering the incidence of income tax, or relieving any person from his liability to pay income tax."

If this section has the effect contended for by the commissioner then the " paddock trusts " must be considered as non-existent. The appellant concedes that in that event the amended assessments would stand because he received the disputed income into his own hands and would be unable to contend that it belonged to trustees. The " annihilating effect " of section 108 does not, in other words, here produce the kind of difficult problem which arose in *Peate* v. *Comr. of Taxation of the Commonwealth of Australia*,[32] and which led to a dissenting judgment of the Board in that case.

The appellant contends, however, that section 108 has no effect in this case for the following reasons:

First, because it has no fiscal effect but operates only as between the parties to the contract, agreement or arrangement.

Second, because if the section does have fiscal effect, that effect is confined to cases where liability to income tax has already accrued.

Third, because in any event the section can operate only on income derived by the taxpayer.

Fourth, because if all else fails, the facts of the present case take it outside the ambit of the section.

These contentions pose the question of the true construction of section 108. Its history will be outlined presently; but it may be useful to recall at the outset some of the rules of interpretation which fall to be applied.

First, the words are to be given their ordinary meaning. They are not to be given some other meaning simply because their object is to frustrate legitimate tax avoidance devices. As Turner J. says in his (albeit dissenting) judgment in *Marx* v. *Inland Revenue Comrs.*,[33] moral precepts are not applicable to the interpretation of revenue statutes.

Secondly, ". . . one has to look merely at what is clearly said. There is no room for any intendment. There is no equity about a tax. There is no presumption as to tax. Nothing is to be read in, nothing is to be implied. One can only look fairly at the language used ": *per* Rowlatt J. in *Cape Brandy*

32 [1967] 1 A.C. 308; [1966] 3 W.L.R. 246.
33 [1970] N.Z.L.R. 182 at p. 208.

Syndicate v. *Inland Revenue Comrs.*,[34] approved by Viscount Simonds L.C. in *Canadian Eagle Oil Co. Ltd.* v. *The King*.[35]

Thirdly, the object of the construction of a statute being to ascertain the will of the legislature, it may be presumed that neither injustice nor absurdity was intended. If therefore a literal interpretation would produce such a result, and the language admits of an interpretation which would avoid it, then such an interpretation may be adopted.

Fourthly, the history of an enactment and the reasons which led to its being passed may be used as an aid to its construction.

. . . The second contention of the appellant is that section 108 refers only to accrued liabilities to tax and not to liabilities which may be expected in futuro. It is said that no contract, agreement or arrangement can alter the incidence of income tax, for that is prescribed by law.[36] This expression in section 108 must therefore be taken to refer to some contract, agreement or arrangement which shifts the burden of some accrued liability to tax. There is, however, another possible meaning. The taxpayer, considering the provisions of fiscal legislation, may discern that by entering into some arrangement he can so distribute the legal incidence of tax on his income that he himself will pay less. In other words the economic incidence is altered. In their Lordships' view this is what is contemplated by section 108.

. . . Both sides relied upon the decision of the Board in *Newton* v. *Comr. of Taxation of the Commonwealth of Australia*.[37] This was a decision upon section 260 of the Australian Income Tax and Social Services Contribution Act 1936–1951—a section apparently copied from section 82 of the New Zealand Act of 1900 above quoted. The judgment was delivered by Lord Denning and in the course of it he said:

> " In order to bring the arrangement within the section, you must be able to predicate—by looking at the overt acts by which it was implemented— that it was implemented in that particular way so as to avoid tax. If you cannot so predicate, but have to acknowledge that the transactions are capable of explanation by reference to ordinary business or family dealing, without necessarily being labelled as a means to avoid tax, then the arrangement does not come within the section."

In their Lordships' view this passage, properly interpreted, does not mean that every transaction having as one of its ingredients some tax saving feature thereby becomes caught by a section such as section 108. If a bona fide business trans-action can be carried through in two ways, one involving less liability to tax than the other, their Lordships do not think section 108 can properly be invoked to declare the transaction wholly or partly void merely because the way involving less tax is chosen. Indeed, in the case of a company, it may be the duty of the directors *vis-à-vis* their shareholders so to act. Again, trustees may in the interests of their beneficiaries, deliberately choose to invest in government securities issued with some tax-free advantage, and to do so for the express purpose of securing it. They do not thereby fall foul of section 108. The clue to Lord Denning's meaning lies in the words " without necessarily being labelled as a means to avoid tax." Neither of the examples above given could justly be so labelled. Their Lordships think that what this phrase refers to is, to adopt the language of Turner J. in the present case,

---

[34] [1921] 1 K.B. 64 at p. 71; *ante*, p. 10.
[35] [1946] A.C. 119; *ante*, p. 10.
[36] A similar argument was considered in *Bromilow and Edwards Ltd.* v. *I.R.C.* [1969] 1 W.L.R. 1180; [1970] 1 W.L.R. 128.
[37] [1958] A.C. 450; *ante*, p. 42.

" a scheme . . . devised for the sole purpose, or at least the principal purpose, of bringing it about that this taxpayer should escape liability on tax for a substantial part of the income which, without it, he would have derived."

The present case clearly exhibits such a scheme; and for the reasons above set out their Lordships will humbly advise Her Majesty that the appeal should be dismissed. . . .

CHAPTER 3

FACT AND LAW

An appeal against an assessment to tax [1] may be made to the General or
Special Commissioners, whose decisions are not reported, and thence, by way
of Case Stated, on a point of law only, to the High Court.[2]

1. The Distinction Between Fact and Law

The distinction between questions of fact and of law is vital, since the
decision of the Commissioners as to the facts is conclusive. To this end, a
distinction is often made between findings of " primary facts " and " conclusions " or " inferences," which may be findings of fact, of law, or
" mixed " findings of fact and law. Since the case stated by the Commissioners should set out the primary facts as found, followed by the conclusions arrived at from those facts, the question for the court on appeal is
whether, given the primary facts stated, the Commissioners were justified
in law in reaching the conclusions they did reach.[3]

BRITISH LAUNDERERS' RESEARCH ASSOCIATION v.
BOROUGH OF HENDON RATING AUTHORITY

Court of Appeal [1949] 1 K.B. 462; [1949] L.J.R. 416; 65 T.L.R. 103; 93 S.J. 58; *sub nom.*
British Launderers' Research Association v. *Central Middlesex Assessment Committee and*
Hendon Rating Authority, 113 J.P. 72; [1949] 1 All E.R. 21; 47 L.G.R. 113

On an appeal from Quarter Sessions with regard to a claim for rating
exemption.

DENNING L.J.: ... Mr. Rowe says, however, that quarter sessions came to
a conclusion of fact in his favour with which the Divisional Court should not
have interfered. On this point it is important to distinguish between primary
facts and the conclusions from them. Primary facts are facts which are observed
by witnesses and proved by oral testimony or facts proved by the production of
a thing itself, such as original documents. Their determination is essentially a
question of fact for the tribunal of fact, and the only question of law that can
arise on them is whether there was any evidence to support the finding. The

---

[1] *i.e.* Income Tax, Corporation Tax or Capital Gains Tax—T.M.A. 1970, ss. 31, 118 (1).
An appeal in respect of liability for Estate Duty is made direct to the High Court, or to
the Lands Tribunal if the dispute is as to the value of land.

[2] For descriptions of appeal procedures, see esp. P. W. de Voil, *Tax Appeals* (1969) and
W. A. Wilson, " The Appeal by Case Stated " [1969] B.T.R. 231.

[3] The distinction is considered at length in the following (*inter alia*): A. Farnsworth,
" Fact or Law in Cases Stated under the Income Tax Acts " (1946) 62 L.Q.R. 248; W. A.
Wilson, " A Note on Fact and Law " (1963) 26 M.L.R. 609; " Questions of Degree "
(1969) 32 M.L.R. 361; C. Morris, " Law and Fact " (1941–42) 55 Harv.L.R. 1303; L. B.
Jaffe, " Judicial Review—Questions of Law " (1955–56) 69 Harv.L.R. 239.

conclusions from primary facts are, however, inferences deduced by a process of reasoning from them. If, and in so far as, those conclusions can as well be drawn by a layman (properly instructed on the law) as by a lawyer, they are conclusions of fact for the tribunal of fact: and the only questions of law which can arise on them are whether there was a proper direction in point of law; and whether the conclusion is one which could reasonably be drawn from the primary facts: see *Bracegirdle* v. *Oxley*.[4] If, and in so far, however, as the correct conclusion to be drawn from primary facts requires, for its correctness, determination by a trained lawyer—as, for instance, because it involves the interpretation of documents or because the law and the facts cannot be separated, or because the law on the point cannot properly be understood or applied except by a trained lawyer—the conclusion is a conclusion of law on which an appellate tribunal is as competent to form an opinion as the tribunal of first instance. . . .

Note
   The case was not, of course, a tax appeal from the Commissioners, but is instructive for the analysis of fact and law. The courts in tax cases have tended to ignore analogous decisions from other areas, *e.g.* appeals from magistrates, county courts and workmen's compensation cases. But see *Usher's Wiltshire Brewery Ltd.* v. *Bruce* [1915] A.C. 433 (H.L.), *post*, p. 168.

GRIFFITHS v. J. P. HARRISON (WATFORD) LTD.

House of Lords [1963] A.C. 1; [1962] 2 W.L.R. 909; 106 S.J. 281; [1962] 1 All E.R. 909;
   sub nom. Harrison (J. P.) (Watford) Ltd. v. *Griffiths*, 40 T.C. 281 (also *post*, p. 129)

As to whether a " dividend-stripping " transaction carried out by the taxpayers constituted an " adventure in the nature of trade."

LORD DENNING: . . . Now the powers of the High Court on an appeal are very limited. The judge cannot reverse the Commissioners on their findings of fact. He can only reverse their decision if it is " erroneous in point of law." Now here the primary facts were all found by the Commissioners. They were stated in the case. They cannot be disputed. What is disputed is their conclusion from them. And it is now settled,[5] as well as anything can be, that their conclusion cannot be challenged unless it was unreasonable, so unreasonable that it can be dismissed as one which could not reasonably be entertained by them. It is not sufficient that the judge would himself have come to a different conclusion. Reasonable people on the same facts may reasonably come to different conclusions, and often do. Juries do. So do judges. And are they not all reasonable men? But there comes a point when a judge can say that no reasonable man could reasonably come to that conclusion. Then, but not till then, he is entitled to interfere. It is just like the position in the old days with juries when questions arose whether goods were " necessaries," whether words were " defamatory " or whether conduct was " negligent." It was a question of law for the judge to rule whether the inference *could* reasonably be drawn, but a question of fact for the jury whether it *ought* to be drawn. Likewise we have nowadays the cases before magistrates whether a speed was " dangerous," or before the Lands Tribunal whether part of a plant was " in the nature of a structure," or before the Commissioners of Inland Revenue whether a transaction was an " adventure in the nature of trade." It is a question of law for the judge whether the conclusion *could* reasonably be drawn, but, given that it

4 [1947] K.B. 349.
5 By the House of Lords in *Edwards* v. *Bairstow*, *post*, pp. 51, 145.

could reasonably be drawn, it is a question of fact for the tribunal whether it *ought* to be drawn. . . .

Note
This was a dissenting judgment, but it is believed that the analysis contained in this passage reflects accurately the attitude of their Lordships as a whole. Lord Reid, however, perhaps takes a wider view of the scope of " law " as opposed to " fact ": see [1963] A.C. 1, 15–16.

I.R.C. v. FRASER

Court of Session (1942) 24 T.C. 498; 1942 S.C. 493

The Court of Session reversed a finding of the Commissioners that the purchase and resale by a woodcutter of a large quantity of whisky in bond did not constitute an " adventure in the nature of a trade."

THE LORD PRESIDENT (NORMAND): . . . Therefore, it is now authoritatively decided, as far as this Court is concerned, that these matters are open to review. In cases where it is competent for a tribunal to make findings in fact which are excluded from review, the Appeal Court has always jurisdiction to intervene if it appears either that the tribunal has misunderstood the statutory language—because a proper construction of the statutory language is a matter of law—or that the tribunal has made a finding for which there is no evidence or which is inconsistent with the evidence and contradictory of it. It is not as a rule possible to say whether the tribunal, in any particular case where the Court finds that it has erred, has failed to appreciate the meaning of the statute or whether it has made a finding without having evidence to support it. But it appears to me that, in most such cases, the error is really one at law, and results from a misunderstanding of the statute rather than from any perversity. . . .

BEAN v. DONCASTER AMALGAMATED COLLIERIES LTD.

Court of Appeal [1944] 2 All E.R. 279; 27 T.C. 296 (decision affirmed by the House of Lords [1946] 1 All E.R. 642; 175 L.T. 10; 27 T.C. 310)

The taxpayers claimed to deduct from the profits of their coal mining business the cost of payments towards a drainage improvement scheme. The General Commissioners allowed the claim on the ground that the payments were made under an agreement to fulfil a statutory obligation. On appeal, the Court of Appeal held that, on the facts found by the Commissioners, the payment was *in law* made to discharge a *capital* liability and was not therefore deductible.

DU PARCQ L.J.: . . . The facts of the present case have been found by the Commissioners and are set out in the case stated. There is no doubt that this court is bound, as was Macnaghten J., to accept those findings of fact as correct. No appeal lies from the Commissioners unless their determination is " erroneous in point of law."
. . . A borderline case is one in which the opinions of traders and even of accountants may be expected sometimes to differ. In such cases the task of assigning a sum expended to income or capital may, as Lord Macmillan said, " become one of much refinement." Apart from authority, it might have been thought that the answer given by Commissioners to the question propounded

in these doubtful cases would be a finding of fact which the courts would have no jurisdiction to disturb. There might even be found some persons bold enough to say that a judge was not to be assumed to be better qualified to resolve such a problem than a skilled trader or accountant, or a body of Commissioners. It seems clear, however, that in both the cases to which I have referred, the House of Lords regarded the question as one which, although its solution depended (as the solution of every problem must depend) on the facts found, was ultimately a question of law. This view of the matter may be expressed by saying that, when once the facts have been ascertained, then only one answer to the question posed can be right.[6] Opinions may differ, but that is not to say that more than one of the differing opinions can be correct. Unless the Commissioners, having found the relevant facts and put to themselves the proper question, have proceeded to give the right answer, they may be said, on this view, to have erred in point of law. If an inference from facts does not logically accord with and follow from them, then one must say that there is no evidence to support it. To come to a conclusion which there is no evidence to support is to make an error in law. . . .

2. The Findings of the Commissioners as to the Facts is Final

The court is restricted to considering whether, on the facts found as set out in the case stated, the Commissioners have erred in law. The facts themselves are not open to challenge. When, as in such important questions as " residence " or " trade," the legislature has employed a term with comparatively wide and general meaning, the power of the courts to review the findings of the Commissioners is considerably restricted.

APTHORPE v. PETER SCHOENHOFEN BREWING CO. LTD.

Court of Appeal (1899) 4 T.C. 41; 80 L.T. 395; 15 T.L.R. 245

SMITH L.J.: . . . Mr. Scrutton in his very excellent argument suggested that the facts were all wrong. Well, they may be all wrong. I cannot help it. The only thing sent to us is these facts, and it is points of law upon these facts that we have to decide. If in after assessment years other facts can be shown and other cause stated, well and good; we have not to decide upon that now; we have only to decide upon this case, and I am of opinion therefore that the Appellants fail.

LEVENE v. I.R.C.

House of Lords (ante, p. 33; post, pp. 438, 444)

VISCOUNT SUMNER: . . . In substance persons are chargeable or exempt, as the case may be, according as they are deemed by this body of Commissioners or that to be resident or the reverse, whatever resident may mean in the particular circumstances of each case. The tribunal thus provided is neither bound by the

---

[6] This is not necessarily so. In some cases, on the facts as found, one or more conclusions may be possible. In which case, the court will not disturb one of these conclusions simply because it would prefer a different conclusion.

findings of other similar tribunals in other cases nor is it open to review, so long as it commits no palpable error of law, and the Legislature practically transfers to it the function of imposing taxes on individuals, since it empowers them in terms so general, that no one can be certainly advised in advance, whether he must pay or can escape payment. The way of taxpayers is hard, and the Legislature does not go out of its way to make it any easier. If it had been possible in this case to apply the principle that a taxing statute must impose a charge in clear terms or fail, since it is to be construed contra proferentem, our duty would have been plain, but since the words are plain and it is only their application that is haphazard and beyond all forecast, Mr. Levene has no remedy in your Lordships' House. . . .

Note
This passage should be contrasted with the passages quoted in Chapter 1.

3. Appeals from the Conclusions of the Commissioners

I.R.C. v. LYSAGHT

House of Lords [1928] A.C. 234; 97 L.J.K.B. 385; 139 L.T. 6; 44 T.L.R. 374; 72 S.J. 270; [1928] 2 All E.R.Rep. 575; *sub nom. Lysaght* v. *I.R.C.*, 13 T.C. 911 (also *post*, pp. 441, 443)

The Commissioners held that L., who lived in Ireland but retained a post as a company director in England and came to England for meetings every month, staying in hotels here, was resident in England for the purposes of income tax. On appeal, it was held that there was evidence upon which the Commissioners could properly arrive at that conclusion.

VISCOUNT SUMNER: . . . It is well settled that, when the Commissioners have thus ascertained the facts of the case and then have found the conclusion of fact which the facts prove, their decision is not open to review, provided (*a*) that they had before them evidence, from which such conclusion could properly be drawn, and (*b*) that they did not misdirect themselves in law in any of the forms of legal error, which amount to misdirection. . . .

Note
See also *De Beers Consolidated Mines Ltd.* v. *Howe, post*, p. 447. As to misdirection in law, see *Thomson* v. *Gurneville Securities Ltd.* [1970] 1 All E.R. 691, 700, where a decision of the House of Lords in an appeal on a different case, involving a similar issue, *subsequent* to the decision of the Commissioners, meant that the Commissioners inevitably directed themselves wrongly as to the law.

CURRIE v. I.R.C.

Court of Appeal [1921] 2 K.B. 332; 90 L.J.K.B. 499; 125 L.T. 33; 37 T.L.R. 371; 12 T.C. 245

LORD STERNDALE M.R.: . . . In this case this gentleman was carrying on the business of accountancy and at the same time of advising as to income tax claims, either for reduction or for repayment. He carried on also the business of communicating with the Inland Revenue authorities in order to get these deductions or allowances made. Speaking for myself, I have not the slightest doubt that the Special Commissioners are far better qualified to judge whether or not that is professional work than I am myself. They know far better what is the ordinary work done by an accountant or a person who specialises in income tax, like this gentleman, and it seems to me that the question is one of degree and one for them to decide. For that reason, I cannot see my way to interfere with their finding by saying that there is no evidence upon which they could find as they did. . . .

SCRUTTON L.J.: . . . I think, therefore, in considering the question in this case that if there is any evidence on which the Commissioners could come to the conclusion that this gentleman did not carry on a profession, their decision is final, and that the fact that on that evidence I might have come to a different conclusion is absolutely immaterial, because I am not the judge of fact but only of law. They are the judges of fact, and whether a man carried on a profession is in the last resort a question of fact. . . .

(A) THE "ONLY REASONABLE CONCLUSION"
EDWARDS v. BAIRSTOW AND HARRISON

House of Lords [1956] A.C. 14; [1955] 3 W.L.R. 410; 99 S.J. 558; [1955] 3 All E.R. 48; 36 T.C. 207 (also *post*, p. 145)

This was an appeal from an order of the Court of Appeal dated May 10, 1954, dismissing an appeal by the appellant, Harold Lewis Edwards (Inspector of Taxes), from an order of the High Court (Wynn-Parry J.) dated February 17, 1954, whereby an appeal from a determination of the Commissioners for the General Purposes of the Income Tax for the Division of West Morley in the County of York on a case stated by them was dismissed and their determination was affirmed. The question in the appeal arose on two assessments to income tax made on the respondents, Harold Bairstow and Fred Harrison, in respect of certain operations carried on by them as a joint venture in partnership in the years 1946–47 and 1947–48 whereby certain spinning plant was acquired by them and disposed of at a profit. . . . The commissioners discharged the assessments and, the appellant having declared dissatisfaction, a case was stated.

Paragraph 3 of the case stated was as follows: " The following facts were admitted or proved:—(1) Mr. Harrison became aware in 1946 that a complete spinning plant was for sale at Messrs. Whitworths at Luddenden Foot and had reason to believe that the plant could be purchased for a reasonable figure. He communicated this information to Mr. Bairstow as he himself was not in a position to finance any purchase. Mr. Bairstow expressed himself to be interested but both he and Harrison agreed that they had no intention of holding the plant—what they desired was a quick purchase and re-sale. Mr. Bairstow therefore arranged for a valuation to be made by a professional valuer in order that he might be satisfied that the price asked by Whitworths was one on which he could make a quick profit. He also immediately and before purchasing the plant made inquiries as to whether he could arrange to sell the plant even before it had been purchased. Mr. Harrison was in touch with an Indian by name Wattal who was very anxious to purchase some of the plant, namely, the botany spinning section; for this he was prepared to pay £17,000 but both Harrison and Bairstow were quite decided that they had no intention of selling the plant piece-meal; they wanted to sell it as a complete unit. Then Mr. Bairstow began negotiations with the International Export Co. They said they were prepared to buy the whole of the plant. On November 14 the International Export Co. wrote to Mr. Bairstow saying that they were prepared to buy the plant which was on the fourth floor which was the botany spinning plant for £15,000 this, of course, being £2,000 less than the price offered for the same section of the plant by the Indian Wattal. The reason why the International Export Co. were prepared to pay £15,000 immediately for that particular section of the plant was because although they were willing to purchase the whole of the plant it was their intention to export it and whilst they were confident that an import licence into China would be forthcoming for the asking in respect of the botany spinning section they were not willing to complete the purchase of the remainder of the plant until the import licences for such remainder were in fact forthcoming. On November 20 Mr. Bairstow on behalf of himself and Harrison having negotiated the purchase of the spinning plant together with two small items of warping plant completed the purchase by the payment to Whitworths of £12,000. On November 27, one week later, the International Export Co. paid Mr. Bairstow the sum of £15,000 for the botany spinning plant. Subsequently Messrs. Bairstow and Harrison were informed by the International Export Co. that unfortunately the import licences relating to the remainder of the plant could not be obtained and therefore it was regretted that they could not purchase the remainder of the plant. Thus Mr. Bairstow and Mr. Harrison found themselves with the remainder of the plant on their hands (which they had endeavoured to avoid) and this left them no alternative but to sell that remainder in whatever market they could. (2) The rest of the plant was sold in two other principal and two smaller lots by February 1948, though owing to difficulties the last plant was not removed until March 1949. The two smaller lots consisted of the two items of warping plant. (3) Mr. Bairstow was a director of a company manufacturing leather. Mr. Harrison was an employee of a spinning firm. Neither of them had had any transactions in machinery or any other commodity before. (4) The profits shown by the accounts (which form part of this case and are annexed hereto, marked ' A ') was £18,225 11s. 3d. (5) The respondents' sole purpose in the transaction was to sell the plant at a profit. (6) With regard to the manner in which the sales were effected :—(A) Some commissions were paid for assistance received in effecting sales. (B) There was no advertising. Customers principally learnt of the existence of the plant for sale when they came to inspect the premises which were being advertised by the original owners as becoming vacant. (c) About 400 spindles out of the 220,000 which the plant represented were replaced because they were missing or damaged. (D) Insurance risks were covered by the respondents while the plant was in their hands. (E) Some costs for renovation were incurred because of damage by floods during their ownership. (F) When it was seen that the transaction would not be over in a matter of weeks, wages were paid to Mr. Bairstow's secretary who kept books and did other office jobs in connexion with these transactions. (G) The respondents incurred expense in travelling and entertainment in meeting both the actual persons who would eventually buy the plant and others who did not in fact become customers. A number of advertisements asking for plant, which appeared in trade papers, were answered by the respondents in an attempt to sell the plant remaining after the first main sale. (H) Owing to the delay in removing the plant, rent was paid to the landlords for the last six months during which the plant was housed, and it is thought that a further amount will have to be paid to put the premises in order."

. . . The respondents contended that this was a transaction the profits of which could not be liable to tax under Case I of Schedule D, because, as they said, in the case of *Jones* v. *Leeming*,[7] " four conditions had been approved by the court, one of which must be present to establish liability; (A) the existence of an organization, or (B) activities which led to the maturing of the asset to be sold, or (c) the existence of special skill, opportunities, in connexion with the article dealt with, or (D) the fact that the nature of the asset itself should lend itself to

---

[7] [1930] A.C. 415, *post*, p. 221.

commercial transactions." And they contended that none of these conditions was present in the transaction in question. They distinguished certain cases upon which the appellant relied and urged that the profit was a capital one and that there was no concern in the nature of trade that could be taxed.

On behalf of the appellant it was contended " that the buying and selling of the plant constituted a trade or adventure in the nature of a trade and that the profits and gains arising therefrom were assessable " accordingly.

The commissioners expressed their original determination in these terms: " We, the commissioners, having considered the facts and evidence submitted to us, are of opinion that this was an isolated case and not taxable and discharge the assessments."

When the matter came before Upjohn J. on the case stated, he remitted it to the commissioners with the intimation that they were to consider and answer the question whether the transaction, being an isolated transaction, was nevertheless " an adventure in the nature of trade " which was assessable to tax under Case I of Schedule D, and he further directed that they should be assisted in their finding by legal argument.

The commissioners accordingly met again and, having heard legal argument and further considered the matter, signed a supplemental case in which they stated their further decision as follows:—" We find that the transaction, the subject-matter of this case, was not an adventure in the nature of trade."

The case thus supplemented came once more before the High Court, this time before Wynn-Parry J., who took the view that he was bound by authority to hold that the question before the court was purely one of fact and that the finding of the commissioners could not be upset unless it was so perverse that as a matter of law it could not stand, and, holding that it was not possible for him to take that view of their decision, dismissed the appellant's appeal with costs.

From the decision of Wynn-Parry J. the appellant appealed to the Court of Appeal, which unanimously dismissed the appeal for the reasons given by Wynn-Parry J. . . .

VISCOUNT SIMONDS, having stated the facts, continued: My Lords, it is clear that the revenue authorities were anxious to bring this case to your Lordships' House largely because it was apprehended that the courts of England and Scotland had to some degree diverged in their treatment of this subject. That there is some ground for this apprehension will be clear from a comparison of (for example) the observations of Atkin and Warrington L.JJ. in *Cooper* v. *Stubbs*,[8] with those of Lord Russell in *Inland Revenue Commissioners* v. *Reinhold*[9]: " In the Scottish courts, however, it is clear that such a question " (*i.e.* whether a transaction is an " adventure in the nature of trade ") " is regarded as a question of law, or at least of mixed fact and law." It is not to be doubted that, particularly in a matter of taxation, any possible conflict, even if it be only an apparent conflict, should be resolved, and that is the task which now falls to your Lordships.

Before, however, examining the authorities in any detail, I would make it clear that in my opinion, whatever test is adopted, that is, whether the finding that the transaction was not an adventure in the nature of trade is to be regarded as a pure finding of fact or as the determination of a question of law or of mixed law and fact, the same result is reached in this case. The determination cannot stand: this appeal must be allowed and the assessments must be confirmed. For it is universally conceded that, though it is a pure finding of fact, it may be set aside on grounds which have been stated in various ways but are, I think, fairly

---

[8] [1925] 2 K.B. 753, *post*, pp. 61, 223.   [9] 1953 S.C. 49, 56; 34 T.C. 389, 394; *post*, p. 148.

summarized by saying that the court should take that course if it appears that the Commissioners have acted without any evidence or upon a view of the facts which could not reasonably be entertained. It is for this reason that I thought it right to set out the whole of the facts as they were found by the Commissioners in this case. For, having set them out and having read and re-read them with every desire to support the determination if it can reasonably be supported, I find myself quite unable to do so. The primary facts, as they are sometimes called, do not, in my opinion, justify the inference or conclusion which the Commissioners have drawn: not only do they not justify it but they lead irresistibly to the opposite inference or conclusion. It is therefore a case in which, whether it be said of the Commissioners that their finding is perverse or that they have misdirected themselves in law by a misunderstanding of the statutory language or otherwise, their determination cannot stand. I venture to put the matter thus strongly because I do not find in the careful and, indeed, exhaustive statement of facts any item which points to the transaction not being an adventure in the nature of trade. Everything pointed the other way. When I asked learned counsel upon what, in his submission, the Commissioners could have reasonably founded their decision, he could do no more than refer to the contentions which I have already mentioned. But these upon examination seemed to help him not at all. For, if it is a characteristic of an adventure in the nature of trade that there should be an " organization," I find that characteristic present here in the association of the two respondents and their subsequent operations. I find " activities which led to the maturing of the asset to be sold " and the search for opportunities for its sale, and, conspicuously, I find that the nature of the asset lent itself to commercial transactions. And by that I mean, what I think Rowlatt J. meant in *Leeming* v. *Jones*,[10] that a complete spinning plant is an asset which, unlike stocks or shares, by itself produces no income and, unlike a picture, does not serve to adorn the drawing room of its owner. It is a commercial asset and nothing else.

Your Lordships have examined a large number of cases in some of which the Commissioners have found an adventure or concern in the nature of trade and in others have not. And in each category will be found cases in which the court has upheld and others in which the court has reversed the Commissioners' decision. I do not think it necessary to review them. It is inevitable that the boundary line should not be precisely drawn, but I think that there has been no case cited to us in which the question, however framed, whether the determination of the Commissioners was maintainable, could be answered more clearly and decisively than in the present case.

I must turn now to the question of the apparent divergence between the English and Scottish Courts and venture to approach it by a brief consideration of the nature of the problem which has many aspects, *e.g.* the finding of a jury, the award of an arbitrator, or the determination of a tribunal which is by statute made the judge of fact. And the present case affords an exact illustration of the considerations which I would place before your Lordships.

When the Commissioners, having found the so-called primary facts which are stated in paragraph 3 of their case, proceed to their finding in the supplemental case that " the transaction, the subject-matter of this case, was not an adventure in the nature of trade," this is a finding which is in truth no more than an inference from the facts previously found. It could aptly be preceded by the word " therefore." Is it, then, an inference of fact? My Lords, it appears to me that the authority is overwhelming for saying that it is. Such cases as *Cooper* v. *Stubbs*,[8] *Jones* v. *Leeming*[7] and *Inland Revenue Commissioners* v. *Lysaght*[11]

10 [1930] 1 K.B. 279.
11 [1928] A.C. 234, *ante*, p. 50, *post*, pp. 441, 443.

(a case of residence) amongst many others are decisive. Yet it must be clear that to say that such an inference is one of fact postulates that the character of that which is inferred is a matter of fact. To say that a transaction is or is not an adventure in the nature of trade is to say that it has or has not the characteristics which distinguish such an adventure. But it is a question of law, not of fact, what are those characteristics, or, in other words, what the statutory language means. It follows that the inference can only be regarded as an inference of fact if it is assumed that the tribunal which makes it is rightly directed in law what the characteristics are and that, I think, is the assumption that is made. It is a question of law what is murder: a jury finding as a fact that murder has been committed has been directed on the law and acts under that direction. The Commissioners making an inference of fact that a transaction is or is not an adventure in the nature of trade are assumed to be similarly directed, and their finding thus becomes an inference of fact.

If this is, as I hope it is, a just analysis of the position, the somewhat different approach to the question in some, but by no means all, of the Scottish cases is easily explicable. For as the Lord President (Lord Normand) put it in *Inland Revenue Commissioners* v. *Fraser* [12]: " . . . the Commissioners here have either misunderstood the statutory language (which I think is the probable explanation of their error) or, having understood it, have made a perverse finding without evidence to support it." He might equally well have said that the assumption that they were rightly directed in law was displaced by a finding which was upon that assumption inexplicable. The misdirection may appear upon the face of the determination. It did so here, I think, in the case as originally stated: for in effect that determination was that the transaction was not an adventure in the nature of trade because it was an isolated transaction, which was clearly wrong in law. But sometimes, as in the case as it now comes before the court, where all the admitted or found facts point one way and the inference is the other way, it can only be a matter of conjecture why that inference has been made. In such a case it is easy either to say that the Commissioners have made a wrong inference of fact because they have misdirected themselves in law or to take a short cut and say that they have made a wrong inference of law, and I venture to doubt whether there is more than this in the divergence between the two jurisdictions which has so much agitated the revenue authorities.

But, my Lords, having said so much, I think it right to add that in my opinion, if and so far as there is any divergence between the English and Scottish approach, it is the former which is supported by the previous authority of this House to which reference has been made. It is true that the decision of the Commissioners is only impeachable if it is erroneous in law, and it may appear paradoxical to say that it may be erroneous in law where no question of law appears on the face of the case stated. But it cannot be, and has not been, questioned, that an inference, though regarded as a mere inference of fact, yet can be challenged as a matter of law on the grounds that I have already mentioned, and this is I think the safest way to leave it. We were warned by learned counsel for the respondent that to allow this appeal would open the floodgates to appeals against the decisions of the General Commissioners up and down the country. That would cause me no alarm, if decisions such as that we have spent some time in reviewing were common up and down the country. But nothing, I think, will fall from your Lordships to suggest that there is not a large area in which the opinion of the Commissioners is decisive. I would myself say nothing to detract from what was said by Lord Sterndale M.R. and Scrutton L.J. in *Currie* v. *Inland Revenue Commissioner* [13] upon the kindred

12 1942 S.C. 493, 501; 24 T.C. 498, 504; *ante*, p. 48.
13 [1921] 2 K.B. 332; *ante*, p. 50.

question whether the taxpayer was carrying on a profession, for I do not think that any more precise guidance can be given in the infinitely complex and ever-changing conditions of commercial adventures. . . .

LORD RADCLIFFE: . . . My Lords, I think that it is a question of law what meaning is to be given to the words of the Income Tax Act " trade, manufacture, adventure or concern in the nature of trade " and for that matter what constitute " profits or gains " arising from it. Here we have a statutory phrase involving a charge of tax, and it is for the courts to interpret its meaning, having regard to the context in which it occurs and to the principles which they bring to bear upon the meaning of income. But, that being said, the law does not supply a precise definition of the word " trade ": much less does it prescribe a detailed or exhaustive set of rules for application to any particular set of circumstances. In effect it lays down the limits within which it would be permissible to say that a " trade " as interpreted by section 237 of the Act does or does not exist.

But the field so marked out is a wide one and there are many combinations of circumstances in which it could not be said to be wrong to arrive at a conclusion one way or the other. If the facts of any particular case are fairly capable of being so described, it seems to me that it necessarily follows that the determination of the Commissioners, Special or General, to the effect that a trade does or does not exist is not " erroneous in point of law "; and, if a determination cannot be shown to be erroneous in point of law, the statute does not admit of its being upset by the court of appeal. I except the occasions when the Commissioners, although dealing with a set of facts which would warrant a decision either way, show by some reason they give or statement they make in the body of the case that they have misunderstood the law in some relevant particular.

All these cases in which the facts warrant a determination either way can be described as questions of degree and therefore as questions of fact.

. . . I think that the true position of the court in all these cases can be shortly stated. If a party to a hearing before Commissioners expresses dissatisfaction with their determination as being erroneous in point of law, it is for them to state a case and in the body of it to set out the facts that they have found as well as their determination. I do not think that inferences drawn from other facts are incapable of being themselves findings of fact, although there is value in the distinction between primary facts and inferences drawn from them. When the case comes before the court it is its duty to examine the determination having regard to its knowledge of the relevant law. If the case contains anything ex facie which is bad law and which bears upon the determination, it is, obviously, erroneous in point of law. But, without any such misconception appearing ex facie, it may be that the facts found are such that no person acting judicially and properly instructed as to the relevant law could have come to the determination under appeal. In those circumstances, too, the court must intervene. It has no option but to assume that there has been some misconception of the law and that this has been responsible for the determination. So there, too, there has been error in point of law. I do not think that it much matters whether this state of affairs is described as one in which there is no evidence to support the determination or as one in which the evidence is inconsistent with and contradictory of the determination, or as one in which the true and only reasonable conclusion contradicts the determination. Rightly understood, each phrase propounds the same test. For my part, I prefer the last of the three, since I think that it is rather misleading to speak of there being no evidence to support a conclusion when in cases such as these many of the facts are likely to be neutral in themselves, and only to take their colour from the combination of circumstances in which they are found to occur.

If I apply what I regard as the accepted test to the facts found in the present case, I am bound to say, with all respect to the judgments under appeal, that I can see only one true and reasonable conclusion. The profit from the set of operations that comprised the purchase and sales of the spinning plant was the profit of an adventure in the nature of trade. . . .

(B) WHERE THE CONCLUSIONS OF THE COMMISSIONERS ARE NOT ERRONEOUS IN LAW AND CAN BE SUPPORTED ON THE FACTS, THE COURT MAY NOT SUBSTITUTE ITS OWN CONCLUSION

PILKINGTON v. RANDALL

Court of Appeal (1966) 42 T.C. 662; 110 S.J. 132

CASE

Stated under the Income Tax Act 1952, s. 64, by the Commissioners for the Special Purposes of the Income Tax Acts for the opinion of the High Court of Justice.

1. At a meeting of the Commissioners for the Special Purposes of the Income Tax Acts held on July 22 and 23, 1963, D. C. Pilkington (hereinafter called "the Appellant") appealed against [assessments to Income Tax for sums totalling £47,500 over the years 1953–63].

...5. As a result of the evidence both oral and documentary adduced before us we find the following facts proved or admitted:

(1) The Appellant's father died on February 15, 1929; part of his estate consisted of land near Sutton Coldfield. Under his will his widow received a life interest. Subject to the life interest of their mother the Appellant and his sister were co-beneficiaries of the land. Their mother died on March 10, 1945.

(2) During the period from 1929 until the outbreak of the war the father's executors made several roads and sold approximately 30 acres of the land in plots, some freehold and some leasehold. In 1939 there were about 70 acres unsold, comprising land in the middle of the plan marked exhibit 1 and the plots coloured yellow, brown and purple on the said plan.

(3) After the death of the mother the father's executors (the Appellant and a solicitor named Mason, who died in 1947) distributed that part of the estate that then consisted of ground rents; the plots marked red on the said plan went to the Appellant, and those marked blue went to his sister; but a large part of the land remained in the name of the executors. No land was sold during the years 1940 to 1948 inclusive.

(4) From 1949 onwards several sales were made by the Appellant and by his sister and some were made by the executor. In letters dated October 9, 1953, and October 29, 1953 (exhibit 5), the sister's solicitors informed the Appellant's solicitors that she desired that all the land remaining in the name of the executor should be sold at the earliest possible moment.

(5) On March 31, 1954, an assent was made between the executor of the one part and the Appellant and his sister of the other part (exhibit 3) and on the same date a conveyance was made (exhibit 4) whereby the Appellant purchased from his sister her share in approximately eleven acres of the land.

(6) On March 3, 1955, an assent was made (exhibit 6) and on March 4, 1955, a conveyance was made (exhibit 7) whereby the Appellant purchased from his sister her share in most of the balance of the land, approximately 35 acres, previously held in the name of the executor. The intention was to convey the whole of the balance of the land, but it was later discovered that a small piece of about

half an acre had been overlooked. No evidence was furnished to us concerning the disposal of the said half an acre.

(7) Outline planning permission had been given in respect of the whole of the land many years before the transactions in March 1954, and March 1955. After the purchase of his sister's share of the eleven acres in March 1954, the Appellant constructed a service road (described as East View Road on the said plan) in order to sell plots numbered 30 to 38 and he also had drains constructed and services installed. The Appellant also constructed other roads and installed services in order to sell plots of the whole area of land to the best advantage. He continued to employ the same estate agent who had been employed by the executors. The agent advertised plots for sale in the local press, and erected a board on the land saying that plots were for sale. The Appellant also bought back a single plot that he had sold to an architect, and subsequently the Appellant sold it again at a profit.

(8) Exhibit 10, attached to this Case, contains a list of sales of plots by the Appellant from March 1954 to August 1957, and exhibit 10 (a), attached to this Case, contains a list of sales for the two years ended April 5, 1960, and April 5, 1961. From March 1954 to March 1955, the Appellant sold 20 plots; from May 1955 to January 1956, he sold fourteen plots and from April 1956 to August 1957, he sold seven plots. Many of these plots were large areas sold to builders; one plot was sold for £18,000, another for £12,825 and another for £7,777, but there were many sales of single plots. Exhibit 11, attached to this Case, contains approximate accounts of sales and expenses for the years ending March 31, 1954, to March 31, 1961, inclusive.

6. It was contended on behalf of the Appellant that he improved and developed inherited property, and that the sales were merely realisations of an inheritance and were not trading sales.

7. It was contended on behalf of the Inspector of Taxes that a trade as estate developer was commenced by the Appellant on March 31, 1954, when he purchased the eleven acres from his sister and that that trade continued and embraced (in addition to the land inherited under his father's will) all purchases and sales of land thereafter.

8. We the Commissioners who heard the appeal found against the Appellant. Neither side had made an alternative submission inviting us to exclude from the ambit of the Appellant's trading activities the proportionate part of the land that he inherited personally. On behalf of the Appellant it had been contended that there was no trade at all; and on behalf of the Inspector of Taxes it had been contended that a trade was commenced on March 31, 1954, and that the commencing stock of that trade included not only the share of land bought from the sister but the Appellant's share as well. The answer to this case depended on a review of all the facts. In considering all the facts we bore in mind, in particular, the following matters. The land in question had long ago been designated by the appropriate authority as land to be developed for building houses. There was an interval of a year between the two purchases from the Appellant's sister. The Appellant had bought back and resold a plot previously sold to an architect. He had made roads, constructed drains, had had services installed. He had employed an agent to sell the land in plots, and the process of selling and developing continued over a number of years. While it was apparent from the two letters in October 1953, that the sister wanted the executor to sell all the land quickly, we did not take the view that the subsequent purchases by the Appellant from his sister were merely transactions effected for the purpose of realising the Appellant's inheritance. The Appellant gave evidence before us, and we are in no doubt that the reason why he bought his sister's share was to make a profit by reselling it after development. Having regard to all the facts that we have found in the Case, we hold that as from March 1954, when he

made the first purchase from his sister, the Appellant commenced to trade as a property developer in respect of the whole area of land then owned by him, and that the second purchase from his sister and the repurchase of the architect's plot were all transactions forming part of his trade. We left figures to be agreed.

... 10. The Appellant immediately after the determination of the appeal declared to us his dissatisfaction therewith as being erroneous in point of law and on May 22, 1964, required us to state a Case for the opinion of the High Court pursuant to the Income Tax Act 1952, s. 64, which Case we have stated and do sign accordingly.

The question of law for the opinion of the Court is whether on the facts found by us there was evidence upon which we could properly arrive at our decision.

F. Gilbert   { Commissioners for the
N. F. Rowe   { Special Purposes of the
    { Income Tax Acts.

Turnstile House,
94–99, High Holborn,
London, W.C.1.
February 3, 1965.

DANCKWERTS L.J.: I am not at all satisfied with the result to which I have to come in this case. I would quote the statement by an authority on taxation, Rowlatt, J., in *Rand* v. *Alberni Land Co., Ltd*. (1920) 7 T.C. 629, where he said, at pages 638–639:

" If a land-owner, finding his property appreciating in value, sells part of it, and uses part of his money still further to develop the remaining parts, and so on, he is not carrying on a trade or business; he is only properly developing and realising his land."

That is the conclusion which I think is properly applicable to the present case.

I find myself in disagreement with almost all the facts found by the Special Commissioners in para. 8 of the Stated Case. What they say is: " The answer to this case depends on a review of all the facts." Of course it does.

" In considering all the facts we bore in mind, in particular, the following matters. The land in question had long ago been designated by the appropriate authority as land to be developed for building houses."

That seems to me to be no more than a condition which enables the land to be developed and sold no doubt in accordance with the value of the land in the market. Then they say:

" There was an interval of a year between the two purchases from the Appellant's sister."

That seems to me to be utterly irrelevant.

" The Appellant had bought back and resold a plot previously sold to an architect."

That seems to be a very minor case and we do not really know the facts relating to the purchase back.

" He had made roads, constructed drains, had had services installed."

That seems to me to be all part of the proper development of his land which was referred to by Rowlatt, J., in the case which I quoted.

" He had employed an agent to sell the land in plots, and the process of selling and developing continued over a number of years."

That seems to me to be no more than one would naturally expect when a land-owner wishes to sell his land to the best advantage. He would hardly be able to do the selling himself, and he would necessarily have to employ an estate agent to sell it to the best advantage like any other owner of land.

" While it was apparent from the two letters in October 1953, that the sister wanted the executor to sell all the land quickly, we did not take the view that the subsequent purchases by the Appellant from his sister were merely transactions effected for the purpose of realising the Appellant's inheritance."

It seems to me from the letters that the sister was wishing for an immediate sale and that the object of the Appellant in purchasing her interest was so that the land need not be sold at once but could be retained for the purpose of sale on a market which was constantly rising.

" The Appellant gave evidence before us and we are in no doubt that the reason why he bought his sister's share was to make a profit by reselling it after development."

I should have thought he bought her interest for the reason I have just mentioned. But of course we are at a disadvantage. We do not know what in fact the evidence given by the Appellant was. The Commissioners heard his evidence and one of course accepts that they were in a better position than we could possibly be to appreciate what he said.

Then they continue:

" Having regard to all the facts that we have found in the Case, we hold that as from March 1954, when he made the first purchase from his sister, the Appellant commenced to trade as a property developer in respect of the whole area of land then owned by him, and that the second purchase from his sister and the repurchase of the architect's plot were all transactions forming part of his trade."

My observation in regard to that is that the facts are not in accordance with the statement which was made. It does not follow, as I have indicated, from the way in which the sister's interest was bought out that the transactions with the sister were in any manner transactions in the course of or for the purposes of trade.

However, it is for the Commissioners to find the facts, as has been repeated many times. We are not at liberty to reverse a decision of the Commissioners unless we can say that it was a decision which could not reasonably have been reached on the facts and the evidence. I am unable to say that the Commissioners could not reasonably have reached that result, particularly in view of the result which has been reached by Lord Denning M.R.

Reluctantly I am compelled to agree that the appeal should be dismissed.

SALMON L.J.: . . . Now, as was restated by the House of Lords in *Edwards* v. *Bairstow and Harrison*,[14] the decision of the Commissioners on any question of this sort must be accepted and cannot be overruled unless it is plain from the primary facts found that " no person acting judicially and properly instructed as to the relevant law could have come to the determination under appeal," or unless one comes to the conclusion that no reasonable person could have arrived at the same conclusion as the Commissioners. I agree that this case is very close to the borderline, and I am by no means certain that if I had been sitting as a Commissioner and had had to draw inferences of fact, I should have come to the

14 [1956] A.C. 14, *ante*, p. 51.

same conclusion as the Commissioners. But it is important to guard oneself against the temptation, to which I suppose we are all prone, and which is happily put by Cross J., in *Lucy & Sunderland, Ltd.* v. *Hunt*, 40 T.C. 132 (at page 138). When we think a conclusion of fact is one at which we would not have arrived ourselves, we are tempted to say that it follows that no reasonable person could have come to that conclusion. I think the facts here were evenly balanced. On the whole I think I would have come down the other way, but I cannot say that the view at which the Commissioners arrived is not a possible view for a reasonable man to take.

Note
   For a similar reluctant decision, see *Iswera* v. *C.I.R.* [1965] 1 W.L.R. 663, P.C. Cases such as these demonstrate how little value, as a precedent, a decision of the court has if it merely upholds the conclusions of the Commissioners.

COOPER v. STUBBS

Court of Appeal [1925] 2 K.B. 753; 94 L.J.K.B. 903; 133 L.T. 582; 41 T.L.R. 614; 69 S.J.
   743; [1925] All E.R.Rep. 643; 10 T.C. 29 (also *post*, p. 223)

As to whether a single transaction amounted to an " adventure in the nature of a trade."

WARRINGTON L.J.: . . . The Commissioners are the judges of fact, and this Court, and every Court on appeal from the Commissioners, which has jurisdiction in questions of law only, is very much tempted, when it feels that it cannot agree with the Commissioners in their finding of fact, to find some reason in law by which that finding may be reversed. In my opinion the Court of Appeal ought to be careful not to yield to that temptation, or to interfere with the decision of the Commissioners on a question of fact except in a very clear case, where either the Commissioners have come to their conclusion without evidence which should support it, that is to say, have come to a conclusion which on the evidence no reasonable person could arrive at, or have misdirected themselves in point of law. I do not say for one moment that Rowlatt J. was wrong in the conclusion at which he arrived, if he had been a judge of facts. On the contrary, although it is purely irrelevant as to what my own opinion is, I should have been inclined to agree with him; but he is not the judge of facts; nor am I; and I am not prepared to go so far as to say that there was no evidence upon which a tribunal such as the Commissioners could have arrived at the conclusion they did. . . .

LUCY AND SUNDERLAND LTD. v. HUNT

Chancery Division [1962] 1 W.L.R. 7; 106 S.J. 35; [1961] 3 All E.R. 1062; (1961) 40 T.C. 132

CROSS J.: . . . It is essentialy, a question of degree. When a judge thinks— as I certainly do—that he himself would not have arrived at the conclusion that the commissioners have arrived at, there is a temptation for him also to think that the conclusion at which the commissioners have arrived must be an unreasonable one. I must guard myself against that. But, while bearing that in mind I have come to the conclusion that here there was no evidence upon which the Commissioners could have properly reached the conclusion that they did reach.

Part Two

TAXES ON INCOME AND GAINS

Chapter 4

" INCOME "

"Income tax, if I may be pardoned for saying so, is a tax on income. . . ."
This famous aphorism of Lord Macnaghten [1] has been frequently quoted, usually out of its proper context. If, however, one includes in the expression " income," for the purposes of the taxing statutes, those accretions to wealth which the statutes specifically provide shall be so treated, whether or not such items would normally be regarded as " income," then the statement is broadly true. Income tax is a tax upon that which is properly regarded as " income " for the purposes of the appropriate taxing acts, that is to say " taxable income." [2]

Not all receipts of what is normally regarded as being income are necessarily taxable; income tax is a tax upon certain *types* of income,[3] and certain types of income may therefore fall outside the tax net, *e.g.* gambling winnings,[4] or a voluntary " allowance." [5] But no receipt which is not properly " taxable income " may be taxed as such; in order to be taxed it must be:

    (i) of a type which is taxable, *i.e.* it must fall within one of the heads of charge; and

    (ii) of an " income " nature.

Otherwise, it will not be subject to income tax unless specifically made subject by some charging provision.[6]

1. The Concept of Income

" Income " is a word which has different meanings for different people. The views of economists differ and, if there is at any given time a widely accepted view, this too changes over the years. In addition, the view commonly held by the layman may differ from that of the economist. The judge, attempting to give the word its " natural meaning," [7] is therefore

---

[1] *London County Council* v. *Att.-Gen.* [1901] A.C. 26, 35. See *post*, p. 87.
[2] For a full discussion, see G. S. A. Wheatcroft, " What is taxable income? " [1957] B.T.R. 310.
[3] *Post*, Chap. 5.
[4] *Graham* v. *Green* [1925] 2 K.B. 37; *cf. Burdge* v. *Pyne* [1969] 1 W.L.R. 364, *post*, p. 132.
[5] *Stedeford* v. *Beloe* [1932] A.C. 388, now reversed by I.C.T.A. 1970, s. 113 (2), as to the type of allowance in that case. The principle remains valid.
[6] For example, by some anti-avoidance provision which specifically treats as taxable income an item which would otherwise be regarded as of a capital nature, *e.g.* I.C.T.A. 1970, ss. 460, 487, 488, *ante*, Chap. 2.
[7] See *ante*, p. 5.

faced with a most difficult task. Further, the natural meaning of " income " for one purpose may not be the same as for another purpose.[8]

The traditional view of income, as opposed to capital, likens it to the fruit from the tree. This view still seems to find favour with the judges. A more modern approach regards income as an accretion to wealth or to economic power.

ADAM SMITH—" THE WEALTH OF NATIONS " (1776)

BOOK I; CHAPTER 6

Whoever derives his revenue from a fund which is his own, must draw it either from his labour, from his stock, or from his land. The revenue derived from labour is called wages. That derived from stock, by the person who manages or employs it, is called profit. That derived from it by the person who does not employ it himself, but lends it to another, is called the interest or the use of money. It is the compensation which the borrower pays to the lender, for the profit which he has an opportunity of making by the use of the money. . . . The revenue which proceeds altogether from land, is called rent, and belongs to the landlord. . . . All taxes, and all the revenue which is founded upon them, all salaries, pensions, and annuities of every kind, are ultimately derived from some one or other of those three original sources of revenue, and are paid either immediately or mediately from the wages of labour, the profits of stock, or the rent of land.

BOOK II; CHAPTER 1

When the stock which a man possesses is no more than sufficient to maintain him for a few days or a few weeks, he seldom thinks of deriving any revenue from it. He consumes it as sparingly as he can, and endeavours by his labour to acquire something which may supply its place before it be consumed altogether. His revenue is, in this case, derived from his labour only. This is the state of the greater part of the labouring poor in all countries.

But when he possesses stock sufficient to maintain him for months or years, he naturally endeavours to derive a revenue from the greater part of it, reserving only so much for his immediate consumption as may maintain him till his revenue begins to come in. His whole stock, therefore, is distinguished into two parts. That part which, he expects, is to afford him this revenue, is called his capital. The other is that which supplies his immediate consumption; and which consists either, first, in that portion of his whole stock which was originally reserved for this purpose; or, secondly, in his revenue, from whatever source derived, as it gradually comes in; or, thirdly, in such things as had been purchased by either of these in former years, and which are not yet entirely consumed; such as a stock of clothes, household furniture, and the like. In one, or other, or all of these three articles, consists the stock which men commonly reserve for their own immediate consumption.

There are two different ways in which a capital may be employed so as to yield a revenue or profit to its employer.

First, it may be employed in raising, manufacturing, or purchasing goods, and selling them again with a profit. The capital employed in this manner

---

[8] The meaning given to " income " for the purposes of National Insurance contributions, *i.e.* " that which comes in " (gross), would be unacceptable for income tax purposes, see *Longsdon* v. *Minister of Pensions and National Insurance* [1956] 2 W.L.R. 176. On the other hand, the meaning for tax purposes seems to correspond fairly closely with its meaning in relation to trusts and succession, see *Bouch* v. *Sproule* (1887) 12 App.Cas. 385.

yields no revenue or profit to its employer, while it either remains in his possession, or continues in the same shape. The goods of the merchant yield him no revenue or profit till he sells them for money, and the money yields him as little till it is again exchanged for goods. His capital is continually going from him in one shape, and returning to him in another, and it is only by means of such circulation, or successive exchanges, that it can yield him any profit. Such capitals, therefore, may very properly be called circulating capitals.

Secondly, it may be employed in the improvement of land, in the purchase of useful machines and instruments of trade, or in such-like things as yield a revenue or profit without changing masters, or circulating any further. Such capitals, therefore, may very properly be called fixed capitals.

Different occupations require very different proportions between the fixed and circulating capitals employed in them.

The capital of a merchant, for example, is altogether a circulating capital. He has occasion for no machines or instruments of trade, unless his shop, or warehouse, be considered as such.

Some part of the capital of every master artificer or manufacturer must be fixed in the instruments of his trade. This part, however, is very small in some, and very great in others. A master taylor requires no other instruments of trade but a parcel of needles. Those of the master shoemaker are a little, though but a very little, more expensive. Those of the weaver rise a good deal above those of the shoemaker. The far greater part of the capital of all such master artificers, however, is circulated, either in the wages of their workmen, or in the price of their materials, and repaid with a profit by the price of the work.

In other works a much greater fixed capital is required. In a great iron-work, for example, the furnace for melting the ore, the forge, the slitt-mill, are instruments of trade which cannot be erected without a very great expense. In coal-works, and mines of every kind, the machinery necessary both for drawing out the water and for the other purposes, is frequently still more expensive.

JOHN SMITH & SON v. MOORE

House of Lords [1921] 2 A.C. 13; 90 L.J.P.C. 149; 125 L.T. 481; 37 T.L.R. 613; 65 S.J. 492; 12 T.C. 266

The taxpayer bought a coal business, which included certain forward contracts, worth £30,000, to supply colliery owners. He claimed to be entitled to deduct the cost of the contracts from the profits of the business. *Held,* deduction was not permitted, the expenditure being of a capital nature.

VISCOUNT HALDANE: . . . My Lords, it is not necessary to draw an exact line of demarcation between fixed and circulating capital. Since Adam Smith drew the distinction in the Second Book of his Wealth of Nations, which appears in the chapter on the Division of Stock, a distinction which has since become classical, economists have never been able to define much more precisely what the line of demarcation is. Adam Smith described fixed capital as what the owner turns to profit by keeping it in his own possession, circulating capital as what he makes profit of by parting with it and letting it change masters. The latter capital circulates in this sense.

My Lords, in the case before us the appellant, of course, made profit with circulating capital by buying coal under the contracts he had acquired from his father's estate at the stipulated price of fourteen shillings and reselling it for more, but he was able to do this simply because he had acquired, among other assets of his business, including the goodwill, the contracts in question. It was not by selling these contracts, of limited duration though they were, it was not by parting with them to other masters, but by retaining them, that he was able to employ his circulating capital in buying under them. I am accordingly of opinion that, although they may have been of short duration, they were none the less part of his fixed capital. . . .

Note
The contracts are here treated as a part of the business acquired. See also *Kauri Timber Co. Ltd.* v. *Commissioner of Taxes* [1913] A.C. 771; *cf. Hopwood* v. *C. N. Spencer Ltd.* (1964) 42 T.C. 169. The same principle may be applied to expenditure on newly acquired capital assets: see *Law Shipping Co. Ltd.* v. *I.R.C.* (1924) 12 T.C. 621, *post*, p. 178; *cf. Odeon Associated Theatres Ltd.* v. *Jones* [1972] 2 W.L.R. 331, *post*, p. 100.

EISNER v. MACOMBER

Supreme Court of the United States (1919) 252 U.S. 189

The case arose out of the 16th Amendment to the First Article of the United States Constitution. Under the First Article, Congress had no power to impose taxes on rents, profits etc., without apportioning them among the States according to population. The 16th Amendment gave Congress the power to lay and collect taxes on *incomes*, from whatever source derived, without such apportionment.

Mark Eisner, collector of U.S. Internal Revenue for the Third District of the State of New York, claimed tax in respect of certain stock dividends (*i.e.* a bonus issue of shares) received by one Myrtle H. Macomber. The taxpayer contended that the dividends were not " income " and that accordingly there was no power to raise tax in respect of them. This contention was upheld by the court.

MR. JUSTICE PITNEY (delivering the opinion of the court): In order, therefore, that the clauses cited from article 1 of the Constitution may have proper force and effect, save only as modified by the Amendment, and that the latter also may have proper effect, it becomes essential to distinguish between what is and what is not " income," as the term is there used; and to apply the distinction, as cases arise, according to truth and substance, without regard to form. Congress cannot by any definition it may adopt conclude the matter, since it cannot by legislation alter the Constitution, from which alone it derives its power to legislate, and within whose limitations alone that power can be lawfully exercised.

The fundamental relation of " capital " to " income " has been much discussed by economists, the former being likened to the tree or the land, the latter to the fruit or the crop; the former depicted as a reservoir supplied from springs, the latter as the outlet stream, to be measured by its flow during a period of time. For the present purpose we require only a clear definition of the term " income," as used in common speech, in order to determine its meaning in the Amendment; and, having formed also a correct judgment as to the nature of a stock dividend, we shall find it easy to decide the matter at issue.

After examining dictionaries in common use (Bouvier's Law Dict.; Standard Dict.; Webster's Int. Dict.; Century Dict.), we find little to add to the succinct definition adopted in two cases arising under the Corporation Tax Act of August 5, 1909 [36 Stat. at L. 11, chap. 6], (*Stratton's Independence* v. *Howbert*, 231 U.S. 309, 415, 58 L. ed. 285, 292, 34 Sup.Ct.Rep. 136; *Doyle* v. *Mitchell Bros. Co.*, 247 U.S. 179, 185, 62 L. ed. 1054, 1059, 38 Sup.Ct.Rep. 467): " Income may be defined as the gain derived from capital, from labor, or from both combined," provided it be understood to include profit gained through a sale or conversion of capital assets, to which it was applied in the Doyle Case (pp. 183, 185).

Brief as it is, it indicates the characteristic and distinguishing attribute of income, essential for a correct solution of the present controversy. The government, although basing its argument upon the definition as quoted, placed chief emphasis upon the word " gain," which was extended to include a variety of meanings; while the significance of the next three words was either overlooked or misconceived,—" derived—from—capital,"—" the gain—derived—from—capital," etc. Here we have the essential matter : not a gain accruing to capital, not a growth or increment of value in the investment; but a gain, a profit, something of exchangeable value proceeding from the property, severed from the capital, however invested or employed, and coming in, being " derived," that is, received or drawn by the recipient (the taxpayer) for his separate use, benefit, and disposal; that is income derived from property. Nothing else answers the description.

Note
This passage has been considered and quoted with approval in a number of English cases, notably by Viscount Finlay in *I.R.C.* v. *Blott* [1921] 2 A.C. 171, 195.

H. C. SIMONS—" PERSONAL INCOME TAXATION " (1938) [9]

Personal income may be defined as the algebraic sum of (1) the market value of rights exercised in consumption and (2) the change in the value of the store of property rights between the beginning and end of the period in question. In other words, it is merely the result obtained by adding consumption during the period to " wealth " at the end of the period and then subtracting " wealth " at the beginning. The *sine qua non* of income is *gain,* as our courts have recognised in their more lucid moments—and gain *to* someone during a specified time interval. Moreover, this gain may be measured and defined most easily by positing a dual objective or purpose, consumption and accumulation, each of which may be estimated in a common unit by appeal to market prices.
. . . The essential connotation of income, to repeat, is *gain*—gain *to* someone during a specified period and measured according to objective market standards.

FINAL REPORT OF THE ROYAL COMMISSION ON THE TAXATION OF PROFITS AND INCOME

Memorandum of Dissent, by Mr. G. Woodcock, Mr. H. L. Bullock and Mr. N. Kaldor, 1955 Cmd. 9474

THE DEFINITION OF INCOME

5. In our view the taxable capacity of an individual consists in his power to satisfy his own material needs, *i.e.* to attain a particular living standard. We know of no alternative definition that is capable of satisfying society's prevailing sense of fairness and equity. Thus the ruling test to be applied in deciding whether any particular receipt should or should not be reckoned as taxable income is whether it contributes or not, or how far it contributes, to an individual's " spending power " during a period. When set beside this standard,

[9] University of Chicago Press (1938), pp. 50–51.

most of the principles that have been applied, at one time or another, to determine whether particular types of receipt constitute income (whether the receipts are regularly recurrent or casual, or whether they proceed from a separate and identifiable source, or whether they are payments for services rendered, or whether they constitute profit " on sound accountancy principles," or whether, in the words of the Majority, they fall " within the limited class of receipts that are identified as income by their own nature ") appear to us to be irrelevant. In fact no concept of income can be really equitable that stops short of the comprehensive definition which embraces all receipts which increase an individual's command over the use of society's scarce resources—in other words, his " net accretion of economic power between two points of time."

2. Income as a Tax Base : The Problem of Definition

There is no single concept of what constitutes " income." Nevertheless, income is commonly used, especially in the more " advanced " nations, as a basis for taxation. The reasons for this may be in part historical, based upon the Victorian view that it was anti-social to live on one's capital. But, as one commentator has pointed out, there is also the very good reason that " the tax collector requires his money next year as well as this one. He does not want to kill the goose that lays the golden eggs." [10]

It is consequently necessary for a country's tax laws to define, in one way or another, what is to be included as income in the tax base. Such a definition may be expressly and comprehensively spelled out in a statute, it may have to be distilled entirely from decided cases, or it may be derived in part from non-exhaustive statutory provisions and in part from the cases.

In any event, two essential decisions have to be made :

(a) What items are intended to be included in the tax base?

(b) How is the tax to be defined in law so that all those items, and only those items, are so included?

REPORT OF THE ROYAL COMMISSION ON TAXATION

[Carter Commission, Canada, 1966]

VOLUME 1 : OBJECTIVES

All resident individuals and families should be taxed on a base that measures the value of the annual net gain or loss in the unit's power, whether exercised or not, to consume goods and services. Such a base would ignore the form of the gain or what was done to obtain the gain. We call this the comprehensive tax base. We also refer to it as " income " because this term is so commonly used. Income to us has, however, a much broader meaning than that ascribed to it under current law.

We are completely persuaded that taxes should be allocated according to the changes in the economic power of individuals and families. If a man obtains increased command over goods and services for his personal satisfaction we do not believe it matters, from the point of view of taxation, whether he earned it through working, gained it through operating a business, received it because he held property, made it by selling property or was given it by a relative. Nor do we believe it matters whether the increased command over goods and services

---

[10] G. S. A. Wheatcroft, " What is taxable income? " [1957] B.T.R. 310.

was in cash or in kind. Nor do we believe it matters whether the increase in economic power was expected or unexpected, whether it was a unique or recurrent event, whether the man suffered to get the increase in economic power or it fell in his lap without effort.

All of these considerations should be ignored either because they are impossible to determine objectively in practice or because they are irrelevant in principle, or both. By adopting a base that measures changes in the power, whether exercised or not, to consume goods and services we obtain certainty, consistency and equity.

FINAL REPORT OF THE ROYAL COMMISSION ON THE TAXATION OF PROFITS AND INCOME

1955 Cmd. 9474.   Chapter 1

INCOME AS A SUBJECT OF TAXATION

What Constitutes Taxable Income

26. It is no use to undertake a review of a tax that is designed to be a tax on income without forming some conception of what is meant by " income " for this purpose. The established distinctions that separate taxable from non-taxable receipts represent the gradual development of a theory of income: and without some account of the theory itself it is difficult to decide whether the reasons upon which these distinctions are founded are adequate to support their weight. For the purpose that is here to be considered in relation to income is the purpose of assessing and collecting tax upon it (a) as an annual tax, (b) imposed upon, at any rate, many millions of the population, (c) in respect of the very different kinds of income that make up the total income of all the tax-payers. Each of these incidents of the tax has had its influence in forming the ruling conception of what constitutes taxable income. . . .

28. The tax code contains no general definition of income. It is often said that it is impracticable or undesirable that it should. We do not feel it necessary to subscribe to either of those epithets. The codes of other countries have achieved the work of definition without any known ill-effects. What seems to us more important is that no real advantage could possibly result from the introduction of a general definition that had to cover so multifarious a subject as taxable income. If it were expressed in very general terms the work of deciding how to apply it to particular instances would have to be done by deductions drawn from other parts of the code's framework or with the help of general principles imported from without. To a large extent the United Kingdom system itself has proceeded by this method of interpretation. On the other hand, the more particular the definition, the more it tends to become a mere list of different classes of receipt, and the anxiety not to exclude some class by inadvertence or omission leads to the addition of a comprehensive " sweeping up " clause at the end which, in effect, raises over again the problem of interpreting the general phrase in the light of a particular instance. The United Kingdom code has in fact established the limits of what it will regard as taxable income by formulating a list of different classes of income grouped under five Schedules: and the interpretation of the wording and significance of these lists has been the subject of copious decisions of the Courts of law during the course of some three generations. Their interpretation has been governed by the principle, in itself unexceptionable, that income tax is a tax on income. We have not looked to refine upon this principle by producing a more precise definition. What we have looked for in the course of our review is to see whether the rules that determine

the existing classifications and their application to all the varied forms of possible receipt fall short of or exceed a true conception of income for the purposes of a widely distributed annual tax.

29. Generally speaking, no income is recognised as arising unless an actual receipt has taken place, although a receipt may take the form of a benefit having money's worth received in kind as well as of money or of a payment made to a third party in discharge of another's legal debt. The main exception from this general rule lies in the taxation of the owner-occupier of a house or land in respect of the annual value represented by his occupation. The case for the exception is generally rested upon the evident benefit that he receives from his investment in the house or land and the inequality of burden as between himself and other taxpayers if he were not taxed. The same treatment is not accorded to an owner's possession of durable chattels, if only because of the very great complications that would attend the assessment and collection of such a tax. But, putting aside the occupation of land as requiring special consideration, no mere improvement of a person's financial or material position is recognised as constituting income. Thus an increase in value of property that he owns, even a net increase in value of his total resources, is excluded from the computation of his income. We shall refer more fully to this point in the Chapter on Capital Gains.

30. Since the tax code identifies income by a process of classification, a receipt, to constitute taxable income, must be capable of being referred to one of those classes. The classification itself takes two forms: either it specifies a kind of receipt which is regarded as being inherently of an income nature, e.g. interest, annuity, public revenue dividends, or, more often, it specifies a kind of source which is regarded as being inherently productive of income, e.g. land, trade, profession, securities, employment, and charges the income from that source. The identification of a receipt of the first kind presents little difficulty, once the material facts are ascertained. But very great difficulty arises from time to time in deciding whether a particular receipt is or is not to be regarded as income of the second kind. For it has to be determined, first, whether the recipient owns one of the specified sources to which the receipt can be related, and, secondly, whether the relation of the receipt to that source is such that it can be said to grow out of it by way of annual increment. The difficulties are added to by the fact that in most cases the income to be taxed is not receipts themselves but profits representing the balance between receipts and deductible expenses.

31. We have here one of the basic conceptions of the tax code, that referability to a defined source is essential to permit of a receipt being categorised as income, unless it falls within the limited class of receipts that are identified as income by their own nature. The source provides the capital substance from which income can emerge. Since the division of classifiable income into five Schedules dates back to the Income Tax Act of 1803, the adaptation of increasingly complex forms of income to the general structure of the tax code has not proceeded without strain. For instance, though offices and employments appeared in the original list of 1803 as a categorised source of income, it is not always easy to recognise that it is the office or employment itself that constitutes the source of income, not the services rendered or the contract that secures the payment. While the fundamental structure remains signally unaltered, additions and alterations have, of course, been made from time to time either by changing or enlarging the list of sources or by ad hoc provisions to the effect that a particular kind of receipt is to rank as taxable income.

32. The conversion of a flat-rate tax into a steeply progressive graduated tax which has taken place in the last 50 years may have had a tendency to limit

the scope of permissible additions to the conception of taxable income. All obvious forms of recurrent receipt are already within the tax net. The debatable items are mainly within that range of receipt which does not admit of a clear dividing line between capital and income. It is possible to expose any payment made for the right to own an income-producing asset as a commutation of the future income which the vendor would have received had he retained it. Even the purchase of a freehold of land is a purchase of the right to enjoy its future income in perpetuity. Payments for rights of lesser duration—premiums on leases, moneys paid for the surrender of leases, moneys paid to acquire various terminable rights of enjoyment or possession—are all capable of being described as anticipations of future income in the hand of the recipient and, as such, as partaking of the nature of income. Yet a steeply graduated tax has so heavy an incidence upon any single receipt which is in substance the equivalent of the discounted income of several years that common fairness argues against its inclusion in the range of taxable income, unless some formula can be applied to it which will artificially spread it out again over the taxable income of several years. And, if these formulas prove incapable of application on any general scale owing to the practical and administrative complications that they cause, no solution is likely to emerge which will satisfactorily relate the debatable income-capital receipt to the requirements of our system of taxing personal income.

33. Another consequence of the conversion of income tax into a progressive tax is that the identification of a receipt as a receipt of taxable income must be made in relation to its character in the hands of the recipient. It is possible to trace a different conception in the history of the tax: a conception that there is, so to speak, a body of income in gross and taxable as such however it may be distributed among its different owners. Such a conception is consistent with a flat-rate tax and is not unreasonable at a period when the bulk of national income is derived from land and public stock: though it could never be applied with complete consistency by any system that recognised exemptions and personal allowances. But it becomes altogether inconsistent with a system that graduates the effective rate of tax according to an individual's total income and admits substantial variations of the effective rate according to personal circumstances. Under such a system income tax is nothing but the sum of all the taxes on each individual, each computed separately according to the total income and personal circumstances of that individual.

34. It follows that a receipt is treated as income or not according to its status in the hands of the recipient. To determine its status it is not relevant to enquire whether the payer charges it to his income or his capital account, from what resources of his it may have been drawn, or whether it would be a deductible expense in his own computation of taxable income. Thus, it is a mistake to import into the conception of income for this purpose any principle to the effect that a receipt cannot be income in the hands of recipient A unless it is drawn from the income resources of payer B, or, conversely, that a payment cannot be deductible in the computation of the income of B unless it is taxable as a receipt of income in the hands of A.

Ibid. Memorandum of Dissent by Mr. G. Woodcock, Mr. H. L. Bullock and Mr. N. Kaldor

9. . . . . The current legal definition of what constitutes taxable income has been arrived at by a process of piecemeal statutory revision and judicial interpretation of the provisions of Five Schedules, introduced by the Income Tax Act of 1803, under which the various kinds of taxable receipts and benefits are enumerated and which collectively define the limits of taxable income. As the Majority state, " While the fundamental structure remains signally unaltered, additions and alterations have, of course, been made from time to time either by changing or enlarging the list of sources or by ad hoc

provisions to the effect that a particular kind of receipt is to rank as taxable income." But the original Act of 1803 already included a " sweeping up clause," in Case VI of Schedule D, under which " any annual profit or gain " is taxable which is not enumerated under any of the other Cases or Schedules. Since the law employs the terms " income," " profit " or " gain " interchangeably, the very insertion of such a clause is incongruous within a system which identifies income only by a process of categorisation and which in consequence nowhere defines what it is that is to be swept up.

10. The circularity inherent in this legal conception is well illustrated by the juxtaposition of two well-known judicial interpretations of the statute. " Income tax," according to Lord Macnaghten's famous dictum,[11] " is a tax on income." But " as regards the word income " said Lord Wrenbury,[12] " it means such income as is within the Act taxable under the Act." The law faces the same dilemma as the medieval Schoolmen who were forced to deny to exotic birds and beasts, captured by travellers in strange lands, the status of birds and beasts, since they relied for their definition on an exhaustive list of birds and beasts reported by tradition to have entered the Ark with Noah.

11. The inclusion or exclusion of particular types of receipts assumed an entirely different significance as income tax was gradually transformed from a small flat-rate impost to a steeply graduated tax calculated with reference to an individual's total income from all sources. Yet the trend towards the comprehensive tax base implied in the very notion of progressive taxation has been checked at various points, mainly on the basis of two distinct considerations. First, as the Majority point out there has been a tendency to avoid the special problem of the heavy incidence of a steeply graduated tax on receipts which by their very nature are realised irregularly, instead of being spread evenly over the years in which they may be regarded as accruing, by the simple expedient of excluding such receipts altogether from the tax charge. Secondly, the ancient constricted conception of income as something which recurrently emerges and is separated off from its perpetual source, like the harvest from the soil, has lingered in the tax code from times when, by and large, income was the harvest from the soil. It has only been abandoned gradually, through the piecemeal adoption of basically inconsistent provisions, and without the consequences of its abandonment ever having been systematically taken into account. Thus the old view of the rigid separation between the income flow and its permanent source has been blurred by the allowances introduced for capital wastage and even losses, as permissible deductions in the calculation of income. The old boundary-line afforded by the regularity or recurrence criterion has been discarded in judicial decisions which have established that casual or isolated gains are taxable provided that they are not of the character of " capital profits."

OXFORD MOTORS LIMITED v. MINISTER OF NATIONAL REVENUE

Supreme Court of Canada [1959] C.T.C. 195; 18 D.L.R. (2d) 712

ABBOTT J.: . . . No one has ever been able to define income in terms sufficiently concrete to be of value for taxation purposes. In deciding upon the meaning of income, the Courts are faced with practical considerations which do not concern the pure theorist seeking to arrive at some definition of that term, and where it has to be ascertained for taxation purposes, whether a

---

[11] In *London County Council* v. *Att.-Gen.* [1901] A.C. 26, 35, *post*, p. 87.
[12] *Whitney* v. *I.R.C.* [1926] A.C. 37.

gain is to be classified as an income gain or a capital gain, the determination of that question must depend in large measure upon the particular facts of the particular case.

UNITED STATES OF AMERICA: INTERNAL REVENUE CODE 1954

SECTION 61: GROSS INCOME DEFINED

(a) General Definition

Except as otherwise provided in this subtitle, gross income means all income from whatever source derived, including (but not limited to) the following items:

(1) Compensation for services, including fees, commissions, and similar items;
(2) Gross income derived from business;
(3) Gains derived from dealings in property;
(4) Interest;
(5) Rents;
(6) Royalties;
(7) Dividends;
(8) Alimony and separate maintenance payments;
(9) Annuities;
(10) Income from life insurance and endowment contracts;
(11) Pensions;
(12) Income from discharge of indebtedness;
(13) Distributive share of partnership gross income;
(14) Income in respect of a decedent; and
(15) Income from an interest in an estate or trust.

Note
The Code does not define " income " but merely provides a non-exhaustive list of examples. For an example of taxable income falling outside the list, see especially *Commissioner of Internal Revenue* v. *Glenshaw Glass Co.* (1955) 348 U.S. 426, U.S. Supreme Court. A sum, equal to treble the amount of loss suffered by the taxpayers, awarded to them as exemplary and punitive damages for fraud, was held to be taxable income.

3. Capital and Income : The Importance of the Distinction

The tendency in English tax law has been to prefer the " fruit of the tree " concept of income, rather than the wider " accretion to economic power " concept.[13] Consequently, whether a particular receipt (or, in certain circumstances, item of expenditure) is regarded as being of an income or a capital nature, may determine whether income tax at steeply progressive rates is imposed or no tax at all, or capital gains tax at a considerably lower rate, is paid. The distinction, though vitally important, is often a fine one.[14]

It is especially important in the following instances:

[13] See *Ryall* v. *Hoare* (*post*, p. 76). See also *Riches* v. *Westminster Bank Ltd*. [1947] A.C. 390, 398, *per* Viscount Simon; and *John Smith and Son* v. *Moore* [1921] 2 A.C. 13, 34 (*ante*, p. 67), *per* Viscount Cave.
[14] See *Bean* v. *Doncaster Amalgamated Collieries Ltd*. (*ante*, p. 48). And see P. G. Whiteman, " The Borderline between Capital and Income " [1966] B.T.R. 115.

(a) Income from land. The distinction between rental payments and "capital" payments, such as lease premiums (*post*, Chap. 6).

(b) "Annual" income. The distinction between instalments of capital and income payments (*post*, Chap. 7).

(c) Trading income. The distinction between a trading profit and an isolated capital gain (*post*, Chap. 8). Also, the distinction between receipts or expenditures of a revenue nature, which enter into the computation of the profits of the trade, and those of a capital nature, which do not (*post*, Chap. 9).

(d) Income from foreign possessions (*post*, Chap. 12).

(e) Tax avoidance. Many avoidance schemes depend upon the successful conversion of income into capital, or vice versa (*ante*, Chap. 2).

The consequences of the distinction will be considered in the appropriate later chapters. However, the distinction is one of general application and, in a number of cases, has been discussed in general terms.

RYALL v. HOARE

King's Bench Division [1923] 2 K.B. 447; 92 L.J.K.B. 1010; 129 L.T. 505; 39 T.L.R. 475; 67 S.J. 750; [1923] All E.R.Rep. 528; 8 T.C. 521 (also *post*, p. 219)

An isolated commission paid to a company director in consideration for guaranteeing the company's bank overdraft was held to be properly assessed to tax under Case VI of Schedule D.

Rowlatt J.: . . . Two kinds of emolument may be excluded from Case 6. First, anything in the nature of capital accretion is excluded as being outside the scope and meaning of these Acts confirmed by the usage of a century. For this reason, a casual profit made on an isolated purchase and sale, unless merged with similar transactions in the carrying on of a trade or business is not liable to tax. " Profits or gains " in Case 6 refer to the interest or fruit as opposed to the principal or root of the tree. The second class of cases to be excluded consists of gifts and receipts, whether the emolument is from a gift inter vivos, or by will, or from finding an article of value, or from winning a bet. All these cases must be ruled out because they are not profits or gains at all. . . .

I.R.C. v. MALLABY-DEELEY

Court of Appeal [1938] 4 All E.R. 818; 55 T.L.R. 293; 82 S.J. 1049; 23 T.C. 162 (also *post*, p. 118)

Payments made to a publishing firm under a seven year covenant, replacing a previous obligation to pay a lump sum to finance the publishing of a literary work, were held to be payments of a capital nature. The covenantor was consequently not permitted to deduct tax from the payments.

Sir Wilfrid Greene M.R.: . . . The distinction which is to be drawn for the purposes of the Income Tax Acts between payments of an income character and payments of a capital nature is sometimes a very fine and rather artificial one. It may—in fact it does—depend upon the precise character of the transaction. To take a simple case, if the true bargain is that a capital sum shall be paid, the fact that the method of payment which is adopted in the document is a payment by instalments will not have the effect of giving to those instalments the character of income. Their nature is finally determined by the circumstance that the obligation is to pay a capital sum, and instalments are merely a method of effecting that payment. On the other hand, to take another simple case, where there is no undertaking to pay a capital sum and no capital obligation in existence, and all that exists is an undertaking to pay annual sums, those may, in the absence of other considerations, be annual payments of an income nature for the purposes of the Income Tax Acts. The operation of that distinction in individual cases may present some appearance of unreality. Nevertheless, it is a distinction which is now well-founded. . . .

Notes
    See also *I.R.C.* v. *National Book League* [1957] Ch. 488 (*post*, p. 114); *Campbell* v. *I.R.C.* [1970] A.C. 77 (*post*, p. 123); and see *post*, p. 118.

    In determining the nature of the payment, the Master of the Rolls was prepared to have regard to the substance of the deed, rather than to the mere form, and discussed the limitations of the doctrine in *I.R.C.* v. *Duke of Westminster* [1936] A.C. 1 (*ante*, p. 23). In considering the capital or income question, the courts have on a number of occasions found it necessary or desirable to go behind the form and consider the substance of a transaction, see *Campbell* v. *I.R.C.* [1967] Ch. 651, *per* Harman L.J.: "There are occasions, even in Revenue cases, when what you come to look for is substance and not form." And see *Perrin* v. *Dickson* [1930] 1 K.B. 107, 114, *per* Lord Hanworth M.R.
    Annual payments may consist of both an income and a capital element, see *Secretary of State in Council of India* v. *Scoble* [1903] A.C. 299, *post*, p. 119; *Lord Howard de Walden* v. *Beck* (1940) 23 T.C. 384.

DUCKER v. THE REES ROTURBO DEVELOPMENT SYNDICATE LTD.

House of Lords [1928] A.C. 132; 97 L.J.K.B. 317; 138 L.T. 598; 44 T.L.R. 307; 72 S.J. 171; [1928] All E.R.Rep. 682; *sub nom. Rees Roturbo Development Syndicate Ltd.* v. *Ducker*, 13 T.C. 366

    The proceeds of sale of certain patents were held to be profits of the taxpayers' trade rather than the proceeds of capital assets.

    ROWLATT J. [at first instance] : —This is one of those cases which raise great difficulty in applying a principle which in itself is perfectly clear. It has been said before in this Court, and in more important Courts, and it is perfectly clear, that where profit accrues from the sale of property a question arises whether that forms the basis of liability to Income Tax. Now Income Tax is not attracted by the mere circumstance that there is a profit; because the profit may be a mere accretion of the value of the article, and the profit may not accrue in the course of any trade at all. On the other hand the circumstance that the profit is due to an accretion in the value of the article does not negative the application of Income Tax, because the accretion of value to the article may have been the very thing that a trade within Case I was established to secure. In that case you have a trade which is going to be in articles with a view to securing the accretion of value to those articles, and the accretion of value does not negative the incidence of Income Tax. Nor does the circumstance that the accretion of value can be described as an accretion of capital in one sense; because you may have an adventure, such a case as the recent linen case,[15] and

15 *Martin* v. *Lowry* [1927] A.C. 317, *post*, pp. 149, 152.

such a case as of companies which are formed to nurse assets, salvage companies of all sorts; you may have a case where the whole capital of the concern is put into property, and the whole object of the concern is to sell that property at a higher price; and if the accretion of value comes about, it affects the assets that represent the whole capital of the company, and it is profit of trading in the clearest possible way. But if it is an accretion of value of what is described as a capital asset, of course the matter is different. In one sense the words " capital asset " are words of art, because you do not have one set of assets representing capital and another set of assets representing income, of course; but what is meant by the phrase " capital asset " is that this is an asset which represents fixed capital as opposed to circulating capital, that is to say, that this is an article which is possessed by the individual in question, not that he may turn it over and make a profit by the sale of it to his advantage, but that he may keep it and use it and make a profit by its use. Then if an article of that sort is sold at a profit, that profit is not a profit of trade. For instance, if a bank or a mercantile company finds it is more expensively housed than it needs, and sells its counting house and its offices, that is not part of the business of banking; and any profit which comes does not come into its profit and loss account, it is represented in the diminution of assets grouped as Premises, and so on, in its accounts.

Note

Rowlatt J.'s judgment was reversed in the Court of Appeal and unanimously restored by the House of Lords, where his test was expressly approved by Lord Buckmaster.

I.R.C. v. BRITISH SALMSON AERO ENGINES LTD.

Court of Appeal [1938] 2 K.B. 482; 107 L.J.K.B. 648; 159 L.T. 147; 54 T.L.R. 904; 82 S.J. 433; [1938] 3 All E.R. 283; 22 T.C. 29

In consideration for an exclusive licence to use a foreign patent the taxpayers received a lump sum payment of £25,000 and further royalties spread over ten years. The lump sum was held to be a capital payment, the royalties income.

SIR WILFRID GREENE M.R.: . . . Income tax, as has been said over and over again, is a tax on income. It does not tax capital. As the corollary to that, in ascertaining profits, payments of a capital nature may not be deducted. It is income all the time which has to be considered under the Income Tax Acts, . . . There were in 1925, and there have been since, many cases where this matter of capital or income has been debated. There have been many cases which fall on the border-line. Indeed, in many cases it is almost true to say that the spin of a coin would decide the matter almost as satisfactorily as an attempt to find reasons. But that class of question is a notorious one, and has been so for many years.

. . . It seems to me that in the case of patents, as in the case of any other matters, the fundamental question remains, in respect to any particular payment: Is it capital or is it income? and that question has to be decided, as it has to be decided in reference to other subject-matters, on the particular facts of each case, including in those facts the contractual relationships between the parties. It has been said that the question is one of fact, and it is, when one gets to the bottom of it, an accountancy question. In saying that it is a question of fact, it does not mean that, in deciding it, questions of law may not have to be discussed and decided. . . .

Note
    The position is now governed, as regards the royalties, by I.C.T.A. 1970, ss. 52 and 53, and, as regards the lump sum, by section 380.

HARRY FERGUSON (MOTORS) LTD. v. I.R.C.

Court of Appeal, Northern Ireland [1951] N.I. 115; 33 T.C. 15; 33 A.T.C. 422

Sums were received by the taxpayers for the exploitation of a patent. *Held*, reversing the Special Commissioners, the payments were of an income nature and should be included in profits.

LORD MACDERMOTT C.J.: . . . During the debate many cases were cited in which a decision was reached as to whether particular payments were capital or income. We do not propose to review these authorities. They set up no conclusive test of general applicability and it is fruitless to argue from the facts of one instance to the differing facts of another. There is so far as we are aware no single infallible test for settling the vexed question whether a receipt is of an income or a capital nature. Each case must depend upon its particular facts and what may have weight in one set of circumstances may have little weight in another. Thus the use of the words " income " and " capital " is not necessarily conclusive; what is paid out of profits may not always be income; and what is paid as consideration for a capital asset may on occasion be received as income. One has to look to all the relevant circumstances and reach a conclusion according to their general tenor and combined effect.

Note
    The inconclusiveness, or even arbitrariness, of any test is emphasised by Lord Sands in *Burmah Steam Ship Co. Ltd.* v. *I.R.C.* (1930) 16 T.C. 67, 73 : " The distinctions between income and capital under the Income Tax system are somewhat artificial, and some of the decisions may appear to be arbitrary," and by the Lord President (Normand) in *Barr, Crombie and Co. Ltd.* v. *I.R.C.* (1945) 26 T.C. 406 : " It has been truly said that every case must be considered on its own facts, and that no legal criterion for distinguishing between capital payments and income payments is readily applicable."

BRITISH INSULATED AND HELSBY CABLES LTD. v. ATHERTON

House of Lords [1926] A.C. 205; 95 L.J.K.B. 336; 134 L.T. 289; 42 T.L.R. 187; [1925] All E.R.Rep. 623; *sub nom. Atherton* v. *British Insulated & Helsby Cables Ltd.*, 10 T.C. 155 (also *post*, p. 169)

The taxpayer company made a lump sum payment to form the nucleus of a pension fund for the benefit of the company's staff. The payment was held to be expenditure of a capital nature and not deductible in calculating taxable profits.

VISCOUNT CAVE L.C.: . . . But there remains the question, which I have found more difficult, whether, apart from the express prohibitions, the sum in question is (in the words used by Lord Sumner in *Usher's* case [16]) a proper debit item to be charged against incomings of the trade when computing the profits of it; or, in other words, whether it is in substance a revenue or a capital expenditure. This appears to me to be a question of fact which is proper to be decided by the Commissioners upon the evidence brought before them in each case; but where, as in the present case, there is no express finding by the Com-

---

[16] *Usher's Wiltshire Brewery Ltd.* v. *Bruce* (*post*, p. 168).

missioners upon the point, it must be determined by the Courts upon the materials which are available and with due regard to the principles which have been laid down in the authorities. Now, in *Vallambrosa Rubber Co.* v. *Farmer* [17] Lord Dunedin, as Lord President of the Court of Session, expressed the opinion that " in a rough way " it was " not a bad criterion of what is capital expenditure—as against what is income expenditure—to say that capital expenditure is a thing that is going to be spent once and for all, and income expenditure is a thing that is going to recur every year "; and no doubt this is often a material consideration. But the criterion suggested is not, and was obviously not intended by Lord Dunedin to be, a decisive one in every case; for it is easy to imagine many cases in which a payment, though made " once and for all," would be properly chargeable against the receipts for the year. Instances of such payments may be found in the gratuity of 1500*l.* paid to a reporter on his retirement, which was the subject of the decision in *Smith* v. *Incorporated Council of Law Reporting for England and Wales*,[18] and in the expenditure of 4994*l.* in the purchase of an annuity for the benefit of an actuary who had retired, which, in *Hancock* v. *General Reversionary and Investment Co.*,[19] was allowed, and I think rightly allowed, to be deducted from profits. But when an expenditure is made, not only once and for all, but with a view to bringing into existence an asset or an advantage for the enduring benefit of a trade, I think that there is very good reason (in the absence of special circumstances leading to an opposite conclusion) for treating such an expenditure as properly attributable not to revenue but to capital.[20]

. . . My Lords, in my opinion the present case falls within the same principle. The payment of 31,784*l.*, which is the subject of dispute, was made, not merely as a gift or bonus to the older servants of the appellant company, but (as the deed shows) to " form a nucleus " of the pension fund which it was desired to create; and it is a fair inference from the terms of the deed and from the Commissioners' findings that without this contribution the fund might not have come into existence at all. The object and effect of the payment of this large sum was to enable the company to establish the pension fund and to offer to all its existing and future employees a sure provision for their old age, and so to obtain for the company the substantial and lasting advantage of being in a position throughout its business life to secure and retain the services of a contented and efficient staff. I am satisfied on full consideration that the payment was in the nature of capital expenditure, and accordingly that the deduction of the amount from profits, although not expressly prohibited by the Act, was rightly held by the Court of Appeal not to be admissible. . . .

GOLDEN HORSE SHOE (NEW) LTD. v. THURGOOD

Court of Appeal [1934] 1 K.B. 548; 103 L.J.K.B. 619; 150 L.T. 427; 18 T.C. 280; [1933] All E.R.Rep. 402

The taxpayer company claimed to be entitled to deduct, in computing profits,

---

[17] (1910) 5 T.C. 529, 536.
[18] [1914] 3 K.B. 674, *post*, p. 180.
[19] [1919] 1 K.B. 25.
[20] This passage has received approval on numerous occasions, see especially *Van den Berghs Ltd.* v. *Clark* [1935] A.C. 431, *per* Lord MacMillan (*post*, p. 156) and *Anglo-Persian Oil Co. Ltd.* v. *Dale* [1932] 1 K.B. 124, 145, where Romer L.J. was " unduly optimistic " in claiming that it " placed beyond the realms of controversy the law applicable to the matter." The case should be compared with *Green* v. *Cravens Railway Carriage and Wagon Co. Ltd.* (1951) 32 T.C. 359. Accounting evidence enabled the decision to be distinguished in *Heather* v. *P.E. Consulting Group Ltd.* [1972] 2 All E.R. 107.

the purchase price of dumps of "tailings" from gold mines. Their claim that the dumps were not capital assets but formed part of the stock-in-trade was upheld.

ROMER L.J.: . . . The question to be decided in this case is whether the dumps are to be regarded as fixed capital or as circulating capital. If they are the former, it is conceded by the appellants that the assessment made on them is correct. If, on the other hand, they are floating or circulating capital, it is conceded that the cost of them to the appellants must be debited in the profit and loss account, the account being credited with the cost price of what was left of the dumps at the end of the year of assessment. The dumps, in other words, must be dealt with in the profit and loss account as stock in hand has to be dealt with in the profit and loss account of any other trader. The reason for this distinction being drawn between fixed and floating or circulating capital is not far to seek. In assessing a trader to income tax under Schedule D, Case I, the revenue authorities are only concerned with his annual gains and profits; that is, gains and profits in the year of assessment or whatever may be the other material interval of time. They are not in the least concerned with his financial position as a whole at the end of the time as compared with his financial position at the beginning. Changes in the value of his fixed capital are therefore disregarded except where it is otherwise expressly provided in the Act. On the other hand, changes in his floating or circulating capital must be taken into consideration in ascertaining his annual gains and profits. For the profits or losses in a year of trading cannot be ascertained unless a comparison be made of the circulating capital as it existed at the beginning of the year with the circulating capital as it exists at the end of the year. It is, indeed, by causing the floating capital to change in value that a loss or profit is made.

Unfortunately, however, it is not always easy to determine whether a particular asset belongs to the one category or the other. It depends in no way upon what may be the nature of the asset in fact or in law. Land may in certain circumstances be circulating capital. A chattel or a chose in action may be fixed capital. The determining factor must be the nature of the trade in which the asset is employed. The land upon which a manufacturer carries on his business is part of his fixed capital. The land with which a dealer in real estate carries on his business is part of his circulating capital. The machinery with which a manufacturer makes the articles that he sells is part of his fixed capital. The machinery that a dealer in machinery buys and sells is part of his circulating capital, as is the coal that a coal merchant buys and sells in the course of his trade.

. . . It seems to follow from these considerations that the question to be decided in the present case resolves itself into this: Are the dumps the raw material of the appellant's business or do they merely provide the means of obtaining that raw material? In my opinion they are the raw material itself. . . .

Note
   This case should be contrasted with *John Smith & Son* v. *Moore* [1921] 2 A.C. 13, *ante*, p. 67.

4. " Income " Means " Taxable Income "

Where the word "income" is used in a taxing Act, it means, unless the context otherwise requires, taxable income, *i.e.* that income which is income chargeable to tax under the tax laws of this country.

BECKER v. WRIGHT

Chancery Division [1966] 1 W.L.R. 215; 110 S.J. 151; [1966] 1 All E.R. 565; 42 T.C. 591

The taxpayer was assessed to income tax on payments received by his wife under a covenant made by her father, Mr. Hoadley, which was not a covenant which could exceed six years. Mr. Hoadley was resident abroad.

STAMP J.: . . . The taxpayer's contention is a simple one. He says that section 392 [21] applies in terms to the income assessed upon him. By virtue or in consequence of the disposition made by the covenantor [his father-in-law] the income is payable or applicable for the benefit of the taxpayer's wife [Mrs. Wright] for a period which cannot exceed six years, and accordingly it is, for all the purposes of the Income Tax Acts, to be deemed to be the covenantor's income and not that of the taxpayer's wife or the taxpayer. It is true that section 392 is not an exempting section, but if the income does fall within its terms, the taxpayer is entitled to have it applied notwithstanding that the effect will be to exempt the income in question altogether from income tax.

. . . The contention of the taxpayer is simple and only really needs to be stated to be understood, and I confess that at an early stage of this case I thought it was right. I am, however, satisfied by the arguments advanced by the Crown that those arguments ought to be accepted and that the Crown is right when it says that the argument on behalf of the taxpayer is not only simple but deceptive. What is said by the Crown is that when one examines the language of section 392 it cannot apply to any income which, if one did apply that section, would cease to be " income " within the meaning of the Income Tax Acts. If, here, the income in question is to be deemed to be the income of the covenantor, it will be altogether outside the ambit of the Income Tax Acts, whereas the express words of section 392 direct that it is to be deemed to be the covenantor's income " for all the purposes of " the Income Tax Act 1952. It is emphasised, with reference to the wording of the section, that it does not provide that the income shall be deemed to belong to the covenantor but that it shall be deemed to be his income for all the purposes of this Act, and that to construe it in the former sense would be to do violence to its terms. And if, urges Mr. Warner on behalf of the Crown, income with which one is concerned is not susceptible to such a deeming, then despite the opening words of the section, " any income which "—words which on the face of it are all-embracing—that income is not within it.

Of course, section 392 must be read in the context of the Income Tax Acts. . . . It is clear that the words " any income " at the beginning of the section do not refer to that which is not income within the meaning of the Income Tax Acts but might be treated as income in another context, e.g. income derived from playing bridge or backing horses or income received by a man by way of allowance from his father: the section is confined to income which, under the Income Tax Acts, is taxable under those Acts: for this purpose, see the speech of Lord Wrenbury in *Whitney* v. *Commissioners of Inland Revenue* [10 T.C. 88, at page 113]. It is also clear from that same speech, where Lord Wrenbury quotes Lord Herschell in *Colquhoun* v. *Brooks* [2 T.C. 490], that there is a territorial limit to the Income Tax Acts, which do not purport to tax income which is " neither derived from property in the United Kingdom nor income received by a person resident in the United Kingdom." It follows that whatever may be the effect of section 392, it does not subject the covenantor to United Kingdom income tax. There is no machinery for that purpose to be

[21] Income Tax Act 1952, s. 392. Now I.C.T.A. 1970, s. 434 (1).

found within section 392, and in order to subject him to liability there would have to be something to bring the income within the one or other of the Schedules of the Income Tax Act. Case V of Schedule D does not apply to income arising or accruing to a foreign resident, and, as Mr. Warner points out, there is no such thing as an assessment under section 392.

In *Astor* v. *Perry* [19 T.C. 255], the phrase " any income " fell to be considered by the House of Lords. There it was sought to treat the words " any income " as extending to income of trustees who were resident abroad. Lord Macmillan, in the leading speech of the majority in the House of Lords, pointed out a number of anomalies which would result if such a view of the section was adopted, and, in considering those anomalies he asked how a British Income Tax Act could impute to an American citizen " for the purposes of the enactments relating to income tax "—and I underline the words " for the purposes of the enactments relating to income tax "—an income of which that American citizen had divested himself under the law of his own country and to which the provisions of the Income Tax Acts, of course, in no way applied. But if the taxpayer is right in the present case that is precisely what section 392 does. Lord Macmillan concluded that the words " any income " should be construed to mean " any income chargeable with tax under the British Finance Act of that year " and not in the wider sense which Lord Russell of Killowen, in his dissenting speech, thought they ought to bear.

. . . Paying regard to the considerations to which I have alluded, I find sufficient in section 392 itself to lead me to the inevitable conclusion that the section is concerned only with any income which, when the deeming process contemplated by the section has taken place, can be, for all the purposes of the Income Tax Acts, the income of the person by whom the disposition was made. For the reasons that I have given—that the covenantor is resident abroad, that Case V cannot apply to subject him to tax, and that there is no such thing as a section 392 assessment—it is impossible to deem this income to be " for all the purposes of " the Income Tax Act 1952, the income of the covenantor. Paraphrasing the rhetorical question which Lord Macmillan asked and to which I have referred, how can a British Income Tax Act impute to a foreign resident, " for the purposes of " that Act, an income of which a foreigner has divested himself under the foreign law and which in his hands is altogether outside all the provisions of the Income Tax Act? . . .

MAPP v. ORAM

House of Lords [1970] A.C. 362; [1969] 3 W.L.R. 557; 113 S.J. 797; [1969] 3 All E.R. 215; 45 T.C. 651

LORD UPJOHN: My Lords, this appeal raises a short but important question on the true construction of section 212 (4) [22] of the Income Tax Act 1952. The facts are fully set out in the case stated and I shall not attempt to restate them. The whole question is whether a parent, having a child of 16 years of age receiving full-time instruction at a University or College, is, therefore, prima facie entitled to make a deduction of income tax on the amount of £165 from the tax with which he is chargeable, or whether, having regard to subsection (4) he has to permit a deduction and, if so, of how much.

. . . The point could hardly be shorter. The claimant's son earned an income of about £150 as a lecturer in France for a year in order to improve his French. As he spent that modest income in France and no part of it was remitted to this

[22] Now I.C.T.A. 1970, s. 10.

country that income in the boy's hands was not subject to British income tax, and the whole question therefore is whether these earnings while in France were properly described for the purposes of section 21 (3) as income to which the child was entitled in his own right. The only point that has been argued before your Lordships and in the courts below was whether, on the one hand, income meant income in a broad sense—and if that be the proper construction, there can be no doubt that this was income of the child—or, on the other hand, whether it meant income subject to assessment for the purposes of British income tax, in which case it was quite plainly not income of the child.

. . . The question, then, is whether the son's income was income for the purposes of section 212 or not. My Lords, it is a trite remark that income has many different meanings in as many different contexts. But in my opinion, in an Income Tax Act, the approach to the construction of that word is that it is income chargeable to tax under our system of taxation laws. This was so stated by Lord Macmillan in *Astor* v. *Perry (Inspector of Taxes)* [23] and by Lord Wrenbury in the case of *Whitney* v. *Inland Revenue Comrs.*[24] But this is only an approach: it is not a rule of construction only to be displaced if the context otherwise requires. There are many cases, as my noble and learned friend, Lord Hodson, has pointed out in his speech, where the word " income " in a taxing Act is used to include income not chargeable to tax.

So I approach the words of section 212 with this in mind and I think it was perfectly clear that the legislature was dealing only with income which in the hands of the son was subject to British tax. If the statute is limiting the right of the taxpaper to make a statutory deduction on proving the primary facts and does so by reference to the income of the infant, it is extremely difficult to see how the income of that infant can be calculated for this purpose save upon income tax principles. Indeed, the appeal of the Crown was based on the fact that this income of the son should be calculated in accordance with Schedule E which it is now common ground has absolutely nothing to do with the case, so that there was no method of ascertaining the relevant income of the son. So if " income " means income in a broad sense, how do you calculate it to see if it exceeds £115? It cannot mean gross receipts, for every person earning an income has expenses but there is no machinery in the Acts for calculating the permissible deductions. This consideration strongly supports the view that " income " means income subject to British tax. So, my Lords, I entirely agree with the judgment of Ungoed-Thomas J., and the dissenting judgment of Danckwerts L.J. In my view, the majority of the Court of Appeal proceeded on a basis which, with all respect to them, is entirely unsound in approaching the construction of a taxing statute. The majority in the Court of Appeal relied upon the anomaly that the father whose son has a tax-free income is presumably in a better position in regard to his son's maintenance than the father whose son's income is chargeable to tax, and this weighed decisively with them. My Lords, I have said on many occasions that in taxing statutes, reliance on hardships or anomalies is a very unsound basis of construction. The complexities of income tax law today are bound to give rise to cases of anomalies and hardships, sometimes even injustices, not always against the subject, sometimes, though less often, against the Crown. Unless there is some real ambiguity in the language used, and I do not think that there is here, it is quite unsafe to allow anomaly, hardship and injustice to control the language Parliament has used.[25] . . .

[23] [1935] A.C. 398, 419, *ante*, p. 15.
[24] [1926] A.C. 37, 56.
[25] See Chap. 1. Lord Upjohn went on to quote with approval the words of Rowlatt J. in *Cape Brandy Syndicate* v. *I.R.C.* [1921] 1 K.B. 64, 71 (*ante*, pp. 10, 18).

Chapter 5

THE SCHEDULES

The taxing Acts are divided into Schedules, of which there are presently six. The schedular system dates back to Addington's Act of 1803 and has always been a feature of our income tax system.

1. The " Source " Concept

In considering, in the previous chapter, the concept of " income," the analogy was drawn with the " fruit of the tree," *i.e.* all taxable income must be derived from some source. These sources, or " trees," are specified in the respective Schedules. For an item of income to be taxed at all it must fall within an express taxing provision contained in the Acts; that is to say, it must fall within one of the Schedules and be derived from a specified source. The Schedules, for the most part, classify income according to the source from which it is derived.[1] Consequently, if a taxpayer has ceased to possess a particular source of income before the year of assessment in question, income from that source cannot be taxed.[2]

BROWN v. NATIONAL PROVIDENT INSTITUTION

House of Lords (*ante*, pp. 5, 16; *post*, p. 205)

The appellants were assessed to income tax under Case III of Schedule D on profits derived from discounts on certain Treasury Bills. According to the " preceding year " method of computing profits, the assessment for the year 1917–18 was based on the profits of an earlier period.[3] Prior to the commencement of that year of assessment, the appellants had ceased to hold any of the Treasury Bills.

Held, in order to be chargeable to income tax for a particular year in respect of income from any source, a person must possess that source of income in that year.

Viscount Haldane: . . . The remaining question is one of considerable difficulty. It is that of the chargeability by assessment for the year 1917–18, in which there were no transactions in bills, of the transactions during the previous year. The Court of Appeal, differing from Rowlatt J., thought that profits on discounts could only be charged under the Third Case of Sched. D in a year

---

[1] This is not entirely true of Cases III and VI of Sched. D, but even in such cases a " source " is necessary before income can be taxed. See *Scott* v. *Ricketts* [1967] 2 All E.R. 1009, *post*, p. 226; *Dickinson* v. *Abel* [1969] 1 All E.R. 484.

[2] The effect of this principle is seen most clearly in the treatment of foreign income taxable only on a remittance basis (*post*, Chap. 12) which escapes tax entirely if the source has dried up prior to the year of remittance. The principle has been considerably modified by statutory provisions relating to post-cessation receipts of trades or professions (*post*, Chap. 10) and " golden handshakes " to former holders of office (*post*, Chap. 11).

[3] The " preceding year " basis of assessment is considered in Chap. 9.

when the source of such profits still continued to exist, and that in consequence the profits on discounts of a previous year escaped taxation under that case if in the succeeding year no such profits had been made. My Lords, this question, the most important in the appeal brought before us, can only, I think, be answered if the principle on which the income-tax legislation is based has been first defined, and to this principle I therefore turn. The case is governed, not by the general Income Tax Act of 1918, an Act which has superseded the older legislation, but by the Income Tax Act of 1853, and the provisions of the Act of 1842, which it kept alive. The Finance Acts of 1916, 1917, and 1918 rendered those the governing statutes for the purposes of the question before us. My Lords, in *London County Council* v. *Attorney-General* [4] it was decided by this House that the Income Tax Acts of 1842 and 1853, as modified by the Customs and Inland Revenue Act 1882, do no more than impose a single tax on profits and gains brought into charge by the Income Tax Acts. There is no special or peculiar tax under each case of Sched. D and the other schedules or their branches, whatever be the idiosyncrasies of the methods prescribed for collection. The expression " income tax," as used by the Legislature, was a generic description of the tax which was levied under all the schedules alike, and it was not meant to be anything but a tax on income. There was imposed under the schedules no collection of taxes distinct from each other, but simply one tax, with standards for assessment which varied according to the sources from which the taxable income was derived.

. . . It is to be observed that, speaking broadly at all events, the general principle of the Acts is to make the tax apply only to a source of income existing in the year of assessment.

. . . If a man carries on business by buying and discounting bills, this is, I think, as much a source of profit as any other for the purposes of the words employed. As in the case before us it is agreed that there was no such source, I think that we have to assume that there was no income on which to base the tax. . . .

LORD ATKINSON : . . . From this legislation one sees clearly what was the true nature of income tax. It was a single tax divided into different parts merely for the convenience of collection. It was a tax assessed, levied, and collected yearly on the profits and gains arising and accruing during the year in which it was collected from one or more of the sources named. If this be so, as in my opinion it clearly is, it necessarily follows that if in the year of assessment a source of income should dry up and no income accrue, then no tax could be levied or collected in respect of a non-existing income. . . .

Note

See also *Grainger* v. *Maxwell* [1926] 1 K.B. 430 (C.A.) for an application of this principle in similar circumstances, and see *post*, p. 205.

BENNETT v. OGSTON

King's Bench Division (1930) 15 T.C. 374

ROWLATT J. : . . . When a trader or a follower of a profession or vocation dies or goes out of business—because Mr. Needham is quite right in saying the same observations apply here—and there remain to be collected sums owing for goods supplied during the existence of the business or for services rendered by the professional man during the course of his life or his business, there is no question of assessing those receipts to Income Tax; they are the receipts of

4 [1901] A.C. 26, *post*, p. 87.

the business while it lasted, they are arrears of that business, they represent money which was earned during the life of the business and are taken to be covered by the assessment made during the life of the business, whether that assessment was made during the life of the business, whether that assessment was made on the basis of bookings or on the basis of receipts. But this is not that case; because here the interest in question is not the accrued earnings of the capital during the life of the deceased or the time the business was carried on; it is the earnings of the capital, or so much as is left of it since the death, and this interest has been earned over the time which has elapsed since the death. . . .

Note

This passage was quoted with approval in the House of Lords in *Stainer's Executors* v. *Purchase* [1952] A.C. 280, 290 by Lord Asquith of Bishopstone and in *Carson* v. *Cheyney's Executor* [1959] A.C. 412, 428 by Lord Reid.

The case also demonstrates that the identity of the recipient may determine the correct source of the income. During the lifetime of the deceased moneylender, interest on promissory notes held by him was treated as being derived from his business and taxable under Case I of Schedule D. After his death the notes were held by his administrator and the source of the interest was held to be the debts themselves, with Case III being applicable.

STAINER'S EXECUTORS v. PURCHASE

House of Lords [1952] A.C. 280; *sub nom. Gospel* v. *Purchase* [1951] 2 T.L.R. 1112; 95 S.J. 801; [1951] 2 All E.R. 1071; *sub nom. Purchase* v. *Stainer's Executors*, 32 T.C. 367

A well-known actor had entered into contracts to direct, produce or act in films, for which he was to receive certain sums by way of initial payments and, in addition, shares of profits from the films. He died before receiving the shares of profits. His executors were assessed in respect of these profits when received. *Held*, the source of these profits was the deceased's profession and, as he was no longer carrying on the profession when the sums were received, they were not taxable under Case II of Schedule D.

LORD ASQUITH OF BISHOPSTONE: . . . It seems clear that the payments whose liability to tax is in issue were exclusively the fruit or aftermath of the professional activities of Mr. Leslie Howard during his lifetime. This was, as a matter of historical fact, their source, and their only source. The fact that he died before some of this fruit had been garnered or its amount could be ascertained cannot alter that historical fact. He, and he alone, had done everything necessary to provide the harvest. . . .

Note

This passage was approved by Viscount Simonds in *Carson* v. *Cheyney's Executor* [1959] A.C. 412, 424.

The effect of this decision is largely nullified by I.C.T.A. 1970, s. 143.

2. Interrelationship of the Schedules

(i) *Income Tax is a single tax*

LONDON COUNTY COUNCIL v. ATTORNEY-GENERAL

House of Lords [1901] A.C. 26; 70 L.J.Q.B. 77; 83 L.T. 605; 4 T.C. 265

The taxpaying authority received rents, from which income tax under Schedule A had been deducted, and interest, from which income tax under Schedule D had been deducted. On paying interest on its Consolidated Stock it deducted income tax under Schedule D. *Held*, it was only liable to account to the Revenue for the tax which it had deducted *less* the tax it had suffered under both Schedules A and D on its income.

LORD MACNAGHTEN : . . . The question depends upon the meaning and effect of subsection 3, section 24, of the Customs and Inland Revenue Act 1888, which enacts that " upon payment of any interest of money or annuities charged with income tax under Schedule D and not payable or not wholly payable out of profits or gains brought into charge to such tax," the rate of income tax in force at the time shall be deducted and an account rendered to the Commissioners of Inland Revenue " of the amount so deducted or of the amount deducted out of so much of the interest or annuities as is not paid out of profits or gains brought into charge, as the case may be." And then the amount deducted is declared to be a debt due to the Crown and recoverable accordingly.

It will be observed that there is a change of language, and that the word " paid " takes the place of the word " payable " which occurs in the earlier part of the sentence. The result, therefore, is that so far as interest of money or annuities chargeable under Schedule D are in fact paid out of profits or gains " brought into charge," whether in law payable thereout or not, the person who makes the payment and deducts the rate of income tax is not accountable to the Crown for the duty deducted.

The difficulty which has given rise to the present claim on the part of the Crown is created by the use of the words " profits or gains brought into charge to such tax " in the earlier part of the subsection, and the words " profits or gains brought into charge " in the latter part. What is the meaning of " such tax "? And what is the meaning of " brought into charge "? The Divisional Court and the Court of Appeal have both held that the expression " such tax," referring back to the foregoing words, means " income tax under Schedule D," and that the expression " profits or gains brought into charge " in the latter part of the subsection means " profits or gains brought into charge under that schedule," and not " profits or gains brought into charge by virtue of the Income Tax Acts."

Now, if one had to construe the enactment with nothing but the words of the subsection to go upon, ignoring the state of the law at the time when the enactment was passed, and supposing, as one might possibly suppose from the language used, that there was a special or peculiar sort of income tax which could be properly described as " income tax under Schedule D," still I think it would be difficult to give any satisfactory reason why the expression " such tax " should mean " income tax under Schedule D " rather than " income tax " simply, or why the expression " brought into charge " should be limited to what is brought into charge under one particular schedule. But the subsection in question, as the Act itself declares, is introduced by way of amendment. And how can you understand the true meaning and effect of an amendment unless you bear in mind the state of the law which it is proposed to amend? It is necessary, therefore, to take a wider survey, and then, I think, the meaning of the enactment becomes plain enough. I cannot help thinking that the advisers of the Crown have somewhat misapprehended the scope and leading principles of our income tax legislation and have not paid sufficient attention to the state of the law at the time when the Act of 1888 was passed. The consequence is that now, when the Act of 1888 has been in force for a number of years, it is discovered that a provision described in the Act as an " amendment " has worked a radical change in the law.

Income tax, if I may be pardoned for saying so, is a tax on income. It is not meant to be a tax on anything else. It is one tax, not a collection of taxes essentially distinct. There is no difference in kind between the duties of income tax assessed under Schedule D and those assessed under Schedule A or any of the other schedules of charge. One man has fixed property, another lives by his wits; each contributes to the tax if his income is above the prescribed limit. The standard of assessment varies according to the nature of the source from which taxable income is derived. That is all.

. . . It is interesting and, I think, instructive to trace the development of income tax legislation. A very clear account of it is to be found in Mr. Stephen Dowell's excellent work. I turn at once to the original Act—the Act of 1799, 39 Geo. 3, c. 13, as amended by 39 Geo. 3, c. 22. For the purposes of the tax the income for the current year of persons to be assessed was ranged under four divisions: " I. Income arising from lands, tenements, and hereditaments. II. Income arising from personal property and from trades, professions, offices, pensions, stipends, employments, and vocations. III. Income arising out of Great Britain. IV. Income not falling under any of the foregoing rules." In the form of return required from the taxpayer, which is given in a schedule, these four heads of income were represented by nineteen " cases," of which the first fourteen fell under Division I. The taxpayer had to return his total income under each and all of these cases. From this total income the taxpayer was allowed to make a great many deductions under various heads also specified in the schedule. There were deductions for rents of all sorts. There was a deduction for " annual interest for debts," whether " personal " or charged on property enumerated in the several " cases," a deduction for " allowance to children or other relations," and a deduction for " annuities." The total amount of deductions was to be subtracted from the total amount of income, and the difference was the " income chargeable." That general return, as Mr. Dowell observes, was regarded as the most objectionable feature in the income tax. By the Act of 1803, in lieu of a general return, particular returns of income from particular sources were required. That was the origin of the five schedules of charge with which we are now so familiar. It was not that there was any difference in kind between the income arising from the different sources. The alteration was made in order to avoid disclosure of the taxpayer's circumstances. This new method was found to work so well that it has been continued in every Income Tax Act ever since. . . .

LORD DAVEY : . . . In my opinion, this construction of the section is entirely wrong. Grammatically I think it wrong. I think that the words " charged with income tax under Schedule D " mean " charged under Schedule D with income tax," and the words " such tax " mean the tax which is called in the Act " income tax." It is said that the tax imposed on property within Schedule A is not strictly an income tax, because it is levied on the annual value of property and not on the profits received by the owner. That, no doubt, is so, and if one were writing a treatise on taxation it would be proper to refer to this distinction. But the question is, What do the words " income tax " mean in the language of the Legislature, and in this Act?

. . . I come to the conclusion that the expression " income tax," in the language of the Legislature, is a generic description of the tax which is levied under all the schedules alike, and is so used in section 24. . . .

(ii) *The Schedules are mutually exclusive*

If a particular item of income is specifically charged under one Schedule, the Crown cannot elect to charge it under some other Schedule which might also be appropriate.

FRY v. SALISBURY HOUSE ESTATE LTD.

House of Lords [1930] A.C. 432; 99 L.J.K.B. 403; 143 L.T. 77; 15 T.C. 266

Viscount Dunedin: My Lords, this is an important case with probably far-reaching consequences, and we had the benefit of a very full and able argument from the Attorney-General on behalf of the Crown, but in the end I have come to the conclusion, though not without difficulty, that the judgment appealed from is right and should be affirmed. The facts which give rise to the question are as follows:

Salisbury House is a building of considerable size in the City of London and is owned by a limited company, which was formed for the purpose of acquiring the property known as Salisbury House, and utilising it. The house contains about 800 rooms. These rooms are let to tenants as offices. There is no residential occupation. No furnishings are provided. The company maintain a staff of servants to operate the lifts and act as porters and look after the building, and there is also a large staff of cleaners all under the orders of a housekeeper paid by the company. The tenants have the exclusive use of the rooms let, but are bound to leave the keys at night with the housekeeper so as to allow access in the case of fire breaking out. The company retain certain rooms as an office. By the terms of the leases the company have to pay all rates and taxes. The company were assessed to income tax under Schedule A upon the gross value of the premises as appearing in the valuation roll in accordance with the Valuation (Metropolis) Act 1869.

. . . The inspector of taxes then served on the company a notice of assessment under Schedule D. He arrived at the assessment by calculating the amount of profit as brought out in the profit and loss account of the company, after deducting expenses of management and upkeep, and then he proposed to deduct from the assessment so brought out the amount of assessment already paid under Schedule A. The company admitted that they had to pay under Schedule D upon the amount of profits which they made from the cleaning and other services, but contended that, so far as the proceeds of the property were concerned, that had already been taxed under Schedule A and could not again be brought in computo under Schedule D and demanded a case. A case was stated by the Commissioners, which sets out the above facts. The figures, apart from the question of principle, have been agreed on.

. . . My Lords, this is one of those cases which may be approached, so to speak, from very different angles, and according as you approach it from one angle or another a different conclusion may seem to be the one that is right to follow. I can only say that, after the best consideration I could give it, my opinion is that the angle from which I now approach it is the right one. Now, the cardinal consideration in my judgment is that the income tax is only one tax, a tax on the income of the person whom it is sought to assess, and that the different Schedules are the modes in which the statute directs this to be levied. In other words, there are not five taxes which you might call income tax A, B, C, D and E, but only one tax. That tax is to be levied on the income of the individual whom it is proposed to assess, but then you have to consider the nature, the constituent parts, of his income to see which Schedule you are to apply. Now, if the income of the assessee consists in part of real property you are, under the statute, bound to apply Schedule A.

. . . Of course that does not mean that the assessee may not be liable in respect of other income under other Schedules.

. . . But he might be liable under any of the other Schedules if he has income to which they apply, and in particular he might be liable under Schedule D. It is a mere commonplace to remark that a man who possesses real property and is assessed under Schedule A, may also have investments and other forms of property which will be assessed under Schedule D.

Now, turning to this case. The income of the respondents, as represented by rents, is admittedly assessed and properly assessed under Schedule A. " But then," says the appellant, " you are carrying on a business, and a business falls to be assessed under Schedule D." To which the respondent replies, " Quite so; and I am willing to pay on the profits which I make on the cleaning and other services." To this the appellant replies, " No; that is not enough. Your business is one business not a congeries of businesses, and if I estimate your profits from your own profit and loss account, I will get the higher figure which I ask." The answer to that is: " You cannot bring out that balance of profit without taking the rents I receive in computo. Now, these rents are also part of my income or property, and the statute says that any income which represents the the value of real property is to be assessed in the manner directed under Schedule A." My Lords, I think the final answer is good. The rents, having been assessed under Schedule A, are, so to speak, exhausted as a source of income, and the so-called concession made by the appellant that there should not be double taxation, and that therefore he would be willing to allow deduction of the sum paid under Schedule A, is a concession which is beside the mark. It is a concession to avoid double taxation, but the concession cannot come into being where double taxation does not exist, and here it does not exist, because, it being imperative to deal with the rents under Schedule A, there is no possibility of subsequently dealing with them under Schedule D.

My Lords, I have preferred to consider this question on the statute alone, without reference to authority, but I am far from anxious to put my judgment on a mere ipsi dixit, and I will therefore analyse my own argument to see if it is supported by authority. Now, the cardinal proposition is that income tax is one tax, and the Schedules merely the different means of collecting it, and that there are not so many taxes as there are Schedules. This point was raised in the most distinct manner in the case of the *London County Council* v. *Attorney-General*.[5]

. . . The next proposition is that when income is dealt with in the proper Schedule the same income cannot be dealt with again under another Schedule. There is no stronger foundation for this proposition than may be found in the fact of the option given not to the Crown but to the taxpayer who is assessed under Schedule B to be assessed under Schedule D.[6] This obviously points to the fact that, once assigned to its appropriate Schedule, the same income cannot be attributed to another Schedule. . . .

LORD ATKIN: . . . My Lords, I think that this case should be decided in favour of the respondents upon the simple ground that annual income derived from the ownership of lands, tenements and hereditaments can only be assessed under Schedule A and in accordance with the rules of that Schedule. In my opinion it makes no difference that the income so derived forms part of the annual profits of a trading concern. For the purpose of assessing such profits for the purpose of Schedule D the income so derived is not to be brought into account. The option of the Revenue authorities to assess under whichever Schedule they prefer in my opinion does not exist, and is inconsistent with the provisions of the Income Tax Acts throughout their history.

. . . My Lords, nothing could be clearer to indicate that the Schedules are mutually exclusive; that the specific income must be assessed under the specific Schedule; and that D is a residual Schedule so drawn that its various Cases may

[5] [1901] A.C. 26, *ante*, p. 87.
[6] The option referred to no longer exists in the same form, but an option of this sort does exist in relation to woodlands, *post*, p. 105.

carry out the object so far as possible of sweeping in profits not otherwise taxed. . . .

LORD MACMILLAN : . . . Once it is determined that the annual value of all lands and houses must be assessed to income tax under Schedule A it follows that this annual value cannot be assessed to income tax under any other Schedule, for it is elementary that the same source of income cannot be twice taxed. Income tax is one tax, not several taxes (*London County Council* v. *Attorney-General* [5]), and the annual value of a particular property having been once assessed to income tax cannot be reassessed to the same tax. . . .

Note
    In some cases it may be difficult to determine which Schedule is applicable, *e.g. Lowe* v. *J. W. Ashmore Ltd.* [1971] Ch. 545. At the time of that decision, the question was whether the profits from the sale of turf by a farmer fell under Case I or Case VIII of Schedule D. Both cases were held to be applicable, it making no difference which applied, although the Revenue can choose the appropriate Case, *post*, p. 95. However, what was then Case VIII of Schedule D is now Schedule A.

LORD GLANELY v. WIGHTMAN

House of Lords [1933] A.C. 618; 102 L.J.K.B. 456; 149 L.T. 121; 17 T.C. 634

The appellant owned a stud-farm, on the profits of which he was assessed under Schedule B. Among the stud was the 1919 Derby winner, " Grand Parade," whose services were rendered thirty or forty times a year, at 400 guineas a time. The assessment under Schedule B was related to the annual value of the land. The Revenue sought to tax additionally under Schedule D the profits derived from the services of the stallion. *Held*, the fees were profits in respect of the occupation of the farm and as such were taxed under Schedule B. Accordingly, no further assessment could be raised under Schedule D.

LORD RUSSELL OF KILLOWEN : . . . All those portions of the appellant's lands which are occupied and used by him for the purpose of a thoroughbred stud farm have been assessed to income tax under Schedule B. In other words, the appellant has thereby been assessed to tax upon his gains in respect of his occupation of the land which he occupies for that purpose, and solely for that purpose.
    It was conceded by the Crown, and necessarily conceded, that the normal receipts of a thoroughbred stud farm include stud fees received for the service by the stud farm stallions of mares which belong to other people and which are brought on to the stud farm for that purpose. Those stud fees are therefore in my opinion part of the gains of the appellant in respect of his occupation of this land.
    By what right can the Crown then claim to pick out one item from the various gains of the appellant in respect of that occupation, and say that it is not covered with the other gains by the assessment under Schedule B but is available as a separate item for a separate assessment under Schedule D? I can envisage no principle which would justify such a course.
    . . . These stud fees are in my opinion merely one item among the gains of the appellant in respect of his occupation of the lands and are, with all such gains, franked by the assessment under Schedule B. . . .

LORD WRIGHT : . . . The tax under Schedule B is expressed to be charged in respect of the occupation of lands, tenements and hereditaments in the United Kingdom for every twenty shillings of their assessable value. It is, like other taxes under the Income Tax Act 1918, a tax on income or profits; but, save in the special cases otherwise provided by the Act, it is a tax not varying with the actual profits or depending on there being profits at all, but the amount of the tax is fixed by relation to the arbitrary or conventional standard of the annual value. In this respect it resembles the landlord's or property tax under Schedule A, which also is on the annual value. There is, under the Income Tax Acts, only one tax; there are not as many taxes as there are schedules, but the schedules are merely the different ways of collecting it. This was clearly set forth by Lord Dunedin in his speech in *Fry* v. *Salisbury House Estate, Ltd.*,[7] where he quotes and relies on the well known judgment of Lord Macnaghten in *London County Council* v. *Attorney-General*.[8]

. . . Schedule B exhausts all profits that come within occupation of the land; such profits are dealt with once for all by the assessment and cannot be taxed otherwise or again : Schedule D has no application to such profits. . . .

Note
　Profits of farming are now assessed under Case I of Schedule D. Similar problems, however, can arise in relation to woodlands under Schedule B; see *post*, p. 105.

THOMPSON v. TRUST AND LOAN COMPANY OF CANADA

Court of Appeal [1932] 1 K.B. 517; 101 L.J.K.B. 342; 16 T.C. 394

The taxpayers, a Finance Company, had dealings in the course of their business in stocks and shares and received interest on Treasury Bonds from which income tax under Schedule C had already been deducted. *Held,* the net interest, having already been taxed under Schedule C, could not again be brought into account for the purposes of assessment under Schedule D in respect of profits of the Company's business.

LORD HANWORTH M.R.: . . . In other words, the Crown seek to bring back into charge something which has already met its fate under the Income Tax Acts, something that has already been dipped into by the tax gatherer and depleted to the extent of the tax deducted under Schedule C. It is the sum remaining after deduction of tax under Schedule C which, it is said by the Crown, ought to be brought back into consideration for the purpose of the estimation of income tax under Schedule D.

. . . In the present case it is plain that this subject-matter of tax, coupons on Government bonds payable out of the Government funds, has got to be taxed under Schedule C. It cannot be taxed under any other Schedule. When the total sum received out of public revenue has been subjected as a totality to the incidence of tax under Schedule C, it is removed from being taxed under Schedule D, for Schedule D in terms provides that it is only to apply under Case I. (which applies here) " in respect of any trade not contained in any other Schedule." . . .

Note
　It is this principle which made possible bond-washing and dividend-stripping transactions. See *post*, p. 135.

MITCHELL AND EDON v. ROSS

House of Lords [1962] A.C. 813; [1961] 3 W.L.R. 411; 105 S.J. 608; [1961] 3 All E.R. 49; 40 T.C. 56

VISCOUNT SIMONDS: My Lords, these consolidated appeals and cross-appeals raise a question of general importance to medical specialists who hold appoint-

---

[7] [1930] A.C. 432, *ante*, p. 90.　　　　　　　　[8] [1901] A.C. 26, *ante*, p. 87.

ments as part-time consultants under the National Health Service and also have
private patients. The appeals relate to assessments to income tax of five such
specialists who held part-time appointments, respectively as consultant radiologist,
ophthalmologist, pathologist, psychiatrist and thoracic surgeon, and also engaged
in private practice. I will consider the case of Dr. Harold Leslie Ross, a consultant radiologist to the Birmingham Regional Hospital Board. The other cases
stand or fall with his.

Dr. Ross, having been assessed to income tax under Schedule E in respect of
the profits and gains arising from his part-time appointment, and under Schedule
D in respect of the profits and gains arising from his private practice, appealed
against the assessments to the special commissioners on two grounds. He
claimed, in the first place, that he should be assessed in respect of the whole of
his profits and gains under Schedule D, and, in the second place, that if this
claim was not upheld, he was entitled in the computation of his liability under
Schedule D to deduct the expenses incurred in the exercise of his appointment
to the extent that they were not allowed under Schedule E. The first of these two
claims was not maintained before this House, learned counsel conceding that an
appointment under the National Health Service to such a post as that held by Dr.
Ross fell within Schedule E, and that an assessment to tax must, accordingly, be
made under that schedule. In my opinion the concession was rightly made and
the opposite view was not arguable. I may add here that some subsidiary questions were raised as to the category into which the fees earned by so-called
domiciliary visits and " locum-tenens " services fell. But these matters also are
no longer in issue.

The single question therefore that remains is whether expenses incurred in
earning the profits and gains which are assessable under Schedule E are, so far
as they are not allowed in that assessment, deductible for the purpose of the
assessment under Schedule D. The special commissioners held that they are,
Upjohn J. upon case stated that they are not, and the Court of Appeal upon
appeal from him that they are.

My Lords, in my opinion Upjohn J. was right, and I can state my reasons
shortly.

I regard it as fundamental and well settled law that the Schedules to the
Income Tax Acts are mutually exclusive, and that the specific Schedules A, B, C
and E, and the rules which respectively regulate them, afford a complete code
for each class of income, dealing with allowances, deductions and exemptions
relating to them respectively. Accordingly, when it is conceded, as it has to be
conceded, that Dr. Ross was assessable under Schedule E and also Schedule D, I
cannot look further than the rules under Schedule E to determine his liability
under that schedule and the rules under Schedule D to determine his liability
under that schedule. It was found by the special commissioners, and much
importance was attached to the finding, that " at all material times Dr. Ross
exercised the profession of consultant radiologist, his part-time hospital appointments being a necessary part of the exercise of that profession and merely
incidental thereto, notwithstanding that a great deal of his time was thereby
taken up." But this means no more than that it was necessary, if he was to
carry on his profession, that he should accept a post, in respect of which he
would be assessable under Schedule E. He would therefore have two taxable
sources of income, but that fact lends no support to the view that he can deduct
expenses incurred in respect of income assessed under one schedule from income
assessed under another. It appears to me, if I may say so with the greatest
respect to the Court of Appeal, that they have given undue weight to the
undoubted fact that Dr. Ross carried on the profession of a radiologist whether
he was exercising his appointment or seeing private patients, but ignored the

fact that for income tax purposes he was, no less undoubtedly, not engaged in a single activity. He may be called a consultant radiologist and so he is, but his activities (and that is what matters) are for tax purposes those of a radiologist holding an employment and a radiologist engaging in private practice. In respect of the former, the amount that he can deduct from his emoluments for tax purposes is governed by the seventh rule in the Ninth Schedule to the Income Tax Act 1952; in respect of the latter, section 137 [9] of the same Act, which is expressed in negative terms, affords no grounds for the claim that expenses incurred in earning profits or gains under another schedule can be brought into account. . . .

Note
See also *post*, Chap. 11, *cf. I.R.C.* v. *Brander and Cruickshank* [1971] 1 W.L.R. 212; *post*, p. 232.

(iii) *The Revenue can choose the appropriate Case of a Schedule*

Although the Schedules are mutually exclusive, where an item falls within one Schedule, but may be taxed under more than one Case of that Schedule, the Revenue is entitled to select the Case which is most favourable to it.

LIVERPOOL AND LONDON AND GLOBE INSURANCE COMPANY v. BENNETT

House of Lords [1913] A.C. 610; 82 L.J.K.B. 1221; 109 L.T. 483; 29 T.L.R. 757; 57 S.J. 739; 20 Mans. 295; 6 T.C. 375

The taxpayer company received interest from its investments abroad which were not remitted to this country. Under Case I of Schedule D these " profits " of the taxpayers' business were taxable, under Case IV they escaped tax if not remitted. *Held*, the Revenue was entitled to elect for assessment under Case I.

LORD SHAW OF DUNFERMLINE : . . . The facts thus appear to answer, in terms, Case I of Schedule D of the Income Tax Act. The duties under that schedule are " to be charged in respect of any trade, manufacture, adventure, or concern in the nature of trade not contained in any other schedule of this Act." No other schedule is put forward by the surveyor. And " the duty to be charged in respect thereof shall be computed on a sum not less than the full amount of the balance of the profits or gains." Prima facie, it is difficult to figure a case so plainly covered by a statute.

But it was argued that the investment of funds abroad placed this company in the position of being only liable to be taxed under the fourth case of Schedule D, which covers " the duty to be charged in respect of interest arising from securities " abroad, and that the duty was restricted accordingly to duty upon the amount of interest " received in Great Britain in the current year." My Lords, it is not necessary to decide whether that case applies or not. The assessment has been laid on, not in respect of it, but has been laid on in respect of the first case in Schedule D, which is applicable to the balance of profit of trade. The argument as to the fourth case, therefore, drops out, because it is well settled that if a sufficient warrant be found in the statute for taxation under alternative heads the alternative lies with the taxing authority. They have selected Case I. It appears to me that this selection is not only justified in law, but is founded upon the soundest and most elementary principles of business. . . .

[9] Now I.C.T.A. 1970, s. 130.

Chapter 6

INCOME FROM LAND

1. Schedule A

SCHEDULE A charges to income tax the annual profits or gains arising in respect of rents under leases, rentcharges and other annual payments, and other receipts arising out of the ownership of an estate or interest in or right over land in the United Kingdom.[1]

(A) RELATIONSHIP OF SCHEDULE A TO OTHER SCHEDULES

REPORT OF THE LAW COMMISSION AND THE SCOTTISH LAW COMMISSION

" Taxation of Income and Gains Derived from Land," 1971 Cmnd. 4654

60. The trading profits of a dealer in land are assessed to tax under Case I of Schedule D; but all rents are (strictly) assessable under Schedule A, whether they arise from land which is stock-in-trade or from other land held by the dealer as an investment. The rental income is often merely incidental to the trade and in practice, if the rents are small in relation to the dealing profits, the Inspector will permit all the rents (and deductions) to be carried into the Case I computation, thus avoiding the necessity of raising a Schedule A assessment as well. This is a useful simplification and we considered recommending its enactment. We decided against it, however, because any transfer from Schedule A to Case I of Schedule D would be limited to rents arising from stock-in-trade and a positive enactment would make it difficult to allow any small investment rents to be carried over as well (as is now the practice). Paradoxically, legislation might result in the making of more, rather than fewer, small Schedule A assessments.

61. Some rental income, namely that from furnished lettings, is assessed under Case VI of Schedule D instead of under Schedule A. It would be superficially tidier if this were transferred to Schedule A, but there are three reasons for not doing so, and we do not recommend it. First, such rent is not wholly derived from land: part of it is attributable to the use of furniture etc., and part may also be for services. Secondly, such rents tend to be irregular and the method of assessing and collecting tax under Schedule A (described in paragraph 55 above) is, in consequence, less appropriate than the more flexible basis adopted for Case VI. Finally, if it is to his advantage, the taxpayer may be able to have the liability transferred from Case VI to Case I, on a trading basis.

62. Two other aspects of the taxation of profits derived from land fall within Case VI. They are, first, certain sums received by persons other than the land-

---

[1] I.C.T.A. 1970, s. 67.

lord, in lieu of premiums (sections 80–82); and, secondly, certain gains falling within section 488. Both sets of provisions are anti-avoidance and they have been very largely successful in discouraging certain abnormal transactions. Needless to say, they are fairly complicated provisions; they are intended to be deterrents and it would be no simplification to bring them under Schedule A.

63. When we considered mining (etc.) rents, the question arose whether they should all be transferred from Schedule D to Schedule A, whether they are paid in kind or in cash. In theory, it would be tidier to do so; but we accepted that where cash payments are involved the collection advantages of Schedule D (and deduction at source) are overwhelming, and we therefore excluded cash rents from our recommendation in paragraph 26. For similar reasons we recommend no change in the treatment of rents payable under electric line wayleaves (section 157).

Note
References are to the I.C.T.A. 1970.

(B) Rents and Lease Premiums

Rents, rentcharges and like payments are payments of an income nature. On the other hand, premiums for a lease have always been regarded as being of a capital nature. In the case of a lease for a short term, the effect of a lease at a low premium (or none at all) and a high rent differs little from that of a lease at a high premium and a correspondingly reduced rent. In consequence, when in 1963 the present system of taxing the profits from land was introduced,[2] provisions were introduced whereby a premium under a " short " lease was to be treated, in part, as rent.[3] These provisions are complex, and alternative methods of dealing with premiums have been suggested.[4]

FINAL REPORT OF THE ROYAL COMMISSION ON THE TAXATION OF PROFITS AND INCOME

1955 Cmd. 9474

Nature of the Problem

851. Over the years there has been considerable controversy regarding the appropriate tax treatment of a premium paid in order to secure a lease of property. The payer acquires an asset of limited life but receives no tax relief in respect of it. A man who lets property at a premium forgoes the whole or part of the rent he might otherwise have received over the term of the lease, and the premium which he receives instead is normally treated as a capital receipt not subject to taxation. It has long been asked whether a lessee should not receive some relief for his wasting asset and it is also a question whether a lessor should be required to include his receipt in his taxable income.

---

[2] Previously, a landowner was taxed upon a notional income from land based upon its annual value.
[3] Now I.C.T.A. 1970, s. 80, as amended by Finance Act 1972, s. 81.
[4] For a full discussion of the problems of taxing premiums, see C. N. Beattie, " Premiums for Leases " [1963] B.T.R. 243. The taxation of leaseholds generally, and the relationship of Sched. A to other taxes, is comprehensively dealt with by A. E. W. Park and D. A. Landau, " The Taxation of Leases " [1969] B.T.R. 265, 368.

865. One line of approach is to enquire: What is the real nature of a premium? For if it is rent in advance, as it is sometimes called, there would be a strong theoretical argument for making the recipient of the premium liable to an equivalent share of the tax on the income of the land and for giving a corresponding measure of relief to the payer.

866. We do not think it possible to assert that a premium can be categorised as rent in advance. If paid in respect of a very short term of lease, it is no doubt practically indistinguishable from rent: if paid in respect of a long term, it has no natural equivalence with rent: and if afforded in kind not in money, as in the case of buildings or improvements to buildings, it is not like rent at all. And even if a premium for the grant of a lease could be treated as rent in advance, it would be a great deal more difficult to say that a sum paid to purchase the assignment of a lease is rent. Therefore we consider that a premium is best treated as a sum of money paid upon a sale, the thing bought being the beneficial right or part of the beneficial right of occupation for the period of years in question. From this point of view the transaction differs in degree, but not in substance, from the purchase and sale of a freehold, which is the right of beneficial occupation in perpetuity.

Note

The Report here states the problem, and the conclusion that lease premiums should continue to be treated as of a capital nature.

It should be remembered, however, that at that time income tax was related to the annual value of land and not to the actual rental income.

Chapter 28 of the Report, and especially paras. 826–827, should be studied for the discussion of the question of whether the " notional income " derived from the enjoyment of land by an owner-occupier should be taxed.

REPORT OF THE LAW COMMISSION AND THE SCOTTISH LAW COMMISSION

" Taxation of Income and Gains derived from Land," 1971 Cmnd. 4654

18. A premium for the grant of a lease exceeding 50 years is regarded for tax purposes as a wholly capital payment and receipt; but a premium paid for a lease of any lesser duration is treated as containing a rental element, and this element is taxable under Schedule A as if it were rent payable in the year of the grant (section 80). Certain other sums are treated as premiums for this purpose. The taxable element is the whole premium less 2 per cent. thereof for each year of the lease other than the first. A premium for a 21-year lease is thus taxable as to 60 per cent., and one for a 7-year lease as to 88 per cent. Since the taxable sum is not (from the recipient landlord's point of view) spread over the term of the lease, there are special provisions relating to the rate at which surtax thereon is payable (section 85 (2) and Schedule 3).

19. The position of the tenant who has paid such a premium (and of his successors in title) is also affected (section 83). He is treated as if he were paying in each year an additional sum by way of rent equal to the sum charged on his landlord spread over the term of the lease; and if he grants an underlease, that " rent " is deductible from the rent received by him, for the purposes of his own liability to tax under Schedule A. If the underlease is also granted at a premium, the taxable amount of that premium will be reduced by reference to the taxable amount of the headlease premium.

20. These provisions are by no means simple and it was represented to us that if Capital Gains Tax had existed in 1963 they might never have been enacted. We think, however, that it would be going too far to abolish the taxation of premiums (as income) altogether: a premium for a very short lease is not

sensibly distinguishable from rent in advance and should be taxed as such at income tax rates.

21. An alternative method of taxing premiums would be to provide that those for terms not exceeding X years wholly constitute payments of rent chargeable under Schedule A (thus excluding any charge to Capital Gains Tax); premiums for longer terms being treated as wholly capital, outside the scope of Schedule A.

22. This alternative method would seriously affect the revenue yield if X were pitched too short, and it would be hard on the taxpayer if it were too long. At 14 years, the premium on a 14-year lease would be wholly taxed; at present only 74 per cent. of it is taxed. Nevertheless, there is no doubt that a change in the law in favour of this alternative method would represent a considerable simplification and *we RECOMMEND it*. Because of the conflicting considerations, we do not make any positive recommendation as to the term which we have called X, but if the change is to win general acceptance we think that X would have to lie in the 7–10 years range.

(C) Permissible Deductions

Schedule A does not charge rents and other receipts as such, but the " annual profits or gains." From the taxpayer's gross rental and other income may be deducted certain items of expenditure on the property, in respect of maintenance, repairs, insurance or management, certain services provided by the taxpayer and payments made by the taxpayer in the form of rates, rent to a superior landlord and similar payments.[5]

(i) Expenditure on Repairs

REPORT OF THE LAW COMMISSION AND THE SCOTTISH LAW COMMISSION

" Taxation of Income and Gains derived from Land," 1971 Cmnd. 4654

31. It is not unusual for difficulties to arise in connection with the deduction of expenditure in respect of deferred repairs to property which has been recently acquired. The problem is of a general nature, and is by no means limited to the field of Schedule A: indeed, the principal authorities relate to the computation of trading profits under Schedule D. The leading case of *Law Shipping Co. Ltd.* v. *I.R.C.*, 1924 S.C. 74; 12 T.C. 621[6] has generally been taken to establish the proposition that a purchaser may not deduct expenditure incurred to make good dilapidations referable to the period of the previous ownership. This is supported on two grounds: first, that such expenditure is not sufficiently related to the earning of the purchaser's profits from which the deduction is sought; and, secondly, that although expenditure on repairs is prima facie of a revenue nature, in such circumstances it should be treated as an outgoing on capital account as an addition to the purchase price of the asset. So far as Schedule A is concerned, it seems that statutory force has been given to this view—section 72 (2) (*b*).

32. In the recent case of *Odeon Associated Theatres Ltd.* v. *Jones,*[7] however,

---

5 I.C.T.A. 1970, ss. 71–77.
6 *Post,* p. 178.   7 [1971] 1 W.L.R. 442; [1971] 2 All E.R. 407.

Pennycuick V.-C. held that certain deferred repairs referable to the pre-acquisition period were deductible in computing the purchaser's trading profits. In that case the nature of the repairs was not such that they had to be carried out before the assets were commercially viable in the purchaser's hands and the *Law Shipping* case was distinguished on that ground, and on the ground that in the earlier case there had been no evidence of accountancy practice.

33. If the decision in *Odeon Associated Theatres* is not reversed on appeal and is allowed by the legislature to stand as authority,[8] there will be a potentially more extensive right to deduct expenditure in respect of pre-acquisition dilapidations for Schedule D purposes than for Schedule A. We would not support the existence of any avoidable distinction of principle between the Schedules and *we suggest* that section 72 (2) (*b*) should if necessary be reviewed.

THE LAW SHIPPING CO. LTD. v. I.R.C.

Court of Session (*post*, p. 178)

Note
    This is a decision on the deductibility of expenditure in calculating trading profits for the purposes of Case I of Schedule D and is discussed in Chapter 9. It is, however, of fundamental importance to the problem of deductibility of expenditure on repairs. (See the extract from the Law Commission Report, above.)

ODEON ASSOCIATED THEATRES LTD. v. JONES

Court of Appeal [1972] 2 W.L.R. 331; (1971) 115 S.J. 850; [1972] 1 All E.R. 681

SALMON L.J.: . . . On January 8, 1945, Odeon bought what had formerly been called the Regal Cinema at Marble Arch for £240,000. During the war years, owing to the then current restrictions, it had been impossible to spend more than comparatively small sums on keeping cinemas in repair. Accordingly in 1945 the cinema at Marble Arch, like all cinemas in this country, was somewhat run down. During the previous five years many repairs and replacements which would normally have been effected had necessarily been deferred, because it had been impossible to obtain licences to carry them out.

Nevertheless, the Marble Arch cinema at the date of its acquisition was a fully effective profit-earning asset, and the price which Odeon paid for it had not been diminished nor in any way affected by reason of its lack of repair.

During the period 1945–54 Odeon spent considerable sums of money in making additions to building plant and equipment at this cinema. All these items were charged as capital expenditure by Odeon in their accounts. In each year from 1945 to 1954 Odeon also spent substantial sums of money on repairs and renewals at this cinema. Some of this money was charged in their accounts as revenue expenditure spent on current repairs and renewals; it was allowed without question by the Inland Revenue as a charge against Odeon's profits. On the other hand, some of the money spent during this period on repairs and renewals was charged in Odeon's accounts as revenue expenditure spent on deferred repairs and renewals.

. . . The Crown contends that the several sums amounting in all to £7,969 are not revenue expenditure but capital expenditure and therefore cannot be taken into account in assessing Odeon's liability for income tax in respect of any of the fiscal years in question.

. . . It is also perhaps worth noting that the work comprised in these items includes, for example, renewing carpets, decorating, rewiring, etc. It does not

---

[8] The decision has been affirmed in the Court of Appeal [1972] 2 W.L.R. 331, *infra*.

seem to me that any of this expenditure can, prima facie, properly be regarded as being in the nature of capital expenditure.

. . . The evidence of a number of exceptionally distinguished accountants, accepted by the Special Commissioners, was that in accordance with the established principles of sound commercial accounting the disputed items of expenditure were a charge to revenue. The Vice-Chancellor [Pennycuick V.-C.[9]] held that in law these items were properly chargeable to revenue and that the profits for the years in question should be assessed for tax on that basis. From that judgment the Crown now appeals.

. . . In my view, the money laid out in respect of the disputed items was indubitably laid out by Odeon wholly and exclusively for the purposes of their trade.[10]

. . . I, of course, accept that if any of the disputed items in truth constituted capital expenditure they would be excluded by section 137 (f) and (g).[11] But no help can be derived from the statute in deciding the question of what is capital expenditure. The statute does not give even the faintest hint as to how this question should be answered. I am therefore wholly unable to accept the argument that the established commercial accounting practice (found by the Special Commissioners) of charging the disputed items to revenue and not to capital in any way conflicts with the statute.[12] . . .

BUCKLEY L.J.: . . . I need not restate the facts, but these points need to be stressed. First, all the disputed expenditure was of a kind which, if the theatres had remained in the ownership of the owners from whom they were acquired by the taxpayer company and the expenditure had been incurred by those owners, would have been deductible as revenue expenditure. Secondly, the amount of dilapidation which occurred before the acquisition by the taxpayer company of a theatre (in the case stated called " deferred repairs ") did not in any case significantly affect the price paid by the taxpayer company for the theatre. Thirdly, the deferred repairs were not for the most part such as to require immediate remedy, and there was no question of danger to the public or of any theatre having to be closed for repairs. Fourthly, all cinema theatre owners were in a like position of being unable, on account of wartime restrictions, to carry out any but the most urgent repairs, redecorations or refurnishing of their theatres; there was no competition in this respect: this state of affairs continued until the early 1950s.

The cost of acquiring or creating a physical capital asset for use in a trade or business is clearly capital expenditure. The cost of improving such an asset by adding to it or modifying it may well be capital expenditure. On the other hand, the cost of works of recurrent repair or maintenance of such an asset attributable to the wear and tear occurring in the course of use of the asset in his trade or business by the person carrying out the works is revenue expenditure, and so constitutes a proper debit item in the profit and loss account of the business. Whether, where there has been a change of ownership, the cost of works of repair or maintenance attributable to wear and tear which occurred before the change of ownership should be regarded as revenue expenditure or capital expenditure is a question the answer to which must, in my opinion, depend on the particular facts of each case. The Solicitor-General has argued that any repair must improve the article repaired and, avoiding undue cynicism, I think that that proposition must be accepted. He says further that if the state

9 [1971] 1 W.L.R. 442.
10 The appropriate charging provision was, in relation to the years in question, Case I of Sched. D, see *post*, Chap. 9. The important question, for the purposes of Sched. A, is whether the repairs are of a capital or revenue nature.
11 Now I.C.T.A. 1970, s. 130.
12 Salmon L.J. went on to consider and to distinguish the *Law Shipping* case.

of the article, when repaired, is better than its state was when it was acquired by the person carrying out the repairs, the cost of repairs should pro tanto be regarded as capital expenditure. A tradesman, for example, who acquires a dilapidated shop in which to carry on his business, and, either before he commences business or as soon thereafter as he can afford to do so, puts the shop into a state of repair and decoration suitable for his business, has incurred the cost not only of acquiring the shop but also of repairing and decorating it in a suitable manner in order to provide himself with a capital asset of a character which he regards as appropriate to his business. The whole of this expenditure, it is said, is capital expenditure because it constitutes the cost of acquiring such a capital asset as the trader requires for the purpose of his business. The argument is an attractive one, but should not, in my opinion, be accepted without careful consideration.

The Solicitor-General contends that the expenditure on deferred repairs was what he described as " a once for all jacking-up of the value of the principal asset," and so was non-recurrent expenditure by the taxpayer company for the enduring benefit of its trade. He says that the fact that the prices paid for theatres took no account of the circumstances that at the dates of purchase repairs had already been deferred is of no importance. He contends that the cost of doing the deferred repairs was an additional cost to the taxpayer company of acquiring the capital assets, that is, the theatres. Such expenditure, he says, should be regarded as capital expenditure. As Lord Reid observed in *Strick* v. *Regent Oil Co. Ltd.*[13]:

> " The question [whether a particular outlay can be set against income or must be regarded as a capital outlay] is ultimately a question of law for the court, but it is a question which must be answered in light of all the circumstances which it is reasonable to take into account, and the weight which must be given to a particular circumstance in a particular case must depend rather on common sense than on strict application of any single legal principle."

In answering that question of law it is right that the court should pay regard to ordinary principles of commercial accounting so far as applicable. Accountants are, after all, the persons best qualified by training and practical experience to suggest answers to the many difficult problems that can arise in this field. Nevertheless the question remains ultimately a question of law.

No one, I think, would dispute that the cost of ordinary current repairs in the normal course of maintenance of a fixed capital asset employed in a business is revenue expenditure. Such cost arises out of the wear and tear of the asset in the course of earning the profits of the business and so is a proper debit to be set against the revenue of the business in its profit and loss account. I would myself think that, save in exceptional circumstances, this is true even in the case of the first repairs in the normal course of maintenance of an asset acquired in a part worn condition. A tradesman who acquires a shop, the outside painting of which was last done two years before his purchase, will have to repaint the shop earlier than if it had been redecorated immediately before acquisition, but this, I think, is something which, as a commercial matter, he will take into account in considering the prospective profitability of the shop during the early years of his ownership. In other words, he will regard it as a revenue expense. He will not say to himself: " When I have to repaint the outside of the shop perhaps three years hence, only three-fifths of the cost will be chargeable against revenue in my profit and loss account: the balance will be a capital investment in my business."

13 [1966] A.C. 295, 313.

. . . The *Law Shipping* case is, in my view, more nearly analogous to the case of a trader who has bought a capital asset which at the date of acquisition was not in working order and has to put it into working order before being able to use it in his business. When the Law Shipping Co. bought the ship they knew that in order to be able to use her in their business beyond the one voyage they would need to spend not only the purchase price of the ship but also the cost of the necessary repairs. The facts of the present case are quite different.

Note

See also *Jackson* v. *Laskers Home Furnishers Ltd.* [1957] 1 W.L.R. 69; *Bidwell* v. *Gardiner* (1960) 39 T.C. 31. The decision is considered by G. S. A. Wheatcroft, " The Law Shipping Rule Eroded " [1972] B.T.R. 51. As to the importance of accounting evidence, see also *Heather* v. *P.-E. Consulting Group Ltd.* [1972] 2 All E.R. 107.

EXTRA-STATUTORY CONCESSION B4

B4. *Maintenance and repairs of property obviated by alterations etc.;*
Schedule A assessments

Where maintenance and repairs of property are obviated by improvements, additions and alterations, so much of the outlay as is equal to the estimated cost of the maintenance and repairs is allowed as a deduction in computing liability in respect of rents under Schedule A. This concession does not apply where:
- (i) the alterations, etc. are so extensive as to amount to the reconstruction of the property, or
- (ii) there is a change in the use of the property which would have made such maintenance or repairs unnecessary.

Note

This concession is published in the Board of Inland Revenue's blooklet, I.R. 1 (1970), " Extra-statutory concessions in operation at August 1, 1970." (In certain cases, where a strict interpretation of the appropriate statutory provision would cause hardship or injustice, the Revenue are prepared to relax the law in favour of the taxpayer. Some of these concessions are well-established and published in the booklet. The taxpayer is not, however, entitled to the concession and no appeal lies against its refusal.)

(ii) *Expenditure on Management*

I.R.C. v. WILSON'S EXECUTORS

Court of Session (1934) 18 T.C. 465; 1934 S.C. 244

Payments by the taxpayer as compensation for disturbance and expenses of litigation were held not to be deductible as costs of " management."

THE LORD PRESIDENT (CLYDE): . . . If " management " just means administration, it follows that the cost of management includes some things which, from an accounting point of view, would constitute capital expenditure, as well as a great variety of things which, from an accounting point of view, would constitute revenue expenditure. In short, there is almost no end to the scope of the deductions which would become permissible under the Rule if the word " management " is construed in the wide and general sense to which I have referred—a sense which, as I have said, is consistent with its ordinary use in popular language. It may be, though I express no opinion on the point, that expenditure of a capital kind should be excluded upon the ground that Schedule A tax is truly a tax upon income, in other words, upon net rent, for it has been dealt with in the House of Lords more than once—and prominently in the case of *The London County Council* v. *Attorney-General*,[14] and in the case of

14 [1901] A.C. 26, *ante*, p. 87.

Miller,[15] as a tax on income, as distinct from a tax on property. If it is a tax on income, or to be deemed to be a tax on income, it might be possible to deem all management expenditure, which is of a capital character, as excluded from the category of admissible deductions under the Rule. But, even so, there would remain within the " costs of management " a range of expenditure so extensive as to make it difficult to believe that Parliament meant by the word " management " to include the general administration of the estate.

There is, however, another meaning which the word " management " will bear, much more restricted and also not inconsistent with the use of the word in popular language. If the proprietor of a large estate were asked who it was that managed his estate for him, he might reply that he employed a factor to whom he paid an annual salary (with perquisites perhaps) to manage the estate for him. There might, of course, be no factor upon the estate, but I imagine that the costs of managing the estate, in the sense in which I am now using the word, would include any cost in having the estate accounts properly kept, in collecting the rents and in making the necessary disbursements. Broadly, from this point of view, the " cost of management " would be restricted either to the fee or salary paid to a factor, or to the costs incurred for such purposes as I have mentioned. The difficulty about this construction of the word " management " is that it appears to be almost too restricted.

There are two aids to the choice between these alternative constructions of the Rule which occur to me. To the first of them I have already referred, namely, the alarmingly large scope of costs which would be included if the wider construction were adopted. I cannot think Parliament meant that. The other aid is that " management " appears in the Rule alongside of " maintenance, repairs " and " insurance." If " management " were given its larger meaning, it would be superfluous to make special mention of maintenance, repairs and insurance, for these are merely particular heads of the cost of administering an estate. Since " management " is put in as a separate head, it is natural to suppose that it was not intended to embrace the others, but, on the contrary, to designate something relatively as limited as each of the others, but different from them. The narrower construction of the Clause is consistent with this supposition. I wish I felt more confident than I do in drawing from these considerations a conclusion that the narrower construction is the preferable one. . . .

Note

Subsequent cases have agreed with Lord Clyde in rejecting the " wide " interpretation of " management." However, it is generally considered that his alternative " restricted " interpretation is too narrow, see *Southern* v. *Aldwych Property Trust Ltd*. [1940] 2 K.B. 266, *infra*. An item may be allowed *in part* as a proper expense of management, *e.g.* salary or fees paid to a surveyor or to directors of an investment company, in so far as the payments relate to duties performed in respect of the property in question; see *London and Northern Estates Co. Ltd*. v. *Harris* [1939] 1 K.B. 335; *L. G. Berry Investments Ltd*. v. *Attwool* [1964] 1 W.L.R. 693.

SOUTHERN v. ALDWYCH PROPERTY TRUST LTD.

King's Bench Division [1940] 2 K.B. 266; 109 L.J.K.B. 719; 163 L.T. 364; 56 T.L.R. 808; 84 S.J. 584; 23 T.C. 707

LAWRENCE J.: . . . Lord Clyde [16] in particular, whose judgment it was suggested was most in favour of the respondent, said that the costs of managing the estate " would include any cost in having the estate accounts properly kept,

---

[15] *I.R.C.* v. *Lady Miller* [1930] A.C. 222; 15 T.C. 25.
[16] In *I.R.C.* v. *Wilson's Executors*, 1934 S.C. 244, *supra*.

in collecting the rents and in making the necessary disbursements." The question is, is the cost of advertising a " necessary disbursement " in managing the property? In my opinion it is perfectly clear that it is. No property which is let can be managed in an ordinary business sense without advertisement of the property when it is about to become vacant.

Upon the whole, I find myself unable to agree with the decision of the Special Commissioners in this case that the word " management " in rule 8 ought to be narrowed down by its association with the words " maintenance, repairs and insurance." I do not think that the words " maintenance, repairs and insurance " form any class which excludes the word " management " in the sense which I put upon that word. I think that the word " management " has its ordinary meaning, and includes all the ordinary expenses of management of the property which falls to be taxed under Schedule A. I am, therefore, of opinion that the expenses in question in this case do not fall within section 33, subsection 1,[17] because they are excluded by [*ibid.* subs. 3], and in consequence the appeal must be allowed with costs.

2. Schedule B

Tax under Schedule B is charged on the occupier of woodlands in the United Kingdom managed on a commercial basis with a view to the realisation of profit.[18] Tax is charged on the assessable value of the occupation in the chargeable period, and this amount, which is equal to one-third of the woodlands' annual value, is *deemed* for all tax purposes to be the income arising from the occupation.[19] Thus tax is charged on an amount deemed to be income, rather than the actual income from the woodlands. However, the occupier may elect instead to be assessed under Case I of Schedule D on his actual profits.[20] A distinction must be drawn between occupying woodlands on a commercial basis and carrying on a trade in relation to the products of woodlands; it may be difficult to ascertain where occupation ceases and a separate trade begins.

REPORT OF THE ROYAL COMMISSION ON THE INCOME TAX

Colwyn Commission, 1920 Cmd. 615

459. Our investigations have led us to the belief that there are few more difficult subjects of assessments than woodlands. The direct return from property of this kind arises when the timber is cut, and the period of maturity varies greatly and is sometimes a very long one. The difficulty of dealing with the resulting profits under a system of taxation which has regard to profits of a more or less annual character will be obvious.

COATES v. HOLKER ESTATES CO.

Chancery Division (1961) 40 T.C. 75; [1961] T.R. 249

An election by the occupier to be taxed under Schedule D does not have the effect that growing timber is to be treated as the stock of a trade.

---

[17] The references are to the Income Tax Act 1918.
[19] *Ibid.* s. 92.

[18] I.C.T.A. 1970, s. 91.
[20] *Ibid.* ss. 91 (2), 111.

PLOWMAN J.: . . . What section 125 (2) [21] is saying, in my judgment, is not that the occupation of woodlands managed on a commercial basis and with a view to the realisation of profit shall be deemed to be a trade, but that the profits or gains arising from such occupation " shall for all purposes be deemed to be profits or gains of a trade." In other words, merely by deeming the offspring to be something which it is not, the section does not change the nature of the parent. Merely to deem the profits or gains arising from the occupation of the woodlands to be the profits or gains of a trade is not, in my judgment, to say that the occupation of the woodlands is to be deemed to be a trade; and on the construction of the sections which I have read up to this point I see nothing to lead to the conclusion that the occupation of woodlands is to be deemed to be a trade. . . .

I.R.C. v. WILLIAMSON BROTHERS

Court of Session (1950) 31 T.C. 370; 1950 S.C. 391; [1949] T.R. 249

On the distinction between occupation of woodlands and separate trade.

LORD KEITH : This case, in my opinion, is balanced on a very narrow edge. An attractive solution might seem to be that this is not the case of a landowner exploiting his land, but the case of a trader acquiring land to supply him with the raw materials of his trade. But the case of *Back* v. *Daniels*,[22] which has been quoted more than once in the House of Lords with approval, or at least with no sign of disapproval, is adverse to a decision proceeding on any such distinction. The respondents there were *inter alia* potato merchants, and under a peculiar form of agreement which was held to constitute an occupation of lands, they grew potatoes for the purposes of their business on lands hired from farmers. It was held nonetheless that they fell to be treated as occupiers liable to assessment in respect of their occupation under Schedule B and not under Schedule D. In the case before us the Respondents have acquired land on which there is a growing crop of trees for the purpose of using the same in their business as timber merchants and sawmillers. Part of the trees have been cut down by them and so used. So far on its facts this case is in my opinion indistinguishable from *Back* v. *Daniels* except for the immaterial difference that in the latter the respondents were only occupiers, whereas here they are both owners and occupiers.

If this be so the only question seems to be, is what the Respondents are doing referable to their right of occupation? We are told very little of the manner in which the Respondents have dealt with the timber, but I gather that they cut the timber, haul it to their mills and there saw it and mill it. I am not clear whether these milling operations are confined to turning the timber into pit-props and poles as seems to be suggested by the first finding in the Case. It may be that the Special Commissioners considered the nature or extent of the treatment immaterial so long as the timber came from the Respondents' property. In my opinion however, all operations on the timber are not franked by the Schedule B assessment. To take an example at one end of the scale, the manufacture of the timber into furniture would in my opinion constitute a trade rendering the Respondents liable in assessment to tax under Schedule D as well as to assessment under Schedule B in respect of their occupation of the woodlands. On the other hand the mere felling of the timber, putting it

---

[21] Now I.C.T.A. 1970, s. 111 (2).
[22] [1925] 1 K.B. 526; 9 T.C. 183. At that time, the occupation of farmlands was treated in a manner similar to the present treatment of woodlands.

into a fit condition for transport, transporting it and selling it would be all operations referable to the occupation of the land. They would be operations as normal and natural to the ownership and occupation of ripe growing timber, as the harvesting, threshing and transport of grain would be in the case of an arable farm. But there comes a point, in my opinion, where an owner and occupier of woodlands or a farmer may pass beyond normal exploitation of his land and crop and deal with the fruits of his lands so as to attract to himself tax as a trader under Schedule D. In *Back* v. *Daniels* Scrutton L.J. gave as illustrations of operations unconnected with the occupation of the land a cheese factory dealing with the milk of a dairy farm, or a butcher's shop dealing with the beasts of a cattle farm. In the same category, I think, might be cases of a cannery dealing with the fruit of a fruit farm, a flour mill dealing with the grain of a farm, and the case already given of a furniture factory dealing with the timber of land. I say might be, because I can conceive of cases where such methods were adopted on a domestic scale merely for the use of the owner, his servants or tenants and would not attract tax under Schedule D; but that I think would be because the owner or occupier was not engaging in trade.

. . . I would observe that while Rule 7 of Schedule B refers to woodlands managed by the occupier on a commercial basis and with a view to the realisation of profits and so shows that such woodlands are assessable under Schedule B unless the occupier elects to be assessed under Schedule D, this reference is confined to woodlands and does not necessarily cover the cut timber. Many, if not most, owners and occupiers of woodlands manage them on a commercial basis by selling the growing timber to a timber merchant to be felled within a stipulated period. But other cases where owners and occupiers retain the cutting and selling in their own hands would also fall under Schedule B. And as I see it the only circumstances in which the possibility of assessment under Schedule D (apart from the election of the occupier) could fall to be considered would be where the occupier's operations with the cut timber extended beyond what could legitimately be regarded as normal preparation for the market and disposing of the fruits of his lands. The use of saw-milling plant for such normal purposes would be only reasonable and would still leave him under Schedule B.

. . . In my opinion accordingly the case should be remitted to the Special Commissioners to consider on the whole facts of the case whether the Respondents' operations can properly be regarded as wholly referable to their right of ownership or occupation, or whether they fall to be treated in whole or in part as separable trading activities. The question may be a question of degree and may be difficult of decision but, in my opinion, we are entitled to the decision of the Special Commissioners on the matter untrammelled by the decision of *Christie* v. *Davies* [23] and when the case returns to us it will, I expect, be amplified by a more detailed account of the extent and nature of the operations to which the timber is subjected. . . .

COLLINS v. FRASER

Chancery Division [1969] 1 W.L.R. 823; 113 S.J. 308; [1969] 3 All E.R. 524; 46 T.C. 143

MEGARRY J.: This is a case upon drawing the line. It arises in relation to Schedule B income tax on woodlands. The taxpayer claims that certain activities

[23] [1945] 1 All E.R. 370; 26 T.C. 398. In that case it was held that the working of a sawmill was an ordinary method of rendering the timber marketable and the woodlands commercially successful. The profits therefrom, to the extent to which timber from the estate was dealt with, arose from the occupation of the woodlands and were covered by the assessment under Sched. B.

of his are liable only under Schedule B. The Crown, on the other hand, say that he is caught by Schedule D.

. . . The particular point which arises before me is this. At what stage in the process of converting a tree into wooden manufactured articles does the wood pass from the cover of Schedule B and become exposed to Schedule D?

. . . The facts are set out in the case stated, and for present purposes I need only summarise certain of the matters. The case is stated by way of an appeal by the taxpayer against certain assessments under Case I of Schedule D in respect of the profits arising from the trade of timber merchant and dealer for the years 1963–64 to 1965–66 inclusive, to a total amount of £10,000. The assessment is in respect of this saw-mills, the Chipnal Saw Mills at Cheswardine, Shropshire. The business commenced there in the year ended March 31, 1953, and at first the main activity was the production and sale of converted timber, including thin boards. These he manufactured from round timber, mainly purchased from outside suppliers but to a small extent provided by some woodland at Chipnal which he owned, being less than half an acre in extent. In the year ended March 31, 1958, the taxpayer embarked upon a policy of box and crate making, and he purchased further stitching, nailing and other machines necessary to this activity. He had previously been making certain fencing posts and panels, and he had been selling his thin boards to customers who made them into wooden crates.

In the year ended March 31, 1959, the woodland that the taxpayer owned at Chipnal had become exhausted, and he purchased a woodland at Prees, which is some 12 miles away, containing rather over 33 acres. These are the woodlands in question in this case. He has been drawing timber from these woodlands, at first merely thinnings but later more substantial fellings. The real issue that has emerged in the argument before me is whether Schedule B covers the timber only to the point when it has become felled round timber, stripped, cut and hauled to the roadside, as the Crown contended (though I may add that they also concede that the transport to the saw-mills would be covered), or whether Schedule B covers the timber up to and including the stage when it is converted into planking, as the taxpayer contends.

The case stated gave me little picture of the processes involved, and for my enlightenment, and not, of course, as a matter of evidence, I asked the taxpayer to describe the stages of operation. Broadly stated, there are seven stages. First, there is the felled tree. Secondly, there is that tree trimmed of its branches. Thirdly, that trimmed tree is reduced either to what is called cross-cut timber, perhaps some 20 or 30 ft. long, or to 5 ft. lengths. This is a process which may be done at the woodland site or may be done at the mill. One then leaves the woodland for the mill, and if the timber has arrived at the mill in the cross-cut timber form it will then be reduced to the 5 ft. length; that is stage four. At stage five, these lengths are then reduced to planking an inch or an inch and a half thick. Stage six consists of the conversion of this planking into what is variously described as thin boards, thin wood or box boards. These are one-eighth of an inch thick, an inch or an inch and a half wide and some 12 to 20 inches long. Stage seven is the conversion of these box boards into the boxes which are the main product of the taxpayer's mill. The extent to which Schedule B covers these stages is accordingly until after stage two, on the Crown's contention, or after stage five, on the taxpayer's contention.

. . . On that footing, the matter stands thus. I have been unable to discover in the case stated any reason (and Mr. Medd was unable to refer me to any) why what the taxpayer does up to and including the planking stage shows that he has done more than market his timber. In saying that, I adapt the words of Lord Cooper in the *Williamson* case,[24] at p. 380. Nor, if I turn to Lord Keith's words, at p. 378, can I see what there was to take the planked timber beyond what could legitimately be regarded as normal preparation for the market and disposing of the fruits of the land. I accept, of course, that the fact that the saw-mill operates on land some 12 miles away from the woodlands is a fact that must be borne in mind; but the *Williamson* case makes it clear that this does not carry the point.

I am anxious not to usurp the functions of the commissioners or interfere in any improper way with their jurisdiction; but on the whole it seems to me that the right course to adopt in this case is to send the case back to the commissioners for amendment under section 64 (7),[25] directing them to state what, if anything, was done with the timber up to and including the planking stage which extended beyond what could legitimately be regarded as normal preparation for the market and disposing of the fruits of the taxpayer's land. . . .

[24] 31 T.C. 370, 380; 1950 S.C. 391; *ante*, p. 106.
[25] Now T.M.A. 1970, s. 56 (7).

Chapter 7

INTEREST, ANNUITIES AND OTHER ANNUAL PAYMENTS

1. The Charge to Tax

INCOME tax is charged under Schedule C upon profits arising from certain public revenue dividends and dividends from foreign government securities.[1] Tax under Schedule C is deducted at source.

Under Case III of Schedule D, tax is charged on:

  (a) any interest of money, whether yearly or otherwise, or any annuity or other annual payment;

  (b) all discounts; and

  (c) income, except income charged under Schedule C, from securities bearing interest payable out of the public revenue.[2]

The interest, annuity or annual payment must be paid pursuant to some legal obligation[3] and voluntary gifts, although they may be annual, are not within the charge.[4] Consequently, it may be said that, for income to be chargeable under these provisions, it must have a " source "; the " source " being the property or interest out of which the payment is charged or reserved, by virtue of any deed or will or otherwise, or the personal debt or obligation which supports it.

(A) QUALITY OF RECURRENCE

Case III charges " any interest, whether yearly or otherwise "[5]: but for an annual payment to be chargeable it must possess the quality of recurrence.

WHITWORTH PARK COAL CO. LTD. v. I.R.C.

House of Lords [1961] A.C. 31; [1959] 3 W.L.R. 842; 103 S.J. 938; [1959] 3 All E.R. 703; 38 T.C. 531

The appellants, an investment company which had, prior to nationalisation, been a coal mining company, received certain payments from the Ministry of Fuel and Power as a form of interim compensation. The payments were held to be subject to direct assessment under Case III.

---

[1] I.C.T.A. 1970, s. 93.

[2] *Ibid.* s. 109.

[3] *Ridge Securities Ltd.* v. *I.R.C.* [1964] 1 W.L.R. 479.

[4] See *Peters' Executors* v. *I.R.C.* [1941] 2 All E.R. 620. As to payments to a beneficiary under a discretionary trust, see *Drummond* v. *Collins* [1915] A.C. 1011; *post*, pp. 286, 372.

[5] For an analysis of the meaning of " interest," see *Lomax* v. *Peter Dixon & Son Ltd.* [1943] K.B. 671; see also *Riches* v. *Westminster Bank Ltd.* [1947] A.C. 390 and *Bennett* v. *Ogston* (1930) 15 T.C. 374; *ante*, p. 86.

VISCOUNT SIMONDS: . . . " Annual payment " must, it is said, be read in its context and must in some way resemble or be ejusdem generis with interest or annuities, but these payments are sui generis. That argument appears to me to be no more than a play on words. One must look at the true nature of the payments. It is well recognised that many payments which in the ordinary sense of the words might well be called annual payments do not come within Case III. One limitation is that Case III only applies to payments received as pure profit income [6]; that is, because no deductions are permitted under Case III. And further, the payments must recur or at least be of a recurring character. I think that the payments in this case comply with both these requirements. . . .

Note
This decision established that Case III is not restricted to payments from which tax has been deducted, or is deductible at source under I.C.T.A. 1970, ss. 52–54; see *post*, p. 125.
The relationship between two Cases of the same Schedule (here, Cases III and VI of Schedule D) are considered by Lord Radcliffe ([1961] A.C. 31, 66) who considered Case VI more appropriate.

MOSS' EMPIRES LTD. v. I.R.C.

House of Lords [1937] A.C. 785; 106 L.J.P.C. 138; 157 L.T. 396; 53 T.L.R. 867; 81 S.J. 667; [1937] 3 All E.R. 381; 21 T.C. 295

The appellants entered into a guarantee to pay a sum to another company each year for five years of an amount sufficient to bring the recipient company's yearly profits up to a stated sum in order to enable a dividend to be paid of certain preference shares. The amounts paid varied each year.
Held, the payments were " annual payments," despite being contingent and variable in character, and were the chargeable income of the recipient company under Case III. Consequently, the appellants were entitled to deduct the payments from their own profits.

LORD MAUGHAM: . . . The sole difficulty in the case, as I see it, is the question whether sums paid under the agreement of January 31, 1928, were annual payments within the language of rule 21 of the General Rules of the Income Tax Act 1918.[7] The sentence runs: " Upon payment of any interest of money, annuity or other annual payment, etc."; and the charging section is to be found in Schedule D, 1 (*b*), taken with the words of rule 1 applicable to Case III of that Schedule as stated by his Lordship.
It is, I think, to be noted that we are not concerned here with the case of annual profits or gains arising from a trade, as to which the decision in *Martin* v. *Lowry* [8] would be decisive to show that in that context " annual " means " in any one year." In rule 21 " annual " must be taken to have, like interest on money or an annuity, the quality of being recurrent or being capable of recurrence. The payments we are concerned with were to continue for five years, subject to their being required to make up the guaranteed annual dividend, and were plainly payments intended to supplement so far as necessary the income of the recipients during each of the years in question. In these circumstances I am of opinion that they had the necessary quality of recurrence. . . .

Note
Annual payments which varied in amount were also covenanted in *I.R.C.* v. *Black* [1940] 4 All E.R. 445; *post*, p. 386; and *I.R.C.* v. *Wolfson* [1949] 1 All E.R. 865; *post*, p. 388; *ante*, p. 7.

[6] *Post*, p. 112.
[7] Now I.C.T.A. 1970, s. 53.
[8] [1927] A.C. 312; *post*, p. 152.

(B) PURE INCOME PROFIT

In order to fall within Case III, the payment must be " pure income profit " in the hands of the recipient; in particular, it is necessary to distinguish " annual payments " from " trading receipts." The former constitute *income* of the recipient (and therefore, as a general rule, are not included in the income of the payer and may be deducted by him in computing his total income [9]); the latter merely enter into the computation of the recipient's *profits* (and are not deductible by the payer as such, though they may, of course, be deductible for some other reason, *e.g.* as a proper expense of the payer's own trade [10]).

EARL HOWE v. I.R.C.

Court of Appeal [1919] 2 K.B. 336; 88 L.J.K.B. 821; 121 L.T. 161; 35 T.L.R. 461; 63 S.J. 516; 7 T.C. 296 (also *post*, p. 341)

Premiums on a policy of life assurance were held to be profits of the recipient company rather than " annual payments," and therefore not deductible by the payer in determining his total income.

SCRUTTON L.J.: . . . It is not all payments made every year from which income tax can be deducted. For instance, if a man agrees to pay a motor garage 500*l.* a year for five years for the hire and upkeep of a car, no one suggests that the person paying can deduct income tax from each yearly payment. So if he contracted with a butcher for an annual sum to supply all his meat for a year. The annual instalment would not be subject to tax as a whole in the hands of the payee, but only that part of it which was profits. I never heard the suggestion that income tax could be deducted from premiums on a life policy till I saw it in the judgments of Kenny J. and Madden J. in the Irish case of *Lord Massy* v. *Inland Revenue Commissioners*,[11] and I respectfully concur with Palles C.B. in disapproval of the suggestion. As said by Bramwell B. in *Foley* v. *Fletcher*,[12] it cannot be taken that the Legislature meant to impose a duty on that which is not profit derived from property, but the price of it. These premiums are either payments of capital to obtain on the death a sinking fund—the policy moneys—or the price of such a payment or fund. They do not seem to me to be annual payments *ejusdem generis* with annual interest or annuities, and as income tax on them cannot be deducted against the recipient, I see no reason why the person paying should deduct them from his taxable income. To allow this would be to establish a kind of profits which would escape taxation in the hands of the person paying because he could deduct it as an annual payment; in the hands of the recipient because it did not represent his profits. From this point of view it is immaterial whether the payment is charged or not; it is not an " annual payment " within sections 102, 163 or 164. . . .

Note
    A taxpayer may claim relief in respect of certain life assurance premiums, I.C.T.A. 1970, ss. 19–21.

[9] See *post*, pp. 121 *et seq.*
[10] See *post*, Chap. 9.
[11] Report reproduced in [1919] 2 K.B. 354.
[12] (1858) 3 H. & N. 769.

Re HANBURY, DECD.

Court of Appeal (1939) 38 T.C. 588; 20 A.T.C. 333

In proceedings in connection with a settlement, an executor was awarded a sum of money in respect of the remainderman's use and enjoyment, for a period of years, of certain mining plant. *Held*, the payment was not pure income profit in the hands of the recipient but merely an element in ascertaining profit. Thus, it was not within Case III and tax was not deductible from the payment.

SIR WILFRID GREENE M.R.: . . . There are two classes of annual payments which fall to be considered for Income Tax purposes. There is, first of all, that class of annual payment which the Acts regard and treat as being pure income profit of the recipient undiminished by any deduction. Payments of interest, payments of annuities, to take the ordinary simple case, are payments which are regarded as part of the income of the recipient, and the payer is entitled in estimating his total income to treat those payments as payments which go out of his income altogether. The class of annual payment which falls within that category is quite a limited one. In the other class there stand a number of payments, none the less annual, the very quality and nature of which make it impossible to treat them as part of the pure profit income of the recipient, the proper way of treating them being to treat them as an element to be taken into account in discovering what the profits of the recipient are. This matter was dealt with in a very well-known passage in the judgment of Scrutton L.J. in *Earl Howe* v. *Commissioners of Inland Revenue*,[13] which, if I may say so, I have always found particularly illuminating on questions of this kind. The type of example he gives is that of a yearly payment made, for instance, to the proprietor of a garage for the hire of a motor car. Nobody would suggest that on making that payment the hirer would be entitled to deduct tax, and yet it is annual payment, the reason being that the very nature of that payment itself, having regard to the circumstances in which it is made, necessarily makes the sums paid in the hands of a recipient an element only in the ascertainment of his profits.

These then are the two broad classes of yearly payments: the first class falls within Rules 19 and 21[14]; the second class does not. Some light on the nature of a payment may, I think, also be ascertained by looking at it from the point of view of the payer. If the owner of a business has for the purpose of carrying on that business hired chattels under an agreement under which he is liable to make annual payments, I should have thought it was beyond the possibility of doubt that the sum which he so paid was a sum which merely came into computation in ascertaining the profits of his trade. In the present case, upon the assumption that I make throughout, that this is a payment with which Income Tax is concerned, so far as regards the payers the position that they are in is that they have paid a sum of money for the use of chattels which they have used in a profit-making business. That seems to me to stamp that payment so far as the payer is concerned with a particular quality. From the point of view of the recipient, his position may be summarised. Being the owner of chattels the use and enjoyment of which has been had by the Respondents against payment, is he bound to submit to having the sum he so receives treated as pure income profit in relation to which as between himself and the Revenue he would be entitled to no item of deduction at all on the

---

[13] [1919] 2 K.B. 336, *supra*.
[14] Now I.C.T.A. 1970, ss. 52, 53.

other side of his profits account, or is it a sum in respect of which he is liable to direct assessment and upon such assessment would be entitled to put forward such claim, if any, as he may have on the other side of the account? It seems to me that the nature of the payment brings it within the second class quite clearly. The matter, I think, can be tested in this way. If the Appellant had been carrying on a business of letting out plant for reward, the receipt which he obtains under the present circumstances would have been an item to be taken into account in ascertaining the profits of that business for the purpose of assessment under Case I of Schedule D. Nobody could suggest in such a case, it seems to me, that this payment would be a thing which must be segregated from the receipts of his business and subjected to some special treatment. If that be right—and I have no doubt that it is right—it appears to me to show the quality of this payment to be such that by its nature it is merely an element in the ascertainment of profits and is not a pure profit to be taken by itself. . . .

I.R.C. v. NATIONAL BOOK LEAGUE

Court of Appeal [1957] Ch. 488; [1957] 3 W.L.R. 222; 101 S.J. 553; [1957] 2 All E.R. 644; 37 T.C. 455

LORD EVERSHED M.R.: The National Book League is a company limited by guarantee which was formed in the year 1925. It was not disputed that since September 1951, the league has been a body established for charitable purposes only. The question on the appeal arises in relation to some 2,000 or more deeds of covenant in a common and well-recognised form entered into by persons who were members—I have emphasised that word for reasons which will later appear—of the league whereby the covenantors covenanted to pay for a period of seven years,[15] if they so long lived, such a sum as after deduction of income tax would leave the net figures of either one guinea or 10s. 6d. The National Book League sought to recover the amount of tax which had been deducted from the notional gross sums named in the deeds of covenant pursuant to section 447 (1) (b) of the Income Tax Act 1952 [16] [which his Lordship read].

It is not in doubt that the tax chargeable falls under Schedule D. It is the contention of the league that the case is one which is comprehended by Case III of Schedule D, now enshrined in section 123 (1) of the Income Tax Act 1952,[17] where it is stated: " Case III—tax in respect of—(a) any interest of money, whether yearly or otherwise, or any annuity, or other annual payment. . . ." It is the contention of the National Book League that the gross sums in question are annual sums within the comprehension of Case III or section 123, and that the league is entitled, according to the terms of paragraph (b) of section 471 (1),[18] to recover the tax which has been deducted by the covenantors.

I confess I have found the case somewhat troublesome, not least because of the conclusions to which the extremes of the argument on either side might appear to lead. It was, for example, on the one side observed by Mr. Cross that, if the argument for the league were sustained, it might be possible for a charity which, in accordance with well-known practice, may require each year to augment its funds or increase public interest by holding a dance, to invite well-disposed persons to enter into deeds of covenant for seven years for a figure in return for which they would be supplied with dance tickets for the charity dance in each of the following seven years. In such a case I do not myself feel

---

15 For the significance of the seven-year period, see I.C.T.A. 1970, s. 434, and *post*, Chap. 15.
16 Now I.C.T.A. 1970, s. 360 (1) (c), (3).
17 Now I.C.T.A. 1970, s. 109.
18 This should refer to s. 447 (1) (b) of the 1952 Act, now I.C.T.A. 1970, s. 360 (1) (c), (3).

much doubt that the substance of the matter would be an arrangement for buying in advance dance tickets for charity dances by means of a covenanted payment of that kind. That being the substance of the matter, it would be difficult to see, as it seems to me, how it could be brought within Case III and entitle the charity to recover tax.

On the other side and at the other extreme, the instance was taken of well-known charities, of which the National Art-Collections Fund may be taken as an example. In such cases, as is well known, the donors, the covenantors in favour of such charities, get certain privileges. They may be allowed the use of certain reading rooms; they may be given the privilege of attending private exhibitions in private houses or elsewhere; and to many I do not doubt these privileges are by no means negligible. But although that case, again, is not before us, it seems to me, as at present advised, that it would altogether offend good sense and good law to say that the sums covenanted in such cases were not gifts to the charity in question, that they were not pure income profit, to use Lord Greene M.R.'s phrase, in the hands of the charity. But the present case (and this is, of course, a truism applicable in all cases) must turn upon its own special facts; and the facts in the present case are special in a marked degree.

. . . The question, therefore, as I see it, turns first upon this. Looking at the substance and reality of the matter, can it be said that those who entered into these covenants have paid the sums covenanted without conditions or counter stipulations; and, on the whole, I have come to the conclusion that they cannot so say. It seems to me that against the special background of this case, and, having regard to the terms of the letter, there was here, in a real sense, a condition or counter stipulation on the part of the league against which the covenant was entered into. I must guard myself against saying that whenever one finds a covenantor in favour of a charity getting allowed to him certain privileges, it therefore follows that such a covenantor no longer can say that he has paid without conditions or counter stipulations. If the test be, as I venture to think it is, whether in all the circumstances, and looking once more at the substance and reality of the matter, these covenantors can be treated as donors of the covenanted sums to the charity, I have come to the conclusion that the answer must be in the negative, subject to the point to which I will now come as to the extent of the conditions or counter stipulations. The aspect of the matter, with which I have so far dealt, does not appear, as I follow the case stated and the judgment of Vaisey J., to have taken at all a prominent part in the argument before the matter was debated in this court. The matter seems rather to have been dealt with before the Special Commissioners and before the judge solely upon the question whether the privileges which the covenantor members admittedly obtained were of so illusory and negligible a character as to be properly disregarded on the principle of *de minimis non curat lex*.

It was observed by Sir Reginald Hills that, if one looks at the case and the arguments which are there recorded, that particular point, namely, that the privileges, the amenities, offered were—and I will use the words of the Special Commissioners—trifling and illusory, was not in fact ever put forward by those responsible for the league, and I can well appreciate his point that it would hardly lie in the mouths of those responsible for the league so to contend. But undoubtedly the Special Commissioners decided this case on the view they formed that in truth they " were so trifling "—again I am quoting—" as to justify us in describing them as affording no advantage of a substantial character."

It was upon that point, whether that decision could be sustained, that the matter went before Vaisey J., and he came to the conclusion that, upon the evidence, such a conclusion could not be justified in law.

The question whether particular advantages or promises can be dismissed on the principle of *de minimis non curat lex* must, I think, be a matter for the lawyer rather than for him who has to find facts, and, on the facts as they are here presented, I am unable to see any proper justification for the conclusion which the Special Commissioners upon this point reached. Particularly I refer to the fact that the covenantors, I think, did get at the very least a clear promise from which the league could not draw back without gross breach of faith and, as I am inclined to think, without also a breach of contract, that they would continue to have advantages of membership at a lower subscription rate than other persons, and that they would be immune from the possibility of increase of subscription rates during the whole period of the covenant. It seems to me impossible to dismiss that matter as being trifling and illusory, and to disregard it on the principle of *de minimis non curat lex*. I am, therefore, upon this point unable to accept the argument of Mr. Brennan that it is a pure question of fact upon which the conclusion of the Special Commissioners must be found. Upon that matter I agree entirely with the conclusion of Vaisey J. to which, indeed, I cannot usefully add anything.

Taking that view, and also concluding, as I do, that in the circumstances of this case the league failed to establish that the sums paid under the covenants can be regarded, to use again Lord Greene M.R.'s phrase, as pure income profit within Case III of Schedule D, and such as to entitle under section 447 [16] the league to recover the tax, I would dismiss the appeal.

Note
    This decision was followed in *Taw and Torridge Festival Society Ltd.* v. *I.R.C.* (1959) 38 T.C. 603, where subscription by covenant to a charity carried with it the privilege of admission to concerts and other performances at reduced prices. Contrast *Barclays Bank Ltd.* v. *Naylor* [1961] Ch. 7, where payments by the bank under a deed of covenant to trustees for education of children of certain employees were held to be annual payments, there being no obligation upon the recipient to do anything in return. (See now *Ball* v. *National and Grindlays Bank Ltd.* [1971] 3 All E.R. 485.)
    For discussions of the meaning of " pure income profit," see also *Asher* v. *London Film Productions Ltd.* [1944] 1 K.B. 133; the *Epping Forest* case (1953) 34 T.C. 293, *infra*, especially Lord Normand at p. 320; *Campbell* v. *I.R.C.* [1967] Ch. 651; *post*, p. 123; and J.G.M., " Annual Payments and Pure Income " [1969] B.T.R. 68.

I.R.C. v. CITY OF LONDON
(AS EPPING FOREST CONSERVATORS)

House of Lords [1953] 1 W.L.R. 652; 117 J.P. 280; 97 S.J. 315; [1953] 1 All E.R. 1075; 34 T.C. 293

LORD REID: . . . It is, I think, clear that the sums payable by the City have all the necessary characteristics of annual payments, taking " annual " in the sense in which that word is generally used in the Income Tax Act; but it is equally clear that by no means all payments which have those characteristics fall within the scope of Case III. There is no qualification or limitation of the words " annual payments " expressed in the rules applicable to Case III, but a limitation must be implied so as to exclude certain kinds of annual payments. The Act must be read as a whole and construed so as to produce, so far as possible, a coherent scheme; and it is settled that Case III does not apply to payments which are in reality trading receipts in the hands of the recipients although such payments take the form of annual payments. One reason is that income tax is a tax on income and trading receipts are not income: a trader's income from his trade can only be determined after he has deducted his expenditure from his receipts and it cannot be supposed that sums which are not income are to be taxable under Case III. But in my judgment the payments in this case are not trading receipts in the hands of the conservators even if they are carrying on a trade or something in the nature of a trade. Trading receipts are generally received in return for something done or provided by the recipient for the payer, but, as I have said, that does not appear to me to be the case here. . . .

Note
    See also *British Commonwealth International Newsfilm Agency Ltd.* v. *Mahany* [1963] 1 W.L.R. 69.

(C) CAPITAL OR INCOME?

Case III charges to tax annual payments of an income nature; instalments of a capital sum, not being income at all, are not taxable.[19] Some payments may consist, in part, of a payment of capital and, in part, of interest on that capital, in which case only the interest portion of the payment is taxable. Special rules relate to purchased annuities.[20]

JONES v. I.R.C.

King's Bench Division [1920] 1 K.B. 711; 89 L.J.K.B. 129; 121 L.T. 611; 7 T.C. 310

    The taxpayer sold his interest in certain inventions and letters patent for a cash sum and a "royalty" payable over ten years. The "royalty" was held to be taxable income.

    ROWLATT J.: In my judgment this appeal fails. It has been urged by Mr. Latter that the annual payment now in question being 10 per cent. upon the sales of machines for ten years is part of the consideration which was paid for the transfer from the appellant of his property. So it is, but there is no law of nature or any invariable principle that because it can be said that a certain payment is consideration for the transfer of property it must be looked upon as price in the character of principal. In each case regard must be had to what the sum is. A man may sell his property for a sum which is to be paid in instalments, and when that is the case the payments to him are not income: *Foley* v. *Fletcher*.[21] Or a man may sell his property for an annuity. In that case the Income Tax Act applies. Again, a man may sell his property for what looks like an annuity, but which can be seen to be not a transmutation of a principal sum into an annuity but is in fact a principal sum payment of which is being spread over a period and is being paid with interest calculated in a way familiar to actuaries—in such a case income tax is not payable on what is really capital: *Secretary of State for India* v. *Scoble*.[22] On the other hand, a man may sell his property nakedly for a share of the profits of the business. In that case the share of the profits of the business would be the price, but it would bear the character of income in the vendor's hands. *Chadwick* v. *Pearl Life Assurance Co.*[23] was a case of that kind. In such a case the man bargains

[19] It is necessary to have regard to the character of the payments in the hands of the recipient. Payments made out of a capital fund may nevertheless take on the character of income and be taxable in the hands of the recipient, see *Brodie's Will Trustees* v. *I.R.C.* (1933) 17 **T.C.** 432; *post,* p. 377; *Williamson* v. *Ough* [1936] A.C. 384; *Cunard's Trustees* v. *I.R.C.* [1946] 1 All E.R. 159; *post,* p. 379.
[20] I.C.T.A. 1970, s. 230.
[21] (1858) 3 H. & N. 769.
[22] [1903] A.C. 299; *post,* p. 119.
[23] 1919 S.C. 147.

to have, not a capital sum but an income secured to him, namely, an income corresponding to the rent which he had before. I think, therefore, that what I have to do is to see what the sum payable in this case really is. . . .

I.R.C. v. MALLABY-DEELEY

Court of Appeal (*ante*, p. 76)

Sir Wilfrid Greene M.R.: . . . What was the nature of the obligation under which Sir Harry Mallaby-Deeley lay under the document of November 29, 1926? If his obligation, on the true construction of that document, was an obligation to pay a lump sum by instalments, and, therefore, an obligation of a capital, and not of an income, nature, and if, by the later deed, that obligation was changed, so far as regards the outstanding payments, by a variation of the amounts and dates of payment of instalments, the only effect of the deed of March 10 1930, would have been to provide for payment, by different instalments at different times of different amounts, of an existing capital obligation, the payment of which, under the original document, was to be by other instalments in different amounts at different times.

. . . It seems to me that the cases to which we have been referred, and, indeed, the principle of the thing, must depend upon there being a real existing capital sum, not necessarily pre-existing but existing in the sense that it represents some kind of capital obligation. If you had a case where a man merely made up his mind that he would like a covenantee to have a certain sum of money more than he had got at present, and then effectuated that intention by entering into a covenant to make annual payments, the sum which he thought of, which in no real sense would be a sum at all, would be no more than the motive for entering into the covenant to make the annual payments. On the other hand, if there is a real liability to pay a capital sum, either pre-existing or then assumed, that capital sum has got a real existence, and, if the method adopted of paying it is a payment by instalments, the character of these instalments is settled by the nature of the capital sum to which they are related. If there is no pre-existing capital sum, but the covenant is to pay a capital sum by instalments, the same result will follow.

Proceeding upon that basis, the position, at the date when the deed of March 10, 1930, was executed, was that Sir Harry was under an obligation to pay a capital sum, or what was left of a capital sum, of £28,000 by certain annual instalments. That obligation he got rid of, substituting for it the obligation under the deed. It seems to me that, putting all those circumstances together, what he was doing under the deed of March 10, 1930, was liquidating a capital obligation of his own, an obligation which, it is true, was only to be carried out by instalment payments, but which, nevertheless, was of a capital nature, and he was liquidating that obligation by a series of instalments differing in amounts and times from those which were referred to in the pre-existing document. On that basis, it seems to me that the case is one where it is not possible to say of the payments made under this document that they are of an income nature. They are given the character of capital. That character is stamped upon them by the circumstance that they are the means of liquidating a capital obligation, and it is quite wrong to say that you must look at the documents alone, and disregard the other elements in the legal relationship between the parties and the legal results which that transaction achieved. . . .

SECRETARY OF STATE IN COUNCIL OF INDIA v. SCOBLE

House of Lords [1903] A.C. 299; 72 L.J.K.B. 617; 89 L.T. 1; 51 W.R. 675; 19 T.L.R. 550; 4 T.C. 618

The purchase price for a railway was expressed to be payable by annual sums. *Held*, that part of the payments which represented payment of the capital sum was not subject to tax; tax was only deductible in respect of the interest portion.

EARL OF HALSBURY L.C.: My Lords, I am not satisfied after hearing the very ingenious arguments of the Attorney-General and Solicitor-General that the Court of Appeal is not right in this case; and, inasmuch as it is the duty of those who assert and not of those who deny to establish the proposition sought to be established, I think the Crown must fail in the contention that this is " an annuity " within the meaning of the Act.

I do not at all say that the question is not surrounded by some difficulties; I think it is. The loose use of the word " annuity " undoubtedly renders a great many of the observations that have been made by the Attorney-General and Solicitor-General very relevant to the question under debate. Still, looking at the whole nature and substance of the transaction (and it is agreed on all sides that we must look at the nature of the transaction and not be bound by the mere use of the words), this is not the case of a purchase of an annuity; it is a case in which, under powers reserved by a contract, one of the parties agrees to buy from the other party what is their property, and what is called an " annuity " in the contract and in the statute is a mode of making the payment for that which had become a debt to be paid by the Government. That introduces this consideration: Was it the intention of the Income Tax Acts ever to tax capital as if it was income? I think it cannot be doubted, upon the language and the whole purport and meaning of the Income Tax Acts, that it never was intended to tax capital—as income at all events.

Under the circumstances I think I am at liberty so far to analyse the nature of the transaction as to see whether this annual sum which is being paid is partly capital, or is to be treated simply as income; and I cannot disagree with what all the three learned judges of the Court of Appeal pointed out, that you start upon the inquiry into this matter with the fact of an antecedent debt which has got to be paid; and if these sums, which it cannot be denied are partly in liquidation of that debt which is due, are to be taxed as if they were income in each year, the result is that you are taxing part of the capital. As I have said, I do not think it was the intention of the Legislature to tax capital, and therefore the claim as against part of those sums fails.

My Lords, as I have already said, I do not think it is a matter on which one can dogmatise very clearly. Where you are dealing with income tax upon a rent derived from coal, you are in truth taxing that which is capital in this sense, that it is a purchase of the coal and not a mere rent. The income tax is not and cannot be, I suppose from the nature of things, cast upon absolutely logical lines, and to justify the exaction of the tax the things taxed must have been specifically made the subject of taxation, and looking at the circumstances here and the word " annuity " used in the Acts, I do not think that this case comes within the meaning which (using the Income Tax Acts themselves as the expositors of the meaning of the word) is intended by the word " annuity," and that is the only word that can be relied upon here as justifying what would be to my mind a taxation of capital. . . .

Note
This decision was followed in *Vestey* v. *I.R.C.* [1962] Ch. 861, but some doubt was cast upon the principle of apportionment into capital and interest elements in *I.R.C.* v. *Land*

Securities Investment Trust Ltd. [1969] 1 W.L.R. 604; see J. G. M., " Annual Payments or Instalments of Capital " [1965] B.T.R. 328; and R. S. Nock, " Form or Substance? " [1969] B.T.R. 256.

REPORT OF THE COMMITTEE ON THE TAXATION TREATMENT OF PROVISIONS FOR RETIREMENT

[1954 Cmd. 9063]

PURCHASED ANNUITIES

477. This matter was the subject of more representations to us than any other. They took the now well-known form of urging that, in the case of a purchased annuity, whether for life or otherwise, part of each annuity payment is in reality a return to the purchaser of part of the capital originally laid out by him in its purchase, the remainder being in effect interest on that capital. The witnesses all claimed, therefore, that income tax should only be charged on that interest content and not on the capital content. We must make it clear at the outset that for this purpose we are discussing annuities purchased by the annuitant himself, whether by a series of annual payments or by a single lump sum payment, although we do include the case of the subsequent assignment of such an annuity to some other person. We entirely exclude annuities which become payable as the result of the operation of any of the types of pension scheme dealt with in the foregoing parts of this Report, for these must always be fully taxable.

496. We now come to our own consideration of the problem, and of the validity of the various grounds upon which splitting of purchased life annuities has consistently been resisted in the past. We take first the argument that a person who buys such an annuity sinks his capital and takes an income in exchange. Logically this must be based on the conception that after the purchase of the annuity the annuity is the income and the " source " of it is the contract of the assurance company or other grantor who undertakes to pay it. No doubt it is then said that, since the underlying principle of our present income tax legislation is to tax the income in full but not to tax its source, the imposition of liability on the whole of the annuity fully accords with that principle and in no way offends against it.

497. Looking at the matter from a purely legalistic aspect the above arguments may perhaps be accepted; but in our view the reality and substance of the matter are that the original capital sum paid to acquire the annuity still remains a part of the source of the annuity, the remaining part being the interest earned by that capital, or by so much of it as from time to time remains not repaid to the annuitant. This seems to us to be recognised in the present-day treatment of annuities-certain. Indeed it appears to be the very basis upon which those annuities are at present split for tax purposes into the two different elements.

503. Our conclusion is that the arguments in favour of the splitting of purchased annuities outweigh those against it, and we therefore recommend that in the taxation of purchased life annuities, the part of each periodical annual payment representing the estimated capital content should be exempted from tax, and only the difference should constitute taxable income. In the case of purchased " annuities-certain," the present practice under which they are not taxed on their capital content should be given statutory force. Neither of these recommendations extends to annuities purchased by a concern carrying on a trade, where the purchase of those annuities forms part of the trade and where the cost of their acquisition consequently falls to be treated as a trade

expense. Nor do they extend to annuities becoming payable as the result of the operation of any of the types of pension scheme dealt with in the earlier Chapters of this Report.

Note
   These proposals were implemented in 1956 and are now incorporated in I.C.T.A. 1970, s. 230.

2. Transfers of Income

The distinction between "annual payments," chargeable under Case III, and other types of receipt is important not only as regards the recipient but as regards the payer. Where an item is regarded as the income of the recipient it will not, according to general principles, form a part of the income of the payer.[24] In consequence, it is possible for income to be transferred from one person to another (*e.g.* from a high surtax payer to a low tax payer or exempt body) by the payer incurring a legal obligation to pay.

FINAL REPORT OF THE ROYAL COMMISSION ON THE TAXATION OF PROFITS AND INCOME

[1955 Cmd. 9474]

Covenants as Transfers of Income

144. The original system of income tax was constructed on the principle that annual payments made under covenant should be treated for tax purposes as the income of the recipient and not as the income of the payer. It seems natural enough to regard such payments as income of the recipient; but it is not so obvious that it is in accordance with correct principle to treat that fact as warranty for regarding the taxable income of the payer as reduced by an equivalent amount. For an income is taxed, generally speaking, without allowance for the fact that part of it is regularly paid over to this or that recipient or for this or that purpose, as rent or wages; and there is only a fine distinction between a charge on income, which is treated as reducing it, and an application of income, which is not. In some aspects it is important that the line should be drawn correctly.

145. According to the original conception, which is reflected in the provisions of the Income Tax Act of 1842, any annual payment, whether payable by virtue of a charge on the property of the payer or merely as a personal debt or obligation by virtue of a contract, was to be treated as income of the recipient and not as income of the payer, provided that it was payable "out of profits or gains brought into charge to tax." The machinery of deduction at source was employed, the whole of the income of the payer being assessed to tax in the first place without allowance for the annual payment but with a statutory right in him to recoup himself by deducting and retaining tax at the standard rate (as it became) when he made his payment. For the purposes of any reliefs or allowances due to the recipient deduction at the standard rate was merely

---

[24] In 1969 special rules were introduced governing the deductibility of interest payments, described by J. G. Monroe, "The Non-Deduction of Interest" [1969] B.T.R. 222. In many respects, the earlier law has now been restored by the Finance Act 1972, s. 75. The manner in which transfers of income operate is described by J. G. Monroe, "Annual and other Periodical Payments" [1956] B.T.R. 136, 281.

provisional and he was entitled to claim an adjustment of tax from the Revenue according to his true marginal rate.

146. It has never been very clear precisely what constituted " annual payments . . . as a personal debt or obligation by virtue of any contract " for the purpose of this rule. It is fairly obvious that they did not include remuneration for services rendered, if only because the system required such payments to be taxed as income of the recipient by direct assessment and not by the process of deduction at source. Nor did they cover such payments as would enter into a computation of the profits of the recipient's trade, those profits again being taxable by direct assessment, under Case I of Schedule D. Moreover, the distinction between a charge on income and an application of income would have become almost meaningless if payments of this kind could have ranked as deductions from the income of the payer. Since we are not concerned to arrive at any precise definition of annual payment, it is enough to say that the kind of payment under contract which fell within the rule was of the nature of an annuity and that the class did not extend to payments in exchange for value received from the recipient. It is just because the payments in question arise from obligations voluntarily undertaken that they are habitually made in the form of covenants, a covenant being a promise made under seal. For the law treated a promise under the seal of a promisor as a binding obligation even if voluntarily undertaken without value received in exchange, whereas a bare promise not so secured had no obligatory force.

147. So long as income tax remained essentially a flat-rate tax it was a matter of comparative indifference to the Exchequer whether the burden of the tax on the annual payment fell upon the payer or the recipient. The law had settled that the payment itself was to be regarded as a piece of income " in its own right," and that it was to be taxed as such as income of the latter. What mattered was that it was not to be taxed twice over and therefore could not be taxed as the income of the former as well. The deduction follows reasonably enough once the idea is accepted that such payments constitute an identifiable " slice " of income. But the 20th century introduction of an extensive scheme of graduation by way of allowance and relief and progressive rates of tax brought with it a new importance to the theory governing annual payments under covenant. For it becomes of considerable significance to the general yield of revenue to determine whether this form of income is still to be reckoned as the income of the recipient and not of the payer for all tax purposes if the marginal rate of the one is one of the higher rates of surtax and of the other one of the reduced rates of income tax: or if the recipient is exempt from tax altogether, as in the case of a charity.

148. In these circumstances it was to be expected that attention would be given to the question within what limits it would be fair to allow annual payments to be regarded as a transfer of income from the payer to the recipient. Accordingly, from the year 1922 onwards various statutory conditions have been laid down with which covenants must comply if they are to be entitled to recognition, complete or partial, for this purpose.[25]

149. As the matter stands today, therefore, voluntary annual payments secured by deed of covenant are recognised as transfers of income, but subject to a fairly elaborate network of conditions that limit their recognition. Their review raises two questions. The first is: Ought such instruments to be recognised at all for this purpose? The second is: Are the present limiting conditions adequate or satisfactory?

150. To the first question our answer is Yes.

[25] For the limitations, see I.C.T.A. 1970, s. 434.

Note
In the view of the Canadian Royal Commission (Carter Commission), non-charitable gifts should not be deducted from the tax base of those who make them (Vol. 3, Chap. 17). In certain circumstances, income under a covenant or settlement is treated as the income of the settlor; *post*, Chap. 15.

CAMPBELL v. I.R.C.

Court of Appeal [1967] Ch. 651; [1967] 2 W.L.R. 1445; 111 S.J. 155; [1967] 2 All E.R. 625; 45 T.C. 444; affirmed by the House of Lords [1970] A.C. 77; [1968] 3 W.L.R. 1025; [1968] 3 All E.R. 588; 45 T.C. 541

The facts are set out in the judgment of Harman L.J., *infra*.

LORD DENNING M.R.: . . . It is a common practice nowadays for a man to make a seven-year covenant in favour of a charity. The object is to enable the charity to recover tax from the revenue. The theory on which it works is best shown by an illustration. Take a man who has a taxable income of £1,000 a year. He is taxed on the whole of the £1,000 at the standard rate of 8s. 3d. in the pound.[26] It comes to £412 10s. Now suppose he makes a covenant in favour of his parochial church council to pay them £10 a year for seven years. He is entitled to deduct tax at source before he pays the church council. He deducts tax at 8s. 3d. in the pound, which comes to £4 2s. 6d., and pays the church council £5 17s. 6d. a year. Now that £10 a year payable under the covenant is really the income of the church council. If you look at it from their point of view, it is £10 a year coming to them forming part of their income. Being their income, it ceases to be the income of the payer. So the £10 a year becomes the income of the church council, thus reducing the income of the payer to £990. That means that when the taxpayer pays tax on the full £1,000, he pays it both on his own income of £990 and on the church council's income of £10. In so far as he pays tax on the £990, he pays it on his own account. It is over and done with. In so far as he pays tax on the £10, he pays it on behalf of the church council. The church council has suffered tax by deduction of £4 2s. 6d. at source. But being a charity, the church council are not liable to tax on that £10. They are exempt. They can, therefore, recover it from the revenue.

That illustration points the moral of this whole case. In order to be an " annual payment " within these sections, the payment must be such that it can be truly regarded as the income of the recipient taxable by deduction at source. Typical instances are mentioned in the statute. " Yearly interest " can be illustrated by interest payable on loans. " Annuities " can be illustrated by annuities granted by will or obtained by purchase from an insurance company. The words " other annual payments " are *ejusdem generis*. They are payments which recur each year in which nothing remains to be done by the recipient except to receive the money. The recipient is not to supply goods or services or give or do anything in return for the payment. If he does so, it is no longer an " annual payment." This appears from *Howe (Earl)* v. *Inland Revenue Commissioners*[27] and *In re Hanbury, decd., Comiskey* v. *Hanbury*.[28] In *Inland Revenue Commissioners* v. *City of London* (the *Epping Forest* case)[29] Lord Normand indicated that a sum would be an " annual payment " if it was paid " without conditions or counter-stipulations out of taxed income "; and

---

[26] The standard rate then in force.
[27] [1919] 2 K.B. 336; *ante*, p. 112, *post*, p. 341.
[28] (1939) 38 T.C. 588; *ante*, p. 113.
[29] [1953] 1 W.L.R. 652; [1953] 1 All E.R. 1075; *ante*, p. 116.

this was adopted by Lord Evershed M.R. as a good guide in *Inland Revenue Commissioners* v. *National Book League.*[30]

Mr. Desmond Miller, Q.C., submitted that Lord Normand was referring only to conditions or counter-stipulations which were *legally enforceable*; he argued that, even where there was only a *private understanding* that the covenantor should receive a counter-benefit (which was not legally enforceable), it was nevertheless an " annual payment." I cannot accept this submission in the least. A seven-year covenant is nullified for tax purposes by a private understanding, just as much as by a contractual stipulation. Take the common case of a covenant by a father to pay his son, who is over 21, £400 a year. If it is wholly the son's income without reservation, it is an " annual payment." But if there is a private understanding that the son should return it or part of it to his father in cash or in kind, then it is not an " annual payment " so as to qualify for tax benefits. The Royal Commission [Royal Commission on The Taxation of Profits and Income (1955), Cmd. 9474] over which Lord Radcliffe presided made a caustic reference to private understandings of this kind. They said: " We feel little doubt that a number of such understandings do exist and that they are no better than a fraud on the system ": see para. 159.

In the present case the judge held that there was a legally binding obligation on the trustees to use the sums in paying for the purchase of Davies's. I decline to go into the question whether it was legally binding or not. I care not one way or the other. There was, as the commissioners found, a clear understanding that they should be so used. That is enough. The moneys payable by the covenantors were being returned to them as part-payment of the purchase price. It is said that it was a fair price and is no different from their buying another school. But I think there is all the difference in the world. By having the money returned to them, even in payment of the price, the covenantors were receiving a counter-benefit. Suppose a man gives a covenant for seven years to his old school, and in return there is a private understanding that his son, who is a dunce, will be given a place. The sum payable under the covenant does not qualify as an " annual payment," even though he pays the full fees for his son. The return benefit disqualifies. It cannot be ignored except when it is minimal and negligible: see the *National Book League* case,[30] *per* Morris L.J. and *Taw and Torridge Festival Society Ltd.* v. *Inland Revenue Commissioners.*[31] . . .

HARMAN L.J.: There are occasions, even in revenue cases, when what one comes to look for is substance and not form. Here were corporators owning a first-class educational business which paid 800 per cent. on its ordinary shares and made a living also for the majority shareholders. It paid tax, of course, like any other commercial concern. The object of the corporators was to sell this business at its full value without losing control of it. They left it to their accountant to find the best means, and what we have is his plan, which smells a little of the lamp. His plan was (1) to sell the goodwill to a concern still controlled by the vendors; (2) to find the price out of the profits of the business; (3) to get back the income tax which was being paid by the vendors, thus accelerating the payment of the purchase-money.

What were the steps taken to carry it out? The first was that a trust was set up, a trust for educational purposes only, and, therefore, a charitable trust, but as its name implies, it was to be tied to Davies's, the name of the business. The object of the charitable trust was to take over the business from Davies's. The second step in this was the covenant which Tutors entered into the day after its formation, which was a convenant for seven years to pay 80 per cent. of its profits to the trust. The third step was that the trust was to use the money to

[30] [1957] Ch. 488, *ante*, p. 114.
[31] (1959) 38 T.C. 603.

pay for the business. I care not at all, like my Lord, whether this was a legally binding transaction or merely one that was morally binding on everybody. After all, all the participators in this scheme were on one side of the table. They were the corporators in this business. They were the people who were making a living out of it and who were hoping to get a good price for it. There is nothing wrong with that. But it makes a formal agreement quite unnecessary because it was to everybody's interest and it was everybody's intention to carry it out in this way if it would get back Tutors' income tax. The fourth step was that the trust, being a charity, was to apply to get back the income tax payable by the vendors and return it to the vendors directly it was got back and so hasten the payment of the purchase price.

It is on this last rock that the ship founders. If I pay my college at Oxbridge income payments over seven years, these are annual payments because I expect and get no return from my outlay. If I make conditions, such as a free place for my son, no tax is reclaimable. Judge the present case by this test. The covenantor makes his payment to the trust. Everyone concerned knows the object of it: it is to get back the payments as instalments of the purchase-money for the business—item to recover through the trust the tax it has paid and return it to themselves as further instalments. No doubt when the seven years are up, there is to be a further covenant on a further understanding that the covenanted sums will go to pay for the vendor's physical assets, freeholds and leaseholds. The prospect is that no one in this business will pay any tax for years. It is a splendid scheme. Meanwhile the business will remain under the control of the majority shareholders and provide them with salaries as managers of the business. It is almost too good to be true. In law quite too good to be true. It won't do.

That is enough in my opinion to deal with this appeal. I follow the judge until he reaches this point precisely; but his further reasoning I cannot follow, and so far as I can follow it, I do not accept it; but it makes no difference.

As to the second point, that the payments were applied for charitable purposes only, being payments made to buy an educational business, when looked at it is essentially the same point at a different stage. The payments to be made by the covenantor are not in my opinion for charitable purposes only because they are paid in pursuance of the understanding that they shall be devoted to the purchase of the business. Therefore it does not matter that the business is an educational business and therefore within the objects of the charitable trust because the objects of the charitable trust are not wholly charitable in this case but to pay for a business, of which they themselves are the controllers.

On both points, therefore, I would dismiss the appeal.

SALMON L.J.: . . . In order for the money paid under the covenant to constitute " annual payments " in the hands of the trustees so that they can recover the tax that has been deducted, it is clearly established by such authorities as the *Epping Forest* case [29] and the *National Book League* case [30] that the money must have been paid to the trustees without " conditions " or " counter-stipulations " and as a " pure gift " or " pure bounty." . . .

3. Deduction at Source

An integral part [32] of the imposition of tax under Case III of Schedule D is the method of collection by means of deduction at source; when making

[32] Though not an essential part—*Whitworth Park Coal Ltd.* v. *I.R.C.* [1961] A.C. 31; *ante*, p. 110.

the payment, the payer deducts income tax at the standard rate and, if the payment is made out of income which has already borne income tax in his hands, keeps the tax deducted [33] and otherwise accounts to the Revenue for the tax.[34]

FINAL REPORT OF THE ROYAL COMMISSION ON THE TAXATION OF PROFITS AND INCOME

1955 Cmd. 9474

988. From the administrative point of view the advantages of the system must be greatest when a single payer makes relevant payments to a large number of recipients most of whom are liable to a marginal rate of tax at least equal to the standard rate. Conversely, the administrative savings are smallest—indeed, the operation of the system may even give rise to some additional work—when a single recipient receives relevant payments from a large number of payers many of whom are liable to a marginal rate of tax less than the standard rate. Collection of tax by deduction at source is not always a completely automatic process, for in some cases it may entail an adjustment of the amount of tax collected from the payer himself in order to ensure that the tax he deducts is duly accounted for; and the standard rate tax collected by deduction at source is only a provisional payment in the account between the recipient and the Revenue which may require later adjustment according to the facts of his case— *e.g.* by way of repayment if his liability is at one of the reduced rates only. It is considerations of this sort that must be looked at in any attempt to estimate where the balance of administrative advantage lies in respect of a proposal to bring under the deduction at source rules a class of payments now outside those rules or vice versa. One of the difficulties of making this kind of estimate is that it has to proceed upon the basis of a rather uncertain generalisation as to the level of income and other circumstances of the typical maker or recipient of payments of the class in question; it is, however, worth pointing out that the standard rate is normally the effective rate of income tax finally chargeable on the incomes of taxpayers other than individuals, and that the form of the various instruments by which graduation has been introduced into the system of personal taxation has the result that there is a relatively wide range of personal incomes for which the marginal rate of tax (on investment income) coincides with the standard rate.

ALLCHIN v. COULTHARD

House of Lords [1943] A.C. 607; [1943] 2 All E.R. 352; 112 L.J.K.B. 539; 107 J.P. 191; 59 T.L.R. 396; 87 S.J. 309; 41 L.G.R. 207; *sub nom. Allchin* v. *South Shields County Borough,* 169 L.T. 238; 25 T.C. 445

The respondent corporation paid interest on loans out of a general rate fund, into which had been paid both taxed and untaxed receipts. Tax was deducted from the interest in the (then) usual way. *Held,* the interest should be deemed to have been paid out of profits brought into charge, in so far as there were sufficient such profits, unless there was any legal impediment to so deeming.

---

[33] I.C.T.A. 1970, s. 52.
[34] I.C.T.A. 1970, s. 53. Special provisions now apply to payments of interest (I.C.T.A. 1970, s. 54; Finance Act 1972, s. 75) and to certain other annual payments, *e.g.* small maintenance payments (I.C.T.A. 1970, s. 65).

VISCOUNT SIMON L.C.: . . . The three heads under which the existing scheme of collection of income tax embodied in rules 19 and 21 [35] may be stated are as follows: (a) A person liable to pay any yearly interest of money, annuity or any other annual payment to a recipient is not entitled to deduct this payment in arriving at his profits or gains to be assessed and charged with income tax. If the amount is payable and paid out of his profits or gains, he is assessed on a sum which includes such payments, while the recipient is not directly assessed in respect of the amount at all. Consequently, the Crown gets from the payer both the tax at the standard rate which would otherwise be due from the recipient of the annual payment and the tax due from himself in respect of what is left of his profits and gains after the payment is made. (b) If the annual payment is payable and paid out of his profits and gains, the payer is *entitled* to deduct from the payment he makes to the recipient income tax at the current rate, and the recipient is bound to allow the deduction on receipt of the residue and to treat the payer as acquitted of liability to him in respect of the amount thus deducted. By this means, the payer recoups himself for the tax which he has paid or will pay on the annual payment. (c) If and in so far as the annual payment is not payable and paid out of profits or gains brought into charge, the person making the payment is *bound* to deduct from it income tax at the current rate and to account to the Crown for the amount deducted. In effect, the payer in such a case acts as collector for the Crown of the tax due from the recipient. The requirement that the recipient must allow the deduction and treat the payer as acquitted of liability in respect of this amount is not repeated in rule 21, but must be implied. Subject to the difficulty which I am about to state, this scheme seems reasonably clear. The receiver of the annual payment is chargeable in respect of annual profits or gains arising from " all interest of money, annuities, and other annual profits or gains " under Schedule D, para. 1 (b), but under rules 19 and 21 the tax is collected at the source before payment to him. If the payment is made out of the profits or gains of the payer, he is entitled to reduce his payment by the amount of the tax, but the legislature is not concerned to insist that he shall do so, as the Crown will get the tax whether he does so or not. If and so far as the payment is not made out of profits or gains, the legislature insists that the payer must deduct tax and account for it, for otherwise the Crown might not receive it.

. . . The proper interpretation of rules 19 and 21 is to hold that annual payments paid in a particular year, which, if the profits or gains brought into charge for that year were large enough, would have been properly payable thereout, are to be treated as having notionally been paid out of the payer's assessed income for that year, and the payer is to be allowed to deduct and retain the tax on the annual payments, provided that the amount so deducted and retained does not exceed the amount of tax payable by him in that year on his assessed income.[36] Any such excess he may not retain, but he must account for it to the Crown. . . .

[35] Now I.C.T.A. 1970, ss. 52, 53.
[36] See *Birmingham Corporation* v. *I.R.C.* [1930] A.C. 307; *I.R.C.* v. *Oswald* [1945] A.C. 360. But where, although there are taxable profits sufficient to support the annual payments, but these are specifically made out of a *capital* fund, the payer must account for the tax deducted under s. 53: *Chancery Lane Safe Deposit and Offices Company Ltd.* v. *I.R.C.* [1966] A.C. 85; *B. W. Nobes & Co. Ltd.* v. *I.R.C.* [1966] 1 W.L.R. 111. These cases are discussed by H.C.E., " Tax and Company Accounts " [1966] B.T.R. 67; and see G.S.A.W. [1964] B.T.R. 200, 437.

Chapter 8

TRADE, PROFESSION OR VOCATION

TAX under Schedule D is charged, *inter alia*, in respect of " the annual profits or gains arising or accruing . . . to any person residing in the United Kingdom from any trade, profession or vocation, whether carried on in the United Kingdom or elsewhere, and . . . to any person, whether a British subject or not, although not resident in the United Kingdom, . . . from any trade, profession or vocation exercised within the United Kingdom . . ." [1] In particular, the following are charged:

Case I—tax in respect of any trade carried on in the United Kingdom or elsewhere;

Case II—tax in respect of any profession or vocation not contained in any other Schedule. [2]

It is the annual profits or gains which are charged to tax, and the next chapter will deal with the computation of chargeable profits. But, in accordance with the " source " principle, it is first necessary to establish:

(a) that the taxpayer is carrying on a " trade, profession or vocation," and

(b) if so, that the item of income which it is sought to tax derives from that source.

A person may be carrying on one particular trade which embraces a number of activities,[3] or he may carry on two or more distinct trades.[4] A trader may also pursue activities which fall outside the scope of his trade and do not themselves constitute trading.[5]

1. Case Law

In Chapter 3 was discussed the distinction between findings of fact and conclusions of law. A number of the cases dealt with concerned the question of whether or not the taxpayer was carrying on a trade, profession or vocation.[6] Considerable caution must be exercised in citing decided cases

---

[1] I.C.T.A. 1970, s. 108. [2] *Ibid.* s. 109.

[3] *Spiers & Son Ltd.* v. *Ogden* (1932) 17 T.C. 117; *Gloucester Railway Carriage and Wagon Co. Ltd.* v. *I.R.C.* [1925] A.C. 469.

[4] *Hawes* v. *Gardiner* (1957) 37 T.C. 671; *Lewis Emanuel & Son Ltd.* v. *White* (1965) 42 T.C. 369. The distinction may be important for the purposes of relief for trading losses: *Cannon Industries Ltd.* v. *Edwards* [1966] 1 W.L.R. 580. See J. Silberrad, " A Stated Case states the Case " [1966] B.T.R. 203.

[5] *Dunn Trust Ltd.* v. *Williams* (1950) 31 T.C. 477; *West* v. *Phillips* (1958) 38 T.C. 203.

[6] In particular, *Edwards* v. *Bairstow and Harrison* [1956] A.C. 14; *ante*, p. 51; *Pilkington* v. *Randall* (1966) 42 T.C. 662; *ante*, p. 57; *Griffiths* v. *J. P. Harrison (Watford) Ltd.* [1963] A.C. 1; *ante*, p. 47; *I.R.C.* v. *Fraser* (1942) 24 T.C. 498; *ante*, p. 48; *Currie* v. *I.R.C.* [1921] 2 K.B. 332; *ante*, p. 50; *Cooper* v. *Stubbs* [1925] 2 K.B. 753; *ante*, p. 61; *Lucy and Sunderland Ltd.* v. *Hunt* [1962] 1 W.L.R. 7; *ante*, p. 61. See also *Jones* v. *Leeming* [1930] A.C. 415; *post*, p. 221.

as precedent when the question concerns a finding of trade or otherwise. Of greatest value are those cases where the court has reversed the finding of the Commissioners and held that the facts as found point to only one possible conclusion.[7] Of least value are those cases where the court, if left to itself, would have drawn the opposite conclusion to that drawn by the Commissioners, but holds reluctantly that there do exist facts to justify the findings of the Commissioners.[8]

2. Definitions

(A) TRADE

INCOME AND CORPORATION TAXES ACT 1970

Section 526 (5): In the Tax Acts, except in so far as the context otherwise requires—
. . . " trade " includes every trade, manufacture, adventure or concern in the nature of trade, . . .

Note
The Act does not define " profession " or " vocation." In *Liverpool and London and Globe Insurance Company* v. *Bennett* [1912] 2 K.B. 41, 55 (*ante*, p. 95), Fletcher Moulton L.J. expressed the view that the words " in the nature of trade " qualify only the word " concern." However, the expression " adventure in the nature of a trade " is commonly used and Goff J., in *Johnston* v. *Heath* [1970] 1 W.L.R. 1567, 1574, considered that view to be " inconsistent " with the decision of the House of Lords in *Edwards* v. *Bairstow and Harrison*.

GRIFFITHS v. J. P. HARRISON (WATFORD) LTD.

House of Lords (*ante*, p. 47)

LORD DENNING: . . . Try as you will, the word " trade " is one of those common English words which do not lend themselves readily to definition, but which all of us think we understand well enough. We can recognise a " trade " when we see it, and also an " adventure in the nature of trade." But we are hard pressed to define it. Donovan L.J. gave an apt illustration.[9] Is a monkey a " human being " or an animal " in the nature of a human being "? It has a head, a body, two legs and two arms. What detail does it lack? Or nearer still, take a gang of burglars. Are they engaged in trade or an adventure in the nature of trade? They have an organisation. They spend money on equipment. They acquire goods by their efforts. They sell the goods. They make a profit. What detail is lacking in their adventure? You may say it lacks legality, but it has been held that legality is not an essential characteristic of a trade. You cannot point to any detail that it lacks. But still it is not a trade, nor an adventure in the nature of trade. And how does it help to ask the question: If it is not a trade, what is it? It is burglary and that is all there is to say about it. So here it is dividend-stripping and nothing else.

[7] As in *Edwards* v. *Bairstow and Harrison*. See also, for example, *Eames* v. *Stepnell Properties Ltd.* [1967] 1 W.L.R. 593; *Dunn Trust Ltd.* v. *Williams* (1950) 31 T.C. 477; and *Snell* v. *Rosser, Thomas & Co. Ltd.* [1968] 1 W.L.R. 295.
[8] As in *Pilkington* v. *Randall* and in *I.R.C.* v. *Reinhold* (1953) 34 T.C. 389; *post*, p. 148. See also *Jenkinson* v. *Freedland* (1961) 39 T.C. 636; *Iswera* v. *I.R.C.* [1965] 1 W.L.R. 663; *Page* v. *Pogson* (1954) 35 T.C. 545, and the remarks of Cross J. in *Lucy and Sunderland Ltd.* v. *Hunt, ante*, p. 61.   [9] In the Court of Appeal (1962) 40 T.C. 286.

Short of a definition, the only thing to do is to look at the usual characteristics of a "trade" and see how this transaction measures up to them. Usually in trade, the trader makes many trading transactions. But that is not essential. An isolated transaction may do. Usually the object of the trader is to make a trading profit. But that is not invariable.[10] Remember the hobby-farmer. But when you find that it was an isolated transaction, as this was, and it was not the object to make a trading profit, as there was none here, you at least have some grounds, and reasonable grounds at that, for thinking there was not a trade nor an adventure in the nature of trade. . . .

MANN v. NASH

King's Bench Division [1932] 1 K.B. 752; 101 L.J.K.B. 270; 147 L.T. 154; 48 T.L.R. 287; 76 S.J. 201; [1932] All E.R.Rep. 956; 16 T.C. 523

Although profits are derived from an illegal trade they are still chargeable to income tax.

The appellant, in the course of his business as an amusement caterer, provided automatic "Fruit" and "Diddler" machines for use for unlawful gaming.

ROWLATT J.: . . . I cannot see why the letting out of these machines in a commercial way with a view to the reception of profits in a commercial way is not a "trade, manufacture, adventure or concern in the nature of trade" so that the profits of it are chargeable to tax. It clearly is. The question really is whether, as a matter of construction, those words are to be cut down by the overriding consideration that the trade is tainted with illegality.

The mainstay of Mr. Field's argument was *Hayes* v. *Duggan*.[11] That decision seems to have gone on the principle that no construction should be adopted which involved that the State should seek to take a profit from what it had prohibited, because it ought to have prevented the prohibited act. It was asked: "Will the Executive keep its revenue eye open and vigilant and its eye of justice closed to crime, if the crime be lucrative?" I must say that I do not feel the force of that observation. Would it have made any difference if the State had kept both its eyes open, prosecuted the individual for the illegal lottery and also taxed him on the profits of it? In truth, it seems to me, all that consideration is misconceived. The revenue authorities, representing the State, are merely looking at an accomplished fact. It is not condoning it, or taking part in it. It merely finds profit made from what appears to be a trade, and the revenue laws say that profits made from a trade are to be taxed.

Reliance was also placed on the maxim *nemo allegans turpitudinem suam est audiendus*. I cannot see that the State is alleging its own turpitude in the present case. It is the appellant who is alleging his turpitude. It is also said that the State are coming forward to take a share in the profits of unlawful gaming. That is mere rhetoric. The State is doing nothing of the kind. It is merely taxing the individual with reference to certain facts. It is not a partner or a sharer in the illegality. . . .

Note

See also *Minister of Finance* v. *Smith* [1927] A.C. 193 and *Southern* v. *A.B.* [1933] 1 K.B. 713. As to gambling in general, see *Graham* v. *Green* [1925] 2 K.B. 37; *post*, p. 132; and K. Day, "The Tax Consequences of Illegal Trading Transactions" [1971] B.T.R. 104.

[10] See *post*, pp. 132–140.
[11] [1929] I.R. 406.

(B) Profession

I.R.C. v. MAXSE

Court of Appeal [1919] 1 K.B. 647; 88 L.J.K.B. 752; 120 L.T. 680; 35 T.L.R. 348; 63 S.J. 429; 12 T.C. 41

The Excess Profits Duty then in force applied to " all trades and businesses." The taxpayer claimed that a part of his activities at best constituted a " profession " and was not subject to the Duty. His contention was upheld.

SCRUTTON L.J.: . . . The next question is what is a " profession "? I am very reluctant finally to propound a comprehensive definition. A set of facts not present to the mind of the judicial propounder, and not raised in the case before him, may immediately arise to confound his proposition. But it seems to me as at present advised that a " profession " in the present use of language involves the idea of an occupation requiring either purely intellectual skill, or of manual skill controlled, as in painting and sculpture, or surgery, by the intellectual skill of the operator, as distinguished from an occupation which is substantially the production or sale or arrangements for the production or sale of commodities. The line of demarcation may vary from time to time. The word " profession " used to be confined to the three learned professions, the Church, Medicine and Law. It has now, I think, a wider meaning. It appears to me clear that a journalist whose contributions have any literary form, as distinguished from a reporter, exercises a " profession "; and that the editor of a periodical comes in the same category. It seems to me equally clear that the proprietor of a newspaper or periodical, controlling the printing, publishing and advertising, but not responsible for the selection of the literary or artistic contents, does not exercise a " profession " but a trade or business other than a profession. . . .

Note
As profits of professions (and vocations) are computed in the same manner as those of trades, the distinction is generally of no importance. But see I.C.T.A. 1970, s. 487. Whether or not an activity constitutes a " profession " is primarily a question of fact: *Currie* v. *I.R.C.* [1921] 2 K.B. 332; *ante*, p. 50.

More important is the distinction between carrying on a profession and holding an office or employment, see *Davies* v. *Braithwaite* [1931] 2 K.B. 628; *post*, p. 230; *Household* v. *Grimshaw* [1953] 1 W.L.R. 710.

(C) Vocation

PARTRIDGE v. MALLANDAINE

Queen's Bench Division (1886) 18 Q.B.D. 276; 56 L.J.Q.B. 251; 56 L.T. 203; 35 W.R. 276; 3 T.L.R. 192; 2 T.C. 179

The appellant made a living through betting, " systematically and annually carried on." This was held to be a " vocation."

DENMAN J.: . . . But the word " vocation " is analogous to " calling," a word of wide signification, meaning the way in which a person passes his life. . . .

HAWKINS J.: " Vocation " and " calling " are synonymous terms, and if anyone were asked what was the calling of the appellants, the answer would be that they were professional bookmakers. What that means is well known, and is fully described in the case. Mere betting is not illegal. It is perfectly lawful for a man to bet if he likes. He may, however, have a difficulty in getting the amount of the bets from dishonest persons who make bets and will not pay. The appellants, in fact, make considerable profits, and I cannot see why they should not be taxed as those made in any other profession or calling.

GRAHAM v. GREEN

King's Bench Division [1925] 2 K.B. 37; 94 L.J.K.B. 494; 133 L.T. 367; 41 T.L.R. 371; 69 S.J. 478; [1925] All E.R.Rep. 690; 9 T.C. 309

ROWLATT J.: . . . Now we come to the other side, the man who bets with the bookmaker, and that is this case. These are mere bets. Each time he puts on his money at whatever may be the starting price. I do not think he could be said to organise his effort in the same way as a bookmaker organises his, for I do not think the subject matter from his point of view is susceptible of it. In effect all he is doing is just what a man does who is a skilful player at cards, who plays every day. He plays today, and he plays tomorrow, and he plays the next day, and he is skilful on each of the three days, more skilful on the whole than the people with whom he plays, and he wins. But it does not seem that one can find in that case, any conception arising in which his individual operations can be said to be merged in the way that particular operations are merged in the conception of a trade. I think all you can say of that man, in the fair use of the English language, is that he is addicted to betting. It is extremely difficult to express, but it seems to me that people would say he is addicted to betting, and could not say that his vocation is betting. The subject is involved in great difficulty of language, which I think represents great difficulty of thought. There is no tax on a habit. I do not think " habitual " or even " systematic " fully describes what is essential in the phrase " trade, adventure, employment, or vocation." All I can say is that in my judgment the income which this gentleman succeeded in making is not profits or gains, and that the appeal must be allowed, with costs.

Note

The real reason for the reluctance to treat habitual gambling as a '' vocation '' may be, as Rowlatt J. said earlier in the same judgment (at p. 40), that to do so '' would entitle a person, where he wastes his earnings by betting, to make the state a partner in his gambling,'' by setting his *losses* against other income; see G. B. Graham, '' Taxes on Betting and Gaming '' [1966] B.T.R. 309.

Compare *Down* v. *Compston* (1937) 21 T.C. 60 and *Burdge* v. *Pyne* [1969] 1 W.L.R. 364.

3. The Profit Motive

The intention to make a profit may be relevant in determining whether or not an activity constitutes trading,[12] but it is not decisive.

(A) NON-PROFIT MAKING ORGANISATIONS [13]

Re DUTY ON THE ESTATE OF THE INCORPORATED COUNCIL OF LAW REPORTING FOR ENGLAND AND WALES

Queen's Bench Division (1888) 22 Q.B.D. 279; 58 L.J.Q.B. 90; 60 L.T. 505; 3 T.C. 105

Under the Memorandum of the Council, all property and income of the Council was applicable solely to the objects of publishing reports, etc. and no part could be paid as dividend, bonus or otherwise to any member.

---

[12] *Post*, p. 144.   [13] For the tax treatment of charities, see I.C.T.A. 1970, s. 360.

Lord Coleridge C.J.: . . . The question is simply whether the Council of the Law Reports are established for carrying on a trade or business. If they are, it follows that they are exempted in respect of their property, howsoever and from whomsoever acquired, from the duty imposed by section 11.[14]

. . . I may ask, as I asked during the course of the argument, what is it that the Incorporated Council of the Law Reports do if they do not carry on a business? They do something; they carry on something; they are very actively engaged in something. I confess I should have thought it capable of strong argument that they carried on a trade, because it is not essential to the carrying on of a trade that the persons engaged in it should make, or desire to make, a profit by it. Though it may be true that in the great majority of cases the carrying-on of a trade does, in fact, include the idea of profit, yet the definition of the mere word " trade " does not necessarily mean something by which a profit is made. But putting aside the question whether they carry on a trade, how can it be denied that the Council carry on a business? They are incorporated; they have a secretary; they employ editors, reporters, and printers; they print books; they sell those books; they do all that is ordinarily done in carrying on the business of a bookseller. It is said that though they make a profit, they cannot, by the terms of their memorandum of association, put that profit into their own pockets. Be it so; they are carrying on a business in which, by the terms of its constitution, they are prevented from making a profit to their own benefit. One can suppose the case of co-operative stores founded upon the this or that way, but prevent the members putting any money into their own principle that no profit shall be made by the members. They buy and sell, and if any profit is made, their articles of association compel them to dispose of it in pockets. They also would probably employ secretaries, and other persons engaged in their warehouses and in buying and selling goods all over the country. Could it possibly be denied that such an association of persons were not carrying on a business? . . .

MERSEY DOCKS AND HARBOUR BOARD v. LUCAS

House of Lords (1883) 8 App.Cas. 891; 53 L.J.Q.B. 4; 49 L.T. 781; 48 J.P. 212; 32 W.R. 34; 2 T.C. 25

The Board was established by Act of Parliament which provided that moneys received by the Board should be applied in payment of expenses, construction of works, etc. and for any surplus to be applied to sinking funds to extinguish certain debts. *Held*, the Corporation was liable to income tax in respect of any surplus.

Earl of Selborne L.C.: . . . but to my mind it is reasonably plain that the gains of a trade are that which is gained by the trading, for whatever purposes it is used, whether it is gained for the benefit of a community, or for the benefit of individuals. . . .

Note
Followed in *Sowrey* v. *Harbour Mooring Commissioners of King's Lynn* (1887) 2 T.C. 201; *Paddington Burial Board* v. *I.R.C.* (1884) 13 Q.B.D. 9; and see *Religious Tract and Book Society of Scotland* v. *Forbes* (1896) 3 T.C. 415.

---

[14] Of the Customs and Inland Revenue Act 1885, now repealed.

BRIGHTON COLLEGE v. MARRIOTT

House of Lords [1926] A.C. 192; 95 L.J.K.B. 356; 134 L.T. 417; 42 T.L.R. 228; 70 S.J. 245;
[1925] All E.R.Rep. 600; 10 T.C. 213

The surplus income of a charitable company had to be devoted, under the company's objects, to improvements and could not be distributed in any way among the members.

VISCOUNT CAVE L.C.: . . . First, it is said that the appellant company, being admittedly a charity, cannot carry on a trade, and that a surplus of receipts over expenditure arising in the execution of a charitable trust is not properly described as profit; and stress is laid on the fact that, having regard to the provisions of the company's memorandum of association, no part of its income can be distributed among the members. I am unable to agree with this contention. It has long been decided that, if a trade is in fact being carried on at a profit, it is immaterial that the profits must, under the constitution of the trading corporation, be devoted to public objects: *Mersey Docks* v. *Lucas* [15]; *cf. In re Incorporated Council of Law Reporting.*[16] It has also been decided, both in the courts and in this House, that a charitable institution which carries on a trade at a profit is chargeable with income tax in respect of its profits or gains in that trade, notwithstanding that they are and can only be applied to the purposes of the charity. Thus, in *St. Andrew's Hospital, Northampton* v. *Shearsmith* [17] a hospital for the care of insane persons was charged with income tax on the profits earned by receiving wealthy patients, although such profits were applied only for the benefit of the poorer patients and the improvement of the hospital. In *Religious Tract and Book Society of Scotland* v. *Forbes* [18] a society whose object was to promote religion by the circulation of tracts and books was held chargeable with tax in respect of profits earned by carrying on a bookseller's business. In *Grove* v. *Young Men's Christian Association* [19] a society formed for the improvement of young men was held liable to tax on profits made by carrying on a restaurant which was open to the public as well as to its members. And in *Coman* v. *Governors of the Rotunda Hospital, Dublin* [20] the governors of a hospital were held to have been rightly assessed to tax under Schedule D in respect of profits earned by letting certain rooms for entertainments. In all these cases the profits earned by the particular trade or business were applicable and applied only to the general purposes of the charities, but this was held to make no difference. . . .

Note
School fees paid to the Company were held to be trading receipts and not annual payments; see also *Campbell* v. *I.R.C.* [1967] Ch. 651; *ante*, p. 123.

(B) MUTUAL TRADING

NEW YORK LIFE INSURANCE COMPANY v. STYLES

House of Lords (1889) 14 App.Cas. 381; 59 L.J.Q.B. 291; 61 L.T. 201; 5 T.L.R. 621;
2 T.C. 460

The only members of the Company were holders of participating insurance policies. Any surplus of premium income over outgoings was held to the credit

---

[15] (1883) 8 App.Cas. 891, *supra*.
[16] (1888) 22 Q.B.D. 279; *ante*, p. 132.
[17] (1887) 19 Q.B.D. 624.
[18] (1886) 3 T.C. 415.
[19] (1903) 4 T.C. 613.
[20] [1921] 1 A.C. 1.

of the general body of members. *Held*, such surplus did not constitute a taxable profit.

LORD WATSON: . . . When a number of individuals agree to contribute funds for a common purpose, such as the payment of annuities, or of capital sums, to some or all of them, on the occurrence of events certain or uncertain, and stipulate that their contributions, so far as not required for that purpose, shall be repaid to them, I cannot conceive why they should be regarded as traders, or why contributions returned to them should be regarded as profits. . . .

LORD BRAMWELL: My Lords, I am of opinion that this judgment should be reversed. The appellants do not carry on a profession, trade, employment, or vocation from which profits or gains arise or accrue within the meaning of the Income Tax Act. It is for the respondent to make out that they do. I think it can be shown negatively that they do not. I speak, of course, of the mutual insurance business. They are a corporation, but the case may be, as is admitted, dealt with as though they were an unincorporated association of individuals. Take it that they were; take it that half-a-dozen persons so associated themselves at the beginning of the year; they each put into a common purse £10, to be given to the executors of any one who dies, or divided, if more than one dies, among the executors of those having died. In fact, no one dies, and the money is returned, or carried on for the next year. Is it possible to say that this is an association for the purpose of profit, or that it has made any profit? But that, with less complexity, is the present case. Instead of six, there are many hundreds, perhaps thousands, associated; instead of the arrangement being for one year, it is for the respective lives of the associated; instead of all the subscriptions being given to the executors of one or more deceased, there is an agreed sum given to them, the rest being carried on to meet the case of future deaths, of which there will be a proportionate increase as the associates grow older. Instead of the money subscribed being returned, it is applied to the reduction of future payments by the associates, or to the increase of the sum they will be entitled to. It cannot be a profit if added to the sum insured, unless it would be if returned. . . .

LORD MACNAGHTEN: . . . I do not understand how persons contributing to a common fund in pursuance of a scheme for their mutual benefit—having no dealings or relations with any outside body—can be said to have made a profit when they find that they have overcharged themselves, and that some portion of their contributions may be safely refunded. . . .

Note

As to the taxation of mutual trading, see now I.C.T.A. 1970, ss. 345–347, and *I.R.C.* v. *Ayrshire Employers Mutual Insurance Association Ltd.* [1946] 1 All E.R. 637; *ante*, p. 11. Similar principles apply to other types of mutual associations and clubs, see *I.R.C.* v. *The Eccentric Club Ltd.* (1925) 12 T.C. 657; *Jones* v. *South-West Lancashire Coal Owners' Association Ltd.* [1927] A.C. 827; and *National Association of Local Government Officers* v. *Watkins* (1934) 18 T.C. 499. Where a members' club trades with non-members, the profits attributable to such trade are taxable: *Carlisle and Silloth Golf Club* v. *Smith* [1913] 3 K.B. 75; *Fletcher* v. *Income Tax Commissioner* [1972] A.C. 414.

(C) DIVIDEND-STRIPPING

The relevance of the profit motive has been considered in a number of cases where the transaction in question, usually taking the form of the purchase by a dealing company of shares, the extraction of accumulated profits in the form of dividends and the subsequent resale of the shares, has been entered into primarily to secure a tax advantage.

BISHOP v. FINSBURY SECURITIES LTD.

House of Lords [1966] 1 W.L.R. 1402; 110 S.J. 636; [1966] 3 All E.R. 105; 43 T.C. 621

LORD MORRIS OF BORTH-Y-GEST: . . . There may be occasions when it is helpful to consider the object of a transaction when deciding as to its nature.

. . . A consideration of the transactions now under review leads me to the opinion that they were in no way characteristic of nor did they possess the ordinary features of the trade of share-dealing. The various shares which were acquired ought not to be regarded as having become part of the stock-in-trade of the company. They were not acquired for the purpose of dealing with them. In no ordinary sense were they current assets.

. . . In my opinion neither argument is correct. For the reasons I have already given, this transaction on its particular facts was not, within the definition of section 526 [of the I.T.A. 1952, see now s. 526, I.C.T.A. 1970] " an adventure or concern in the nature of trade " at all. It was a wholly artificial device remote from trade to secure a tax advantage. . . .

PETROTIM SECURITIES LTD. v. AYRES

Court of Appeal [1964] 1 W.L.R. 190; 107 S.J. 908; [1964] 1 All E.R. 269; 41 T.C. 389

LORD DENNING M.R.: . . . It seems to me that, when there is a sale at a gross undervalue by one associated company to another, the commissioners are entitled to find that it is not a transaction made in the course of trade. Whoever would suppose that any trader in his right senses would enter into transactions of this kind? That he would sell at a gross undervalue—were it not that he had in mind some benefit out of making a loss? It is just on a par with a case where a company gives its money away. . . .

Note
In this case, securities were sold by the taxpayer Company to an associated Company at a price considerably below their market value. It was held that the transactions were not trading transactions and, under the rule in *Sharkey* v. *Wernher* [1956] A.C. 58, *post*, p. 161, market value was substituted for the actual consideration in the accounts of the taxpayer Company. See also *Ridge Securities Ltd.* v. *I.R.C.* [1964] 1 W.L.R. 479.

JOHNSON v. JEWITT

Court of Appeal (1961) 40 T.C. 231; 105 S.J. 987; [1961] T.R. 321

LORD EVERSHED M.R.: . . . I come unhesitatingly, myself, to the same decision. I am quite unpersuaded that these transactions can properly, fairly or sensibly be called anything but fantastic to the degree almost, perhaps, of impudence. I am bound to say that were it otherwise, it would seem to me that the English law, and particularly the Companies Act, would have been made mock of; and I only, in conclusion, express great regret that the engineer of this extraordinary scheme should be a member of the profession of solicitor. . . .

DONOVAN, L.J.: . . . I entirely agree with the finding of the Commissioners and with Buckley J.'s judgment. We were asked, what was this if it were not trading? If I had to give an answer, I would call it a cheap exercise in fiscal conjuring and book-keeping phantasy, involving a gross abuse of the Companies Act and having as its unworthy object the extraction from the Exchequer of an

enormous sum which the Appellant had never paid in tax and to which he has
no shadow of a right whatsoever. . . .

LUPTON v. F.A. & A.B. LTD.

House of Lords [1972] A.C. 634; [1971] 3 W.L.R. 670; 115 S.J. 849; [1971] 3 All E.R. 948;
[1971] T.R. 285

LORD MORRIS OF BORTH-Y-GEST: . . . My Lords, this is one more case in
which the question which arose for consideration was whether certain transactions should fairly and reasonably be regarded as share-dealing transactions
resulting in the acquisition of shares by a company as a dealer in shares so that
they become part of its stock-in-trade or whether the transactions could not fairly
and reasonably be so regarded.

At all relevant times the appellant company was trading as a dealer in stocks
and shares. It entered into numerous transactions in stocks and shares. The
proceedings which culminate in your Lordships' House related only to five
transactions. It does not follow that because a person is carrying on a trade as
a dealer in shares every transaction into which he enters will be a dealing in
shares in the course of his trade. So the question arose in regard to five
particular transactions. The way that the question arose was that there was an
assessment to income tax made upon the company for the year 1960–61. The
company appealed and claimed relief from tax under section 341 of the Income
Tax Act 1952, for the years 1959–60, 1960–61 and 1961–62 in respect of losses
claimed by the company to have been sustained by it in those years in its trade
as a dealer in stocks and shares.

In the case stated the Special Commissioners carefully summarised the five
transactions (which were in relation to shares in five separate companies) which
were entered into by the appellant company. The commissioners had in mind
the decision in *Griffiths (Inspector of Taxes)* v. *J. P. Harrison (Watford) Ltd.*[21]
and the decision of the Court of Appeal on July 7 1965, in *Finsbury Securities
Ltd.* v. *Inland Revenue Commissioners* [22] (which was later reversed in this
House [23]). They found that the five transactions, which they described as
" dividend-stripping transactions," had formed part of the trade of the company
of dealing in shares.

The learned judge (Megarry J.[24]) reversed the decision of the Special Commissioners. Though with some hesitation in regard to one of the five transactions he held in the case of all of them that they were not trading transactions
in the course of the company's trade; rather were they to be regarded as artificial
devices remote from trade in order to secure tax advantages.

The appellants did not appeal against the decision of the learned judge in
regard to four of the five transactions. Their appeal in relation to the fifth was
dismissed by the Court of Appeal [25] (Lord Denning M.R. and Phillimore L.J.;
Sachs L.J. dissenting).

So it becomes necessary carefully to examine this fifth transaction. Ought it,
when viewed fairly and rationally, to be classed as a trading transaction coming
within the trade of a dealer in shares? Ultimately this becomes a matter of
judgment. In such cases as these some help may be derived from considering
the decisions of courts as to how other transactions have been regarded. One

21 [1963] A.C. 1, *ante*, pp. 47, 129.
22 [1965] 1 W.L.R. 1206.
23 [1966] 1 W.L.R. 1402, *ante*, p. 136.
24 [1968] 1 W.L.R. 1401.
25 [1969] 1 W.L.R. 1627. See A. D. W. Pardoe, " Is Dividend Stripping a Trade? "
[1969] B.T.R. 418; [1970] B.T.R. 211.

transaction with certain features may have been held to have been a transaction properly to be regarded as being within the trade of a dealer in shares. Another transaction with other features may have been held not to have been one which could properly be so regarded. Deriving such help as a consideration of other cases may yield—the question for decision will be whether the particular transaction under review can and should be regarded as a trading transaction within the course of the trade of a dealer in shares.

This enquiry may or may not involve or necessitate a consideration of the profitability of a transaction or of the tax results of a transaction. One trading transaction may result in a profit. Another may result in a loss. If each of these, fairly judged, is undoubtedly a trading transaction its nature is not altered according to whether from a financial point of view it works out favourably or unfavourably. Nor is such a transaction altered in its nature according to how the revenue laws determine the tax position which results from the financial position.

. . . The question then arises whether a trading transaction which is entered into with a view to the obtaining subsequently of such benefit as may or could result from the application of revenue law will cease to be such a trading transaction or will never have been such a transaction once the motive which inspired it is known. In the *Harrison* case the decision (by a majority) of your Lordships' House affirming the majority decision of the Court of Appeal which affirmed the decision of the learned judge was that trading transactions do not cease to be trading transactions merely because they are entered into in the hope of later taking advantage of the revenue law by making a claim for recovery of tax. The making of such a claim would not be a part of any trading transaction and would not itself be a trading transaction.

The approach of Mr. Monroe [counsel for the Crown] was as follows. He submitted that if there is a trading transaction the fact that the motive which inspired it was that fiscal benefit might be made to result does not transform the trading transaction into something else. To that extent Mr. Monroe accepted and supported the principle which guided the decision in *Harrison's* case. Stated otherwise Mr. Monroe submitted that if there is a transaction which is unambiguously a trading transaction the circumstance that a tax benefit is in view does not alter the fact that the transaction is and remains a trading transaction. The motive which inspires a transaction must of course exist before the transaction. It follows that the presence or absence of a motive securing a tax benefit is irrelevant when deciding whether a transaction is or is not a trading transaction. In spite of this, it was contended that the transaction in *Harrison's* case was not a trading transaction. When the reason for this contention was advanced it lay only in the circumstance that the motive that inspired the transaction was that of later securing a tax benefit. But, my Lords, once it is accepted, as it must be, that motive does not and cannot alter or transform the essential and factual nature of a transaction it must follow that it is the transaction itself and its form and content which is to be examined and considered. If the motive or hope of later obtaining a tax benefit is left out of account, the purchase of shares by a dealer in shares and their later sale must unambiguously be classed as a trading transaction.

The transactions in the *Harrison* case were solely and unambiguously trading transactions. There was a purchase of shares and after receipt of a dividend a sale of shares. There was no term, express or implied, in any contract or any transaction which in any way introduced any fiscal element. No fiscal consideration or arrangement intruded itself in any way into any bargain that was made. There was merely an acknowledged reason which inspired one party to enter into certain trading transactions. If that party later made some tax claim that claim would be no part of a trading activity. The transactions in the *Harrison* case not only had all the characteristics of trading, there was no characteristic which was not trading. There was nothing equivocal. There was no problem to be solved as to what acts were done. To the question—quid actum est? there could be but one answer. The question—quo animo? was irrelevant. As Lord Reid said in giving the judgment of the Board in *Iswera* v. *Inland Revenue Commissioners* [26]:

> " If, in order to get what he wants, the taxpayer has to embark on an adventure which has all the characteristics of trading, his purpose or object alone cannot prevail over what he in fact does. But if his acts are equivocal his purpose or object may be a very material factor when weighing the total effect of all the circumstances."

The somewhat loose phrase " dividend-stripping transaction " has acquired a certain emotive force but if it is used its meaning must be examined. It has been suggested that the *Harrison* case decided that a transaction can be a trading transaction even though it is a pure dividend-stripping transaction entered into with the sole object of making a fiscal profit without any view to a commercial profit. Analysis will show that such a suggestion is illfounded and misleading. The word " transaction " generally suggests some arrangement between two or more persons. In the *Harrison* case there was a purchase of shares from a seller of them. That was a trading transaction. Later there was a sale of the shares to a new purchaser. That was a trading transaction. In between there had been the declaration and receipt of a dividend. But there was no arrangement whatsoever under which the sellers to Harrisons of the shares or the purchasers from them of the shares were concerned as to whether Harrisons would or would not later make some claim which under the law as it then stood they might be able to make. There was, therefore, no dividend-stripping " transaction " in the *Harrison* case in the sense that any other person had any control or concern or interest as to what Harrisons would do once they had bought the shares.

If, therefore, as in my view is clear, the presence of a motive of securing tax recovery does not cause a trading transaction to cease to be one then reliance on motive must disappear. And if reliance on motive is either voluntarily or reluctantly but compulsively jettisoned it is not saved even if the language of rhetoric is used to characterise it.

It is manifest that some transactions may be so affected or inspired by fiscal considerations that the shape and character of the transaction is no longer that of a trading transaction. The result will be not that a trading transaction with unusual features is revealed but that there is an arrangement or scheme which cannot fairly be regarded as being a transaction in the trade of dealing in shares. The transactions which were under review in *Finsbury Securities Ltd.* v. *Inland Revenue Commissioners* were of this nature. The transactions have only to be looked at for it to be seen that they were wholly and fundamentally different from the transactions in the *Harrison* case. Whereas in the *Harrison* case there is not a trace of any fiscal " arrangement," in the *Finsbury* case certain fiscal arrangements were inherently and structurally a part of the transactions which it was sought to describe as trading transactions. The *Harrison* case and the *Finsbury* case are wholly different from each other. In the *Harrison* case the transactions contained no fiscal arrangements whatsoever; in the *Finsbury* case such arrangements were central to and pivotal of the transactions under review.

There are, therefore, cases where, as Megarry J. indicated, the fiscal element has so invaded the transaction itself that it is moulded and shaped by the fiscal elements. This was helpfully expressed by Megarry J. as follows [24]:

[26] [1965] 1 W.L.R. 663, 668.

" If upon analysis it is found that the greater part of the transaction consists of elements for which there is some trading purpose or explanation (whether ordinary or extraordinary), then the presence of what I may call ' fiscal elements,' inserted solely or mainly for the purpose of producing a fiscal benefit, may not suffice to deprive the transaction of its trading status. The question is whether, viewed as a whole, the transaction is one which can fairly be regarded as a trading transaction. If it is, then it will not be denatured merely because it was entered into with motives of reaping a fiscal advantage. Neither fiscal elements nor fiscal motives will prevent what in substance is a trading transaction from ranking as such. On the other hand, if the greater part of the transaction is explicable only on fiscal grounds, the mere presence of elements of trading will not suffice to translate the transaction into the realms of trading. In particular, if what is erected is predominantly an artificial structure, remote from trading and fashioned so as to secure a tax advantage, the mere presence in that structure of certain elements which by themselves could fairly be described as trading will not cast the cloak of trade over the whole structure."

. . . It was submitted that the truly strange arrangements which I have summarised were but the arrangements of a trading transaction of a dealer in shares. It was further submitted that the elaborate and unusual provisions which were entered into merely reflected the fact that the shares possessed a special value if sold to a dealer in shares. I cannot accept these submissions. It would be a complete delusion to regard the transaction in this case as a share dealing transaction coming within the area of trade of a dealer in shares. It was something very different. . . .

Note

Applied by the House of Lords in another decision, delivered on the same day: *Thomson* v. *Gurneville Securities Ltd.* [1972] A.C. 661.

The effect of the decision is to deny relief in respect of a " loss " on the basis that it was not incurred in a trading transaction. Relief in respect of a loss incurred in an admitted trade may also, in certain circumstances, be denied: see *post,* Chap. 9, and J. P. Lawton, " Hobby Trading " [1960] B.T.R. 241.

4. The Badges of Trade

Prior to the introduction of tax upon Capital Gains [27] the question whether or not a person had engaged in trade was of fundamental importance. A particular transaction might be held to be a trading transaction, and the profit derived therefrom fully subject to income tax and surtax; if it was not trading, the gain escaped tax altogether.[28] Even now, the difference is between the full rates of income tax and surtax on the one hand and the lower rate applicable to Capital Gains on the other.

The problem is at its most acute in the case of casual profits derived from more-or-less isolated transactions.[29]

[27] Income tax upon short-term gains was introduced in the Finance Act 1962 (and abolished in the Finance Act 1971) and tax upon capital gains generally by the Finance Act 1965. *Post,* Chap. 13.

[28] *Jones* v. *Leeming* [1930] A.C. 415; *post,* p. 221.

[29] Some aspects of the problem have been discussed in Chap. 4.

REPORT OF THE ROYAL COMMISSION ON THE INCOME TAX

Colwyn Commission, 1920 Cmd. 615

86. There are many categories of transactions the profits arising from which seem, to the ordinary mind, eminently proper subjects for Income Tax, although they are not at present charged because it cannot be successfully asserted that they are " annual profits ". There are cases where a person may deliberately set out to make a profit, may quite properly treat his profit as income and spend it as income, his taxable capacity may be undoubtedly greater because of the result of his venture; his gains may even be the reward of services rendered, but yet his profits may entirely escape Income Tax under the present law.

87. Many Dominions and foreign States endeavour to bring within the ambit of their Income Tax these non-recurring or occasional profits, often by enumerating the particular sources which are to be regarded as producing assessable income, though this method leaves loopholes of escape for particular forms of profit that happened not to be present to the minds of the framers of the Acts.

88. Several witnesses have called our attention to the possibility and the desirability of increasing the revenue by widening the doors of the tax so as to admit profits which at present are not regarded as assessable income. We are satisfied that the narrow scope of the existing charge cannot be justified and should be enlarged. We feel very strongly that at a time like the present, when taxation is necessarily high, to allow whole classes of sometimes highly profitable transactions to lie outside the range of the Income Tax, on the narrow technical ground that the resulting profits are not of a recurring character, should no longer be permitted, and we have been made aware that the existence of this exemption is felt to be a real grievance by other taxpayers whose profits are taxed to the full. The difficulty will be to open the doors wide enough to bring in what it is desired to include and yet not so wide as to admit what should be left outside, but we consider that an attempt should be made to overcome this difficulty in view of the importance and desirability of the object sought to be achieved.

89. It is not easy by legal definition to discriminate between two transactions, having many superficial points in common, one of which would be generally admitted to be a capital transaction, while the profits of the other would at once strike the ordinary mind as a suitable and proper subject for Income Tax. If A, having occupied his own house for 20 years, sells it at a profit, it would generally be thought unfair to charge that profit to Income Tax. If B, on the other hand, either by himself or with other co-adventurers, buys an estate, not for occupation but with the intention of disposing of it as soon as possible, sells it in six weeks, and makes a profit on the deal, most people would think it unreasonable that his profit should escape Income Tax.

90. In general we consider that such powers should be given by law as would enable the taxing authorities to deal with any cases of casual or non-recurring profits arising from a transaction that is prima facie a profit-seeking business transaction, since on the score of equity practically nothing can be said for the present exemption of these profits. Profits that arise from ordinary changes of investments should normally remain outside the scope of the tax, but they should nevertheless be charged if and when they constitute a regular source of profit.

91. We are of opinion that any profit made on a transaction recognisable as a business transaction, i.e. a transaction in which the subject matter was acquired with a view to profit-seeking, should be brought within the scope of the Income Tax, and should not be treated as an accretion of capital simply because the

transaction lies outside the range of the taxpayer's ordinary business, or because the opportunities of making such profits are not likely, in the nature of things, to occur regularly or at short intervals.

FINAL REPORT OF THE ROYAL COMMISSION ON THE TAXATION OF PROFITS AND INCOME

1955 Cmd. 9474

109. If the law is not to be altered in any such radical fashion,[30] it is necessary to enquire whether the existing treatment of what, for convenience, we will call capital profits rests on a satisfactory basis. All profits that arise from the utilisation of property are made in a sense out of capital; but, as we have explained above, the law has established a distinction between the profit that arises when property has been committed to a trade or " an adventure or concern in the nature of trade " as part of its merchantable stock and is then realised in the course of trading operations and the profit that arises from a realisation of property not so committed. The one is taxable income, the other not. The one is regarded as a detachable surplus arising from a source of income which is one of the sources listed by the tax code, namely, the trade, adventure or concern: the other has no source unless it be the mere fact of realisation, and is spoken of as " an accretion to capital." The conception causes no difficulty in the case of profits from ordinary trading: but it is evident that it requires the drawing of a very fine line when it has to be applied to the case of the isolated transaction which may be on the one hand the product of a trading venture or on the other hand a mere change of investment.

110. In our view the line of distinction represents a real difference between two kinds of profit, which we do not wish to see abolished, so long as we can feel satisfied that the distinction is capable of being given effect to with reasonable certainty in its application to actual cases. This seems to be the crux of the matter. For, when each case has to be decided on an assessment of the available evidence, one person may be exempted through the sheer absence of any determining circumstance, even though he has been just as much a dealer in fact as another who is found to be liable. Moreover, cases of this sort, though some of them may reach the High Court on appeal on a point of law, are usually decided by the various bodies of General Commissioners in the various divisions or by the Special Commissioners. If there could be laid down some uniform test that they could apply in order to determine on which side of the line a case lay the charge of tax would be likely to fall more evenly, and therefore more satisfactorily, upon the persons whose transactions brought them to the fringe of this liability.

111. With this end we set ourselves to enquire whether there was any general rule that could advantageously be propounded as a simple test that would separate the taxable case from the non-taxable one. Two suggestions seemed worthy of detailed consideration.

112. One was that profit arising from any realisation of property should be declared by law to be taxable income if the property had been acquired with a view to profit-seeking. This seems to have been the kind of test envisaged by the 1920 Commission where they speak of " any profit made on a transaction recognisable as a business transaction, *i.e.* a transaction in which the subject matter was acquired with a view to profit-seeking." [31] The difficulty about

---

[30] In the previous paragraph the Commission had recommended against the introduction of a capital gains tax, or bringing all such gains within the income tax net, see *post*, Chap. 13.
[31] 1920 Cmd. 615, para. 91, *supra.*

applying this is that, in any normal sense of the words, a " view to profit-seeking " may accompany many transactions that would not be called business transactions. Since few investors can expect that their investment will remain exactly stable in value in their hands they are bound to contemplate the probabilities of rise or fall and it is hardly to be expected that they will not choose one for which they hope or expect a rise. Yet hitherto the law has refused to treat the presence of this expectation as conclusively identifying a taxable profit. " An accretion to capital," said Lord Buckmaster in the House of Lords [32] " does not become income merely because the original capital was invested in the hope and expectation that it would rise in value."

113. Lord Buckmaster's dictum is perhaps too frequently invoked, since it is expressed in very guarded form. But we regard a test that depends on the motive or view of a person at the date of acquisition (which may have occurred years before the question comes under review) as a bad general test for the purpose that we have in mind. There are many fields in which the law has to concern itself with ascertaining motive, but a tax appeal is not well suited for this kind of enquiry. We are afraid that the result would be not to achieve a more even-handed application of the tax charge but to give a helping hand to the person who can make a plausible defence of himself in the witness chair. Indeed the Revenue's experience in the administration of those provisions of the excess profits tax (" E.P.T.") and profits tax which make certain tax consequences depend on motive suggest that, if motive is to be ascertained, it is better ascertained by being imputed as the automatic result of prescribed conditions than by an attempt to search the mind of the taxpayer himself. When we add to this the inescapable vagueness of any such phrase as a " view to profit-seeking," we feel no doubt that it would be a mistake to introduce any general rule that sought to solve the matter by the presence or absence of a particular motive in the taxpayer's mind.

114. If, as we conclude, the only useful test must be one of an objective kind, there is much to be said for a rule that treats as taxable income every profit that arises from a realisation made within some fixed period after the acquisition. It is natural to think of a period of twelve months. Such a rule would go a very long way towards identifying the " deal," which is just the " adventure in the nature of trade " that we have in mind. For if a person has become and ceased to be the owner of some piece of property within the space of twelve months, he is unlikely to have been concerned with it as an investment or as an asset for personal enjoyment and he is much more likely to have been engaged in that employment of resources for the purpose of making profit which constitutes the basis of a deal.

115. But, on the whole, the drawbacks of such a fixed rule seem to us to outweigh its advantages. If all profitable realisations achieved within the period are income then unprofitable realisations are losses which according to our present conceptions would be allowable against other income: and this would amount to an invitation to take the losses within the twelve months and to defer the gains. If on the other hand the scheme was to be that a profit made after the close of the period might still be, though would not necessarily be, a taxable profit, depending on its circumstances, there would be no simple general rule for deciding such cases and the position as a whole would not be much advanced. Moreover, it is likely that the introduction of a twelve months' rule would give rise to a presumption—even if an unreasonable presumption—that a realisation effected outside the period was not taxable; and on balance the hand of the Revenue would be weakened instead of being strengthened by the recognition of the fixed period. Finally, there would be some cases of hardship in which

an unexpected change of circumstance had brought about a forced sale shortly after purchase; and the further problem of dealing with settled property where a surplus on realisation is reinvested as part of the capital and is not available to be paid to the life-tenant who receives the income.

116. We concluded that it was better that there should be no single fixed rule. This means that each case must be decided according to its own circumstances. The general line of enquiry that has been favoured by appeal Commissioners and encouraged by the Courts is to see whether a transaction that is said to have given rise to a taxable profit bears any of the " badges of trade." This seems to us the right line, and it has the advantage that it bases itself on objective tests of what is a trading adventure instead of concerning itself directly with the unravelling of motive. At the same time we have noticed that there has been some lack of uniformity in the treatment of different cases according to the tribunals before which they have been brought. This seems to us unfortunate and, for the sake of clarity, we have drawn up and set out below a summary of what we regard as the major relevant considerations that bear upon the identification of these " badges of trade."

(1) *The subject matter of the realisation.* While almost any form of property can be acquired to be dealt in, those forms of property, such as commodities or manufactured articles, which are normally the subject of trading are only very exceptionally the subject of investment. Again property which does not yield to its owner an income or personal enjoyment merely by virtue of its ownership is more likely to have been acquired with the object of a deal than property that does.

(2) *The length of the period of ownership.* Generally speaking, property meant to be dealt in is realised within a short time after acquisition. But there are many exceptions from this as a universal rule.

(3) *The frequency or number of similar transactions by the same person.* If realisations of the same sort of property occur in succession over a period of years or there are several such realisations at about the same date a presumption arises that there has been dealing in respect of each.

(4) *Supplementary work on or in connection with the property realised.* If the property is worked up in any way during the ownership so as to bring it into a more marketable condition; or if any special exertions are made to find or attract purchasers, such as the opening of an office or large-scale advertising, there is some evidence of dealing. For when there is an organised effort to obtain profit there is a source of taxable income. But if nothing at all is done, the suggestion tends the other way.

(5) *The circumstances that were responsible for the realisation.* There may be some explanation, such as a sudden emergency or opportunity calling for ready money, that negatives the idea that any plan of dealing prompted the original purchase.

(6) *Motive.* There are cases in which the purpose of the transaction of purchase and sale is clearly discernible. Motive is never irrelevant in any of these cases. What is desirable is that it should be realised clearly that it can be inferred from surrounding circumstances in the absence of direct evidence of the seller's intentions and even, if necessary, in the face of his own evidence.

117. On the whole we think that it would be a desirable reform if all tax appeals that raise this issue, whether a particular transaction took place in the course of a trade, profession or vocation within the meaning of Case I or Case II of Schedule D, should be heard by the Special Commissioners instead of going before the various bodies of General Commissioners. Such appeals depend on a

delicate balance of facts and we think that it would be more satisfactory that they should be dealt with regularly by one body of judges. We recall that appeals involving an issue of residence or non-residence, which require a comparable weighing of facts, are frequently dealt with by the Special Commissioners. In fact, the Codification Committee recommended that they should have exclusive jurisdiction on this subject.[33]

EDWARDS v. BAIRSTOW AND HARRISON

House of Lords (*ante*, p. 51)

LORD RADCLIFFE: . . . This seems to be, inescapably, a commercial deal in secondhand plant. What detail does it lack that prevents it from being an adventure in the nature of trade, or what element is present in it that makes it capable of being aptly described as anything else? Well, to judge by the respondents' contentions as recited in the case, there were some circumstances lacking in this deal of which the presence has been regarded as of importance in other cases. I do not think that this line of argument is ever very conclusive; but, in any event, it breaks down completely on the facts that are found. It is said that there was no organisation for the purposes of the transaction. But in fact there was organisation, as much of it as the transaction required. It is true that the plant was not advertised for sale, though advertisements asking for plant were answered by the respondents. But why should they incur the cost of advertising if they judged that they could achieve the sale of the plant without it? It is said that no work had been done on the maturing of the asset to be sold. But such replacement and renovation as were needed were in fact carried out, and I can see no reason why a dealer should do more work in making his plant saleable than the purposes of sale require. It is said that neither of the respondents had any special skill from his normal activities which placed him in an advantageous position for the purposes of this transaction. It may be so, though one of them was the employee of a spinning firm. In any case the members of a commercial community do not need much instruction in the principles and possibility of dealing, and I think that, given the opportunity, the existence or non-existence of special skill is of no significance whatever. It is said, finally, that the purchase and sale of plant lent itself to capital, rather than commercial, transactions. I am not sure that I understand what this is intended to mean. If it means that at the relevant period there was no market for secondhand plant in which deals could take place, there is no finding to that effect and all the facts that are recited seem to be against the contention. If it means anything else, it is merely an attempt to describe the conclusion which the respondents would wish to see arrived at on the whole case.

There remains the fact which was avowedly the original ground of the commissioners' decision—" this was an isolated case." But, as we know, that circumstance does not prevent a transaction which bears the badges of trade from being in truth an adventure in the nature of trade. The true question in such cases is whether the operations constitute an adventure of that kind, not whether they by themselves or they in conjunction with other operations, constitute the operator a person who carries on a trade. Dealing is, I think, essentially a trading adventure, and the respondents' operations were nothing but a deal or deals in plant and machinery. . . .

[33] 1936 Cmd. 5131.

(A) NATURE OF THE SUBJECT MATTER [34]

RUTLEDGE v. I.R.C.

Court of Session (1929) 14 T.C. 490; 1929 S.C. 379

THE LORD PRESIDENT (CLYDE): This is an appeal against an assessment to Income Tax and also an assessment to Excess Profits Duty on certain profits arising or accruing to the Appellant in the following circumstances. The Appellant is a business man with many interests; he lends money, he is connected with film business, and he deals in real property. He happened to be in Berlin in connection with one of these interests a few years ago, and while there had the opportunity of making a purchase of a very large quantity of toilet paper from a bankrupt German firm for £1,000. He had the paper sent over to this country and endeavoured to market it. He ultimately found a purchaser for the whole quantity at the price of £12,000. He has now been assessed to Income Tax and Excess Profits Duty on the profit of about £11,000 which thus arose or accrued to him.

The question in the case is whether the profits thus assessed are, or are not, profits of an " adventure . . . in the nature of trade " within the meaning of section 237 of the Income Tax Act 1918.

An adventure it certainly was; for the Appellant made himself liable for the purchase of this vast quantity of toilet paper obviously for no other conceivable purpose than that of re-selling it at a profit; and that is just what he did. The element of adventure accordingly entered into the purchase from the first. It has been said, not without justice, that mere intention is not enough to invest a transaction with the character of trade. But, on the question whether the Appellant entered into an adventure or speculation, the circumstances of the purchase, and also the purchaser's object or intention in making it, do enter, and that directly, into the solution of the question. An adventure, then, the Appellant's speculation certainly was, and a most successful adventure.

The question remains whether the adventure was one " in the nature of trade." The Appellant's contention is that it could not be such, because it is essential to the idea of trade that there should be a continuous series of trading operations; and an observation made in the course of my opinion in *Inland Revenue* v. *Livingston*,[35] 1927 S.C. 251, at p. 255, was founded on, according to which " a single transaction falls as far short of constituting a dealer's trade, as the appearance of a single swallow does of making a summer. The trade of a dealer necessarily consists of a course of dealing, either actually engaged in or at any rate contemplated and intended to continue." But the question here is not whether the Appellant's isolated speculation in toilet paper was a trade, but whether it was an " adventure . . . in the nature of trade "; and in the opinion referred to I said that, in my opinion, " the profits of an isolated venture . . . may be taxable under Schedule D provided the venture is ' in the nature of trade.' " I see no reason to alter that opinion. It is no doubt true that the question whether a particular adventure is " in the nature of trade " or not must depend on its character and circumstances, but if—as in the present case—the purchase is made for no purpose except that of re-sale at a profit, there seems little difficulty in arriving at the conclusion that the deal was " in the nature of trade," though it may be wholly insufficient to constitute by itself a trade. It is not difficult, on the other hand, to imagine circumstances in which the question might become very narrow; and in *Inland Revenue* v. *Livingston*

[34] The first of the " badges of trade " referred to by the Royal Commission in para. 116, *ante*, p. 144.
[35] (1927) 11 T.C. 538.

I instanced such a case which it may be worth while to expound. Suppose the Appellant on the occasion of his visit to Berlin had seen a picture for sale which he admired and which he thought likely to appreciate in value in the course of years; he might buy it—and might be conclusively influenced to buy it—because of an anticipated rise in its value. After using it to embellish his own house for a time, he might sell it if the anticipated appreciation in value ultimately realised itself. In such a case, I pointed out that it *might* be impossible to affirm that the purchase and sale constituted an " adventure . . . in the nature of trade," although, again, the crisis of judgment might turn on the particular circumstances.

Reverting to the facts of the present case, it seems to me to be quite plain (1) that the Appellant, in buying the large stock of toilet paper, entered upon a commercial adventure or speculation; (2) that this adventure or speculation was carried through in exactly the same way as any regular trader or dealer would carry through any of the adventures or speculations in which it is his regular business to engage; and therefore (3) that the purchase and re-sale of the toilet paper was an " adventure . . . in the nature of trade " within the meaning of the Income Tax Act 1918. If that is right the appeal cannot succeed.

LORD SANDS: . . . The nature and quantity of the subject dealt with exclude the suggestion that it could have been disposed of otherwise than as a trade transaction. Neither the purchaser nor any purchaser from him was likely to require such a quantity for his private use. . . .

COOKE v. HADDOCK

Chancery Division (1960) 39 T.C. 64; [1960] T.R. 133

The Appellant, a solicitor, bought a piece of land which he subsequently resold. He was assessed to income tax under Case I of Schedule D on the profit of the transaction, but claimed that the land had been purchased as a long-term investment. *Held*, it was a trading transaction.

PENNYCUICK J.: . . . There are a number of circumstances in the present case which justify the finding of the Commissioners. In particular, (i) the land was ripe for building subject to the necessary licences being obtained; (ii) the land was unsuitable for occupation by the Appellant or for retention as an income-producing investment by the Appellant; (iii) the Appellant obtained planning permission for the development of the estate (although this was to safeguard himself against the threat of compulsory purchase and not with a view to developing the estate himself); (iv) the Appellant sold parts of the land piece-meal; and (v) the Appellant has been concerned in companies and a partnership firm engaged in dealings in land. I think all these elements have been referred to in other reported decisions on this particular question as to what constitutes the carrying on of a trade of a dealer in land. It seems to me that those circumstances amply warrant the conclusion to which the Special Commissioners came.

Note
Land, and other property, such as shares, capable of producing an income and therefore being suitable for holding as a long-term investment, present special problems: see J. Pearce, " The Characteristics of Trade in relation to Property Deals " [1962] B.T.R. 144, where many of the cases are examined. Conversely, the inference of trade will be strongest where the subject-matter in question is unsuitable as a long-term investment, producing little or no income, and unlikely to be held for personal use or enjoyment, *e.g. Wisdom* v. *Chamberlain* [1969] 1 W.L.R. 275; *post*, p. 148.

I.R.C. v. REINHOLD

Court of Session (1953) 34 T.C. 389; 1953 S.C. 49; 1953 S.L.T. 94; [1953] T.R. 11

The Respondent bought and resold four houses. The General Commissioners were equally divided and allowed the appeal against the assessment. *Held*, the fact that the properties were purchased with a view to resale did not of itself establish trade, and it was not possible to say that the Commissioners were not justified in their conclusion.

LORD CARMONT: . . . The Lord Advocate suggested in the present case that the admission of the Respondent, that he had bought for ultimate sale and instructed that sale whenever a suitable opportunity occurred, was as plain an intention of trade as was shown by the terms of a company memorandum. But the mere setting up of a company points to a trading intention because of its implied continuity, whereas a single transaction, albeit one in which a sale is contemplated whenever a suitable opportunity for disposal arrives, has no such implication. A disclosed intention not to hold what was being bought might, as Lord Dunedin said, provide an item of evidence that the buyer intended to trade, and if the commodity purchased in the single transaction was not of a kind normally used for investment but for trading, and if the commodity could not produce an annual return by retention in the hands of the purchaser, then the conclusion may easily be reached that the venture was a trading one. If, however, the subject of the transaction is normally used for investment— land, houses, stocks and shares—the inference is not so readily to be drawn from an admitted intention in regard to a single transaction to sell on the arrival of a suitable preselected time or circumstance and does not warrant the same definite conclusion as regards trading or even that the transaction is in the nature of trade. . . .

(B) LENGTH OF THE PERIOD OF OWNERSHIP

WISDOM v. CHAMBERLAIN

Court of Appeal [1969] 1 W.L.R. 275; (1968) 112 S.J. 946; [1969] 1 All E.R. 332; 45 T.C. 103

The appellant purchased a quantity of silver ingots as a " hedge " against an anticipated devaluation. He sold the silver at a profit within little more than a year. *Held*, the profit was taxable as a trading profit.

HARMAN L.J.: . . . For myself I cannot take that view at all. In the first place it seems to me that, supposing it was a hedge against devaluation, it was nevertheless a transaction entered into on a short-term basis for the purpose of making a profit out of the purchase and sale of a commodity, and if that is not an adventure in the nature of trade I do not really know what is. The whole object of the transaction was to make a profit. It was expected that there would be devaluation, and the reason for wanting to make a profit was that there would be a loss on devaluation, but that does not make any difference, it seems to me, to the fact that the motive and object of the whole transaction was to buy on a short-term basis a commodity with a view to its resale at a profit. That, as it seems to me, is an adventure in the nature of trade. . . .

Note
    See also *Johnston* v. *Heath* [1970] 1 W.L.R. 1567, where a material fact in the finding of trade was that the taxpayer contracted to sell land before he had purchased it.

(C) FREQUENCY OR NUMBER OF SIMILAR TRANSACTIONS BY THE SAME PERSON

PICKFORD v. QUIRKE

Court of Appeal (1927) 13 T.C. 251

A syndicate was formed to buy and resell cotton mills. There were four such transactions. *Held*, although any one transaction by itself would not have constituted a trade, together they did so.

LORD HANWORTH M.R.: . . . It must be remembered that under the interpretation clause trade " includes every trade, manufacture, adventure or concern in the nature of trade." When, however, you come to look at four successive transactions you may hold that what was, considered separately and apart, a transaction to which the words " trade or concern in the nature of trade " could not be applied, yet when you have that transaction repeated, not once nor twice but three times, at least, you may draw a completely different inference from those incidents taken together. That is what the Commissioners have done. . . .

Note
  The membership of the syndicate was not identical for each transaction. It is possible for one member of a partnership or syndicate to have participated in one transaction only, whereas other members have participated in repeated transactions. In *Burrell, Webber and others* v. *Davis* (1958) 38 T.C. 307, where three " inexperienced adventurers " joined in a venture with two others who had previously engaged in similar transactions, it was held that they became " joint speculators " in a trading venture and were all assessable.
  There is also the problem of the effect of subsequent repetitions upon the *first* isolated transaction, see *Leach* v. *Pogson* (1962) 40 T.C. 585; *cf. Page* v. *Pogson* (1954) 35 T.C. 545; *Hudson* v. *Wrightson* (1934) 26 T.C. 55.

MARTIN v. LOWRY

House of Lords [1927] A.C. 312; 96 L.J.K.B. 379; 136 L.T. 580; 11 T.C. 320 (also *post*, p. 152)

A wholesale machinery merchant purchased a large quantity of Government surplus aircraft linen. He rented an office and set up an organisation to dispose of it in lots. *Held*, he was carrying on a trade.

VISCOUNT CAVE L.C.: . . . My Lords, the Commissioners have found as a fact that he did carry on a trade, and they set out in the case ample material upon which they could come to that conclusion. Indeed, having regard to the methods adopted for the resale of the linen, to the number of operations into which the appellant entered, and to the time occupied by the resale, I do not myself see how they could have come to any other conclusion. . . .

Note
  Considering the nature of the subject-matter and the other factors which Viscount Cave stressed, this case bears most of the " badges of trade."

(D) SUPPLEMENTARY WORK

CAPE BRANDY SYNDICATE v. I.R.C.

King's Bench Division (*ante*, pp. 10, 18)

The taxpayers bought a quantity of brandy, which was blended, recasked and sold in lots. It was held to be a trading transaction.

ROWLATT J.: . . . But this case presents some curious features. It is quite clear that these gentlemen did far more than simply buy an article which they thought was going cheap, and re-sell it. They bought it with a view to transport it, with a view to modify its character by skilful manipulation, by blending with a view to alter, not only the amounts by which it could be sold as a man might split up an estate, but by altering the character in the way it was done up so that it could be sold in smaller quantities. They employed experts—and were experts themselves—to dispose of it over a long period of time. When I say over a long period of time I mean by sales which began at once but which extended over some period of time. They did not buy it and put it away, they never intended to buy it and put it away and keep it. They bought it to turn over at once obviously and to turn over advantageously by means of the operations which I have indicated. Now under those circumstances the Commissioners have held that they did carry on a trade, and I think it is a question of fact, and I do not think, by telling me all the evidence, that the Commissioners can make me, or indeed give me authority—because they cannot give me authority if I do not possess it by law—to determine the question of fact. I think it is a question of fact, and a question of degree which generally is a question of fact. I need not say any more than that. I am not prepared to say that there was no evidence before the Commissioners. I think it is just one of those cases where there was evidence. I can conceive people deciding the other way. I do not say which way I should decide myself. But I certainly think that there were materials upon which they could find as they did. . . . (quoted from Tax Cases).

Note

Supplementary work, indicative of trading, may take the form of work, *e.g.* renovation, done to the article which is resold: see *I.R.C.* v. *Livingston* (1927) 11 T.C. 538; *cf. Jenkinson* v. *Freedland* (1961) 39 T.C. 636; or of work, *e.g.* setting up an organisation, advertising, performed in the course of resale: see *Martin* v. *Lowry, supra*; *cf. Hudson* v. *Wrightson* (1934) 26 T.C. 55.

(E) Circumstances Responsible for the Realisation

THE HUDSON'S BAY COMPANY v. STEVENS

Court of Appeal (1909) 5 T.C. 424; 101 L.T. 96; 25 T.L.R. 709

Over a number of years the Company sold off a large quantity of land which it had acquired in return for the surrender of its charter. The sales were held not to be trading transactions.

Sir H. H. Cozens-Hardy M.R.: . . . The real question is whether this money can be regarded as profits or gains derived by the Company from carrying on a trade or business. In my opinion it cannot. The Company are doing no more than an ordinary landowner does who is minded to sell from time to time, as purchasers offer, portions suitable for building of an estate which has devolved upon him from his ancestors. I am unable to attach any weight to the circumstance that large sales are made every year. This is not a case where land is from time to time purchased with a view to resale; the Company are only getting rid by sale as fast as they reasonably can of land which they acquired as part of a consideration for the surrender of their Charter. . . .

Note

Where the subject-matter in question was acquired otherwise than by purchase and is later sold a finding of trading seems less likely than in the normal purchase and resale situation: see *McClelland* v. *Commissioner of Taxation of the Commonwealth of Australia* [1971] 1 W.L.R. 191; *cf. Balgownie Land Trust Ltd.* v. *I.R.C.* (1929) 14 T.C. 684.

COHAN'S EXECUTORS v. I.R.C.

(1924) 12 T.C. 602; 131 L.T. 377

The deceased was a partner in a firm of shipbrokers. Before his death he had entered into a shipbuilding contract. The contract was completed by his executors and the ship sold. It was held that the executors did not continue the trade but were merely performing their duty to realise the deceased's assets to the best advantage.

POLLOCK M.R.: . . . I think it is clear that the Commissioners in the case did find that the deceased carried on a trade or business within the meaning of the words used in the Finance Act of 1915, and perhaps one may say, although it is not in one's province to do so, that I should certainly agree with them in that finding. But it is quite a different question as to whether or not after his death that business, which had been carried on by him, now in the relevant period was carried on by his executors. The executors would have the duty of getting in the estate, of winding up the deceased's affairs and concluding his business, and they would necessarily have to deal with the business situation created by the testator in his lifetime; and the fact that the Commissioners have found that the testator was carrying on a business clearly indicates that the executors were presented with a business being carried on at that time which they had to handle in a business-like way for the purpose of the realisation of the estate. . . .

ATKIN L.J.: . . . Now, from the facts I have stated, and those are the whole of the facts, what is there to indicate that these executors, dealing with this one asset, were in fact carrying on business? It seems to me there is nothing. I have asked myself, in what way did their conduct differ from the conduct of executors who determined not to carry on business, and made up their minds not to carry on business; and I find nothing that would differentiate their conduct from that state of things. It is said that they ought to have released the ship in its incomplete form straightaway. I apprehend that there is no obligation upon an executor at once to deal with executory contracts and terminate them in that way. It is a question of what is the best way of dealing with the estate, and if there is an executory contract which will result in the creation of a chattel which will form part of the estate, and the executors are under a contract which binds them to complete that executory contract, it appears to me it is well within their power to do so, and that in so doing there is no evidence that they are carrying on a business. That must happen very often in the case where the testator did in fact carry on business, and I can imagine many cases in which there are executory contracts which would result in the property belonging to the estate, as, for instance, in the case of a contract entered into by a testator on the hire-purchase system, where it might be of the worst possible disadvantage to the estate that the executors should not complete the contract by paying the remaining instalments of hire so as to secure the eventual property. . . .

Note
   Cf. Weisberg's Executrices v. *I.R.C.* (1933) 17 T.C. 696. Similar problems arise where assets are sold by a company in liquidation: *I.R.C.* v. *The " Old Bushmills " Distillery Co. Ltd.* (1927) 12 T.C. 1148; *cf. I.R.C.* v. *Toll Property Co. Ltd.* (1952) 34 T.C. 13; *Baker* v. *Cook* (1937) 21 T.C. 337; by surviving partners on the death of a partner: *Marshall's Executors* v. *Joly* (1936) 20 T.C. 256; *cf. Hillerns and Fowler* v. *Murray* (1932) 17 T.C. 77; *Newbarn's Syndicate* v. *Hay* (1939) 22 T.C. 461; and by a trader on retirement from business: *I.R.C.* v. *Nelson* (1939) 22 T.C. 716; *cf. J. & R. O'Kane & Co.* v. *I.R.C.* (1922) 12 T.C. 303. Each case turns upon its own facts.

(F) MOTIVE

The relevance of motive has already been discussed.[36]

[36] *Ante,* pp. 132–140.

CHAPTER 9

PROFITS

Tax under Cases I and II of Schedule D is charged in respect of the " annual profits or gains " of the trade, profession or vocation.[1] The expression is not defined in the taxing statutes.

ERICHSEN v. LAST

Court of Appeal (1881) 8 Q.B.D. 414; 51 L.J.Q.B. 86; 45 L.T. 703; 46 J.P. 357; 30 W.R. 301; 4 T.C. 422

Sir George Jessel M.R.: . . . The next point is the question of profits. Now what is profit? It is, as I understand, the difference between the price received on a sale and the cost price of what is sold. . . .

GRESHAM LIFE ASSURANCE SOCIETY v. STYLES

House of Lords [1892] A.C. 309; 62 L.J.Q.B. 41; 67 L.T. 479; 56 J.P. 709; 41 W.R. 270; 8 T.L.R. 618; 3 T.C. 185

The Society granted annuities in return for lump sum payments. In determining its profits, the Society was held to be entitled to deduct sums paid in discharge of annuity contracts.

Lord Halsbury L.C.: . . . Profits and gains must be ascertained on ordinary principles of commercial trading, and I cannot think that the framers of the Act could be guilty of such confusion of thought as to assume that the cost of the article sold to the trader which he in turn makes his profit by selling was not to be taken into account before you arrived at what was intended to be the taxable profit. . . .

Note
The case illustrates that that which is an " annuity " in the hands of the recipient may be a trading expense as regards the payer, see Chap. 7, *ante*.

MARTIN v. LOWRY

Court of Appeal [1926] 1 K.B. 550; 95 L.J.K.B. 497; 135 L.T. 523; 42 T.L.R. 233; 70 S.J. 301; 11 T.C. 297 (*ante*, p. 149)

Pollock M.R.: . . . It is thus necessary to examine the use of the word " annual," and its meaning in the Income Tax and Finance Acts where it is freely used.
. . . The Finance Act each year imposes the tax, and by its terms revives and continues the system under which provision is made for the collection of the tax. The system is maintained by the operation of section 210 of the

[1] I.C.T.A. 1970, ss. 108, 109.

Income Tax Act 1918, which ensures its application to income tax for the succeeding year. It is clear, therefore, that the Acts contemplate and impose a tax for one year only. Since 1842, when the Act was passed which is the fore-runner of the consolidated Act of 1918, this has been the system adopted.

. . . I cannot find any authority to support the contention made by the appellant that the characteristic of repeating the profits or gains in other years beyond the year of assessment and charge must be attached to the trade carried on so as to make the gains annual.

In my judgment Rowlatt J. was right.[2] " Annual " means in the current year, occurring in the year of the assessment to taxation. For these reasons the appellant fails on this point also as to the income tax. The assessment was rightly made, and the appeal must be dismissed with costs.

Note
Consequently, the profit derived from an isolated trading transaction is taxable as an " annual " profit.

REPORT OF THE COMMITTEE ON THE TAXATION OF TRADING PROFITS

1951 Cmd. 8189

133. It is desirable to set out at the beginning what we understand to be the present general state of the law as to the computation of business profits for tax purposes. For the majority of businesses the main rules governing the computation of taxable profits are either the Rule applicable to Case I or the Rule applicable to Case II, together with the Rules applicable to both Cases I and II of Schedule D, although scattered here and there over the many Acts of Parliament dealing with Income Tax are other rules relating to items of a more or less special nature. Each of the first two main Rules expresses the taxable profit as being " the full amount of the balance of the profits . . ." so that in order to compute that balance a profit and loss account is necessary. It is at this stage that questions arise as to what particular items qualify for inclusion in either side of the account or fall to be excluded from it altogether.

134. Except in relation to a comparatively few special items, however, the Income Tax Acts themselves contain no rules which lay down affirmatively what sums are to be treated as receipts and what as expenses in the compilation of such an account. In the main the Acts merely set out various classes of expenses which cannot be included, or the maximum extent to which a par-ticular kind of expense is to be allowed. It has therefore been for the Courts to lay down the general principle to be observed.

135. The decision in the House of Lords in the case of *Usher's Wiltshire Brewery Ltd.* v. *Bruce* [3] can be taken as the one which first expressed that general principle in definite terms. As a result of this case and of decisions in subsequent cases we think it can now be taken as settled that the profits or losses of a business for tax purposes are to be computed in accordance with established commercial accountancy principles as they apply to the particular business in question, subject nevertheless to a number of qualifications.

[2] In *Ryall* v. *Hoare* [1923] 2 K.B. 447; *ante*, p. 76, *post*, p. 219.
[3] [1915] A.C. 433, *post*, p. 168.

WHIMSTER & CO. v. I.R.C.

Court of Session (1926) 12 T.C. 813; 1926 S.C. 20

An anticipated loss on the hiring of certain ships was held not to be a proper deduction, not being actually incurred in the relevant accounting period.

THE LORD PRESIDENT (CLYDE): . . . In computing the balance of profits and gains for the purposes of Income Tax, or for the purposes of Excess Profits Duty, two general and fundamental commonplaces have always to be kept in mind. In the first place, the profits of any particular year or accounting period must be taken to consist of the difference between the receipts from the trade or business *during such year or accounting period* and the expenditure laid out to earn *those receipts*. In the second place, the account of profit and loss to be made up for the purpose of *ascertaining that difference* must be framed consistently with the ordinary principles of commercial accounting, so far as applicable, and in conformity with the rules of the Income Tax Act, or of that Act as modified by the provisions and schedules of the Acts regulating Excess Profits Duty, as the case may be. For example, the ordinary principles of commercial accounting require that in the profit and loss account of a merchant's or manufacturer's business the values of the stock-in-trade at the beginning and at the end of the period covered by the account should be entered at cost or market price, whichever is the lower; although there is nothing about this in the taxing statutes. . . .

Note
The relevance of the Accounting Period and the problems of valuation of stock are discussed later in this Chapter. The question of provision for an anticipated liability is discussed more fully in *Southern Railway of Peru Ltd.* v. *Owen* [1957] A.C. 334; *post*, p. 204.
As to the " ordinary principles of commercial accounting," see S. T. Crump, " Accounting Profits and Tax Profits " [1959] B.T.R. 323. Recent cases have demonstrated the importance of evidence as to correct accounting principles, *e.g. B.S.C. Footwear Ltd.* v. *Ridgway* [1972] A.C. 544, *post*, pp. 191, 196, 201; *Odeon Associated Theatres Ltd.* v. *Jones* [1972] 2 W.L.R. 331, *ante*, p. 100; *Heather* v. *P.-E. Consulting Group Ltd.* [1972] 2 W.L.R. 918.

1. Receipts

The above extracts have stressed that " profits " are arrived at in accordance with accounting principles by determining the " balance," or difference, between certain receipts on the one hand and certain outgoings on the other. It is therefore necessary to consider, first, which receipts are to enter into the computation.

(A) RECEIPTS OF THE TRADE, PROFESSION OR VOCATION

Not all receipts of a trader are trading receipts.[4]

HIGGS v. OLIVIER

Court of Appeal [1952] Ch. 311; [1952] 1 T.L.R. 441; 96 S.J. 90; 33 T.C. 136

A well-known actor received a payment of £15,000 in consideration of his agreeing not to act in, produce or direct any film anywhere for a period of eighteen months, except for the paying company. *Held*, the payment was not a receipt of his profession.

[4] *Davies* v. *The Shell Company of China Ltd.* (1951) 32 T.C. 133. See also p. 128, *ante*.

LORD EVERSHED M.R.: . . . I think Sir Frank Soskice was disposed to agree that, if a trader, or a professional man, for a money consideration covenanted to give up his trade or profession for the rest of his life, then it would be difficult to say that the money received was " profits or gains accruing or arising from his trade or profession." On the other hand, it is not difficult to see that a restriction of a very limited or partial character might less easily be taken out of the ambit of the taxing provision. One example in the argument was that of an actor who covenanted for a limited period not to act for one particular company out of a large number. I myself gave the example of an actor who covenanted for a limited period not to act under his own or well-known stage name. But between the two extremes there is a large area, and for myself I am disposed to think that within that area it may well be a matter of degree. In so far as it is a matter of degree it would be, I think, a question of fact.

In this case the Special Commissioners concluded that the £15,000 was not within the taxing provisions I have quoted. " We found it impossible to say that the sum of £15,000 under the deed came to the taxpayer as part of the income from his vocation. On the contrary, it came to him for refraining from carrying on his vocation, and in our opinion was a capital receipt." I agree that in questions of this kind which involve a consideration of the true import and scope of the trading provisions, it is not possible to say that the whole matter is one of fact. It is, I think, a question of mixed law and fact. But I think that, if I am right in saying that in such a case as this it may well be a matter of degree, then so long as it does not appear that the Special Commissioners have misapprehended the effect of the taxing provisions their decision should not be disturbed. That was Harman J.'s first approach to this case, and I am of the same opinion. . . .

(B) CAPITAL AND REVENUE [5]

Income tax, as we have seen is concerned with income; recepts of a *capital* nature consequently do not enter into the computation of profits.[6]

LOTHIAN CHEMICAL CO. LTD. v. ROGERS

Court of Session (1926) 11 T.C. 508

THE LORD PRESIDENT (CLYDE): . . . My Lords, it has been said times without number—it has been said repeatedly in this Court—that in considering what is the true balance of profits and gains in the Income Tax Acts—and it is not less true of the Act of 1918 than of its predecessors—you deal in the main with ordinary principles of commercial accounting. They do expressly exclude a number of deductions and allowances, some of which according to the ordinary principles of commercial accounting might be allowable. But where these ordinary principles are not invaded by Statute they must be allowed to prevail. It is according to the legitimate principles of commercial practice to draw distinctions, and sharp distinctions, between capital and revenue expenditure, and it is no use criticising these, as it is easy to do, upon the ground that if you apply logic to them they become more or less indefensible. They are matters of practical convenience, but practical convenience which is undoubtedly embodied in the generally understood principles of commercial accounting. . . .

---

[5] See Chap. 4, generally.
[6] *I.R.C.* v. *British Salmson Aero Engines Ltd.* [1938] 2 K.B. 482, *ante*, p. 78; *Harry Ferguson (Motors) Ltd.* v. *I.R.C.* (1951) 33 T.C. 15, *ante*, p. 79.

VAN DEN BERGHS LTD. v. CLARK

House of Lords [1935] A.C. 431; 104 L.J.K.B. 345; 153 L.T. 171; 51 T.L.R. 393; [1935]
All E.R.Rep. 874; 19 T.C. 390

The appellants, who manufactured margarine, had entered into an agreement
with a competing Dutch company to restrict competition between them, share
profits, etc. Subsequently, a dispute arose and finally the Dutch company paid
the appellants £450,000 as " damages " and in consideration of the termination
of the agreement. *Held*, the payment was for the cancellation of a capital asset
and as such was not to be treated as a trading receipt for the purposes of
calculating the taxable profits of the trade.

LORD MACMILLAN: . . . My Lords, the problem of discriminating between an
income receipt and a capital receipt and between an income disbursement and
a capital disbursement is one which in recent years has frequently engaged your
Lordships' attention. In general, the distinction is well recognised and easily
applied, but from time to time cases arise where the item lies on the borderline
and the task of assigning it to income or to capital becomes one of much refinement, as the decisions show. The Income Tax Acts nowhere define " income "
any more than they define " capital "; they describe sources of income and
prescribe methods of computing income, but what constitutes income they
discreetly refrain from saying. Nor do they define " profits or gains "; while
as for " trade," the " interpretation " section [7] only informs us, with a fine
disregard of logic, that it " includes every trade, manufacture, adventure or
concern in the nature of trade." Consequently, it is to the decided cases that
one must go in search of light. While each case is found to turn upon its own
facts, and no infallible criterion emerges, nevertheless the decisions are useful
as illustrations and as affording indications of the kind of considerations which
may relevantly be borne in mind in approaching the problem.

The reported cases fall into two categories, those in which the subject is
found claiming that an item of receipt ought not to be included in computing
his profits, and those in which the subject is found claiming that an item of
disbursement ought to be included among the admissible deductions in computing his profits. In the former case the Crown is found maintaining that the
item is an item of income; in the latter, that it is a capital item. Consequently,
the argumentative position alternates according as it is an item of receipt or
an item of disbursement that is in question, and the taxpayer and the Crown
are found alternately arguing for the restriction or the expansion of the
conception of income.

I propose to refer first to the case of *British Insulated and Helsby Cables, Ltd.*
v. *Atherton.*[8] This case has been generally recognised as the leading modern
authority on the subject, though I fear that Romer L.J. was unduly optimistic
when he said that it " placed beyond the realms of controversy " the law
applicable to the matter: *Anglo-Persian Oil Co.* v. *Dale.*[9] The facts were that
the appellant company claimed to deduct in the computation of its trade profits
a sum which it had provided to form the nucleus of a pension fund for its
employees. The Crown argued that the sum ought to be debited to capital on
the ground that it " was not in its nature recurrent but was made once for all "
and that it was a case of the " provision of a capital sum which will for ever
after relieve the company from making any further payment whatsoever." This
argument prevailed. The Lord Chancellor (Viscount Cave) found in the deci-

---

[7] Income Tax Act 1918, s. 237. Now I.C.T.A. 1970, s. 526 (5).
[8] [1926] A.C. 205, *ante*, p. 79.
[9] [1932] 1 K.B. 124, 145.

sions "considerable authority" for the view which he recommended to the House to adopt—namely, that " when an expenditure is made, not only once and for all, but with a view to bringing into existence an asset or an advantage for the enduring benefit of a trade . . . there is very good reason (in the absence of special circumstances leading to an opposite conclusion) for treating such an expenditure as properly attributable not to revenue but to capital." Lord Atkinson indicated that the word " asset " ought not to be confined to " something material " and, in further elucidation of the principle, Romer L.J. has added that the advantage paid for need not be " of a positive character " and may consist in the getting rid of an item of fixed capital that is of an onerous character : *Anglo-Persian Oil Co.* v. *Dale.*

My Lords, if the numerous decisions are examined and classified, they will be found to exhibit a satisfactory measure of consistency with Lord Cave's principle of discrimination. Certain of them relate to excess profits duty and not to income tax, but for the present purpose this distinction is immaterial. A sum provided to establish a pension fund for employees, as has already been seen, is a capital disbursement : *British Insulated and Helsby Cables, Ltd.* v. *Atherton*; so is a sum paid by a coal merchant for the acquisition of the right to a number of current contracts to supply coal : *John Smith & Son* v. *Moore* [10]; so is a payment by a colliery company as the price of being allowed to surrender unprofitable seams included in its leasehold : *Mallet* v. *Staveley Coal & Iron Co.* [11] Similarly, a sum received by a fireclay company as compensation for leaving unworked the fireclay under a railway was held to be a capital receipt : *Glenboig Union Fireclay Co.* v. *Commissioners of Inland Revenue.* [12]

On the other hand, a sum awarded by the War Compensation Court to a company carrying on the business of brewers and wine and spirit merchants in respect of the compulsory taking over of its stock of rum by the Admiralty was held to be a trade or income receipt : *Commissioners of Inland Revenue* v. *Newcastle Breweries, Ltd.* [13]; so was a sum paid to a shipbuilding company for the cancellation of a contract to build a ship : *Short Brothers, Ltd.* v. *Commissioners of Inland Revenue* [14]; so was a lump sum payment received by a quarry company in lieu of four annual payments in consideration of which the company had relieved a customer of his contract to purchase a quantity of chalk yearly for ten years and build a wharf at which it could be loaded : *Commissioners of Inland Revenue* v. *Northfleet Coal and Ballast Co.* [15]; so was a sum recovered from insurers by a timber company in respect of the destruction by fire of their stock of timber : *J. Gliksten & Son* v. *Green.* [16] Conversely, where a company paid a sum as the price of getting rid of a life director, whose presence on the board was regarded as detrimental to the profitable conduct of the company's business, the payment was held to be an income disbursement : *Mitchell* v. *R. W. Noble Ltd.* [17]; so was the payment made in the case of the *Anglo-Persian Oil Co.* v. *Dale* in order to disembarrass the company of an onerous agency agreement. There are further instances in the reports, but I have quoted enough for the purposes of illustration.

With the guidance thus afforded I now address myself to the question whether the 450,000*l.* received by the appellants in the circumstances already narrated can properly be described as an item of profit arising or accruing to

[10] [1921] 2 A.C. 13, *ante*, p. 67.
[11] [1928] 2 K.B. 405.
[12] (1922) 12 T.C. 461, *post*, p. 159.
[13] (1927) 12 T.C. 927.
[14] (1927) 12 T.C. 955.
[15] (1927) 12 T.C. 1102.
[16] [1929] A.C. 381.
[17] [1927] 1 K.B. 719, *post*, p. 172.

them from the carrying on of their trade, which ought to be credited as an income receipt. It is important to bear in mind at the outset that the trade of the appellants is to manufacture and deal in margarine, for the nature of a receipt may vary according to the nature of the trade in connection with which it arises. The price of the sale of a factory is ordinarily a capital receipt, but it may be an income receipt in the case of a person whose business it is to buy and sell factories.

My Lords, the learned Attorney-General stated that he was content to take the agreements of 1927 as meaning what they say. The sum of 450,000l. is accordingly to be taken as having been paid by the Dutch Company to the appellants in consideration of the appellants consenting to the agreements of 1908, 1913 and 1920 being terminated at December 31, 1927, instead of running their course to December 31, 1940. If the payment had been in respect of a balance of profits due to the appellants by the Dutch Company for the years 1914 to 1927, different considerations might have applied, but it is agreed that it is not to be so regarded.

Now what were the appellants giving up? They gave up their whole rights under the agreements for thirteen years ahead. These agreements are called in the stated case " pooling agreements," but that is a very inadequate description of them, for they did much more than merely embody a system of pooling and sharing profits. If the appellants were merely receiving in one sum down the aggregate of profits which they would otherwise have received over a series of years the lump sum might be regarded as of the same nature as the ingredients of which it was composed. But even if a payment is measured by annual receipts, it is not necessarily itself an item of income. As Lord Buckmaster pointed out in the case of the *Glenboig Union Fireclay Co.* v. *Commissioners of Inland Revenue*: " There is no relation between the measure that is used for the purpose of calculating a particular result and the quality of the figure that is arrived at by means of the test."

The three agreements which the appellants consented to cancel were not ordinary commercial contracts made in the course of carrying on their trade; they were not contracts for the disposal of their products, or for the engagement of agents or other employees necessary for the conduct of their business; nor were they merely agreements as to how their trading profits when earned should be distributed as between the contracting parties. On the contrary the cancelled agreements related to the whole structure of the appellants' profit-making apparatus. They regulated the appellants' activities, defined what they might and what they might not do, and affected the whole conduct of their business. I have difficulty in seeing how money laid out to secure, or money received for the cancellation of, so fundamental an organisation of a trader's activities can be regarded as an income disbursement or an income receipt. Mr. Hills very properly warned your Lordships against being misled as to the legal character of the payment by its magnitude, for magnitude is a relative term and we are dealing with companies which think in millions. But the magnitude of a transaction is not an entirely irrelevant consideration. The legal distinction between a repair and a renewal may be influenced by the expense involved. In the present case, however, it is not the largeness of the sum that is important but the nature of the asset that was surrendered. In my opinion that asset, the congeries of rights which the appellants enjoyed under the agreements and which for a price they surrendered, was a capital asset.

I have not overlooked the criterion afforded by the economists' differentiation between fixed and circulating capital which Lord Haldane invoked in *John Smith & Son* v. *Moore* [10] and on which the Court of Appeal relied in the present case, but I confess that I have not found it very helpful. Circulating capital is capital which is turned over and in the process of being turned over yields profit or loss. Fixed capital is not involved directly in that process, and remains unaffected by it. If this is to be the test, I fail to see how the appellants could be said to have been engaged in turning over the asset which the agreements in question constituted. The agreements formed the fixed framework within which their circulating capital operated; they were not incidental to the working of their profit-making machine but were essential parts of the mechanism itself. They provided the means of making profits, but they themselves did not yield profits. The profits of the appellants arose from manufacturing and dealing in margarine. . . .

Note
But not every payment or receipt of compensation for cancellation of a contract will be regarded as capital. It depends upon all the circumstances of the case—see *Kelsall Parsons & Co.* v. *I.R.C.* (1938) 21 T.C. 608; *Bush, Beach & Gent Ltd.* v. *Road* (1939) 22 T.C. 519; *Elson* v. *James G. Johnston Ltd.* (1965) 42 T.C. 545; cf. *Barr Crombie & Co. Ltd.* v. *I.R.C.* (1945) 26 T.C. 406.

GLENBOIG UNION FIRECLAY CO. LTD. v. I.R.C.

House of Lords (1922) 12 T.C. 427; 1922 S.C. 112

The Appellants received compensation from a railway company for the exercise of the railway company's statutory power to require the Appellants to leave unworked certain fireclay deposits underneath the railway. *Held*, the compensation was a capital receipt in return for the sterilisation of an asset.

LORD BUCKMASTER: My Lords, the Finance (No. 2) Act of 1915 imposed a duty, known as the Excess Profits Duty, to be levied and paid upon profits arising from trade or business. The method provided for assessment was by comparing the profit in the particular business for the period known as the accounting period with the average pre-war standard of profit, determined by taking the average of any two of the three last pre-war trade years, the difference between the two being liable to duty, which was imposed at the rate of 50 per cent.

The Appellant Company here, The Glenboig Union Fireclay Company, Limited, in making their return for the purpose of this Statute, included as one of the two pre-war years the year that ended August 31, 1913, and into the accounts of that year they brought as items of profit a sum of £15,316 received from the Caledonian Railway Company on April 9, 1913, and a further sum of £4,500 received from the same Company on August 29, 1913. The question that is raised upon this appeal is whether or no the Company are entitled to increase the amount of their pre-war profits by these two sums and thereby reduce the amount of the Excess Profits Duty payable under the Statute. There is no question whatever about the bona fides of the Appellant's case in this case. Both those sums had been included in their balance sheet as profit for the year 1913, and upon them they had paid Income Tax without demur.

The circumstances in which those moneys were paid may be shortly stated. The Appellants, the Glenboig Union Fireclay Company, carry on business as manufacturers of fireclay goods and as merchants of raw fireclay. Part of their property consisted of mining rights over certain beds of fireclay at Gartverrie, Glenboig, and in the course of working these fields they were at the end of 1907 approaching the line of the Caledonian Railway, and due notice was given on January 25, 1908, to the Railway Company of the intended extension of their working. The Railway Company, being apprehensive as to the result, required the Fireclay Company to desist from working. A dispute arose as to whether or no the fireclay in question was a mineral and litigation ensued, during which the Railway Company were able to obtain against the Fireclay Company interdicts which operated for two periods, one from February 29, 1908, to April 15, 1910, and the second from November 12, 1910, to April 28, 1911, when the interdict was finally recalled. Upon the recall of the interdict the Railway Company accordingly became liable to pay the Fireclay Company the damages that had been caused to them by the order, and the sum of £4,500, to which I have made reference, was the sum that was paid under that head. The Railway Company now proceeded to treat with the Fireclay Company for the purpose of preventing any further working of this fireclay adjacent to their railway, and arbitration proceedings ensued for the purpose of determining what sum the Railway Company were bound to pay for this privilege, and ultimately the sum of £15,316 was fixed as the sum payable by the Railway Company, and this was accordingly paid on April 9, 1913.

My Lords, these two sums require some different consideration for the purposes of this appeal, but your Lordships are relieved with regard to the second sum of £4,500, because the parties to this appeal have very wisely made an arrangement upon the point, with the terms of which it is unnecessary to trouble your Lordships. The sum of £4,500 is therefore removed from your consideration.

It therefore only remains to consider whether the sum of £15,316 was properly included as a profit in the Appellants' balance sheet for the year ending August 31, 1913. The argument in support of its inclusion can only be well founded if the sum be regarded as profits, or a sum in the nature of profits, earned in the course of their trade or business. I am quite unable to see that the sum represents anything of the kind. It is said, and it is not disputed, that the amount in fact was assessed by considering that the fireclay to which it related could only be worked for some two and a half years before it would be exhausted, and it is consequently urged that the amount therefore represents nothing but the actual profit for two and a half years received in one lump sum. I regard that argument as fallacious. In truth the sum of money is the sum paid to prevent the Fireclay Company obtaining the full benefit of the capital value of that part of the mines which they are prevented from working by the Railway Company. It appears to me to make no difference whether it be regarded as a sale of the asset out and out, or whether it be treated merely as a means of preventing the acquisition of profit that would otherwise be gained. In either case the capital asset of the Company to that extent has been sterilised and destroyed, and it is in respect of that action that the sum of £15,316 was paid. It is unsound to consider the fact that the measure, adopted for the purpose of seeing what the total amount should be, was based on considering what are the profits that would have been earned. That, no doubt, is a perfectly exact and accurate way of determining the compensation, for it is now well settled that the compensation payable in such circumstances is the full value of the minerals that are to be left unworked, less the cost of working, and that is, of course, the profit that would be obtained were they in fact worked. But there is no relation between the measure that is used for the purpose of calculating a particular result and the quality of the figure that is arrived at by means of the application of that test. I am unable to regard this sum of money as anything but capital money, and I think, therefore, it was erroneously entered in the balance sheet ending August 31, 1913, as a profit on the part of the Fireclay Company.

It has been stated before your Lordships that the Income Tax which was paid upon that sum will be returned by the Crown with interest, but that consideration forms no part of the matter that is now before this House, and I have only to ask your Lordships to dismiss this appeal with costs.

Note

Compensation paid in respect of loss, or sterilisation, of trading stock, on the other hand, will be an income receipt: *Glicksten & Son Ltd.* v. *Green* [1929] A.C. 381; *Shadbolt* v. *Salmon Estate (Kingbury) Ltd.* (1943) 25 T.C. 52.

(C) Notional Receipts

A "receipt" is credited in the trader's accounts when it is earned, or when it is actually paid if accounts are made up on the "cash basis"[18]; in certain cases, however, a trader who disposes of stock-in-trade otherwise than in the course of his trade may be treated as though he had made a sale at market value and be credited with a "notional" receipt.[19]

SHARKEY v. WERNHER

House of Lords [1956] A.C. 58; [1955] 3 W.L.R. 671; 99 S.J. 793; [1955] 3 All E.R. 493; 36 T.C. 294

Viscount Simonds: My Lords, this appeal arises upon an assessment to income tax for the year 1949–50 made upon the respondent, Sir Harold Wernher, in respect of profits made by his wife, Lady Zia Wernher, from a stud farm owned and carried on by her. The question in dispute is what amount should be entered on the credit side of the trading account of the stud farm in respect of animals bred there and transferred to a racing establishment also carried on by her.

It is common ground between the parties that some amount must be credited in respect of these animals upon their transfer (a matter upon which I shall say something later) and the issue has been whether this amount should be the cost of production of the animals so transferred or their market value at the date of transfer.

. . . Before I examine the rival contentions, and the authorities by which they are supported, I must make certain further observations which are not, I think, controversial.

It is not in dispute that the enterprise of a stud farm carried on by Lady Zia Wernher is what has been called a taxable activity, which is another way of saying that the respondent is chargeable in respect of any profits arising therefrom in accordance with the Rules of Case I of Schedule D of the Income Tax Act 1918, relating to trades. Nor is it in dispute that the racing establishment carried on by Lady Zia is not a taxable activity: her profits, if any, of that activity are not subject to taxation; her losses, if any, cannot be set off against any other taxable income. This has been called a recreational activity.

Further, it is common ground that the stud farm enterprise is a farming enterprise which is by virtue of section 10 of the Finance Act 1941, and section 31 (1) (a) of the Finance Act 1948,[20] to be treated as the carrying on of a trade, and, accordingly, that its profits are chargeable in the way that I have mentioned.

Again, it is not disputed that (to take the year ending December 31, 1948, as an example) Lady Zia transferred five horses from her stud farm to her racing

[18] *Post*, pp. 202–209.
[19] *Petrotim Securities Ltd.* v. *Ayres* [1964] 1 W.L.R. 190, *ante*, p. 136. See also *Skinner* v. *Berry Head Lands Ltd.* [1970] 1 W.L.R. 1441. A similar problem arises where assets are disposed of for a consideration other than cash, *e.g. Gold Coast Selection Trust Ltd.* v. *Humphrey* [1948] A.C. 459; *Lamport & Holt Line Ltd.* v. *Langwell* (1958) 38 T.C. 193.
[20] Now I.C.T.A. 1970, s. 110.

establishment and that their then market value exceeded their cost of production. Nor, I think, is it in doubt that a main purpose, if not the main purpose, of the stud farm was to supply the racing establishment.

These, my Lords, are the simple facts of the case, and it is perhaps surprising that in the year 1955 there should be any room for doubt about a position which cannot in its essentials differ from a great many other cases. I wish at the outset to say that I attach no importance to the fact that of Lady Zia's two activities to which I have referred the one is taxable and the other is not. I do not understand how her taxable profits in respect of the stud farm can in principle be the greater or the less because the profits of the racing establishment are or are not taxable. The problem, therefore, in all its simplicity, is whether a person, carrying on the trade of farming or, I suppose, any other trade, who disposes of part of his stock in trade not by way of sale in the course of trade but for his own use, enjoyment, or recreation, must bring into his trading account for income tax purposes the market value of that stock in trade at the time of such disposition. But for the fact that this case has throughout proceeded upon the footing as stated in paragraph 2 of the special case that " some figure in respect of the transferred horses fell to be brought into the stud farm accounts as a receipt," I should have stated the problem differently. I say this because, since it is the respondent's case that Lady Zia did not dispose of the transferred horses in the way of trade, I do not understand why it is admitted that she should be credited as a receipt with the cost of production. In fact as a trader she received no more the cost of production than the market value: I do not understand, therefore, why the argument did not proceed that, as she received nothing, her trading account should be credited with nothing; that she suffered, so far as her trade was concerned, a dead loss in respect of these animals, and that the accounts of the stud farm should be made up so as to show this like any other dead loss. I do not understand how the adjustment could take the form of the fictitious entry of a receipt which had not been received.

My Lords, I am the more puzzled by the basis on which this case has proceeded because learned counsel for the respondent has throughout insisted on what is an elementary principle of income tax law that a man cannot be taxed on profits that he might have, but has not, made: see, *e.g. Dublin Corporation* v. *M'Adam* [21]; *Gresham Life Assurance Society* v. *Styles.* [22] But this is only saying in another way that a trader is not to be charged with the receipt of sums that he might have, but has not, received, and this is equally true whether the sum with which it is sought to charge him is market value or production cost, whether it will result in a notional profit or a notional balancing of receipts with expenditure and whether the reason for his not in fact receiving such a sum is that the goods which are his stock in trade have perished in the course of nature or that he has chosen to use them for his own pleasure or otherwise dispose of them. The true proposition is not that a man cannot make a profit out of himself but that he cannot trade with himself. The question is whether and how far this general proposition must be qualified for the purposes of income tax law.

An attempt has been made to justify the notional receipt of a sum equal to the cost of production by treating such a receipt as the equivalent of an expenditure which in the event proved not to have been for the purpose of trade, since the article was not disposed of in the way of trade. But this is pure fiction. Up to the very moment of disposition (in this case the transfer of a horse from stud farm to racing stable) the article was part of the trader's stock in trade and the cost of its production was properly treated as part of his

[21] (1887) 2 T.C. 387.
[22] [1892] A.C. 309, *ante*, p. 152.

expenditure for income tax purposes. I see no justification for an *ex post facto* adjustment of account which in effect adds to a fictional receipt a false attribution of expenditure.

This is, however, the position with which we are faced. Your Lordships may not think it necessary to express any opinion on the question whether, if the Crown is not right in requiring market value to be brought into account in the present case, it is nevertheless entitled to require the cost of production to be brought in. This is said to be of no importance in this case, though it might well be of great importance in other cases. Yet I cannot refrain from calling attention to what must be fundamental to the solution of the question. For I cannot escape from the obvious fact that it must be determined whether and why a trader, who elects to throw his stock in trade into the sea or dispose of it in any other way than by way of sale in the course of trade, is chargeable with any notional receipt in respect of it, before it is asked with how much he should be charged.

It is, as I have said, a surprising thing that this question should remain in doubt. For unless, indeed, farming is a trade which in this respect differs from other trades, the same problem arises whether the owner of a stud farm diverts the produce of his farm to his own enjoyment or a diamond merchant, neglecting profitable sales, uses his choicest jewels for the adornment of his wife, or a caterer provides lavish entertainment for a daughter's wedding breakfast. Are the horses, the jewels, the cakes and ale to be treated for the purpose of income tax as disposed of for nothing or for their market value or for the cost of their production?

It is convenient at this stage to refer to the case of *Watson Brothers* v. *Hornby*,[23] which I have already mentioned. In that case the taxpayers, who were the appellants in the appeal, carried on a business of poultry dealers and breeders of poultry at a hatchery belonging to them which was conceded to be an enterprise chargeable as a trade under Case I of Schedule D of the Income Tax Act 1918. The business of the hatchery was to produce and sell day-old chicks. They also carried on farming activities which were conceded to be, for income tax purposes, a separate enterprise from the hatchery business and, as the law then stood, were an income tax source chargeable under Schedule B of the Income Tax Act 1918. Most of the produce of the hatchery was sold, but a substantial number of day-old chicks were from time to time transferred to the farm and became part of the stock of poultry of the farm. The question in the appeal was whether, in computing the profits of the hatchery business, the day-old chicks transferred to the farm should be brought in at cost or market value. The market value was at the material times much below cost, *viz.* 4d. as against 7d. per chick. It was contended for the taxpayers that market price and for the Crown that cost of production should be adopted as the appropriate figure in the accounts. It was decided by Macnaghten J. that the taxpayers' contention was right, and they were accordingly chargeable upon the footing that as traders in respect of their hatchery business they received 4d. only per chick. This decision, which your Lordships were told has ever since been adopted as the basis of assessment by the Revenue in similar cases, involves two things, first, that the taxpayer may in certain cases be subject to a sort of dichotomy for income tax purposes and be regarded as selling to himself in one capacity what he has produced in another, and, secondly, that he is regarded as selling what he sells at market price. It is a decision upon which the appellant relies in the present case, and which, as I have said, Vaisey J. regarded as an authority binding him. The learned judge also derived some assistance from *Inland Revenue*

---

[23] (1942) 24 T.C. 506. The problem in that case is very similar to that in *Collins* v. *Fraser* [1969] 1 W.L.R. 823, *ante*, p. 107.

Commissioners v. *William Ransom & Son Ltd.*,[24] in which it was at least recognised that for tax purposes two parts of an enterprise carried on by a taxpayer should be treated as distinct. But it was not, I think, an issue in that case at what price goods should be deemed to be transferred from one part of the enterprise to the other. . . .

. . . For I repeat that I see no valid distinction between a trader crediting himself with a price (market value) which produces a profit or with a price (production cost) which strikes a balance or reduces his loss. Yet it is the basis equally of the judgment of Macnaghten J. in *Watson Brothers* v. *Hornby* [23] and of the observations of Lord Greene in the *Laycock* [25] and the *Briton Ferry* [26] cases that something has to be brought into account where the legislature recognises a sort of artificial dichotomy and a taxpayer is regarded as carrying on more than one taxable activity. And so also, as I have more than once pointed out, in this case it is conceded by the taxpayer that some figure must appear in the stud farm account as a receipt in respect of the transferred horses, though Lady Zia in her capacity as transferee did not carry on a taxable activity. In the same way, it would, I suppose, be claimed that, if Lady Zia were to transfer or re-transfer a horse from her racing establishment to her stud farm, some figure would have to appear in the stud farm accounts in respect of that horse, though it cost her nothing to make the transfer: if it were not so and she subsequently sold the transferred horse and the proceeds of sale were treated as receipts of the stud farm, she could justly complain that she had been charged with a fictitious profit.

My Lords, how far is this principle, which is implicit in the judgments that I have cited and in the admission upon which this case has proceeded, supportable in law? That it conflicts with the proposition taken in its broadest sense, that a man cannot trade with himself is, I think, obvious. Yet it seems to me that it is a necessary qualification of the broad proposition. For, if there are commodities which are the subject of a man's trade but may also be the subject of his use and enjoyment, I do not know how his account as a trader can properly be made up so as to ascertain his annual profits and gains unless his trading account is credited with a receipt in respect of those goods which he has diverted to his own use and enjoyment. I think, therefore, that the admission was rightly made that some sum must be brought into the stud farm account as a receipt though nothing was received and so far at least the taxpayer must be regarded as having traded with himself. But still the question remains, what is that sum to be? I suppose that in the generality of cases in which the question arises in a farming or any other business, *e.g.* where the farmer supplies his own house with milk, or a market gardener with vegetables, an arbitrary or conventional sum is agreed. The House was not given any information as to the prevailing practice. Now the question precisely arises. In answering it I am not influenced by the fact that a change in the law has made the farmer liable to tax under Schedule D instead of under Schedule B, nor does section 10 of the Finance Act 1941,[20] affect my mind beyond the fact that it emphasises the artificial dichotomy which the scheme of income tax law in many instances imposes. But it appears to me that, when it has been admitted or determined that an article forms part of the stock in trade of the trader and that upon his parting with it so that it no longer forms part of his stock in trade some sum must appear in his trading account as having been received in respect of it, the only logical way to treat it is to regard it as having been disposed of by way of trade. If so, I see no reason for ascribing to it any other sum than that which he would normally have received for it in the due course of trade, that is to say,

[24] [1918] 2 K.B. 709.
[25] [1939] 2 K.B. 1.
[26] [1940] 1 K.B. 463.

the market value. As I have already indicated, there seems to me to be no justification for the only alternative that has been suggested, namely, the cost of production. The unreality of this alternative would be plain to the taxpayer, if, as well might happen, a very large service fee had been paid so that the cost of production was high and the market value did not equal it.

In my opinion, therefore, the judgment of the Court of Appeal was wrong and should be reversed, and the judgment of Vaisey J. restored.

LORD OAKSEY (dissenting): . . . In my opinion, the Court of Appeal and the commissioners were right in holding that the respondent is not liable, His wife has not, in my opinion, made a profit or gain on the horses in question within the meaning of section 10 of the Act of 1941.

I think this follows from two principles which have long been established on the construction of the Income Tax Acts. The first principle is that the " profits or gains " taxed are actual commercial profits and not mere benefits (see *Tennant* v. *Smith* [27] and *Gresham Life Assurance Society* v. *Styles* [22]). The second is that a man cannot trade with himself in the sense in which the word " trade " is used in the Income Tax Acts.

. . . In my opinion Palles C.B. was right [28] and no authority inconsistent with his view was cited to your Lordships. The idea of a person trading with himself is inconsistent with the idea of ownership. An owner can do as he likes with his own property apart from legislation : he cannot be compelled to sell his own property to himself either at the market or any other value apart from legislation to that effect. Any sale so called which a trader makes to himself must be " notional " and not " actual." He cannot make a commercial profit or loss by transferring an asset from himself to himself or by a gift to someone else no matter what price he notionally ascribes to the transaction.

It may be said that such things rarely happen, and that the maxim *de minimis* is applicable, but it is impossible to answer the difficulty in that way because a trader's assets may be of great value, *e.g.* a diamond tiara or, for that matter, a thoroughbred two-year-old. It follows from this that an owner in trade can withdraw any asset he chooses from his trade for his own use provided, of course, that he does so bona fide and not with the intention of selling it outside his trade to someone else.

. . . The argument of the Crown was also supported on the ground that Lady Zia Wernher's stud account, which had been debited with the cost of rearing the yearlings which she subsequently transferred to her racing stable, was then credited with the same figure.

In my opinion, there is no substance in this argument. Traders must show in their trading accounts the value of their assets. If they sell those assets they must credit the price obtained. If they do not sell them but get rid of them, either by using them themselves or in any other way, they must credit the figure at which the assets stand in their accounts or the profits of the account will be improperly diminished by the amount entered in the account as the value of the asset. Taxation under Schedule D is imposed on the balance of profits and gains. Profits and gains are actual commercial profits and gains, and similarly the deductions allowed by the Act which produce the balance are deductions which are considered to be properly attributable to the profits as being commercial expenses incurred in order to earn the profits. It follows, in my opinion, that such expenses as have been incurred to produce an asset which is withdrawn from the trade cannot properly be deducted and must therefore be withdrawn

27 [1892] A.C. 150, *ante*, p. 3, *post*, p. 255.
28 In *Dublin Corporation* v. *M'Adam* (1887) 2 T.C. 387.

from the account, which can only be done in accordance with accounting practice by crediting the amount of the expenses.

For these reasons I am of opinion that the findings of the commissioners and the judgment of the Court of Appeal were right.

Note

The *Sharkey* v. *Wernher* principle may apply equally to an *acquisition* of trading stock, treated as a notional *purchase*, with a corresponding *debit* in the trader's account. For an interesting attempt to apply the principle in this manner, see *Jacgilden (Weston Hall) Ltd.* v. *Castle* [1971] Ch. 408; *cf. Julius Bendit Ltd.* v. *I.R.C.* (1945) 27 T.C. 44.

For a criticism of the decision, see D. C. Potter, " Reflections on *Sharkey* v. *Wernher* " [1964] B.T.R. 438.

MASON v. INNES

Court of Appeal [1967] Ch. 1079; [1967] 3 W.L.R. 816; 111 S.J. 376; [1967] 2 All E.R. 926; 44 T.C. 335

LORD DENNING M.R. : Mr. Hammond Innes is a writer of distinction who has for many years carried on the profession of an author. He has written many novels and travel books. He has kept his accounts on a cash basis and has submitted these to the revenue for tax purposes. On the one side, he has included his receipts from royalties and so forth. On the other side, he has included the expenses of his travels overseas to gather material; the expenses of his study at home; and a small salary to his wife for her work for him.

In this case we are concerned with one particular novel which he wrote called The Doomed Oasis. It was based on material which he gathered in the Persian Gulf in 1953. He started to write it in September 1958, and worked on it up till 1959. He charged all the expenses in his accounts for those years. In 1960 he was about to publish it. But he felt he would like to do something to support his father, who had retired on modest resources. So Mr. Hammond Innes decided to transfer the copyright in the book The Doomed Oasis to his father as a gift. By an assignment made on April 4, 1960, he assigned to his father, " in consideration of natural love and affection," the copyright, performing rights and all other rights in The Doomed Oasis.

The question arises whether he is liable to tax on the value of those rights in The Doomed Oasis. If he had sold the rights at that time in 1960 their market value would have been £15,425. The Crown say that that sum ought to be brought into his accounts and that he should be taxed on it, although he did not receive a penny for the rights because he had given them away. I may add that Mr. Hammond Innes had also before publication assigned rights in two others of his novels, one to his mother and the other to his mother-in-law. So a like question may arise there.

I start with the elementary principle of income tax law that a man cannot be taxed on profits that he might have, but has not, made: *Sharkey* v. *Wernher*.[29] At first sight that elementary principle seems to cover this case. Mr. Hammond Innes did not receive anything from The Doomed Oasis.

But in the case of a trader there is an exception to that principle. I take for simplicity the trade of a grocer. He makes out his accounts on an " earnings basis." He brings in the value of his stock-in-trade at the beginning and end of the year: he brings in his purchases and sales; the debts owed by him and to him; and so arrives at his profit or loss. If such a trader appropriates to himself part of his stock-in-trade, such as tins of beans, and uses them for his own purposes, he must bring them into his accounts at their market value. A trader who supplies himself is accountable for the market value. That is established

[29] [1956] A.C. 58, *supra.*

by *Sharkey* v. *Wernher* itself. Now, suppose that such a trader does not supply himself with tins of beans, but gives them away to a friend or relative. Again he has to bring them in at their market value. That was established by *Petrotim Securities Ltd.* v. *Ayres.*[30]

Mr. Monroe, on behalf of the Revenue, contends that that exception is not confined to traders. It extends, he says, to professional men, such as authors, artists, barristers, and many others. These professional men do not keep accounts on an " earnings basis." They keep them on a " cash basis," by which I mean that on one side of the account they enter the actual money they expend and on the other side the actual money they receive. They have no stock-in-trade to bring into the accounts. They do not bring in debts owing by or to them, nor work in progress. They enter only expenses on the one side and receipts on the other. Mr. Monroe contended that liability to tax does not and should not depend on the way in which a man keeps his accounts. There is no difference in principle, he says, between a trader and a professional man. And he stated his proposition quite generally in this way: The appropriation of an asset, which has been produced in the ordinary course of a trade or profession, to the trader's or professional man's own purposes, amounts to a realisation of that asset or the receipt of its value, and he must bring it into account.

I cannot accept Mr. Monroe's proposition. Suppose an artist paints a picture of his mother and gives it to her. He does not receive a penny for it. Is he to pay tax on the value of it? It is unthinkable. Suppose he paints a picture which he does not like when he has finished it and destroys it. Is he liable to pay tax on the value of it? Clearly not. These instances—and they could be extended endlessly—show that the proposition in *Sharkey* v. *Wernher* does not apply to professional men. It is confined to the case of traders who keep stock-in-trade and whose accounts are, or should be, kept on an earnings basis, whereas a professional man comes within the general principle that, when nothing is received, there is nothing to be brought into account.

I would only add that the legislature seems to have acted on this footing. Section 471 of the Income Tax Act 1952,[31] applies where an author has spent more than twelve months in writing a book and sells it for a lump sum. He can " spread " the lump sum over two or three years so that his tax on it does not fall all in one year. That provision only applies to lump sums received by him. If the legislature had thought he was liable for market value of books given away, surely they would have extended the " spread " to those cases also.

Take next *Carson* v. *Cheyney's Executor.*[32] The House of Lords held that when an author dies or discontinues his profession, he is not taxable on moneys received after the date of discontinuance. That was altered by section 32 of the Finance Act 1960.[33] He becomes chargeable on sums arising from his profession, even though he receives them after he had discontinued it. This provision does not apply when he gives a book away. If the legislature had thought he was chargeable on its value, I should have thought it would have covered that case too.

I hold that Mr. Hammond Innes is not chargeable with tax on gifts which he makes of copyright in his books. I think that Goff J. and the Commissioners came to a right decision. I would dismiss this appeal.

Note
    The distinction between this case and *Sharkey* v. *Wernher* is discussed by M. A. Pickering, " How far can *Sharkey* v. *Wernher* be taken?" [1967] B.T.R. 209.

30 [1964] 1 W.L.R. 190, *ante*, p. 136.
31 Now I.C.T.A. 1970, s. 389.
32 [1959] A.C. 412.
33 See now I.C.T.A. 1970, ss. 143, 144.

2. Expenditure

As in the case of receipts, it is necessary to determine which items of expenditure are to enter into the computation of the profits of a trade, profession or vocation.

USHER'S WILTSHIRE BREWERY LTD. v. BRUCE

House of Lords [1915] A.C. 433; 84 L.J.K.B. 417; 112 L.T. 651; 31 T.L.R. 104; 59 S.J. 144; 6 T.C. 399

The Appellants acquired premises which they let to tied tenants. The tenants were under an obligation to repair the premises, but the Appellants in fact saw to repairs, paid rates, insurance, etc. *Held*, the Appellants were entitled to deduct all this expenditure in computing their profits.

LORD SUMNER: . . . If a subject engaged in trade were taxed simply upon " the full amount of the balance of the profits or gains of such trade," there can be no doubt that, upon the facts found in this special case, he would be entitled to deduct all the items which are now in debate before arriving at the sum to be charged. To do otherwise would neither be to arrive at a balance between two sets of figures, a credit and a debit set, which balance is the profit of the trade, nor to ascertain the profits of the trade, for trade incomings are not profits of the trade till trade outgoings have been paid or allowed for and deducted.

Rule 1 of the First Case of Schedule D does not, however, leave matters to the taking of a commercial account simpliciter; it provides that the duty shall be " assessed, charged, and paid without other deduction than is hereinafter allowed," and this must mean, though it is not strictly expressed, " without other deductions in the computation of the sum on which the duty is charged." Section 159 [34] states it thus: " In the computation of duty to be made under this Act in any of the cases before mentioned . . . it shall not be lawful to make any other deductions therefrom than such as are expressly enumerated in this Act," and here " therefrom " is not from the duty but from the sum, whatever it be, that has to be ascertained before duty can be charged on it. Virtually both provisions mean that in computing the sum which, when ascertained, is to be charged with duty, only the enumerated deductions shall be lawfully allowable.

The paradox of it is that there are no allowable deductions expressly enumerated at all, and there is in words no deduction allowed at all, unless indirectly by the words in rule 3 of the First Case, namely, repairs " beyond the sum usually expended for such purposes according to an average of three years "; loss " not connected with or arising out of such trade "; debts, " except bad debts proved," and average loss " beyond the actual amount of loss after adjustment," and by the words in rule 1 applicable to both the first two cases, namely, expenses " not being money wholly and exclusively laid out or expended for the purposes of such trade "; and rent, " except such part thereof (*i.e.* of the premises) as may be used for the purposes of such trade."

The effect of this structure, I think, is this, that the direction to compute the full amount of the balance of the profits must be read as subject to certain allowances and to certain prohibitions of deductions, but that a deduction, if there be such, which is neither within the terms of the prohibition nor such that the expressed allowance must be taken as the exclusive definition of its area, is to be made or not to be made according as it is or is not, on the facts of the

[34] See now, I.C.T.A. 1970, s. 130.

case, a proper debit item to be charged against incomings of the trade when computing the balance of profits of it. . . .

Note
  The fact that the appellants were not *bound* to incur the expense did not prevent it being deductible. Expenditure voluntarily incurred may be deductible: *Bourne and Hollingsworth Ltd.* v. *Ogden* (1929) 14 T.C. 349, and see also Extra-Statutory Concession B7, " Charitable and benevolent gifts by traders."

(A) CAPITAL AND REVENUE

Only expenditure which is of a revenue nature is deductible.[35]

BRITISH INSULATED AND HELSBY CABLES LTD. v. ATHERTON

House of Lords (*ante*, p. 79)

VISCOUNT CAVE L.C.: . . . But when an expenditure is made, not only once and for all, but with a view to bringing into existence an asset or an advantage for the enduring benefit of a trade, I think that there is very good reason (in the absence of special circumstances leading to an opposite conclusion) for treating such an expenditure as properly attributable not to revenue but to capital. . . .

REGENT OIL CO. LTD. v. STRICK

House of Lords [1966] A.C. 295; [1965] 3 W.L.R. 636; 109 S.J. 633; [1965] 3 All E.R. 174; 43 T.C. 1

Payments made by an oil company to acquire leases were held to be payments for the acquisition of assets for the purpose of carrying on a trade thereon and were therefore capital payments and not deductible in computing profits.

LORD REID: . . . Whether a particular outlay by a trader can be set against income or must be regarded as a capital outlay has proved to be a difficult question. It may be possible to reconcile all the decisions but it is certainly not possible to reconcile all the reasons given for them. I think that much of the difficulty has arisen from taking too literally general statements made in earlier cases and seeking to apply them to a different kind of case which their authors almost certainly did not have in mind—in seeking to treat expressions of judicial opinion as if they were words in an Act of Parliament. And a further source of difficulty has been a tendency in some cases to treat some one criterion as paramount and to press it to its logical conclusion without proper regard to other factors in the case. The true view appears to me to be that stated by Lord Macmillan in *Van den Berghs Ltd.* v. *Clark* [36]:

[35] *John Smith & Son* v. *Moore* [1921] 2 A.C. 13, *ante*, p. 67; *British Insulated and Helsby Cables Ltd.* v. *Atherton* [1926] A.C. 205, *ante*, p. 79; *Golden Horse Shoe (New) Ltd.* v. *Thurgood* [1934] 1 K.B. 548, *ante*, p. 80.
  This question is complementary to that of whether a particular receipt is of a capital or revenue nature, *ante*, p. 155. It should, however, be stressed that a payment does not necessarily possess the same character at each end, *i.e.* a payment by one trader to another may be a revenue expenditure but a capital receipt, or vice versa. The character of the payment at either end may well affect the price paid, see *Saunders* v. *Pilcher* (1949) 31 T.C. 314, 335–336.
[36] [1935] A.C. 431, 438–439, *ante*, p. 156.

"While each case is found to turn upon its own facts, and no infallible criterion emerges, nevertheless the decisions are useful as illustrations and as affording indications of the kind of considerations which may relevantly be borne in mind in approaching the problem."

One must, I think, always keep in mind the essential nature of the question. The Income Tax Act requires the balance of profits and gains to be found. So a profit and loss account must be prepared setting on one side income receipts and on the other expenses properly chargeable against them. In so far as the Act prohibits a particular kind of deduction it must receive effect. But beyond that no one has to my knowledge questioned the opinion of Lord President Clyde in *Whimster & Co.* v. *Inland Revenue Commissioners*,[37] where, after stating that profit is the difference between receipts and expenditure, he said:

"the account of profit and loss to be made up for the purpose of *ascertaining that difference* must be framed consistently with the ordinary principles of commercial accounting so far as applicable . . ."

So it is not surprising that no one test or principle or rule of thumb is paramount. The question is ultimately a question of law for the court, but it is a question which must be answered in light of all the circumstances which it is reasonable to take into account, and the weight which must be given to a particular circumstance in a particular case must depend rather on common sense than on strict application of any single legal principle.

. . . The case which is generally cited and relied on, often by both sides, is *British Insulated and Helsby Cables* v. *Atherton*.[38] In order to understand the passage in Viscount Cave L.C.'s speech, which is always quoted, it is essential to have the facts in mind. The company laid out a sum to assist in the setting up of a pension fund for its staff. It was intended that the fund would endure for the whole life of the company and it was not expected that the company would have to lay out any further sum for this purpose. So when Lord Cave referred to expenditure

"made not only once and for all, but with a view to bringing into existence an asset or an advantage for the enduring benefit of a trade . . . ,"

he was dealing with a case where the payment was made literally once and for all and where the asset or advantage was to last as long as the company lasted. I can find nothing in his speech to indicate that he had in mind or intended to deal with a case where the asset or advantage would only last for a short period of years after which further money would have to be spent if a further corresponding asset or advantage was sought. And when in *Vallambrosa*[39] Lord Dunedin contrasted a thing going to be spent once and for all with a thing going to recur every year, I do not think that he had such a case in mind either.

But so much has been built on Lord Cave's words that I must try to see how they could be applied to a case like the present. In the first place what is the meaning of once and for all? Suppose that an advantage has been achieved by acquiring an asset which will only last for three years so that it will be necessary at the end of that time to acquire another similar asset if the advantage is to be retained. I would not think that a lump sum paid for that asset is paid once and for all, and I see nothing to indicate that either Lord Cave or Lord Dunedin would have thought so. If once and for all is merely to be related to the fact that only one payment, a lump sum, is made for the particular short-lived asset, then the only contrast is between paying a lump sum for it and making a

---

[37] 1926 S.C. 20; 12 T.C. 813, *ante*, p. 154.
[38] [1926] A.C. 205, *ante*, p. 79.
[39] 1910 S.C. 519, 5 T.C. 525. The "once and for all test" has been applied frequently, notably in *Ounsworth* v. *Vickers Ltd.* [1915] 3 K.B. 267.

periodical payment for it. Surely that cannot have been all that was meant. If a further payment to retain the advantage, in this case the outlet for sale of oil resulting from the tie of a particular garage, is necessary in the near future I would hold that the first payment was not once and for all.

There is a good deal of authority on the question of what kind of asset or advantage Lord Cave's words will cover. Broadly it seems to have been accepted that they will not extend to cover a payment to get rid of a handicap or disadvantage. But I do not think it necessary to explore this matter because I am satisfied that the words must cover a tie such as we are concerned with whether it is constituted by a simple obligation or by covenants in a sublease.

Lastly what is meant by "enduring"? I think that Lord Cave intended to link that with once and for all. He was thinking of a single payment for an advantage which would last for an indefinite time. I do not think he had in mind an advantage of limited duration, and I think that any decision about such an advantage must be reached without reference to or reliance on what Lord Cave said.

But it was argued that "enduring" has come to be interpreted so as to include any benefit which lasts for more than one year and that this was recognised in the *Nchanga* case.[40] If this is an interpretation of Lord Cave's words where "once and for all" is coupled with "enduring" then the supposed rule must be that any lump sum paid for a benefit enduring for more than one year must be treated as a capital outlay—not that any asset conferring an enduring benefit is intrinsically a capital asset. For if it were intrinsically a capital asset then any payment for it whether by a lump sum or by a series of periodic payments must be a capital outlay, and so far as I know it has not been suggested that, say, monthly payments for any asset the benefit of which endures for more than a year must all be treated as capital outlays. Certainly that could not be spelled out from Lord Cave's words. I have searched in vain for any rational explanation of this supposed rule, so apparently it must just be an arbitrary rule. But, as I have already explained, arbitrary rules are quite out of place in this matter of capital or income. . . .

Note
See also *B.P. Australia Ltd*. v. *Commissioner of Taxation of the Commonwealth of Australia* [1966] A.C. 224. Both decisions are considered by P. G. Whiteman, "The Borderline between Capital and Income" [1966] B.T.R. 115.

I.R.C. v. CARRON COMPANY

House of Lords (1968) 45 T.C. 65; 1968 S.C. 47; 1968 S.L.T. 305

The expense to a company of obtaining a supplementary charter and of settling an action by a dissenting shareholder was held to be a permissible deduction.

LORD REID: . . . The main argument for the Crown was that by obtaining the new charter the Company obtained an enduring advantage in the shape of a better administrative structure. Of course they obtained an advantage: companies do not spend money either on capital or income account unless they expect to obtain an advantage. And money spent on income account, for example on durable repairs, may often yield an enduring advantage. In a case of this kind what matters is the nature of the advantage for which the money was spent. This money was spent to remove antiquated restrictions which were preventing

40 [1964] A.C. 948.

profits from being earned. It created no new asset. It did not even open new fields of trading which had previously been closed to the Company. Its true purpose was to facilitate trading by enabling the Company to engage a more competent manager and to borrow money required to finance the Company's traditional trading operations under modern conditions. None of the authorities cited is directly in point, and I think that the most apposite general statement in those authorities is that of Lawrence L.J. in *Anglo-Persian Oil Co. Ltd.* v. *Dale* [1932] 1 K.B. 124, at page 141. It "merely effected a change in its business methods and internal organization, leaving its fixed capital untouched." As the Lord President put it in the present case:

> "The benefit was essentially of a revenue character because the Company became able more easily to finance its day-to-day transactions, and more efficiently to carry on its day-to-day manufacture." . . .

MITCHELL v. B. W. NOBLE LTD.

King's Bench Division (affirmed in the Court of Appeal) [1927] 1 K.B. 719; 96 L.J.K.B. 484; 137 L.T. 33; 43 T.L.R. 245; 71 S.J. 175; [1927] All E.R.Rep. 717; 11 T.C. 372

ROWLATT J.: In this case the question is whether there can be deducted in arriving at the profits of the company, as an expense of carrying on the trade, an instalment paid in the year in question on account of the very large sum which was payable to this outgoing director, Mr. Haylor, under the terms of the agreement.

It was said (and perhaps this is the clearest as well as the most authoritative statement on the point), in *British Insulated and Helsby Cables, Ltd.* v. *Atherton*,[41] by the Lord Chancellor that "a sum of money expended, not of necessity and with a view to a direct and immediate benefit to the trade, but voluntarily and on the grounds of commercial expediency, and in order indirectly to facilitate the carrying on of the business, may yet be expended wholly and exclusively for the purposes of the trade." It is only made voluntarily, it may be, but it is under that sort of description that this was said to be an expense incurred wholly and exclusively for the purposes of the trade.

The other point is whether it was capital expenditure.

This point as to the deductibility of a payment made upon the termination of a person's employment was glanced at in the House of Lords in *Royal Insurance Co.* v. *Watson*.[42] Lord Herschell reserved his opinion upon it without expressing any view. Lord Shand said that he thought damages paid to a dismissed servant—and I suppose he would include a sum paid by way of agreement to get rid of a claim for damages—might be a deductible expense. I think that in the ordinary case a payment to get rid of a servant, when it was not expedient to keep him in the interests of the trade, would be deductible expense: I leave out of consideration for the moment special cases, as when a servant is dismissed on the ground of a purely personal quarrel, although his staying on would not affect the trade at all. But it seems to me that a payment to get rid of a servant in the interests of the trade is a proper deduction. A person who carries on a trade has to employ an efficient staff, and he has to employ a staff that will prove satisfactory to the customers of the trade. He has also to cease from employing an inefficient staff and a staff that does not get on with the customers of the trade; and if he has to pay for that cessation, it seems to me that there is no reason why that should not be an expense incurred for the

41 [1926] A.C. 205, 212.
42 [1897] A.C. 1.

purposes of the trade. He has to facilitate people going when they reach the age of retirement, in their own interests and in the interests of their employer. He has to hold that prospect out to them. If he has not held out the prospect, as least he has to deal with the situation and provide in some way, as Lord Cave says, " on the grounds of commercial expediency," for people who may have to leave his employment.

. . . I should not have much difficulty if this were a question of paying a month's wages or six months' wages in lieu of notice to an employee, who from the business point of view could not possibly be retained by the employers, because he was turning away custom. But here we have very special facts and very big figures, and the question is whether there is anything in these facts that makes a difference. . . . They paid it because it was essential in their opinion, as the case finds, to get rid of him for the sake of the good name of the company, and they did not want any litigation or publicity or any scandal or anything of that kind, so they paid it for business reasons. It seems to me that they paid all this sum—although the circumstances are very peculiar—simply to get rid of the director.

. . . Now comes the question whether it was a capital expense. I do not think the cases in which the question of a lump sum payment to avoid a recurring business expense have anything to do with this case. There is no question here of a recurring business expense or payment of a capital sum to get rid of it. I do not think that it can successfully be argued on that ground that this is not a capital expense. But is it a capital expense on any ground? As Lord Cave points out in *British Insulated and Helsby Cables, Ltd.* v. *Atherton* it is a capital expense if you buy an asset or purchase an enduring advantage. This was not that case, or anything like it. What it is more like, perhaps, is the case of a payment made to remove the possibility of a recurring disadvantage. If a business is being carried on under circumstances affecting its property, as a business carried on under circumstances which concern the silting up of a channel, or on premises which involve continual trouble and expense, and a payment is made to put the premises on a different footing, that is a capital expenditure.  There the persons carrying on the business say to themselves: " Instead of having this silting channel, we will have a concrete channel, in which there will be no silting at all." If you say, " I will not have a railing which perpetually falls down or wants repainting; I will abolish it and I will build a brick wall which will not fall down or will not want painting," that is a capital expenditure. But I do not see how that can be said in this case. This gentleman being there as an unsatisfactory servant was not a permanency. He was no doubt there for his life, but I do not think you can say: " By an expenditure of capital I will get rid of this nuisance affecting my business, and have his room rather than his company by making this capital expenditure." I cannot look at it in that way. It seems to me it is simply this, although the largeness of the figures and the peculiar nature of the circumstances perplex one, that this is no more than a payment to get rid of a servant in the course of the business and in the year in which the trouble comes. I do not think it is a capital expense, and I have already held that it is an expense incurred in the conduct of the business. Therefore I am unable to differ from the Commissioners, and this appeal fails.

ASSOCIATED PORTLAND CEMENT MANUFACTURERS LTD. v. KERR

Court of Appeal [1946] 1 All E.R. 68; 62 T.L.R. 115; 27 T.C. 103

LORD GREENE M.R.: In these two appeals the question which arises is whether the appellant company is entitled to deduct for tax purposes, income

tax and National Defence Contribution, two sums of £20,000 and £10,000 which
were paid in the circumstances mentioned in the case. In 1939, two directors
of the appellant company, Stevens and Charleton, retired. They had each spent
a working lifetime in the service of the appellant company, or of other companies engaged in the cement trade. Stevens apparently joined the company in
1900 as secretary, and in 1906 he became a managing director. He continued to
hold that office until he retired on December 31, 1939. He was then of the age
of 69. Charleton had been associated with the company, or its predecessors, for
some 40 years. He became a director in 1931, and from that date he had charge
of an important branch of the company, the coastwise shipping part. In 1939,
at the time of his retirement, he was about 60 years of age.

A person ignorant of the facts might have thought that the retirement of
these two directors, which took place in entirely friendly circumstances, was a
prelude to their enjoying during their declining years the leisure which their
eminent services had earned them. A person who thought that would have been
mistaken. Stevens, although 69 years of age, was in good health. He was a
very hard worker and quite competent to give advice to, or steer the policy of,
any other company. Charleton, although only 60 years of age, does not obtain
in the case the same certificate of robust health as Stevens. No specific mention
of his state of health is made. But it is found that the company thought that
there would be a very definite danger of his acting in opposition to the company
when his connection with it was severed. Of Stevens, it is said that he would
have been free, had no steps been taken to prevent him, to turn his abilities to
account in the way of lending his name to any enterprise, he might compete
with or otherwise act to the disadvantage of the appellant company.

The appellant company, as the case finds, with its associated companies, are
the largest manufacturers of cement in Great Britain. The seriousness of the
threat overhanging the prosperity of the company did not escape the vigilant
eyes of the other members of the board. The fact that the two retiring directors
might in future engage in competitive activities led the board to think that the
appropriate method of protecting the company against such an attack would be
to secure from both of them restrictive covenants which would insure that they
should not enter into competition with the company. I use the phrase " enter
into competition " as a convenient phrase to cover the various types of activities
in connection with cement with which the contracts deal, and in which the two
retiring directors are prohibited from engaging.

The unimpaired nature of their business abilities appears from the type of
activity against which it was thought necessary to protect the company. Stevens,
although 69, was in the position when he might apparently become engaged in
the manufacture of Portland cement in the British Isles, in Canada, in India,
or in the Republic of Mexico, or in the Union of South Africa, or, indeed,
in any other part of the world. Against such activities, and a number of
others, he was precluded by the agreement. The same thing applies to
Charleton because the contracts are the same in both cases. Therefore we have
this position, that the company, having on the retirement of these two directors
before its eyes the prospect of their competition and desiring to protect itself
against that disadvantage, thought that it was worth £30,000 to impose upon
them these restrictions. I should say that the contracts extend apparently during
the rest of the lives of these two directors.

After the execution of the contracts, the two sums of £20,000 and £10,000
were paid. It must be taken, for the purposes of this case, that the benefits
secured to the company, although they might well have been more valuable
than the sums actually paid, were worth not a shilling, indeed not a penny, less
than £20,000 and £10,000 respectively—not inconsiderable sums. It appears that

the board, perhaps through a feeling of modesty, did not expose themselves to the congratulations of the shareholders upon this important achievement. In the company's accounts a rather remarkable entry appears. The accounts laid before the shareholders consisted of a profit and loss account and a balance sheet. In the profit and loss account appears this item on the receipt side: " By profit on trading (including compensation under a working agreement) after deducting management expenses, bad debts, sundry reserves and provision for taxation, £879,282." The words with which we are concerned are the words " sundry reserves." That balance of £879,282 is a balance on trading account carried into the profit and loss account. The trading account was not put before the shareholders. Nobody can complain of that. But when one looks into the trading account, one finds an item entitled: " Sundry special reserves, £30,000." That £30,000 was the sum of the two amounts of £20,000 and £10,000 with which we are concerned. The words " sundry reserves " in the profit and loss account include that item. It was Voltaire (who had a certain dislike of shams) who said of the Holy Roman Empire that it was neither Holy nor Roman, nor an Empire. He perhaps would have been less severe on this particular description. Although he might have quarrelled, and properly quarrelled, with the word " sundry " and with the word " reserves," he might very well have agreed that the expenditure in question was " special." Apart from that possibility I cannot imagine a more inaccurate entry than this. However, we are not directly concerned with that.

I only mention it for one reason. We were invited by counsel for the appellants [Mr. King] to pay particular attention to the evidence of the company's auditors, who expressed the view that these sums could not be treated as a capital item in the accounts. Although there is no auditors' certificate attached to the profit and loss account, or to the trading account, it seems a reasonable inference that this particular entry did not pass the auditors unobserved. In those circumstances, I may not perhaps be thought peculiar if I feel some reluctance in allowing myself to be guided on the theory or practice of accountancy by this company's auditor.

But before I leave the question of accounts I should say this. On the question whether an item of expenditure is of a capital or a revenue nature, it is no doubt helpful to consider the circumstances from the accountancy point of view. But one must be careful to define one's terms. Whether or not an item of expenditure is to be regarded as of a revenue or capital nature must in many, and, indeed, in the majority of cases, I should have thought, depend upon the nature of the asset or the right acquired by means of that expenditure. If it is an asset which properly appears as a capital asset in the balance sheet, then that is an end of the matter. But it must never be forgotten that an asset which may properly, and quite correctly, appear, and only appear, in the balance sheet as an asset may be acquired out of revenue. There is nothing in the world to force a company or a trader who buys a capital asset to debit the cost of it to capital. Conservatively managed companies every day pay for capital assets out of revenue if they are fortunate enough to have the revenue available. It is, therefore, no sufficient test to say that an asset has been paid for out of revenue because the consequence does not, by any means, necessarily follow that it is an asset of a revenue nature as distinct from a capital nature. Similarly, there is nothing to prevent a company or a trader who has acquired a capital asset from refraining from placing any value on that asset in his balance sheet. I put to counsel for the appellants an example which I think is worth repeating. If a trader buys up somebody else's business and pays £10,000 for the goodwill, that being the price on which the vendor insists, there is nothing in the world to prevent the purchaser paying the £10,000 out of revenue and debiting it to revenue account, and then writing down the goodwill in his own balance sheet to nothing. The fact that he has written it down in his own balance sheet does not mean that he has not got an asset. He has; he has the goodwill, but for his own domestic purposes he chooses not to put a value upon it; just in the same way as many companies, who have patents of very great value indeed, are in the habit of valuing them at a pound in their balance sheet, or at some other nominal sum. I venture to think, therefore, when one is considering the nature of an asset acquired by a piece of expenditure, it is by no means conclusive to find that the asset does not have any definite value set upon it in the balance sheet.

When one looks at what happened in the present case, first of all one finds that the company chose to make these payments out of revenue. As I have said, that is by no means conclusive as to their nature. In their balance sheet they did not put any item representing the value, which is £30,000, and not a penny less, of this asset. But that again is by no means conclusive, as I have just ventured to point out. They have not thought that a value could definitely be put upon this particular asset. From the business point of view, that is quite natural. It is not good business to put values on assets of a rather vague and intangible nature like this. A balance sheet does not commonly contain such things, and it might be depreciatory to the company if it did. The fact that you do not find a value put upon it is, to my mind, of comparatively little importance in the present case.

What is the true nature of the asset which the company has acquired? It has acquired two choses in action, the benefit of two restrictive covenants against competition, using that phrase again comprehensively, for which it has paid a total sum of £30,000. The danger against which these covenants protected the company was serious and imminent. It would be quite wrong to allow oneself to think for a moment that the company was not getting its money's worth. When the two directors left the board, they were free to compete, not merely in Great Britain, but in Mexico, and, indeed, in the South Sea Islands. Against that danger the company has protected itself. What is the true business result of all that? When the two directors left the company, the goodwill of the company would immediately have become extremely vulnerable. When the company had the monopoly of their services, it was in a very advantageous position. As soon as they became potential competitors there was ground for thinking that the goodwill of the company would receive a serious shock. The risk of competition and damaging competition was great. The company succeeded in protecting itself against that risk. In effect the company was buying off two potential competitors. It seems to me that the effect of buying off potential competitors must of its very nature affect the value of the company's goodwill. If all potential competitors could be bought off, the goodwill of the business would obviously be very greatly benefited. If some competitors are bought off, if they are dangerous potential competitors, the goodwill is affected substantially. The true nature of what they have done seems to me to be this. They have acquired these rights against these two retiring directors, and, by doing so, they have enhanced the value of an existing asset, to wit, their goodwill. In the balance sheet the company's goodwill is included in the global sum of £5,751,885. There is a note indicating that the amount of goodwill " included in the above figure is not shown in the books and is not otherwise ascertainable." That is a very good example of what I was referring to a moment ago, a capital asset on which no value is placed in the balance sheet at all. As the value of the goodwill was regarded as not ascertainable, it was not to be expected that the directors would treat this £30,000 as an addition to it. Accordingly, it does not appear in the balance sheet. But that cannot affect its nature. The fact that the directors for good business purposes did not choose to value the goodwill of the company in the balance sheet does not prevent the goodwill from being an asset.

Before turning to the authorities which counsel for the appellants principally relied upon, I might perhaps quote the well known words in the judgment of Viscount Cave L.C. in *Atherton* v. *British Insulated and Helsby Cables, Ltd.*,[43] where he says this:

" But when an expenditure is made, not only once and for all, but with a view to bringing into existence an asset or an advantage for the enduring benefit of a trade, I think that there is very good reason (in the absence of special circumstances leading to an opposite conclusion) for treating such an expenditure as properly attributable not to revenue but to capital."

That test which Viscount Cave L.C. propounds is one which, though I think not by any means exhaustive, is an extremely useful test, and in many cases will give the clue to the right answer.

In my opinion, in the present case the language of Viscount Cave L.C. is satisfied by the facts. This was an expenditure made once and for all with a view to bringing into existence " an advantage for the enduring benefit of a trade." There was nothing temporary about this advantage. It was to last during the lives of the two directors in question. That that advantage was a solid one, I have already endeavoured to point out. That it was " for the benefit of the trade " in a very true sense is again quite clear because, when analysed, its effect unquestionably was to add to the value of the goodwill. There was all the difference in the world, as it seems to me, between this case and the case of *Noble* v. *Mitchell*,[44] on which counsel for the appellants principally relied. The payment made in that case was made to procure the retirement of a director who was regarded by the board as a person not desirable to retain on the board. It might have done the company great harm if it had become necessary to dismiss him from the board. But there seems to me to be all the difference in the world between getting rid of an unsatisfactory servant—and that was the principle on which the case was decided—and buying off a potential outside competitor. In the one case you are getting rid of a servant, and the sum you pay for that is no more of a capital nature, nor is the benefit any more permanent, than is the wage that you pay the servant for his services. But when you are buying off an outside competitor, the position is entirely different. Therefore I do not get any assistance from that case at all.

Southern v. *Borax Consolidated, Ltd.*,[45] was a case where the tax-paying company had spent money in defending its title to certain American land which it had acquired. The money that you spend in defending your title to a capital asset, which is assailed unjustly, is obviously a revenue expenditure. There again there is all the difference in the world between defending your assets against the claim of somebody who has no claim against them and acquiring a new asset or adding to an existing asset.

. . . As I have said, these benefits acquired by the company were solid; they were permanent; and they were world-wide. They protected the company against certain risks, and the value to be set on that protection was shown by the company itself in deciding to pay these amounts. No doubt it will be a disappointment to the company that they cannot crown their success in acquiring these solid advantages by passing on to the general taxpayer the privilege of paying for a large part of the expense so incurred. . . .

Note
For the treatment of such payments in the hands of the recipients, see I.C.T.A. 1970, s. 34, and see *Beak* v. *Robson* [1943] A.C. 352; *post*, p. 245.

43 [1926] A.C. 205, 212, *ante*, p. 79.   44 [1927] 1 K.B. 719, *ante*, p. 172.
45 [1941] 1 K.B. 111; *cf. I.R.C.* v. *Carron Company* (1968) 45 T.C. 65, *ante*, p. 171.

LAW SHIPPING CO. LTD. v. I.R.C.

Court of Session (1924) 12 T.C. 621; 1924 S.C. 74

THE LORD PRESIDENT (CLYDE): In December 1919, the Appellants bought for £97,000 a ship, built in 1906, which at the time of the purchase was ready to sail with freight booked. The periodical survey of the ship was then considerably overdue; indeed, for the purposes of the voyage about to commence, exemption from survey had had to be obtained. When the ship returned from the voyage she underwent survey, and the purchaser had to expend a sum of £51,558 on repairs (in addition to certain further expenditure of an admittedly capital character).

The assessment appealed against is for Excess Profits Duty and is made in terms of section 47 of the Finance Act 1916, which specially deals with the case of ships changing hands by purchase. Accordingly, the pre-war profits are calculated with reference to the profits arising from the use of the ship by the purchasers' predecessors during the pre-war trade years.

As required by section 40 of the Finance (No. 2) Act 1915, the *purchasers' own profits* during the accounting period fall to be determined on the same principles as those upon which the profits and gains of their business would be determined for the purpose of Income Tax, subject to the modification contained in Part I of the Fourth Schedule to the said Act. By paragraph 3 of Part I it is enacted: "Deductions for wear and tear, or for any expenditure of a capital nature for renewals, or for the development of the trade or business . . . shall not be allowed except such as may be allowed under the Income Tax Acts. . . ."

The whole question in the case is as to the admissibility of the above mentioned repair account of £51,558 as a deduction in the determination of the purchasers' profits; and it will be seen from the foregoing narrative that that question really turns on the Income Tax Act 1918, and particularly on Rule 3 of Cases I and II of Schedule D of that Act.

The expense laid out in keeping a ship, which is employed in trade, in proper repair is certainly an expense necessary for the purposes of the trade. It is made for the purpose of earning the profits of the trade. Repairs may be executed as the occasion for them occurs; or, if they are such as brook delay, they may be postponed to a convenient season: but, in either case, they truly constitute a constantly recurring incident of that continuous employment of the ship which makes them necessary. They are therefore an admissible deduction in computing profits, and, as is admitted in the case, if the ship had not been sold, the purchasers' predecessors would have been entitled to deduct the whole of the £51,558 in returning their profits for Income Tax. Accumulated arrears for repairs are, in short, none the less repairs necessary to earn profits, although they have been allowed to accumulate.

In the present case, however, the accumulation of repairs, represented by the expenditure of £51,558 required to overtake them, was an accumulation which extended partly over a period during which the ship was employed, not in the purchasers' trade, but in that of the purchasers' predecessors. And the question relates to the computation of the *purchasers' profits only*.

The purchasers started their trade with a ship already in need of extensive repairs. The need was not so clamant as to make it impossible to employ her (as she stood at the time of the purchase) in the voyage she was then about to commence. So much is clear from the fact that she was allowed exemption from survey for the purposes of that voyage. But, while some portion of the repairs executed after her return was no doubt attributable to her employment in the purchasers' trade between the date of their purchase and the return of the ship— and while such portion was therefore necessary to the earning of profits by them in that and subsequent voyages—it seems plain that a large portion of them was attributable solely to her employment by the purchasers' predecessors, in whose profits the purchasers had no interest whatever. The admissibility of deduction of the latter portion thus appears to be negatived by the terms of Rule 3 (*a*) of Cases I and II.

It is obvious that a ship, on which repairs have been allowed to accumulate, is a less valuable capital asset with which to start business than a ship which has been regularly kept in repair. And it is a fair inference that the sellers would have demanded and obtained a higher price than they actually did, but for the immediate necessity of repairs to which the ship was subject when they put her in the market. The additional gains they had made by postponing repairs were thus counter-balanced by the diminished value of the ship on realisation; but it is not relevant to the question of the extent of the purchasers' assessibility to Income Tax on their own profits, that the Revenue may have gained by the inflation of the profits of their predecessors consequent on the postponement of repairs which—if regularly made—would have diminished them.

Again, when the purchasers started trade with the ship, the capital they required was not limited to the price paid to acquire her, but included the cost of the arrears of repairs which their predecessors had allowed to accumulate; because, while their own trading with her would—in ordinary course—provide a revenue out of which the repairs incidental to such trading would be met, it would be unreasonable and abnormal—in any commercial sense—to saddle such trading with the burden of arrears of repairs incidental to the trading of their predecessors from which the purchasers derived no benefit. If the purchasers had " succeeded to the trade " of their predecessors within the meaning of Rule 11 of Cases I and II of Schedule D, the case would have been otherwise; but this view of the purchasers' relation to the sellers is excluded by the case of *Watson Bros.* v. *Lothian* [46] mentioned in the Case.

The Commissioners have allowed deduction of £12,000 (out of the £51,558) as being in their view of the facts applicable to the period during which the purchasers were owners of the ship, and to the extent of the £12,000 thus allowed I think the Company is entitled to deduction, but not to the extent of the whole £51,558.

LORD CULLEN: . . . The Appellants purchased a ship in order to begin and carry on a business with it. If the ship had been a new ship but not completed so as to make it adequate for use, and if the Appellants had laid out on it the money required to complete it, there would, I take it, have been no doubt that the money so laid out would have been properly treated as capital expenditure. The ship actually bought by the Appellants was not a new ship, but it was not complete and adequate for use in their intended business, inasmuch as a large amount of money had to be laid out on necessary repairs. I am unable to see any good ground in principle for differentiating, *quoad* the present question, the money so laid out by the Appellants on necessary repairs from the figured expenditure on completion in the case of the new ship, and I am of opinion that it has been properly treated by the Commissioners as capital expenditure. It is, in substance, the equivalent of an addition to the price. If the ship had not been in need of the repairs in question when bought, the Appellants would, presumably, have had to pay a correspondingly larger price. . . .

Note
This decision has been especially important in considering questions of repairs to property, see *ante*, p. 99. See also *Odeon Theatres Ltd.* v. *Jones* [1972] 2 W.L.R. 331; *ante*, p. 100; *Jackson* v. *Lasker's Home Furnishers Ltd.* [1957] 1 W.L.R. 69; *Bidwell* v. *Gardiner* (1960) 39 T.C. 31.

[46] (1902) 4 T.C. 441.

O'GRADY v. MARKHAM MAIN COLLIERY LTD.

King's Bench Division (1932) 17 T.C. 93

ROWLATT J.: I am of opinion that the Commissioners were right in both these cases. As regards the chimney, I think it is really very clear. Of course, every repair is a replacement. You repair a roof by putting on new slates instead of the old ones, which you throw away. There is no doubt about that. But the critical matter is—as was pointed out in the passage read from Lord Justice Buckley's judgment, in the case which has been referred to [47]—what is the entirety? The slate is not the entirety in the roof. You are repairing the roof by putting in new slates. What is the entirety? If you replace in entirety, it is having a new one and it is not repairing an old one. I think it is very largely a question of degree, but it seems to me the Commissioners have taken the only possible view here. What was this? This was a factory chimney to which the gases and fumes, and so on, were led by flues and then went up the chimney. It was unsafe and would not do any more. What they did was simply this: They built a new chimney at a little distance away in another place; they put flues to that chimney and then, when it was finished, they switched the gases from the old flues into the new flues and so up the new chimney. I do not think it is possible to regard that as repairing a subsidiary part of the factory. . . .

Note
See also *Phillips* v. *Whieldon Sanitary Potteries Ltd.* (1952) 33 T.C. 213; *Conn* v. *Robins Bros. Ltd.* (1966) 43 T.C. 266.

(B) "WHOLLY AND EXCLUSIVELY"

No sum may be deducted, in computing the amount of the profits or gains to be charged under Case I or Case II of Schedule D, in respect of any disbursements or expenses, not being money wholly and exclusively laid out or expended for the purposes of the trade, profession or vocation.[48]

SMITH v. INCORPORATED COUNCIL OF LAW REPORTING FOR ENGLAND AND WALES

King's Bench Division [1914] 3 K.B. 674; 83 L.J.K.B. 1721; 111 L.T. 848; 30 T.L.R. 588; 6 T.C. 477

The respondents gave a gratuity of £1,500 to a reporter on his retirement and sought to deduct the payment as a proper expense. The Commissioners allowed the deduction. *Held*, the question of whether or not the sum was expended wholly and exclusively for the purposes of the trade was a question of fact and there was no reason to interfere with the Commissioners' finding.

SCRUTTON J.: . . . It seems to me that the question whether money is wholly and exclusively laid out or expended for the purposes of a trade is a question of fact. Judges of the High Court may know, by the accident of their previous training, something about a particular trade. To take a personal instance, I may be assumed to know something about shipping, but there are many trades about which I know absolutely nothing, and there are equally many trades about

[47] *Lurcott* v. *Wakely and Wheeler* [1911] 1 K.B. 905: not a revenue case, but an important authority on the duty to repair.
[48] I.C.T.A. 1970, s. 130 (*a*).

which any of my learned brethren would know nothing except what they were told by the Commissioners. In many cases the question whether the money was wholly or exclusively laid out or expended for the purposes of the trade must depend upon a knowledge of the facts of the trade, of the way in which it is carried on, of the effect of payments made in that trade, all of which are questions of fact. There may be cases where it is clear even to a judge who knows nothing about the trade, that a particular payment could not be wholly or exclusively laid out for the purposes of the trade. I do not desire to discuss politics, but I take examples which seem to me fairly clear. Payments for political purposes might conceivably be for the purposes of trade.[49] It might be that a payment by a company to the Tariff Reform League might be of great advantage to its trade. It might be that a payment by a company to a political party which was supposed to be identified with the interests of a particular trade might be to the advantage of the trade; but one can easily imagine cases, such as a payment by a company to the National Service League, where it would be impossible to conceive that anybody could find that such money was wholly or exclusively laid out or expended for the purposes of the trade. There may be cases in which the Court would have to say there is no evidence on which any tribunal could find that this sum was laid out or expended for the purposes of such trade, but in most cases it appears to me that it depends on the facts of the trade of which the Court has no knowledge, and for which it must depend on the findings of the Commissioners. . . .

Note
The question is essentially one of fact—*Bentleys, Stokes & Lowless* v. *Beeson* (1952) 33 T.C. 491; *post,* p. 186; *James Snook & Co. Ltd.* v. *Blasdale* (1952) 33 T.C. 244—and the finding of the Commissioners is most important; but the inference to be drawn involves a mixed question of fact and law—see *Usher's Wiltshire Brewery Ltd.* v. *Bruce* [1915] A.C. 433, 466–467; *ante,* p. 168.

REPORT OF THE COMMITTEE ON THE TAXATION OF TRADING PROFITS

1951 Cmd. 8189

149. We now come to the question of deductible expenses and begin with a consideration of one of the main rules now in operation, namely Rule 3 (*a*) of Cases I and II. This rule provides that in computing profits no sum is to be deducted in respect of " any disbursements or expenses, not being money wholly and exclusively laid out or expended for the purposes of the trade," etc.[50]

150. Since it is the profits of the business itself which are to be computed, and these are in general to be computed in accordance with accountancy principles, it would seem that the charging of any expense not solely attributable to the business itself would in any event be ruled out. It might be thought therefore that a rule of this kind was not necessary at all; but having regard to the considerations to which we have already alluded we think it desirable to retain a specific provision.

151. Nevertheless we do not think the present wording of Rule 3 (*a*) is entirely satisfactory in view of the interpretation which the Courts have placed upon it. The main and perhaps the only difficulty arises from a passage in the speech of Lord Davey in the case of *Strong & Co. of Romsey Ltd.* v. *Woodifield* [51] where, in reference solely to this particular rule, its effect and result, he said :

[49] *Cf. Morgan* v. *Tate & Lyle Ltd.* [1955] A.C. 21, *post,* p. 186.
[50] I.C.T.A. 1970, s. 130 (*a*).
[51] [1906] A.C. 448, 453, *post,* p. 184.

"It is not enough that the disbursement is made in the course of, or arises out of, or is connected with, the trade or is made out of the profits of the trade. It must be made for the purpose of earning the profit."

152. We are satisfied from a scrutiny of many subsequent decisions of the Courts, including those of quite recent times, that the last sentence in that passage has often been taken to be the test of admissibility, and this may continue to be the case. For ourselves we think that as a test it is much too narrow, and in any event it seems clear that the expression " for the purposes of the trade " has a much wider scope than the expression " for the purpose of earning the profits of the trade." Two examples which often arise in practice are sufficient to bring out the distinction. The owners of a transport undertaking may be ordered to pay damages for injury to a pedestrian caused by the negligent driving of one of their vehicles; or the owner of a business may be made to pay damages for the wrongful dismissal of an employee. In practice such payments are always allowed as deductions.[52] But if there is to be accuracy in the use of language it hardly seems possible to describe them as made for the purpose of earning the profits of the undertaking. They are involuntary outgoings due to events incidental to and occurring in the course of carrying on the business, and on this basis are clearly expended for the purpose of the business.

153. These examples, which could be multiplied if space permitted, seem to us to establish that Lord Davey's test is not only unsatisfactory in its operation, but in many respects out of accord with actual practice. Since it seems desirable that law and practice should as far as possible be in accord we think that any rule which does not represent what is actually done in practice ought to be amended.

154. Additional support for our view is provided by the wording of the present Rule 3 (e). This rule provides that no deduction is to be made in respect of " any loss not connected with or arising out of the trade . . ." By implication any loss of a revenue nature which is connected with or does arise out of the business is to be allowed, and it would be odd if the joint effect of Rules 3 (a) and (e) is to allow the deduction of a *loss* connected with or arising out of the business but to deny the deduction of an *expense* equally so connected or arising except where the expense in question satisfies the further requirement of having been incurred for the purposes of earning the profits. We therefore recommend that Rule 3 (a) be qualified in such a manner as to make it clear that the test propounded by Lord Davey is no longer to have any operation.[53]

155. We also considered whether the words " wholly and exclusively " in Rule 3 (a) required some qualification. We did this at the request of some witnesses who suggested that there were expenses which might be said to be incurred partly for the purposes of the business and partly for other purposes, and therefore not wholly and exclusively for business purposes. These witnesses were apprehensive that on a strict construction of the rule the whole of such expenses would be disallowed notwithstanding that some part could truly be said to be incurred for business purposes. One simple illustration taken was that of the owner of a business who went abroad partly for business reasons and partly on holiday. It was suggested that the words " wholly and exclusively " in the rule would prohibit him from charging as a business expense any part of the cost of his passage there and back, as well as any part of the expenses of his

---

[52] But see *Fairrie* v. *Hall* (1947) 28 T.C. 200; *I.R.C.* v. *Alexander von Glehn & Co. Ltd.* [1920] 2 K.B. 553.

[53] The Radcliffe Commission were equally of the opinion that Lord Davey's test " should be explicitly disowned "—1955 Cmnd. 9474, § 127. Nevertheless, no amendment has been made to the statutory provision.

stay abroad, even though he could show that he would never have gone at all had the element of business necessity not been present.[54]

156. In view of these representations we considered two decisions of the Courts which had a bearing on the point, and we also consulted the Board of Inland Revenue on the present practice about expenditure which could be said to have had objects additional to those of a purely business nature. Expenditure of this nature may fall into two classes. As regards one class, an analysis of the purposes for which it was incurred may in itself supply the answer to the question which part of the total sum is attributable solely to business purposes, and which part is attributable solely to other purposes. An instance of expenditure of this class is to be found in the case of *Lochgelly Iron and Coal Company, Ltd.* v. *Crawford* [55] which came before the First Division of the Court of Session. The Company owned and worked a colliery and paid certain levies to a local association of coal-owners. That association spent the total levies received from its members on a variety of objects. It was held to be permissible to analyse the manner in which the company's contribution had been spent by the association, and to allow or disallow a proportion of the levy according to the manner in which it had been so spent.

157. It will be seen from that decision that in a proper case there can be a splitting up of a total sum into that part which is allowable and that which is not. So far as we know the propriety of that decision has never been brought into question, and we think therefore that there is nothing in law which would prevent the due apportionment of expenditure of such a description.

158. The second class of expenditure referred to above cannot be accurately dissected, and it is not possible to say that any particular part of it is attributable to one purpose rather than another. In relation to expenditure of this type we have considered the more recent decision of the High Court in *Copeman* v. *William Flood & Sons Ltd.*[56]

159. That was the case of a private company in which a father, mother and two children aged 17 and 23 years were directors and held between them all the share capital. Remuneration of £2,600 per annum was paid by the company to each of the two children for their services, but having regard to the age and the nature of the duties of each child the Inspector of Taxes contended that only part of the total remuneration paid to each child could be said to have been expended wholly and exclusively for the purposes of the business and that the remainder should be disallowed. On appeal by the company the High Court remitted the matter to the local General Commissioners for them to determine how much of the total remuneration was wholly and exclusively expended for the purpose of the company's business.

160. On a consideration of this decision we think it assumed the existence of the principle that expenditure if in fact attributable to more than one object —and in that particular case it may have been thought to be attributable partly to services rendered and partly to bounty—it should be apportioned in accordance with all the facts which gave rise to it, and, in so far as one of the purposes of the expenditure was truly a business purpose, should be allowed.

161. We were informed by the Board of Inland Revenue that in the case of expenditure which had objects additional to those of a purely business nature it was not the general practice to resist allowance altogether; there were several extensive classes of case in which the present practice is to apportion such expenditure on a fair and just basis. An example was the running and garage expenses of a car used partly for business and partly for private purposes. In the illustra-

---

[54] See *Bowden* v. *Russell and Russell* [1965] 1 W.L.R. 711, *post*, p. 187.

[55] (1913) 6 T.C. 267.

[56] [1941] 1 K.B. 202, *post*, p. 190.

tion already given of the journey abroad for combined business and holiday reasons, if the taxpayer satisfied the Inspector of Taxes that the journey was genuinely undertaken partly for business purposes, the Inspector would agree to a fair apportionment. The actual apportionment would of course be a matter for negotiation and agreement, and in default of agreement would be determined by the Appeal Commissioners concerned.[54]

162. On the whole therefore we do not think that any modification of the words " wholly and exclusively " is necessary.

(i) " For the Purpose of the Trade, etc."

As is seen from the above extract, two requirements must be met if the sum expended is to be deductible; it must be expended " for the purposes of the trade, profession or vocation " and it must be " wholly and exclusively " so expended.

HARRODS (BUENOS AIRES) LTD. v. TAYLOR-GOOBY

Court of Appeal (1964) 41 T.C. 450; 108 S.J. 117

A company, resident in the United Kingdom, carried on business in the Argentine and was liable to pay a tax there based on the share-capital of the company in order to be entitled to carry on business there. *Held*, the tax was incurred to enable the company to trade and was deductible.

DANCKWERTS L.J.: . . . There are a number of authorities upon the question of deductible expenses and the guiding principle appears to me to be that if the expense has to be incurred for the purposes of gaining the company's profits, it is a deductible expense; on the other hand, if the payment of the expenses or charges is made after the profits have been ascertained, then the expense is not deductible, because it is simply an application of the profits which have been earned. . . .

Note
   The important distinction is between an expense incurred in earning profits and an application of those profits: see *Mersey Docks and Harbour Board* v. *Lucas* (1883) 8 App.Cas. 891; *ante*, p. 133. Income tax (or corporation tax) is imposed on a profit which has been ascertained, *i.e.* it is an *application* of profits: *Ashton Gas Co.* v. *Att.-Gen.* [1906] A.C. 10; and see *Smith's Potato Estates Ltd.* v. *Bolland* [1948] A.C. 508; *post*, p. 185.

STRONG & CO. OF ROMSEY LTD. v. WOODIFIELD

House of Lords [1906] A.C. 448; 75 L.J.K.B. 864; 95 L.T. 241; 22 T.L.R. 754; 50 S.J. 666; [1904–07] All E.R.Rep. 953; 5 T.C. 215

LORD DAVEY: My Lords, the question in this appeal is whether a sum of 1490*l*., which the appellants have had to pay for costs and damages occasioned to a person staying in their inn by the fall of a chimney, is a proper deduction in arriving at the profits of the appellants' trade for the purpose of the income tax. The answer to that question, in my opinion, depends on the answer to be given to another question, whether the deduction claimed was a disbursement or expense wholly and exclusively laid out or expended for the purpose of the appellants' trade within the meaning of Rule 1 applying to both Cases 1 and 2 of Schedule D in section 100 of the Income Tax Act 1842.

It has been argued that the deduction claimed was a loss connected with or arising out of the appellants' trade within Rule 3 applying to Case 1 only. Case 1 relates to trades, manufactures, adventures, or concerns in the nature of trade, and I think that the word " loss " in Rule 3 means what is usually known as a loss in trading or in speculation. It contemplates a case in which the result of the trading or adventure is a loss, wholly or partially, of the capital employed in it. I doubt whether the damages in the present case can properly be called a trading loss. I prefer to decide the case upon Rule 1, which applies to profits of trades and also to professions, employments, or vocations. I think that the payment of these damages was not money expended " for the purpose of the trade." These words are used in other rules, and appear to me to mean for the purpose of enabling a person to carry on and earn profits in the trade, etc. I think the disbursements permitted are such as are made for that purpose. It is not enough that the disbursement is made in the course of, or arises out of, or is connected with, the trade, or is made out of the profits of the trade. It must be made for the purpose of earning the profits. In short, I agree with the judgment of the Master of the Rolls.

I therefore think that the appeal should be dismissed with costs.

Note
   Criticised by the Millard Tucker Committee, 1951 Cmd. 8189; *ante*, p. 181.

SMITH'S POTATO ESTATES LTD. v. BOLLAND

House of Lords [1948] A.C. 508; [1948] L.J.R. 1557; 64 T.L.R. 430; 92 S.J. 527; [1948] 2 All E.R. 367; 30 T.C. 267

The appellants claimed to deduct the legal and accountancy expenses of an appeal against an assessment to income tax. *Held*, the expense was incurred to determine the amount of tax payable on the profits, not in order to earn profits.

LORD PORTER: . . . " To my mind," said Lord Selborne L.C. in *Mersey Docks & Harbour Board* v. *Lucas*,[57] " it is reasonably plain that the gains of a trade are that which is gained by the trading, for whatever purposes it is used " and therefore what your Lordships have to determine is whether the expense is incurred in order to earn gain or is the application or distribution of that gain when earned. With all respect to the opposing view, expenditure to ascertain the true amount of tax to be paid, whether it be income tax or excess profits tax and whether successful or unsuccessful, is in my opinion incurred, at any rate in part, in order to determine the correct amount of income tax or excess profits tax as the case may be and not in order to earn gain, even though that phrase be given a broad significance. The same conclusion might be reached by saying in the words of this statute that such expense is not wholly or exclusively laid out for the purposes of trade. It is in truth partially, if not wholly, laid out in order to discover what sum is to be paid to the Crown out of the profits or gains, which have already been earned and computed. . . .

Note
   Legal and other costs incurred in order to facilitate trading and enable profits to be earned may be deductible: *Southern* v. *Borax Consolidated Ltd.* [1941] 1 K.B. 111; *I.R.C.* v. *Carron Company* (1968) 45 T.C. 18; *ante*, p. 171. The American taxpayer is treated more favourably in the matter of tax appeals, see B. Nadel, " Legal and Accounting Expenses to contest Tax Liabilities " [1963] B.T.R. 423.

57 (1883) 8 App.Cas. 891, *ante*, p. 133.

MORGAN v. TATE & LYLE LTD.

House of Lords [1955] A.C. 21; [1954] 3 W.L.R. 85; 98 S.J. 422; [1954] 2 All E.R. 413; 35 T.C. 367

The expenses incurred by the Respondents in a campaign to prevent the nationalisation of their industry were held to have been wholly and exclusively laid out for the purposes of trade and properly deductible.

LORD MORTON OF HENRYTON: . . . My Lords, apart from authority I should have no hesitation in answering the question just posed in the affirmative. Looking simply at the words of the rule I would ask: " If money so spent is not spent for the purposes of the company's trade, for what purpose is it spent? " If the assets are seized, the company can no longer carry on the trade which has been carried on by the use of these assets. Thus the money is spent to preserve the very existence of the company's trade.

(ii) *Duality of Purpose*

To be deductible, a sum must be expended wholly and exclusively for the purposes of the trade and not for any other purpose.

BENTLEYS, STOKES & LOWLESS v. BEESON

Court of Appeal [1952] 2 All E.R. 82; [1952] W.N. 280; [1952] 1 T.L.R. 1529; 96 S.J. 345; 33 T.C. 491

A firm of solicitors incurred expenses in entertaining clients to lunches at which business was discussed. The expenses were held to be deductible.

ROMER L.J.: The relevant words of rule 3 (a) of the Rules applicable to Cases I and II—" wholly and exclusively laid out or expended for the purposes of the . . . profession "—appear straightforward enough. It is conceded that the first adverb—" wholly "—is in reference to the quantum of the money expended and has no relevance to the present case. The sole question is whether the expenditure in question was " exclusively " laid out for business purposes, that is: What was the motive or object in the mind of the two individuals responsible for the activities in question? It is well established that the question is one of fact: and again, therefore, the problem seems simple enough. The difficulty, however, arises, as we think, from the nature of the activity in question. Entertaining involves inevitably the characteristic of hospitality: giving to charity or subscribing to a staff pension fund involves inevitably the object of benefaction: an undertaking to guarantee to a limited amount a national exhibition involves inevitably supporting that exhibition and the purposes for which it has been organised. But the question in all such cases is: Was the entertaining, the charitable subscription, the guarantee, undertaken *solely* for the purposes of business, that is, solely with the object of promoting the business or its profit-earning capacity? It is, as we have said, a question of fact. And it is quite clear that the purpose must be the sole purpose. The paragraph says so in clear terms. If the activity be undertaken with the object both of promoting business and also with some other purpose, for example, with the object of indulging an independent wish of entertaining a friend or stranger or of supporting a charitable or benevolent object, then the paragraph is not satisfied though in the mind of the actor the business motive may predominate. For the statute so prescribes. Per contra, if, in truth, the sole object is business promotion, the expenditure is not disqualified because the nature of the activity necessarily involves some other result, or the attainment or furtherance of some other objective, since the latter result or objective is necessarily inherent in the act.

The matter may be illustrated by simple cases which were given in argument. A London solicitor may hear that an old friend and client whom he has not for a long time seen has arrived in London. He says to himself: "I would like to see my friend again, and I know he may wish to talk business with me. I will ask him to have lunch with me and then we can discuss any business he has at the same time. I can kill two birds with one stone." A London solicitor may hear from the representative of a foreign firm, old clients of his own, that the representative is in London and urgently desires to see him on some matter of business, but that his time is very short—he cannot come to the solicitor's office, and is only free at lunch time. The solicitor, to enable the client to get his advice, asks him to lunch at his club or a restaurant. In the first case it appears to us clear that the expenditure could not be justified under the paragraph even though it turned out that the friend spent the whole of the lunch time seeking the solicitor's advice on his private affairs. On the other hand, it would appear to us reasonably clear that in the second case the expenditure (so far, at any rate, as reasonable) must be allowable. The difficulty, of course, arises in the large area between the two examples when it is a question of fact in each case to determine what was the real motive or purpose of the entertaining. But in both examples we have given there is present inevitably the motive or purpose of hospitality—that is, the solicitor in inviting the friend or the foreign representative to lunch does so with the purpose of giving him lunch. That motive is unavoidably involved in the activity itself. A man, to oblige a friend who is a Roman Catholic priest, may agree to participate in a church bazaar organised for the purpose of promoting the interests of the Catholic Church, though he has himself no desire whatever to support that church to which he may be religiously opposed. In such a case the subsidiary purpose is no part of the conscious or deliberate motive of the actor.

So much, indeed, counsel for the Crown [Sir Frank Soskice] concedes, for otherwise it would follow that all entertaining expenses, all charitable donations, would be necessarily excluded. . . .

Note
See now I.C.T.A. 1970, s. 411, which disallows expenditure on business entertainments except in specified circumstances: *N.B. Fleming* v. *Associated Newspapers Ltd.* [1972] 2 W.L.R. 1273, in particular the remarks of Lord Simon of Glaisdale at p. 1286.

BOWDEN v. RUSSELL AND RUSSELL

Chancery Division [1965] 1 W.L.R. 711; 109 S.J. 254; [1965] 2 All E.R. 258; 42 T.C. 301

A solicitor went to the United States for a holiday and to attend a conference. He claimed to deduct a part of his expenses. *Held*, no part of the expenses was deductible.

PENNYCUICK J.: . . . Mr. Orr, for the inspector of taxes, contended that upon the facts found in the case stated deduction of the expenses of the American visit falls within the prohibition under (*a*) and (*b*) of [the Income Tax Act 1952, s. 137 (now I.C.T.A. 1970, s. 130)] on the ground that these expenses were not wholly and exclusively laid out for the purposes of the taxpayer firm's profession, and further, that these represented sums expended for private purposes distinct from the purposes of the profession. He based this contention under two heads which he conveniently labelled "Remoteness" and "Duality" respectively, namely:

1. *Remoteness.* The expense of attending these conferences in America had only a remote connection with the profession of a solicitor carrying on general practice in Lancashire and could not properly be said to be expenses incurred for the purpose of enabling the taxpayer firm to carry on and earn profits in that profession.

2. *Duality.* The expenses were incurred not only for the purpose of Taylor attending the conferences in America but also for the purpose of his having a holiday there.

I propose to deal with the second contention first since it seems to me that upon Taylor's own evidence before the commissioners there is no answer to it. Taylor conducted his case before me in person and although I put this point to him twice as clearly as I could, he was unable to give any answer to it which carried any conviction to my mind.

The general principle with regard to deductions has been frequently stated and is conveniently summarised by Jenkins L.J. in *Morgan* v. *Tate & Lyle Ltd.*[58]

"Accordingly, it has long been well settled that the effect of these provisions as to deductions is that the balance of the profits and gains of a trade must be ascertained in accordance with the ordinary principles of commercial trading, by deducting from the gross receipts all expenditure properly deductible from them on those principles, save in so far as any amount so deducted falls within any of the statutory prohibitions contained in the revelant rules, in which case it must be added back for the purpose of arriving at the balance of profits and gains assessable to tax."

I confess that the more I read section 137 (*a*) the greater difficulty I find in the expression "money wholly and exclusively laid out or expended for the purposes of trade, profession or vocation."

However, this paragraph has received authoritative analysis recently in *Bentleys, Stokes & Lowless* v. *Beeson.*[59]

. . . To return to the present case, the commissioners in paragraph 4 of the case said that Taylor gave evidence before them that "it was also his intention to have a holiday with his wife at the same time."

It seems to me that this statement by Taylor represents an unequivocal admission by him that the expenses of the American visit were incurred for a dual purpose, namely (i) the advancement of his profession and (ii) the enjoyment of a holiday. This being the case, paragraph (*a*) of section 137 and also paragraph (*b*) of the same section apply and prohibit the deduction of the expenses.

. . . The commissioners, when they came to their conclusion, merely "found that the following expenses were laid out or expended wholly and exclusively for the purposes of the profession of the taxpayer firm," and gave no further reasons as to why they reached that conclusion. That is a form of conclusion which has been commented on in more than one case recently, including the *Bentleys, Stokes & Lowless* case and also the *Tate & Lyle* case.

It seems to me that the commissioners' finding that the expenses were laid out wholly and exclusively for the purposes of the profession is inconsistent with Taylor's evidence in paragraph 4 (*b*) of the case stated, and having regard to that conclusion is, on the face of it, wrong in law.

[58] (1954) 35 T.C. 367, 393, see *ante*, p. 186.
[59] (1952) 33 T.C. 491, *ante*, p. 186. Pennycuick J. then quoted a part of the passage from the judgment of Romer L.J., quoted above.

I was referred to the well-known passages from the speeches of Lord Simonds and Lord Radcliffe in *Edwards* v. *Bairstow*.[60] In the present case the commissioners' decision, to use Lord Radcliffe's words, contained something which is *ex facie* bad law. I do not think I need refer further to that case.

I should only add that, so far as I can see, Taylor's admission on this point accords with the realities of the matter. It is clear from the facts found in the case that this was, at any rate in part, a holiday trip.

Having decided the appeal on the issue of duality, I think it is undesirable for me to express a view upon the issue of remoteness. Although each case turns on its particular facts, the deductibility or otherwise for the purposes of tax of the expense of attending conferences is a matter of wide importance which has not yet, I understand, been judicially considered, and I do not think I ought to make any observations upon it which are not necessary for the determination of the present appeal. Mr. Orr concurs in this view. .

Note
This decision may be compared with that in *Edwards* v. *Warmsley, Henshall & Co.* [1968] 1 All E.R. 1089. See M. C. Flesch, " All Work, No Play? " [1966] B.T.R. 204; R. S. Nock, " Business or Pleasure " [1968] B.T.R. 199.

MURGATROYD v. EVANS-JACKSON

Chancery Division [1967] 1 W.L.R. 423; 110 S.J. 926; [1967] 1 All E.R. 881; 43 T.C. 581

The taxpayer, a trade-mark agent, became ill and needed hospital treatment. He paid to enter hospital as a private patient in order to have a room to himself, from which he continued to run his business, holding conferences and dealing with correspondence there. He claimed to deduct a part of his expenses in respect of the cost of having a private room.

PLOWMAN J.: . . . It seems to me that the claim by the taxpayer [Mr. Evans-Jackson] for 60 per cent. of his expenses is really fatal to his case, because implicit in a claim for only 60 per cent. of the expenses must be an admission that the expenses involved a dual purpose, namely, as to 60 per cent. expenses of conducting an office and as to 40 per cent. something else. I think the taxpayer's claim would have been more plausible had he claimed the whole of his expenses in the nursing home and not merely 60 per cent. of them. But even had he claimed the whole of the expenses, it seems to me that it would not really be a rational view of the situation to conclude that the whole of his expenses in the nursing home were incurred wholly and exclusively for the purposes of his business. The whole object of going into the nursing home in the first place was to receive treatment for the injury which he had sustained, and it seems to me that it would offend common sense to say that at any rate one of his motives or purposes in going into the nursing home was not to receive treatment for that injury—treatment which would enure to his benefit, not merely during the time when he was carrying on his business, but, as Lord Greene M.R. said in the passage I have already read from *Norman* v. *Golder*,[61] " as a living human being."

In those circumstances, both on the ground that the deduction is prohibited by paragraph (*a*) of section 137 of the Act and on the ground that it is prohibited by paragraph (*b*) of the same section, I must allow this appeal.

60 [1956] A.C. 14, *ante*, pp. 51, 145.
61 (1944) 26 T.C. 293.

Note
See also *Prince* v. *Mapp* [1970] 1 W.L.R. 260 where, although there was a finding of duality of purpose and the claim accordingly failed, it appears that a claim in respect of medical expenses may, in certain circumstances, succeed. The implications of the Murgatroyd decision are discussed by J. G. Monroe, " Partly for the purposes of Trade, Profession or Vocation " [1967] B.T.R. 151, and a comparison made with *Copeman* v. *Flood*, *infra*.

Consider also the question of deductible expenditure in computing liability to Capital Gains Tax: *I.R.C.* v. *Richards' Executors* [1971] 1 W.L.R. 571.

COPEMAN v. FLOOD (WILLIAM) & SONS LTD.

King's Bench Division [1941] 1 K.B. 202; 110 L.J.K.B. 215; 24 T.C. 53

A private company, of which the directors were all members of the same family, charged in its accounts two sums of £2,600, as remuneration for two of the directors. One director, the son of the managing director, was aged twenty-four and had worked in the business for several years; the other, a daughter aged seventeen, had no business experience and had rendered some unskilled and inconsiderable services for a few months during the year. The General Commissioners held that they could not interfere with the prerogative of the company to pay such remuneration as it thought fit. On appeal by the Inspector it was held that the duty of the commissioners was to find whether the sums charged were wholly and exclusively laid out for the purposes of the trade.

LAWRENCE J.: I am of opinion that this appeal must be allowed and the case be remitted to the commissioners for them to consider whether the sums paid to these two directors were " money wholly and exclusively laid out or expended for the purposes of the trade " of the company so as to entitle it to deduct them in computing the amount of its profits or gains for income tax purposes. The decision of the commissioners—that they could not interfere with the prerogative of the company to pay such sums as directors' remuneration as it thought fit— does not find that fact, which they were bound to find.

Mr. Donovan has argued that on this appeal no question arises of what amounts should have been paid to the two directors with whom we are concerned, but that the question is whether the company did charge the sums specified as directors' remuneration, and, if it did, it follows that they were wholly and exclusively laid out for the purposes of the company's trade. Therein, in my opinion, lies the fallacy of Mr. Donovan's argument. It does not necessarily follow that, because the sums were charged as remuneration to the directors, they were wholly and exclusively laid out for the purposes of the trade.

Turning again to the Commissioners' decision, it is quite true that they cannot interfere with the prerogative of a company to pay to its directors whatever it thinks fit. The only tribunal which can interfere with the company's prerogative in that matter is the High Court. The Commissioners have nothing to do with the internal economy of the company, but they can find in a proper case that sums paid by a company as remuneration to its directors are not wholly and exclusively laid out or expended for the purposes of the company's trade, and it is their duty to direct their minds to that question. The Commissioners must see whether the sums deducted by the company in computing the amount of its profits or gains for income tax purposes are sums which the company is permitted to deduct by the Income Tax Acts. A company may have paid to its directors sums as remuneration for their services in accordance with the articles of association and a resolution of the company, but it does not follow that those sums are " money wholly and exclusively laid out or expended for the purposes of the trade " of the company so as to render them properly deductible.

The case must, therefore, be remitted to the Commissioners to find as a fact whether the sums in question were wholly and exclusively laid out or expended for the purposes of the company's trade, and, if they were not, to find how much of those sums was so laid out or expended.

Note
    See the remarks of the Millard Tucker Committee, 1951 Cmd. 8189, paras. 158–161, *ante*, p. 183; *cf. Murgatroyd* v. *Evans-Jackson* [1967] 1 All E.R. 881; *ante*, p. 189. The fact that a trader may be contractually bound to make certain payments does not, of itself, make the payments deductible, *per* Megarry J. in *Ransom* v. *Higgs* [1972] 2 All E.R. 817, 844–845.

3. Valuation of Stock

In order to obtain a true picture of the profits of a trade, etc. over any given period, it is necessary to have regard not only to the receipts and the expenditure during that period, but also to any change in the value of trading stock, or of work in progress, between the beginning and the end of the period. The main problem areas are:
    (i) identification of the stock which has been sold and that which remains to be valued;
    (ii) the method of valuation of stock and work in progress;
    (iii) the effects of a change in method of valuation.

B.S.C. FOOTWEAR LTD. v. RIDGWAY

House of Lords [1972] A.C. 544; [1971] 2 W.L.R. 1313; 115 S.J. 408; [1971] 2 All E.R. 534
(also *post*, pp. 196, 201)

The taxpayers claimed to be entitled to value stock at the end of an accounting period by reference to its " replacement value," *i.e.* the amount the taxpayers would be prepared to pay to replace the stock, this amount being less than its original cost. The Revenue contended that it should be valued at cost price, or market value, if lower, market value meaning the price obtainable in the retail market. The method claimed by the taxpayers had been used by them for a number of years and had been accepted by the Revenue. *Held*, the method contended by the Revenue was more appropriate and the taxpayers could be required to adopt that method.

LORD REID: . . . It is commonplace that a trader's profit for tax purposes must be determined by framing a profit and loss account in which there is set against his gross receipts all relevant expenditure. It has often been said that you set against the receipts all expenditure incurred in earning those receipts. But that is not quite accurate. If you manure the field in year one in order to reap the harvest in year two, no one now doubts that the cost of the manure is a proper charge against the receipts in year one although that cost produces no return until the next year. There are no statutory rules about this, and it is well settled that the ordinary principles of commercial accounting must be used except in so far as any specific statutory provision requires otherwise. The question is what is fair to the taxpayer and fair to the revenue.

It has long been recognised that a fair result cannot be achieved without taking into account the trader's stock-in-hand at the beginning and at the end of the year. In the long run it might not much matter how this stock is valued because, if the wrong figure for the stock at the end of year one causes the profit for that year to be too low, the same figure on the other side of the account at the beginning of year two will cause the profit for year two to be to the same extent too high. But for obvious reasons it is desirable that in each separate year the profit should be determined as accurately as possible.

The application of the principles of commercial accounting is, however, subject to one well established though non-statutory principle. Neither profit nor loss may be anticipated. A trader may have made such a good contract in year one that it is virtually certain to produce a large profit in year two. But he cannot be required to pay tax on that profit until it actually accrues. And conversely he may have made such an improvident contract in year one that he will certainly incur a loss in year two but he cannot use that loss to diminish his liability for tax in year one.

This principle is subject to an exception as regards stock-in-trade. If it were applied logically, stock-in-trade must always be valued at the end of the year at cost, even if it could have been bought at the end of the year much more cheaply. But for half a century at least traders have been allowed to value such stock at the end of the year at its market price or market value at that date if that is lower than the original cost price: on the other hand, the trader is not required to value his stock at market value if that is higher than the original cost. So to this extent he can diminish his profit in year one by setting against it an anticipated loss in year two. It is only an anticipated loss because the market price may move upwards before he sells the stock so that when he does sell it he gets a price equal to or greater than the original cost and so never in fact suffers any loss. If that happens the matter is put right in year two. The effect of carrying forward the stock at a valuation below cost is that in the account for year two that valuation and not the actual original cost is deemed to be the cost, and so the profit in year two is increased.

That exception has been expressed by the phrase "cost or market value, whichever is the lower." But that is only a shorthand convenient form of expression. It is not contended by the Crown that it is a rule of law to be interpreted as if the words occurred in a statute. It is I think accurate and adequate where there is a market in the ordinary sense. . . .

Note
　　Lord Reid's was a dissenting judgment but it is considered that his enunciation of the basic principles is not in contention. Further extracts from the judgments appear *post*, pp. 196, 201.

(i) *Identification*

FINAL REPORT OF THE ROYAL COMMISSION ON THE TAXATION OF PROFITS AND INCOME

1955 Cmd. 9474

448. The problem of the proper treatment of stock in trade in the accounts that record the trading profits of the year is usually discussed as another instance of the fact that a rising monetary cost of replacing business assets results in distorting business profits so long as they are computed on the basis of historical cost. It has therefore been put to us as one branch of the argument that a true conception of business profit requires the allowance of a reserve against current receipts in respect of the enhanced cost of their replacement. But we came to the conclusion, after analysing the problem, that the analogy is likely to mislead and that, so far as taxation is concerned, the considerations that are important for one case are not the considerations that are important for another.

449. It is useful to be clear what the problem is. A trader operates with stock in trade. His business revenue consists primarily of his receipts from the disposal of that stock. Against those receipts there must be set the costs appropriate to the stock disposed of before any figure of profit can emerge. Those costs cover not only the costs of acquisition and disposal but also, if the trader processes or manufactures his stock, the cost of process or manufacture, including in that cost the cost of any material consumed during the operation.

450. Since, however, it is necessary that a trader should always have in hand an adequate supply of stock, though not at any unvarying level or volume, there is no obvious way of determining what is the cost appropriate to any particular sale of stock. It has simply been drawn from his pile or pool. Profits, whether for taxation or otherwise, are normally struck on the basis of annual rests. Therefore, at the opening of the accounting period there will be stock in hand, the cost of which will have been carried over from the previous year; there will be stock acquired from time to time during the year, previous to the date of the sale of the parcel in question; and there will be other purchases during the remainder of the year and, at the close, some volume of stock in hand, itself to be carried over to the succeeding year at an appropriate cost. All the different parts of this floating supply may have been acquired at different levels of price.

451. The natural way of meeting this complexity is to make some general assumptions and then to assign cost to particular sales on the basis of those assumptions. It is not as if it were possible to identify the actual cost of the actual item disposed of, except in a few special cases. A jeweller, a picture dealer, some retailers, must match their receipt to the actual cost of acquiring the object sold. But in the majority of cases that would either be impossible or would be possible only with an expenditure of time and labour in accounting records so great as to make the exercise absurd in practice. The general assumption hitherto accepted in this country is that stock is sold in the same order of priority as the order of the dates at which it was acquired. Thus the trader is treated as selling the parcel of stock which has been longest in his hands at the date of sale, and the cost appropriated to it is the cost that has been longest in his books.

452. We do not suppose that this assumption, however convenient, derives its validity from any peculiar correspondence with the trader's physical operations. Strictly speaking, it assumes an order that is likely to be observed only in the case of perishable goods, and only then if all consignments were equally perishable. On the other hand, where successive purchases of stock go into store or pile, the chances are that in practice the more recent arrivals are the earlier drawn upon. In other cases, as for instance in the case of liquids, consignments may become so mixed as to be inextricable in any historical order.

453. We must make a second qualification. While the system of appropriating costs on the basis of " first in, first out " (which has now come to be known as F.I.F.O.) is the generally accepted one in this country, it is not, and probably never has been, the system universally employed. We have already referred to the necessity of appropriating to some articles their actual individual cost—the " unit cost " system. Then there is the " average cost " system, under which the book cost of the opening stock is averaged with the cost of goods added during each succeeding period after deducting consumption at the average price, the periods being determined by rests as frequent as the nature of the business will admit. Other methods are in use, in which the relevant cost is arrived at avowedly by an estimate and no assumption is made that an actual historical cost is involved. One such method is that of " standard cost," by which a predetermined or budgeted cost per unit is taken : another obtains an estimated cost by pricing stock at current selling prices and deducting an

amount equivalent to the normal profit margin and the estimated cost of disposal.

454. There are two systems known respectively as the " base stock " method and the " last in, first out " (L.I.F.O.) method which we shall mention in some detail later. Neither has any considerable currency in this country.

Note

The Royal Commission concluded that no single method could be recommended to the exclusion of all others, but that the FIFO method was generally the most suitable. It was stressed that it did not follow from that conclusion that a trader might use any method he wished in order to reduce tax : 1955 Cmd. 9474, paras. 470, 471.

MINISTER OF NATIONAL REVENUE v. ANACONDA AMERICAN BRASS LTD.

Privy Council [1956] A.C. 85; [1956] 2 W.L.R. 31; 100 S.J. 10; [1956] 1 All E.R. 20; [1955] T.R. 339

VISCOUNT SIMONDS : . . . Their Lordships do not question that the Lifo method or some variant of it may be appropriate for the corporate purposes of a trading company. Business men and their accountant advisers must have in mind not only the fiscal year with which alone the Minister is concerned. It may well be prudent for them to carry in their books stock valued at a figure which represents neither market value nor its actual cost but the lower cost at which similar stock was bought long ago. A hidden reserve is thus created which may be of use in future years. But the Income Tax Act is not in the year 1947 concerned with the years 1948 or 1949 : by that time the company may have gone out of existence and its assets been distributed. Seventy years ago Lord Herschell said in *Russell* v. *Town and County Bank* [62] : " The profit of a trade or business is the surplus by which the receipts from the trade or business exceed the expenditure necessary for the purpose of earning those receipts." This is only one of many judicial observations in which it is implicit that no assumption need be made unless the facts cannot be ascertained, and then only to the extent to which they cannot be ascertained. There is no room for theories as to flow of costs, nor is it legitimate to regard the closing inventory as an unabsorbed residue of cost rather than as a concrete stock of metals awaiting the day of process. It is in their Lordships' opinion the failure to observe, or, perhaps it should be said, the deliberate disregard of, facts which can be ascertained and must have their proper weight ascribed to them, which vitiates the application of the Lifo method to the present case. It is the same consideration which makes it clear that the evidence of expert witnesses, that the Lifo method is a generally acceptable, and in this case the most appropriate, method of accountancy, is not conclusive of the question that the court has to decide. That may be found as a fact by the Exchequer Court and affirmed by the Supreme Court. The question remains whether it conforms to the prescription of the Income Tax Act. As already indicated, in their Lordships' opinion it does not.

. . . So, also, in the United Kingdom an attempt has been vainly made to uphold the base stock method for income tax purposes. In the recent case of *Patrick* v. *Broadstone Mills Ltd.*[63] Singleton L.J., in words that are equally apt if applied to the Lifo method, declined to accept the base stock method as conformable to income tax law, though it might be approved by accountancy practice. . . .

[62] (1888) 13 App.Cas. 418, 424.
[63] [1954] 1 W.L.R. 158.

(ii) *Method of Valuation*

REPORT OF THE COMMITTEE ON THE TAXATION OF TRADING PROFITS

1951 Cmd. 8189

281. The formula which is generally accepted as a description of the proper way to value trading stock (including work in progress) is " cost or market value, whichever is the lower." The theory underlying this formula was well set out in paragraph 8 of the Report of the Committee on Financial Risks attaching to the holding of Trading Stocks in 1919 (Cmd. 9224) in the following terms:

" The custom of business is to ascertain the result of its trading from time to time by a survey of its operations. Commercial practice has fastened upon a year as the most convenient period over which this survey should extend; and the practice of accountancy has been to regard profits (or losses) as arising from *the sales* during this period. (In an economic world otherwise constituted, traders might have preferred to hold that the profit or loss of the year is the result of everything *bought or done* in that year, in which case the profit of the year might not be determinable till some years after.)

The ideal method of making up the Trading Account of the year might be to charge it only with the cost of the goods actually sold in the year (corresponding to the sale prices credited in that year) and to carry to a separate account all expenses relating to goods not sold during that year, as in suspense on account of the next year's trading. In practice this course is inconvenient, for no one can say at the time of purchase when the goods unsold will be sold.

The same effect, however (*viz.* that of confining the trading profit to the sales of the year), is obtained by a contra-entry representing the goods *unsold* at the end of the year. As the entry for stock which appears in a Trading Account is merely intended to cancel the charge for the Goods purchased which have not been sold, it should necessarily represent the *cost* of the goods. If it is more or less than the cost, then the effect is to state the profit on the goods which actually have been sold, at an incorrect figure. . . . From this rigid doctrine one exception is very generally recognised on prudential grounds and is now fully sanctioned by custom, *viz.* the adoption of market value at the date of making up accounts, if that value is less than cost. It is, of course, an anticipation of the loss that may be made on those goods in the following year, and may even have the effect, if prices rise again, of attributing to the following year's results a greater amount of profit than the difference between the actual sale price and the actual cost price of the goods in question."

I.R.C. v. COCK, RUSSELL & CO. LTD.

King's Bench Division [1949] 2 All E.R. 889; 65 T.L.R. 725; 93 S.J. 711; 29 T.C. 387

In valuing its stock of wine, the taxpayer company valued all but two items at cost and the remaining two items at market value, which was, in the case of those two items only, lower than cost. *Held*, they were entitled to do so.

CROOM-JOHNSON J.: . . . It follows that there is nothing to be found anywhere in the statutes which indicates how the valuation is to be made. There is no authority which has been called to my attention which indicates that there is any legal principle which is applicable to the present case other than the general principle regarding the application of ordinary commercial principles. In *Absalom* v. *Talbot*,[64] Lord Porter said:

" What has to be ascertained are the profits and gains of the business, or, as the wording originally stood, the balance of profits and gains—a difference in language which does not affect the meaning of the provision. In order to ascertain that balance one has to determine what sums are to be credited and what debited in the annual accounts. No directions are given in the Income Tax Acts as to how those profits are to be ascertained and in default of direction they must, I think, be arrived at on ordinary commercial principles, subject to such provisions of the Income Tax Acts as require a departure from such ordinary principles."

In these circumstances, it is impossible for me to say that the General Commissioners have failed to have regard to any principle of law which is applicable or that they have misdirected themselves. On the contrary, they appear to have directed themselves accurately and properly. They have accepted the evidence which was before them which was all one way. Profits for income tax purposes are to be computed as a business man, employing sound principles of commercial accountancy, would compute them, subject only to any statutory modification of such principles. I cannot imagine anything which is more clearly a question of fact than what is the value of stock in trade at a particular time. I can see nothing to indicate that the General Commissioners have gone wrong in deciding this matter. There is no justification for a departure now from what admittedly has been the long continued practice of the Inland Revenue Commissioners and their officials.

B.S.C. FOOTWEAR LTD. v. RIDGWAY

House of Lords (*ante*, p. 191; *post*, p. 201)

LORD MORRIS OF BORTH-Y-GEST: . . . My Lords, in approaching the issues which now arise it is right to remember that there is no substantive rule of law which positively decrees that the value of the stock-in-trade (at the beginning and at the end of an accounting period) must be entered at cost or market value whichever is the lower. The formula is, however, a time honoured one. It has often been accepted as providing a convenient business method by the use of which there can be ascertainment of profits or gains. In his speech in *Sun Insurance Office* v. *Clark*,[65] Viscount Haldane said: "It is plain that the question of what is or is not profit or gain must primarily be one of fact, and of fact to be ascertained by the tests applied in ordinary business." He said that questions of law could only arise when some express statutory direction applied which excluded ordinary commercial practice.

Before the special commissioners, as the stated case records, evidence was given by two experienced and eminent accountants. One took the view that the method of accountancy adopted by the taxpayers was appropriate: the other took the contrary view. The evidence did not show that the company's method was to be recognised as being established settled commercial practice though its exponent did consider that it represented a modern and sophisticated form of accounting in contrast with that of the Crown which was stigmatised as being old-fashioned. He accepted that there is more than one method employed by

64 [1944] A.C. 204.
65 [1912] A.C. 443, 455.

accountants and traders in determining market value and he said that one well-accepted method is to take the lower of replacement price and net realisable value. He considered that the replacement price as calculated by the taxpayers produced a fair allocation of profits and losses to different periods because it fairly measured the adverse circumstances regarding the stocks held at the accounting date. The other accountant took the view that the company's method of valuation distorted the company's profits. He agreed that where stock has fallen in value below cost (with the result that a loss would be expected) it would be prudent to have a valuation below cost: for that purpose he considered that market value should be taken and that selling price must be the criterion in arriving at market value (even though there might be occasions when replacement price would afford the best guide to market value or price). He did not accept that it was the function of a profit and loss account to make provision for a diminution of expected profit. Where stock has fallen in value but is still expected to make a profit (even though a smaller one than was originally hoped for) he considered that the appropriate entry was cost price.

Faced with the testimony of two expert witnesses whose evidence conflicted it was in the end the duty of the commissioners to reach a conclusion. Each of the two witnesses expressed a preference for one method and each gave reasons for his particular preference and for his individual opinion. One of the differences of opinion was in relation to the meaning of " market value." Does that denote the value of the goods to the company (*i.e.* the price the company will obtain) or does it denote the price that the company would have to pay to acquire similar goods? Broadly stated the Crown's contention was that the appropriate figure in reference to the stock-in-trade was the figure of cost price but alternatively, and if it were lower, the price (subject in a few cases to one allowance) at which the company would sell the goods: the company, on the other hand, contended that the figure was the lowest of (a) cost price, (b) selling price, (c) replacement price.

While the commissioners gave too exalted a status to the formula " cost or market value " when they described it as " established law " they ultimately had to decide whether the company's method of accounting was one that did or did not truly produce the figure of profits and gains of the company for tax purposes. If the commissioners considered that there were serious objections to the method of accountancy adopted by the company then in spite of the fact that for a long period it was not challenged I think that the commissioners were warranted in declining to endorse it. Ultimately as between the Crown's method and the company's method it has to be decided which of the two is the better calculated to show the full amount of profits and gains.

In my view, there is (for tax purposes) an unreality in taking the calculated figures for which the company contend. They have stock-in-hand at the end of a year. They have planned to have it. Most of it they expect to sell at a profit. They have vast selling organisations. Their main business is to sell. It is an accepted principle that profits are not to be taxed until they are realised. So it would not normally be fitting to enter the stock-in-trade at the figure of selling price. The figure of cost price would be more appropriate. It is an actual figure and a real figure. It may be, however, that it can be seen that some of the stock will be sold at a loss. It has been accepted that in such circumstances the selling price, if it is below cost, may be given as the figure. I agree with the view expressed by Salmon L.J. that this is in the nature of an exception or concession in favour of the taxpayer. This may well be somewhat illogical, as my noble and learned friend, Lord Reid, pointed out in *Duple Motor Bodies Ltd.* v. *Inland Revenue Commissioners* [66] when he said:

[66] [1961] 1 W.L.R. 739, 751, *post*, p. 199.

"Then the question is what figure should be taken to represent the stock-in-trade. If it consists of articles bought for resale the answer is obvious—the price the taxpayer paid for them or their cost to him. If market value were taken that would generally include an element of profit, and it is a cardinal principle that profit shall not be taxed until realised: if the market value fell before the article was sold the profit might never be realised. But an exception seems to have been recognised for a very long time: if market value has already fallen before the date of valuation so that at that date the market value of the article is less than it cost the taxpayer, then the taxpayer can bring the article in at market value, and in this way anticipate the loss which he will probably incur when he comes to sell it. That is no doubt good conservative accountancy but it is quite illogical. The fact that it has always been recognised as legitimate is only one instance going to show that these matters cannot be settled by any hard and fast rule or strictly logical principle."

In his judgment Russell L.J. helpfully described [67] the basis of what he regarded as the "accepted practice" of entering stock-in-hand at cost at the terminal date of the first period and the opening date of the second period. He regarded the practice as arising from the fact that the expenditure has not contributed anything directly to the figures of gross profit in the first period.

I can well appreciate the view of those who purely from accountancy considerations would prefer to place an anticipated shortfall in profits, as well as an anticipated loss, in the year in which stock is purchased, but as a method of ascertaining the actual amount of profit for income tax purposes I consider that the method adopted by the company is open to the objections which have been pointed out in the judgments under review. There is, in my view, an unreality and an artificiality about the figure that the company seek to enter in regard to stock-in-hand. Though the figure to be entered must be notional in the sense that it is entered as a notional receipt, the figure of actual cost (or sale price expected to be received if lower) is not open to the objections that attach to a figure of replacement price as calculated by the company. It may seem strange in the first place to start calculating a replacement price when there is neither need nor desire to replace. The company has goods which it has bought for resale. If it is correct that the alternative to cost price is that by way of concession to the taxpayer market price (if lower) may be taken I would have thought that in this context (the context of the time-honoured formula) market price would denote the price at which the goods held for sale would be marketed. The company are in the best position to know what such market price is. Their very business is to market their goods. The prices which they can obtain in their hundreds of shops must form the surest guide to the prices in the markets which are peopled by the persons to whom they sell. So far as any decided cases throw any light on this matter I would agree with Cross J. [68] that though the decision of Rowlatt J. in *Brigg Neumann & Co.* v. *Inland Revenue Comrs.*[69] may show that there may be some cases in which the wholesale market value may be taken as the appropriate market value the case does not establish that a retailer who on a retail sale will sell at a price above what it cost him to buy may value his unsold stock-in-hand by reference to the wholesale or replacement value if that is less than what it cost him.

But apart from these considerations the figure that the company seek to enter (their valuation figure) is, in my view, otherwise open to objection. If a whole-

[67] [1971] Ch. 427, 435.
[68] [1969] 1 W.L.R. 1488, 1496.
[69] (1928) 12 T.C. 1191. Rowlatt J. appears to have considered "market value" to mean the price at which the appellants could have *purchased* the goods in the market.

sale price (or replacement price) is being sought for it is clear that the company would not be willing to sell their stocks wholesale to other retailers at the valuation figure it puts forward. The case stated finds that the company would never be likely to try to sell off the stock at the company's valuation. As an example, there are items of stock-in-hand which are grouped as window samples. They cost £188,430. Their marked retail prices amounted to £300,000 but the later expected retail selling prices amounted to £285,000. Applying to that figure their mathematical formula (a deduction so as still to yield a gross profit on the basis of their mark-up percentage) the company's valuation would be £178,997. As the case stated finds, the company " would never sell the window samples at its valuation of £178,997 when it expected to obtain £285,000 for them over its own counters." Nor was there any evidence or any suggestion that in a wholesale market the company could in fact have purchased stock at the figures of their valuations. Those figures are wholly unreal. They merely represent the price they would have been prepared to pay if they had been able to find anyone willing to sell at that price, which they were not, and if they had wanted to buy, which they did not. So the company's figures are mathematical figures and not market figures and they are used as a means of adjusting accounts whereby an anticipated diminution of future profit can be brought into current account. The company's methods make a considerable inroad on the broadly accepted principle that neither expected future profits nor expected future losses are to be anticipated.

Whatever merits there may be in the company's accountancy methods for the purposes of its internal affairs I am not persuaded that Cross J. and the Court of Appeal were wrong in finding them unacceptable for tax purposes.

I would dismiss the appeal.

Note
Lord Morris was in the majority, a similar view being taken by Lords Guest and Pearson. Lord Reid, passages from whose dissenting judgment have been quoted, thought the Revenue method more appropriate but did not consider that the taxpayer could be made to change methods, see *post*, p. 201. Viscount Dilhorne preferred the taxpayer's method and also agreed with Lord Reid on the question of change of method.
For a general discussion of the problem, see A. F. Bessemer Clark, " The Valuation of Stock in Trade " [1970] B.T.R. 65.

OSTIME v. DUPLE MOTOR BODIES LTD.

House of Lords [1961] 1 W.L.R. 739; 105 S.J. 346; [1961] 2 All E.R. 167; *sub nom. Duple Motor Bodies* v. *Ostime*, 39 T.C. 537

In valuing work in progress on motor bodies the appellants claimed to use the " direct cost " method, which took into account only the cost of direct materials and labour. The Revenue contended that the " on cost " method should be employed, this taking into account a proportion of the indirect expenditure, *e.g.* factory and office overheads and expenses. The Special Commissioners found that the accountancy profession was satisfied with either method. *Held*, on this finding, the Revenue were not justified in requiring the appellants to change their method.

VISCOUNT SIMONDS : . . . Before doing so, it is proper to say—it is indeed implicit in what I have said—that it is common ground that some value must be attributed to work in progress, and that in ascertaining that value two considerations must be borne in mind : first, that the ordinary principles of commercial accounting must as far as practicable be observed and, secondly, that the law relating to income tax must not be violated: see *Whimster & Co.* v. *Commissioners of Inland Revenue* [70]: that is to say, by one means or another the full amount of the profits or gains of the trade must be determined.

. . . My Lords, I think that in this dilemma the prevailing consideration must be that the taxpayer should not be put to any risk of being charged with a higher amount of profit than can be determined with reasonable certainty. He may concede that stock-in-trade and work in progress must for tax purposes be regarded as a receipt. Upon that professional accountants appear to be universally agreed, though it might not be at once obvious to the layman. But this concession should not be pressed beyond the point at which the profession is widely, if not universally, agreed, and I should, therefore, if I had to choose (which I have not) between two vaguely defined methods, choose the " direct cost " method as the less likely to violate the taxing statute. I should be supported in this choice by the reflection that, if the cost is put at too low a figure, the error will be made good to the advantage of the Crown in the following year.

Another consideration that weighs with me is this. I recognise the force of the contention that, if the cost of work in progress cannot be ascertained with accuracy, at least the attempt should be made to be as accurate as possible. But against this I put at least two powerful considerations. The first is that it is undesirable to indulge in what is no better than guess-work though it may be described as an intelligent estimate, and it appeared to me that a large part of the suggested apportionment of overheads to stock-in-trade and work in progress was the wildest guess-work. It may be from the commercial point of view a desirable practice. But it is a very different thing to impose it upon a trader whether he wants it or not. It is not only unreliable for the purpose of ascertaining the year's profit. It is also an elaborate and costly practice if carried to its logical conclusion. And I see no reason why, once embarked on, it should not be carried to its logical conclusion. There appears to me to be no distinction, except perhaps of convenience, between the many varieties of cost which the exponents of one " on-cost " system or other advocate.

A second and more powerful reason, which the case under appeal illustrates, is that an attempt to get as nearly as possible an accurate estimate of cost may, if it means the consistent application of a theory of costing, lead to what from the taxing point of view is an absurd conclusion. That is not too strong a word. For here, as was well pointed out by the Master of the Rolls (Lord Evershed) and Pearce L.J., the value of the work in progress at the end of the relevant year was £2,000 less than at its beginning if the " direct cost " method is adopted, whereas according to the " on-cost " method it was not £2,000 less but £14,000 more. This difference is due to little else than the fact that the overheads had to be distributed among a smaller number of articles so that each of them bore a greater proportion of such costs. An idle and unprofitable year thus increases for tax purposes the value of the work that has been or is in course of being done. Counsel for the Crown did not shrink from this conclusion and accepted my suggestion that, if owing to a prolonged strike little work was produced, the weight of all the overheads would have to be thrown upon that little. The only course then open to the trader would be to take market value as the test. This, I have pointed out, is an invitation that may be accepted.

My Lords, in my opinion this is fundamentally wrong. Stock-in-trade and work in progress are brought into account because, fictitiously but as a matter of plain common sense, they are treated as a receipt of the year's trading. The words " receipt " and " realised profit " were often on counsel's lips in regard to them. My Lords, I would say, nevertheless, that it is something remote indeed

[70] (1925) 12 T.C. 813, *ante*, p. 154.

from common sense to say that for taxing or any other purpose an inflated value is to be given to stock-in-trade or work in progress because a slump in trade has reduced the articles between which overhead costs can be apportioned. The asset regarded as a receipt is not more valuable nor is a greater profit realised.

For the reasons that I have given I reject the so-called on-cost method as a method which can be imposed on the taxpayer. . . .

(iii) *Change in Method*

B.S.C. FOOTWEAR LTD. v. RIDGWAY

House of Lords (*ante*, pp. 191, 196)

LORD REID: . . . There is one strong reason for not imposing this different system of valuation. The Crown does not seek to re-open the appellants' accounts for tax purposes for the year 1958 where the stock-in-hand on December 31, 1958, was valued by the appellants' method. But if a new method of valuation is to be required for 1959 admittedly that necessarily involves applying the new method in valuing the stock-in-hand at January 1, 1959. So different values will be shown for the same stock, and, again admittedly, that means, according to which way the difference is, that a sum equal to that difference will either be taxed twice or will escape taxation altogether. It is a fundamental principle of income tax law that the same sum shall not be taxed twice. . . .

Note
    Both *B.S.C. Footwear* v. *Ridgway* and *Duple Motor Bodies Ltd.* v. *Ostime* are concerned with whether or not the Revenue can require the taxpayer to change his method of valuation. As to change of accounting methods generally, see *Monthly Salaries Loan Co. Ltd.* v. *Furlong* (1962) 40 T.C. 313. It may, however, be the taxpayer who wishes to change his method.

INLAND REVENUE PRACTICE NOTE

The Accountant, Nov. 17, 1962, p. 648

The following note has been received from the Board of Inland Revenue in answer to inquiries made by the Institute as to the procedure now followed by the Inland Revenue in cases where there has been a change in the method of computing the amount at which stock-in-trade and work in progress are brought into account:

CHANGE IN BASIS OF STOCK VALUATION

1. The Revenue accepts any method of computing the value of work in progress and finished stock, which is recognised by the accountancy profession, so long as it does not violate the taxing statutes as interpreted by the Courts. Such a basis is referred to in this note as a " valid basis." The expression " non-valid basis " is used to denote a basis which does not accord with the standard of acceptability referred to in the first sentence of this paragraph, and includes a valuation which, although in form made on a recognised basis, pays insufficient regard to the facts. Having regard to the principle of consistency, there would need to be good reason for any change in an existing valid basis.

Change from One Valid Basis to Another Valid Basis

2. Where a change from one valid basis to another valid basis is accepted, certain consequences normally follow. The opening stock of the basis year of change is valued on the same basis as the closing stock. Whether the change is to a higher level or to a lower level, the Revenue normally does not seek to revise the valuations of earlier years. It neither seeks to raise additional assessments, nor does it admit relief under the " error or mistake " provisions.

3. It is not possible to define with precision what amounts to a change of basis. It is a convenience, both to the taxpayer and to the Revenue, not to regard every change in the method of valuation as a change of basis. In particular, the Revenue encourages the view that changes which involve no more than a greater degree of accuracy, or a refinement, should not be treated as a change of basis, whether the change results in a higher or a lower valuation. In such cases the new valuation is applied at the end of the year without amendment of the opening valuation.

4. What constitutes a good reason for a change in the existing basis is a question to be answered by reference to the facts of each case. Possible examples of such justified changes are that of a company absorbed by a group and adapting its basis to the group's principles, or a concern adjusting its basis to conform to some alteration in the nature of its trade.

Change from a Non-valid Basis to a Valid Basis

5. When a change in the basis of valuation is first made from a non-valid basis to a valid one, the new basis is applied to both the opening and closing values of the year of change. In addition a review is made of past liabilities, but in cases where there is no question of past irregularities (that is, fraud, wilful default or neglect) the Revenue would not in any event seek to recover tax for past years on an amount greater than that involved in the uplift of the opening valuation of the year of change.

4. The Accounting Period

The profits of a trade, etc. can only be ascertained in relation to a period of time, by reference to the receipts and expenditure during that period and the difference in value of stock and work in progress at the beginning and at the end of the period. Further, income tax is an annual tax and Schedule D taxes the *annual* profits or gains.[71] But it is rarely that a trader makes up his own accounts for a period corresponding precisely to a year of assessment. The main problems are, therefore:

    (i) the determination of the basis of assessment, *i.e.* the identification with a year of assessment of a particular part of the trader's profits; and

   (ii) the timing of items of receipt and expenditure, *i.e.* the correct appropriation of an item to a particular accounting year and year of assessment.

---

[71] I.C.T.A. 1970, s. 108. *Martin* v. *Lowry* [1926] 1 K.B. 550; *ante*, pp. 149, 152.

(i) *The Basis of Assessment*

REPORT OF THE COMMITTEE ON THE TAXATION OF TRADING PROFITS

1951 Cmd. 8189

19. The first question to which we addressed ourselves was the basis of assessment to Income Tax, for on the answer to this question depended many of our other problems. Under the existing law the owner of a business is normally assessed for each year of assessment ending April 5 on the profits of his accounting year ending in the year preceding the year of assessment; thus, if he makes up his accounts to December 31 in each year he will be assessed for the year 1950–51 (ending April 5, 1951) on the profits of the account ending December 31, 1949. There are, however, special provisions, commonly known as the commencement and cessation provisions, applicable to the first three and the last two years of assessment in which the business is carried on. For the first year (normally a broken year, except where the business begins on April 6) he is assessed on the actual profits of the year of assessment; for the next year the assessment is on the profits of the first twelve months of the business. The assessment for the third year is normally on the profits of the preceding accounts year, but the owner of the business may claim that the assessment for both the second and third years, but not one only, should be on the actual profits of those respective years. For the year in which he ceases business (normally also a broken year) he is assessed on the actual profits of the year of assessment; for the penultimate year he is assessed either on the profits of the accounts year ending in the ante-penultimate year, or on the profits of the actual year of assessment, whichever are the greater.

20. The existing system was introduced by the Finance Act 1926, with effect from 1927–28 and in general followed the recommendations of the Royal Commission on the Income Tax of 1920. Up to 1926–27 the normal basis of assessment of businesses had been the average profits of the three accounts years preceding the year of assessment. The Royal Commission received a great deal of evidence on the question of the basis of assessment, practically all of which was antagonistic to the three years average and in favour of the preceding year basis. As the Commission said in their Report, hardly anyone had a good word for the average; they therefore had no hesitation in recommending its abolition and the substitution of the preceding year basis.

21. We received a great deal of evidence, both written and oral, on the question of the basis of assessment, but we did not share the experience of the Royal Commission that opinions in industry were virtually unanimous. In the first place there was a by no means negligible minority which favoured the preservation of the existing system; this was due not so much to its positive advantages, though it was claimed to be beneficial to new and expanding businesses, as to fear of the unknown; as one of our witnesses put it " better the devil they knew than the devil they didn't know." Secondly, while the majority of our witnesses were in favour of a change to some form of current year basis, they were by no means agreed on what the new basis should be. One thing only was clear, that there was no desire to return to the old three years' average; the only merit claimed for this system was that, with a highly progressive Surtax, it was more equitable to those whose incomes fluctuated widely and it was generally recognised that this consideration could not weight the scales in favour of a return to the old average system, and that the question of

giving relief to those with fluctuating incomes is one which requires to be dealt with as a separate problem. We have in fact so dealt with it and our recommendations are set out in paragraphs 84 to 93 below.

22. The main question, therefore, resolved itself into a choice between the existing preceding year basis and some form of current year basis, and, as we have said, the majority of our witnesses favoured a change. It will be desirable to set out, in the first place, the main objections alleged against the present system.

23. *Anomalies in computation of total income.* As a result of the preceding year basis the statutory total income for any year of an individual who derives profits from a business and also has other sources of income (such as the emoluments of an office or employment taxed under P.A.Y.E., or dividends and interest on investments taxed at the source) in general never corresponds, except by accident, with his actual total income for that or any other year. Income from some sources for one year is added to income from other sources for another year, and the result is treated as the total income for one of those years. Thus, an individual's statutory total income for the Income Tax year 1952–53 may be made up of:

(i) business profits for his accounts year ending December 31, 1951;

(ii) income which is taxed under P.A.Y.E. (such as fees from a directorship of a company), income from which tax is deducted at the source and also certain other income; all for the year ending April 5, 1953;

(iii) other income not taxed at the source (such as dividends on overseas investments) for the year ending April 5, 1952.

Where income from different sources fluctuates from year to year, the result in a particular year may differ widely from the actual income for that or the preceding year, and with a highly progressive Surtax the results may be extremely anomalous.

24. *Commencing and ceasing provisions.* These provisions, which have been briefly referred to in paragraph 19 above, are complicated and difficult to understand by the layman. They may result in a considerable discrepancy between the actual profits of the business and the amounts assessed, for their effect is that some profits are assessed more than once while other profits are not assessed at all. In the early years of a business the taxpayer has an option to choose, within certain limits, which profits are to be assessed more than once. Corresponding to this option is the option given to the Inland Revenue in the penultimate year of the business to assess the higher of two periods of profit. Over the life of a business as a whole it is only by accident that the total profits assessed exactly equal the total profits made. In general, the benefit probably lies with the taxpayer, for the duplicated period will belong to the early years of his business when his rate of profit may not have reached its maximum. There can, however, be cases where the trend of profits or their fluctuations are such that he finishes up by having paid tax on substantially more profits than he has made over the life of his business.

Note

The Committee concluded that a true " current year " basis could not be achieved, a conclusion also arrived at by the Radcliffe Committee, 1955 Cmd. 9474, para. 776 who, however, considered that a form of current year basis was appropriate to Companies.

The present statutory rules are contained in I.C.T.A. 1970, ss. 115–128, and, for Corporation Tax, ss. 129, 243.

The problems involved in changing the basis were stressed by the Millard Tucker Committee, paras. 33–34; see also *Monthly Salaries Loan Co Ltd.* v. *Furlong* (1962) 40 T.C. 313; *I.R.C.* v. *Helical Bar Ltd.* [1971] Ch. 813; J. M. Cope, " The Consequences of Changing an Accounting Date " [1970] B.T.R. 338.

The question of commencement is illustrated by *Stephenson* v. *Payne, Stone, Fraser & Co.* [1968] 1 W.L.R. 858; *post*, p. 207; *Westward Television Ltd.* v. *Hart* [1969] 1 Ch. 201; *post*, p. 212.

DUCKERING v. GOLLAN

House of Lords [1965] 1 W.L.R. 680; 109 S.J. 355; [1965] 2 All E.R. 115; 42 T.C. 333

LORD DONOVAN: . . . My Lords, it is a truism which the Crown do not dispute that United Kingdom Income Tax for any year of assessment for which the tax is granted by Parliament is a levy upon the income of that year. It is not a levy upon the income of a preceding year, nor does it become so by virtue of the fact that this latter income may be used to measure the amount of tax payable. . . .

BROWN v. NATIONAL PROVIDENT INSTITUTION

House of Lords (*ante*, pp. 5, 16, 85)

VISCOUNT HALDANE: . . . The question is whether under such circumstances the Institution can, under the words of rule 1, be charged in respect of the amount of the profit and gains which arose within the preceding year, or whether the source of such profits and gains must be one which continued to exist in the year of assessment. So that, whatever the principle of computation or measurement directed to be applied, what is assessable is only profit existing in the year of assessment. My Lords, the language of the rule measures the amount in respect of which the assessment is to be made by that of the profits and gains within the preceding year. But this does not appear to be conclusive. For the principle of retrospective measurement is one which is applied elsewhere in the Acts, limited, however, to cases in which the source of income continues to exist in the year of assessment. It is the profits and gains of a continuing business that are in such cases the subject of assessment, but the amount is measured by reference to preceding years. . . .

(ii) *" Timing "*

J. P. HALL & CO. LTD. v. I.R.C.

Court of Appeal [1921] 3 K.B. 152; 90 L.J.K.B. 1229; 125 L.T. 720; 37 T.L.R. 744; 12 T.C. 382

The profit on the sale of electric control gear was held to be properly included in the accounts for the periods during which deliveries of the goods were effected and not in the pre-war period when the contracts were originally made.

ATKIN L.J.: I agree. The proposition put forward by the respondents in this case seems to me so very unsound that I am really left in doubt whether I have fully appreciated it; but, as I understand it, it appears to me to be quite wrong. The profits for excess profits duty are to be assessed on the same basis as profits for income tax purposes, and the word " profits " for income tax purposes is to be understood in accordance with the words of Lord Halsbury in *Gresham Life Assurance Society* v. *Styles*,[72] " in its natural and proper

[72] [1892] A.C. 309, 315–316; *ante*, p. 152.

sense—in a sense which no commercial man would misunderstand." He further says that " profits and gains must be ascertained on ordinary principles of commercial trading." I need not say anything more after what has been said by the Master of the Rolls. It seems to me that no person here trying to ascertain these profits on the principles of ordinary commercial trading would dream of including in his yearly balance-sheet profits which would not be made until the goods had actually been delivered, in respect of a contract which was to run over a period of at least two years, and possibly more. To my mind, the procedure of the respondents in taking into account the profits that they made as and when the goods were delivered was the ordinary commercial procedure. Any other course would be quite contrary to commercial procedure. I think therefore this appeal should be allowed.

Note
For the timing of receipts, see also *Lincolnshire Sugar Co. Ltd.* v. *Smart* [1937] A.C. 697; *Jays The Jewellers Ltd.* v. *I.R.C.* (1947) 29 T.C. 274; *Elson* v. *Prices Tailors Ltd.* [1963] 1 W.L.R. 287; *cf. Morley* v. *Messrs Tattersall* (1938) 22 T.C. 51.

SOUTHERN RAILWAY OF PERU LTD. v. OWEN

House of Lords [1957] A.C. 334; [1956] 3 W.L.R. 389; 100 S.J. 527; [1956] 2 All E.R. 728; 36 T.C. 602

Under Peruvian legislation, an English company had to pay employees compensation on termination of employment. The Company claimed to be entitled to charge against each year's receipts the cost of making provision for the retirement payments which would ultimately be thrown upon it. *Held*, the Company was not entitled to the deduction claimed as there was no proper estimate of the future liability. (*Semble*, the claim would have succeeded if the Company had allowed proper discounting of the future liability.)

LORD RADCLIFFE: . . . It is true that the company carries on business from one year to another, but it is not charged on the average of its annual profits. Tax rates and allowances themselves vary and, apart from that, to charge tax on a profit unduly accelerated or unduly deferred is, in my opinion, no more respectable an achievement than to admit that the annual accounts of business do in some cases require the introduction of estimates or valuations if a true statement of profit is to be secured.

Another method is that which the appellant is seeking to establish with regard to its assessments for the four years 1947–50. I will say at once that what it aims at (I do not say, what it achieves) appears to me to be a more accurate assessment of true annual profit than that which could be provided by the other method. When I am told, then, that its adoption is banned by some established principle of law, to which your Lordships are bound to give effect, I feel that I must inquire closely what that principle of law is and upon what understanding of accountancy practice the principle is said to be based. For the overriding principle of law is still, I believe, as it was stated by Lord Haldane in *Sun Insurance Office* v. *Clark* [73]:

" It is plain that the question of what is or is not profit or gain must primarily be one of fact, and of fact to be ascertained by the tests applied in ordinary business. Questions of law can only arise when (as was not the case here) some express statutory direction applies and excludes ordinary commercial practice, or where, by reason of its being impracticable to ascertain the facts sufficiently, some presumption has to be invoked to fill the gap."

[73] [1912] A.C. 443, 455.

And our task is not made any easier by the knowledge that, though the law with its system of precedents may sometimes seem to stand still (I hope that it does not), it is quite certain that the techniques and practices of commercial accountancy are very far from static.

. . . But there is no difficulty if we accept the main argument of the Crown. That argument is that, quite simply, there is a rule of law which forbids the introduction of any provision for future payments in or payments out, if the right to receive them or the liability to make them is in legal terms contingent at the closing of the relevant year. The rule, it seems, is absolute and must be adhered to whatever the current principles or practices of commercial accountancy may require as a method of ascertaining the year's profits. And this is the argument which hitherto has prevailed in the High Court and the Court of Appeal. Now, in my opinion, there is no such rule of law governing the ascertainment of annual profits. Where does it come from? Not from anything to be found in the Income Tax Acts, which, indeed, by the well-known rule limiting the exclusion of debts, show a different and, as I think, a more realistic approach to the problem. Not from any decided authority which is binding on your Lordships. On the contrary, there are two decisions of this House which negative the existence of any such rule of law.[74]

. . . But, whatever the legal analysis, I think that for liabilities as for debts their proper treatment in annual statements of profit depends not upon the legal form but upon the trader's answers to two separate questions. The first is: Have I adequately stated my profits for the year if I do not include some figure in respect of these obligations? The second is: Do the circumstances of the case, which include the techniques of established accounting practice, make it possible to supply a figure reliable enough for the purpose? . . .

Note
  See also *Whimster & Co.* v. *I.R.C.* (1925) 12 T.C. 813; *ante*, p. 154; *J. H. Young & Co.* v. *I.R.C.* (1925) 12 T.C. 827.

STEPHENSON v. PAYNE, STONE, FRASER & CO.

Chancery Division [1968] 1 W.L.R. 858; 112 S.J. 443; [1968] 1 All E.R. 524; 44 T.C. 507

PENNYCUICK J.: . . . In order that the issue may be intelligible, it is necessary to bear in mind the provisions as to the basis of computation of the profits of a trade or profession, particularly in regard to the opening years of the trade or profession. These will be found in sections 127 and 128 of the Income Tax Act 1952.[75] I need not read these provisions. It will be sufficient to say that for the first three fiscal years the profit is normally computed by reference to the actual profit of the first yearly period of account. It is, therefore, much to the interests of the taxpayer to keep the profits of the first yearly period as low as possible.

In the present case the taxpayers are in practice as chartered accountants. They have been in practice for a number of years and have made regular profits of substantial amounts. One member of the firm died on October 29, 1960, and thereupon the firm fell to be treated as though the surviving partners had set up a new profession. The taxpayers' period of account runs to November 30

[74] *Sun Insurance Office* v. *Clark*, *supra*, and *Harrison* v. *John Cronk & Sons Ltd.* [1937] A.C. 185.
[75] Now I.C.T.A. 1970, ss. 115, 116.

in each year. Towards the end of 1960 the taxpayers caused to be incorporated a company by the name of Bedford Row Nominees Ltd. (described as " the service company ") for the purpose of providing services to the firm. The service company's first period of account began on December 1, 1960, and ran until May 31, 1962. The partners in the firm are the sole shareholders in the service company and are also the directors of the service company. It was arranged from the start that the service company should make a charge for its services to the taxpayers, but the basis of the charge was not agreed until the summer of 1962, *i.e.* after the end of the taxpayers' period of account ended on November 30, 1961. It was then arranged that the service company's charge should be adjusted to secure what is described as a nominal profit only. But as part of the arrangement, the charge for the period of account ended November 30, 1961, was fixed at a figure in excess by £15,000 of the actual cost of the services which had been rendered during that period, and there was to be a corresponding reduction in the charge thereafter. On this basis the profit for the all-important first period of account of the taxpayers was diminished by £15,000. The Crown contend that this sum of £15,000 is not admissible as an outgoing for that period.

. . . With all respect to the general commissioners I do not think their decision can be supported. The attribution of any given outgoing to one or other period of account for the purpose of striking a true balance of profit or loss is a matter to be determined upon the ordinary principles of commercial accountancy. Here the basis of charge agreed upon in the summer of 1962 by the partners in their dual capacity as such and as directors of the service company was a nominal profit, that is, the actual cost to the service company of the services which it rendered with or without a very small addition which could be described as nominal profit. It is accepted by Mr. Grundy, for the taxpayers, that this basis was to be applicable overall to the whole period for which services had been or were to be rendered, including the period of account already ended on November 30, 1961 (see case stated, paragraph 5 (x) and (xii)). The partners, however, arranged that in calculating the amount of its service charge the service company should add £15,000 to the actual cost of the services rendered in the year of account ended November 30, 1961, and make a corresponding deduction in making its service charges in the subsequent year or years of account. This was in fact done. It seems to me that this misattribution is manifestly contrary to the ordinary principles of commercial accountancy and distorts the true balance of profit of the taxpayers' profession. The point hardly admits of elaboration.

It is clear enough on the findings of the commissioners that during the period of account ended on November 30, 1961, the service company rendered its services on the footing that it would make a charge for them (see case stated, paragraph 5 (viii)). Mr. Carmichael gave evidence in the case stated, paragraph 4 (b), " That in such case the actual cost of providing the services would be irrelevant." The commissioners, while only going so far as to accept Mr. Carmichael's evidence as given bona fide, found that the £47,000 was a commercially reasonable price for the service company to charge anybody for services costing £32,000. I am not concerned to question this finding of the commissioners and I do not do so, but neither Mr. Carmichael's evidence nor the commissioners' findings get over the difficulty in the way of the taxpayers, namely, that overall the £15,000 was not in truth a profit charge at all, but an allocation of part of the actual cost of the services for the subsequent period or periods of account.

I fully recognise that the service company is a different person in law from the taxpayers and that the provision as to the £15,000 was part of the contractual arrangement between them. But on analysis this provision represents no more than a term that each party shall deal with the £15,000 in its own accounts in a particular manner. It does not touch either the amount payable by the taxpayers to the service company or the times at which payments are to be actually made.

I observe the finding in the case stated, paragraph 5 (x), that, " No part of the figure of £47,000 constituted a prepayment." This is literally true. What took place was a misattribution.

I agree with the commissioners that the whole sum of £47,000 was wholly and exclusively expended for the purposes of the taxpayers' profession. The vice in their finding lies in the words " in that year." The expenditure made in the second year could only as to £32,000 properly be attributed to the first year.

. . . So here, there is no doubt that the taxpayers were entitled to bring in as an outgoing for the period of account ended November 30, 1961, an amount owing to the service company in respect of the services rendered during that period of account. Again, no doubt, at the end of the period the amount so owing was still a matter for computation. What was not legitimate was to attribute to the period a disproportionate part of the charge subsequently agreed at a uniform rate. . . .

Note
Cf. *Naval Colliery Co. Ltd.* v. *I.R.C.* (1928) 12 T.C. 1017, esp. Viscount Sumner (at p. 1049): " It seems to me like saying that a man is entitled to charge supper in his expenses for Sunday night because, though he went supperless to bed, he orders something extra for his breakfast on Monday morning."

5. Losses

A loss in an accounting period arises when, in computing " profits," the allowable expenditure exceeds the appropriate receipts, taking into account the changes in stock, etc.[76] If the result of the computation is a minus quantity, then—

   (i) there are *no profits* of the accounting period;
   (ii) there is a *loss* which, in certain circumstances, may be set against other income to reduce the amount of tax payable.

FINAL REPORT OF THE ROYAL COMMISSION ON THE TAXATION OF PROFITS AND INCOME

1955 Cmd. 9474

GENERAL PRINCIPLES

480. The tax system recognises a taxpayer's right to set off losses against what would otherwise be taxable income. We thought it desirable to make some analysis of the conditions that govern the exercise of this right and of the nature of the losses that qualify for recognition.

481. In effect there are only two sources of income that need to be considered as sources of loss. One is a trade, profession or vocation, the profits of which

[76] The relationship is discussed by R. S. Nock, " Loss Relief and Deduction of Expenditure " [1970] B.T.R. 50; see also *I.R.C.* v. *Alexander von Glehn & Co. Ltd.* [1920] 2 K.B. 553.

are assessed under Case I or Case II of Schedule D; the other is land (including buildings), the income from which is assessed under Schedule A. Exceptionally, an employment under Schedule E might throw up a case of loss, in which event a claim for relief would be competent, but, generally speaking, the two classes of source that we have mentioned are the ones in which a problem arises from the fact that in any period of twelve months the expenses of earning the receipts may exceed the receipts themselves.

482. At different times our system has given different answers to the question what allowance should be given for such a loss in the taxation of other income arising in the same year or of income arising in later years. There is today a marked difference in the treatment of losses for the purposes of Case I and II of Schedule D and of losses for the purposes of Schedule A. It is desirable to see how far this difference of treatment depends on a real difference between the two cases.

483. The development of loss provisions under Schedule D in respect of business income—as we will call it for convenience—is of comparatively recent growth, though it is true that the Income Tax Act of 1842 (reproducing a provision that first appeared in the Act of 1805) gave to the business man carrying on two or more distinct trades the right to set off a current loss in one against the current profits of the other. In 1890 the business man received the further right to set off a business loss against any other income of his for the same period, from whatever source arising. In 1926, when the assessment of business profits according to a three-year average was abolished, the system was introduced of allowing a business loss (so far as not already set off against other income of the year) to be carried forward for a period of six years following the year of loss for the purpose of being set off against the assessment on any subsequent profits of the same business. In 1952 the six-year limitation was removed, so that the loss can be carried forward indefinitely until absorbed. In 1953 the right to set off a loss against other income of the year was extended so as to allow it to be set off against other income of the year succeeding the year of loss.

484. A loss may be said to arise in respect of income under Schedule A when the expenses of keeping the building insured and in good tenantable condition exceed the income arising from the property. This income will be the rent, if it is let, or the computed annual value, if it is in the occupation of the owner. With the level of rents and so of Schedule A valuations held back by rent control it is inevitable that the statutory allowance for repairs, the purpose of which is to reduce the gross rental by an amount representing the expense which the recipient has to incur in order to qualify himself to receive it, should be inadequate for the purpose in many cases: for it is measured by fixed minimum sums or a percentage of the rent, whereas the expenses of repair are represented by the uncontrolled prices of the day. If the statutory allowance for repairs were the only relief, there would be no provision at all for loss in respect of income from property. But a modified recognition is provided by the " maintenance " claim, first introduced as long ago as 1910, by virtue of which the owner who can show that over the five preceding years he has expended on " maintenance, repairs, insurance and management " a sum which on the average exceeds the statutory allowance can set off the amount of the excess against his Schedule A liability for the current year. He is not allowed, however, to set it off against other income (unless the excess expenditure relates to agricultural property) or to carry it forward against Schedule A assessments for later years.

485. It is possible to discern in these different provisions different methods of approach to the problem of allowing relief for losses under a system which

employs those general conceptions of the nature of taxable income which are traceable in our own:

(1) One method would be to refuse altogether to recognise an income loss from one source as affecting the taxable income of the year from another source or the taxable income from the same or other sources for a future year.

(2) A second method would be to treat income from each separate source as part of a running account between taxpayer and Revenue and to allow carry-forward of losses against future income from that source, but not to allow them to be set off at all against income from other sources.

(3) A third method would be to allow losses from one source to be set off, primarily, against income from other sources of the same year, but, so far as not absorbed by that allowance, to be carried forward to one or more of the succeeding years and set off either against future income from the same source or against future income from other sources.

It is possible to find even further variants of these methods. For instance, a loss from a source a profit from which would have been a profit taxable under Case VI of Schedule D may be set against a profit from another source if that profit is also taxable under the same Case for the same year, and any balance not so relieved may be carried forward and set against any subsequent profit from the source giving rise to the loss or a subsequent profit from a different source taxable under Case VI; but no other form of carry-forward or set-off against other income is allowed.

486. When these various methods are compared, it seems to us plain that method (1) could not be applied nowadays. It can fairly be said to be the one that, logically, is most consistent with a scheme of taxation that does not make a general principle of allowing capital losses against income or taxing capital gains as income. For, if the idea of a loss of income involves that more money has been spent than has been received on income account during the period, the balance has in some sense been found out of capital: and to set the loss against taxable income, current or future, is to allow the depletion of capital to be made good at the expense of taxable income. On the other hand, the ascertainment of business profits at fixed intervals of twelve months is so arbitrary a process, considering the continuous nature of business operations, that method (2), which allows the carry-forward of loss, is an obvious concession to common sense. Theoretically, a carry-back against the taxed profits of past years would be equally reasonable, but the practical arguments against refunds of tax paid [77] are sufficient to lead us to reject any extension on these lines.

REPORT OF THE COMMITTEE ON THE TAXATION OF TRADING PROFITS

1951 Cmd. 8189

79. We have come to the conclusion that there is no sufficient reason for restricting the period within which business losses can be carried forward, and we accordingly recommend that *the owner of a business should be allowed to carry forward business losses and set them against subsequent profits from the business without time limit.*[78]

[77] Millard Tucker Report, 1951 Cmd. 8189, para. 80, *infra.*
[78] I.C.T.A. 1970, s. 171; N.B. the loss can only be set against subsequent profits of the *same* business: see *Ingram & Son Ltd.* v. *Callaghan* [1969] 1 W.L.R. 456; *Pritchard* v. *M.H. Builders (Wilmslow) Ltd.* [1969] 1 W.L.R. 409; *Wood Preservation Ltd.* v. *Prior* [1969] 1 W.L.R. 1077.

80. A number of our witnesses represented that the owner of a business should be allowed to carry back a loss and set it against earlier profits and thus obtain repayment of tax paid on those earlier profits. Objections of principle can be raised to this suggestion. It would introduce a novel proposition into the Income Tax if tax admittedly due for a particular year and correctly representing the taxpayer's capacity to pay for that year could be reclaimed by reference to circumstances arising in a later year. But whatever the theoretical merits or demerits of the proposal may be, we are of opinion that it must be rejected on practical grounds. In the case of a company there could be no justification for giving relief from tax on the profits of an earlier year where those profits had been distributed to shareholders in the form of a dividend. To meet this objection it might be suggested that the relief should be confined to tax on profits which had not been distributed by the company. Complicated provisions would, however, be necessary to determine out of what profits particular distributions came; in any event the test of distribution is one which could not be applied to a partnership and even less to a " one-man " business. Further, any proposal which involved the reopening of past years' liability is, in our view, exposed to very serious practical objections because of the additional work which it would cause both to the Inland Revenue and to the taxpayer and his advisers. We therefore reject the suggestion that there should be any general power to carry losses backwards.

81. This general conclusion is subject to one reservation. Cases arise where a business incurs a large loss in its last year and unless the taxpayer has a substantial income from other sources for that year he is, under the existing law, unable to obtain any relief. Particular hardship may arise where the loss can be regarded as in some sense artificial, *e.g.* where it arises because he is entitled for the last year to a substantial balancing allowance on the disposal of plant and machinery, industrial buildings, etc. The existing law recognises this problem in the special case of mines, oil wells, etc.; section 27 (3) of the Income Tax Act 1945, enables the annual allowances for capital expenditure on mining works, etc. to be recomputed for the last six years of the life of a mine or foreign concession. We think that the principle underlying this provision merits more general application and we recommend that *there should be a provision under which the owner of a business may carry back a loss incurred in the last year of business and set it against the assessments on that business for the three preceding years.*[79]

Note
Loss relief is now governed by I.C.T.A. 1970, ss. 168–180.

WESTWARD TELEVISION LTD. v. HART

Court of Appeal [1969] 1 Ch. 201; [1968] 3 W.L.R. 480; 112 S.J. 484; [1968] 3 All E.R. 91; 45 T.C. 11

SALMON L.J.: Common sense and even justice are perhaps uncertain guides in ascertaining the highly complicated and artificial rules which govern tax liability. However, I derive some comfort from the fact that the construction which my Lords put upon the relevant statutory provisions, and with which I agree, seems to me to be just and to make sense.

There is no doubt that the taxpayer company made a loss from August 1, 1960, when it started to trade, until April 28, 1961, of some £132,000. Then in the ensuing twelve months up to April 30, 1962, it made a profit of £165,000

[79] I.C.T.A. 1970, s. 174.

odd. It paid no tax in respect of its first year's trading, which ended on July 31, 1961. For the fiscal year 1961–62 its liability to tax was assessed on the basis of its first year's trading ending July 31, 1961. By a time apportionment there was a profit shown from April 29, 1961, to July 31, 1961, of some £41,000. The loss from August 1, 1960 to April 28, 1961, was £132,000. As a result, there was a loss for the first year's trading and accordingly for the fiscal year 1961–62 of some £91,000, and the assessment was a nil assessment. The tax position for the year 1962–63 was assessed on exactly the same basis in accordance with the provisions of section 127 (2) (b) of the Income Tax Act 1952.[80] It is quite plain that if the loss to which I have referred had not been taken into account for the fiscal years 1961–62 and 1962–63, the company would have been assessable to tax on a profit of some £41,000 in each of those years. It is only by taking the loss into account in each year that, at any rate in a broad sense, the company has to that extent been relieved from tax. It is agreed that for the year 1964–65 it was relieved to the tune of nearly £36,000; and it was relieved also, under section 341[81] for 1960–61, in respect of some £4,000. Accordingly, the Crown's case is that, having been relieved to the extent of £41,000 in each of the years 1961–62 and 1962–63, there is now left only £9,000 of the loss in the first year available for relief.

Those figures, as figures, are I think agreed. The real fight is as to whether or not £41,000 can be treated as tax relief in each of the second and third years. As I understand Mr. Rees' very able argument, he says that under section 342[82] there can be relief against nothing except tax liability. Accordingly, before you come to the question of whether there is relief, you have to see whether there is any tax liability in respect of which relief can be claimed; and you can only solve that question by computing the profits or losses for the year. Mr. Rees says that in computing the profit or loss for the year it may be that you take into account the loss from a former year, but that is a method of computation, and if that method of computation shows you that there is no tax payable, there is nothing against which relief can be applied. But in the end this argument seems to me to attach altogether too artificial a meaning to the word " relief " in section 342.

The material words of section 342 are :

> " Where a person has . . . sustained a loss . . . in respect of which relief has not been wholly given . . . any portion of the loss for which relief has not been so given shall be carried forward and, as far as may be, deducted from or set off against the amount of profits or gains on which he is assessed under Schedule D . . . for subsequent years of assessment."

In a real sense it seems to me that this company has used the loss or part of the loss of £132,000 to obtain relief from tax liability for the second and third years of its trading. As I have said, but for using that loss, it would have been assessed in each of those years for tax on profits of £41,000. If Mr. Rees is right, the most astonishing results would follow, for, having taken the loss of £132,000 into account in the second and third years, it shows a trading loss of some £91,000 in each of those years. Although his client company has been magnanimous enough not to claim it, Mr. Rees concedes that if his argument is correct, not only could it benefit from the loss of £132,000 which it utilised in the second and third years, but it could in addition claim relief in respect of the £91,000 loss which it showed in each of those years. So it could in effect utilise not only the £132,000 loss but also about another £180,000 of loss to reduce its liability to tax. That seems a very startling result.

[80] Now I.C.T.A. 1970, s. 115.
[81] Now I.C.T.A. 1970, s. 168.
[82] Now I.C.T.A. 1970, s. 171.

I do not feel disposed to construe the word " relief " in section 342 so strictly and so artificially as to lead to such a result, unless compelled to do so by authority. Far from being obliged to do so, the very point that has arisen for decision in this case fell to be decided some 36 years ago in the Court of Session in Scotland in *Commissioners of Inland Revenue* v. *Scott Adamson.*[83] In that case the argument which has been advanced here on behalf of the taxpayer company was rejected. So far as I know, during the last 36 years that decision has never been questioned in any reported case, and it is of considerable persuasive authority. Lord Evershed M.R. pointed out in *Abbott* v. *Philbin* [84] that it is of great importance that, if possible, the Income Tax Acts which apply equally to Scotland as they do to England, should be interpreted in the same way on both sides of the border. Therefore, unless there is some compelling reason for differing from the decision of the Court of Session, we ought to follow it. There is no such reason. The judge entertained some doubt about it. I confess that I have some slight doubts myself, but they certainly are not such doubts as would justify me in refusing to follow it. I would, accordingly, dismiss the appeal.

6. Capital Allowances

For an item of expenditure to be deductible by a trader it must be of a revenue, rather than of a capital nature. However, relief from taxation may be given in respect of capital expenditure by means of the system of capital allowances, the appropriate allowance being set against taxable profits rather as in the manner of relieving losses. The system of capital allowances, which has been subjected to frequent changes, is the product of two distinct motives.[85] There is the political, or economic, object of encouraging investment, and the fiscal motive, which recognises that depreciation of capital assets has to be made good from revenue profits, justifying the setting off of the cost of investment against income tax. Two types of problem have to be solved in any system of capital allowances:

  (i) the form which the system takes, *i.e.* cash grant or allowance against tax, the apportionment of relief as between initial expenditure and periodic writing-down, etc.
  (ii) the definition of the classes of expenditure which qualify for relief.

GOVERNMENT WHITE PAPER—" INVESTMENT INCENTIVES "

1970 Cmnd. 4516

1. It is the Government's objective to secure an improvement in the long-term rate of growth of the economy. This calls for the creation of an economic climate within which individual firms can plan with confidence an expansion of their output and for the removal of obstacles which are likely to discourage or impede such expansion. A sustained improvement in the rate of economic

---

[83] (1933) 17 T.C. 679.
[84] [1960] Ch. 27.
[85] " Indeed the existing relief springs as much from economic policy as from any considera-tion of the correct principles of computing profits." Report of the Committee on the Taxation of Trading Profits, 1951 Cmd. 8189, § 192. For the most recent proposals, see the White Paper, " Industrial and Regional Development," 1972 Cmnd. 4942.

growth, while at the same time keeping Britain competitive, depends on both the level and the effectiveness of investment, and the Government intend to create the conditions which are essential to achieving this. Investment incentives can play some part in stimulating investment both by increasing the profitability after tax of new projects and by reinforcing the cash flow needed to finance those projects. Experience has shown, however, that their effect is uncertain, and they cannot by themselves be expected to create the conditions under which new investment is likely to be profitable and therefore attractive to firms. In the Government's view investment incentives should be seen as one element of their general economic policies intended to create an economic climate favourable to investment. It is against this background that the Government have been considering the desirable future pattern of investment incentives.

Note
See also now the White Paper, "Industrial and Regional Development," 1972 Cmnd. 4942.

REPORT OF THE COMMITTEE ON THE TAXATION OF TRADING PROFITS

1951 Cmd. 8189

194. In considering the question we have borne in mind that Income Tax is a tax on income; the existing Income Tax code neither taxes capital gains nor gives relief for capital losses. Nevertheless we do not think that there is any real contradiction between the general principle we have enunciated and the rule that no relief should be given in respect of capital losses. Assets may either diminish or increase in value as the result of wholly extraneous circumstances having no connection with their use in the business. On the other hand, the wastage which we have in mind is that which is caused by the natural process of decay or exhaustion through use, for example, the physical deterioration suffered by a building or the exhaustion of mineral deposits. If a manufacturer buys a piece of land and erects a factory on it, the factory will depreciate over a period of years, and on our principle he ought to get an allowance in respect of that depreciation. The site of the factory, however, may not depreciate in value at all; even if it does, the depreciation will not be through use. He may indeed find that after a period of years the site is not so valuable as it was when he bought it because, owing to a change in population, the value of land in that particular locality has gone down. If on winding up his business, or moving his business to some other place, he incurs a loss on the sale of that site, the loss is not a loss incurred in the course of business but is a capital loss in respect of which the existing Income Tax code should give no relief. Relief in respect of such a loss would be appropriate only if the tax system imposed liability on any appreciation in the value of the site.

. . . 195. The translation into practice of this distinction between depreciation through use and fluctuation in value is not always easy. Where there is a reduction in the value of plant and machinery, the existing law does not in general attempt to draw any distinction between the two factors. Thus under Rule 7 of Cases I and II, the owner of a business is in certain circumstances entitled to an allowance in respect of the cost of replacing obsolete machinery or plant; the allowance is computed by deducting from the cost of the replaced machinery or plant (*a*) any wear and tear allowances given on it and (*b*) any proceeds of sale; but cannot exceed the cost of the new machinery or plant. This Rule has largely been superseded by the more recent system of balancing allowances introduced by the Income Tax Act 1945, the effect of which is that, when plant or machinery is discarded or sold, any part of the net cost in respect of which relief has not already been given can be written off; it is irrelevant that part of the fall in value may be attributable not to physical depreciation, but to changes in fashion or methods of manufacture or to movements of population. Any attempt to take account of the distinction in computing depreciation allowances would, of course, be quite impracticable in the case of plant and machinery and we are not suggesting that the attempt should be made. The distinction is, however, important because it points to the complete exclusion from relief of those classes of assets which, though their value may fluctuate, cannot in any sense be said to be used up or consumed in the course of carrying on the business, thus making it clear from the outset that they cannot qualify for a writing-off or depreciation allowance of any kind. An obvious and important class of asset of this kind is land, and it is perhaps desirable to emphasise that, subject to certain special cases with which we shall deal separately later, we do not recommend any writing-off allowance for land as such. A further example is the goodwill of a business. This may also fluctuate in value, but we do not think it can be said to be used up or consumed wholly or partly in the course of carrying on the business. We do not, therefore, recommend any writing-off allowance in respect of goodwill.

196. With regard to other types of expenditure which, under the present law, fall to be treated as capital expenditure, some general observations will indicate how we have approached the question.

197. The main reason for disallowing any deduction in respect of capital expenditure, using that expression in its strict meaning, is, of course, that no initial loss is incurred by such expenditure; it represents merely the conversion of one asset, usually money, into another asset which presumably is of the same value as the price paid. The meaning of capital expenditure has, however, been extended to cover expenses which are incidental to the acquisition of a capital asset, for example, stamp duties and legal costs on the acquisition of property. In effect those incidental expenses are treated as part of the total cost of the asset acquired, and, generally speaking, this treatment is sanctioned by established accountancy principles.

198. There are two other types of expenditure which taxation law also treats as capital expenditure and for which, in general, it refuses any allowance. One is expenditure incurred to acquire or create what has been described as " an enduring benefit "; the other is expenditure incurred in an unsuccessful attempt to acquire a capital asset, so that the expenditure has in effect been abortive. These two types require examination and are dealt with in more detail later in this chapter.

Note
There have been many changes in the system since 1951, and the view taken was considered too narrow by the Radcliffe Committee, 1955 Cmd. 9474, paras. 322–325. The extract quoted does, however, illustrate some of the inherent problems.

HINTON v. MADEN & IRELAND LTD.

House of Lords [1959] 1 W.L.R. 875; 103 S.J. 812; [1959] 3 All E.R. 356; 38 T.C. 391

Knives and lasts used in the manufacture of shoes were held to be " plant " and the expenditure was of a capital nature, despite their comparatively short life.

LORD REID: . . . Under subsection (1) an investment allowance can only be made in respect of capital expenditure on new assets. It is not disputed that these knives and lasts were new assets: the word " new " is used in contrast to second-hand. The contention of the Crown is that the cost of acquiring these assets was not capital expenditure. Subsection (3) contains a further limitation: the new assets must be new machinery or plant.

. . . I am certainly not going to attempt a definition of capital expenditure on the one hand or of revenue expenditure on the other. Like most ordinary English words or expressions they are probably incapable of exact definition, and I must look at the whole circumstances and determine as a matter of construction into which class this expenditure falls. As the first step I would ask what is the practical difference between treating an item of expenditure as capital or as revenue expenditure. I claim no expert knowledge of accountancy or of business methods, and the only practical difference that occurs to me— and none other was suggested in argument—is that if you treat a sum as capital expenditure you do not write it all off in one year or set it all against the income of one year, whereas if you treat it as revenue expenditure the whole of it is set off against the revenue of the year when it is expended.[86] If the money had been expended on stock-in-trade and the thing bought is still there at the end of the year, you carry forward the value of the stock-in-trade at the end of the year. But these knives and lasts were not stock-in-trade and I do not know how their value at the end of the year could be carried forward in a profit and loss account if they are plant, and the cost of them has been treated as revenue expenditure.

. . . Subject to one point, I have no doubt that these knives and lasts are plant in the ordinary sense of the word. It is true that they are numerous, small and cheap. But one trader may have to use a few large articles while another may have to use a large number of small articles, and I see no good ground for distinguishing between them as regards investment allowance. The one point is the durability of these articles. When Lindley L.J. used the phrase " permanent employment in the business "[87] he was using it in contrast to stock-in-trade which comes and goes, and I do not think that he meant that only very long-lasting articles should be regarded as plant. But the word does, I think, connote some degree of durability and I would find it difficult to include articles which are quickly consumed or worn out in the course of a few operations. There may well be many borderline cases, but these articles have an average life of three years, and if their cost can fairly be called capital expenditure I cannot refuse to them the description of " plant " unless the Act discloses some special reason for doing so. The word " invest-ment " may indicate a rather longer duration than what might be sufficient in other cases, but it seems to me that machinery could not be disqualified for investment allowance because it only had a life of three years, and I see no reason why a stricter test as to durability should be applied to plant than to machinery when the Act appears to treat them on an equal footing. . . .

Note

It was the taxpayer in this case who claimed that the expenditure was of a capital nature. Sometimes the capital allowance system has given total relief *greater* than the amount of actual expenditure and it may then be actually more advantageous to treat expenditure as capital than as revenue.

---

[86] *Cf.* Lord Reid's own remarks in *Regent Oil Co. Ltd.* v. *Strick* [1966] A.C. 295, *ante*, p. 169.

[87] In *Yarmouth* v. *France* (1887) 19 Q.B.D. 647.

I.R.C. v. BARCLAY CURLE & CO. LTD.

House of Lords [1969] 1 W.L.R. 675; 113 S.J. 245; [1969] 1 All E.R. 732; 45 T.C. 237

Expenditure on the construction and excavation of a dry dock was held to be expenditure on " machinery or plant."

LORD GUEST: . . . To qualify for the allowance of three-tenths under Chapter II the expenditure must be incurred on the provision of plant. There is no definition of the word " plant " in the Act. The *locus classicus* for the definition of " plant " is in the words of Lindley L.J. in *Yarmouth* v. *France* [88]:

" . . . in its ordinary sense, it includes whatever apparatus is used by a business man for carrying on his business—not his stock-in-trade which he buys or makes for sale; but all goods and chattels, fixed or moveable, live or dead, which he keeps for permanent employment in his business. . . ."

This definition has been accepted as accurate for income tax purposes as recently as 1959 by Lord Reid in *Hinton* v. *Maden & Ireland Ltd.*[89] In the case of *Yarmouth* v. *France* it was held that a horse was " plant " in a question under the Employers' Liability Act 1880. It has been suggested that for that reason the definition is not apposite when considering " plant " in its present context. But, without attempting to elaborate the definition, it appears to me satisfactory. The emphasis is on " an apparatus used for carrying on business." . . .

[88] (1887) 19 Q.B.D. 647, 658.
[89] [1959] 1 W.L.R. 875, *supra*.

CHAPTER 10

SCHEDULE D, CASE VI

CASE VI of Schedule D is the " sweeping-up " Case, charging tax in respect of " any annual profits or gains not falling under any other Case of Schedule D, and not charged by virtue of Schedule A, B, C, or E." [1] Case VI fulfills a dual purpose: as a residual Case charging certain " annual profits or gains " not otherwise charged, and as the Case under which certain special types of income, or receipts which are to be treated as income, are specifically directed to be charged, *e.g.* post-cessation receipts,[2] balancing charges and capital profits on sale of patent rights,[3] tax chargeable in respect of revocable settlements,[4] assets transferred to persons abroad,[5] receipts under certain other anti-avoidance provisions,[6] and certain balancing charges in respect of capital allowances.[7]

1. Annual Profits or Gains

RYALL v. HOARE

King's Bench Division (*ante*, p. 76)

ROWLATT J.: In these two cases the question for decision is whether two directors of a limited company who received sums by way of commission for guaranteeing the company's overdraft with its bankers are liable to be assessed to income tax under the Sixth Case of Schedule D in respect of those commissions. The Special Commissioners for Income Tax have discharged the assessment, and from their decision the Crown appeals.

The facts are that the company, which was in want of money at the time, asked the directors to give a personal guarantee to the company's bankers in consideration of an increase from 5,000*l.* to 10,000*l.* in the company's overdraft. The directors, although unwilling to do this, ultimately consented. The transaction was not one in which the directors were interested as a matter of business, and one of them, who is a solicitor, declares that he never previously entered upon such a transaction and in all probability would never again do so. Therefore, although the circumstances are that they are men of affairs and that the company is engaged in business, in view of the facts found by the Special Commissioners and included in the case stated I must treat the case as if a person who was not connected with business at all received a commission from another person also not connected with business, in return for the favour of

---

[1] I.C.T.A. 1970, s. 109. For the relationship with other Cases and Scheds., see *Asher* v. *London Film Productions Ltd.* [1944] K.B. 133; *Fry* v. *Salisbury House Estate Ltd.* [1930] A.C. 430; *ante*, p. 90.
[2] *Ibid.* ss. 143, 144.
[3] *Ibid.* ss. 379, 380, 385.
[4] *Ibid.* ss. 445–449; *post*, Chap. 15.
[5] *Ibid.* ss. 478–480.
[6] *Ibid.* ss. 486–488.
[7] Capital Allowances Act 1968, ss. 6, 12, 46.

guaranteeing his account at a bank. In these circumstances are these commissions received as "annual profits or gains" under Case 6? Two kinds of emolument may be excluded from Case 6. First, anything in the nature of capital accretion is excluded as being outside the scope and meaning of these Acts confirmed by the usage of a century. For this reason, a casual profit made on an isolated purchase and sale, unless merged with similar transactions in the carrying on of a trade or business is not liable to tax. "Profits or gains" in Case 6 refer to the interest or fruit as opposed to the principal or root of the tree. The second class of cases to be excluded consists of gifts and receipts, whether the emolument is from a gift *inter vivos*, or by will, or from finding an article of value, or from winning a bet. All these cases must be ruled out because they are not profits or gains at all. Without giving an exhaustive definition, therefore, we may say that where an emolument accrues by virtue of service rendered whether by way of action or permission, such emoluments are included in "Profits or gains." Assuming then that these commissions constitute "profits or gains," the further question for consideration is whether they are "annual" profits or gains. The word "annual" may mean "annually recurring," as applied to the seasons of the year, or "recurring over a long period of years": or it may mean "lasting only for one year," as we speak of certain flowers as annuals which must be sown afresh every year: or, as in the case of interest on a sum of money, it may mean "calculated with reference to a year." In the present case the transaction did last for a year and was renewed for another year, although it did not so continue of its own accord, but by agreement between the parties. I do not think that any of those meanings are applicable to the word "annual" as used in Case 6. Now one is not entirely left without guidance, at any rate as a matter of practice. It has been recognised that if a furnished house is let even for a few weeks during the season in any one year, the letting will attract income tax under Case 6 on the profit so made: the principle of this has never been ruled upon by decision of the Courts, but it has been tacitly assumed that this is so by the Courts in Scotland, and I do not think it is now open to a Court of first instance, at any rate, to say that this practice is wrong. The letting in such a case is not recurring yearly, nor does it last for a year, nor is it calculated with reference to a year, but only with reference to the requirements of a few weeks. Similarly, when a person is appointed for a few weeks to an office to perform some services not in the nature of a trade or business in consideration of a lump sum (as for instance a Judge's marshal) income tax is deducted. Nor does it afford a clear explanation of this to say that the servant is taxed in such cases as being the holder of an "office"; for the tax on an office is calculated on the annual amount of profits. The word "annual" here can only mean "calculated in any one year," and "annual profits or gains" mean "profits or gains in any one year or in any year as the succession of years comes round." [8]

This case raises the whole question of the meaning of the expression "casual profits." I have already referred to the case of the letting of a furnished house, and other illustrations were referred to in the course of argument. I need only mention the case of casual authorship, as where a person who is neither a journalist nor an author by profession is called in by a firm of publishers to write a single book or a single article for reward. There again the amount which it is sought to tax is an instance of casual profits, but yet is liable to tax under Case 6 in the same way as the rent received in the letting of a furnished house, or as the commissions paid to the directors who gave the guarantee in the present case.

[8] For a similar view of the word "annual," see *Martin* v. *Lowry* [1927] A.C. 312; *ante*, pp. 149, 152. See also *Lyons* v. *Cowcher* (1926) 10 T.C. 438; *Sherwin* v. *Barnes* (1931) 16 T.C. 278; *Wilson* v. *Mannooch* (1937) 21 T.C. 178.

2. Capital and Income

For a profit or gain to be taxable under Case VI, it must be of an income nature. A capital profit on an isolated transaction does not fall within the Case.

JONES v. LEEMING

House of Lords [1930] A.C. 415; 99 L.J.K.B. 318; 143 L.T. 50; 46 T.L.R. 296; 74 S.J. 247; [1930] All E.R.Rep. 584; *sub nom. Leeming* v. *Jones*, 15 T.C. 333

LORD THANKERTON : My Lords, the respondent was one of a syndicate of four who in August 1925, secured an option of purchase—apparently without any payment for the option—of a rubber estate in the Federated Malay States at the price of 26,000*l*.; their object was the promotion of a company to whom the estate should be sold at a profit to the syndicate. Finding the estate too small for their purpose, they acquired in September 1925, an option of purchase on a neighbouring estate, again apparently without any payment, at the price of 35,000*l*. The company was thereafter formed and the options transferred to it. The result of the syndicate's operations was a net profit, after deduction of expenses, of which the respondent's share was 603*l*. 10*s*., which is claimed by the Crown as chargeable to income tax as being profits or gains comprised in Schedule D of the Income Tax Act 1918, that is to say, either profits or gains from a trade, adventure or concern in the nature of trade within the category of Case I of Schedule D or other profits or gains within the category of Case VI of Schedule D.

The General Commissioners upheld the assessment, but their finding was inconclusive as to whether the case fell within Case I or Case VI of Schedule D, and Rowlatt J., before whom the respondent's appeal came, remitted the stated case to the Commissioners for them " to find whether there was or not a concern in the nature of trade." The Commissioners then made a supplementary finding as follows—namely: " The Commissioners having considered the evidence and arguments submitted as to what took place in the nature of organising the speculation, maturing the property and disposing of the property and after due consideration of the facts and arguments submitted to them find that the transaction in question was not a concern in the nature of trade."

I agree with the view taken in both the Courts below that that finding was a finding in fact which excludes the application of Case I of Schedule D.

There remains Case VI, which brings into charge " any annual profits or gains not falling under any of the foregoing Cases and not charged by virtue of any other Schedule."

It is now settled that annual profits and gains taxable under Schedule D may be satisfied by profits falling within the year of charge and accruing during a period of less than a year: see *Martin* v. *Lowry*,[9] in which the opinion of Rowlatt J. on this point in *Ryall* v. *Hoare*[10] was approved. In that case Rowlatt J. said: " The word ' annual ' here can only mean ' calculated in any one year,' and ' annual profits or gains ' mean ' profits or gains in any one year or in any year as the succession of years comes round.' " While this is so, the isolated nature of a transaction, as opposed to a series of transactions of the same kind, will have a material bearing not only on the question as to whether it was a " trade, adventure or concern in the nature of trade," but also as to whether the profit arising therefrom was an accretion of capital or " profits or

9 [1927] A.C. 312; *ante*, pp. 149, 152.
10 [1923] 2 K.B. 447; *ante*, pp. 76, 219.

gains " within the meaning of the Income Tax Act, which connotes the idea of revenue or income.

In the present case two options for the purchase of real estate were acquired and disposed of within two months; the estates themselves were not taken up or dealt with in any way. This was a simple case of purchase and sale, once the Commissioners had decided that the transaction was not a concern in the nature of trade. I agree with Lawrence L.J. when he says [11]: " I have the greatest difficulty in seeing how an isolated transaction of this kind, if it be not an adventure in the nature of trade, can be a transaction *ejusdem generis* with such an adventure and therefore fall within Case VI. All the elements which would go to make such a transaction an adventure in the nature of trade, in my opinion, would be required to make it a transaction *ejusdem generis* with such an adventure. It seems to me that in the case of an isolated transaction of purchase and re-sale of property there is really no middle course open. It is either an adventure in the nature of trade, or else it is simply a case of sale and re-sale of property." . . .

VISCOUNT DUNEDIN: . . . Now, Case VI sweeps up all sorts of annual profits and gains which have not been included in the other five heads, but it has been settled again and again that that does not mean that anything that is a profit or gain falls to be taxed. Case VI necessarily refers to the words of Schedule D, that is to say, it must be a case of annual profits and gains, and those words again are ruled by the first section of the Act, which says that when an Act enacts that income tax shall be charged for any year at any rate, the tax at that rate shall be charged in respect of the profits and gains according to the Schedules.

The limitations of the words " profits and gains " were pointed out by Blackburn J. long ago in the case of *Attorney-General* v. *Black*,[12] when he said that profits and gains in Case VI must mean profits and gains *ejusdem generis* with the profits and gains specified in the preceding five Cases. And then there came the memorable and often quoted words of Lord Macnaghten in the *London County Council* case,[13] when he begged to remind people " that income tax is a tax on income." The only question, therefore, here was—Was there in any sense income? It is quite true that, as the counsel for the Crown said, the word " annual " does not mean something that recurs every year, but none the less the receipt must be of the nature of income. Lawrence L.J. put the matter very succinctly when he said [11]: " It seems to me that in the case of an isolated transaction of the sale and re-sale of property, there is really no middle course open. It is either an adventure in the nature of trade, or else it is simply a case of sale and re-sale of property." It was sought to assail this dictum by quoting *Cooper* v. *Stubbs*,[14] where there was a finding, as here, that no trade had been carried on and yet the tax was imposed. But the answer is simple, the whole point of *Cooper* v. *Stubbs* was that the transaction was not an isolated transaction. Warrington L.J. says that the transactions extended over a considerable period of years, and Atkin L.J. says that an annual profit or gain must be something which is of the nature of revenue or income, and he points out that the transactions in that case had been going on for eight years running. . . .

[11] [1930] 1 K.B. 279, 301, 302.
[12] (1871) L.R. 6 Ex. 308, 309. See also *Severn Fishery Board* v. *O'May* [1919] 2 K.B. 484, 490, *per* Rowlatt J.
[13] [1901] A.C. 26, 35; *ante*, p. 87.
[14] [1925] 2 K.B. 753, *infra*.

COOPER v. STUBBS

Court of Appeal (*ante*, p. 61)

Partners in a firm undertook a series of speculations by way of buying and selling cotton futures. The Special Commissioners held that the dealings were not so habitual and systematic as to constitute the carrying on of a trade, thus the profits were not assessable under Case I of Schedule D. They further held that the dealings were gambling transactions so that Case VI did not apply. On appeal, it was held that the Commissioners had directed themselves wrongly in regard to Case VI and that the profits were taxable under that Case.

WARRINGTON L.J.: . . . In my opinion this is not a case in which it can be said that there was no evidence upon which the Commissioners could arrive at that conclusion. I think, therefore, if it be material, that the finding of the Commissioners with regard to Case I is one which ought to be accepted.[15]

But then arises the second question, and on that, I think, the conclusion ought to be that the profits arising from the dealings in question are annual profits or gains under paragraph 1 (*b*) of Schedule D, and would be classified under Case VI, which is this: " Tax in respect of any annual profits or gains not falling under any of the foregoing Cases and not charged by virtue of any other Schedule." The Commissioners have come to the opposite conclusion, and I think they have done so on the ground, and on the ground alone, that these dealings were gambling transactions. In a sense they were gambling transactions,[16] but in my view that circumstance, on the facts of the present case, at any rate, is irrelevant. They were gambling transactions so far as the appellant is concerned, because, as the Commissioners have said, he entered into them without any intention of taking up actual cotton, or using the contracts as hedges for actual transactions; but they were not wagering contracts, for the reason to which I have already alluded, that, so far as the other parties to the contracts were concerned, there was no evidence whatever that from their point of view they were not real contracts for the purchase or sale of cotton. The question therefore is simply this, were these dealings and transactions entered into with a view to producing, in the result, income or revenue for the person who entered into them? If they were, then in my opinion profits arising from them were annual gains or profits within the meaning of paragraph 1 (*b*) of Schedule D. On the findings of the Commissioners themselves they were contracts entered into with a view to making a profit on a rise or fall, as the case may be, in the market price of the contracts. They extended over a considerable number of years. There were large numbers of transactions in each of those years, from which in some years the appellant derived considerable revenue; and for myself I cannot see what there is to exclude that revenue from the tax which is charged under Schedule D. It seems to me, therefore, that, in this case, whatever may be the case under different facts, at all events the profits made by these transactions are annual profits or gains, and must be assessable to income tax.

Note

This decision is rather unsatisfactory, but has been followed in a number of cases, *e.g. Townsend* v. *Grundy* (1933) 18 T.C. 140; *Leader* v. *Counsell* [1942] 1 K.B. 364, *infra.*; *cf. Whyte* v. *Clancy* (1936) 20 T.C. 679. The case was distinguished in *Jones* v. *Leeming* [1930] A.C. 415; *ante*, p. 221 (see the passage quoted from the speech of Viscount Dunedin).

[15] At first instance, Rowlatt J. concluded that the Commissioners' finding as to Case I ought *not* to be accepted. It is unlikely nowadays that there would not be a finding of trade.
[16] *Cf.* Atkin L.J., who held that they were not.

LEADER v. COUNSELL

King's Bench Division [1942] 1 K.B. 364; 111 L.J.K.B. 390; 167 L.T. 156; [1942] 1 All E.R.
435; 24 T.C. 178

Racehorse owners subscribed sums to purchase a stallion. Subscribers were entitled to send their nominated mares free of charge or to sell their " nominations " to other owners. The appellant sold his rights to nominate. It was held that he was not carrying on a trade but that the receipts were of an income nature and properly assessed under Case VI.

LAWRENCE J.: . . . As appears from the authorities, where the commissioners have found that there is no trade, the true question to be considered is whether the receipts in question are of the nature of income or revenue. That is indicated in *Ryall* v. *Hoare*.[17]

. . . In my opinion, however, there is nothing like a purchase and re-sale of goods or of any other property to be found in the transactions which gave rise to the receipts in question in the present case. The appellants did not buy the right to their nominations. They bought the horse. It is accurate to say that they sold the right to the nominations, but that was merely a way of realising the fruit of the purchase of the horse. In *Jones* v. *Leeming*,[18] another case of the purchase and re-sale of real estate, the Law Lords put the matter in very much the same way, though they referred to the dictum of Lawrence L.J. which I have quoted. Lord Buckmaster said : " Can the profits made in this case be described as income? "

. . . The true principle applicable here is that laid down in *Cooper* v. *Stubbs*,[19] namely, that where there is no trade it must be seen whether the receipts are of an income or revenue nature, and, if they are, they can be taxed under Case VI although they may be said to be from some aspects the purchase and re-sale of property. In the case before the court the transactions in question were not a purchase and a re-sale of property, but were merely a realisation of the reproductive faculties of Solario. . . .

Note
See also *Norman* v. *Evans* [1965] 1 W.L.R. 348.

3. Sale of Asset or Performance of Services?

Case VI has been said to apply to an " adventure in the nature of a profession," *i.e.* to charge remuneration received for the rendering of casual services.[20] In certain instances it may be difficult to say whether a receipt is in respect of the sale of an asset, and is of a capital nature, or is in respect of services, and chargeable as a revenue receipt.

HOBBS v. HUSSEY

King's Bench Division [1942] 1 K.B. 491; 111 L.J.K.B. 404; 167 L.T. 155; [1942] 1 All E.R.
445; 24 T.C. 153

LAWRENCE J.: In this case the commissioners have held that the appellant,

---

17 [1923] 2 K.B. 447; *ante*, pp. 76, 219.
18 [1930] A.C. 415; *ante*, p. 221.
19 [1925] 2 K.B. 753; *ante*, pp. 61, 223.
20 As in *Ryall* v. *Hoare* [1923] 2 K.B. 447; *ante*, pp. 76, 219; *Sherwin* v. *Barnes* (1931) 16 T.C. 278; *Wilson* v. *Mannooch* (1937) 21 T.C. 178.

a solicitor's clerk, who has never carried on the profession of an author, is assessable under Case VI of Schedule D in respect of a sum of money received from the People newspaper for the serial rights in his life story.

It was contended for the appellant that the transaction was a sale of the copyright of the series of articles and, therefore, resulted in the realisation of capital and was not a revenue receipt, and the case of *Earl Haig's Trustees* v. *Inland Revenue Commissioners* [21] was relied on. The Solicitor-General, while not admitting that *Earl Haig's Trustees* v. *Inland Revenue Commissioners* was rightly decided, argued that it is distinguishable and that it was settled by *Ryall* v. *Hoare* [22] so far as courts of first instance are concerned, that profits from a single article by a person who is not an author are assessable under Case VI of Schedule D. He also submitted that the true question in such cases is whether the transaction in question is really a sale of property or the performance of services, that the present transaction falls into the latter category, and that profits therefrom are therefore of a revenue nature.

In my opinion, the test suggested is correct. Any sale of property where no concern in the nature of trade is carried on must result in the realisation of capital: compare *Ryall* v. *Hoare, per* Rowlatt J.: and it is also true, in my opinion, that the performance of services, although they may involve some subsidiary sale of property (*e.g.* dentures sold by a dentist) are in their essence of a revenue nature since they are the fruit of the individual's capacity which may be regarded in a sense as his capital but are not the capital itself. Does then the fact that the present transaction involved the sale of the copyright in the appellant's series of articles constitute the profits therefrom capital, or is such sale merely subsidiary to what was in its essence a performance of services by the appellant? In my opinion, the true nature of the transaction was the performance of services. The appellant did not part with his notes or diaries or his reminiscences. He could re-publish the very articles themselves so long as they were not in serial form, and, on the whole, I am of opinion that the profits he received were of a revenue nature and not the realisation of capital. In the case of *Earl Haig's Trustees* the facts were totally different. The trustees possessed diaries of unique importance and great value, and the view of the Court of Session was that these diaries were capital assets and that the trustees had realised some part of such assets. The court had not to consider the profits received by the author of the book, nor could it be said that from the point of view of the trustees the sale was subsidiary to the performance of services by them.

In any event, in view of the decision of *Ryall* v. *Hoare* approved, as it was, by the Court of Appeal in *Martin* v. *Lowry* [23] and adhered to by Rowlatt J. in *Sherwin* v. *Barnes*,[24] I consider that I ought to follow the dicta of Rowlatt J.[22] which are directly in point and were approved by the Court of Appeal. The appeal will, therefore, be dismissed, with costs. . . .

Note

See also *Housden* v. *Marshall* (1958) 38 T.C. 233; *cf. Withers* v. *Nethersole* [1948] 1 All E.R. 400.

[21] 1939 S.C. 676. It is perhaps surprising that the receipt in that case was held to be of a capital nature since there was no outright sale of the diaries, which were retained by the Trustees.

[22] [1923] 2 K.B. 447; *ante*, pp. 76, 219.

[23] [1926] 1 K.B. 550; *ante*, pp. 149, 152.

[24] (1931) 16 T.C. 278.

SCOTT v. RICKETTS

Court of Appeal [1967] 1 W.L.R. 828; 111 S.J. 297; [1967] 2 All E.R. 1009; 44 T.C. 319

LORD DENNING M.R.: . . . Mr. Ricketts is an auctioneer and estate agent in Bristol. In 1959 a company called Ravenseft Properties Ltd. paid him the sum of £39,000. The question is whether he is taxable on it or not. The revenue sought to charge him under Case I or Case II of Schedule D. They said it was part of the profits of his trade or profession. That claim was rejected by the special commissioners. The Crown accepts their decision on that point. Alternatively, the revenue sought to charge him under Case VI of Schedule D. They said that the £39,000 was an " annual profit or gain " not falling under any other head. The Special Commissioners rejected this claim. They held that it was a gratuitous payment of a non-revenue nature. The judge reversed their decision. He held that the £39,000 was taxable under Case VI as an annual profit. Mr. Ricketts appeals to the court.

The facts relating to it are set out in the special case and in the report of the court below.[25] I need only summarise them here.

The Bristol Co-operative Society employed Mr. Ricketts in very complicated negotiations with the Bristol Corporation. The Bristol Co-operative Society's shop in Castle Street had been destroyed by bombs. The corporation proposed to acquire that site compulsorily for £575,000. Having been bombed out of Castle Street, the co-operative society had a strong claim that the corporation should provide them with another site. The corporation realised this and offered to let the co-operative society a site in Merchant Street for 99 years at a rent of £25,000. But before the deal went through, Mr. Ricketts discovered a site, called the " Jacey " site, which would suit the co-operative society much better. The rent was half that of the proposed Merchant Street site. So the co-operative society got Mr. Ricketts to negotiate for the Jacey site in his own name. If they were successful in getting the Jacey site, they would not need the Merchant Street site. So Mr. Ricketts proposed that he, with his father, should form a company to take over the Merchant Street site. But about the same time there was another company interested in the Merchant Street site, called Ravenseft Properties Ltd., and it was proposed that they might come in jointly with the Ricketts in acquiring it. Eventually a settlement was reached whereby: (i) the corporation paid over £500,000 to the co-operative society for the old Castle Street site; (ii) the corporation let the Jacey site to the co-operative society; (iii) the corporation let the Merchant Street site to Ravenseft Properties Ltd. The co-operative society paid Mr. Ricketts's fees for his professional services in these respects. These fees were included in his profits and gains, and he has paid tax on them. But, in addition to that remuneration, Ravenseft Properties Ltd. also paid him a sum of £39,000. The reason for this payment appears to be as follows: the parties thought that Mr. Ricketts had some sort of claim to an interest in the Merchant Street site. The reason was because at one stage in the negotiations it was proposed that he should take over the Merchant Street site, either on his own or jointly with Ravenseft. In the result Ravenseft took over the site themselves, and Mr. Ricketts was left with no interest in it. His ensuing claim may have been a business claim, a moral claim, or a legal claim. But whatever it was, he was bought out for £39,000. The reason for this payment was stated in this way in a letter of November 18, 1958, from Ravenseft to Mr. Ricketts:

> " In consideration of your withdrawing any claim you might have had to participate, and accepting the settlement between the Bristol Corporation and the Bristol Co-operative Society Limited on the terms outlined above

25 [1967] 1 W.L.R. 90; [1966] 3 All E.R. 791; 44 T.C. 303.

and agreeing at our request to execute such documents as we may be advised are necessary to record such withdrawal and acceptance, we are prepared to compensate you for the loss of your investment on the following basis "

and then there follow terms under which the sum of £39,000 was to be payable to Mr. Ricketts. Mr. Ricketts signed the letter accepting that proposal. So he withdrew any claim he might have had to participate in this proposed investment in return for the sum of £39,000. The one point now is whether this £39,000 is chargeable under Case VI. That Case is a " sweeping up " provision. It catches " annual profits or gains " which have not been caught by the other provisions. It is difficult to construe and we have to go by the decided cases.

In *Ryall* v. *Hoare* [26] Rowlatt J. staked out the guide-lines: and there have been other cases following it. Some things are clear. " Annual " profits does not mean profits which are made year by year. It is satisfied by profits made in one year only. " Profits and gains " include remuneration for work done, services rendered or facilities provided. They do not include gratuitous payments which are given for nothing in return. Nor do they include profits in the nature of capital gains. So they do not include gains made on purchase and sale of an asset. Such gains (except for recent legislation) are only taxable if the transaction was an adventure in the nature of trade.

The crux of the present case is that Mr. Ricketts had no legal ground to be paid anything. All he had—to use the judge's words—was a moral claim or a nuisance value. Ravenseft paid him £39,000 in order that he should not feel aggrieved, and to get rid of any possible claim. If they had paid this sum over to him as a gratuitous payment, it would not have come within Case VI. But because it was " dressed up " as a contract—to use the judge's own words—he has held that it is caught by Case VI. I do not think that is right. Take the case where a man has a good legal claim which he agrees to forgo in return for a sum of money, such as a claim for personal injuries which is compromised by payment of a lump sum. That is not an annual profit or gain within Case VI. It is the sale of an asset—namely, his legal claim—for a price. Next, suppose that the man has a claim which he believes to be good but which is in fact unfounded—and he agrees to forgo it in return for a sum of money. It might be a claim for personal injuries when has has no evidence of negligence. It is not strictly an " asset," because it would not stand up in the courts. But the compromise is binding. The payment has the same quality as if the claim were well founded. It is not an annual profit or gain within Case VI. Finally, take a man who has a moral claim but knows that he has no legal claim. He tries it on so as to see if the defendants will pay him something. They agree to buy him out so as to save the cost of fighting it. It seems to me that the payment for tax purposes has the same quality as that in a compromise. It is not an annual profit or gain within Case VI.

The judge seems to have thought that, as the payment was made under a contract, that was enough to bring it within Case VI. I cannot agree with him. It must be a contract for services or facilities provided, or something of that kind.

The present case is rather like *Leeming* v. *Jones*.[27] If the sum was taxable at all, it was taxable as part of the profits of Mr. Ricketts' trade or profession. Once that is negatived, it becomes simply a sum received in compromise of a disputed claim: whether legal or moral makes no difference.

I think that this case does not fall within Case VI. I would allow the appeal and restore the decision of the commissioners.

[26] [1923] 2 K.B. 447, 454; 39 T.L.R. 475; 8 T.C. 521; *ante*, pp. 76, 219.
[27] [1930] A.C. 415; *ante*, p. 221.

Note

This case presents a number of difficulties. A gratuitous payment, *e.g.* in respect of some past service and not in pursuance of any contract, would not normally be regarded as " income " at all: *Dickinson* v. *Abel* [1969] 1 W.L.R. 295; *Bloom* v. *Kinder* (1958) 38 T.C. 77; but see *post,* Chap. 11. If there is an enforceable contract for services, the remuneration is assessable: *Brocklesby* v. *Merricks* (1934) 18 T.C. 576; and see *Bradbury* v. *Arnold* (1957) 37 T.C. 665. It is, however, difficult to accept that a payment in respect of an enforceable contract for services can be dressed as a capital payment to extinguish a contractual right and thereby escape tax.

CHAPTER 11

EMOLUMENTS OF EMPLOYMENT

TAX under Schedule E is charged on the emoluments of any office or employment which fall under one of the three Cases into which the Schedule is divided. Cases II and III apply where some foreign element is involved; Case I applies to any emoluments for the chargeable period:

"where the person holding the office or employment is resident and ordinarily resident in the United Kingdom, and does not perform the duties of the office or employment wholly outside the United Kingdom in the chargeable period (and the emoluments are not excepted as foreign emoluments). . . ." [1]

The basic problems to be considered in relation to Schedule E are as follows:

(1) The meaning of "office" or "employment";
(2) the meaning of "emoluments";
(3) the deductions which are permitted to be made in determining the amount of the taxable emoluments.

1. "Office" or "Employment"

For an individual to be assessed to tax under Schedule E he must be the holder of an "office" or "employment." Despite the lack of statutory definition, it is, in most cases, not difficult to determine whether or not the performance of a particular activity constitutes the holding of an office or employment. Nevertheless there may be problems, particularly where the taxpayer concerned works for more than one person, either concurrently or consecutively. He may be the holder of a number of offices, or be employed by a number of persons; alternatively, his work may all be part of one profession which is carried on by him. It is clearly possible for a person to hold a number of offices or employments consecutively; it is equally possible to hold more than one at the same time and for a person who is carrying on a trade or profession simultaneously to hold one or more offices or employments in addition. Whichever is the case, it is essentially a question of *fact*.

McMILLAN v. GUEST

House of Lords [1942] A.C. 561; 111 L.J.K.B. 398; 167 L.T. 329; [1942] 1 All E.R. 606; 24 T.C. 190

The taxpayer, M., was a director of an English company. Under the Articles

[1] I.C.T.A. 1970, s. 181 (1).

of Association he was entitled to remuneration of 15 per cent. of the net profits. M. was resident in the U.S.A. and at no time attended board meetings in England. An assessment was made under Schedule E.

LORD ATKIN: . . . Schedule E to the Income Tax Act 1918, provides that " tax under Schedule E shall be charged in respect of every public office or employment of profit." By rule 6: " The tax shall be paid in respect of all public offices and employments of profit within the United Kingdom . . . *viz.* . . . offices or employments of profit under any company or society whether corporate or not corporate." It is necessary to consider whether the appellant (1) held an office; (2) held a public office [2]; (3) held a public office within the United Kingdom.[3]

(1) On the first point there was no dispute. There is no statutory definition of " office." Without adopting the sentence as a complete definition one may treat the following expression of Rowlatt J. in *Great Western Ry. Co.* v. *Bater*,[4] adopted by Lord Atkinson,[5] as a generally sufficient statement of the meaning of the word: " an office or employment which was a subsisting, permanent, substantive position which had an existence independent of the person who filled it, which went on and was filled in succession by successive holders." There can be no doubt that the director of a company holds such an office as is described. . . .

DAVIES v. BRAITHWAITE

King's Bench Division [1931] 2 K.B. 628; 100 L.J.K.B. 619; 145 L.T. 693; 47 T.L.R. 479; 75 S.J. 526; [1931] All E.R.Rep. 792; 18 T.C. 198

Miss Braithwaite was a well-known actress who, in the year of assessment in question, appeared on stage, film and radio in the United Kingdom and in the U.S.A.

ROWLATT J.: The question of principle in this case is whether the respondent ought to be assessed under Schedule D of the Income Tax Act 1918, as following her profession of an actress, or whether she ought to be assessed under Schedule E as exercising certain employments under the particular engagements which she makes.[6] The question is a difficult one, mainly because of the want of precision in the meaning of the term " employment " as it comes into this controversy.

The scheme of the Income Tax Acts used to be to include under Schedule D " profession, employment, or vocation." That was held to be a fairly comprehensive definition of the persons who carried on business on their own account. Under Schedule E were public offices. It was recognised that where a person was in a permanent situation it was much better to assess his salary as the salary

---

[2] The requirement that the office be a " public " office was removed by the Finance Act 1956. The requirement had, in any event, come to mean very little, *viz.* Rowlatt J. in *Great Western Ry. Co.* v. *Bater* [1920] 3 K.B. 266.

[3] It is not now the *office* which must be within the United Kingdom but the *duties* which must be performed here, if a non-resident is to be taxable under Case II of Sched. E: I.C.T.A. 1970, s. 181 (1).

[4] [1920] 3 K.B. 266, 274.

[5] [1922] A.C. 1, 15.

[6] The point of the case was that, if Sched. E applied to each engagement, the taxpayer's earnings abroad would only be taxable if remitted to this country. On the other hand, if she was carrying on one profession and Sched. D applied, then, as the profession was being carried on in this country, *all* the profits of the profession would be assessed.

of the situation than to go to him personally, and assess him in respect of his earnings. There were persons, like railway clerks, who were hired for an indefinite period. For the purposes of assessment to income tax they were treated as holders of offices. That was a very convenient method of assessment to income tax. Then a case arose (*Great Western Ry. Co.* v. *Bater*), in which I pointed out that these railway clerks were not holders of offices at all. I said that my own view was that Parliament in using this language in 1842 meant by an office a substantive thing that existed apart from its holder. It was something which had an existence independent of the person who filled it. It was something which was held by tenure and title rather than by contract and which continued to exist, though the holders of it might change and it was filled in succession by successive holders. The House of Lords decided that my view was right. It was, therefore, found convenient to put " employment " expressly in Schedule E.

When the word " employment " is used in connection with a profession or vocation in Schedule D it means the way in which a man employs himself. But " employment " in Schedule E means something different. In that Schedule it means something analogous to an office and which is conveniently amenable to the scheme of taxation which is applied to offices as opposed to the earnings of a man who follows a profession or vocation.

That unhappy word " employment " has now to be construed with reference to this case. The respondent is an actress, and, of course, the contract which an actor or actress, or any person whose livelihood is earned in that sort of way, has, is rather different from other contracts, as has been pointed out, because it involves that the employer under the contract is bound to let the actor or actress appear. But what is the criterion? The Solicitor-General has said a good deal with regard to the degree of skill and attainment which is required of a lady who is in a position to enter into agreements of this kind. I do not think that the question turns on the degree of skill at all. It seems to me that the most skilful and distinguished persons, whose qualifications are very rare in art or medicine, or any other profession where distinction is difficult to obtain, may well enter an " employment," and, if they take a situation for years and made it their life occupation, it would be no answer to a claim to assess them under Schedule E to say that they are very skilled and distinguished persons, because such very skilled and distinguished persons would be exercising an " employment " in the sense of Schedule E as much as anybody else who holds an office. On the other hand, if a very humble person takes a series of jobs for an hour or so each, he would be carrying on a trade. Nor is the mere duration of the engagement the criterion. An actress may make a contract for the run of a play, which might be a considerable time, but it would not necessarily thereby become " employment " within Schedule E.

It seems to me quite clear that a man can have both an employment and a profession at the same time, in different categories. A man may have the steadiest employment in the world by day and he may do something quite different in the evening and make some more money by the exercise of a profession or vocation. I cannot doubt that that would be so, and even if it were in the same sphere, I do not see why he should not have both an employment as well as a profession. For instance, a musician who holds an office or employment under a permanent engagement can at the same time follow his profession privately.

I have to formulate some line of cleavage and it seems to me that what I must glean my inspiration from is the purpose of the change from Schedule D to Schedule E in the Finance Act 1922, s. 18. I have to consider the effect of the change which was made in the different methods of raising income tax. It seems to me that when the Legislature took " employment " out of Schedule

D, and put it into Schedule E, alongside " Offices," the Legislature had in mind employments which were something like offices, and I thought of the expression " posts " as conveying the idea required. When a person occupies a post resting on a contract, and if then that is employment as opposed to a mere engagement in the course of carrying on a profession, I do not think that is a very difficult term of distinction, though perhaps a little difficult to apply to all cases. But I would go further than that and say that it seems to me that where one finds a method of earning a livelihood which does not consist of the obtaining of a post and staying in it, but consists of a series of engagements and moving from one to the other—and in the case of an actor's or actress's life it certainly involves going from one to the other and not going on playing one part for the rest of his or her life, but in obtaining first one engagement, then another, and a whole series of them—then each of those engagements cannot be considered an employment, but is a mere engagement in the course of exercising a profession, and every profession and every trade does involve the making of successive engagements and successive contracts and, in one sense of the word, employments.

In this case I think it is quite clear that the respondent must be assessed to income tax under Schedule D, because here she does not make a contract with a producer for a post. She makes a contract with a producer for the next thing that she is going to do, and then with another producer, and then a third producer, and at any time she may make a record for a gramophone company or act for a film. I think that whatever she does and whatever contracts she makes are nothing but incidents in the conduct of her professional career. Therefore, I think she is taxable under Schedule D.

With regard to the question whether the respondent's American earnings ought to be included in the assessment, I am not in a position to decide that, because I have no decision on it from the Commissioners. But the point was raised because it was contended on her behalf on the appeal to the General Commissioners against the Schedule D assessments that, as no remittances had been made to this country, she could not be assessed under Case V of Schedule D. I shall allow this appeal, but I shall send the case back to the Commissioners, at Miss Braithwaite's option, to have a decision by them on the question whether her American earnings ought to be included in the assessment under Schedule D.[7]

Note
See further, *Household* v. *Grimshaw* [1953] 1 W.L.R. 710, where an author's contract with a film company to spend twelve weeks each year producing novels, scenarios and adaptations *as directed* was held, by Upjohn J., to be an engagement forming part of his profession as author, rather than a separate office or employment.

I.R.C. v. BRANDER AND CRUICKSHANK

House of Lords [1971] 1 W.L.R. 212; (1970) 115 S.J. 79; [1971] 1 All E.R. 36; 46 T.C. 574

The taxpayers were a firm of Scottish advocates who, in addition to their general legal business, acted for some thirty to forty companies as secretaries and/or registrars. In the case of two particular companies, on ceasing to act as registrars the taxpayers received a terminal payment of £2,500.

LORD MORRIS OF BORTH-Y-GEST: My Lords, the special commissioners came to the conclusion, on the basis of the facts which they found, that the respondents'

---

[7] In a supplemental case, Finlay J. held that the American profits must be included.

appointments as registrars of Robert Lawson & Sons (Holdings) Ltd., and of its subsidiary company, Robert Lawson & Sons (Dyce) Ltd., were appointments to offices. The respondents were appointed as secretaries and registrars of both companies. In the case of one company the salary was £750 and in the case of the other it was £500. In regard to the time the respondents spent as secretaries and registrars of these two companies one-third of it related to their duties as secretaries and two-thirds to their duties as registrars. When proposals were made for taking over the shares held in the two companies the respondents were informed that, in the event of a take-over, they would be relieved of their secretaryships and registrarships. The arrangement that was later made, when the take-over took place, was that the respondents should cease to be registrars, should receive £2,500 upon such termination of their appointments as registrars but should continue for some time as secretaries of the two companies. They did so continue for some time and then voluntarily resigned their secretaryships.

A duty is imposed on a company to keep a register of members (Companies Act 1948, s. 110). Even though the Companies Act does not require that there should be an appointment as registrar, a company must arrange that some person or persons should on its behalf perform the statutory duties of maintaining its register. In doing so, it may establish a position which successively will be held by different persons. If it does so the company may have created what could rationally for income tax purposes be called an office. In *McMillan* v. *Guest* Lord Atkin, while pointing out that there is no statutory definition of " office," was prepared to accept what Rowlatt J. had said in *Great Western Ry. Co.* v. *Bater* (as adopted by Lord Atkinson) as being a generally sufficient statement of meaning. Rowlatt J. had referred to " a subsisting, permanent, substantive position, which had an existence independent of the person who filled it, and which went on and was filled in succession by successive holders." Lord Wright, in his speech in *McMillan* v. *Guest*, pointed out that regard must be had to the facts of any particular case and to the ordinary use of language and the dictates of common sense.

In my view, the special commissioners were warranted on the facts as they found them in deciding that the respondents' appointments as registrars of the two companies were appointments to offices.

Though in fact the fees which certain partners in the respondent firm received as directors of certain companies were, by reason of some arrangement that they made between themselves, included in the partnership income and though in fact the respondents' net receipts from all activities (including legal fees, directors' fees, secretarial salaries, managerial fees, business commissions and registrars' fees) were assessed to income tax under Case II of Schedule D, I think that it must follow from the decision of this House in *Mitchell and Edon* v. *Ross* [8] that tax was chargeable under Schedule E on the emoluments in respect of the two registrarships.

The payment of £2,500 was clearly made " in consideration or in consequence of or otherwise in connection with " the termination of the holding of the offices of registrar (see s. 37 (2) of the Finance Act 1960).[9] Unless it was a payment " otherwise chargeable to income tax " it would be a payment in respect of which income tax would be charged under Schedule E (see s. 37 (1)) but for the fact that by virtue of section 38 (3) tax is not to be charged in respect of a payment of an amount not exceeding £5,000. So the question arises

---

[8] [1962] A.C. 813; *ante*, p. 93. In that case, the taxpayers, who carried on the profession of medical practitioners also held " offices " as part-time consultants under the National Health Service. See also *Fuge* v. *McClelland* (1956) 36 T.C. 571, a case of two separate employments.

[9] Now I.C.T.A. 1970, s. 187.

whether the payment of £2,500 was "otherwise" chargeable to income tax. The presence of the words "not otherwise chargeable to income tax" in subsection (2) of section 37 (unless they were introduced unnecessarily or for reasons of caution) would appear to recognise that there could be payments coming within the words of subsection (2), which, independently of subsection (1) would be chargeable to tax. The words do not necessarily denote chargeability under a Schedule other than Schedule E. The contention of the appellants is that the offices were assets of the respondents' profession or vocation obtained in the course of carrying on such profession or vocation and that compensation for the loss of those assets should be treated as a receipt of the profession or vocation and taxable under Case II of Schedule D.

My Lords, I cannot think that the appointments to the offices of registrar were in any real sense to be regarded as assets of the respondents in respect of their profession. . . .

LORD DONOVAN: . . . One asks, therefore, why there should not be one global assessment under Case II of Schedule D? And the answer is the decision of this House in *Mitchell and Edon* v. *Ross*. I think it is to be clearly gathered from that decision that even if offices like these registrarships are collected and exercised by a taxpayer as part of his trade or profession, nevertheless, under the rule that each Schedule to the Income Tax Acts is completely self-contained and autonomous, the offices must be separately assessed under Schedule E.

In relation to a case like the present I cannot refrain from saying that I think this rule is quite unreal and serves no useful purpose. Indeed, its application to cases like the present will cause administrative chaos unless the law is changed. There can be no relevant difference between secretaryships and registrarships. Both are offices: and henceforth, if this decision is acted upon, there will have to be 30 to 40 separate Schedule E assessments in the present case, and the same number of claims for expenses "wholly exclusively and necessarily" incurred in the performance of the duties of each office. In England the position will be worse. There a partnership is not a separate legal entity, and cannot be separately assessed in one assessment except under Schedule D upon trading or professional profits. Accordingly, a firm of chartered accountants with, say, 20 partners, will have to be assessed in respect of the profits of each office as auditor by means of separate Schedule E assessments in each individual partner, who likewise will have to prove his deductible expenses. . . .

2. Emoluments

Emoluments are defined as including " all salaries, fees, wages, perquisites and profits whatsoever." [10] Thus not only money payments are included, but also other benefits which are not received in the form of cash. But not every payment made by an employer to an employee [11] is a taxable emolument.

(A) THE EMOLUMENTS MUST BE DERIVED FROM THE OFFICE OR EMPLOYMENT

Tax under Schedule E is charged " in respect of any office or employment

[10] I.C.T.A. 1970, s. 183 (1).
[11] For simplicity, the words "employment" and "employee" will be used to include " office " and " office-holder."

on emoluments therefrom." [12]   It is therefore necessary, in considering any
payment or benefit received by an employee, whether from his employer or
from some other person, to determine whether that payment or benefit is
derived from the employment or whether it is derived from some other
source. For example, a payment or benefit may be:

(i) a personal gift from the employer;

(ii) a gift made by some person other than the employer, again made
for personal reasons;

(iii) a contractual receipt not arising from the employment;

(iv) a payment made on or after termination of employment, which is
not made in consideration of past services or under the terms of
a service agreement, but is, for example, gratuitous or paid as
compensation or in respect of damages for wrongful termination of
the contract of service. [13]

HOCHSTRASSER v. MAYES

House of Lords [1960] A.C. 376; [1960] 2 W.L.R. 63; 104 S.J. 30; [1959] 3 All E.R. 817;
38 T.C. 673

The employer operated a scheme to assist employees to purchase a house.
If an employee was transferred within the company, he had the option to sell
his house to the company at a fair valuation and, in addition, the company
guaranteed him against any capital loss on the sale provided the house had
been kept in good repair. The taxpayer, M., bought a house in 1951 for £1,850.
In 1954 he was transferred to another factory and was only able to sell the
house for £1,500. The company paid him £350 under the guarantee. M. was
assessed on this amount under Schedule E.

VISCOUNT SIMONDS: . . . My Lords, if in such cases as these the issue turns,
as I think it does, upon whether the fact of employment is the *causa causans*,
or only the *sine qua non*, of benefit, which perhaps is only to give the natural
meaning to the word " therefrom " in the statute, it must often be difficult to
draw the line and say on which side of it a particular case falls. But I think that
the approach should not be exactly that of Parker L.J. It is for the Crown,
seeking to tax the subject, to prove that the tax is exigible, not for the subject
to prove that his case falls within exceptions which are not expressed in the
statute but arbitrarily inferred from it. Thus, in the present case it is for the
Crown to establish that a payment made under the housing agreement is a
reward for the employee's services. Let me interpolate that the addition of the
words " as such " adds nothing to the proposition. How, then, does the Crown
seek to prove its case? It does not, and could not, suggest that the agreement
is in any way colourable. Nevertheless it is driven to the argument that a payment made under it is a reward for services and nothing else. This argument
it fortifies by a close analysis of the benefit or detriment accruing to or suffered
by the employee, and concludes that no substantial consideration for the payment moves from the employee.

My Lords, I altogether dissent from this argument and conclusion. There
is nothing express or implicit in the agreement which suggests that the payment

[12] I.C.T.A. 1970, s. 181 (1).
[13] Certain payments of this nature made on retirement or removal from office or employment,
though not properly " emoluments," may nevertheless be taxed under Sched. E by virtue
of the provisions of I.C.T.A. 1970, ss. 187, 188; Finance Act 1972, s. 73.

is a reward for services except the single fact of the relationship of the parties, and it is clear enough from *Inland Revenue Commissioners* v. *Duke of Westminster* [14] that that fact alone will not justify such a conclusion. On the other hand, there is the significant fact that the salary earned by the employee compares favourably with salaries paid by other employers not operating a housing scheme, and is the same whether or not he takes advantage of the housing scheme. This at once suggests that there is some other reason for the payment than services rendered or to be rendered. . . .

LORD RADCLIFFE: . . . The test to be applied is the same for all. It is contained in the statutory requirement that the payment, if it is to be the subject of assessment, must arise " from " the office or employment. In the past several explanations have been offered by judges of eminence as to the significance of the word " from " in this context. It has been said that the payment must have been made to the employee " as such." It has been said that it must have been made to him " in his capacity of employee." It has been said that it is assessable if paid " by way of remuneration for his services," and said further that this is what is meant by payment to him " as such." These are all glosses, and they are all of value as illustrating the idea which is expressed by the words of the statute. But it is perhaps worth observing that they do not displace those words. For my part, I think that their meaning is adequately conveyed by saying that, while it is not sufficient to render a payment assessable that an employee would not have received it unless he had been an employee, it is assessable if it has been paid to him in return for acting as or being an employee. It is just because I do not think that the £350 which are in question here were paid to the respondent for acting as or being an employee that I regard them as not being profits from his employment.

The money was not paid to him as wages. The wages of employees are calculated independently of anything which they get under the housing scheme, and the I.C.I. salaries compare favourably with salaries paid by other employers in the chemical industry who do not operate a housing scheme. We are bound to say on the facts found for us that the source of the £350 was the housing agreement into which the respondent had entered on June 1, 1951, and that the circumstance that brought about his entitlement to the money was not any services given by him but his personal embarrassment in having sold his house for a smaller sum than he had given for it.

. . . The essential point is that what was paid to him was paid to him in respect of his personal situation as a house-owner, who had taken advantage of the housing scheme and had obtained a claim to indemnity accordingly. In my opinion, such a payment is no more taxable as a profit from his employment than would be a payment out of a provident or distress fund set up by an employer for the benefit of employees whose personal circumstances might justify assistance. . . .

LORD COHEN: . . . My Lords, on the facts of the present case I am satisfied that Jenkins L.J. was right when he said [15]: " I think it may well be said here that while the employee's employment by I.C.I. was a *causa sine qua non* of his entering into the housing agreement and, consequently, in the events which happened, receiving a payment from I.C.I., the *causa causans* was the distinct contractual relationship subsisting between I.C.I. and the employee under the housing agreement, coupled, of course, with the event of the declining in value." . . .

---

14 [1936] A.C. 1; *ante*, p. 23.
15 [1959] Ch. 22, 53–54.

Note
  Quaere whether I.C.T.A. 1970, s. 187, might apply to payments of this type. See G. S. A. Wheatcroft, " A Guide to Golden Handshakes " [1961] B.T.R. 23.
  See also *Jarrold* v. *Boustead* (*post*, p. 244); *Laidler* v. *Perry* (*post*, p. 239).

CLAYTON v. GOTHORP

Chancery Division [1971] 1 W.L.R. 999; 115 S.J. 266; [1971] 2 All E.R. 1311; [1971] T.R. 103

Under the terms of an agreement with her employer, the taxpayer's wife received a " loan " during a period of study for further qualifications, the " loan " becoming absolute, *i.e.* not repayable, if she returned to her former employment and remained for at least eighteen months. This she did.

Held, the amount of the " loan " was assessable as an emolument of her employment.

PLOWMAN J.: . . . The question therefore arises: when at the expiration of eighteen months, namely, on January 15, 1968, the £637 ceased to be repayable, what was it which turned the loan into an absolute payment? The consideration for the county council's making the loan in the first instance was the promise by Mrs. Gothorp [the taxpayer's wife] to follow the course of training and at its completion to serve the county council for a period of at least eighteen months. But what turned the loan into an absolute payment was that eighteen months' service. Clearly, in my judgment, it was a reward for past services and, as such, an emolument arising from Mrs. Gothorp's employment.

I think that the commissioners made the mistake of asking themselves the wrong question. They considered the question whether Mrs. Gothorp's right not to repay the loan stemmed from the loan agreement or from her contract of service, as if the answer to that question concluded the matter. But, in my opinion, it does not, because the right not to repay the loan might well stem from the loan agreement and yet be taxable as a reward for services, and that in my opinion is the true position. . . .

(i) *Gifts from Employers*

SEYMOUR v. READ

House of Lords [1927] A.C. 554; 96 L.J.K.B. 839; 137 L.T. 312; 43 T.L.R. 584; 71 S.J. 488; [1927] All E.R.Rep. 294; *sub nom. Reed* v. *Seymour*, 11 T.C. 625

VISCOUNT CAVE L.C.: . . . In the year 1920 the appellant, who had been for many years in the employment of the Kent County Cricket Club at a salary and had played fine cricket, was allowed by the club to have a benefit match, the match selected being the Kent v. Hampshire match played in the Canterbury week. The club's regulations for the staff contained the following provision:

" Benefits and Tours.

The committee reserve to themselves an absolute and unfettered discretion as regards benefit matches, the collection of subscriptions in connection with such matches, and dealing with the net proceeds of such matches in any way they may think desirable in the interest of the beneficiaire [*sic*]. The committee also reserve the like discretion in regard to granting permission to any player to go on winter tour and in regard to dealing with remuneration receivable by him on account of such tour."

The gate money received at the match in question, less some expenses, amounted to £939 16s. 11d., and this sum, together with other sums obtained by public subscription, was invested by the direction of the committee in certain securities, of which the income (less tax) for the years 1921, 1922 and 1923, was paid to the appellant. In the year 1923 the securities were realised and the proceeds, amounting (with the addition of certain other moneys) to £1914 14s. 5d., were paid to the appellant with a view to their being applied, with the approval of the committee, to the purchase of a farm. Thereupon the respondent, the inspector of taxes, made an assessment upon the appellant under Schedule E of the Income Tax Act 1918, in the sum of £939 16s., being the net gate money received from the benefit match, for the tax year 1920–21, and the question for your Lordships to determine is whether this assessment was valid.

In considering this question, I will assume that the appellant was assessable (if at all) under Schedule E of the Act. It would appear that in the year 1920–21 any assessment upon him must have been made, not under Schedule E, but under Schedule D (see *Great Western Ry Co.* v. *Bater* [16]); but the law was altered by the Finance Act 1922, and it has not been disputed that the assessment in the year 1923, if allowable at all, was properly made under Schedule E.

The question, therefore, is whether the sum of £939 16s. fell within the description, contained in rule 1 of Schedule E, of "salaries, fees, wages, perquisites or profits whatsoever therefrom " (*i.e.* from an office or employment of profit) "for the year of assessment," so as to be liable to income tax under that Schedule. These words and the corresponding expressions contained in the earlier statutes (which were not materially different) have been the subject of judicial interpretation in cases which have been cited to your Lordships; and it must now (I think) be taken as settled that they include all payments made to the holder of an office or employment as such, that is to say, by way of remuneration for his services, even though such payments may be voluntary, but that they do not include a mere gift or present (such as a testimonial) which is made to him on personal grounds and not by way of payment for his services. The question to be answered is, as Rowlatt J. put it: "Is it in the end a personal gift or is it remuneration? " If the latter, it is subject to the tax; if the former, it is not.

Applying this test, I do not doubt that in the present case the net proceeds of the benefit match should be regarded as a personal gift and not as income from the appellant's employment. The terms of his employment did not entitle him to a benefit, though they provided that if a benefit were granted the committee of the club should have a voice in the application of the proceeds. A benefit is not usually given early in a cricketer's career, but rather towards its close, and in order to provide an endowment for him on retirement; and, except in a very special case, it is not granted more than once. Its purpose is not to encourage the cricketer to further exertions, but to express the gratitude of his employers and of the cricket-loving public for what he has already done and their appreciation of his personal qualities. It is usually associated, as in this case, with a public subscription; and, just as those subscriptions, which are the spontaneous gift of members of the public, are plainly not income or taxable as such, so the gate moneys taken at the benefit match, which may be regarded as the contribution of the club to the subscription list, are (I think) in the same

---

[16] [1922] 2 A.C. 1.

category. If the benefit had taken place after Seymour's retirement, no one would have sought to tax the proceeds as income; and the circumstance that it was given before but in contemplation of retirement does not alter its quality. The whole sum—gate money and subscriptions alike—is a testimonial and not a perquisite. In the end—that is to say, when all the facts have been considered —it is not remuneration for services, but a personal gift.

I am of opinion that this appeal should succeed, and that the order of Rowlatt J. should be restored with costs here and below, and I move your Lordships accordingly.

Note

Cf. Moorhouse v. *Dooland* (*post*, p. 242) and *Corbett* v. *Duff* [1941] 1 K.B. 730, where benefit payments to a professional footballer were held to be taxable, being clearly made in respect of and as remuneration for the employment.

LAIDLER v. PERRY

Court of Appeal [1965] Ch. 192; [1964] 3 W.L.R. 709; 108 S.J. 480; [1964] 3 All E.R. 329; 42 T.C. 351; affirmed by House of Lords [1966] A.C. 16; [1965] 2 W.L.R. 1171; 109 S.J. 316; [1965] 2 All E.R. 121; 42 T.C. 351

LORD DENNING M.R.: This case raises the question whether Christmas presents which are made by an employer to an employee are taxable in the hands of the employee. In the lead industry there are a number of family businesses with long histories. For many years they have made Christmas gifts in kind to the staff. Before the war they gave turkeys to the office workers. They entertained the manual workers at Christmas festivities. When the lead industry was formed into a big concern, the group followed the same policy through the individual companies. They did it so as to maintain a feeling of happiness among the staff and goodwill. During the war these gifts in kind could not be continued, and National Savings Certificates vouchers were given instead. After the war, in 1948, a resolution was passed by the directors that they would revert to gifts in kind but obtainable by the staff through vouchers from various shops. Each of the employees was allowed a voucher for £10. Anyone who had worked for more than a year would get, at Christmas-time, a voucher for the sum of £10, which he could use at a shop of his choice and get an article as his Christmas gift. If he had not served ten months, he did not get a £10 voucher. The newcomers only got a voucher according to the number of months they had served. There were 2,300 people in the group who got a £10 voucher at Christmas.

The question arises whether each individual member of the staff is chargeable with tax under Schedule E in respect of his £10. We have two cases before us. Dr. Laidler, who is on the research side and who earns more than £2,000 a year; and Morgan, who earns less than £2,000 a year. The question in each case is whether this money's worth of £10 a year can properly be said to be emoluments from the employment. "Emoluments therefrom," are the words of section 156 of the Income Tax Act 1952. Emoluments includes "all salaries, fees, wages, perquisites and profits whatsoever," see Schedule 2, 1 (1) of the Finance Act 1956.

We have been taken through the cases. It was urged before us by Mr. Heyworth Talbot that the approach to these cases has been altered altogether by the House of Lords recently in *Hochstrasser* v. *Mayes*.[17] Mr. Heyworth Talbot said that before that case the test in the courts was simply this: Was

[17] [1960] A.C. 376; see *ante*, p. 235.

it a personal gift, or was it remuneration for services? It was assumed that it
must be one or the other. Whereas *Hochstrasser* v. *Mayes*, he said, showed
that there was a third possibility. The employers there did not make a personal
gift to the employee. They only made up to him his loss on selling his house.
It was held not to be taxable.

As I read the cases, however, including *Hochstrasser* v. *Mayes*, the one
question in all these cases is this: Was the payment made, or the money's
worth given, to the employee as a reward or remuneration or in return for his
services? If it was, it is taxable in his hands. That test explains the case of
the Easter offerings [18] (which are by custom a return for the services of the
parson), and the cricketer's benefit [19] (where a collection would be made for his
benefit if he had scored more than fifty runs), and the case of the huntsman's
tips (where money was collected for the huntsman on Boxing Day), see *Wright*
v. *Boyce*.[20]

In this case the commissioners made this finding: " The first question for
decision is whether the appellant is assessable under Schedule E in respect of
vouchers given to him annually at Christmas. As we understand the authorities
the value of the vouchers is so assessable only if they represent ' money's worth '
which was made available to the appellant in return for acting as or being an
employee, *i.e.* as a reward for his services "—a test which they took from the
very words of Lord Radcliffe's judgment in *Hochstrasser* v. *Mayes*. Having
asked themselves that question, they said: "After reviewing all the evidence and
the arguments based on the many authorities cited to us we hold that the
vouchers were made available in return for services rather than as gifts not
constituting a reward for services."

That finding of the commissioners can only be upset by this court if it is a
finding to which they could not have reasonably come. So I ask myself the
question whether this finding was unreasonable. I put this case in the course
of argument: Suppose it had been £100 a year which had been given to all
the staff of these companies each year at Christmas. In that case it would
clearly be open to the commissioners to find that it was a reward, a remuneration or a return for services rendered. But now suppose that, instead of £100,
it was a box of chocolates or a bottle of whisky or £2, it might be merely a
gesture of goodwill at Christmas without regard to services at all. So it is a
question of degree. It seems to me that in this case when one finds that £10
a year was paid to each of the staff year after year, each of them must have
come to expect the £10 as a regular payment, which went with their services.
It was, I think, open to the commissioners to find that it was made in return for
services. It is, therefore, taxable in the hands of the recipient. That is sufficient
to decide both cases.

I would only add in regard to Dr. Laidler (who was paid over £2,000), that
if there was any doubt on this point it is clear to me that this gift would be a
" benefit " within section 161 of the Income Tax Act 1952,[21] which would be
chargeable in his hands under the terms of that section.

For these reasons I think the judgment of Pennycuick J. was right and I
would dismiss the appeals.

LORD HODSON (in the House of Lords): . . . In this case the vouchers of £10
each were given every year to each member of the staff, including ex-members
who drew pensions. They were regular gifts, not gifts of an exceptional kind

[18] *Blakiston* v. *Cooper* [1909] A.C. 104, *infra.*
[19] *Moorhouse* v. *Dooland* [1955] Ch. 284; *post*, p. 242.
[20] [1958] 1 W.L.R. 832 (C.A.). For an interesting discussion of this and other cases, see
H. H. Monroe, " Fees, Wages, Perquisites and Profits Whatsoever " [1959] B.T.R. 25.
[21] Now I.C.T.A. 1970, s. 196.

to meet exceptional circumstances. In 1960 about 2,300 vouchers for £10 were so given. The fact that they were given at Christmas and accompanied in each case by appreciative letters from the chairman sending Christmas greetings on behalf of the company does not destroy their character as reward for services. . . .

(ii) *Gifts from Persons other than the Employer*

BLAKISTON v. COOPER

House of Lords [1909] A.C. 104; 78 L.J.K.B. 135; 100 L.T. 51; 25 T.L.R. 164; [1908–10] All E.R.Rep. 682; *sub nom. Cooper* v. *Blakiston*, 53 S.J. 149; 5 T.C. 347

The vicar of East Grinstead was assessed in the sum of £56, being the amount of the voluntary Easter offerings from his parishioners, which were customarily devoted to the personal use of the incumbent. The assessment was upheld.

LORD LOREBURN L.C.: My Lords, I agree with the Court of Appeal. The only question is whether or not a sum given by parishioners and others to the vicar at Easter 1905 is assessable to income tax as being " profits accruing " to him " by reason of such office."

In my opinion, where a sum of money is given to an incumbent substantially in respect of his services as incumbent, it accrues to him by reason of his office. Here the sum of money was given in respect of those services. Had it been a gift of an exceptional kind, such as a testimonial, or a contribution for a specific purpose, as to provide for a holiday, or a subscription peculiarly due to the personal qualities of the particular clergyman, it might not have been a voluntary payment for services, but a mere present.

In this case, however, there was a continuity of annual payments apart from any special occasion or purpose, and the ground of the call for subscriptions was one common to all clergymen with insufficient stipends, urged by the bishop on behalf of all alike. What you choose to call it matters little. The point is, what was it in reality?

It was natural, and in no way wrong, that all concerned should make this gift appear as like a mere present as they could. But they acted straightforwardly, as one would expect, and the real character of what was done appears clearly enough from the papers in which contributions were solicited.

LORD ASHBOURNE: . . . These offerings had been made for several years to the appellant, the vicar of East Grinstead. They were made in response to a systematic appeal initiated by the bishop and supported by the churchwardens to induce collections to eke out slender stipends. People were urged, it is true, to subscribe as a personal freewill gift, the contributions were wholly voluntary, and the amount given was regulated entirely by the discretion of the subscribers. But in what character did the appellant receive them? It was suggested that the offerings were made as personal gifts to the vicar as marks of esteem and respect. Such reasons no doubt played their part in obtaining and increasing the amount of the offerings, but I cannot doubt that they were given to the vicar as vicar and that they formed part of the profits accruing by reason of his office. The bishop was naturally anxious to increase the scanty stipends of ill-paid vicars. The whole machinery was ecclesiastical—bishops, churchwardens, church collections—and I am unable to see room for doubt that they were made for the vicar because he was the vicar, and became, within the statute, part of the profits which accrued to him by reason of his office. . . .

Note
   See also *Archbishop of Thyateira* v. *Hubert* (1942) 25 T.C. 249. Voluntary contributions
to the Metropolitan of the Orthodox Church, resident in England, from churches in Britain
and abroad and from the Greek Government held to be assessable under Schedule E. And
see *Herbert* v. *McQuade* [1902] 2 K.B. 631 and *Calvert* v. *Wainwright, infra.*

CALVERT v. WAINWRIGHT

King's Bench [1947] K.B. 526; [1947] L.J.R. 1335; 177 L.T. 159; 63 T.L.R. 199; [1947]
1 All E.R. 282; 27 T.C. 475

ATKINSON J.: This case raises the comparatively simple point: Are tips
which are received by taxi drivers in the ordinary way assessable to income tax?
. . . In *Blakiston* v. *Cooper*, which was the Easter offerings case, the principle
was stated by the Lord Chancellor in this way: " In my opinion, where a sum
of money is given to an incumbent substantially in respect of his services as
incumbent, it accrues to him by reason of his office. Here the sum of money
was given in respect of those services. Had it been a gift of an exceptional
amount, such as a testimonial, or a contribution for a specific purpose, as to
provide for a holiday, or a subscription peculiarly due to the personal qualities
of the particular clergyman, it might not have been a voluntary payment for
services, but a mere present." To my mind, that puts the principle very clearly.
The distinction would apply to a taxi driver in this way, to give an illustration.
Suppose somebody who has the same taxi every day, which comes in the
morning as a matter of course to take him to his work, and then takes him home
at night. The ordinary tip given in those circumstances would be something
which would be assessable, but supposing at Christmas, or, when the man is
going for a holiday, the hirer says: " You have been very attentive to me, here
is a £10 note," he would be making a present, and I should say it would not be
assessable because it has been given to the man because of his qualities, his
faithfulness, and the way he has stuck to the passenger. In those circumstances,
it would, in my opinion, be a payment of an exceptional kind. But a tip given
in the ordinary way as remuneration for services rendered is well within the
principles defined in that case. . . .

MOORHOUSE v. DOOLAND

Court of Appeal [1955] Ch. 284; [1955] 2 W.L.R. 96; 99 S.J. 60; [1955] 1 All E.R. 93;
36 T.C. 1

The taxpayer, D., was a well-known professional cricketer in the Lancashire
League. Under his contract with the East Lancashire Cricket Club he was
entitled to have made on his behalf collections from spectators whenever he
scored fifty runs or took six wickets or a hat trick in an innings. He appealed
against an assessment under Schedule E made upon the proceeds of such collections. *Held*, he was properly assessed.

SIR RAYMOND EVERSHED M.R.: . . . But, in my judgment, the facts on
which *Seymour's* [22] case was determined are different in vital respects from
those in the present case. The terms of Seymour's contract nowhere appear,
but quite plainly they did not include any right in any circumstances to a
" benefit." At most, as Sargant L.J. observed, it was said to be a settled practice
of the Kent Club to arrange a " benefit " for a professional, who had rendered

[22] *Seymour* v. *Reed* [1927] A.C. 554 (*ante*, p. 237).

long and distinguished service to the club, so that there might be some claim on
the part of a cricketer after such service to expect a donation of that kind. But
the grant or arrangement of a benefit was a matter entirely in the discretion of
the club—as was also the method of disposition of the sum subscribed, which,
according to the evidence, was not handed over to the professional but invested
on his behalf as a means for providing for him after his retirement from the
game. These circumstances, plus the facts that (according to the evidence)
except in the rarest instances, a player had only one benefit and that one towards
the end of his career as a professional, and that the sum subscribed was very
large by comparison with the professional's regular salary (the converse of the
present case) were the basis of the decision and have no correspondence with
the facts of the present case. . . .

JENKINS L.J.: . . . From these citations [23] I deduce the following principles:
(i) The test of liability to tax on a voluntary payment made to the holder of
an office or employment is whether, from the standpoint of the person who
receives it, it accrues to him by virtue of his office or employment, or in other
words by way of remuneration for his services.
(ii) If the recipient's contract of employment entitles him to receive the
voluntary payment, whatever it may amount to, that is a ground, and I should
say a strong ground, for holding that, from the standpoint of the recipient, it
does accrue to him by virtue of his employment, or in other words, by way of
remuneration for his services.
(iii) The fact that the voluntary payment is of a periodic or recurrent
character affords a further, but I should say a less cogent, ground for the same
conclusion.
(iv) On the other hand, a voluntary payment may be made in circumstances
which show that it is given by way of present or testimonial on grounds
personal to the recipient, as, for example, a collection made for the particular
individual who is at the time vicar of a given parish because he is in straitened
circumstances, or a benefit held for a professional cricketer in recognition of his
long and successful career in first-class cricket. In such cases the proper conclusion is likely to be that the voluntary payment is not a profit accruing to
the recipient by virtue of his office or employment but a gift to him as an
individual, paid and received by reason of his personal needs in the former
example and by reason of his personal qualities or attainments in the latter
example.
Applying these principles to the facts of the present case, I find: (i) that
under his contract of service with the East Lancashire Cricket Club Mr. Dooland
was entitled to make, or have made on his behalf, collections from spectators
on the ground, whenever he achieved one of the performances in batting or
bowling which carried the right to a collection according to the rules of the
Lancashire Cricket League; and (ii) that occasions on which he attained one
or other of the stipulated performances, and enjoyed a collection accordingly,
recurred with considerable frequency, there having been no less than eleven
of such occasions during the 1951 season. According to the principles above
stated, these facts afford cogent grounds for holding that the present case falls
within the line of tax liability. . . .

Note
This case contains elements common to cases in a number of different categories. Thus,
there is an element of a gift from the employer, in that he was permitted to have collections

---

[23] Jenkins L.J. was referring to passages from *Seymour* v. *Reed, Blakiston* v. *Cooper* (*ante*,
p. 241) and *Herbert* v. *McQuade* [1902] 2 K.B. 631.

made, *cf. Seymour v. Reed*; the gifts were made by persons other than his employer; he had a contractual right to have collections made, *cf. Jarrold v. Boustead, infra.*

The cases in this section should be compared with *I.R.C. v. Morris* (1967) 44 T.C. 685. See also [1969] B.T.R. 331.

(iii) *Contractual Receipts not Arising from the Employment*

JARROLD v. BOUSTEAD

Court of Appeal [1964] 1 W.L.R. 1357; 108 S.J. 500; [1964] 3 All E.R. 76; 41 T.C. 701

LORD DENNING M.R.: These three cases raise the question whether a " signing-on fee " received by three Rugby footballers is taxable in their hands. I must first explain that Rugby *Union* football is exclusively an amateur game. It is played much in Wales. But Rugby *League* football is played by professionals as well as amateurs. It is played mostly in the north of England.

Take the first case of the first taxpayer, Richard Boustead. He was a man of twenty-five who was living in Monmouthshire. He had played a considerable amount of Rugby Union football for Newport and other clubs. He had a good chance of becoming an international player. Whilst in Monmouthshire he was approached by representatives of a professional club in the north of England. They wanted him to become a professional and play Rugby League football for the club. A fee of £3,000 was discussed. He actually played in a trial match at the Hull Rugby Football Club, but he did so under an assumed name so that he should not lose his amateur status. Then terms were agreed. On September 22, 1958, documents were signed. The first was an agreement between Bousted and the Hull Football Club whereby he agreed to play for them during the next playing season. He was to be paid a specified sum for each match in which he played. The amount depended on whether the club won or lost. He agreed, of course, to observe all the bylaws and rules of the Rugby Football League. Finally, there was a clause: " The club shall pay the player the sum of £3,000 less Income Tax on signing professional forms for the club." On the self-same day he signed the professional forms. One was a form applying to be registered with the Northern Rugby Football League as one of their league players. The other was a form consenting to be registered as a professional football player. The £3,000 was paid to him as the signing fee; and the question is whether that £3,000 is taxable in his hands or not.

In order to understand the nature of the agreement, it is necessary to look at the bylaws of the Rugby League. Bylaw No. 24 says that " A player who relinquishes his amateur status is permitted to receive a signing-on fee from the club with which he first registers as a professional player. No club shall pay, or offer to pay a signing-on fee to a player who has previously been registered as a professional player with the league." So it is quite clear that on this occasion Richard Boustead relinquished his status as an amateur; he became a professional. The fee of £3,000 was paid to him once-and-for-all. Thereafter he could not return to amateur football. Nor, indeed, could he return to athletics. Apparently, he was a very good runner, but under the rules of the Amateur Athletic Association, when he became a professional in the Rugby League, he ceased to be an amateur for athletics and could not take part in amateur athletics at all.

Furthermore, it is found as a fact that on becoming a professional he found some degree of social discrimination against him by some people. Apparently he was not allowed to visit Rugby Union Clubs and if he was discovered on a Rugby Union ground as a spectator he might be asked to leave.

The other two cases were similar: but in Kenneth Large's case, £1,000 was paid and in Anthony Simm's case £200 was paid as a signing-on fee. In each of the cases the commissioners came to the same conclusion and expressed it in the same way. They said (I am taking Boustead's case): "In our opinion the payment of £3,000 to [Boustead] was quite separate from the engagement of his services and was not the payment of remuneration in advance. It was we think, merely an inducement to [him] which he accepted, to put himself into a position in which he could be employed by the Hull Football Club and to relinquish his amateur status." So they held it was not taxable in his hands. It was not remuneration for service but a payment for relinquishing his amateur status. Pennycuick J. took a different view. He construed the agreements as meaning that the payment was a consideration for signing the forms. It was part of the footballer's duty to sign the forms and therefore it was remuneration for his services. He did not express any views as to what would have been the position if the agreement had in terms said that it was in consideration of the relinquishment of his amateur status for the rest of his life.

I construe the agreements differently from the Judge. When read with the bylaws, I think they should be interpreted as saying that the £3,000 was paid as a consideration for relinquishing his amateur status, which meant relinquishing it for the whole of his life. The other payments were payments per match and were only for the next playing season. They might only last for seven months. But the relinquishment of his amateur status was for life.

In the course of the argument an illustration was taken by counsel on both sides. Suppose there was a man who was an expert organist but was very fond of playing golf on Sundays. He is asked to become organist of the parish church for the ensuing seven months at a salary of £10 a month for the seven months. But it is expressly stipulated by this strange parish council that, if he takes up the post, he is to give up Sunday golf for the rest of his life. Thereupon he says that, if he is to give up golf, he wants an extra £500, and they agree to pay it. In such a case the £500 is not a payment for his services as an organist for seven months; it is a payment for relinquishing what he considered to be an advantage to him.

So here it seems to me in the cases of these three footballers; each was an amateur, playing Rugby Union football with all the advantages that attached to amateur status, such as the prospect of gaining an international cap; each gave up all the advantages of being an amateur for the rest of his life and in return got his payment of the lump sum at the beginning. It seems to me that the commissioners were quite entitled to find that it was a capital sum in compensation for what was a permanent asset in his hands. The remuneration for services of so much a match was an entirely different thing. It was remuneration for services, whereas the signing-on fee was for giving up a permanent advantage.

I do not think the commissioners made any error in point of law. I think that they have directed themselves properly and I would allow the appeal accordingly.

Note
   This case should be compared with *Riley* v. *Coglan* [1967] 1 W.L.R. 1300 where, in slightly different circumstances, a Rugby League signing-on fee was held to be taxable remuneration. In that case, part of the £500 fee was repayable if the player failed to serve for the stipulated period. In the opinion of Ungoed-Thomas J., "the £500 was to be a running payment for his making himself available to serve the club when required to do so."
   See also *Hochstrasser* v. *Mayes* [1960] A.C. 376 (*ante*, p. 235), and *Pritchard* v. *Arundale* [1972] 1 Ch. 229.

BEAK v. ROBSON

House of Lords [1943] A.C. 352; 112 L.J.K.B. 141; 169 L.T. 65; 59 T.L.R. 90; 87 S.J. 13; [1943] 1 All E.R. 46; 25 T.C. 33

   The taxpayer, R., was employed by a company as manager and director for a term of five years. In addition to salary, his contract of service provided for a payment of £7,000 in consideration of his entering into a restrictive covenant not to compete with the company after his service terminated.

VISCOUNT SIMON L.C.: My Lords, in this case the Crown contends that a payment of £7,000, to the respondent by a private company called William Mathwin & Son (Newcastle), Ld., under a written agreement between them dated October 4, 1937, was a profit from the office of director and manager of that company within the meaning of rule 1 applicable to Schedule E to the Income Tax Act 1918. Lord Greene M.R. has indicated the answer to this claim in very clear language. In the agreement before us the obligations flowing from the contract of service and the remuneration to be received by the respondent in respect of that service are entirely separate from the restrictive covenant and the consideration which is given for it. The sum of £7,000 is not paid for anything done in performing the services in respect of which he is chargeable under Schedule E. The consideration which he has to give under the covenant is to be given not during the period of his employment, but after its termination. He is giving to the company for a sum of £7,000 the benefit of a covenant which will only come into effect when the service is concluded. I agree with Lord Greene M.R. in the view that to treat this £7,000 as a profit arising from the respondent's office " is to ignore the real nature of the transaction." It is quite true that, if he had not entered into the agreement to serve as a director and manager, he would not have received £7,000, but that is not the same thing as saying that the £7,000 is profit from his office of director so as to attract tax under Schedule E.

Note
    For the treatment of payments for restrictive covenants received by employees and former employees see now I.C.T.A. 1970, s. 34, as amended by Finance Act 1971, Sched. 6, para. 15. As to the deductibility of such payments by the employer, see *Associated Portland Cement Manufacturers Ltd.* v. *Kerr* [1946] 1 All E.R. 68; *ante*, p. 173.

(iv) *Payments Made on or after Termination of Employment*

The fact that a payment is made after termination of employment does not prevent its being an emolument of that employment if it has been made in consideration of past services and under the terms of the contract of employment. However, it may be a gratuitous payment (in which case it is necessary to consider it as a gift from the employer, and it may or may not be taxable as such; see *ante*, p. 237) or it may be a contractual payment, *e.g.* compensation for loss of office (in which case one must determine whether or not the contractual receipt arises from the employment; see *ante*, p. 244). It is also necessary to bear in mind that a payment which is not an emolument as such may nevertheless be chargeable under I.C.T.A. 1970, ss. 187, 188, as what is commonly referred to as a " golden handshake."

HENLEY v. MURRAY

Court of Appeal [1950] 1 All E.R. 908; [1950] W.N. 241; 31 T.C. 351

    H., the managing director of a company, resigned his office by agreement with his employer before the expiration of his contract. He received a lump sum of £2,202, which approximated to the remuneration to which he would have been entitled from the date of his resignation until the expiration of his contract. He was held not to be taxable on the lump sum.

SOMERVELL L.J.: . . . We are concerned with a sum of £2,202 14s. 4d. which was paid to him (I will use neutral words for the moment) on that resignation. It is common ground that that sum was not in respect of remuneration for past services. It was in respect of the salary that he could have earned if he had not resigned and the agreement had continued.

. . . It is conceded by the Crown that in a case where damages for wrongful dismissal are sued for, the sum awarded as damages is not only not within Schedule E—as I think it plainly could not be—but also is not taxable as income under any other Schedule. If in the case of dismissal where the employee says "I am wrongfully dismissed" and sues for damages he is admittedly outside Schedule E and untaxable, it seems to me to follow from that, if one goes by stages, that if you take a case where equally the employer dismisses his employee and the damages are agreed without litigation, the fact that they are agreed instead of being awarded by a judge or jury cannot affect their legal position in regard to the Income Tax code. It seems to me on the evidence that that is what happened here. The employer said, "You must go." I think it is perhaps clear from the position that he held that he need not have gone, but he, as he said, was forced into it; he did it at the request of the employers. The sum which he stipulated for according to his letter, it seems to me, must legally be in precisely the same position as would have been a sum for damages for wrongful dismissal. . . .

JENKINS L.J.: . . . I agree.

As the many cases on this topic show, it is often very difficult to determine the character of a payment made to the holder of an office when his tenure of the office is determined or the terms on which he holds it are altered, and the question in each case is whether, on the facts of the case, the lump sum paid is in the nature of remuneration or profits in respect of the office or is in the nature of a sum paid in consideration of the surrender by the recipient of his rights in respect of the office. . . . (this extract is quoted from Tax Cases).

Note
This type of case would now fall within the provisions of I.C.T.A. 1970, ss. 187, 188. A similar decision was reached, on rather unusual facts, in *Hunter* v. *Dewhurst* (1932) 16 T.C. 605 (H.L.). In that case, a director of a company, whose Articles provided that he should be entitled to "compensation" for loss of office should he resign or die, agreed with the company to abandon his intention to resign and to remain as a consultant in return for the payment of a reduced rate of remuneration and a lump sum. The lump sum was held not to be taxable; in the opinion of Lord Atkin (16 T.C. 605 at p. 645): "It seems to me that a sum of money paid to obtain a release from a contingent liability under a contract of employment cannot be said to be received 'under' the contract of employment, is not remuneration for services. . . ." *Per* Lord Thankerton (at p. 650): "They were payments for release from the obligations of article 109 and they did not arise from the contract of service; in my opinion, accordingly, they did not arise from the office of director, but in spite of it."
Again, in *Tilley* v. *Wales* [1943] A.C. 386, so much of a lump sum as was paid to a managing director in commutation of his pension rights was held not to be assessable. In both these cases, the provisions of sections 177 and 178 would now apply.
These cases should be contrasted with *Cameron* v. *Prendergast* [1940] A.C. 549. A director wishing to resign was paid a lump sum of £45,000 if he would remain on the Board in an advisory capacity. The sum was held to be taxable, being paid in consideration of his agreeing to *continue* to serve.
The general principle is also illustrated by *Dale* v. *de Soissons* (1950) 32 T.C. 118 (C.A.) and by *Henry* v. *Foster* (1930) 16 T.C. 605 (C.A.). In each case, the lump sum on termination was paid by virtue of a contractual right contained in the agreement of service. As Sir Raymond Evershed M.R. said in the former case (32 T.C. 118 at p. 126) ". . . the Colonel surrendered no rights. He got exactly what he was entitled to get under his contract of employment." See also H. H. Monroe, "Compensation for Loss of Office" [1956] B.T.R. 252 and "The Silver Handshake—1960 Pattern" [1960] B.T.R. 277.

Payments made on or after termination of employment may also be gratuitous: see *Bridges* v. *Hewitt* [1957] 1 W.L.R. 674 (C.A.) (a transfer of shares to a company director held to be a *personal* gift and not remuneration); also *Cowan* v. *Seymour* [1920] 1 K.B. 500 (C.A.) (money voted in general meeting by shareholders to the company secretary on winding-up as " best thanks " held to be a " tribute or testimonial " rather than remuneration. *N.B.* the " gift," as Lord Sterndale M.R. pointed out, came not from the employer (the company) but from third parties).

The distinctions between some of these cases are fine and the situation created somewhat anomalous and open to abuse. In the opinion of the Royal Commission on The Taxation of Profits and Income (Final Report—(1955) Cmd. 9474 at p. 78, para. 245):

" It is clear from the rather startling instances cited to us that what is ostensibly a payment in compensation for loss of office is sometimes used merely as a cloak for additional remuneration. Contractual rights are created in order to be lost, and nothing is lost which was ever intended to be retained."

As a result, wide provisions were introduced by the Finance Act 1960 (now I.C.T.A. 1970, ss. 187, 188) to bring into charge certain of these payments which had hitherto escaped tax. It is nevertheless necessary to consider whether or not a payment constitutes an emolument as such; if it does, it is already taxable and is unaffected by the special statutory provisions. If not, the payment may be exempt, *e.g.* under the £5,000 limit section 188 (3): as in *I.R.C.* v. *Brander and Cruickshank* (*ante*, p. 232).

(B) What Constitutes Emoluments?

In the majority of cases the employee receives a stated " wage " or " salary." In some instances, however, he may receive a stated sum *less* some deduction, or a stated sum *plus* some cash " allowance," or a stated sum *plus* some benefit received in a form other than cash.

(i) *Deductions from Remuneration*

MACHON v. McLOUGHLIN

Court of Appeal (1926) 11 T.C. 83

The taxpayer was a male attendant at an asylum. He received a weekly salary subject to fixed deductions, before payment, for board and lodging and for laundry. He contended that only the net amount of salary was assessable. *Held*, he was assessable in respect of the gross amount.

ROWLATT J.: . . . I think this appeal on behalf of the Crown must be allowed. I do not want to repeat what I said in *Cordy* v. *Gordon* (9 T.C. 304), although I still look at the matter in the same way. If a person is paid a wage with some advantage thrown in, you cannot add the advantage to the wage for the purpose of taxation unless that advantage can be turned into money. That is one proposition. But when you have a person paid a wage with the necessity—the contractual necessity if you like—to expend that wage in a particular way, then he must pay tax upon the gross wage, and no question of alienability or inalienability arises.[24] . . .

HEATON v. BELL

House of Lords [1970] A.C. 728; [1969] 2 W.L.R. 735; 113 S.J. 245; [1969] 2 All E.R. 70; 46 T.C. 211 (also *post*, p. 256)

The taxpayer agreed to participate in a car loan scheme initiated by his

---

[24] Judgment of Rowlatt J. in the King's Bench Division, upheld by the Court of Appeal. *Quaere* the position if the taxpayer had been entitled to a smaller salary and " free " board and lodging.

employers. In return for the use of a car, he was to receive an amended lower wage. Two questions were considered: (1) whether the wage was reduced or whether there was merely a deduction from his gross wage, the gross wage remaining taxable; and (2) whether the benefit of the car-loan scheme was a taxable perquisite and, if so, what was the value. *Held*, (1) (Lord Reid dissenting) it was a deduction and the gross wage was taxable; (2) (Lord Hodson and Lord Upjohn dissenting) in any event, the benefit was a taxable perquisite.

LORD REID: . . . My lords, the question of general importance in this case relates to the proper method of taxing perquisites. The respondent is a craftsman. His employers introduced a scheme under which they provided private cars for certain classes of their employees at moderate cost to them. A man who took advantage of the scheme, which was optional, could use the car to travel to and from his work but he was under no obligation to do so; and he could use the car otherwise in any way he chose provided that he drove it himself. We are not concerned with the effect of this scheme on the tax position of the employers. The respondent is assessed to income tax under Schedule E, and the question which the Special Commissioners had to determine was whether sums of £2 10s. per week and later of £2 18s. per week " being the amount of car loan scheme adjustments " were correctly included in computing the amount of his emoluments. The commissioners held that " the use of the car is not in our view money's worth " and that therefore these sums were not part of the respondent's emoluments. Their decision was reversed by Ungoed-Thomas J. but restored by the Court of Appeal.

The first question to be decided is the true construction of the agreement made between the respondent and his employers when he came into the scheme. This agreement is not embodied in any document and its terms must be inferred from what the parties said and did. The appellant says that there was no variation of the existing wage and that the respondent merely authorised his employers to deduct from that wage the weekly sum which he had to pay them for the use of the car which they provided. If that is right then no question as to perquisites arises. It is well settled that a taxpayer's liability to tax on his emoluments is not diminished by the fact that he has authorised his employer to make a deduction from his wages or salary before paying it to him and to apply the part deducted in an agreed manner. What he chooses to do with the wage or salary to which he is entitled is of no moment.

But the respondent says that that is not what the parties agreed. He says that he agreed to accept a reduced wage and that as a counterpart his employers agreed to give him the use of a car. If that is right then he became entitled to two things—first the reduced wage and secondly the use of the car. Then the question arises whether the use of the car was a perquisite within the meaning of the Income Tax Acts so that he had to pay tax in respect of it. . . .

LORD MORRIS OF BORTH-Y-GEST: . . . It is necessary, in the first place, to decide as to the true interpretation of the agreement subsisting at the relevant time between the respondent and his employers. When he joined the car loan scheme did he vary his terms of employment by agreeing to accept a reduced wage or did he agree that from his wage there would be deducted such sum as represented the sum payable to him in respect of his hiring of a car?

. . . In my view, there can be no doubt that the respondent obtained from his employers the right to use a car on terms which involved that he should pay to them whatever was from time to time an appropriate hire charge. As a matter of convenience he agreed that his payment was to be set off or deducted week by week from the amount which by his labour he had earned and which his employers therefore owed him. To dress that up as a wage reduction seems to me to be fanciful. The terms and conditions relating to the method of computing the respondent's earnings were in no way changed. If two crafts-men worked under precisely the same conditions so that they earned precisely the same amount and if one joined the car loan scheme while the other did not, it would, in my view, be a mere delusion to treat the former as having agreed to a wage reduction (being a wage reduction which was to vary from time to time according as to how the cost of hiring the car varied). In truth there would have been an arranged and agreed deduction from wages. A deduction by any other name would be a payment just the same.

To speak of a wage reduction increase brought about by new charges affecting a car the loan of which is free involves a measure of verbal distortion which suggests tax adjustments rather than " wage adjustments." . . .

Note
    As the majority held that the gross wage before deduction was taxable, it was not strictly necessary to consider whether, had this not been so, participation in the scheme was a taxable " perquisite." Nevertheless, this was done, and is considered below (p. 256).

(ii) *Additional " Allowances "*

FERGUSSON v. NOBLE

Court of Session (1919) 7 T.C. 176, 1919 S.C. 534

The taxpayer, N., a detective-sergeant in the Glasgow police force, was assessed to tax on £11 paid to him in cash as an allowance for clothing. He was obliged to spend this sum to provide " plain clothes." The payment was held to accrue to him by reason of his office and to be assessable under Schedule E.

LORD SALVESEN: . . . Therefore, it does not seem to me, if this is part of the salary or emoluments of this man's office, that it is the least degree con-clusive against assessment that he has to employ it in a particular way prescribed by his employers. He agrees to that when he accepts employment from them. It appears to me that such a money allowance is in a totally different position from the case where the employer supplies a uniform to be worn only when the man is on duty and which remains the employer's property.

. . . Now, in that view, I think one avoids a number of the very difficult and perplexing cases which were put by way of analogy by Mr. Brown. We are not dealing here with any case of what constitutes money's worth. We are dealing with a payment of money. It seems to me to be a payment accruing to the respondent by reason of his office. Whether he may be entitled to get a deduction in respect of its being an expense to which he is put in the necessary discharge of his duties is not a matter before us, but as the Solicitor-General stated quite properly that he did not foreclose that question, I think we should indicate that it would be quite open to the Commissioners to consider that question with reference to the assessment of the respondent for the year in question. I am pronouncing no opinion at all as to whether there might be such a deduction,[25] but it seems to me that once we have reached the conclusion that this money allowance is part of the salary or wages, perquisites, profits or other emoluments which are derived from his office, we must hold that it is assessable to Income Tax whatever deductions may be claimable by the

[25] *Cf. Owen* v. *Pook, infra*; *Nolder* v. *Walters* (*post*, p. 274).

respondent in terms of section 51 of the Act 16 and 17 Vict. c. 34, or any other legislation entitling him to make a claim. . . .

Note
   The payment for the clothes might have been made in a number of ways; the employer might have bought the clothes for N., or given him a voucher exchangeable only for clothes at a particular tailor (see *Wilkins* v. *Rogerson, post,* p. 258); he might have reimbursed N. for the money, or part of it, already expended (see *Owen* v. *Pook*); or N. might simply have charged the cost of the clothes to his employer's account. In each case the approach, though not necessarily the result, would be different.

OWEN v. POOK

House of Lords [1970] A.C. 244; [1969] 2 W.L.R. 775; 113 S.J. 267; [1969] 2 All E.R. 1;
45 T.C. 582 (also *post,* p. 273)

LORD GUEST: . . . My Lords, Dr. Owen is a general medical practitioner in practice at Fishguard. He also holds two part-time appointments with the South Wales Hospital Management Committee as obstetrician and anaesthetist at a hospital in Haverfordwest some fifteen miles from Fishguard. Under the terms and conditions of these appointments he was on " stand-by duty " as obstetrician, one weekend a month and as anaesthetist on Monday and Friday nights and one weekend a month. At such times he was required to be accessible by telephone, apart from being on call at all times for obstetric " flying squad " duties in any part of Pembrokeshire. He had no other duties at the hospital; all were concerned with emergency cases. The flying squad duties were very rare. On receipt of a telephone call from the hospital he gives instructions to the hospital staff. He usually sets out immediately by car to the hospital. He may advise treatment by telephone and await a further report. Sometimes the telephone call is received when he is out on his medical rounds. It is found in the stated case that his responsibility for a patient begins as soon as he receives a telephone call.
   Under the terms and conditions of service of hospital staff the management committee pay to the appellant travelling expenses as a part time officer at a fixed rate per mile, said to be 8d., for single journeys between Fishguard and the hospital, limited to a single journey of ten miles. The appellant pays the cost of the additional five miles travel himself.
   The appellant in 1962–63 made about 140 journeys to the hospital and received payment of expenses amounting to £100. This sum was included in his income assessable for that year. In 1963–64 he made about 115 journeys receiving £82 which was also included in his assessment for 1963–64. Before the commissioners he sought to deduct the whole cost of travelling incurred, which for 1962–63 amounted to £150 and for 1963–64 to £123 for income tax purposes.
   The general commissioners sustained his appeal and allowed the deductions sought under rule 7 of Schedule 9 to the Income Tax Act 1952. Stamp J. reversed that determination and his judgment was upheld by the Court of Appeal (Diplock and Edmund Davies L.JJ., Lord Denning M.R. dissenting).
   Two questions arise: (1) whether the travelling allowances were properly included in the appellant's emoluments for income tax purposes under Schedule E and (2) was the actual cost of the journeys deductible from his emoluments under the relevant rule.[26]
   . . . The Court of Appeal, certainly the Master of the Rolls, appear to have treated the payments as allowances payable to the appellant whether he incurred the expenses or not. But Edmund Davies L.J. would have decided the case

[26] This point is further considered below (p. 273).

the same way whether the payments were actual reimbursement for expenses incurred or allowances. From their reliance on *Fergusson* v. *Noble*,[27] I take it that the case was treated as one where the payment was truly an allowance and not a reimbursement.

There is, in my view, a distinction between the two cases. If the allowance was, as in *Fergusson* v. *Noble*, a clothing allowance payable whether it was expended or not, I can see the argument that it was an emolument in the sense of a profit or gain and I do not wish to question the authority of that case; but if the payment was merely a reimbursement for actual expenditure, different considerations arise. This case is, in my view, distinguishable. . . .

LORD PEARCE: . . . There is a further point raised by the appellant in the Court of Appeal. He contends that reimbursements such as that which is here in question do not come within the "emoluments" of an appointment or employment under Schedule E. They therefore never fall to be charged, and it is unnecessary to consider whether they are allowable under rule 7. In my opinion, that contention is correct. "Emoluments" are charged. These are defined as including "all salaries, fees, wages, perquisites and profits whatsoever."

The reimbursements of actual expenses are clearly not intended by "salaries," "fees," "wages" or "profits." It is contended that they are "perquisites." The normal meaning of the word denotes something that benefits a man by going "into his *own* pocket." It would be a wholly misleading description of an office to say that it had very large perquisites merely because the holder had to disburse very large sums out of his own pocket and subsequently received a reimbursement or partial reimbursement of these sums. If a school teacher takes children out for a school treat, paying for them out of his (or her) own pocket, and is later wholly or partially reimbursed by the school, nobody would describe him (or her) as enjoying a perquisite. In my view, "perquisite" has a known normal meaning, namely, a personal advantage, which would not apply to a mere reimbursement of necessary disbursements. There is nothing in the section to give it a different meaning. Indeed, the other words of the section confirm the view that some element of personal profit is intended. . . .

LORD WILBERFORCE: . . . I agree, therefore, with the judgment of Lord Denning M.R.,[28] and would allow the appeal. I should add that, if I had not reached this conclusion, I should have difficulty in seeing how the appellant could succeed, on his alternative point, in establishing that reimbursement of a non-deductible expense is something other than an emolument.

LORD PEARSON: . . . The other question in the appeal is whether the travelling allowance which the appellant receives from the hospital authorities constitutes an "emolument" of his employment. I would arrive at the answer in this way. Suppose that A, B and C are employed each at a salary of £500 per annum, and in the first year each has to pay entirely out of his own pocket the expenses of travelling between his home and his place of work. Then, in the second year the employer reimburses to A the cost of his season ticket or gives him an allowance of (say) 8d. per mile for coming to work and returning home by car. A is better off financially by the amount of the reimbursement or allowance.

---

[27] *Ante*, p. 250. Lord Donovan distinguished *Fergusson* v. *Noble* on the ground that in that case there was a " benefit or advantage " to the taxpayer.

[28] In the Court of Appeal [1968] 2 W.L.R. 591; [1968] 1 All E.R. 261. This judgment, a dissenting one, was that the expenditure incurred by Dr. Owen was an allowable deduction. It was on this ground that Lord Wilberforce found for the taxpayer.

He is better off than he himself was in the first year, and better off than B and C who still have to pay entirely out of their own pockets the expenses of travelling between their homes and their places of work. As A has effectively a better income than B and C, he ought to pay more income tax than they do. The reimbursement or car allowance is a benefit to A and is a sum of money. In my opinion, it is a perquisite, a profit, an emolument.

There is a quite different position when the employee incurs an expense in performing the duties of his employment—e.g. making a journey from head office to branch office and back to head office, or buying stamps and stationery for the firm—and has it reimbursed to him. In such a transaction there is no benefit—no profit or gain—to the employee. He does not receive any emolument. . . .

Note

Lord Wilberforce appears to equate the question of whether an "allowance" paid to reimburse an employee for an expense constitutes taxable remuneration to that of whether the expense is an allowable deduction. This clearly *ought* to be the position, but, it is submitted, is not necessarily the case—see the note on this case by J. G. M. in [1969] B.T.R. 190 and see the extract from the Final Report of the Royal Commission on the Taxation of Profits and Income (*post*, p. 261).

Lord Pearson, dissenting, held that the expenditure by the taxpayer was not an allowable deduction and found the case indistinguishable from *Ricketts* v. *Colquhoun* [1926] A.C. 1 (*post*, p. 272). Like Lord Wilberforce he appears to equate the taxability of an allowance with the deductibility of an expense.

See also *Nolder* v. *Walters* (1930) 15 T.C. 380 (*post*, p. 274). The taxpayer's claim, which was allowed, was for the amount by which his actual expenses when away from home *exceeded* the subsistence allowance granted by his employer, i.e. the same type of claim as was made by Dr. Owen. The question of the taxability of the allowance was not raised. Similarly, the question was not raised in *Marsden* v. *I.R.C.* [1965] 1 W.L.R. 734, where the employee (an Investigator in the Inland Revenue!) claimed (and failed) to deduct the amount by which his actual travelling expenses exceeded his allowance. *Quaere* if his allowance had been over-generous.

(iii) "*Benefits in Kind*"

In addition to cash payments to an employee, i.e. salaries, fees and wages, the expression "emoluments" also includes "perquisites and profits." Thus a payment "in kind" and a benefit received in a form other than money may be taxable, but only if such benefit is "convertible" into cash. It is necessary to consider:

(a) the convertibility of benefits;
(b) the valuation of benefits; and
(c) the special statutory provisions in respect to certain types of benefit.

Akin to the question of benefits in kind is that of payments made by the employer to some person other than the employee but made on behalf of, or to discharge some liability of, the employee. In *Richardson* v. *Lyon* [29] a company paid premiums on an endowment policy on the life of its manager to secure an annuity on his retirement. The policy belonged to the manager and he was held to be properly assessed on the payments made by his employer to the insurance company.[30] Subscriptions to a club paid

---

[29] (1943) 25 T.C. 497.
[30] This case can be contrasted with *Barclays Bank Limited* v. *Naylor* [1961] Ch. 7, where payments made by the employer bank to *trustees* for the benefit of the employee's child, and applied to pay the child's school fees for which the employee was liable, were held *not* to be part of his remuneration but to be the income of the child. Payments under "approved" pension schemes and other retirement arrangements are governed by special rules: see esp. I.C.T.A. 1970, ss. 208–231.

by a Bank on behalf of its manager were considered to be " remuneration " in *Brown* v. *Bullock*.[31] The provision of free accommodation, and of many other benefits to employees, usually involve a cash payment from the employer to some other person.[32]

REPORT OF THE ROYAL COMMISSION ON THE INCOME TAX

Colwyn Commission, 1920 Cmd. 615

101. Remuneration in kind is not charged under the present law unless it is capable of being turned into money. The anomaly exists, therefore, that one employee A may have to pay Income Tax on the salary which constitutes his sole remuneration, while his fellow employee B, who receives board and lodging or the free use of a residence in addition to the same salary, pays only the same amount of tax. From the point of view of ability to pay there is no doubt that B is capable of paying more tax than A.

102. There is obviously much to be said on the grounds of equity for the suggestion that the total benefits which accrue to an employee should be taken into consideration for Income Tax purposes, both for the purpose of fixing the net amount of his assessable income, and for determining the rate of tax at which he is liable. We recognise that there may be considerable administrative difficulties in carrying this principle into effect, but, unless those difficulties are greater than we believe them to be, we think that an attempt should be made to charge income tax on the true remuneration of employment, including subsidiary benefits arising out of the employment, although these may not be capable of being turned into money.

FINAL REPORT OF THE ROYAL COMMISSION ON THE TAXATION OF PROFITS AND INCOME

1955 Cmd. 9474

208. We have already noted that the law includes in its conception of income a benefit having money's worth even though it is only received in kind. We found it necessary to give our full attention to this subject, since a period of high taxation gives it an importance that it would not otherwise possess. If advantage can be taken of any weakness in the tax treatment of such benefits, there is an obvious temptation to resort to them as a means of part remuneration. And the harm that results is not merely the absolute loss of revenue : it is unfairness in the distribution of tax as between one taxpayer and another.

209. A benefit in kind may be convertible or inconvertible. It is convertible if it is of such a nature that the recipient can turn it into money: for instance, employees of many factories which produce consumer goods are allowed a free or reduced rate issue of such goods; the coal miner was, traditionally, allowed a free issue of coal. A benefit is inconvertible if it is of such a nature that it can

---

[31] [1961] 1 W.L.R. 1095, (C.A.). The amount paid by the bank was considered to be clearly an " emolument." The case turned on whether the manager was entitled to deduct it as an allowable expenditure. *Cf. Elwood* v. *Utitz* (1965) 42 T.C. 482 (C.A. Northern Ireland) where a different conclusion was reached on slightly different facts, and *Brown* v. *Bullock* distinguished. These two cases equate the taxability of an emolument with the non-deductibility of an expense. See the *Notes* to *Owen* v. *Pook* (*ante*, p. 253).

[32] See, in particular, the discussion of the special statutory provisions (*post*, p. 260); and see *Nicoll* v. *Austin* (1935) 19 T.C. 531.

only be enjoyed by the recipient: for instance the domestic servant's board and lodging, an employee's free meals, a railwayman's free travel, a bank manager's living accommodation at the bank, a teacher's free education for his children. Subject to certain special legislation in 1948,[33] the inconvertible benefit is not treated as taxable income apparently because it is not regarded as being equivalent to money's worth. At any rate there is no ready means of assigning to it a monetary equivalent; and, whatever administrative expedients might be adopted, the task of assessing the annual value of every such benefit and collecting tax upon it strikes us as a singularly formidable and laborious one. This is the fundamental difficulty in any treatment of the matter that seeks to be consistent. And the fact that non-convertible benefits are not taxed has led, not unnaturally, to a relaxation of the rule about convertible benefits. Where the volume of goods allowed to an employee by way of perquisite does not exceed what is reasonable for his own consumption, no tax charge is made in respect of them. Nor is tax charged on cash payments which coal miners receive in lieu of their former perquisite of free coal. The idea seems to be that perquisites of this kind are primarily intended for the consumption of the recipient and his family and, though they are of a nature that is convertible, the general understanding is that they are for personal enjoyment. They are therefore analogous to the inconvertible benefit. Since, however, the concession depends upon the volume of goods not being larger than would be needed for personal requirements, it does not go so far as to make it possible for any one individual to escape anything beyond a very small amount of tax.

210. On the other hand a taxable benefit arises whenever an employer discharges a pecuniary liability of an employee that he has not incurred in the course of performing the duties of his employment. Usual instances are the payment of the rent of a dwelling-house where its occupation is not part of the employment,[34] or the provision of a season ticket for travel from home to work. Sometimes children's school fees or holiday expenses are provided. This rule cuts across the distinction between convertible and inconvertible benefits, since the payment of a particular bill for a man gives him no option between personal enjoyment and realisation. But any different rule would be contrary to commonsense; and, presumably, the same difficulties of valuation do not occur as those that tend to defeat the assessment of the ordinary inconvertible benefit. However, liability is not attached to an employee's occupation of a house if the occupation is incidental to the duties of his employment, as it would be in the case of a lodge-keeper or level-crossing keeper or a colliery manager required to live in the neighbourhood of the mine.

211. What we have said is sufficient to illustrate the very great difficulty of applying any logically consistent treatment to this subject. Theoretically, all benefits in kind received in the course of employment and attributable to it are a form of remuneration and should rank as taxable income, since otherwise one taxpayer's income is not equitably balanced against another's.

(A) The Convertibility of Benefits

TENNANT v. SMITH

House of Lords (*ante*, p. 3)

The taxpayer, a bank-manager, occupied rent-free a house belonging to the Bank. He was required by his employers to live there, not allowed to sub-let

---

[33] Now contained in I.C.T.A. 1970, ss. 195–203 (*post*, p. 260).
[34] Special rules now apply to the provision of free accommodation: I.C.T.A. 1970, s. 185.

and bound to quit if he ceased to manage the Bank. He was assessed to income tax on the annual value of the house and appealed, claiming that this did not form part of his income, which was consequently less than £400 a year and not, under the law then in force, subject to tax. He was successful.

LORD HALSBURY L.C.: . . . I am of opinion . . . that the thing sought to be taxed is not income unless it can be turned into money. . . .

LORD HANNEN: My Lords, the question for consideration is whether the appellant is entitled under the Customs and Inland Revenue Act 1876, s. 8, to an abatement on the amount of income on which he has been assessed, on the ground that his total income from all sources is under £400. His undisputed income is £374; if to this should be added the annual value of the house he resides in rent free, his assessable income exceeds £400, otherwise not.

The appellant is agent for the Bank of Scotland at Montrose. He is bound as part of his duty as such agent to live in the bank house as custodier of the whole premises, and to transact business there after bank hours. He cannot temporarily vacate the house without special consent of the directors, and he cannot sublet or use the premises for other than bank business. Is such an occupation as this to be regarded as a part of the appellant's income? It certainly does not come within the natural meaning of the word "income." It saves the appellant from the expenditure of income on house rent, but it is not in itself income. That it is a suitable residence for the appellant is an accident which ought not to affect the determination of a question of principle as to the incidence of taxation. The income tax is imposed, not on the personal suitableness of a man's surroundings, which must vary with each man, and with the same man in different circumstances, but on his income capable of being calculated. The appellant occupies the bank house as a part of his duty, and I do not see how the case can be distinguished from that, so aptly put by Lord Young, of the master of a ship who is spared the cost of house rent while afloat. His cabin does not on that account become a part of his income.

Different considerations would apply to the case of an agent who as part of his remuneration has a residence provided for him which he might let. That which could be converted into money might reasonably be regarded as money—but that is not the case before us. . . .

Note
See now I.C.T.A. 1970, s. 185.

HEATON v. BELL

House of Lords (*ante*, p. 248)

As to whether the benefit of membership of the car-loan scheme was a taxable perquisite. The House of Lords held by a majority of 3–2 that it was.

LORD MORRIS OF BORTH-Y-GEST: . . . How, then, should the well-established principles be applied if it be assumed that since 1961 the respondent was employed on the terms that his wage was a reduced one but that he was to have the free use of a car? In my view, his free use of a car was a perquisite which represented money's worth and was taxable. It is true that his right to use the car could not be assigned (just as the option in *Abbott* v. *Philbin* [35]

[35] [1961] A.C. 352, *infra*.

could not be transferred) but the right could be converted into money. The option in *Abbott* v. *Philbin* could be exercised and the shares acquired by its exercise could then be sold. It was recognised that by such process the option was by its nature capable of being turned into money. In the present case the respondent's right to use the car could be converted into money or .was capable of being turned into money by a much simpler process. The respondent could at any time (subject only to giving two weeks' notice) and without making any new contract say to his employers that he relinquished in their favour his right to use the car and in exchange could require that an ascertained sum of money should be paid to him. His employers would be bound to accept the use of the car which was all that the respondent had a right to. They would then be bound to pay him a sum which (on the basis now being considered) was equal to the amount by which he had agreed that his wage was to be reduced. His employers, for their part, could at any time (subject only to giving two weeks' notice) require him to give up his right to use the car and require him to accept a sum of money in exchange. At all times and at any time since 1954 the respondent was in a position to decide whether he would choose to have from his employers a particular and ascertained sum of money and no car or whether he would choose not to have that particular and ascertained sum of money but to have a car. The fact that two weeks' notice of change of will was needed does not, in my view, alter the fact that the perquisite represented money's worth.

At any time since 1961 the respondent, after giving notice, could have had money rather than the use of a car. . . .

LORD UPJOHN (dissenting): . . . So is this perquisite a taxable perquisite?

Of course you can sensibly value it at £2 13s. 6d. per week, but that plainly is not the test; you must be able (and I care not what expression is used, for we are not now construing an Act of Parliament) to turn it into money.

Ungoed-Thomas J. was of opinion that as the respondent could terminate the car loan scheme so far as he was concerned by giving fourteen days' notice he could convert the perquisite into money by receiving higher wages thereafter.

My Lords, powerful reasons were advanced by the judges of the Court of Appeal for disagreeing with and overruling that reasoning. I agree with them. The respondent could not turn the perquisite, which was no more than the personal use of the car, into money or anything which could be equated to money; all he could do would be to give up his perquisite and obtain higher wages. In my opinion, this personal unassignable right for use of the car was not equivalent to money while it continued and that, surely, must be the test. . . .

ABBOTT v. PHILBIN

House of Lords [1961] A.C. 352; [1960] 3 W.L.R. 255; 104 S.J. 563; [1960] 2 All E.R. 763; 39 T.C. 82

The taxpayer, A, was secretary to a company. He was offered, for a small consideration, an option to purchase shares in the company at the then market price of £3 8s. 6d. per share. About eighteen months later he exercised the option, at which time the shares were worth £4 2s. each.

He was assessed on a sum equal to the difference. He contended that any benefit he had received had been conferred at the time he acquired the option and that any excess in value was not an emolument but represented an appreciation in the value of property (the option) owned by him. His contention was upheld; it was held that the benefit of the option contract was a perquisite which fell to be taxed only in the year in which it was granted.

E.R.L.—9

Lord Radcliffe: . . . I think that it has been generally assumed that this decision [36] does impose a limitation upon the taxability of benefits in kind which are of a personal nature, in that it is not enough to say that they have a value to which there can be assigned a monetary equivalent. If they are by their nature incapable of being turned into money by the recipient they are not taxable, even though they are in any ordinary sense of the word of value to him. It is obvious that this conception raises many attendant uncertainties which are not, so far as I know, cleared up except where some particular class of benefit in kind has offended the eye of the legislature and has been dealt with by special legislation. Must the inconvertibility arise from the nature of the thing itself, or can it be imposed merely by contractual stipulation? Does it matter that the circumstances are such that conversion into money is a practical, though not a theoretical, impossibility; or, on the other hand, that conversion, though forbidden, is the most probable assumption? [37]

I do not think that the decision of this case can go very far, if any distance, to clear up such points as these. I think that the Revenue are right in saying that a line has to be drawn somewhere between convertible and non-convertible benefits and that somehow we have to put a general meaning on the not very precise language used in *Tennant* v. *Smith*. What I do not think, however, is that a non-assignable option to take up freely assignable shares lies on that side of the line which contains the untaxable benefits in kind. The option, when paid for, was thereafter a contractual right enforceable against the company at any time during the next ten years so long as the holder paid the stipulated price and remained in its service. That right is, in my opinion, analogous for this purpose to any other benefit in the form of land, objects of value or legal rights. It was not incapable of being turned into money or of being turned to pecuniary account within the meaning of these phrases in *Tennant* v. *Smith* merely because the option itself was not assignable. What the option did was to enable the holder at any time, at his choice, to obtain shares from the company which would themselves be pieces of property or property rights of value, freely convertible into money. Being in that position he could also at any time, at his choice, sell or raise money on his right to call for the shares, even though he could not put anyone he dealt with actually into his own position as option holder against the company. I think that the conferring of a right of this kind as an incident of service is a profit or perquisite which is taxable as such in the year of receipt, so long as the right itself can fairly be given a monetary value, and it is no more relevant for this purpose whether the option is exercised or not in that year, than it would be if the advantage received were in the form of some tangible form of commercial property. . . .

(B) The Valuation of Benefits

WILKINS v. ROGERSON

Court of Appeal [1961] Ch. 133; [1961] 2 W.L.R. 102; 105 S.J. 62; [1961] 1 All E.R. 358; 39 T.C. 344

Lord Evershed M.R.: . . . Mr. Rogerson, the respondent, at the relevant date in 1955–56 was in the service of a company known as the Anglo-Oriental &

---

[36] *Tennant* v. *Smith* [1892] A.C. 150 (*ante*, p. 255).
[37] These questions remain largely unanswered. But see *Heaton* v. *Bell* (*ante*, p. 256). *Cf. Weight* v. *Salmon* (1935) 19 T.C. 191 (H.L.) where there was an immediate benefit, directors being permitted to take up at par (£1) shares then worth more than £3. See now I.C.T.A. 1970, s. 186, as amended by F.A. 1972, ss. 77–79, Sched. 12.

General Investment Trust Limited. As the season of goodwill approached in the year 1955 the company, of which he was the servant, wrote to him, and to some twenty or twenty-one fellow servants, a letter which, so far as material, was as follows: " The Board have decided to make a Christmas present to all male members of the staff of clothes suitable for wear at the office up to the value of £15. Arrangements have been made with Messrs. Montague Burton Ltd., 112, Cheapside, E.C.2, for you to be able to acquire from them a choice from or combination of the following: Suit, overcoat, raincoat. The bill will be sent to the Trust, and it is stressed that no cash payment either way can be made between £15 and the actual cost of the goods.

" Please take this letter with you when you visit Messrs. Montague Burton, which can be done on or after Thursday, November 10, 1955. Messrs. Montague Burton will provide a fitting if this is required and asked for. They will also make alterations if required. Both fittings and alterations will take additional time."

On the same date the company wrote to Montague Burton Ltd. of 112, Cheapside, and the letter is as follows: " We write with reference to the visit of Mr. W. Peter Spens on November 4, 1955. This company, a subsidiary of London Tin Corporation Ltd., has decided to give its male staff a Christmas present (purchased from Messrs. Montague Burton Ltd.) up to the value of £15 of clothes suitable for wear at the office drawn from a choice from or combination of a suit, overcoat or raincoat. We enclose a copy of a letter which we will write to each male member of the staff whose names are given below," and then there follows the list of names. " Please supply them with suits, overcoats or raincoats as above, and send us your account in due course. We stress that the bill will be paid by this company, and no cash payment either way can be made between £15 and the actual cost of the clothes. We have advised the staff to call on you on or after Thursday, November 10, 1955," etc.

The only other document to which I need refer is a receipt in favour of the company in February of the following year for a total sum of £311 12s. 6d. which was the cost of the suits, overcoats or raincoats which had been supplied to the various members of the company's staff.

It has been necessary to read in full those documents because, in the end, much turns upon the exact nature of what was done. The taxpayer availed himself of the generosity of his employers, and acquired clothing from Montague Burton for which the bill was delivered to the company, the price in his case being not quite £15, but £14 15s.

The claim of the Crown has been that that figure, £14 15s., is to be treated as part of the taxable income of the taxpayer for the tax year in question. It is said that it falls within the terms of paragraph 1 of the Ninth Schedule to the Income Tax Act 1952: " Tax under Schedule E shall be annually charged on every person having or exercising an office or employment of profit mentioned in Schedule E or to whom any annuity, pension or stipend chargeable under that Schedule is payable, in respect of all salaries, fees, wages, perquisites or profits whatsoever therefrom for the year of assessment. . . ." It is the Crown's case that the £14 15s. must be treated as a perquisite or profit from the employment for the year of assessment 1955–56.

On behalf of the taxpayer it was said that any perquisite or profit was limited in this case to the value expressed in money of the thing which he got, namely, the clothing. For the purposes of this case, the value of the clothing, treated, of course, as second-hand the moment it had been delivered, has been agreed at £5. Let me say at once that this involves no reflection upon Messrs. Montague Burton Ltd., who are not before the court; and it should not, of course, be assumed that goods which they supply are worth only one-third of the price which they charge. But it is, of course, notorious that, apart from purchase tax, the value of clothing is very much reduced the moment it can be called second-hand. In any case, the value is one which has been mutually accepted and agreed, and nothing turns upon it. It may have been agreed at a low figure to discourage any cross-appeal by the taxpayer. If so, it has achieved its purpose, for it is now accepted on his behalf that he is rightly taxed, as the judge in the court below held, upon the money value of what he got.

. . . It seems to me that the taxpayer never acquired any rights against anybody. He received this letter; armed with it, he went to Messrs. Montague Burton's establishment, and Montague Burton expressed themselves as willing to supply him with the clothes he ordered. When the clothes were delivered, then (and then only) the taxpayer got something which was his own. He acquired at that point of time a suit, albeit he had no right against anyone to get the suit. Nor had he, as I conceive, any right against the company, though as a matter of ordinary decency as between master and servant he could no doubt rely upon the company doing what they said they would do. But this was not a case in which he was entitled to call upon the company to pay some sum of money on his behalf, as that phrase is ordinarily understood.

If I have incurred a debt—for example, my debt due for income tax comparable to *Hartland* v. *Diggines* [38]—and my employer chooses to discharge that debt for me, then it is no doubt true that what I have received in money or money's worth is the equivalent of the debt; and the sum of money is, therefore, properly brought within the scope of the charge. But as I think in this case, and in accordance with Mr. Heyworth Talbot's argument, what the taxpayer got—what the company intended to give him, what the letter to him and Montague Burton said would be done, and was done—was a present of a suit. Until he got it, he got nothing; and when he got it, the thing which came in (which was his income expressed in money's worth) was the value of the suit. . . .

REPORT OF THE ROYAL COMMISSION ON TAXATION

Carter Commission, Canada, 1966.   Chapter 14 : Recommendations

17. Free, subsidised or discounted goods and services provided to employees should be taxable as benefits to them or subject to the special tax on the employer as described above. When the good or service is of a kind sold by the employer, the value of the benefit should be based on the market value of the good or service. In all other cases, the value of the benefit should be the full cost to the employer. Among the more obvious goods and services provided by employers that should be treated in this way are : meals, housing, schools for children of employees, loans, transportation passes and recreational facilities including summer cottages, lodges, fishing and hunting camps, yachts and golf courses.

(C)   SPECIAL STATUTORY PROVISIONS

Part VIII of the Income and Corporation Taxes Act 1970 contains special provisions relating, *inter alia*, to the provision of accommodation (s. 185), the granting of rights to acquire shares (s. 186), and expenses allowances and benefits in kind provided for directors and certain other employees (ss. 195–203).

[38] [1926] A.C. 289.

FINAL REPORT OF THE ROYAL COMMISSION ON THE TAXATION OF PROFITS AND INCOME

1955 Cmd. 9474

213. All that has been said above must be read subject to the effect of the special legislation introduced in 1948 by Part IV of the Finance Act of that year.[39] Speaking generally, the persons to whom the legislation applies are directors of trading companies and employees whose gross remuneration (salary plus expenses payments and benefits in kind) amounts to £2,000 per annum. It makes every benefit in kind, convertible or inconvertible, chargeable to tax as part of the remuneration of the director or employee who has received it, except for certain limited services which are specified in the Act. Thus, neither director nor employee is chargeable with (a) accommodation, supplies and services used wholly for business purposes on the business premises, or (b) meals taken in canteens where meals are provided for the staff generally: and an employee, but not a director, receives a further exemption in respect of living accommodation provided on the employer's premises, if the employee is required to live there for the purpose of his duties. But, these exceptions apart, all benefits are brought in, even though some of them would not be taxable under the general law: the provision of a motor car, free accommodation and entertainments, free travel, personal services, the expenses of foreign travel. The Act directs that the measure of liability is to be the expense which the company or employer has been put to in providing the benefit in question.

224. An employee who has expenses to meet in the performance of his duties may have those expenses met in one of several ways. He may have a gross salary out of which his employer requires him to meet them. His problem, then, is to get those expenses allowed against his gross salary for the purpose of determining his taxable income.[40] Or he may incur the expenses on the understanding that the charges will be met by the employer, or that, if he pays them in the first instance, the employer will reimburse him. In those cases, his problem is not a tax one, since neither the moneys paid nor the moneys reimbursed can form any part of his taxable income, unless they are in reality, contrary to what they appear, a provision of personal benefit to him, instead of a payment of expenses necessary to his work.[41] Lastly, the employer may provide the employee with a round sum to cover his expenses of the year, thus eliminating the necessity of any detailed accounting between them.

225. So far as the general law goes, an expense allowance is not treated as taxable income of the recipient if it is no more than a reasonable estimate of the expenses which he would have to incur in the performance of his duties.[42] Theoretically this must be so, since it would be aimless first to add the allowance to the remuneration and then to deduct an equivalent amount as permissible expenses under rule 9. The Board do not treat an expense allowance as necessarily constituting taxable income even if it is intended to cover some expenses which are not of a nature to qualify as deductible expenses under the rule. If this practice is right,[43] it creates a curious no-man's land between taxable income and deductible expenses. In any event the uncertainty of the frontier line contributes another reason for regarding the expense allowance system, though in itself a reasonable and, indeed, unavoidable business arrangement, as one that invites special precautions at a time of high taxation of personal incomes.

---

[39] Now I.C.T.A. 1970, ss. 195–203.
[40] The problem discussed below (post, p. 267).
[41] See, in particular, Owen v. Pook (ante, p. 251).
[42] But see Fergusson v. Noble (ante, p. 250).
[43] Cf. the remarks of Lord Wilberforce and Lord Pearson in Owen v. Pook (ante, p. 252).

226. It is obvious that a payment by way of expense allowance or in reimbursement of expenses could be used to cover more than those expenses which would be deductible under rule 9. If such a payment really amounted to a concealed personal benefit to the recipient the law would treat the quantum of benefit as part of his taxable income. But in the nature of things it would be very difficult for the Revenue to challenge any but the most obvious cases of disguised remuneration or to make good their challenge before appeal Commissioners. The purpose of the special legislation of 1948 was to reverse the position to the extent that the onus of showing that any payment made in respect of expenses covers no more than deductible expenses is placed upon the recipient instead of the onus being placed upon the Revenue to show that the allowance in fact covered a quantum of personal benefit.

227. The method by which this was brought about was to declare that, for directors and employees affected, all sums " paid in respect of expenses " should be treated as part of the assessable income (Income Tax Act 1952, s. 160): and to leave the recipient free to make good such deductions from that income as he could show to be represented by money expended, wholly, exclusively and necessarily in performing the duties of the office or employment. He is not put by this under any rule different from that which governs the expenses of all incomes assessable under Schedule E. What he loses is the possibility of escaping the full rigour of the rule by becoming the recipient of a payment in respect of expenses without being called upon to itemise and prove them as complying with the terms of rule 9.

Memorandum of Dissent, by Messrs. G. Woodcock, H. L. Bullock and N. Kaldor

181. In our view the form in which a person obtains a receipt—whether it is called a wage or a salary, or an expense allowance—ought not to make any difference to the question of whether the receipt is taxable or not. Equally the extent to which a taxpayer is able to claim expenses against his receipts should be the same, irrespective of whether these expenses are met out of his regular salary or out of a special allowance provided by the employer for the purpose. If different rules apply to the deductibility of expenses according to whether the employer makes provision for those expenses in fixing the basic salary of the employee, or whether he makes a special provision in the form of supplementary payments, avenues are opened for tax avoidance through the masquerading of remuneration as expense allowances.

182. The 1948 legislation was intended to eliminate such differences of treatment by providing that all allowances received by certain classes of taxpayers should be added to their taxable incomes, and deductions could be claimed for expenses actually incurred, in so far as those expenses satisfied the general rule of expenses applicable to Schedule E. The provisions of this legislation were limited however to directors of companies and to employees with emoluments (including the expense allowance received) of over £2,000 a year. We understand that this limitation did not rest on any principle but on administrative considerations. It was thought that the circumstances, in which the opportunity and temptation occurred to pay or receive remuneration under the guise of an expense allowance, were broadly limited to those in which members of the boards of companies were in a position to determine the form of their own remuneration: or those in which companies might seek to attract and recruit high salary earners by the offer of tax-free expense allowances. We understand it to be the view of the Revenue authorities that these two classes do, in fact, cover most of the likely recipients of regular expense allowances.

BUTTER v. BENNETT

Court of Appeal [1963] Ch. 185; [1962] 3 W.L.R. 874; 106 S.J. 548; [1962] 3 All E.R. 204; 40 T.C. 402

LORD DENNING M.R.: In this case the taxpayer is employed by the Bridgend Paper Mills Ltd. as the manager of a paper mill. He is paid more than £2,000 a year. He has a house near the mill in which he is required by the company to live and in which it is necessary for him to live in order to carry out his duties as manager. The company not only provide him with the house but they also provide him with coal for heating the house, they provide him with electricity, which is run by cable from the mill to the house, and their own grounds-man cuts the grass in the garden and clips the hedges; and that expense falls on the company.

The question is whether the taxpayer is chargeable to tax with the cost of the coal, the electricity and the part-time services of the gardener.

This question depends on a series of sections, sections 160, 161 [44] and following sections, in the Income Tax Act 1952. They were first enacted in 1948. They applied to directors of companies and employees earning more than £2,000 a year. The mischief which they were designed to remedy is well known. One mischief was this: at that time directors and senior employees used to have large expense accounts in which they debited the company with expenses incurred in entertaining, and the like. Those expenses were repaid to the director or employee by the company which was allowed them as a tax deduction, and the director or employee got the benefit of it all tax-free. So, in section 160 of this Act it was provided that all expense accounts were to be treated as perquisites of the office or employment and that the director or employee was assessable for them to tax except in so far as he could show that it was money expended wholly, necessarily and exclusively in the performance of his duties.

The other mischief which had to be remedied was not expense accounts proper, but the provision by the company of living accommodation or other benefits of which the director or employee had the benefit but which the company paid for itself: for instance, the company might provide a flat in London which would be useful for overseas visitors or for other purposes of the company and might allow the director to stay there and have all the benefit of it. He could not turn it to money or money's worth; he could not sub-let it, or anything like that, so he was not liable to tax on it, and the company used to put down the outlay as part of its own expenses. So it really meant a tax-free benefit to the director or employee, as the case may be. In order to deal with that mischief, section 161 (1) provided that where the company incurred expense in or in connection with the provision for any of its directors (or for any person employed by it of the over £2,000 a year level) " of living or other accommodation, of entertainment, of domestic or other services or of other benefits or facilities of whatsoever nature," then in those circumstances it was to be treated as if the director or the servant had paid out the money himself in that provision, and that it had been regarded as paid on an expense account and that the money had been refunded to him by the company by means of a payment of expenses. The result was that he became chargeable for the value of the provision of living or other accommodation, of entertainments, of domestic or other services and of other benefits or facilities which he got, except again in so far as it could be shown to be wholly, exclusively and necessarily incurred for the performance of his duties.

[44] Now I.C.T.A. 1970, ss. 195, 196.

... There was an exception to section 161 (1). By subsection (3), an employee was not accountable for expenses incurred by the company for his benefit in these cases: where the expense was incurred by the company " in or in connection with the provision of living accommodation for an employee in part of any of its business premises " and the employee was required to live in the premises and—I will put it shortly—that it was necessary for him to do so.

The taxpayer certainly is entitled to the benefit of subsection (3). He was required to live in this mill house, the manager's house; it was necessary for him to do it in respect of his duties; and, therefore, he is exempt from taxation in regard to expenses incurred by the company " in or in connection with the provision of living accommodation " for him.

So we come to the short point in this case. Was the cost of the coal, the electricity and the part-time services of the gardener an expense incurred by the company " in or in connection with the provision " of living accommodation for the taxpayer? In considering this question, I do not think we need to go back to the state of the law before this Act was passed. These sections form a comprehensive code which cover the tax position of a man such as the taxpayer. The only question is what is the meaning of the words " in or in connection with the provision of living accommodation." To my mind " living accommodation " is to be construed here in a narrow sense. The expense which is exempt is the expense of providing accommodation (including the expense of maintaining it) so as to make it habitable for the employee, as distinct from the expense of inhabiting the accommodation. I gather this by looking back to section 161 (1). Parliament there draws a distinction between " living accommodation " and " other accommodation." It draws a distinction between " living accommodation " and " domestic or other services or other benefits or facilities whatsoever," so it seems to me that in this situation " living accommodation " must be narrowly construed as meaning the premises themselves which the employee occupies. The expense of providing his accommodation certainly includes the expense of the rent. It also includes the expense of the rates. But Mr. Bucher points to the words " in connection with." He asks, what expense is covered by the words " in connection with " the provision of living accommodation? I would say that repairs to the house would certainly be covered. But do those words go so far as to extend to the coal, the electricity and the gardener such as we have to consider here? In my judgment they do not. It seems to me that when an employee gets his coal provided for heating the house or for cooking, and when he gets his electricity for light to read by, that is not the cost of making the premises habitable. It is part of the cost of inhabiting the premises. I would agree that, in so far as he has used the heat or light for his actual work, it might come within the words " used or expended wholly, exclusively and necessarily in the performance of his duties." It might in that regard come within the exemption. But there is no evidence to that effect in this case.

As to the gardener, Mr. Bucher said that was his best point of the three, but I do not think it is a good one. The services of a gardener in mowing the lawn and keeping the hedges clipped seem to me to be simply the cost of keeping the place tidy—the cost of inhabiting it—and not the expense of keeping or rendering it habitable.

In my judgment the judge was right in the view which he took in this case and I would dismiss the appeal.

I ought only to add that a point was raised in argument as to the possibility of apportioning this expenditure, but I do not see that the evidence warrants any apportionment in this case. The point was not taken before the judge nor in the notice of appeal, and in the absence of evidence I see no ground for apportionment under section 161 (6). I would, therefore, dismiss the appeal.[45]

LUKE v. INLAND REVENUE COMMISSIONERS

House of Lords (*ante*, p. 16)

The taxpayer occupied a large house which he had earlier sold to the company of which he was a director. It was considered desirable that he should have an imposing residence as he frequently entertained overseas customers of the company. He paid a proper rent, but in the year in question the company expended £950 on rates, feu duties, insurance, and repairs, which included the installation of a new boiler and water main and renewal of the plumbing and the roof. *Held,* the expenditure by the company did not form part of L's emoluments, conferring upon him no benefit beyond what he had under his pre-existing rights under the lease.

LORD DILHORNE L.C.: . . . The first question that falls for consideration is whether the sum which was spent by the company in discharge of owners' rates, feu duty and for insurance can properly be regarded as expended in the provision of living accommodation for the appellant or in connection therewith. In my opinion, it cannot properly be so regarded. As owners of the property "Deaseholm" the company had to pay owners' rates and feu duty and it was to their interest to see that the property was insured.

. . . Nor can I reach the conclusion that any letting by a company to a director at a full rent with the normal obligations of a tenant is to be regarded as subjecting the tenant to tax in respect of such outgoings as fall upon the company as owner of the property. On the other hand, the expense of repairs to a property so let cannot, in my opinion, be regarded otherwise than as expense incurred in, or in connection with, the provision of living accommodation, and so, in my view, that expense will be subject to tax unless taken out of section 161 (1) [46] by a subsequent provision.

. . . It follows that unless the amounts spent by the company on repairs are to be regarded as coming within section 162 (1),[47] the appellant is liable to be taxed on an amount equivalent to the annual value and also on the expenditure on repairs.

Many instances can be given of the manifest unfairness of this. I will content myself with one. If the roof of the house had been blown off in a gale and the repair effected in one financial year, the appellant would have been liable to pay tax for that year on the annual value and on the entire cost of putting on a new roof. The more expensive the repair, the greater is the amount to be notionally added to his income. It must be borne in mind that it is to the interest of the owner of the premises that repairs of the character for which a landlord is normally responsible should be carried out, so that the value of the premises may be maintained, and, also, while the effect of the expenditure may last for several years, the whole cost has on this interpretation to be regarded as taxable income of the year in which it was spent.

I cannot believe that it was the intention of Parliament that these provisions should have this effect. As I have said, the object of this chapter appears to

---

[45] On the question of apportionment, see *Rendell* v. *Went* (*post*, p. 266), *Westcott* v. *Bryan* [1969] Ch. 324 and R. S. Nock: "Company Houses" [1969] B.T.R. 253. See also *McKie* v. *Warner* [1961] 1 W.L.R. 1230 and *Doyle* v. *Davison* (1961) 40 T.C. 140.
[46] Now I.C.T.A. 1970, s. 196 (1).
[47] Now I.C.T.A. 1970, s. 197 (1).

have been to prevent avoidance of tax liability by the payment of expenses allowances and, as a corollary to that, to bring into tax the value of benefits in kind. I cannot believe that it was the intention of Parliament to treat the cost of carrying out repairs for which a landlord is normally responsible and the carrying out of which is to both his and the tenant's advantage as a benefit in kind to the tenant. But, unless such expenditure can be regarded as incurred in the acquisition or production of an asset, that, in my opinion, is the effect of these provisions.

. . . I think, having regard to the context, that this phrase should not be narrowly interpreted. As I have pointed out, if it is to be understood to exclude the cost of repairs of the character executed in this case, the result will be manifestly unjust.

I do not think that one is constrained to consider each item of expenditure separately and say whether or not that particular item of expenditure produced an asset which remained the property of the company. I think one is entitled to look at the position before the repairs are executed and to contrast it with that after their execution. Before they were executed the company owned premises with a defective water main, defective plumbing, a defective chimney, defective fireplaces and a defective roof. After their execution they owned premises of a very different character. The creation of premises of such a different character can, I think, legitimately be regarded as constituting the production of an asset.

For these reasons, in my view, the commissioners were right in holding that the sums involved in this case were not liable to tax. The case would, I think, be different if the company had executed repairs the cost of which is normally borne by a tenant [48]; then it might well be said that the tenant had received a benefit in kind. . . .

RENDELL v. WENT

House of Lords [1964] 1 W.L.R. 650; 108 S.J. 401; [1964] 2 All E.R. 464; 41 T.C. 641

LORD REID: My Lords, the appellant is a whole time director of Peter Merchant Ltd. On July 23, 1958, the car which he was driving on the company's business struck and killed a pedestrian. The next day while in hospital he instructed his secretary to get legal advice from the Automobile Association. But when his managing director heard of this he countermanded that instruction and consulted the company's solicitors. He was advised that the appellant might be charged with causing death by reckless or dangerous driving, that if convicted he would be sent to prison and that the company might be involved in liability. The appellant was the only director in a position to negotiate contracts with certain customers and his services were also needed in connection with a reorganisation. So the managing director instructed the solicitors to spare no reasonable expense in his defence. This appears to have been fully justified in the interests of the company, as they might have lost much business if the appellant had been convicted and sent to prison.

A partner of the solicitors' firm went immediately to see the appellant in hospital and told him that the managing director had given instructions that he was not to have anything further to do with the provision of his defence, and the appellant was very relieved by this information. The solicitors made full preparation for the defence, instructing an expert and senior and junior

---

[48] See *Doyle* v. *Davison* (1961) 40 T.C. 140 (N.I.). The money expended by the employer company on repairs was held to form part of its managing director's remuneration. *Per* McVeigh J.: " . . . provided it is reasonable tenant's repair, it seems to me to be taxable."

counsel. On November 3, 1958, the appellant was tried at the Old Bailey and acquitted. The cost of the defence, £641, was paid by the company.

The appellant was then assessed to income tax for the year 1958–59 in the sum of £3,919 in respect of his emoluments as director. This sum included the sum of £641 spent by the company on his defence. The question in this appeal is whether that sum ought to have been included in the assessment.

. . . The facts make it quite clear that the company did incur expense in the provision of a legal defence for their director, the appellant. And it appears to me to be equally clear that the provision of that defence was a benefit within the meaning of this subsection. It was argued that the expense had been incurred solely for the purpose of protecting the interests of the company. That may be so. But it cannot be doubted that in fact the provision of his defence was a benefit to him: if it had not been provided by the company he would have had to pay for his own defence or take the risk that lack of a proper defence might lead to his being convicted and sent to prison. No one suggests that he could have obtained free legal aid. And I can find nothing in the Act to support an argument that a benefit in fact provided by the company ceases to be a benefit within the meaning of the section if it is proved that the company's sole reason, motive or purpose was to protect itself and was not to favour its director.

The main argument for the appellant was that, although he had received a benefit, it was not worth £641 to him and that that sum should be apportioned. I could understand a case being made for apportionment if the expenditure had been made for two objects, only one of which was of benefit to the director. But here there was only one object—to prevent conviction of the appellant. The company's reason for trying to achieve that object may have been different from the appellant's. The company did not want to be deprived of his services, while he wanted to avoid going to prison. But the whole of the money was spent for the purpose of avoiding that.

It is found as a fact that the appellant would not have spent so much on his own defence: he mentioned a sum of £60. But then he would not have got the same benefit. His defence would not have been prepared in the way it was and he would not have been defended by experienced counsel. There is nothing to suggest that the £641 was extravagantly spent or that the benefit which he actually received could have been got for less. This is not a case of the company spending without the director's knowledge a large sum to procure a benefit which he did not want, and I do not intend to consider how such a case ought to be dealt with. The appellant knew and accepted what was being done on his behalf though he may not have realised how much it was costing.

Where there is in fact a benefit and, therefore, a perquisite the Act provides that the measure of the perquisite shall be the expense incurred by the company in providing it. Whether there can ever be circumstances in which it would be possible to depart from that rule in a case where the money was wholly spent to provide the benefit is a matter which it is unnecessary to consider. I can see nothing in the facts of this case to justify any reduction of the sum in which the appellant has been assessed, and accordingly I would dismiss this appeal.

VISCOUNT RADCLIFFE: . . . But an expenditure is not the less advantageous to a director because it suits or advantages his company to make it. . . .

3. Allowable Expenditure

" If the holder of an office or employment is necessarily obliged to incur and defray out of the emoluments thereof the expenses of travelling in the performance of the duties of the office or employment, or of keeping and maintaining a horse to enable him to perform the same, or otherwise to expend money wholly, exclusively and necessarily in the performance of the said duties, there may be deducted from the emoluments to be assessed the expenses so necessarily incurred and defrayed." [49]

As may be seen from the preceding part of this Chapter, the deductibility or otherwise of an item of expenditure may determine whether or not a payment made to, or on behalf of, an employee constitutes an emolument of that employee. [50] Where an expense is to be incurred in respect of an employee, the employer may pay him a wage or salary and leave him to bear the expense himself. The question then is simply whether or not the employee is entitled to deduct from his emoluments the amount of the expense. Alternatively, the employer may pay the expense himself. The question then should be whether the payment by the employer constitutes a taxable benefit to the employee, i.e. is it a "perquisite or profit"? [51] Whether it is or not *may* depend upon whether, if the employee had incurred it himself, he would have been able to deduct it. Again, the employer may pay the employee an " allowance " out of which the employee is to pay the expense, [52] or, the employee having already incurred the expense, he may " reimburse " him. In these cases, also, it is submitted that the correct question is whether or not the payment constitutes an emolument; this *may* be determined according to whether the expense would be deductible by the employee.

FINAL REPORT OF THE ROYAL COMMISSION ON THE TAXATION OF PROFITS AND INCOME

1955 Cmd. 9474

129. It seems to be the general impression that the rule governing the deduction of expenses in respect of offices or employments under Schedule E is too narrow. It will be convenient to refer to it by its old name as rule 9. We had before us a great many representations complaining of the operation of the rule in various respects, to which we gave our careful attention. In making these criticisms our witnesses were doing no more than apply to their own particular circumstances the substance of a series of comments which have been made by Courts of law during the last thirty years. There can have been no part of the income tax code which has been so regularly the subject of unfavourable notice.

130. Rule 9 has been variously described as " jealously restricted," " strictly limited " and " a very narrow and strict rule." Its words are said to be " notoriously narrow in their application " and " notoriously rigid, narrow and restricted in their operation . . . stringent and exacting." Nor has judicial

---

[49] I.C.T.A. 1970, s. 189 (1).
[50] See especially *Owen* v. *Pook* (ante, p. 251).
[51] As, for example, in *Richardson* v. *Lyon* (1943) 25 T.C. 497, in *Luke* v. *I.R.C.* [1963] A.C. 557; ante, p. 265, and in *Rendell* v. *Went* [1964] 1 W.L.R. 650; ante, p. 266. The approach to this problem in *Brown* v. *Bullock* [1961] 1 W.L.R. 1095 (C.A.), namely to treat the payment by the employer to a third party on the employee's behalf as being " clearly an emolument " and then to consider whether the employee is entitled to deduct the expense (which was not actually incurred by him) appears to the author to be misconceived. It is surely either a " profit " or it is not.
[52] *Fergusson* v. *Noble*, 1919 S.C. 534; 7 T.C. 176; ante, p. 250.

sympathy been withheld from those to whom the " very strict words laid down in rule 9 " have been applied. " This case raises a question of hardship. I may go further and say the position really is unreasonable "; " A great number of these cases have produced, in my judgment, extremely hard results "; " a . . . rule . . . which undoubtedly causes a considerable amount of hardship when applied to particular cases." It has been compared unfavourably with the rule for Schedule D: " much more limited and severe as regards allowances of expenses than the rules applicable in the case of Schedule D assessments. . . ."

132. On the other hand, despite all that has been said in criticism of rule 9, nothing has ever been done to alter it.[53] Moreover, the Board submitted to us evidence, both written and oral, to the effect that the existing rule drew the line as fairly as could be expected of any general rule and that no other form of wording would be an improvement upon it. If we felt that we must recommend some alteration, they urged upon us that special allowances should be made for special circumstances rather than that any general rewording should open the way for wider claims.

133. In dealing with this difficult question it is essential to establish clearly what rule 9 does require. Its reputation has suffered partly from its verbiage, and there has been a tendency to exaggerate the significance of certain words. The two determining phrases are " obliged . . . to expend " and " in the performance of the said duties." " Necessarily obliged " means no more than " obliged." " Wholly and exclusively " are the same words as those that occur in the Schedule D rule [54] and, given the recognition of a right to apportion whatever is apportionable, they impose no unfair limitation. " Necessarily," again, adds no further force, once it has been laid down that the only allowable expenses are those which the holder of the office or employment is obliged to incur in the performance of the duties of his office or employment. Stripped of its verbiage, that is all that the rule requires.

134. The use of the word " obliged " is defended on the ground that the subject of tax is income from office or employment. Consequently it must be possible to ascertain from the terms of the employment what expenses the employee was bound to incur in the performance of his duties. It was that performance that qualified him to receive the remuneration which forms the taxable income, and therefore the only expenses that can properly be set against that income are those which had to be met in order to earn it. Normally, indeed, it is the employer who pays for proper expenses, directly or by reimbursement and a claim that involves an employee's uncovered expenses is prima facie suspect. On the other hand, if the taxpayer were left free to decide for himself what expenses it was reasonable or proper to incur for the purpose of performing his duty, regardless of whether he was actually obliged to incur them in order to earn his salary, there would be no common measure to apply to the allowance of expenses and all sorts of claims would become admissible which it would be very difficult to scrutinise effectively in the course of administration.

135. We do not quarrel with this as a formal presentation of the problem. It is quite true that the nature of income from employment is such that it does not admit a wide range of individual choice as to the expenses to be incurred. Put it as a series of questions: Are personal tools to be allowed for, if used in preference to those provided by the employer? books additional to those so provided? overalls where their use is optional? a private car where alternative travelling facilities are provided free? wife's or secretary's wages where the terms of employment do not require their assistance? It would be possible, we

[53] This is still true.
[54] See *ante*, Chap. 9, p. 180, where the effect of these words is discussed. See also M. Flesch: " All Work, No Play? " [1966] B.T.R. 204.

think, to return the answer No to most, if not all, of these questions without concluding that the best available test is provided by asking whether it was obligatory to incur the expenses in the performance of the duties. For it does not seem to us that the contrast between what the employer or the employment requires and what the employee decides to do is nearly so absolute as is assumed by the orthodox line of argument. For that argument does not take sufficient account of the fact that there are many offices and employments the true obligations of which are not capable of being precisely defined. It is not enough therefore to ask whether the terms of the office or employment specifically require the employee to incur the expense, and, if not, to disallow the expense as a tax deduction.[55] In many cases the taxpayer himself must be the interpreter of the obligations of his office. To take one instance from several that came under our notice: what rule is to determine with precision the limits of a clergyman's duty to his parish? How far is it part of his duty to show hospitality, to aid the sick, to organise or support benevolent activities, to supplement his ministry with visiting preachers? . . .

137. The present form of the rule bears hardly upon persons of professional status in another way. We do not use the word " professional " here in any precise sense: we have in mind all those persons in office or employment whose work is of such a kind that they are expected to employ in it an equipment of expert or specialised knowledge. Doctors, teachers, lawyers, scientific workers, clergymen fall into this category. Such persons require to maintain and often to increase their professional equipment of knowledge, and it must often be quite impossible to relate the expenses of so doing to any specific obligation in performing the duties of a particular period. Their obligation is not only to be skilled in learning but to remain skilled in learning as conditions change. The expenses of so doing are represented by subscriptions to professional and learned societies, purchases of books and magazines, attendance at conferences, travel for research, purchase of instruments, etc. Yet, under the present rule, the Revenue is forced into taking what seems to us rather unreal distinctions between what an employer insists upon and what he does not, between what a person is obliged to do in the performance of his duty and what it is desirable that he should do in order to be able to perform his duty: and between current expenses of maintaining knowledge or skill for one post and capital expenses of acquiring improved knowledge or skill to qualify for another post. It is not to be wondered at that the administration of rule 9 is attended by rather widespread dissatisfaction. What remains to be seen is how much of that dissatisfaction is curable.

138. We have come to certain general conclusions. One is that the form of rule 9 is calculated to provide a narrower allowance for expenses than that provided by the Schedule D rule, and that, although there are a great many employments in which its operation creates no hardship because there are no debatable expenses, there is a number to which it fails to do justice. The second is, that there is no good reason for treating Schedule E expenses less generously than Schedule D expenses, except to the limited extent that some difference of treatment is inherent in the nature of the two kinds of income. The third is, that we are bound to recommend some form of adjustment. If the matter stood by itself, it might be the wiser course to leave the Schedule E rule unaltered, since no completely satisfactory form of words is likely to be discovered. But we do not regard that as a possible course of action, having regard to the rule's disconformity with the Schedule D rule and the constant critical attack to which it has been subjected.

---

[55] But that is *not* the proper test: see the *Note* to *Lupton* v. *Potts* (*post*, p. 276).

139. We considered a variety of possible methods of carrying out a change. One method would be to allow for Schedule E income a higher rate of earned income relief than for Schedule D income and thereby afford to it some compensation for what might be thought to be its lower taxable quality. We rejected this proposal, partly because the earned income relief centres round the idea of precariousness and precariousness is certainly no more a feature of Schedule E income than of Schedule D profits; and partly because it did not seem right to give a general preference to all Schedule E incomes on account of disadvantages which affected only certain classes of them. Another form of compensation would be to give a lump-sum or percentage allowance to Schedule E income, without proof of actual expenditure, in the hope that thereby a rough justice would be done and a concession made that would be sufficient to cover the marginal items of expenditure, including " capital " expenditure on self-improvement.[56] We had to abandon this idea, since we could see no possibility of deciding what to suggest as the amount of such a lump sum or percentage. A more hopeful line of inquiry seemed to lie in investigating the possibility of drawing up specific rules for identifying certain types of permissible expenditure to be allowed if bearing on the employment. It was suggested, for instance, that figures could be fixed for expenditure on books and periodicals, on subscriptions to named learned societies, on maintaining and furthering the employee's skill in his calling. In the end we decided that a method of this kind would not work. Admittedly, it would give some additional relief, particularly in those classes of employment in which the pinch is felt the sharpest today. But a code of rules of this kind would have to be extremely detailed and comprehensive, if it was really to cover the circumstances of every kind of employment and do justice to them; and the opportunities for debate as to what was or what was not to be included seemed to us to threaten to be virtually without end. Moreover, we saw objections on grounds of principle to any listing of named organisations for this purpose.

140. Finally, we came to the conclusion that the best solution was to recommend a rewording of rule 9 on less restricted lines. The wording that we propose would allow the deduction of " all expenses reasonably incurred for the appropriate performance of the duties of the office or employment." We have chosen this wording in order to bring the wording of rule 9 into a closer conformity with the wording of the Schedule D rule and to remove the genuine cause of complaint that the Legislature deliberately imposes upon those in employment a narrower form of allowance for expenses than it accords to those who are deriving a profit income from their own efforts.

REPORT OF THE ROYAL COMMISSION ON TAXATION

Carter Commission, Canada, 1966

CHAPTER 14: RECOMMENDATIONS

. . .

3. Because of the stringent limitations in the present law, employees are unable to deduct many expenses that are deductible by the self-employed. Skilled manual workers and employed professionals in particular are unfairly treated relative to the self-employed.

4. Equity requires that both types of unfair discrimination be eliminated from the tax system by effectively bringing all significant non-cash benefits into

---

[56] Cf. the suggestions of the Carter Commission, infra. This solution is also considered by L. Lazar: " Nearly nothing at all " [1970] B.T.R. 95.

tax and by putting the deduction of expenses on the same basis for employees and the self-employed.

. . .

23. The same rules with respect to deductibility of expenses should apply to employees and to the self-employed. Expenses reasonably related to the earning of income should be deductible. There should be a general prohibition against the deduction of personal living expenses. For greater certainty, deductibility should be explicitly denied to such expenses as commuting expenses, fees or dues for social or recreational clubs and expenses related to the use of recreational facilities or pleasure boats. Also, travelling and entertainment costs in excess of the designated limits should be deemed to be personal expenditures.

24. To reduce the administrative burden, there should be an optional deduction of 3 per cent. of employment income up to a maximum deduction of $500. This could be taken in lieu of the deduction of actual expenses.

LOMAX v. NEWTON

Chancery Division [1953] 1 W.L.R. 1128; 97 S.J. 573; [1953] 2 All E.R. 801; 34 T.C. 558

The taxpayer, a major in the Territorial Army, claimed a deduction in respect of mess expenses. *Held*, except as to the cost of hotel accommodation in excess of his allowance, no deduction was permitted.

VAISEY J.: Before coming to the particular items of expenditure, I would observe that the provisions of rule 9 of Schedule E are notoriously rigid, narrow and restricted in their operation. In order to satisfy the terms of the rule it must be shown that the expenditure incurred was not only necessarily, but wholly and exclusively incurred in the performance of the relevant official duties. And it is certainly not enough merely to assert that a particular payment satisfies the requirements of the rule, without specifying the detailed facts upon which the finding is based. An expenditure may be " necessary " for the holder of an office without being necessary to him in the performance of the duties of that office; it may be necessary in the performance of those duties without being exclusively referable to those duties; it may perhaps be both necessarily and exclusively, but still not wholly so referable. The words are indeed stringent and exacting; compliance with each and every one of them is obligatory if the benefit of the rule is to be claimed successfully. They are, to my mind, deceptive words in the sense that when examined they are found to come to nearly nothing at all. . . .

RICKETTS v. COLQUHOUN

House of Lords [1962] A.C. 1; 95 L.J.K.B. 82; 134 L.T. 106; 90 J.P. 9; 42 T.L.R. 66; 10 T.C. 118

The appellant, R, held the office of Recorder of Portsmouth. He claimed to deduct his travelling expenses to and from London, where he lived and practised as a barrister. His claim failed.

VISCOUNT CAVE L.C.: As regards the appellant's travelling expenses to and from Portsmouth, with which may be linked the small payment for the carriage to the Court of the tin box containing his robes and wig, the material words of the rule are those which provide that, if the holder of an office is " necessarily obliged to incur . . . the expenses of travelling in the performance of the duties of the office " the expenses so " necessarily incurred " may be deducted from the emoluments to be assessed. The question is whether the travelling expenses in question fall within that description. Having given the best consideration that I can to the question, I agree with the Commissioners and with the Courts below in holding that they do not. In order that they may be deductible under this rule from an assessment under Schedule E, they must be expenses which the holder of an office is necessarily obliged to incur—that is to say, obliged by the very fact that he holds the office and has to perform its duties—and they must be incurred in—that is, in the course of—the performance of those duties.

The expenses in question in this case do not appear to me to satisfy either test. They are incurred not because the appellant holds the office of Recorder of Portsmouth, but because, living and practising away from Portsmouth, he must travel to that place before he can begin to perform his duties as Recorder and, having concluded those duties, desires to return home. They are incurred, not in the course of performing his duties, but partly before he enters upon them, and partly after he has fulfilled them. No doubt the rule contemplates that the holder of an office may have to travel in the performance of his duties, and there are offices of which the duties have to be performed in several places in succession, so that the holder of them must necessarily travel from one place to another. That was no doubt the case of the minister whose expenses were in question in the case of *Jardine* v. *Gillespie*.[57] But it rarely, if ever, happens that a Recorder is in that position, and there is no suggestion that any such necessity exists in the case of the present appellant. It is said that a barrister normally lives in London, or in some great city where there is a local Bar, and that the Legislature, in enacting in the Municipal Corporations Act that only a barrister shall be appointed Recorder,[58] must have contemplated that he would usually incur some expenses in travelling to and from his Court. That may be so, but the question is, not what expenses a Recorder or the holder of some other office may be expected to incur, but what expenses he may deduct from his assessment, and upon this point rule 9 appears to be conclusive.

I may add that in the case of *Cook* v. *Knott*,[59] decided in the year 1887, it was held by Pollock B. and Hawkins J., sitting as judges of the Queen's Bench Division, that travelling expenses of this character could not be deducted under a similar rule contained in section 51 of the Income Tax Act 1853. Since that decision the rule has been re-enacted in the same terms, and I should hesitate long before overruling a decision which has stood for thirty-eight years, and upon which subsequent legislation may have been based. . . .

OWEN v. POOK

House of Lords (*ante*, p. 251)

LORD GUEST: . . . In *Ricketts* v. *Colquhoun* there was only one place of employment, Portsmouth. It was not suggested that any duties were performed in London. In the present case there is a finding of fact that Dr. Owen's duties commenced at the moment he was first contacted by the hospital authorities.

---

[57] (1906) 5 T.C. 263. It was necessary for the Minister to travel around his parish in the performance of his duties. He was permitted to deduct his expenditure on a horse and carriage.

[58] In the words of Rowlatt J., at first instance, " The Statute, however, does not say that a Recorder must be a practising barrister; still less does it say that he must be a barrister practising in London." [1924] 2 K.B. 347, 350.

[59] (1887) 2 T.C. 246. In that case, a solicitor residing and carrying on his profession in Worcester held the office of Clerk to the Justices at Bromyard. He was held not to be entitled to deduct the cost of travelling from Worcester to Bromyard.

This is further emphasised by the finding that his responsibility for a patient began as soon as he received a telephone call and that he sometimes advised treatment by telephone. It is noteworthy that under section 19 (*b*) (3) (iv) of his terms and conditions of service the hospital is referred to " where his principal duties lie." There were thus two places where his duty is performed, the hospital and his telephone in his consulting room. If he was performing his duties at both places, then it is difficult to see why, on the journey between the two places, he was not equally performing his duties. Indeed Mr. Heyworth Talbot did not contend to the contrary. It follows that he had to get from his consulting room to the hospital by car to treat the emergency. The travelling expenses were, in my view, necessarily incurred in the performance of the duties of his office. . . .

Note
Contrast the treatment of travelling expenses under Cases I and II of Schedule D: *Newsom* v. *Robertson* [1953] Ch. 7; *cf. Horton* v. *Young* [1972] 1 Ch. 157.

NOLDER v. WALTERS

King's Bench Division (1930) 15 T.C. 380; 46 T.L.R. 397; 47 S.J. 337

The taxpayer, W., was an aircraft pilot. He claimed deductions (i) in respect of the upkeep and running of a car to take him to and from the airfield and his home, (ii) in respect of the excess of his actual subsistence expenses when away from home on duty over the subsistence allowance granted to him by his employer. The first claim was disallowed, but the second was allowed.

ROWLATT J.: It seems to me that, as a matter of principle the rule to be applied in these cases is clear. What the statute allows to be deducted are expenses of travelling in the performance of the duties of the office, or employment, or money wholly, exclusively, and necessarily expended in the performance of the duties. As regards the latter branch, it seems quite clear that what is to be allowed to be deducted are expenses " wholly, necessarily," and so on, incurred in doing the work of the office. " In the performance of the duties " means in doing the work of the office, in doing the things which it is his duty to do while doing the work of the office. A man who holds an office or employment has, equally necessarily, to do other things incidentally, and spend money incidentally, because he has the office. He has to get to the place of employment, for one thing. If he had not got the employment he could stay at home. As he has got the employment he has necessarily got to get there, and it costs him something, if it is only shoe leather, to get there; but that is not in the performance of the office, because in getting there he is not doing the duties, or doing the work of the office.
. . . Then I come to the other part of the case. Some offices and employments do involve the duty of travelling. It is not a question of getting to the place of employment, but the employment may be actually to travel, as in the common case of the commercial traveller, and, as some people say, in the case of the Member of Parliament. The duties may actually be to travel, and this gentleman's duty is to travel; therefore both, I should have thought, under the general words of the latter part of the section, and, I think, under the head of travelling expenses, he is allowed the expenses of so travelling. The Solicitor-General and Mr. Hills very fairly agree, and I think it always has been agreed, that when you get a travelling office, so that travelling expenses are allowed, those travelling expenses do include the extra expense of living

which is put upon a man by having to stay at hotels and inns, and such places, rather than stay at home. Of course his board and lodging in a sense, eating and sleeping, are the necessities of a human being, whether he has an office, or whether he has not, and therefore, of course, the cost of his food and lodging is not wholly and exclusively laid out in the performance of his duties, but the extra part of it is. The extra expense of it is, and that is the quite fair way in which the Revenue look at it. In this case, therefore, he would be entitled to charge something for the extra expense which he is put to by having to go and spend all the day, and often the night, away from home, because that is part of his duty; . . .

Note
As in *Owen* v. *Pook* (*ante*, pp. 251, 273) the claim was for the amount by which actual expenditure exceeded an allowance. *Cf. Marsden* v. *I.R.C.* (see *ante*, p. 253).

SIMPSON v. TATE

King's Bench Division [1925] 2 K.B. 214; 94 L.J.K.B. 817; 133 L.T. 187; 41 T.L.R. 370; 69 S.J. 460; 9 T.C. 314

The taxpayer was the Medical Officer of Health for Middlesex. To assist him in keeping-up with medical and scientific developments he joined certain learned societies and sought to deduct the subscriptions. *Held,* he was not *obliged* so to expend his money.

RowLATT J.: . . . The respondent qualified himself for his office before he was appointed to it, and he has very properly endeavoured to continue qualified by joining certain professional and scientific societies, so that by attending their meetings and procuring their publications he may keep abreast of the highest developments and knowledge of the day. He seeks to deduct from his assessable income the subscriptions paid by him to these societies as money expended necessarily in the performance of the duties of the office. When one looks into the matter closely, however, one sees that these are not moneys expended in the performance of the official duties. He does not incur these expenses in conducting professional inquiries or get the journals in order to read them to the patients. If he did, the case would be altogether different. He incurs these expenses in qualifying himself for continuing to hold his office, just as before being appointed to the office he qualified himself for obtaining it. . . .

Note
See now I.C.T.A. 1970, s. 192.

LUPTON v. POTTS

Chancery Division [1969] 1 W.L.R. 1749; 113 S.J. 569; [1969] 3 All E.R. 1083; 45 T.C. 643

A solicitor's articled clerk claimed to deduct a fee paid by him for sitting the Law Society's examination. The claim failed.

PLOWMAN J.: . . . In my judgment, the duties of the taxpayer under the contract of employment were perfectly capable of being performed without incurring the particular outlay with which I am concerned in this case. I find it impossible to say that that outlay was necessarily incurred in the performance of those duties.

Moreover, I am not satisfied that the expenditure was incurred exclusively in the performance of his duties under the contract of employment. If Mr. Nolan is right in submitting that the purpose of the taxpayer in paying the fees is involved in this question, then it seems to me that the purpose of paying the fees for the Part I subjects for which he sat after being articled cannot have been radically different from his purpose in paying the fees for the Part I subjects for which he sat before being articled. This was not to benefit or fulfil an obligation to an employer but to benefit himself because he wanted to become a solicitor. . . .

Note

In addition to the expenditure being incurred " wholly and exclusively " in the performance of the taxpayer's duties (and the remarks of Plowman J. suggests that this was not so), it must be " necessarily incurred."

This is illustrated by this case and by *Simpson* v. *Tate, supra.* See also *Humbles* v. *Brooks* (1962) 40 T.C. 500, where a school teacher was not permitted to deduct fees paid by him to attend lectures in the subject he taught. He was not " necessarily obliged " to do so: *per* Ungoed-Thomas J. And see *Owen* v. *Burden* [1972] 1 All E.R. 356.

It is also not enough that the employer requires his employee to incur certain expenses: see *Bolam* v. *Barlow* (1949) 31 T.C. 136 and *Brown* v. *Bullock* [1961] 1 W.L.R. 1095, *per* Donovan L.J., " The test is not whether the employer imposes the expense but whether the duties do, in the sense that, irrespective of what the employer may prescribe, the duties cannot be performed without incurring the particular outlay."

CHAPTER 12

INCOME FROM FOREIGN SOURCES

SOME income from foreign sources falls within the Schedules and Cases discussed in earlier Chapters. Thus, while Schedules A and B charge profits in respect of land and woodlands in the United Kingdom,[1] Schedule C relates to overseas public dividends,[2] Case I of Schedule D to any trade carried on in the United Kingdom or elsewhere[3] and Schedule E to emoluments of an office or employment, whether performed in the United Kingdom or elsewhere.[4]

Other income, from foreign securities and possessions, is charged to tax under Cases IV and V of Schedule D.[5]

ROYAL COMMISSION ON THE TAXATION OF PROFITS AND INCOME

First Report, 1953 Cmd. 8761

8. The United Kingdom tax system asserts two distinct claims as the basis of tax jurisdiction:

(1) It taxes income arising in the United Kingdom no matter to whom it belongs.

(2) It taxes residents in the United Kingdom no matter where their income arises.

1. Profits of a Foreign Trade

Although Case I applies to " any trade carried on in the United Kingdom or elsewhere,"[5] it does not charge the profits of a trade carried on entirely outside the United Kingdom.[6] Whether a trade is being carried on wholly abroad, or partly in this country, is in part a question of fact.[7]

COLQUHOUN v. BROOKS

House of Lords (1889) 14 App.Cas. 493; 59 L.J.Q.B. 53; 61 L.T. 518; 54 J.P. 277; 38 W.R. 289; 5 T.L.R. 728; [1886–90] All E.R.Rep. 1063; 2 T.C. 490

The respondent, who resided in the United Kingdom, was partner in a firm in Australia. Part only of his share of profits was remitted to this country.

[1] I.C.T.A. 1970, ss. 67, 91.   [2] Ibid. s. 93.
[3] Ibid. s. 109.
[4] Ibid. s. 181. See Davies v. Braithwaite [1931] 2 K.B. 628; ante, p. 230.
[5] Ibid. s. 109.
[6] Colquhoun v. Brooks (1889) 14 App.Cas. 493, infra.
[7] Firestone Tyre & Rubber Co. Ltd. v. Llewellin [1957] 1 W.L.R. 464; Mitchell v. Egyptian Hotels Ltd. [1915] A.C. 1022; post, p. 280. Although the question of where a trade is being carried on and that of where a trading company is resident may be related, the two questions are not the same and it is possible for a trading company to be resident in the United Kingdom although trading exclusively abroad: Swedish Central Railway Co. Ltd. v. Thompson [1925] A.C. 495; post, p. 448.

Held, as no part of the firm's business was carried on in this country, Case I of Schedule D did not apply, but Case V did apply.

LORD HERSCHELL: ... If the result of rejecting the argument presented on behalf of the Crown [8] were to land your Lordships in the conclusion that profits arising from a business carried on abroad, even though received here, were not subject to the tax it would present a formidable obstacle to yielding to the argument of the respondent, though I am not sure that the difficulties you would have to encounter in refusing your assent to it would not even then be greater. But I do not think your Lordships are driven to this conclusion. The rule, styled the fifth case, which I have already referred to, deals with the duty to be charged in respect of possessions in any of Her Majesty's dominions out of Great Britain and foreign possessions. Now the word " possessions " is not used in the part of the Schedule D which describes the subjects of the tax. Speaking generally they are defined to be the profits arising from property and those arising from trades and professions. When therefore the term " possessions " is employed it seems to indicate an intention to cover by it something more than " property." And it is difficult to see why, unless the intention were to embrace something more, the latter word was not used. " Possessions " is a wide expression, it is not a word with any technical meaning; the Act supplies no interpretation of it. I cannot see why it may not fitly be interpreted as relating to all that is possessed in Her Majesty's dominions out of the United Kingdom or in foreign countries and which is a source of income. And if so I do not think any violence would be done to the language if it were held to include the interest which a person in this country possesses in a business carried on elsewhere. So to construe the Act would have the advantage of removing the glaring anomaly to which I have referred as inevitably flowing from the rival construction and of taxing alike such portion only of the profits arising abroad whether from property or trade as is received in the United Kingdom.[9] ...

SAN PAULO (BRAZILIAN) RAILWAY CO. LTD. v. CARTER

House of Lords [1896] A.C. 31, 65 L.J.K.B. 161; 73 L.T. 538; 60 J.P. 84; 44 W.R. 336; 12 T.L.R. 107; 3 T.C. 407

LORD HALSBURY: ... My Lords, I think one proposition has been conclusively established by the various cases that have come under your Lordships' consideration, and that is, that where the trade is wholly or partially carried on in this country the trader is liable to pay income tax on the profits of his trade.

Now, in this case the appellant company is an English company residing (so far as that abstraction a corporation can reside at all) in England. It has an office in London, and I am disposed to think (though it is unnecessary for the purposes of this case to say so) that its trade, if the word " trade " is strictly construed, is wholly carried on in England. It seems to me that, as was said by Cockburn C.J. in the case of *Sulley* v. *Attorney-General,*[10] " it is probably a question of fact where the trade is carried on," and it is probably true to say that that phrase may be understood in two different senses. It may mean where the goods in respect of which trading is carried on are conveyed, made, bought, or sold; or, speaking of land, where it is cultivated or used for any other purpose of profit. That makes the locality of the goods or the land

---

[8] *i.e.* that Case I applied.
[9] Such profits are, and were then, taxable only on a remittance basis: I.C.T.A. 1970, s. 122 (2) (*b*), (3); see *post,* pp. 290–295.
[10] (1860) 5 N. & H. 711; 2 L.T. 439.

which are the subjects of the trade to be in a certain sense the place where the trade is carried on, because it is the place where the things corporeally exist, or are dealt with. But there is another sense, in which the conduct and management, the head and brain of the trading adventure, are situated in a place different from that in which the corporeal subjects of trading are to be found. It becomes, therefore, a question of fact, and according to the answer to be given to the question where is the trade in a strict sense carried on, will the assessment be.

My Lords, it is therefore necessary to determine upon these principles where this appellant company carries on its business. It deals, undoubtedly, with land in the Brazils. In Brazil the payments are received, and in Brazil the passengers and goods are carried; but the form of trading can make no difference. If it were a mine, as in the *Cesena Case*,[11] or a jute mill, equally with a railway, the person who governs the whole commercial adventure, the person who decides what shall be done in respect of the adventure, what capital shall be invested in the adventure, on what terms the adventure shall be carried on, in short, the person who, in the strictest sense, makes the profits by his skill or industry, however distant may be the field of his adventure, is the person who is trading. That person appears to me, in this case, to be the appellant company. Every one of the tests I have applied are applicable to its proceedings. A shipowner, or indeed a shipbroker, may not have any one of the ships or the charterparties which he negotiates in England; but by correspondence or by agency he may have both charterparties and ships, not necessarily British ships, all over the globe. But if he lives in London, and by his direction governs the whole of this commercial adventure, could it be properly said that he is not carrying on his trade in London? So it appears to me that this appellant company is carrying on the trade in London, from which it issues its orders, and so governs and directs the whole commercial adventure that is under its superintendence.

I am, therefore, of opinion that the appeal must be dismissed with costs, and I move your Lordships accordingly.

OGILVIE v. KITTON

Court of Exchequer (Scotland) (1908) 5 T.C. 338; 1908 S.C. 1003

The Appellant, resident in the United Kingdom, was the sole owner of a business carried on on his behalf by managers in Canada. *Held,* the trade was being carried on in part in this country and Case I of Schedule D applied.

LORD STORMONTH DARLING : . . . It is settled by the judgment of the House of Lords in *The San Paulo (Brazilian) Railway Company, Limited* [12] that where a trade is carried on either wholly in the United Kingdom, or partly within and partly outside it, and profits accrue therefrom to a person or a corporation residing in the United Kingdom (in this case the profits accrue to a person residing in Aberdeen) the assessment for Income Tax falls under the First Case of Schedule D of [the Income Tax Act 1842, s. 100], and does not fall under the Fifth Case, and the duty is to be computed upon the full amount of the balance of the profits or gains of the trade, and not only upon the actual sums received in the United Kingdom. Therefore the question is whether the trade is carried on either wholly in the United Kingdom, or partly within and

---

11 *Cesena Sulphur Co.* v. *Nicholson* (1876) 1 Ex.D. 428; 1 T.C. 88.
12 [1896] A.C. 31; *supra.*

partly outside it, and it is enough for the view that the assessment for Income Tax falls under the First Case and not under the Fifth, if the necessary inference from the facts is that the trade is carried on partly in the United Kingdom and partly outside it.

. . . Now, apply this judgment to the case in hand, and what do you find? The " head and brain of the trading adventure " in Toronto are undoubtedly to be found in Aberdeen, where Mr. Thomas Ogilvie, senior, resides, to which weekly statements of the transactions of the Toronto business in all its departments are sent, and where the sole right to manage and control every department of its affairs is central. Mr. Ogilvie, senior, is Board of Directors and Company all in one, for the case states that " the managers and other employees associated and employed in the carrying on of said business of Thomas Ogilvie & Sons have no power to act in the carrying on of the trade apart from the authority, express or implied, which they hold from the said Thomas Ogilvie, senior."

It is said that, although all this may be true, although Mr. Thomas Ogilvie, senior, may have in theory the absolute control of the business or trade locally situated in Toronto, since it is carried on for his sole benefit and he could do with it what he likes with no one to say him nay, yet not a single instance has ever occurred in which he has, as a matter of fact, attempted to exercise his control, or to give directions even about the smallest detail. Yet the right of control is there all the time, and might be exercised at any moment. It is a matter, as it seems to me, of power and right, and not of the actual exercise of right or power. The necessary inference from forbearance to exercise the right of control is that the man who possesses it is content for the time being with the way in which his wishes are being carried out, and his interests attended to by his employees.[13] . . .

MITCHELL v. EGYPTIAN HOTELS LTD.

House of Lords [1915] A.C. 1022; 84 L.J.K.B. 1772; 113 L.T. 882; 31 T.L.R. 546; 59 S.J. 649; *sub nom. Egyptian Hotels Ltd.* v. *Mitchell*, 6 T.C. 542

LORD PARKER OF WADDINGTON: . . . My Lords, in considering whether the principle of *Colquhoun* v. *Brooks* [14] applies to any particular circumstances, it is also necessary to bear in mind your Lordships' decision in the case of *San Paulo (Brazilian) Ry. Co.* v. *Carter,*[15] to the effect that a trade or business cannot be said to be wholly carried on abroad if it be under the control and management of persons resident in the United Kingdom, although such persons act wholly through agents and managers resident abroad. Where the brain which controls the operation from which the profits and gains arise is in this country the trade or business is, at any rate partly, carried on in this country.

I will now invite your Lordships' attention to the facts in this case. Since August 28, 1908, the affairs of the company have been regulated by the articles as altered by the special resolutions confirmed on August 27, 1908. According to these articles all the company's affairs and business whatsoever in Egypt and the Sudan are under the control of a local board, to the exclusion of the board

---

13 It has been doubted whether the mere power to exercise control, without any actual exercise, should suffice to make the trade carried on where that power exists. In *Mitchell* v. *Egyptian Hotels, Ltd.* [1915] A.C. 1022, *infra*, Lord Parmoor left the question open, whilst Lord Parker of Waddington appears to have considered that there must be actual interference and not merely a power to interfere (at p. 1037); *cf.* Lord Sumner (at pp. 1040–1041).

14 (1889) 14 App.Cas. 493; *ante*, p. 277.

15 [1896] A.C. 31; *ante*, p. 278.

of directors of the company, and of all general meetings of the company not held in Egypt. The local board holds its meetings in Egypt and not elsewhere. It is found by the special case that the business carried on by the company during the year of assessment was the carrying on of two hotels in Egypt, these hotels being under the direct management of servants of the company under the orders of the local board, and the profits of the company being derived wholly from such hotels. All the members of the local board reside in Egypt. Since August 27, 1908, the board of directors of the company have met once only. At this meeting a day was fixed for the annual meeting of shareholders, it was decided to recommend a dividend of 5 per cent., a draft of the directors' report and the accounts for the year ending April 30, 1909, was submitted and approved, and the secretary was authorised to obtain a loan from the company's bankers to enable the dividend to be paid. The annual meeting of the shareholders was held on June 29, 1909, when the directors' report and the accounts for the year ending April 30, 1909, were adopted and the dividend recommended by the directors declared.

Under these circumstances it appears to me indisputable that no single act has been done in or directed from this country by way of participation in or furtherance of the trade or business of the company from which the profits or gains said to be chargeable to income tax since August 28, 1908, have arisen. It was argued that a company can only have one business and that such business necessarily includes the passing of annual accounts, the declaration of a dividend if circumstances admit, and the financial arrangements necessary to enable such dividend to be paid. I cannot accept this argument. The trade or business we have to consider is a trade or business from which profits or gains can arise and not the business of disposing of and dividing such profits and gains when they have arisen, and I can see no reason why a corporation any less than an individual should not be engaged in more than one trade or business at the same time.

The Attorney-General further insisted on the various powers which, even under the altered articles, are still retained by the board of directors of the company. He pointed out that the board of directors of the company have power to determine the remuneration of the members of the local board, to decide when the Egyptian profit and loss account is to be made out, what is to be done with the available cash in Egypt, how cash is to be provided for the Egyptian business if none be available, and generally to determine all questions of finance. It may well be possible that the board of directors of the company still retain powers by virtue of which they could, if occasion arises, so interfere with the company's business in Egypt that such business would cease to be carried on wholly outside this country, but, as I have already pointed out, it is not what they have power to do, but what they have actually done, which is of importance for determining the question which now arises for decision. In the absence of any act done or directed by any person resident here in participation or furtherance of the business operations in Egypt from which the profits and gains in question arose, I think your Lordships are bound to come to the conclusion that this trade or business was carried on wholly outside the United Kingdom, and, therefore, is within case 5 rather than case 1. If this be so the decision of the Court of Appeal must be confirmed and the appeal dismissed with costs.

LORD PARMOOR: . . . The respondents are an English company having its registered office in England, and, subject to the special provisions affecting the Egyptian business, the general management of the affairs of the company is, in the ordinary way, entrusted to the directors. The control of the share capital of the company was left with the directors, including the question of its increase or reduction. It was within the power of the directors to say when the profit and loss account of the Egyptian business should be made out and in what manner the available assets should be allocated. The directors decided how much the Egyptian managers should be paid, and if the Egyptian business should be carried on at a loss in any particular year, the responsibility rested with them of making any necessary financial arrangements. On this evidence the Commissioners found that before and after August 27, 1908, the directors of the respondents were empowered to, and did, deal with the general affairs of the company, including all general financial arrangements of the company.

In my opinion there was evidence before the Commissioners on which within reason they could come to the above finding. It was open to the Commissioners to find that a business is not exclusively carried on outside the United Kingdom when all the general financial arrangements are dealt with and controlled at meetings held from time to time at the offices of the company in England. The Commissioners further found that the head and seat and controlling power of the company remained in England with the board of directors of the company. How far, in any particular case, the power over finance gives controlling power is a question for the Commissioners, but I find it difficult to appreciate how any trade or business can be exclusively carried on outside the United Kingdom by a company which has its offices in England and whose directors are empowered to and do deal with all the general financial arrangements of the company. I agree with Horridge J., that it is not possible to sever the business of the respondents in such a way as to hold that there is a cleaving line between general questions of finance and the local management in Egypt.

It was said in argument that although the directors in England had general controlling powers in matters of finance, there was no evidence that they exercised this power in relation to the Egyptian business. For the reasons already stated, I think that there was evidence on which the Commissioners could find that the directors of the respondents had not only the power to deal with all general financial arrangements of the company, but also exercised this power. It becomes, therefore, unnecessary to decide how far the reservation of a power of control which has not been exercised, is in itself sufficient to negative a claim.[16] . . .

Note

Earl Loreburn agreed with Lord Parmoor that there was evidence to support the Commissioners' finding. Lord Sumner agreed with Lord Parker of Waddington. As the House divided equally, the decision of the Court of Appeal (which held that Case V, rather than Case I applied) was affirmed.

GRAINGER & SON v. GOUGH

House of Lords [1896] A.C. 325; 65 L.J.Q.B. 410; 74 L.T. 435; 60 J.P. 692; 44 W.R. 561; 12 T.L.R. 364; 3 T.C. 462

LORD HERSCHELL: . . . All that the appellants have done in this country on behalf of M. Roederer has been to canvass for orders, to transmit to him those orders, when obtained, and in some cases to receive payment on his behalf. Beyond this he has done nothing in this country, either personally or by agents. Does he, then, exercise his trade within the United Kingdom? It has been some times said that it is a question of fact whether a person so exercises his trade. In a sense this is true; but, in order to determine the question in any particular case, it is essential to form an idea of the elements which constitute the exercise of a trade within the meaning of the Act of Parliament. In the first place,

---

[16] *Cf. Ogilvie* v. *Kitton* (1908) 5 T.C. 338; *ante*, p. 279.

I think there is a broad distinction between trading *with* a country and carrying on a trade *within* a country. Many merchants and manufacturers export their goods to all parts of the world, yet I do not suppose any one would dream of saying that they exercise or carry on their trade in every country in which their goods find customers. . . .

Note

    Followed in *Greenwood* v. *F. L. Smidth & Co.* [1922] 1 A.C. 417; *cf. Firestone Tyre & Rubber Co. Ltd.* v. *Llewellin* [1957] 1 W.L.R. 464.

2. Securities and Possessions

Neither the term " securities " nor the term " possessions," as used in Cases IV and V of Schedule D, are defined in the Tax Acts. " Securities " has been given, by the courts, a restricted meaning [17]; " possessions," on the other hand, has a very wide meaning.[18] The distinction between " securities " and " possessions " was formerly of importance, income from possessions being charged on a three-years average basis and, for the most part, only on a remittance basis.[19] This is no longer so.

    In determining liability to income tax, two particular problems present themselves:

  (i) the *location* of the securities or possessions has to be determined, *i.e.* the income therefrom is charged under Cases IV and V only if they are " out of the United Kingdom ";

  (ii) the *source* of the income has to be determined, *i.e.* as the taxpayer is charged on the income from " possessions " it is necessary to know precisely what those possessions are.[20]

BRADBURY v. ENGLISH SEWING COTTON CO. LTD.

House of Lords [1923] A.C. 744; 92 L.J.K.B. 736; 129 L.T. 546; 39 T.L.R. 590; 67 S.J. 678; [1923] All E.R.Rep. 427; 8 T.C. 481

VISCOUNT CAVE L.C.: . . . And the question, therefore, arises, whether the locality of the shares or stock of a company is to be determined by its place of incorporation and registration or by its place of residence and trading. After some doubt, I have come to the conclusion that the latter is the true view. " Shares in a company," said Sir James Hannen in *In the Goods of Ewing*,[21] " are locally situate where the head office is "; and I think this means that they are locally situate where the company's principal place of business is to be found. A share or a parcel of stock is an incorporeal thing, carrying the right

---

[17] According to Viscount Cave, in *Singer* v. *Williams* [1921] 1 A.C. 41, 49, " securities " denotes " a debt or claim, the payment of which is in some way secured." It does not include shares in a foreign company, which are " possessions."

[18] Including profits from a trade carried on wholly abroad: *Colquhoun* v. *Brooks* (1889) 14 App.Cas. 493; *ante*, p. 277; *Bartholomay Brewing Company Ltd.* v. *Wyatt* [1893] 2 Q.B. 499.

[19] See *post*, p. 290.

[20] The " source " principle (see Chap. 5) is especially important where the remittance principle applies, since income remitted in a tax year after the source has ceased to exist escapes tax; *N.B. Joffe* v. *Thain* (1955) 36 T.C. 199; *Lilley* v. *Harrison* (1952) 33 T.C. 344; *Inchyra (Baron)* v. *Jennings* [1966] Ch. 37.

[21] (1881) 6 P.D. 19.

to a share in the profits of a company; and where the company is, there the share is also, and there is the source of any dividend paid upon it. It was decided in *Joyce's Case* [22] that during the first three years the American company was here for all the purposes of income tax; and the company being here, I find it impossible to hold that its stock was abroad. In any case I am unable to understand how the Crown, having in 1913 successfully maintained that the American company was then resident and trading in England, can now be heard to say that the profits of that trading when divided among the stockholders were income from foreign possessions. The fact that the dividends were declared in America and remitted by American cheque cannot, in my opinion, displace the inference to be drawn from the fact that the company resided and traded in England. The result may be unfortunate for the Crown, which will lose duty on some part of the later dividends; but the Crown succeeded in 1913 in establishing that for income tax purposes the American company was here, and must accept the consequences of its victory. . . .

BAKER v. ARCHER-SHEE

House of Lords [1927] A.C. 844; 96 L.J.K.B. 803; 137 L.T. 762; 43 T.L.R. 758; 71 S.J. 727; 11 T.C. 749

LORD WRENBURY: . . . The result of the above may be shortly stated by saying that in the case of a person residing in the United Kingdom all his property whatever, situate in the United Kingdom or elsewhere, is charged to tax, but if he shows that a particular part of his property is within Case V (2) then the tax is computed only upon so much of the income as is actually received in the United Kingdom.[23]

In this case the taxpayer is a British subject resident in England. The property from which the income is derived is in America. The income is not remitted to this country. The case states that the income has been paid to Lady Archer-Shee's order at Messrs. J. P. Morgan & Co.'s bank in New York. It stops there, and does not go on to state that it has not been remitted by New York to this country but it is admitted at the Bar that this is the case. Under these circumstances the question is whether the income is such as that in that state of facts it is taxable to income tax.

The income in question is income of Lady Archer-Shee under a gift in the will of her father Mr. Arthur Pell of New York in the following terms: " I direct that all my real and personal estate except what is herein before disposed of be held in trust by my Executors and Trustees as follows. . . . (3) that " (in an event which happened) " the whole of the said income and profits shall thereafter be applied to the use of my said daughter Frances during her life." Lady Archer-Shee is the said daughter Frances.

The date of Mr. Pell's death does not appear, but it was before 1904. It is not disputed that the estate has been fully administered. The Trust Company of New York have been appointed as and now are trustees of the fund, and it is not disputed that the funds are now in their hands as trustees upon the trust above stated.

The securities, stocks and shares are liable to American income tax and the Trust Company of New York are entitled to commission or other payment for their services. Subject to these Lady Archer-Shee is during her life entitled

---

[22] *American Thread Company* v. *Joyce* (1913) 6 T.C. 163. A wholly-owned subsidiary of the respondent company, which, in the earlier case in the House of Lords had been held to be resident in the United Kingdom, being managed from London. *Cf. Brassard* v. *Smith* [1925] A.C. 371.
[23] This is no longer the case; see *ante*, p. 283.

to the income arising from the securities, stocks and shares and foreign possessions.

In this state of facts Lady Archer-Shee's interest under her father's will is beyond all question " property." The question for determination is what is the nature of that property, is it a " possession out of the United Kingdom other than stocks, shares, or rents " within Case V (2)? To escape taxation the respondent must establish that it is.

What, then, is the property to which Lady Archer-Shee is entitled? The will is an American will. The law of America is in an English Court question of fact. In the case stated by the Commissioners there is no finding as to what is the American law in the light of which the construction of Mr. Pell's will is to be ascertained. We have not heard that there has been any agreement between the parties on the point, and I have not traced that there has been any reference to it in the course of the proceedings. The members of the Court of Appeal do not appear to have considered the matter. They, and in particular Warrington L.J., seem to have treated the question for decision as purely a question of fact and, without any finding as to the American law as question of fact, they contented themselves with referring to paragraph 4 of the case and founded themselves upon the statement that there is paid over to Lady Archer-Shee's account only such part of the sums which the trustees have received from the funds as they considered to be income. My Lords, the question is not what the trustees have thought proper to hand over and have handed over (which is question of fact) but what under the will Lady Archer-Shee is entitled to (which is question of law). The trustees, of course, have a first charge upon the trust funds for their costs, charges and expenses, and American income tax will be a tax which they would have to bear and which would fall upon the beneficiary.

But this does not reduce the right of property of the beneficiary to a right only to a balance sum after deducting these. If an owner of shares deposits them with his banker by way of security for a loan he is not reduced to being the owner of a balance sum being the difference between the dividends on the shares and the interest on the loan. He is the owner of the equity of redemption of the whole fund. If a landowner employs an agent to collect his rents and authorises him to deduct a commission he does not cease to be owner of the rents. Under Mr. Pell's will Lady Archer-Shee (if American law is the same as English law) [24] is, in my opinion, as matter of construction of the will, entitled in equity specifically during her life to the dividends upon the stocks. If, say, in January £100, after deduction of American income tax, was received for a dividend and there was nothing owing to the trustees which they were entitled to deduct, Lady Archer-Shee could, in my opinion, call upon them to pay her that £100. If such a property is not taxable it results that a person residing here (whether a British subject or not) can by creating a foreign trust of stocks and shares and accumulating or spending the income abroad escape taxation upon that income.

If the estate had not been fully administered I could well understand a contention that the right to whatever in administration might turn out to be the fund the subject of this gift was a " foreign possession," and fell under Case V (2). But that is not the case. I have to read the will and see what is Lady Archer-Shee's right of property in certain ascertained securities, stocks and shares now held by the Trust Company " to the use of my said daughter."

---

[24] Subsequently, in *Archer-Shee* v. *Garland* [1931] A.C. 212, the taxpayer successfully appealed against further assessments, expert evidence being adduced that, under the appropriate law in the United States, his wife had no estate or interest in the securities, stocks or shares; her sole right was to compel the Trustees to discharge their duties. This was a " possession " to which Case V, r. 2 applied, and consequently tax was chargeable on a remittance basis only. See also *Nelson* v. *Adamson* [1941] 2 K.B. 12.

It is, I think, if the law of America is the same as our law, an equitable right in possession to receive during her life the proceeds of the shares and stocks of which she is tenant for life. Her right is not to a balance sum, but to the dividends subject to deductions as above mentioned. Her right under the will is " property " from which income is derived.

DRUMMOND v. COLLINS

House of Lords [1915] A.C. 1011; 84 L.J.K.B. 1690; 113 L.T. 665; 31 T.L.R. 482; 59 S.J. 577; 6 T.C. 538 (also *post*, p. 372)

The Appellant, an infant resident in the United Kingdom, received advances from Trustees in the U.S.A., under the provisions of a discretionary trust contained in the will of an American testator. *Held*, although the recipient child had no control of the property comprised in the trust, the advances arose from " possessions " within the meaning of Case V and the remittances were properly assessed.

LORD PARKER OF WADDINGTON: . . . As I understand the appellants' argument, it depends on the proposition that case 5 applies only to profits or gains from foreign possessions when these possessions belong to the person sought to be assessed, and that this property did not in the present case belong either to the infants or to their guardian.

In my opinion it is enough for case 5 to apply that the person to be assessed has such an interest in the property as to entitle him to the profits or gains in question. The infants had in my opinion such an interest. Though they might be incapable because of their age of giving a receipt for the money, it is in my opinion none the less clear that the money in question was, as soon as the Trustees had exercised their discretionary trust, held in trust for these infants as beneficiaries. . . .

LORD WRENBURY: . . . It is, however, contended that the case is not within the fifth case of the Act of 1842, for that this is not a foreign possession. This argument, if I rightly understand it, is that property, *e.g.* income derived from assets in another country is not a foreign possession unless the person taxed owns the corpus of the foreign possession. If this were true no life tenant or other person having a limited interest in property abroad would be assessable under the fifth case. The test is not, I think, whether there is an absolute interest in a foreign possession, but whether there is such an interest in a foreign possession that the party assessed derives income from it. The case is, I think, within the fifth case, and whether this is so or not, it is, I think, within Schedule D of the Act of 1853. The income is annual profits arising to a person residing in the United Kingdom from property situate elsewhere than in the United Kingdom. For these reasons I submit to your Lordships that the remittances are income subject to income tax. . . .

Note

The case is important in establishing that advances under a discretion nevertheless arise from a " source." See also, A. E. W. Park, " Section 478 and Foreign Discretionary Trusts " [1970] B.T.R. 88.

Payments made under a court order for alimony and under a deed of separation have been held to derive from foreign " possessions ": *I.R.C.* v. *Anderstrom* 1928 S.C. 224; *Chamney* v. *Lewis* (1932) 17 T.C. 318.

3. Capital and Income

Cases IV and V can only impose a charge to tax upon receipts which are of an income nature. In the case of foreign property, in order to determine whether a receipt is of a capital or an income nature, it is first necessary to establish the nature of the recipient's rights in the property according to the appropriate foreign law, and then to determine, according to English law, whether the entitlement is to capital or income.

I.R.C. v. REID'S TRUSTEES

House of Lords [1949] A.C. 361; [1949] L.J.R. 701; 93 S.J. 146; [1949] 1 All E.R. 354; 30 T.C. 431; 1949 S.C. (H.L.) 71; 1949 S.L.T. 217

A South African company declared a dividend payable from capital profits and a dividend was remitted to a shareholder resident in the United Kingdom. *Held,* the receipt was income arising from a possession out of the United Kingdom and Case V applied.

LORD SIMONDS : My Lords, I do not understand it to be denied by the Crown, that the dividend of 20 per cent. was in fact paid out of what are conveniently called " capital profits," that is to say, profits which were derived from a sale of capital assets at an enhanced value, and would not, if the company were being assessed to tax under Case I of Schedule D be included in the computation of its trading profits. It is in these circumstances that the question arises whether the Court of Session, affirming the special commissioners, has rightly held that tax is not exigible.

The claim of the appellants is founded on Case V of Schedule D. They say that this sum of £6,866 is " income arising from possessions out of the United Kingdom," that the shares in a South African company are possessions out of the United Kingdom and that the sum in question is income arising from those shares. They say that there is no tertium quid. This sum is either capital or income. How can it be capital, if the shares remain intact, so many shares of £10 each in the capital of the company? There is a way of distributing a dividend, while leaving the capital intact, and there is a way of returning part of the capital: it is the former course that has here been taken. This then, they say, is income.

. . . My Lords, this is the short and simple case made by the appellants and I see no answer to it. The learned Lord President accepted an answer which he thus stated [25] : " The short answer of the respondents, accepted by the special commissioners after investigating the facts, is that this sum is not the income of anyone, and never was. I agree." My Lords, I must say with great respect that I think that this conclusion can only be reached by ignoring that what may be regarded as capital in the hands of the payer may yet be income in the hands of the payee. It is begging the question to say that this sum is not income in the hands of the shareholders: by every practical test it has proved to be income. I will assume that the money out of which the dividend was paid was capital in the hands of the company for the purpose, at any rate, of ascertaining its taxable profit. I think that the commissioners were entitled to find that as a fact; but it was not the fact, and they were not entitled to find as a fact, that the dividend in the hands of a recipient shareholder was not his income.

[25] 1947 S.C. 700, 707.

But, it was urged, this will create a strange anomaly. If this was an English company, carrying on its trade in the United Kingdom, and the same series of events occurred, an appreciation of capital assets, a realisation of those assets and a distribution by way of dividend of so called capital profits, no income tax would be exigible in respect of them in the hands of the company or of its shareholders. My Lords, let it be so. I think it should not be necessary to repeat what has so often been said in this House that the position of a company resident in the United Kingdom (I will call it an English company) and its shareholders is wholly different from that of a foreign company and its shareholders, who, being resident here, are taxable in respect of income from their foreign possessions.

. . . And here too I would remind your Lordships of the observation of Lord Phillimore in *Bradbury* v. *English Sewing Cotton Co. Ltd.*,[26] that, in regard to the income arising from foreign possessions, " the officers of the Crown do not know and do not care what is the character of the sources from which the money comes." I must not be taken as suggesting any inaccuracy or insufficiency in the information which has in this case been furnished by the South African company, but it is obvious that as a general rule the Inland Revenue authorities cannot have the same facilities for investigating the affairs of a foreign company and checking its statement that a dividend is paid out of " capital profits." They must work upon a broader basis and I cannot imagine a safer or better one, where the question is as to income arising from a foreign possession, than to ask whether the corpus of the asset remains intact in the hands of the taxpayer. That question can in the case of the shares here in question only be answered in the affirmative. The shares the respondents held before the distribution of dividend they still hold intact. The dividend they received was income arising out of those shares. . . .

RAE v. LAZARD INVESTMENT CO. LTD.

House of Lords [1963] 1 W.L.R. 555; 107 S.J. 474; 41 T.C. 1

An investment company resident in the United Kingdom received a distribution in respect of shares held in a company in Maryland, U.S.A. Under the law of Maryland the payments were made under a " distribution on partial liquidation " and constituted a return of capital. *Held,* the payment was of a capital nature and not assessable under Case V.

LORD REID: . . . In deciding whether a shareholder receives a distribution as capital or income our law goes by the form in which the distribution is made rather than by the substance of the transaction. Capital in the hands of the company becomes income in the hands of the shareholders if distributed as a dividend, while accumulated income in the hands of the company becomes capital in the hands of the shareholders if distributed in a liquidation. In the present case the form of the distribution was one unknown to our law—distribution in a partial liquidation. By the law of Maryland which governs the company and which authorised this distribution the shares distributed were capital in the hands of the shareholders. Why, then, should we regard them as income? It is said that if this had been an English company and it had done what Certain-teed did these shares would have been income in the hands of the shareholders. But an English company could not do what Certain-teed did for it could not distribute in a partial liquidation. No doubt an English com-

---

[26] [1923] A.C. 744, 770; *ante*, p. 283.

pany could have reached the same result by using a different method—declaring a dividend. But it is found as a fact that it would not have been possible in Maryland to effect this transaction by way of a declaration of dividend. So why are we to hold something to be a dividend which by the law of Maryland was not and could not be a dividend? There is no question here of the foreign law producing a result which is unreasonable or contrary to our idea of justice.

The argument for the Crown was based to a large extent on what was said in this House in *Inland Revenue Commissioners* v. *Reid's Trustees*.[27] In that case a dividend in the form of cash was received from a South African company by a taxpayer in Scotland. It is clear from several of the speeches that this dividend was received as income but its source was profit from appreciation of capital assets of the company. It was assumed, in the absence of evidence to the contrary, that the law of South Africa was the same as the law of England: so the dividend would be received in South Africa as income. But the taxpayer maintained that it was not taxable income founding on the fact that a similar dividend paid by a British company would not be subject to income tax. This was held to be irrelevant: the dividend was income from a foreign possession and was therefore within Case V.

. . . Accepting that test,[28] as I do without reservation, the question is whether " the corpus of the asset " or " shares of the company " or " the capital of the possession " did or did not remain intact after the Bestwall shares were distributed: or whether the Bestwall shares were merely fruit or had in their fall taken part of the tree with them.

It is not disputed that the nature of a taxpayer's right to his foreign possession must be determined by the foreign law: *Archer-Shee* v. *Garland*.[29] So we must go to the law of Maryland to find whether the taxpayer's capital asset remained the same, and it is found as a fact " (6) As a result of the distribution by Certainteed in partial liquidation under Maryland law Lico's original interest in Certainteed did not remain intact," and then the reason is given followed by the statement that the shareholder received capital. The plain meaning of that appears to me to be that after the partial liquidation the corpus of the respondent's capital asset did not remain intact. . . .

LAWSON v. ROLFE

Chancery Division [1970] 1 Ch. 613; [1970] 2 W.L.R. 602; 114 S.J. 206; 1 All E.R. 761; 46 T.C. 199

Under the will of a Californian testator a beneficiary resident and domiciled in England was entitled to a life interest in a trust fund. Bonus shares were received by the fund and transferred into the name of the beneficiary, but were not remitted. In Californian law, under the " Pennsylvania Rule," stock dividends of this nature pass to the life tenant. *Held*, although the shares passed to the life tenant they were nevertheless of a capital nature and not assessable under Case V.

FOSTER J.: . . . I accept the principle that the court first considers the nature of the taxpayer's interest under the foreign disposition. Under Californian law the nature of Mrs. Lawson's interest is that she is entitled to the income of her share and to bonus shares of a certain nature. But the court must then consider

---

[27] [1949] A.C. 361; *ante*, p. 287.
[28] *i.e.* the test in *I.R.C.* v. *Reid's Trustees*, namely, whether the corpus of the asset remained intact.
[29] [1931] A.C. 212; 15 T.C. 693. See also *Inchyra (Baron)* v. *Jennings* [1966] Ch. 37.

whether those bonus shares when issued have the character of capital or income in accordance with the law of England. In English law it was decided by the House of Lords in *Inland Revenue Commissioners* v. *Blott* [30] that shares credited to a shareholder in respect of a bonus being distributed by the company as capital were not income in the hands of that shareholder. . . .

4. The Remittance Basis

In general, tax is charged upon foreign income when it arises. However, in certain instances tax is only charged upon so much of the income as is remitted to the United Kingdom and received by the taxpayer.[31] It is therefore necessary to consider when a remittance is made and what constitutes a remittance.[32]

THOMSON v. MOYSE

House of Lords [1961] A.C. 967; [1960] 3 W.L.R. 929; 104 S.J. 1032; [1960] 3 All E.R. 684; 39 T.C. 291

The respondent, a British subject resident in the United Kingdom but domiciled in the U.S.A., was entitled to income from the estates of his parents in the U.S.A. The money was paid by trustees into an account in the respondent's name in a New York bank. The respondent drew cheques in dollars on the New York bank in favour of English bankers; the English bankers purchased the cheques and credited the respondent's English bank account with the sterling equivalent of the cheques, which they sold for dollars. *Held,* the sterling credits were sums received and the respondent had " brought over " his income to the United Kingdom.

LORD REID: . . . At first sight it would seem that the requirements of these provisions are satisfied. As regards Case IV, the respondent undoubtedly received in the United Kingdom the sums paid to him as the price of the cheques and in each case, by virtue of the contract under which he received the sum, the amount of accrued income held by him in New York was diminished by a corresponding amount. And as regards Case V again he undoubtedly received such sums and they would appear to be money arising from property not imported, that is, his accrued income in New York which he assigned in order to get these sums. But obviously this case cannot be disposed of as easily as that. There is a wealth of authority about these provisions,[33] and on the strength of that authority the commissioners, Wynn-Parry J. and the majority of the Court of Appeal all held that the facts of this case do not satisfy the statutory provisions.

The main ground of judgment in each case was that the sums paid to the respondent had not been brought into the United Kingdom, and that there is

---

[30] [1921] 2 A.C. 171; 8 T.C. 101; *cf. Brodie's Trustees* v. *I.R.C.* (1933) 17 T.C. 432; *post,* p. 377.

[31] I.C.T.A. 1970, ss. 122, 181. Relief is given in respect of income assessable on an " arising " basis which cannot be remitted to the United Kingdom, *ibid.* s. 418.

[32] It is also necessary to identify the source of a remittance and to determine whether it is a remittance of income or of capital: *Kneen* v. *Martin* [1935] 1 K.B. 499; *Scottish Provident Institution* v. *Allan* [1903] A.C. 109; *Patuck* v. *Lloyd* (1944) 26 T.C. 284; *Duke of Roxburghe's Exors.* v. *I.R.C.* (1936) 20 T.C. 711.

[33] In particular, *Gresham Life Assurance Society* v. *Bishop* [1902] A.C. 287; *Forbes* v. *Scottish Provident Institution* (1895) 3 T.C. 443 on the question of " constructive remittance."

nothing to show that any money was ever brought into the United Kingdom in connection with these transactions. That is quite true. But there is nothing in Case IV requiring that money should be brought into the United Kingdom, and this requirement is only attached to one head of Case V which does not apply to the present case. . . .

LORD RADCLIFFE: My Lords, I do not need to travel again over the facts of this case which have been stated already. It is a straightforward story of a resident of this country selling dollars in his bank account in New York in exchange for sterling which the bankers in London were ready to provide. The American bank account was fed only by the receipt of income arising from his American securities or possessions. I should say that in the plain meaning of language the sterling credits were sums received by him in this country out of his American income, which had *pro tanto* been used to acquire them, and that in this sense he had " brought over " his American income to the United Kingdom. That being so, the sums so received are, in my opinion, properly computed in assessing his tax under Case IV and Case V to Schedule D.

What has puzzled me throughout is to see how or why the banking transactions for effecting the remittance of his money from America to which the respondent resorted should be regarded as insufficient to constitute the sterling proceeds received as assessable sums for the purpose of these two cases. He did not, of course, invest his American income in bullion or commodities to be shipped over here and sold or in United States dollar bills for similar realisation: but then nobody says or supposes that assessability is confined to such transactions. Nor did he instruct his bankers or agents to use his dollar income in buying a bill on London which could have been discounted or presented here for payment. These would have been possible methods of " bringing " the money here, and, no doubt, have all been resorted to in their time. But what he did do seems to me to have been in all essentials a similar transaction and to have amounted just as much to a " bringing " in the relevant sense. He wrote out his cheques on his New York bankers directing them to hand over his dollars to or to the order of his United Kingdom purchasers and these purchasers in return acknowledged a sterling debt to him calculated at the current rate of exchange between New York and London. He parted with his dollars: he got his sterling. He emptied one pocket of dollars in order to fill another pocket with sterling. It is true that the cheques in question were written out and signed in London and, if you please, sold here, so that the instruments themselves did not cross the Atlantic until he had made this sale and even then only in the outward direction; but what importance can there be in the actual place of making the instrument or in its physical movements if the direct result of the mechanism employed was to turn the taxpayer's income in one country into money or value in the other country to which he had decided to transfer it?

LORD DENNING: . . . Let me first consider the tax chargeable under Case IV. Clearly tax is only to be computed on the sums received in England. These sums must be directly referable to Mr. Moyse's New York income, in this sense, that they must come out of his New York income or be deductible from it or be traceable to it, so that, in the end, his New York income is seen to be the provider of the sums received in England. If Mr. Moyse receives the sums out of that income in England himself, he must, of course, pay tax on those sums. But he need not receive them himself. It is sufficient if the sums are received in England by some third person by his authority. Thus, if Mr. Moyse, instead of receiving the money himself, tells his New York banker to send a remittance direct to his butcher or baker or candlestick-maker in England, he is chargeable with tax on it: for the simple reason that he was " entitled " to the income which has been used to pay the debt, and he must pay the tax on it when it is received in England, no matter by whom it is received, so long as it is received by his authority, see rule 1 of the Miscellaneous Rules applicable to Schedule D and *Timpson's Executors* v. *Yerbury*.[34] Nor is it necessary that Mr. Moyse or the third party should receive the sums in coins or dollar notes or treasury notes. It is sufficient if he or the third party receives the sums in England in any of the other forms of money recognised by commercial men, such as bills of exchange, cheques, promissory notes or cash at bank, see *Gresham Life Assurance Society* v. *Bishop*[35] by Lord Lindley. Thus if Mr. Moyse, whilst in New York, draws a cheque in dollars on his New York bank in favour of his butcher or baker or candlestick-maker in England, and brings the cheque over himself—or sends it over by post—and hands it to the tradesman in payment of the debt, then Mr. Moyse is chargeable with tax on it. So much is conceded. But the reason is not because Mr. Moyse brought the cheque over from New York, or posted it in New York. It is because the tradesman received it here in payment of his account on the authority of Mr. Moyse himself. The position would be just the same if Mr. Moyse, with Treasury permission, wrote out the same cheque in England and handed it over himself to the tradesman here. For the dollar cheque itself would be a " sum received " in England by the tradesman on the authority of Mr. Moyse: and as it was payable out of his New York income, Mr. Moyse is chargeable with tax on it.

My Lords, I have just said that the dollar cheque itself would be a " sum received " in England by the tradesman: and this is, I think, a cardinal point in the case. It is immaterial how the tradesman cashes the cheque. He may, with Treasury permission, cash the cheque in the United States and keep the dollars there: or he may sell the cheque to an authorised dealer in England and receive the proceeds in sterling: or the cheque may be stolen from him and cashed by a wrongdoer: in which case he may sue the wrongdoer in conversion. None of that concerns the man who pays by cheque: for he has got the goods and paid his debt. True it is that the payment is conditional on the cheque being met but that is only a condition subsequent. If the cheque is met, it ranks as an actual payment from the time it was given and not a conditional one. If the cheque is not met, the tradesman can have recourse to the debtor, because then there has been no payment. But subject to it being defeated by that condition subsequent the payment is complete at the time when and the place where the cheque is accepted by the creditor. . . .

TIMPSON'S EXECUTORS v. YERBURY

Court of Appeal [1936] 1 K.B. 645; 105 L.J.K.B. 749; 154 L.T. 283; 80 S.J. 184; [1936] 1 All E.R. 186; 20 T.C. 155

A beneficiary under a foreign trust, who resided in the United Kingdom, directed the Trustees to pay allowances to her children in the United Kingdom. *Held,* the drafts sent to the United Kingdom in respect of the voluntary allowances did not become the property of the children until cashed. Until then their mother was " entitled " to the income and was therefore properly assessed on it.

LORD WRIGHT M.R.: . . . It is convenient in the first place to analyse the legal effect of these transactions. Each remittance was a voluntary allowance or

---

[34] [1936] 1 K.B. 645, *infra*.   [35] [1902] A.C. 287, 296.

gift, with the consequence that the donee only acquired the remittance when the gift was perfected. No distinction was drawn by the appellants, indeed any distinction was expressly disclaimed between the drafts before the merger and the drafts after the merger. I accordingly discuss only the latter, in which the trustees were drawers. It is clear that at any time before the drafts were cashed the trustees could countermand payment, and hence there was no completed gift until payment, just as much as in the case of a cheque there is no completed gift, at least *inter vivos,* of the money until the cheque is cashed.

No doubt when the draft reached the child there was a completed gift of the piece of paper, but that paper had only a nominal value unless and until the money was collected by, or credited to, the child. Hence until that was done the money represented by the cheque remained the income of Mrs. Timpson, that is, income to which she was beneficially entitled under the trust and as such arrived in England and was received by the child or his or her agent. . . .

Note
   Followed in *Walsh* v. *Randall* (1940) 23 T.C. 55, where the gift was to a hospital in this country. The income had been accumulated and invested abroad. The investments were later sold and the proceeds of sale remitted. It was nevertheless held to be a remittance of the income. If the gift to a donee is complete *before* the income reached the United Kingdom, no assessment may be made: *Carter* v. *Sharon* (1936) 20 T.C. 229.

SCHIOLER v. WESTMINSTER BANK LTD.

Queen's Bench Division [1970] 2 Q.B. 719; [1970] 3 W.L.R. 68; 114 S.J. 513; [1970] 3 All E.R. 177; [1970] T.R. 167

MOCATTA J.: The claim in this action arises out of somewhat novel facts and raises questions of importance to the parties of some difficulty.

The plaintiff, a married woman, is of Danish nationality. She resides in Hampshire, but is domiciled in Denmark. In May 1962 she opened an account with the defendants' branch in St. Peter Port, Guernsey. It appears that from then onwards until the crucial events of June and July 1968, substantially the only sums paid into that account derived from dividends to which she was entitled from her shareholding in a company called United Plantations Ltd. carrying on business in Malaysia, with its registered office at Teluk Anson in the States of Malaya. At some date unknown to me, but presumably in 1962, she gave instructions to the company to forward her dividends to the defendants' Guernsey branch for the credit of her account there. From June 1962, until June 1967, dividends were so forwarded in sterling either in the form of a banker's draft drawn on the Hong Kong and Shanghai Banking Corporation in London, or occasionally in the form of cheques in the plaintiff's favour drawn by the company on the same bank and sent to Guernsey by the plaintiff. In all these cases her account in the defendants' Guernsey branch was duly credited with the appropriate sterling sum without deduction of United Kingdom income tax. . . . On June 15, 1968, the company sent to the defendants' Guernsey branch for the account of the plaintiff a dividend voucher in respect of the year ending December 31, 1967, with dividend warrant attached for 17,848.80 Malaysian dollars, a sum arrived at after deduction of Malaysian income tax at 40 per cent. I have not seen the warrant, but it appears to have been a draft drawn by the company on the Hong Kong and Shanghai Banking Corporation, Teluk Anson, for 17,848.80 Malaysian dollars. It seems likely that the draft was made payable to bearer, though there was no direct evidence of this.

The voucher and warrant were received by the bank in Guernsey on June 19 and were on the same day sent by the securities clerk in the branch to the defendants' stock office at Crawley for realisation.

. . . The defendants' stock office at Crawley provides any services which the defendants' numerous branches may require in relation to stocks and shares. The stock office sold the draft in London to an appropriate bank operating in Malaysia for £2,412 7s. 6d., deducted United Kingdom income tax at 8s. 3d. in the pound totalling £995 2s. 1d., and returned the form to Guernsey as a credit for the net sum of £1,417 5s. 5d. The plaintiff's account was credited with this sum by the Guernsey branch on July 2, 1968.

When the plaintiff discovered that £995 2s. 1d. had been deducted in respect of income tax, she and her accountant, Mr. Littledale, complained to the manager of the branch of this on the grounds that not being domiciled in the United Kingdom she was not liable to income tax on income derived from the Malaysian company, save in so far as any part of that income was remitted to the United Kingdom: see Income Tax Act 1952, s. 132 (2) and (3).[36]

. . . The plaintiff claims damages for breach of contract from the defendants in the sum of £995 2s. 1d. in that in breach of duty as bankers to take due care of the dividend warrant received by them on her behalf they remitted it to London thereby subjecting it to a deduction of income tax at 8s. 3d. in the pound without first obtaining specific instructions.

. . . It is desirable that I should now state a number of additional facts and matters that are not in dispute. In the first place it is clear from the documents that the plaintiff, although resident in Hampshire, was domiciled in Denmark, and that the provisions of section 132 (2) and (3) of the Income Tax Act 1952 [36] applied in her case so that her income from the Malaysian company was only liable to income tax pursuant to those subsections to the extent that it was received in the United Kingdom in the year preceding the year of assessment. This was made clear to the then manager of the defendants' Guernsey branch in letters from the plaintiff and Mr. Littledale to him dated November 13 and 16, 1964, in which the assistance of the manager was requested as to the details of any remittances from the plaintiff's account to the United Kingdom in previous years required for a hearing before the appropriate tax commissioners. These two letters remained upon the plaintiff's file kept by the Guernsey branch. Secondly, it was common ground between counsel that, pursuant to the provisions of section 189 (b) of the Income Tax Act 1952 [37] the defendants were obliged to deduct income tax at the standard rate from the proceeds of the sale of the dividend warrant in London and account therefor to the Inland Revenue. Section 190 [38] provides for exemption for the dividends of non-residents, but this was not of course applicable to the plaintiff.

. . . I have found this a difficult issue to determine and feel considerable sympathy for the plaintiff. I would much have welcomed the guidance of some authority nearer to the facts here than the two cases mentioned. I accept that some banks in similar circumstances might have taken the course suggested by Mr. Payne [counsel for the plaintiff] before sending the dividend warrant to England for realisation in sterling. It is, however, quite another matter to hold that the defendants were under a contractual obligation so to do. They had implied authority and a contractual duty to credit the plaintiff's account with dividends received by them on her behalf. In sending the dividend warrant to England for realisation in sterling, they were, on the evidence, not doing anything unusual and there was no alternative method available to them of crediting the plaintiff's account. I think there is great force in the argument that to hold that they were negligent in acting as they did without first consulting the plaintiff or her accountant, because of the possible tax repercussions, would be

---

[36] Now I.C.T.A. 1970, s. 122 (2) (3).
[37] Now I.C.T.A. 1970, s. 159 (3) (b).
[38] Now I.C.T.A. 1970, s. 159 (4) (5).

to place an impossible and unreasonable burden on banks generally. In the absence of any express instructions to the defendants on the matter, I find myself unable to hold that, in acting as they did, they were negligent or exceeded their implied authority.

Accordingly there must be judgment for the defendants.

Note

Cf. *Duke of Roxburghe's Executors* v. *I.R.C.* (1936) 20 T.C. 711, where a bank's mistake was less costly.

5. Double Taxation

The practice of states taxing all income arising in the state, no matter to whom it belongs, and all income of residents, no matter where it arises,[39] must necessarily involve the double taxation of " foreign income ": once in the state where the income arises and again in the state where the person entitled to such income resides. To mitigate this effect, a number of reliefs have been evolved.

ROYAL COMMISSION ON THE TAXATION OF PROFITS AND INCOME

First Report, 1953 Cmd. 8761

25. It seems to be generally accepted that the United Kingdom practice of taxing a resident trader on the whole of his profits wherever made was adopted at a time when income or profits taxes were not a regular feature of the revenue systems of other countries. Consequently the problems raised by double taxation—the claims of two distinct taxing jurisdictions to tax the same piece of property, income or profit—are, comparatively speaking, of recent growth. Under present conditions there are very few countries in the world that do not impose some form of income or profits tax on profits made within their own territories. Therefore if both the claim of the local jurisdiction to tax profits because they are made there and the claim of the jurisdiction of the maker's residence to tax them because he is resident there are to be regarded as valid claims the high rates of taxation which rule in the contemporary world would have the result of going far to eliminate the profit altogether, so far as the maker was concerned.

26. We think that international usage has now settled that not only has the country in which profits arise a valid right to tax those profits, no matter to whom they belong, but that it has the prior right to exact the tax as against the country in which the owner resides. Consistently with this view the United Kingdom has entered into numerous double taxation agreements with other countries in recent years, which have for their purpose the harmonisation of conflicting tax claims of this sort.

[39] *Ante*, p. 277.

O.E.C.D. DRAFT MODEL DOUBLE TAXATION CONVENTION

CHAPTER I

SCOPE OF THE CONVENTION

Article 1

Personal Scope

This Convention shall apply to persons who are residents of one or both of the Contracting States.

Article 2

Taxes Covered

1. This Convention shall apply to taxes on income and on capital imposed on behalf of each Contracting State or of its political subdivisions or local authorities, irrespective of the manner in which they are levied.

2. There shall be regarded as taxes on income and on capital all taxes imposed on total income, on total capital, or on elements of income or of capital, including taxes on gains from the alienation of movable or immovable property, taxes on the total amounts of wages or salaries paid by enterprises, as well as taxes on capital appreciation.

3. The existing taxes to which the Convention shall apply are, in particular:

    (*a*) In the case of (State A): ....

    (*b*) In the case of (State B): ....

4. The Convention shall also apply to any identical or substantially similar taxes which are subsequently imposed in addition to, or in place of, the existing taxes. At the end of each year, the competent authorities of the Contracting States shall notify to each other any changes which have been made in their respective taxation laws.

CHAPTER II

DEFINITIONS

Article 3

General Definitions

1. In this Convention, unless the context otherwise requires:

    (*a*) the terms " a Contracting State " and " the other Contracting State " mean (State A) or (State B), as the context requires;

    (*b*) the term " person " comprises an individual, a company and any other body of persons;

    (*c*) the term " company " means any body corporate or any entity which is treated as a body corporate for tax purposes;

    (*d*) the terms " enterprise of a Contracting State " and " enterprise of the other Contracting State " mean respectively an enterprise carried on by a resident of a Contracting State and an enterprise carried on by a resident of the other Contracting State;

    (*e*) the term " competent authority " means:

1. in (State A) ....
2. in (State B) ....

2. As regards the application of the Convention by a Contracting State any term not otherwise defined shall, unless the context otherwise requires, have the meaning which it has under the laws of that Contracting State relating to the taxes which are the subject of the Convention.

Article 4

Fiscal Domicile

1. For the purposes of this Convention, the term "resident of a Contracting State" means any person who, under the law of that State, is liable to taxation therein by reason of his domicile, residence, place of management or any other criterion of a similar nature.

2. Where by reason of the provisions of paragraph 1 an individual is a resident of both Contracting States, then this case shall be determined in accordance with the following rules:

(a) He shall be deemed to be a resident of the Contracting State in which he has a permanent home available to him. If he has a permanent home available to him in both Contracting States, he shall be deemed to be a resident of the Contracting State with which his personal and economic relations are closest (centre of vital interests);

(b) If the Contracting State in which he has his centre of vital interests cannot be determined, or if he has not a permanent home available to him in either Contracting State, he shall be deemed to be a resident of the Contracting State in which he has an habitual abode;

(c) If he has an habitual abode in both Contracting States or in neither of them, he shall be deemed to be a resident of the Contracting State of which he is a national;

(d) If he is a national of both Contracting States or of neither of them, the competent authorities of the Contracting States shall settle the question by mutual agreement.

3. Where by reason of the provisions of paragraph 1 a person other than an individual is a resident of both Contracting States, then it shall be deemed to be a resident of the Contracting State in which its place of effective management is situated.

Article 5

Permanent Establishment

1. For the purposes of this Convention, the term "permanent establishment" means a fixed place of business in which the business of the enterprise is wholly or partly carried on.

2. The term "permanent establishment" shall include especially:

(a) a place of management;
(b) a branch;
(c) an office;
(d) a factory;
(e) a workshop;
(f) a mine, quarry or other place of extraction of natural resources;
(g) a building site or construction or assembly project which exists for more than twelve months.

3. The term " permanent establishment ". shall not be deemed to include:

    (*a*) the use of facilities solely for the purpose of storage, display or delivery of goods or merchandise belonging to the enterprise;

    (*b*) the maintenance of a stock of goods or merchandise belonging to the enterprise solely for the purpose of storage, display or delivery;

    (*c*) the maintenance of a stock of goods or merchandise belonging to the enterprise solely for the purpose of processing by another enterprise;

    (*d*) the maintenance of a fixed place of business solely for the purpose of purchasing goods or merchandise, or for collecting information, for the enterprise;

    (*e*) the maintenance of a fixed place of business solely for the purpose of advertising, for the supply of information, for scientific research or for similar activities which have a preparatory or auxiliary character, for the enterprise.

4. A person acting in a Contracting State on behalf of an enterprise of the other Contracting State—other than an agent of an independent status to whom paragraph 5 applies—shall be deemed to be a permanent establishment in the first mentioned State if he has, and habitually exercises in that State, an authority to conclude contracts in the name of the enterprise, unless his activities are limited to the purchase of goods or merchandise for the enterprise.

5. An enterprise of a Contracting State shall not be deemed to have a permanent establishment in the other Contracting State merely because it carries on business in that other State through a broker, general commission agent or any other agent of an independent status, where such persons are acting in the ordinary course of their business.

6. The fact that a company which is a resident of a Contracting State controls or is controlled by a company which is a resident of the other Contracting State, or which carries on business in that other State (whether through a permanent establishment or otherwise), shall not of itself constitute for either company a permanent establishment of the other.

CHAPTER III

TAXATION OF INCOME

Article 6

Income from Immovable Property

1. Income from immovable property may be taxed in the Contracting State in which such property is situated.

2. The term " immovable property " shall be defined in accordance with the law of the Contracting State in which the property in question is situated. The term shall in any case include property accessory to immovable property, livestock and equipment used in agriculture and forestry, rights to which the provisions of general law respecting landed property apply, usufruct of immovable property and rights to variable or fixed payments as consideration for the working of, or the right to work, mineral deposits, sources and other natural resources; ships, boats and aircraft shall not be regarded as immovable property.

3. The provisions of paragraph 1 shall apply to income derived from the direct use, letting, or use in any other form of immovable property.

4. The provisions of paragraphs 1 and 3 shall also apply to the income from immovable property of an enterprise and to income from immovable property used for the performance of professional services.

Article 7

Business Profits

1. The profit of an enterprise of a Contracting State shall be taxable only in that State unless the enterprise carries on business in the other Contracting State through a permanent establishment situated therein. If the enterprise carries on business as aforesaid, the profits of the enterprise may be taxed in the other State but only so much of them as is attributable to that permanent establishment.

2. Where an enterprise of a Contracting State carries on business in the other Contracting State through a permanent establishment situated therein, there shall in each Contracting State be attributed to that permanent establishment the profits which it might be expected to make if it were a distinct and separate enterprise engaged in the same or similar activities under the same or similar conditions and dealing wholly independently with the enterprise of which it is a permanent establishment.

3. In the determination of the profits of a permanent establishment, there shall be allowed as deductions expenses which are incurred for the purposes of the permanent establishment including executive and general administrative expenses so incurred, whether in the State in which the permanent establishment is situated or elsewhere.

4. In so far as it has been customary in a Contracting State to determine the profits to be attributed to a permanent establishment on the basis of an apportionment of the total profits of the enterprise to its various parts, nothing in paragraph 2 shall preclude that Contracting State from determining the profits to be taxed by such an apportionment as may be customary; the method of apportionment adopted shall, however, be such that the result shall be in accordance with the principles laid down in this Article.

5. No profits shall be attributed to a permanent establishment by reason of the mere purchase by that permanent establishment of goods or merchandise for the enterprise.

6. For the purposes of the preceding paragraphs, the profits to be attributed to the permanent establishment shall be determined by the same method year by year unless there is good and sufficient reason to the contrary.

7. Where profits include items of income which are dealt with separately in other Articles of this Convention, then the provisions of those Articles shall not be affected by the provisions of this Article.

Article 8

Shipping, Inland Waterways Transport and Air Transport

1. Profits from the operation of ships or aircraft in international traffic shall be taxable only in the Contracting State in which the place of effective management of the enterprise is situated.

2. Profits from the operation of boats engaged in inland waterways transport shall be taxable only in the Contracting State in which the place of effective management of the enterprise is situated.

3. If the place of effective management of a shipping enterprise or of an inland waterways transport enterprise is aboard a ship or boat, then it shall be deemed to be situated in the Contracting State in which the home harbour of the ship or boat is situated, or, if there is no such home harbour, in the Contracting State of which the operator of the ship or boat is a resident.

Article 9

Associated Enterprises

Where

    (a) an enterprise of a Contracting State participates directly or indirectly in the management, control or capital of an enterprise of the other Contracting State, or

    (b) the same persons participate directly or indirectly in the management, control or capital of an enterprise of a Contracting State and an enterprise of the other Contracting State,

and in either case conditions are made or imposed between the two enterprises in their commercial or financial relations which differ from those which would be made between independent enterprises, then any profits which would, but for those conditions, have accrued to one of the enterprises, but, by reason of those conditions, have not so accrued, may be included in the profits of that enterprise and taxed accordingly.

Article 10

Dividends

1. Dividends paid by a company which is a resident of a Contracting State to a resident of the other Contracting State may be taxed in that other State.

2. However, such dividends may be taxed in the Contracting State of which the company paying the dividends is a resident, and according to the law of that State, but the tax so charged shall not exceed:

    (a) 5 per cent. of the gross amount of the dividends if the recipient is a company (excluding partnership) which holds directly at least 25 per cent. of the capital of the company paying the dividends;

    (b) in all other cases, 15 per cent. of the gross amount of the dividends.

The competent authorities of the Contracting States shall by mutual agreement settle the mode of application of this limitation.

This paragraph shall not affect the taxation of the company in respect of the profits out of which the dividends are paid.

3. The term " dividends " as used in this Article means income from shares, " jouissance " shares or " jouissance " rights, mining shares, founders' shares or other rights, not being debt-claims, participating in profits, as well as income from other corporate rights assimilated to income from shares by the taxation law of the State of which the company making the distribution is a resident.

4. The provisions of paragraphs 1 and 2 shall not apply if the recipient of the dividends, being a resident of a Contracting State, has in the other Contracting State, of which the company paying the dividends is a resident, a permanent establishment with which the holding by virtue of which the dividends are paid is effectively connected. In such a case, the provisions of Article 7 shall apply.

5. Where a company which is a resident of a Contracting State derives profits or income from the other Contracting State, that other State may not impose any tax on the dividends paid by the company to persons who are not residents of that other State, or subject the company's undistributed profits to a tax on undistributed profits, even if the dividends paid or the undistributed profits consist wholly or partly of profits or income arising in such other State.

Article 11

Interest

1. Interest arising in a Contracting State and paid to a resident of the other Contracting State may be taxed in that other State.

2. However, such interest may be taxed in the Contracting State in which it arises, and according to the law of that State, but the tax so charged shall not exceed 10 per cent. of the amount of the interest. The competent authorities of the Contracting States shall by mutual agreement settle the mode of application of this limitation.

3. The term " interest " as used in this Article means income from Government securities, bonds or debentures, whether or not secured by mortgage and whether or not carrying a right to participate in profits, and debt-claims of every kind as well as all other income assimilated to income from money lent by the taxation law of the State in which the income arises.

4. The provisions of paragraphs 1 and 2 shall not apply if the recipient of the interest, being a resident of a Contracting State, has in the other Contracting State in which the interest arises a permanent establishment with which the debt-claim from which the interest arises is effectively connected. In such a case, the provisions of Article 7 shall apply.

5. Interest shall be deemed to arise in a Contracting State when the payer is that State itself, a political subdivision, a local authority or a resident of that State. Where, however, the person paying the interest, whether he is a resident of a Contracting State or not, has in a Contracting State a permanent establishment in connection with which the indebtedness on which the interest is paid was incurred, and such interest is borne by such permanent establishment, then such interest shall be deemed to arise in the Contracting State in which the permanent establishment is situated.

6. Where, owing to a special relationship between the payer and the recipient or between both of them and some other person, the amount of the interest paid, having regard to the debt claim for which it is paid, exceeds the amount which would have been agreed upon by the payer and the recipient in the absence of such relationship, the provisions of this Article shall apply only to the last-mentioned amount. In that case, the excess part of the payments shall remain taxable according to the law of each Contracting State, due regard being had to the other provisions of this Convention.

Article 12

Royalties

1. Royalties arising in a Contracting State and paid to a resident of the other Contracting State shall be taxable only in that other State.

2. The term " royalties " as used in this Article means payments of any kind received as a consideration for the use of, or the right to use, any copyright of literary, artistic or scientific work, including cinematograph films, any patent, trade mark, design or model, plan, secret formula or process, or for the use of, or the right to use, industrial, commercial, or scientific equipment, or for information concerning industrial, commercial or scientific experience.

3. The provisions of paragraph 1 shall not apply if the recipient of the royalties, being a resident of a Contracting State, has in the other Contracting State in which the royalties arise a permanent establishment with which the right or property giving rise to the royalties is effectively connected. In such a case, the provisions of Article 7 shall apply.

4. Where, owing to a special relationship between the payer and the recipient or between both of them and some other person, the amount of the royalties paid, having regard to the use, right or information for which they are paid, exceeds the amount which would have been agreed upon by the payer and the recipient in the absence of such relationship, the provisions of this Article shall apply only to the last-mentioned amount. In that case, the excess part of the payments shall remain taxable according to the law of each Contracting State, due regard being had to the other provisions of this Convention.

Article 13

Capital Gains

1. Gains from the alienation of immovable property, as defined in paragraph 2 of Article 6, may be taxed in the Contracting State in which such property is situated.

2. Gains from the alienation of movable property forming part of the business property of a permanent establishment which an enterprise of a Contracting State has in the other Contracting State or of movable property pertaining to a fixed base available to a resident of a Contracting State in the other Contracting State for the purpose of performing professional services, including such gains from the alienation of such a permanent establishment (alone or together with the whole enterprise) or of such a fixed base, may be taxed in the other State. However, gains from the alienation of movable property of the kind referred to in paragraph 3 of Article 22 shall be taxable only in the Contracting State in which such movable property is taxable according to the said Article.

3. Gains from the alienation of any property other than those mentioned in paragraphs 1 and 2, shall be taxable only in the Contracting State of which the alienator is a resident.

Article 14

Independent Personal Services

1. Income derived by a resident of a Contracting State in respect of professional services or other independent activities of a similar character shall be taxable only in that State unless he has a fixed base regularly available to him in the other Contracting State for the purpose of performing his activities. If he has such a fixed base, the income may be taxed in the other contracting State but only so much of it as is attributable to that fixed base.

2. The term " professional services " includes, especially independent scientific, literary, artistic, educational or teaching activities as well as the independent activities of physicians, lawyers, engineers, architects, dentists and accountants.

Article 15

Dependent Personal Services

1. Subject to the provisions of Articles 16, 18 and 19, salaries, wages and other similar remuneration derived by a resident of a Contracting State in respect of an employment shall be taxable only in that State unless the employment is

exercised in the other Contracting State. If the employment is so exercised, such remuneration as is derived therefrom may be taxed in that other State.

2. Notwithstanding the provisions of paragraph 1, remuneration derived by a resident of a Contracting State in respect of an employment exercised in the other Contracting State shall be taxable only in the first-mentioned State if:

(a) the recipient is present in the other State for a period or periods not exceeding in the aggregate 183 days in the fiscal year concerned, and

(b) the remuneration is paid by, or on behalf of, an employer who is not a resident of the other State, and

(c) the remuneration is not borne by a permanent establishment or a fixed base which the employer has in the other State.

3. Notwithstanding the preceding provisions of this Article, remuneration in respect of an employment exercised aboard a ship or aircraft in international traffic, or aboard a boat engaged in inland waterways transport, may be taxed in the Contracting State in which the place of effective management of the enterprise is situated.

Article 16

Directors' Fees

Directors' fees and similar payments derived by a resident of a Contracting State in his capacity as a member of the board of directors of a company which is a resident of the other Contracting State may be taxed in that other State.

Article 21

Income Not Expressly Mentioned

Items of income of a resident of a Contracting State which are not expressly mentioned in the foregoing Articles of this Convention shall be taxable only in that State.

Chapter IV

Taxation of Capital

Article 22

Capital

1. Capital represented by immovable property, as defined in paragraph 2 of Article 6, may be taxed in the Contracting State in which such property is situated.

2. Capital represented by movable property forming part of the business property of a permanent establishment of an enterprise, or by movable property pertaining to a fixed base used for the performance of professional services, may be taxed in the Contracting State in which the permanent establishment or fixed base is situated.

3. Ships and aircraft operated in international traffic and boats engaged in inland waterways transport, and movable property pertaining to the operation of such ships, aircraft and boats, shall be taxable only in the Contracting State in which the place of effective management of the enterprise is situated.

4. All other elements of capital of a resident of a Contracting State shall be taxable only in that State.

CHAPTER V

METHODS FOR ELIMINATION OF DOUBLE TAXATION

Article 23A

Exemption Method

1. Where a resident of a Contracting State derives income or owns capital which, in accordance with the provisions of this Convention, may be taxed in the other Contracting State, the first-mentioned State shall, subject to the provisions of paragraph 2, exempt such income or capital from tax but may, in calculating tax on the remaining income or capital of that person, apply the rate of tax which would have been applicable if the exempted income or capital had not been so exempted.

2. Where a resident of a Contracting State derives income which, in accordance with the provisions of Articles 10 and 11, may be taxed in the other Contracting State, the first-mentioned State shall allow as a deduction from the tax on the income of that person an amount equal to the tax paid in that other Contracting State. Such deduction shall not, however, exceed that part of the tax, as computed before the deduction is given, which is appropriate to the income derived from that other Contracting State.

Article 23B

Credit Method

1. Where a resident of a Contracting State derives income or owns capital which, in accordance with the provisions of this Convention, may be taxed in the other Contracting State, the first-mentioned State shall allow:

(*a*) as a deduction from the tax on the income of that person, an amount equal to the income tax paid in that other Contracting State;

(*b*) as a deduction from the tax on the capital of that person, an amount equal to the capital tax paid in that other Contracting State.

2. The deduction in either case shall not, however, exceed that part of the income tax or capital tax, respectively, as computed before the deduction is given, which is appropriate, as the case may be, to the income or the capital which may be taxed in the other Contracting State.

CHAPTER VI

SPECIAL PROVISIONS

Article 24

Non-discrimination

1. The nationals of a Contracting State shall not be subjected in the other Contracting State to any taxation or any requirement connected therewith which is other or more burdensome than the taxation and connected requirements to which nationals of that other State in the same circumstances are or may be subjected.

2. The term " nationals " means:

(*a*) all individuals possessing the nationality of a Contracting State;

(*b*) all legal persons, partnerships and associations deriving their status as such from the law in force in a Contracting State.

3. Stateless persons shall not be subjected in a Contracting State to any taxation or any requirement connected therewith which is other or more burdensome than the taxation and connected requirements to which nationals of that State in the same circumstances are or may be subjected.

4. The taxation on a permanent establishment which an enterprise of a Contracting State has in the other Contracting State shall not be less favourably levied in that other State than the taxation levied on enterprises of that other State carrying on the same activities.

This provision shall not be construed as obliging a Contracting State to grant to residents of the other Contracting State any personal allowances, reliefs and reductions for taxation purposes on account of civil status or family responsibilities which it grants to its own residents.

5. Enterprises of a Contracting State, the capital of which is wholly or partly owned or controlled, directly or indirectly, by one or more residents of the other Contracting State, shall not be subjected in the first-mentioned Contracting State to any taxation or any requirement connected therewith which is other or more burdensome than the taxation and connected requirements to which other similar enterprises of that first-mentioned State are or may be subjected.

6. In this Article the term " taxation " means taxes of every kind and description.

Chapter VII

Final Provisions

Article 29

Entry Into Force

1. This Convention shall be ratified and the instruments of ratification shall be exchanged at .... as soon as possible.

2. The Convention shall enter into force upon the exchange of instruments of ratification and its provisions shall have effect:

(*a*) in (State A): ....
(*b*) in (State B): ....

Article 30

Termination

This Convention shall remain in force until denounced by one of the Contracting States. Either Contracting State may denounce the Convention, through diplomatic channels, by giving notice of termination at least six months before the end of any calendar year after the year .... In such event, the Convention shall cease to have effect:

(*a*) in (State A): ....
(*b*) in (State B): ....

Note
Most modern conventions entered into by the United Kingdom are closely based upon the O.E.C.D. Model.
See J. D. B. Oliver, " Double Tax Treaties in United Kingdom Tax Law " [1970] B.T.R. 388; R. Willis, " Great Britain's Part in the Development of Double Taxation Relief " [1965] B.T.R. 270.

CHAPTER 13

CAPITAL GAINS

EARLIER chapters [1] have stressed the importance of the distinction between " capital " and " income." Income Tax is a tax on income, and gains or accretions of a non-income nature are excluded from the income tax base. The extent of this tax base, however, depends upon the concept of " income " in the particular tax system. [2]

1. Capital Gains and the Tax Base

Before considering the proper approach to the taxation of capital gains, it is necessary to consider:

(a) what is meant by " capital " gains, as opposed to other types of gain;

(b) the extent to which such gains do already fall within the tax base, and

(c) if such gains do fall within the tax base, whether they are to receive special treatment.

Thus, in the British view, a gain made on the purchase and resale of an item of property may be regarded as being within the Income Tax base or outside it [3]; if it falls outside the base, it may nevertheless be subjected to a separate tax, *i.e.* Capital Gains Tax. In the United States of America, on the other hand, a similar gain may come within the concept of " income," but be singled out for special treatment as a special type of income.

FINAL REPORT OF THE ROYAL COMMISSION ON THE TAXATION OF PROFITS AND INCOME

1955 Cmd. 9474

84. It is much less easy to state succinctly what is the present legal theory as to the taxation of realised gains upon the sale of property. In so far as the property consists of stock in trade, there is no question but that a gain on sale enters into a computation of profit. That covers the case of the ordinary trader and his stock. But a man may make a profit from an isolated venture, without being in other respects a trader at all, or from a venture, separate from his regular business, which he does not intend to maintain or to repeat. There is nothing in the law that precludes such a profit from being taxed as his income, so long as the venture in the course of which the sale took place is itself a " trade, manufacture, adventure or concern in the nature of trade." This seems to be the sole relevant test. The idea that a profit to be taxable must be recurrent or at any rate a profit arising from an activity that is likely to yield

---

[1] In particular Chap. 4, *ante*, p. 65.

[2] *Cf.* the concept of income in the United States of America: Internal Revenue Code, 1954, para. 61, *ante*, p. 75; and that of the Carter Commission in Canada, *ante*, p. 70.

[3] See esp. Chap. 8, *ante*, pp. 140–145, and *Jones* v. *Leeming* [1930] A.C. 415; *ante*, p. 221.

recurrent profits is not now part of the legal conception that is applied, however persuasive it may have seemed in the light of the fact that the tax is a tax on " annual " profits. The doctrine that now prevails may be summed up by saying that the profit from an isolated transaction in property is not as such exempt from taxation; but that since only profits that are of the nature of income are to be subjected to an income tax, the law has tended to identify taxable profits as those which arise out of something more substantial than the mere occasion of the profit itself. Income, it has been said, is the fruit that ripens on and can be plucked off the tree. If there is to be income therefore there must not only be fruit but also a tree. This substance is to be found where the person concerned has been conducting a venture or concern in the nature of trade out of which the profit arises. That is equivalent to saying that he was a dealer, even if he made only one deal. But the profit that is taxed in such a case is the income arising from the venture: it is meaningless to say that what is taxed is the profit from the sale itself. It is sometimes said that a person is liable if he acquired the property sold with a view to its resale, and this again serves well enough to express the same general idea, so long as it is remembered how much ambiguity may be concealed by the words " with a view to its resale."

Note
The Report then goes on to consider the recommendations made in 1920 by the Colwyn Committee (*ante*, p. 141). It concludes that, although no action was taken by Parliament pursuant to those recommendations, the manner in which the courts had, over the years, interpreted " adventure in the nature of a trade " had established the taxability of profits from isolated transactions. A paradoxical situation results, whereby, due to British failure to tax " capital gains " at all until 1962, certain isolated profits are fully taxed as income whereas they might well have received favourable treatment in the U.S.A. as gains in respect of " capital assets," though within the definition of " income ": see W. W. Brudno and L. D. Hollman, " The Taxation of Capital Gains in the United States and the United Kingdom " [1958] B.T.R. 26, 134.

REPORT OF THE ROYAL COMMISSION ON TAXATION

[Carter Commission, Canada, 1966]

VOLUME I: INTRODUCTION

The decision to tax the annual changes in the economic power of each tax unit rather than " income," as it is now defined, has dramatic consequences.

For adoption of the comprehensive tax base requires the taxation of not only income from property, but also " capital " gains on the disposition of property. Almost everyone is familiar, at least in a general way, with the difference between " income " and " capital," even though the words seem to be incapable of precise definition. Capital is the source of income. By levying a tax on " income " the distinction between the two concepts takes on great significance, for if the courts find a particular gain to be " capital " the trans-action is not now taxable. There is an enormous incentive for the taxpayer to try to transform " income " gains into " capital " gains.[4] However, it is impossible to draw an unambiguous distinction between " capital " gains and " income " gains and the attempt to do so necessarily results in great uncertainty for the taxpayer because a particular transaction may or may not be found by the courts to fall on one side of the line or the other.

[4] *Cf.* the comments of the minority of the Royal Commission, 1955 Cmd. 9474, Memorandum of Dissent, paras. 45–48; *post*, p. 319.

After the most careful and exhaustive consideration of this complex question, we have arrived at the conclusion that the present distinction between kinds of gain is inconsistent with our concept of what we believe " income " is for purposes of determining the individual's capacity to pay tax.

A dollar gained through the sale of a share, bond or piece of real property bestows exactly the same economic power as a dollar gained through employment or operating a business. The equity principles we hold dictate that both should be taxed in exactly the same way. To tax the gain on the disposal of property more lightly than other kinds of gains or not at all would be grossly unfair.

These radical reforms are advocated because equity can be achieved in no other way, because in our opinion there would be no adverse economic effects through their adoption when combined with our other proposed changes, and because they would simplify the tax system and reduce uncertainty.

If the full taxation of property gains would result in dire economic consequences or hopelessly complex administrative questions, some backing away from equity principles could be justified. We are satisfied that neither result would come about.[5]

Accordingly, we recommend the full taxation of realised property gains. To prevent unwarranted postponement, to minimise the " locking-in " effect, and to stop residents from avoiding the tax altogether by leaving the country, property gains should be deemed to have been realised on the death of the owner [6] (unless the property passes to a surviving spouse or other member of the family unit) or on his leaving the country. For administrative reasons we recommend a lifetime exemption of $25,000 on realised real property gains on residences and farms.

Simply to adopt the full taxation of capital gains as a modification of the present system could be disastrous, as critics of the taxation of these gains assert. This is not what we are recommending. The effects of taxing capital gains in full can only be assessed as one feature of an entirely new system. The new system would have:

1. Much reduced marginal personal rates of tax.
2. Averaging provisions of unparalleled liberality.
3. Loss provisions that would remove any tax bias against risk taking.
4. Full credit to residents for Canadian corporation taxes.
5. More efficient incentives for new and small businesses.

When the taxation of capital gains is only one component of a package with these features, we can dismiss the claims that it would destroy initiative, reduce saving, and drive people out of the country.

We have no intention that the taxation of property gains should be retroactive. Accordingly, we propose that only gains accruing after the effective date of the legislation should be subject to taxation, with a liberal option to avoid the necessity of a multitude of valuations.

UNITED STATES OF AMERICA : INTERNAL REVENUE CODE 1954

§ 1201 ALTERNATIVE TAX

(a) *Corporations*

If for any taxable year the net long-term capital gain of any corporation exceeds

---

[5] *Cf.* the opinion of majority of the Royal Commission, 1955 Cmd. 9474, paras. 104–108; *post*, pp. 318–319.　　　　　　　　　　　　　　　　　[6] *Cf.* F.A. 1971, s. 59.

the net short-term capital loss, then, in lieu of the tax imposed by sections 11, 511, 802 (a), 821 (a) (1) or (b), and 831 (a), there is hereby imposed a tax (if such tax is less than the tax imposed by such sections) which shall consist of the sum of—

(1) a partial tax computed on the taxable income reduced by the amount of such excess, at the rates and in the manner as if this subsection had not been enacted, and

(2) an amount equal to 25 per cent. of such excess, or, in the case of a taxable year beginning before April 1, 1954, an amount equal to 26 per cent. of such excess.

In the case of a taxable year beginning before April 1, 1954, the amount under paragraph (2) shall be determined without regard to section 21 (relating to effect of change of tax rates).

(b) *Other Taxpayers*

If for any taxable year the net long-term capital gain of any taxpayer (other than a corporation) exceeds the net short-term capital loss, then, in lieu of the tax imposed by sections 1 and 511, there is hereby imposed a tax (if such tax is less than the tax imposed by such sections) which shall consist of the sum of—

(1) a partial tax computed on the taxable income reduced by an amount equal to 50 per cent. of such excess, at the rate and in the manner as if this subsection had not been enacted, and

(2) an amount equal to 25 per cent. of the excess of the net long-term capital gain over the net short-term capital loss.

§ 1221 CAPITAL ASSET DEFINED

For purposes of this subtitle, the term " capital asset " means property held by the taxpayer (whether or not connected with his trade or business), but does not include—

(1) stock in trade of the taxpayer or other property of a kind which would properly be included in the inventory of the taxpayer if on hand at the close of the taxable year, or property held by the taxpayer primarily for sale to customers in the ordinary course of his trade or business;

(2) property, used in his trade or business, of a character which is subject to the allowance for depreciation provided in section 167, or real property used in his trade or business;

(3) a copyright, a literary, musical, or artistic composition, or similar property, held by—

(A) a taxpayer whose personal efforts created such property, or

(B) a taxpayer in whose hands the basis of such property is determined, for the purpose of determining gain from a sale or exchange, in whole or in part by reference to the basis of such property in the hands of the person whose personal efforts created such property;

(4) accounts or notes receivable acquired in the ordinary course of trade or business for services rendered or from the sale of property described in paragraph (1); or

(5) an obligation of the United States or any of its possessions, or of a State or Territory, or any political subdivision thereof, or of the District of Columbia, issued on or after March 1, 1941, on a discount basis and payable without interest at a fixed maturity date not exceeding one year from the date of issue.

§ 1222 Other Terms Relating to Capital Gains and Losses

For purposes of this subtitle—

(1) Short-term Capital Gain

The term " short-term capital gain " means gain from the sale or exchange of a capital asset held for not more than 6 months, if and to the extent such gain is taken into account in computing gross income.

(2) Short-term Capital Loss

The term " short-term capital loss " means loss from the sale or exchange of a capital asset held for not more than six months, if and to the extent that such loss is taken into account in computing taxable income.

(3) Long-term Capital Gain

The term " long-term capital gain " means gain from the sale or exchange of a capital asset held for more than six months, if and to the extent such gain is taken into account in computing gross income.

(4) Long-term Capital Loss

The term " long-term capital loss " means loss from the sale or exchange of a capital asset held for more than 6 months, if and to the extent that such loss is taken into account in computing taxable income.

(5) Net Short-term Capital Gain

The term " net short-term capital gain " means the excess of short-term capital gains for the taxable year over the short-term capital losses for such year.

(6) Net Short-term Capital Loss

The term " net short-term capital loss " means the excess of short-term capital losses for the taxable year over the short-term capital gains for such year.

(7) Net Long-term Capital Gain

The term " net long-term capital gain " means the excess of long-term capital gains for the taxable year over the long-term capital losses for such year.

(8) Net Long-term Capital Loss

The term " net long-term capital loss " means the excess of long-term capital losses for the taxable year over the long-term capital gains for such year.

(9) Net Capital Gain

(A) Corporations

In the case of a corporation, the term " net capital gain " means the excess of the gains from sales or exchanges of capital assets over the losses from such sales or exchanges.

(B) Other taxpayers

In the case of a taxpayer other than a corporation, the term " net capital gain " means the excess of—

(i) the sum of the gains from sales or exchanges of capital assets, plus taxable income (computed without regard to the deductions provided by section 151, relating to personal exemptions or any deduction in lieu thereof) of the taxpayer or $1,000, whichever is smaller, over

(ii) the losses from such sales or exchanges.

For purposes of this subparagraph, taxable income shall be computed without regard to gains or losses from sales or exchanges of capital assets. If the taxpayer elects to pay the optional tax under section 3, the term " taxable income " as used in this subparagraph shall be read as " adjusted gross income."

(10) Net Capital Loss

The term " net capital loss " means the excess of the losses from sales or exchanges of capital assets over the sum allowed under section 1211. For the purpose of determining losses under this paragraph, amounts which are short-term capital losses under section 1212 shall be excluded.

2. Taxation of Capital Gains

If it is accepted that certain gains are of a special, " capital," nature, whether falling within the Income Tax base or not, such gains may be treated in a number of ways. They may be:

(a) subjected to tax fully as " income ";

(b) escape tax altogether; or

(c) be taxed according to special provisions.

A distinction may be drawn between " short-term," or " speculative," gains and other gains.[7] The rates applicable to capital gains may differ from those applying to other income. Certain types of property or disposal may receive special treatment and various other special provisions may apply.[8]

BUDGET SPEECH : THE CHANCELLOR OF THE EXCHEQUER, MR. SELWYN LLOYD

April 9, 1962; Hansard, H.C. Debates, Vol. 657, col. 979–980

I have not, therefore, come here today to propose a capital gains tax, but to suggest that what may loosely be called speculative gains should be subject to tax.

---

[7] As in the U.S.A., Internal Revenue Code 1954, para. 1222, *supra*. Thus, in the United Kingdom four approaches have been tried. Until 1962 capital gains were not taxed at all; from 1962 to 1965, short-term gains were taxed as income under Case VII of Sched. D, but other gains were not taxed; from 1965 to 1971, short-term gains were taxed as income, other gains being charged to Capital Gains Tax at a lower rate; from 1971, all chargeable capital gains are taxable at the lower rate to Capital Gains Tax, irrespective of the length of time for which the asset is held.

[8] For a full description of the taxation of capital gains in the United Kingdom, the reader is referred in particular to *Wheatcroft on Capital Gains* (Vol. I of the *British Tax Encyclopaedia*). The economic and policy issues involved are especially well treated in A. R. Ilersic, *The Taxation of Capital Gains* (London, 1962). Reference should also be made to L. Muten, " Some general problems concerning the Capital Gains Tax " [1966] B.T.R. 138; G. S. A. Wheatcroft, " The Problems of a Capital Gains Tax " [1964] B.T.R. 395; and P. G. Whiteman, " The Fundamental Defects in the Capital Gains Tax Structure " [1970] B.T.R. 46.

While the main function of any system of taxation must be to bring in revenue, it must also be designed to produce a feeling of broad equity of treatment between taxpayers. At present, it is pretty widely felt to be inequitable that those who supplement their incomes by speculative gains should escape tax on those gains. I do not think that they should continue to do so; and I tell the Committee frankly that it is on this account, and not mainly for yield, that I put forward this proposal.

Certain types of quick gains secured by those not engaging in such operations as a business, are under the present law treated as capital receipts. Although ordinary people find it difficult to distinguish them from income, and they may often be used as income, they are not taxed. Those engaged in certain types of profit-seeking transactions now escape tax altogether—for example, the man who buys stocks and shares not to invest but in the hope of a quick profit, and the man who buys land in the hope of a quick speculative profit through a sale to a genuine developer.

Those who make a business of such transactions are taxed already as traders. Those to whom the new arrangements will apply are those of whom it cannot be established that they are carrying on a business. In my view, however, it is wrong that such people should escape taxation on such activities.

The problem is not a new one. The 1920 Royal Commission advocated action: the Radcliffe Commission said that it needed consideration. I have said repeatedly that I intended to tackle it. I propose to bring such profits within the existing charge under Schedule D of Income Tax by way of a new Case VII.

I have examined various ways of doing this and have come to the conclusion that the appropriate method is by a time test. What I propose is that if assets are acquired and disposed of within a stated period of time—and the period will differ for different kinds of asset—any gain will be taxable under the new Case VII. The periods fixed will be such that the reasonable inference can be drawn that in general the transactions were of an income-seeking nature. What I am asking the Committee to do is to bring within Schedule D transactions which, some say—wrongly, I am advised—are already within the law.

BUDGET SPEECH: THE CHANCELLOR OF THE EXCHEQUER, MR. JAMES CALLAGHAN

April 6, 1965; Hansard, H.C. Debates, Vol. 710, col. 245

First, I begin with tax reform. The failure to tax capital gains is widely regarded, outside as well as inside the Labour Party, as the greatest blot on our existing system of direct taxation. There is little dispute nowadays that capital gains confer much the same kind of benefit on the recipient as taxed earnings more hardly won. Yet earnings pay tax in full while capital gains go free. This is unfair to the wage and salary earner. It has in the past been one of the barriers to the progress of an effective incomes policy, but now my right hon. Friend the First Secretary of State has carried this policy forward to a point which many did not believe was possible six months ago. This new tax will provide a background of equity and fair play for his work.

Moreover, there is no doubt that the present immunity from tax of capital gains has given a powerful incentive to the skilful manipulator of which he has taken full advantage to avoid tax by various devices which turn what is really taxable income into tax-free capital gains. We shall only make headway against avoidance of this sort when capital gains are also taxed.

FINAL REPORT OF THE ROYAL COMMISSION ON THE TAXATION OF PROFITS AND INCOME

1955 Cmd. 9474

PROBLEMS OF TAXING CAPITAL GAINS

88. There is nothing impossible about the introduction or the operation of a tax on capital gains. Varying forms of such a tax can be found in the codes of several European countries. Capital gains have been taxed in the United States of America since the introduction of an income tax into the Federal code in 1913. As we made it our business to make some study of the history and incidents of this tax, it may be useful by way of introduction to refer to one or two points that seem to be illustrated by the American experience.

89. The definition of income in the U.S. tax code [9] is so expressed that it was from the first interpreted in the Courts as including any realised appreciation in value of any property of the taxpayer, even though the realisation did not take place in the course of business. Consistently with this, such gains were taxable in full as part of the taxpayer's income and at the progressive rates of tax applicable to that income.

(1) In 1922, however, after this interpretation of the code had been confirmed by decisions of the Supreme Court in 1920 and 1921, special provisions were introduced which had the effect of separating the " long-term " capital gains of individuals from the rest of their income: these gains (subject to some exceptions) were taxed at a flat rate of $12\frac{1}{2}$ per cent., if advantageous, while " short-term " gains (on assets held for less than two years) remained fully taxable.

(2) The treatment of capital gains and losses in the tax code has undergone many variations since then. Not only were there substantial changes of treatment in 1933, in 1937, in 1941 and in 1951, but even within these periods there were several modifications of specific provisions. Thus exemptions, rates, qualifying periods, have all been varied from time to time.

(3) The system at present in force (a) accords different treatment to the capital gains of corporations and of individuals, (b) distinguishes between gains made on property held for longer than six months and other gains, (c) accords more favourable treatment to the long-term gain, and imposes upon it a maximum rate of 25 per cent., (d) makes provision for losses as well as gains, and (e) contains exemptions for special categories of property or of certain transactions which are treated as tax-free exchanges. Included in such exchanges are (i) a transfer of any kind of property to a corporation by one or more persons solely in exchange for stock or securities, where immediately after the exchange the person or persons are in control of the corporation, (ii) an involuntary conversion, (iii) a sale of an owner-occupied residence if a new one is bought within twelve months, in which event only any excess of the sale proceeds over the cost of new purchase is chargeable.

90. The present structure of the U.S. system indicates some of the problems that confront any practical application of the theory that capital gains ought to be treated as taxable income. The profit which accrues in the year of realisation has no true relation to the income of that year unless the

---

[9] Art. 61 of the Internal Revenue Code 1954, *ante*, p. 75. See also the other extracts from the Code, at p. 308, and for a further description of the American system, see J. T. Sneed, " Capital Gains Taxation—American Plan " [1968] B.T.R. 394.

appreciation in value can itself be found to have occurred wholly in that year. Yet if the property sold has been held for a period of years there is no reason at all why this should be so. There may have been a steady increase in value spread evenly over the period: more likely, there will have been rises and falls during the years that the period covers. Some of the appreciation, perhaps all of it, may have taken place before the tax ever existed. In a system of highly progressive rates, such as ours, to treat the whole profit as part of the income of the year of realisation and so to tax it at the marginal rate or rates of the taxpayer concerned would seem unjust. Consequently there has to be superimposed upon the simple idea of treating capital gains as taxable income a more or less complex structure of provisions for taxing gains on property acquired before the current year at special abated rates or for spreading back the gains over the years during which the property was held (if that were feasible) and for ascertaining how much of the appreciation is to be attributed to the period before the tax was introduced. The distinction between long-term and short-term gains, which is the basis of one method of trying to cope with these problems, itself involves the introduction of a new group of difficulties.

91. Secondly, to tax capital gains seems to require allowance of capital losses. If a capital gain is to be claimed as taxable income on the ground that the obtaining of it constitutes a real increase of taxable capacity as between the one taxpayer and others, then the suffering of a capital loss constitutes a real decrease of taxable capacity and a system which allows losses generally as a deduction from income of the year ought to admit such a loss among others. But it is almost impossible to suppose that a tax system would accept the logical consequence of this dilemma at a time of high progressive rates of taxation. To do so seems to offer too obvious an invitation to the speculator to share with his fellow citizens the ill results of a speculation that has gone wrong. The point has been made that a simple tax confined to realised gains and losses would allow a taxpayer to set off losses at the marginal rate of tax on his income while retaining other resources which may have appreciated as much or much more in value; just as it would force him to pay tax at the marginal rate on his gain, even though he continued to hold other resources which had depreciated in value to the same or greater extent. To avoid the full allowance of losses which is logically due, various suggestions are made, of which the most usual is that they should be allowed only against capital gains and that, if the allowance is not exhausted in the first year, they should be carried forward on the same account for a limited or unlimited number of years. Some analogy for such a method of treatment can be found in the existing provisions for the treatment of profits arising under Case VI of Schedule D and the allowance of losses against them: but it has to be admitted that the result would not be to hold the balance evenly as between capital gains and capital losses, for, whereas a gain would be chargeable even if there were no realised loss, a loss would not be allowable except so far as there was a realised gain.

92. The third preliminary problem is concerned with the question of exemptions. The logical argument for taxing capital gains as income does not call for distinctions between one kind of capital resource and another or between the different sets of circumstance in which the realisation takes place. But if distinctions are not made, the tax would be found to be applied to " gains " which very few people would regard as fairly the subject of taxation. The case that is, perhaps, most often dwelt upon is that of an owner-occupier who, for personal or business reasons, has to sell his house and find a new home somewhere else. If he bought or built his house before, say, 1939, there is a strong likelihood that he will get more money when he sells it than

he paid for it. But there is an equal likelihood that, to buy another house of the same quality and condition, he will have to pay more than his pre-1939 price. He may well have to pay more than his net proceeds. Is he then to pay tax on his " gain " when the result of the whole transaction is that, in real terms, he is no better off than he was before and has needed all the money representing the gain even to maintain that level? If he does not buy again but has to rent equivalent accommodation it may be doubted whether his gain is not still something of an illusion, for, except so far as the retarding effect of rent restriction can come to his aid, he will need the higher income arising from the investment of the sale proceeds to pay for the enhanced cost of living space.

93. Another crux is found in the treatment of reinvestment generally. Many of these gains on realisation occur to individuals or institutions for whom the act of realisation is merely a change of investment: the proceeds of sale are spent on acquiring a new source of income. Yet it by no means follows that a larger income in money terms results from a gain. To take the field of gilt-edged investments alone, appreciation or depreciation in value of the holding is mainly attributable to changes in the pure rate of interest occurring during the life of the security, omitting for the moment the more specialised question of maturing redemptions. Consequently, if appreciation takes place through a fall in the rate of interest, a reinvestment of sale proceeds has to be made upon the terms that the investor must accept a lower yield upon his money and he needs therefore all or most of his gain to maintain the same nominal income. Frequently, the persons who make such a gain are trustees of settled property. The law does not treat the difference as forming part of the income of the life-tenant; on the contrary it forms part of the capital of the settled property and has to go back into it by way of reinvestment. It seems a difficult proposition to assert that in any such circumstances—and they can occur in many forms—a gain by way of income arises that ought to be taxed upon one recipient or the other as part of his income.

Advantages and Disadvantages

94. We have said enough to show that a tax on capital gains, if put into operation, cannot be expected to prove a tax of simple structure or one that would be free from a number of rather arbitrary solutions of its various problems. It is now necessary to see how strong are the arguments for including such gains in the conception of income, despite the difficulties. It is perhaps the very variety of the forms in which the gains can occur that complicates a general discussion of merits. We have mentioned already the gain that arises from a deliberate acquisition of property with a view to its sale at a profit. This is the kind of case that is probably most often thought of by those who advocate the extended tax. We have pointed out that in many cases the law does include a gain of this sort within the range of taxable income, and we are to consider later whether any further rules, not inconsistent with the principle, are needed for its implementation. Contrasted with this, at the other end of the scale, is the gain from an appreciation in value that was neither anticipated at the time of acquisition nor sought for by the recipient. Compulsory acquisitions of property have thrown up many instances of this. To tax a windfall of this kind would inflict very small proportionate sacrifice on the taxpayer, so long at any rate as the gain realised upon the asset in question is considered in isolation from the state of account of his other resources; but it would still leave the question open whether such

a gain in respect of a single piece of property, isolated and non-recurrent, bore any recognisable sign of being income.

95. On the other hand there are forms of property which carry in themselves the capacity to appreciate in value in the hands of their holders without yielding, under the present system, a corresponding taxable income during the period of appreciation. The reversion on a long lease offers an instance of one sort [10] : a redeemable security, under certain conditions, another. In the first case, it will normally happen that the property can be let at a higher rental when the lease expires, all the more so if the current lease was granted for a monetary premium or is a building lease. Therefore as each year brings the reversion nearer to possession there is likely to be an appreciation of value which is realised in the year of expiry. In the second case a variety of circumstances may bring about a gain. The security may be issued at a discount to be repaid at par or at par to be repaid at a premium: or, alternatively, whatever the terms of issue, it may be bought in the market during its currency at a price less than the amount payable on redemption. In either event a gain occurs in the year of maturity. But an analysis on these lines seems to us to point to the conclusion that there is something equivalent to income accruing each year during the period of maturity and not to the conclusion that the ultimate gain is income of the year in which it is realised. And that is the present point. Although a device could, in theory, be proposed for spreading back the gain, when realised, over the preceding years, long periods of years are normally involved in this kind of case and the administrative task of reopening assessments and recomputing liability for those years would make such a scheme unworkable. On the other hand we are satisfied that it would be wrong to try to charge tax on the unrealised increment for each year of the periods of accretion. To do so would amount to taxing nothing but an imputed income and would contradict the principle of taxing only realised gains: and it would be found in practice that, owing to the influence of other factors such as the current rate of interest and the uncertainties that affect all forms of deferred reward, the true increment represented nothing like a regular annual progression.

96. The taxation of capital gains is sometimes advocated as a corrective of what is said to be the special advantage enjoyed by the holder of ordinary shares in a limited company. In so far as the profits made by the company in any year are not distributed in dividend they are retained in the company's business, thereby making a contribution to an increase in the value of the assets belonging to the corporate body of shareholders. The retentions also contribute to the likelihood of increased profits and, ultimately, increased dividends in the future; and since increased asset cover, increased profit cover for current dividends and the prospect of higher future dividends tend themselves to increase the capital value of shares a process is detected which has the effect of adding to the capital of the shareholder through savings made out of the company's income without his share of the savings ever having been subjected to surtax as income in his hands. From time to time some part of the retained profits may be capitalised by the company and fully-paid shares issued to the equity shareholders in respect of their interest in the profits so capitalised. If that is done, those profits are no longer available for distribution as dividend and must be retained by the company as part of its permanent capital. While the operation of capitalising profits and issuing " bonus " shares in respect of them presents in a dramatic form what is involved in the process of corporate saving, we do not take the view that the issuing of " bonus " shares, which leaves the shareholder's position substantially unaltered,

---

[10] For a criticism of the adopted treatment of leases and reversions, see P. G. Whiteman, " The Fundamental Defects in the Capital Gains Tax Structure " [1970] B.T.R. 46.

is itself an important aspect of the matter. What matters for the present purpose is the improvement of the shareholder's position through corporate saving, without his share of the saving passing through his hands as taxable income.

97. We deal elsewhere with this special aspect of the problem of taxing corporate profits. While it is true that the individual shareholder is not taxed on his share of the undistributed part of those profits as if it formed part of his personal income, it is also true that the whole profits of the corporation are subjected to income tax at the standard rate as well as to profits tax (subject in the latter case to provisions for exemption and abatement). This charge, which is an effective burden on retained profits except in respect of standard rate income tax on distributed profits, has no ascertainable relation to the benefit that some shareholders may obtain from the fact that their share of retained profits is, in effect, saved for them in the corporate pool without first being placed in their hands so as to render it part of their income assessable to surtax. But, when it comes to considering the question whether the peculiar incidents of corporate saving are in themselves sufficient to justify the charging to tax of capital gains, we think that it is impossible to ignore the countervailing circumstances that profits made in corporate form do in fact bear a supplementary charge which is not imposed on other forms of profits or income: or to suppose that these peculiar incidents could support an argument for a capital gains tax in respect of any form of property other than equity shares.

98. We are now in a position to state our general view on the question whether capital gains should or should not be taxed in the field of taxation of income. Those who advocate such taxation are, we think, responding to a feeling which is the product of disappointment at the failure of high taxes on income to restrain all lavish expenditure by the wealthy; but we suspect that this feeling is due to a misunderstanding. It is undoubtedly possible for a person of property to live for a while, perhaps a long while, upon his capital, so that his expenditure is not limited by the income which is left to him after he has paid tax upon it. But he can do this whether or not he is making capital gains. Two persons, one with a capital of £100,000 on which no gains are being made, the other with a capital of £30,000 on which he is making gains, may each of them be selling assets in order to finance their expenditure; but why should the second be taxed on his excess expenditure while the first is untaxed? If a capital gains tax is regarded as a means of taxing expenditure which is left untaxed by the present system, it does not hit that object at all squarely.

99. Thus we are not at all impressed by the argument that the taxation of capitals gains would achieve a more equitable distribution of the tax burden between one taxpayer and another. On the contrary, the considerations to which we have alluded in the foregoing paragraphs seem to show plainly that they could not well be taxed without raising a number of points of principle which are both difficult in themselves and of which the solution would remain debatable. They could, of course, be solved, if they had to be, by the adoption of arbitrary rules: but the rules would be arbitrary ones, without much support from logical principle, and in the result a tax on these lines would be likely to create at least as many inequities as it would remove. Indeed, no form of the tax that was based on realised gains and realised losses—and there is no alternative—would escape the serious objection to its foundation in equity that it would tax to the same extent a man who had realised a gain on one of his assets, though showing a net loss on others that he retained, as the man who had realised a similar gain without any current depreciation of his other assets

to set against it.   Whatever form is proposed for such qualifications and exemptions, their introduction seems to us to show up a central weakness in the
arguments for taxing capital gains as income: if such a gain is fairly to be
regarded as income the recipient ought to be taxed on it at the full progressive
rate, but on the other hand, if it cannot fairly be so regarded, there is no good
reason why his capacity to pay income tax or surtax should be thought to be
increased by its receipt.   In brief, we do not share the view of those advocates
of the charge who maintain that it is called for by the need to correct an
evident inequity between different taxpayers.

100. The next thing that we must say is that, as we have already indicated,
no measure for bringing capital gains under taxation could be a simple
one.   Just because they fit so awkwardly into a scheme of income tax that
is steeply progressive, we must envisage a measure that is complicated by
a number of exemptions and qualifications; that has to provide different treatment for long-term and short-term gains; and that has to establish machinery
for dealing with other problems apart from those that we have mentioned
already, such as the relation of the tax to property acquired by gift or inheritance, the valuation of improvements made upon improvable property, the
valuation of all realisable property as at the opening date of the tax (unless
it is to bring into tax increases of value accrued before the date of its
imposition). . . .

Conclusion

104. The propriety of the tax has received some support on economic grounds,
the view being advanced that the absence of a tax on capital gains contributes
to the course of inflation.   The premise is that the capital gain forms a
resource that is peculiarly likely to be withdrawn from investment and
expended in consumption.   But it seemed to us that no sound conclusion could
be arrived at, one way or the other, on this theme.   We would grant that in a
period of very high taxation of the large incomes and of very high duty on
death the owners of large property resources must find their will to save and
their desire to conserve capital much weakened, so that they will have a general
readiness to draw upon capital in the attempt to preserve an accustomed standard
of living.   Given the two conditions of the existence of private property and
the continuance of these very high rates of taxation on income and capital it is
not easy to see that this tendency will abate.   But this is a different thing from
saying that the obtaining of capital gains makes an identifiable contribution to
inflationary pressure.   The tendency to live upon capital will be there, whether
capital gains are being made or not; the mere fact that capital is increasing
in money value (though in many cases falling in real value) does not in any
obvious way give strong encouragement to spending out of capital.

105. The above does not imply a denial of the probability that spending will
be higher at a time when general conditions are such as to create capital gains
than at a time of steady values or capital losses.   For even if this probability
is granted, the question still remains whether the characteristic form of such
spending involves the actual selling of securities to finance it (so that it would
be directly checked by a tax on *realised* gains); or whether the individual,
finding that his position on capital account is strengthened, becomes less concerned than before to refrain from spending the whole of his current income
or to maintain the level of his bank balance.   We see no reason to suppose
that the greater part of such boom spending as can be traced is of the former,
rather than the latter, character.   If it is of the latter character, it is not evident

that the proposed tax would have much effect upon it. A capital gains tax would indeed have some general effect, in an inflationary phase, as a deterrent to investment in securities and real property; but this effect is the same as that produced by monetary policy, which does the job much more directly and is vastly easier and cheaper to administer.

106. It seems to us much better to assume that, on the whole, capital gains will be saved. Certainly it is the sensible thing that they should be; and we do not see much evidence that this presumption of reasonable conduct fails to correspond, in the main, with the facts. It is a general principle that a tax which falls upon saving does not in itself contribute to the control of inflation. We believe that it is upon savings that a capital gains tax would mainly fall; and, if that is so, the hopes that have been built on its favourable economic effects would be disappointed.

107. In the light of these general considerations we came to the conclusion that we could not safely attach any weight to the economic arguments that were advanced in favour of the tax. On the other hand we felt that we must give weight to the fact that such a tax would have some, even possibly a serious, disincentive effect on the private saving which now takes place: and, though it might discourage a small number of people who were enabled by the obtaining of capital gains to maintain a standard of living out of relation to their income, its general effect would be to tax a very much larger number of persons without the justification of any equitable design.

108. We do not recommend therefore that capital gains should be brought under a general charge to income tax or surtax as constituting income. Nor do we recommend the introduction of any supplementary scheme for charging them or some of them to a flat-rate tax as constituting a special category of income.

Memorandum of Dissent, by Mr. G. Woodcock, Mr. H. L. Bullock and Mr. N. Kaldor.

THE GENERAL CASE FOR THE TAXATION OF CAPITAL GAINS

34. The tax exemption of the so-called capital profits of various kinds represents the most serious omission in our present system of income taxation.

35. The basic reason for the inclusion of capital gains in taxation is that capital gains increase a person's taxable capacity by increasing his power to spend or save; and since capital gains are not distributed among the different members of the taxpaying community in fair proportion to their taxable incomes but are concentrated in the hands of property owners (and particularly the owners of equity shares) their exclusion from the scope of taxation constitutes a serious discrimination in tax treatment in favour of a particular class of taxpayer. The manner in which capital gains (of certain kinds at any rate) augment the taxable capacity of the recipient, has been convincingly shown, in our view, in the memorandum by the Board that is reproduced as an Annexe to the present Memorandum and we do not therefore consider it necessary to argue this at length.

Arguments against Taxing Capital Gains

36. The main arguments habitually used to justify the exclusion of capital gains from taxation are—
   (*a*) that the rise in capital values in the course of, or in consequence of, inflation represents illusory, and not real, gains;

(*b*) equally the capital gains arising as a result of a fall in interest rates may be illusory, since they do not increase the investor's future income;

(*c*) capital gains are not only irregular, but may also be unsought or unexpected, and do not therefore represent the same kind of taxable capacity as regular and expected income;

(*d*) only a tax on realised capital gains is administratively feasible, and this is inequitable because (*i*) it imputes the gains on any realised asset to the particular year in which the realisation takes place, whereas the appreciation may have accrued over a series of years; (*ii*) the realised capital gains of any particular year may be offset by the depreciation in the value of unrealised assets in that year; (*iii*) if in a particular year the realised losses exceed realised gains, it would not be practicable to allow such losses to be set off against other income, and yet it would be unjust merely to allow such losses to be carried forward as an offset against future gains.

The Majority base their recommendations mainly on arguments connected with (*b*), (*c*) and (*d*) above. We shall deal with all four types of argument in turn.

(a) Capital Gains in an Inflation [11]

37. We do not deny that the rise in capital values that occurs in the course of an inflation does not increase the taxable capacity of the recipients in the same way as a rise in capital values during a period of steady prices. But we cannot regard this as a justification for excluding capital gains from taxation within the general framework of a tax system which sets out to tax income and not consumption, and which therefore taxes that part of income which is saved as well as that part which is spent—although, as we shall argue below, it does constitute a case for certain well-defined exceptions. If the proceeds of the gain are spent the recipient derives the same benefit as he does in spending taxed income. If the gains are saved, the argument about their illusory character applies equally to all saving, and not merely to capital appreciation. If a man regularly saves up a part of his earnings by adding to his savings deposits or paying premiums on a life assurance, it may equally happen that as a result of inflation the real value of his accumulated savings is constantly shrinking. He is in no different position from another man who attains the same increase in the money value of his capital as a result of capital appreciation. The fact that in times of inflation money appreciation will not mean a corresponding real appreciation may be regarded as an argument against the taxation of savings as such. It is not an argument for the differential treatment of capital appreciation as against other forms of saving.

38. It must also be remembered that taxable capacity is essentially a relative concept, and those property owners who make capital gains during an inflation are undoubtedly in a better position than those who own fixed interest securities, and who therefore lose part of their real capital as a result of the rise in prices. Equity cannot be secured by ignoring relative changes in the taxable capacities of different property owners; and, if it were held to be desirable (and possible) to exempt that part of capital appreciation which

---

[11] On the question of inflation, see *Secretan* v. *Hart* [1969] 1 W.L.R. 1599; *post*, p. 330; the Introduction to *Wheatcroft on Capital Gains*; and G. C. Hockley, " Capital Gains and Inflation " [1968] B.T.R. 3.

was commensurate with the general price rise, it would follow that any
lesser degree of capital appreciation should be regarded as a loss. It is not
our view that the tax code should be so devised as to insure taxpayers against
the risk of inflation. Indeed, we should consider any such intention singularly
inappropriate, for taxation must be regarded as one of the principal weapons
in the armoury of the central government for combating inflation. In the
event of a drastic depreciation it might become necessary to revise the basis
of all monetary obligations and commitments, including tax payments—as was
done in Belgium after the First World War, and in Belgium and France after
the Second World War. But we do not regard such a situation as within the
foreseeable circumstances which tax regulations, or tax reform, should take into
account.

(b) Capital Gains and Interest Rates

39. An appreciation of capital values which results from a fall in the " pure "
rate of interest is not in the same category as a rise in values which merely
reflects higher prices, since in this case the capital gain is real enough in the
sense that it increases the gainer's command over goods and services. As
the Majority emphasise, however, if the proceeds of the gain are reinvested
" a reinvestment of sale proceeds has to be made upon the terms that the
investor must accept a lower yield upon his money and he needs therefore
all or most of his gain to maintain the same nominal income." This is
true, but ignores the fact that the holders of long-term bonds still gain on
such occasions relatively to other savers who save out of current incomes,
or whose past savings were not invested in long-term bonds. When rates
of interest fall, some savers (e.g. those whose savings are invested in savings
deposits) must accept a reduction of income, whilst other savers manage to
offset the effect of the fall in interest by the capital gains on their existing
holdings. We do not see that equity is better served by ignoring the relative
improvement in the position of the second group of taxpayers altogether
rather than by recognising it; even though we would agree that a capital
gain resulting from a reduction in the yield of long-term bonds does not
add to taxable capacity as much as an equivalent gain on equity shares resulting
from higher dividend payments.

40. Further, it should be noted that whereas general movements in the
price-level tend to be irreversible, there is no reason to suppose that the long-
term trend of interest rates is either falling or rising. Past experience suggests
on the contrary that periods of falling interest rates alternate with periods of
rising interest rates, with little net change on balance. The man or the
beneficiary of a settled estate who is unduly heavily taxed as a result of a
fall in interest rates is correspondingly lightly taxed as a result of a rise in
interest rates.

(c) Capital Gains and Taxable Capacity

41. We wish to emphasise, however, that—ignoring the exceptional periods
following in the wake of great wars or great economic depressions—capital
gains are not, to any important extent, the consequence of either rising prices
or falling interest rates. The great bulk of capital gains in normal periods is
the result of rising real incomes (higher profits and larger dividend payments)
to which therefore none of the above considerations apply. In a modern
industrial community such as ours a high proportion (four-fifths or more if
American experience can be taken as a guide) of all capital gains are derived
from transactions in securities, and mainly in ordinary shares of business

corporations. There is a steady long-run trend of rising share values which simply reflects the growth of the real earning power and the growing dividend payments of companies.

42. We take the view therefore that the great bulk of capital gains is of a kind to which the description " neither anticipated at the time of acquisition nor sought for by the recipient " [12] does not apply. It may be true that at any one time the majority of ordinary shares are held by their owners in the hope of long-term appreciation rather than of any definite expectation of an early sale at a quick profit, but this does not mean that the expectation of such long-run appreciation is not an important part of the benefit which the owners expect to derive from the acquisition or the holding of ordinary shares. The value which successful businesses acquire in the form of " good-will "—the excess of their market capitalisation over their share capital and reserves—is not an isolated windfall like a lucky draw in a sweepstake. It is part of the normal reward of successful enterprise: indeed, under present day conditions it is by far the most important part of that reward, the expectation of which is a crucial factor in the supply of risk capital and business ability to new ventures. We do not wish to deny that the prospect of high rewards to successful enterprise plays an important role in the economic progress of society. But this does not alter the fact that it is grossly unfair to allow the rewards to the successful property owner or business man to remain so largely exempt from taxation when successful authors, actors, inventors, lawyers, surgeons or civil servants are all fully taxed on their earnings.

43. Our first concern has been to show that, in the circumstances of present day Britain, it is not a sensible view to look upon capital profits generally as isolated and non-recurrent windfalls; but we also unreservedly reject the view that by virtue of being a windfall, incidental and unforeseen, a gain ought to be exempt from tax. Windfall gains confer material benefit just as expected gains do. The Majority argue that to tax a pure windfall " would inflict very small proportionate sacrifice on the taxpayer " but it would still leave open the question whether " a gain in respect of a single piece of property, isolated and non-recurrent, bore any recognisable sign of being income." [12] If this is taken to mean that the recipient will not adjust his scale of living, as a result of the receipt of such a non-recurrent gain in the same way as in the case of an increase in his regular receipts, the point is obvious: but it is hardly relevant to a tax system which sets out to tax savings as well as spendings.

44. In paragraph 98, on the other hand, the Majority argue that even if a man does spend his capital gains it would be unfair to tax him on that account so long as spending out of capital in general is left untaxed. " Two persons, one with a capital of £100,000 on which no gains are being made, the other with a capital of £30,000 on which he is making gains, may each of them be selling assets in order to finance their expenditure; but why should the second be taxed on his excess expenditure while the first is untaxed? " Here the Majority seem to be disputing the justice of electing Income as the base for personal taxation. The objective of income taxation is to tax a man, not in accordance with his spendings as such, nor in accordance with his disposable wealth as such, but in accordance with his " increment in economic power " over a given period. Under an income tax capital gains represent taxable capacity precisely because they provide a distinct addition to the amount of goods and services which an individual is in a position to command, quite irrespective of whether he chooses to spend them or save them.

[12] Cf. the majority report, para. 94; ante, p. 315.

Capital Gains and Tax Avoidance

45. The full significance of the omission of capital profits from taxation only becomes clear, however, when it is appreciated that the extent to which rewards take the form of tax-free capital gains rather than taxed dividend income is not something that is fixed by Nature, but is very much subject to manipulation by the taxpayer.[13] . . .

47. . . . No doubt extreme practices of this kind could be stopped by special anti-avoidance provisions. But in our view so long as capital gains remain exempt from taxation it is impossible to deal with the problem of the conversion of income into capital gains in all its possible forms by specific pieces of legislation.

48. All these opportunities, moreover, are far more readily available to the large property owner than to the small saver; and it is well known from American experience that capital gains are a major source of large incomes but unimportant as a source of smaller incomes. The Report, while it pays a great deal of attention to the alleged inequities that the taxation of capital gains would involve as between one property owner and another (discussed in paragraph 61 below), makes no mention of the far more serious inequities that arise as a result of the exclusion of capital gains from taxation as between those who can (and do) manipulate their affairs so as to augment their tax-free gains at the cost of their taxable income and those who are not in a position to minimise their tax liability in this manner. In fact the Majority find no occasion to refer to problems of tax avoidance in connection with capital gains at all.

Capital Gains and Undistributed Profits

49. With regard to the capital profits associated with ordinary shares, the Majority admit that as companies are growing through the steady retention of part of their current profits and the consequent growth of their earnings and dividends, " a process is detected which has the effect of adding to the capital of the shareholder through savings made out of the company's income without his share of the savings ever having been subjected to surtax as income in his hands." [14]

52. . . . We believe, therefore, that if capital appreciation were brought into charge in the form of a capital gains tax there would be a case for reducing the present burden of taxation on undistributed profits and our recommendations in Chapter III below are directed to this purpose.[15]

(d) Realised and Accrued Gains

53. We should now like to turn to the objections against the taxation of capital profits that are particularly directed against a scheme of taxation of realised capital gains. As is explained in the Report [16] it is a basic principle both of the tax system and of business accounting not to take account of profits until they are realised. This means that ordinary trading profits are reckoned as the year's receipts (whether in actual money or in money's worth),

---

[13] The memorandum goes on to consider certain methods of tax avoidance by transactions in securities, made possible by the distinction between capital and income. See now, I.C.T.A. 1970, ss. 460–477, and Chap. 2, *ante.*

[14] These remarks must be read subject to the " shortfall " provisions applicable to close companies, I.C.T.A. 1970, ss. 289, 296–300. See Chap. 16, *post.*

[15] When, in 1965, the Capital Gains Tax was introduced, the taxation of companies was also restructured, one of the effects being to give undistributed profits favourable treatment.

[16] Para. 29, *ante*, p. 72. See also the recommendations of the Carter Commission, *infra.*

less the expenses that are attributable to those receipts, the latter being evaluated by reckoning the difference between the opening and the closing stock at actual cost. Unrealised gains which take the form of an appreciation in the market value of unsold goods relatively to their costs of acquisition are not taken into account; though accountancy principles approve, and the tax system by special concession allows, the anticipation of unrealised losses in permitting stocks to be valued at market prices, when market prices are below cost.

54. We agree with the view expressed in paragraph 12 of the Board's memorandum that both administrative and other considerations make it inevitable that a tax on capital profits should follow analogous principles. From an administrative point of view it would be extremely difficult, if not impossible, to make a periodic valuation of all capital assets with sufficient accuracy to permit a tax to be levied on the change in the market value of all assets between two points of time. A tax on realised capital gains does, however, come to the same as a tax on the profit accruing through capital appreciation : the difference being only that for the purpose of measuring this profit the various assets that compose capital at any one time are valued at cost (and not at current market price) until they are sold or otherwise disposed of by their owners. Hence, but for the special concession of valuing stocks at market prices when these are below costs, the tax on realised capital gains follows the same principles as are followed in the determination of trading profits.

55. We do not share the view that a tax on realised capital gains when considered over a sequence of years is either a less comprehensive or less equitable measure of the benefit derived from capital appreciation, than a tax on accrued gains. As the memorandum of the Board shows (in paragraph 12), if the tax on realised capital gains is so framed that all forms of property transfer are reckoned as " realisation " for tax purposes (the transfer of assets by way of gift or inheritance just as much as by way of sale) the difference between realised capital gains and accrued capital gains can only be one of timing. Over a taxpayer's whole life the accumulated total of realised capital gains must necessarily come to the same as the accumulated total of accrued capital gains; and in consequence, the cumulative tax liability on account of capital gains should also come to the same (provided the tax rates are stable) except in so far as the one measure shows a greater or lesser irregularity in time than the other.

56. In general, taxation based on realised gains means a postponement of liability as compared with taxation based on accrued gains since property owners may not realise some of their assets during their lifetime at all, or not for some years after the appreciation of value has occurred. Moreover, the very existence of a capital gains tax might tempt taxpayers to postpone the realisation of the gains (or encourage the early realisation of losses) since they thereby gain the interest on the taxes payable during the period of postponement. Net realised gains would therefore normally lag behind net accrued gains, though under a progressive system the taxpayer would have an incentive to even out in time the rate of realisation of gains, and this consideration would tend to moderate the extent of the postponement. It may be thought that the fact that an investor normally prefers to realise an individual holding when the market is favourable—selling those assets which have risen in value and holding on to those which have fallen, in the hope of subsequent appreciation— might cause his net realised gains at times to exceed his net capital appreciation on all holdings and thus expose him to a higher liability than that warranted by the net change in his capital assets. However, it is open to an investor to effect a purely formal realisation of losses—by selling depreciated assets and buying them back immediately afterwards—so that he is not likely to incur liability on a higher total of realised gains than his net accrued gains. Hence,

whilst the rate at which gains are realised may lag behind the rate at which they accrue, they are not likely to run ahead of it.

57. There is no presumption, therefore, that the man whose capital is invested in diversified holdings and in easily marketable securities would be more harshly treated under a system of progressive taxation when capital gains and losses are imputed to the year of realisation than under a system which taxes gains as they accrue. Indeed, the contrary is likely to be the case. It is true that a tax on realised gains imputes the gain on any particular asset to the particular year in which realisation occurs, whereas the appreciation in its value may have accrued over a series of years. However, what matters from the taxpayer's point of view is not the gain associated with the realisation of a particular asset but the fluctuation in the annual net total of his taxable gains, since it is only to the extent that his net annual gains fluctuate that he is obliged to incur heavier charges (under a progressive system of taxation) owing to the timing of the gains.

58. These fluctuations would tend to be much greater, however, under a system which taxes all capital appreciation as it accrues than under a system which taxes gains only as they are realised. Under the former system the taxpayer would be exposed to the full incidence of short-period fluctuations in the market prices of securities. In boom years he would be charged on the net appreciation of all his assets (and would presumably have to realise some of his assets in order to meet his tax bill). If the appreciation were subsequently wiped out in a depression year, he would have established a corresponding loss, but—on the hypothesis of a progressive scale of charges— this would not entitle him to a corresponding rebate of tax. He would thus lose on balance as a result of a fluctuation in the market value of unrealised securities over which he had no control and which brought him in the end no net gain.

59. Under a system of taxation which taxes only realised capital gains the very fact that the timing of the realisation of gains is under the taxpayer's own control would serve to even out the fluctuations in his annual liability. If the gains on realised assets are reckoned as the gains of a single year, so are the losses; if losses can be offset against the gains, and unabsorbed losses carried forward against future gains, the taxpayer is given, in fact, full facilities for moderating the effects of fluctuations in his taxable gains over time.

60. On the other hand there are circumstances in which a tax on realised gains inevitably involves a bunching of gains in time, and hence, under a progressive tax, would involve the taxpayer in heavier liability owing to the incidence of timing. This would obviously occur where the capital profits are derived from a single indivisible asset—as, for example, when a man who has gradually built up a business sells it as a going concern or it changes hands at his decease. But it may occur more generally in cases where the capital assets are not easily marketable and can only be realised infrequently or when a wholesale realisation of accrued but unrealised gains is deemed to have occurred through death. This familiar problem in equity under progressive taxation arises in connection with capital gains whenever a property owner is not in a position to spread out or regulate the realisation of his net capital profits. It should be emphasised that the problem disappears under a flat-rate tax, and that it constitutes the main argument, in equity, for a flat rate rather than a progressive rate of tax on capital gains.

61. Independently of the above considerations we recognise the force of the argument which leads to the conclusion that it would be inexpedient to tax

capital gains at the full progressive rate of income tax and surtax combined.[17] The arguments in favour of confining the charge to income tax—which would mean in effect a flat rate of tax once total income (including capital gains) is above the point at which the taxpayer becomes liable to the standard rate— are more powerful in our view when considered from the point of view of expediency than when considered from the strict point of view of equity. The great bulk of capital gains accrue to the higher income groups; the fundamental reason for this is that the accrual of capital gains is closely linked with the investment of capital in risky ventures, and it is the large property owner, and not the small saver, who is able to commit his resources to ventures involving risk. If capital gains were subjected to both income tax and surtax the effect would be that a great part of these gains would be taxed at an extremely high rate (mounting at present to 19s. 0d. in the £) which would be bound to have a destructive effect on the willingness to assume risks. Added to this is the consideration that since a great deal of capital investment is made in the expectation of distant and not immediate appreciation even those investors not currently liable to the higher surtax rates would be in considerable uncertainty as to the rate at which their ultimate gains would be taxed when realised. Finally, the full charging of capital gains to both income tax and surtax would have a negative effect on the incentive to save and encourage capitalists to dissipate their capital. Though we do not share the view of the Majority[18] that capital gains are generally saved and do not contribute to the spending of the property-owning classes, it is true, of course, that the present opportunity to save tax free in the form of capital appreciation must provide an incentive to the large property owner not to dissipate his capital, despite the strong temptations which the high taxation of income combined with the tax exemption on spendings out of capital provides in this direction. We think, therefore, that the taxation of capital gains beyond a certain rate would have highly undesirable effects on risk-bearing, saving and capital formation.

62. We cannot agree, on the other hand, that these considerations of economic expediency justify the continued tax exemption of an important source of income and the consequent grave injustice in the distribution of the tax burden between different groups and different social classes. We certainly do not share the view of the Majority[19] that the gains should either be taxed at the full progressive rate or else not at all. There is no principle of equity which leads us to suppose that if something cannot or should not be taxed at 95 per cent. it should be taxed at zero per cent. We therefore recommend that subject to the qualifications and on the definitions suggested below capital gains should be subjected to income taxation but not to surtax.

Short-term and Long-term Gains

63. Subject to the above recommendation that capital gains should not be liable to surtax we recommend that no distinction should be made between short-and long-term gains. Any such distinction is bound to be arbitrary[20] and an invitation to tax avoidance. The distinction in the U.S. tax system makes it worth while for the taxpayer to realise short-term losses in less than six months and short-term gains in more than six months and has in many cases the effect that the taxpayer's liability is less than it would have been if short-

[17] Cf. the recommendations of the Carter Commission, that gains be taxed fully at income tax rates, with liberal averaging provisions, ante, pp. 307–308.
[18] Para. 106; ante, p. 319.
[19] Para. 99; ante, p. 317.
[20] Illustrated by the problems of ascertaining the time of acquisition and disposal, see [1971] B.T.R. 259.

term gains had been taxed at the long-term rate. We do not share the view that long-term gains have any inherent claim to more favourable treatment than short-term gains. We agree with the view expressed in the memorandum of the Board (paragraph 17) that " looking at the matter purely as one of taxable capacity there may seem little justification for distinguishing between two gains of equal amount simply because in one case the asset was held for a longer period than in the other."

64. As already indicated we strongly support the suggestion that contrary to the existing American practice change of ownership of property by gift or bequest should count as realisation in the same way as the transfer of ownership by way of sale (the property being valued for the purpose by the same rules as apply to stamp duties). Without this provision, not only would a large part of capital gains escape the tax net altogether, but the taxpayer would have every incentive so to manipulate the realisation of his losses and his gains as to make his net unrealised gains as large as possible.[21]

Treatment of Losses

65. We agree with the suggestions made by the Board as to the treatment of losses. Realised losses ought to reckon as an offset to realised gains; net unabsorbed losses ought to be permitted to be carried forward indefinitely as an offset against the taxpayer's future gains. As the Board's memorandum explains (paragraph 13), it is always open to a taxpayer to turn a paper loss— at least in easily marketable securities—into a realised loss, and to cover himself (if he has no real desire to liquidate his investment) by repurchasing the security afterwards. So long as losses only count as an offset against current or future realised gains, the taxpayer's incentive to do so will be confined by the extent of the realisation of his gains, and will tend to have the effect of confining the concept of net taxable gains in any particular year to the excess of net realised gains over net accrued losses. If, however, losses could be offset against past gains, the taxpayer would find it worth while to " realise " paper losses as they accrued, so that the tax would become one where the recognition of accrued losses was not limited to the amount of currently realised gains. In those circumstances the taxpayer could so manipulate his realisations (by formally selling securities whenever their price happened to be low enough to show a loss) that in an extreme case he would avoid paying tax altogether during his lifetime even though he might enjoy a steady appreciation on the total of his assets and/or a growing total of net gains on " genuine " realisations. It is true that all such manipulations will involve a correspondingly higher liability on his estate at death but under a flat-rate tax (unless he has a definite expectation of a rise in the rates of taxation) he can only gain by them, since he saves the interest on the tax during the period of postponement. Analogous considerations apply to the question of allowing capital losses as an offset against other income. In that case the taxpayer would not only be able to avoid paying tax during his lifetime on his capital gains but to " borrow " money from the Revenue during his lifetime to be repaid only when his accounts are closed on his death. These particular considerations might not be so important if capital gains were taxed at a full progressive rate since in that case the taxpayer would have a clear incentive to even out in time the rate of realisation of his gains. But under a flat-rate tax the need to regard the taxpayer's account with the Revenue in respect of liability for net realised capital gains as a separate running account is the more obvious.

[21] Under the present system, a gift counts as a disposal—F.A. 1965, s. 22—but there is no longer a deemed disposal on deaths after March 30, 1971: F.A. 1971, s. 59.

66. The need for such restrictions on the manner and extent to which capital losses are taken into account seems to have weighed heavily with the Majority of the Commission in their rejection of the taxation of capital gains. In paragraph 99, which sums up their general view of the problem, the Majority state that: " indeed no form of the tax that was based on realised gains and realised losses—and there is no alternative—would escape the serious objection to its foundation in equity that it would tax to the same extent a man who had realised a gain on one of his assets, though showing a net loss on others that he retained, as the man who had realised a similar gain without any current depreciation of his other assets to set against it." Here their concern seems to be misplaced, and the reasoning behind it somewhat circular, since the main reason, or one of the main reasons, for restricting the way in which losses are taken into account (which in paragraph 91 the Majority appear to recognise) is precisely the ease with which a man can realise a paper loss, and the likelihood that he will do so whenever by so doing he effects a reduction in his tax bill. The situation described would therefore only be likely to occur, in any particular year, in the relatively rare circumstance of the depreciated asset being of a kind that is not readily saleable. Even so this " serious objection to its foundation in equity " is only an objection if equity is so narrowly conceived as to require full equality of treatment between different taxpayers for each particular year. Under a flat-rate tax a taxpayer's cumulative liability would be unaffected by any delay he experienced in realising his loss.

67. There may be cases, however, in which a taxpayer realises a true loss but has no opportunity during his lifetime to offset that loss against gains, since he makes no subsequent gain. This case may be what the Majority have in mind when they state that the result of the proposed treatment " would not be to hold the balance evenly as between capital gains and capital losses, for, whereas a [realised] gain would be chargeable even if there were no realised loss, a loss would not be allowable except so far as there was a realised gain." [22] We do not believe that such cases are likely to be numerous. But they undoubtedly could occur; and whenever they do, the taxpayer's estate will show net unabsorbed losses at his death. Any possible inequity resulting from this would be mitigated if the tax claim arising out of net unabsorbed capital losses shown by an estate at probate valuation were allowed to be credited against estate duty liabilities. Provided the tax on capital gains is a flat-rate tax (so that the Exchequer is not committed to bearing the major share of unabsorbed losses, in a manner which might indeed tempt the aged into a last speculative fling) we are prepared to recommend that this should be allowed.

Other Considerations

68. We agree with the Majority that in times of inflation a tax on capital gains would inflict hardship on the owner-occupier who for personal or business reasons has to sell his house and find a new home somewhere else, and who may need all the money received from the sale of his old house for the purchase of another house of the same quality and condition. If the scope of the capital gains tax were extended to the case of the owner-occupier this might have the further undesirable effect of hindering mobility since people might be deterred from accepting new jobs if it meant that they had to sell their existing home. We therefore recommend that the gains arising out of the sale of owner-occupied houses, to the extent of one residence for each taxpayer, should be exempted from the capital gains tax.

[22] Para. 91, *ante*, p. 314.

69. We believe, on the basis of the consideration of the various alternatives suggested in the Board's memorandum (paragraph 20) that for the purpose of the capital gains tax assets purchased prior to the appointed day should, in the case of securities quoted on the Stock Exchange, be deemed to have been purchased at the middle price ruling at the appointed day.[23] In the case of other assets, the actual cost of acquisition should reckon as the purchase price, but the taxable gain should be reduced to that fraction of the total gain which the period between the appointed day and the date of realisation bears to the total period of ownership.

70. We do not wish to enter into a detailed consideration of the administrative problems created by a capital gains tax except to record our view that we do not believe that these problems would prove so formidable as is sometimes suggested. The experience of several European countries—such as the Scandinavian countries—as well as of the United States show that a tax on capital gains is by no means beyond the powers of an efficient tax administration. We believe that the institution of an automatic reporting system in connection with property transfers (such as is already in force in some countries, e.g. in Sweden) would greatly ease the administrative task of checking the transactions recorded on the taxpayer's return. We are in accord with the view that for an initial period the tax should be limited to gains arising from the sale of businesses, securities of all kinds and real property and that there should be an exemption limit (of say, £50 or less on any particular sale, when the annual gain is £400 or less) to reduce the administrative task involved.

REPORT OF THE ROYAL COMMISSION ON TAXATION

Carter Commission, Canada, 1966

VOLUME III : TAXATION OF INCOME. CHAPTER 8

Realisation of Gains

10. To be consistent with the principle of the comprehensive tax base net gains on assets should in principle be brought into income annually, whether the gains were realised or not. This would preclude tax postponement, and if time were provided to pay the tax on the gains, serious liquidity problems could be avoided. Taxing gains on a realised basis allows for tax postponement and may induce holders of property not to realise their gain in order to avoid the tax. Furthermore, if gains were taxed annually, whether realised or not, the postponement of tax through the retention of income in corporations, trusts and mutual organisations would not pose a problem. There would be no reason to collect tax from these organisation except to obtain tax from non-residents and to prevent tax avoidance.

11. We are convinced, however, that the annual valuation of all property is not practical at this time, and therefore, that property gains should be taxed on realisation. However, to prevent permanent deferment we recommend that a realisation be deemed to occur on making a gift of property or on giving up Canadian residence. In addition, we recommend that a realisation be deemed to take place when an individual dies, except in the case of property passing to a surviving member of his family unit. There should also be a deemed realisation to a family unit with respect to property which a child takes with him on leaving the unit.

[23] Cf. Crabtree v. Hinchcliffe [1972] A.C. 707.

SECRETAN v. HART

Chancery Division [1969] 1 W.L.R. 1599; 113 S.J. 722; [1969] 3 All E.R. 1196; 45 T.C. 701

BUCKLEY J.: This case raises an interesting point, which appears to be entirely novel, on the law relating to capital gains tax. The taxpayer, Mr. Secretan, between the years 1932 and 1944 inclusive, bought six parcels of shares in a company called Hampton Gold Mining Areas Ltd. at varying prices. The purchases totalled 39,000 shares, and the aggregate price that Mr. Secretan paid for them was £768 7s. 5d. He held those 39,000 shares until October 1967, when he sold them for £80,943 5s. 5d. The investment seems to have been a very successful one.

He was assessed to capital gains tax in respect of this transaction. In the assessment, the deductions that were made from the price which he received, £80,943 5s. 5d., including an allowable loss, which he had incurred in respect of other assets, amounting to £1,404, and the sum of £768 the amount which he had paid for the shares when he bought them. Deducting the sum of these two amounts from £80,943, a figure of £78,771 is arrived at, and Mr. Secretan was assessed as being liable to pay capital gains tax on that figure.

He objects to the assessment because, he says, between the time when he bought the shares and the time when he sold them the value of the pound had seriously decreased; and he has produced a letter from the Central Statistical Office which states that, taking the purchasing power of the pound to be 20s. in 1932, which was the earliest year in which Mr. Secretan bought any of these shares, its value in July 1967, which was a few months before he sold the shares, would be 5s. 3d. So Mr. Secretan says that, instead of deducting the sum of £768 only, in respect of the price he paid for the shares, from the price which he received, the figure of £768 ought to be multiplied by a suitable factor to take account of the change in the value of the pound between the time when he paid the £768 and the time when he received the proceeds of the sale of the shares in October 1967.

It is a point of view with which, I think, any taxpayer would feel a certain degree of sympathy, for it is very irritating to think that if one buys a piece of property—say, for instance, a plot of land—and holds it for a number of years during which nothing occurs to affect its market value and it is then sold for a price which exceeds the price originally paid for it because of a change in the value of money, one will then be taxed on a gain which in terms of sterling one has made but to which one has not contributed in any way and which has not been brought about by any circumstance other than merely a change in the value of money. But one has to look at the statute and see in what way this tax is charged, in what circumstances liability arises and what the liability is.

Capital gains tax was brought into existence by the Finance Act 1965, s. 19 of which provided that there should be a tax charged in accordance with the Act " in respect of capital gains, that is to say chargeable gains computed in accordance with this Act and accruing to a person on the disposal of assets." Section 20 (1) provided that, subject to certain exceptions,

" a person shall be chargeable to capital gains tax in respect of chargeable gains accruing to him in a year of assessment during any part of which he is resident in the United Kingdom, or during which he is ordinarily resident in the United Kingdom."

Section 22, the first of the sections in the part of the Act dealing with chargeable gains, provides in subsection (9) that " The amount of the gains accruing on the disposal of assets shall be computed in accordance with Part I of Schedule 6 to this Act " subject to certain provisions in other schedules. So one turns to Schedule 6 and finds that paragraph 4 provides as follows:

" Subject to the following provisions of this schedule, the sums allowable as a deduction from the consideration in the computation under this schedule of the gain accruing to a person on the disposal of an asset shall be restricted to—(a) the amount or value of the consideration, in money or money's worth, given by him or on his behalf wholly and exclusively for the acquisition of the asset, together with the incidental costs to him of the acquisition or, if the asset was not acquired by him, any expenditure wholly and exclusively incurred by him in providing the asset, (b) the amount of any expenditure wholly and exclusively incurred on the asset by him or on his behalf for the purpose of enhancing the value of the asset, being expenditure reflected in the state or nature of the asset at the time of the disposal, and any expenditure wholly and exclusively incurred by him in establishing, preserving or defending his title to, or to a right over, the asset, (c) the incidental costs to him of making the disposal."

Those are the matters which a taxpayer who has disposed of an asset is entitled to deduct from the consideration which he received upon the disposal.

There are provisions in the Act which allow the taxpayer to elect whether he will be treated as having acquired the asset, if he acquired it before April 6, 1965, at the price which he in fact paid for it or at its value as at April 6, 1965, whichever is more favourable to the taxpayer; but nothing of that kind arises in the present case, for the quoted market value of Mr. Secretan's 39,000 shares in this company as at April 6, 1965, was £731 7s. 5d., and it was, therefore, more advantageous to him to include in the deduction the actual price which he paid rather than the market value at the appointed day.

The argument which has been put forward by Mr. Secretan in support of his appeal is that this tax is a tax on capital gains, that in order to establish that a charge to tax arises, it must be proved that some capital gain has been made by the taxpayer, and that in order to ascertain the amount upon which the tax should be assessed the amount of the gain must be established. He says that " capital gains " must for this purpose mean gains in true money terms, and must be proved. He says that the capital gain which he has made here is not one which can be properly ascertained by deducting from the price which he received for the shares merely the original price that he paid in terms of pounds sterling. I am omitting for the moment consideration of the allowable loss which he was also entitled to deduct in respect of other assets, because that does not affect the question I have to consider. He says that the real gain can be discovered only by comparing like with like, and that in order to compare like with like one has to reassess the price that he paid by taking into account the fact that in the years 1932 to 1944 every pound which he paid for one of these shares was worth much more than the pound which he received on the sale in 1967.

I think the point really turns on the meaning of paragraph 4 of Schedule 6, which deals with the permitted deductions, and particularly on sub-paragraph (1) (a) of that paragraph of the schedule, which refers to " the amount or value of the consideration, in money or money's worth, given by him . . . for the acquisition of the asset." Mr. Secretan draws attention to the reference to " money's worth," and he might also, perhaps, have drawn attention to the use of the words " value of the consideration." The expression " consideration, in money's worth " is, of course, one which is very familiar to lawyers as being a way of expressing the price or consideration given for property where property is acquired in return for something other than money, such as services or other property, where the price or consideration which the acquirer gives for the property has got to be turned into money before it can be expressed in terms of money. The use here of the words " money's worth " does not, I think, indicate that Parliament had any idea in mind, when enacting this part of the statute, of a change in the value of money in the course of the passage of time. Nor, I think, does the reference to " value of the consideration " indicate that any such idea was in mind.

If the intention had been that the effects of inflation were to be taken into account in determining whether or not a capital gain had been made, and the amount of such a gain, there would clearly have been in the Act some explicit statement to that effect and some machinery provided for ascertaining the effect of inflation. There is nothing anywhere in the Act of that kind. What is referred to in sub-paragraph (1) (a) of paragraph 4 of Schedule 6 is " the amount or value of the consideration " given by the taxpayer " for the acquisition of the asset." The time which is looked at for the purpose of discovering what sum is a legitimate deduction is the time when he gave the consideration for the acquisition of the asset; and it is the consideration which he then gave in terms of money, or, if it was not given in money, turned into terms of money as at that date, which is the legitimate deduction.

If support for this view is required, I think some support is to be found in sub-paragraph (1) (b) of the same paragraph in Schedule 6, where there is a reference to the amount of expenditure incurred by the taxpayer " for the purpose of enhancing the value of the asset." The amount of such expenditure can be discovered only by looking at the bills which he paid for whatever he did or had done for the purpose of enhancing the value of the asset. There is no suggestion there that any adjustment is to be made to take account of inflation. Indeed, if Mr. Secretan's submission were the right one, it seems to me that it would lead to conclusions of the utmost difficulty and confusion in the administration of this Act, for the value of the pound fluctuates constantly, and it would involve complicated research and calculation to arrive at the amount of profit made in respect of any particular asset before a capital gain could be discovered on the lines that Mr. Secretan suggests ought to be adopted.

Although I feel sympathy with him in his approach to this problem, I am afraid I feel unable to come to the conclusion that his view is the correct one, and I think that the decision of the commissioners in the present case was right. They dismissed Mr. Secretan's appeal against the assessment that was made upon him, and I think that in doing so they came to the right conclusion. I shall also take a similar course, and dismiss Mr. Secretan's appeal.

Note

    As Buckley J. points out, the original cost of acquisition was taken rather than the value on April 6, 1965, because the shares were worth *less* in 1965. The taxpayer's claim to take into account the fall in the purchasing power of the pound since 1932 consequently loses much of its force as the entire gain must have accrued in a little over two years, between 1965 and 1967.

Part Three

TAXABLE PERSONS

CHAPTER 14

THE INDIVIDUAL AND THE FAMILY

THE previous section has been concerned with the types and sources of taxable income. It is now necessary to consider the persons and entities in respect of whom that income is assessed. The basic taxpaying unit is the individual to whom the income belongs. In certain circumstances, that unit is expanded to comprise a married couple or a family. Further persons or groups of persons may constitute an entity for the purpose of assessment and payment of tax, in particular the Executors or Administrators of an Estate, the Trustees of a Settlement and the Members of a Partnership.[1] Moreover, a Company constitutes a taxable entity in its own right and is liable for Income Tax and for Corporation Tax.[2]

1. Progressive Taxation

In the case of individuals and, where appropriate, the expanded family unit, income tax is chargeable on a progressive basis, that is to say, as the income of the individual increases so the *proportion* of that income which is payable as tax also increases. This is achieved, in the present system, by imposing a standard rate of income tax, from which, at the lower end of the income scale, certain amounts of the taxpayer's income are exempted by means of a system of allowances and reliefs and, at the upper end of the scale, by imposing additional rates of tax.[3]

ROYAL COMMISSION ON THE TAXATION OF PROFITS AND INCOME

Second Report, 1953 Cmd. 9105

PROGRESSIVE TAXATION

101. The system of personal taxation is progressive. The effective rate of tax upon the income of the individual taxpayer, the amount of tax that he pays divided by the amount of his total income, increases as the income increases. By this means the burden of tax is so distributed that the owner of the larger income contributes a larger proportion of it in tax than the owner of the smaller income. But the tax burden is adjusted not only by variations of rate but also by the grant of allowances in respect of (1) certain categories of personal circumstances that affect taxpaying capacity of individual taxpayers and (2) a differentiation between earned income on the one hand and investment income on the other. Before we could come to any conclusion about the extent to which the

---

[1] Chap. 15, *post.*
[2] Chap. 16, *post.*
[3] At present known as " surtax," at one time called " super-tax," and, commencing in the tax-year 1973–74, to be replaced by a new system of " higher rates ": F.A. 1971, s. 32 (1); White Paper, " Reform of Personal Direct Taxation," 1971 Cmnd. 4653; *post,* p. 338.

present distribution is satisfactory, we found it necessary to establish a point of view about the basis upon which the principle of progressive taxation rests.

102. It is plain that progression is not the only possible scheme of tax distribution. It is possible for tax to be levied in such a way that each taxpayer is assessed for an equal amount, whatever the size of his income; taxes have often been levied in such a form that tax is proportional to income; nor do these alternatives exhaust the possibilities. The United Kingdom income tax, as first levied in 1799, was in its main lines (apart, that is, from certain exemptions for small incomes) a proportional tax; it did not begin to acquire a generally progressive character until the year 1907. Today the progressive character of the tax is taken for granted; to return to the old proportional tax would be quite impracticable. It is, however, necessary for our purposes to consider the grounds upon which this great change in opinion can be justified, since it would be insufficient for us to rest our treatment upon the mere historical fact that the change has occurred. We are called upon to judge the scheme of progressive taxation as it now stands, and we must accordingly have some basis for our judgment.

103. The case for progressive taxation has often been argued upon the basis of the following propositions. The aim of government, in taxation as in other matters, is to promote the greatest happiness of the governed. All payment of taxes being in some measure a sacrifice by the taxpayer of the means of happiness, taxation ought to be so adjusted between the payers as to cause as little sacrifice in the aggregate as possible. In general, and in the absence of special needs, there is a presumption that to take £1 from a man with a large income will cause less sacrifice than to take the same sum from a man whose income is smaller. Taxation should therefore be laid predominantly upon the wealthy, and a progressive income tax is justified as a means of bringing about this result.

REPORT OF THE ROYAL COMMISSION ON TAXATION

Carter Commission, Canada, 1966

VOLUME 1: OBJECTIVES

The first and most essential purpose of taxation is to share the burden of the state fairly among all individuals and families. Unless the allocation of the burden is generally accepted as fair, the social and political fabric of a country is weakened and can be destroyed. History has many examples of the severe consequences of unfair taxation. Should the burden be thought to be shared inequitably, taxpayers will seek means to evade their taxes. When honesty is dismissed as stupidity, self-assessment by taxpayers would be impossible and the cost of enforcement high. We are convinced that scrupulous fairness in taxation must override all other objectives where there is a conflict among objectives.

. . . Equity has two dimensions. Horizontal equity requires that individuals and families in similar circumstances bear the same taxes. Vertical equity requires that those in different circumstances bear appropriately different taxes. Two questions therefore, have to be answered. What personal circumstances should be recognised in allocating tax burdens among individuals and families? By how much should tax burdens differ between those in one circumstance relative to those in another? These are both questions of belief rather than of fact. We can do no more than recommend what we believe to be fair.

We believe that horizontal equity is achieved when individuals and families with the same gains in discretionary economic power pay the same amount of tax. By economic power we mean the power to command goods and services for personal use. By discretionary economic power we mean the residual power to command goods and services for personal use after providing the " necessities " of life and after meeting family obligations and responsibilities. To be more concrete, some part of each family's income must be spent to provide food, clothing, medical expenses and other " necessities." The change in the discretionary economic power of the family is the income the family has available to spend or save after meeting these non-discretionary expenses.

We believe that vertical equity is achieved when individuals and families pay taxes that are a constant proportion of their discretionary economic power.

Both horizontal and vertical equity would be achieved by the adoption of a tax system that embodied the following principles:

1. The family and the unattached individual should be recognised as the basic tax-paying units in the system. The family unit would consist of parents and their dependent children. Transactions and transfers between members of a family unit would have no tax consequences.
2. All resident individuals and families should be taxed on a base that measures the value of the annual net gain or loss in the unit's power, whether exercised or not, to consume goods and services. Such a base would ignore the form of the gain or what was done to obtain the gain. We call this the comprehensive tax base. We also refer to it as " income " because this term is so commonly used. Income to us has, however, a much-broader meaning than that ascribed to it under current law.
3. This comprehensive tax base should be subject to progressive rates of tax. The progressive rates would reflect the diminishing relative importance of non-discretionary expenditures for those with larger gains in economic power.
4. The tax burdens of those with particularly heavy family and other obligations and responsibilities should be reduced to reflect the non-discretionary expenditures required to meet them. This would be done through the adoption of separate rate schedules, tax credits and deductions.

Combined with a government expenditure system that provides relatively greater benefits for the poor than for the wealthy, a tax system with these characteristics would redistribute some of the power to consume goods and services in favour of the lowest income groups. We are firmly convinced that this redistribution is necessary if we are to achieve greater equality of opportunity for all Canadians and make it possible for those with little economic power to attain a decent standard of living. However, we are also convinced that the rates of tax which are applicable at any level of income should not be so high as to discourage initiative and thereby reduce the production of goods and services for Canadians.

. . . Should taxation be progressive or proportionate? This is one of the most contentious issues in taxation. Our answer is clear and unequivocal. The tax base of each family and unattached individual should be subject to progressive rate of tax. Because we believe that non-discretionary expenses absorb a much larger proportion of the annual additions to the economic power of those with low income than of the wealthy, in order to attain the proportionate taxation of discretionary economic power, we recommend that a base that measures total economic power be taxed at progressive rates.

Note
The treatment of the family unit is considered in greater detail, *post*, pp. 360–366.

The argument for progressive taxation is one of respectable antiquity; thus Adam Smith—
" It is not very unreasonable that the rich should contribute to the public expense **not only**

in proportion to their revenue, but in something more than proportion "—*The Wealth of Nations*, Book V, Chapter II. There is a considerable volume of literature on the principle of progressive taxation; the reader is referred in particular to A. R. Prest, *Public Finance* (4th ed.) Chapter 6 and W. J. Blum and H. Kalven, Jr., *The Uneasy Case for Progressive Taxation* (Chicago, 1953).

This aspect of the proposals of the Carter Commission is considered by G. C. Hockley, " Fiscal Reform " [1969] B.T.R. 81.

2. The Structure of Personal Taxation

A new method of charging income tax is to apply for the tax year 1973–74 and subsequent years.[4]

WHITE PAPER—" REFORM OF PERSONAL DIRECT TAXATION "

1971 Cmnd. 4653

THE NEW TAX STRUCTURE

3. The present income tax and surtax are constructed in terms of investment income, with a complicated pattern of allowances for earned income (the earned income relief for income tax and for surtax, and the special earnings allowance for surtax). The standard rate of 38·75 per cent. in practice applies primarily to investment income and the effective marginal rate on earned income (up to £4,005) is reduced to 30·14 per cent. by the earned income relief of two-ninths.

4. Unified tax is constructed in terms of earned income. A broad band of income will be charged at a rate corresponding to the standard rate less earned income relief: the Finance Bill provisionally fixes this " basic rate " at 30 per cent. for the tax year 1973–74. There will be higher rates of tax, above the basic rate, applicable to higher incomes. These rates and the bands of income to which each will apply will be fixed by the 1973 Finance Act but the Chancellor stated in his Budget Speech that he envisaged a top rate of tax for earned incomes of 75 per cent., reached at a level of about £20,000 a year.

5. The new tax rates will apply equally to earned and investment income. Earned income relief as such will be abolished but a distinction between earned income and investment income will be retained by the institution of a surcharge on investment income exceeding a specified amount. The amount of this surcharge and the level of income above which it will apply will also be fixed by the 1973 Finance Act, but the Chancellor stated in his Budget Speech that he intended that the first slice of investment income should be taxed at the rate applicable to earned income.

PERSONAL ALLOWANCES IN THE NEW TAX STRUCTURE

6. The existing pattern of personal reliefs will be substantially retained. These reliefs become deductions from income (instead of, as now, being formally given in terms of tax) so that the basic and higher rates will apply to the balance of any individual's income after deducting his personal reliefs (and any other allowable deductions).

. . . 12. The Government believe that the major reform of the personal tax structure will result in substantial benefits under the following headings:

---

4 F.A. 1971, ss. 32–39; Scheds. 6 and 7. The changes are considered by D. C. Potter, " New Personal Taxation " [1971] B.T.R. 204.

(a) *Simplification of tax structure.* Instead of two taxes which have to be assessed separately there will be a single graduated tax.

(b) *Smoother graduation.* Instead of the present uneven graduation, with rates that increase irregularly and steeply, there will be an essentially simple system under which personal allowances are deducted from total income, a " basic rate " (provisionally 30 per cent.) then applies to the majority of taxpayers, while for the higher incomes successive slices of income above the band covered by the basic rate are charged on a smoothly increasing scale of rates.

(c) *Incentive to earnings.* By restructuring the tax in terms of earned income, the unified tax will secure that the nominal rate of tax on earned income is seen to be the true rate. This will remove the cause of the widespread misunderstanding about tax paid on extra earnings.

(d) *Incentive to savings.* The present tax system discriminates severely against investment income. By equating with earned income the tax treatment of investment income up to a certain level, the incentive for personal savings will be materially increased.

(e) *Simplification of administration.* At present, any surtax payer has to deal with at least two Inland Revenue offices—a tax officer for his income tax affairs and the Surtax Office for his surtax. Unified income tax will be handled entirely in tax offices. This will not only be a convenience for taxpayers but will, in due course, save a considerable number of Inland Revenue staff.

Note

As stated above, the existing pattern of personal reliefs will be substantially retained, as will the distinction between earned income and investment income.

Consequently, the existing law relating to reliefs and allowances (*post*, pp. 344–351) continues to be important.

3. Total Income

It is necessary to determine the total income of an individual in order to establish (i) whether the individual has reliefs or allowances which may be set against income which has suffered tax and is thereby entitled to a repayment of tax, and (ii) whether, and to what extent, the higher rates of tax, or surtax, apply. Total income,[5] for income tax purposes, is determined by aggregating the taxpayer's income from all sources, including such income as may already have suffered tax at source, and by deducting therefrom those " charges on income " which are regarded as not properly being the income of the taxpayer at all.

(i) *Receipts*

A sum which, though due, is not paid in a year of assessment is not part of the individual's total income for that year.

LEIGH v. I.R.C.

King's Bench Division [1928] 1 K.B. 73; 96 L.J.K.B. 853; 137 L.T. 303; 43 T.L.R. 528; 11 T.C. 590

ROWLATT J.: . . . It is to be remembered that for income tax purposes " receivability " without receipt is nothing.

[5] I.C.T.A. 1970, s. 528.

Note
    The actual decision is no longer of importance, but the principle remains, with certain reservations, valid.

DEWAR v. I.R.C.

Court of Appeal [1935] 2 K.B. 351; 104 L.J.K.B. 645; 153 L.T. 357; 51 T.L.R. 536; 79 S.J. 522; [1935] All E.R.Rep. 568; 19 T.C. 561

Under the terms of a will the appellant was appointed executor and bequeathed a legacy of £1 million, upon which, from the end of the executor's year, he was entitled to interest, at 4 per cent. per annum, so long as it remained unpaid. The appellant never received, nor demanded, the interest. *Held*, as he had never received the interest he could not be assessed to tax upon it.

ROMER L.J.: . . . Now it is said, and said truly, that it has not been received by Mr. Dewar or placed at his disposal owing to his voluntary act or omission; that is to say, the interest has not been paid, not because the debtor cannot pay it but because Mr. Dewar has not thought fit to ask for payment, and further has intimated the possibility of his releasing the debtor altogether from payment of that interest. But for the purposes of income tax, one does not take an account of income on the footing of wilful default. The question is what income the subject has received, and not what income he has received or but for his wilful default might have received. The truth of the matter is that no one owes a duty to the State to maintain his assessment for surtax at the highest possible figure. If a subject thinks proper so to do, he assuredly may get rid of an income-bearing security for the purposes of avoiding the addition of the income from that security to his assessment for surtax purposes. That is admitted. A tenant for life, if he thinks fit, may surrender his life interest. If he does so, most assuredly he does not remain liable to be assessed to income tax in respect of the income which he has surrendered, and I for myself can see no reason why a subject should not, if he thinks fit, retain the capital of an income-bearing fund and release his right to receive the income, either for one year or two years or altogether. If he does so, in my opinion he does not receive the interest and cannot be assessed for surtax in respect of it. . . .

Note
    The Court of Appeal approved the dictum of Rowlatt J. in *Leigh* v. *I.R.C.* [1928] 1 K.B. 73, quoted above at p. 339. See also Lord Finlay in *I.R.C.* v. *Blott* [1921] 2 A.C. 171 at p. 195: " There can be no supertax upon income unless it has been received by the taxpayer." See also *I.R.C.* v. *Lebus' Executors* [1946] 1 All E.R. 476; *post*, p. 411; *cf. I.R.C.* v. *Hamilton-Russell's Executors, infra.*

I.R.C. v. HAMILTON-RUSSELL'S EXECUTORS

Court of Appeal [1943] 1 All E.R. 474; *sub nom. Hamilton-Russell's Executors* v. *I.R.C.*, 87 S.J. 255; 25 T.C. 200

A beneficiary, who was absolutely entitled under a settlement, left the fund to accumulate in the hands of Trustees. *Held*, although not actually paid to him, the income of the funds was the income of the beneficiary and assessable to surtax.

LUXMOORE L.J.: . . . We are unable to accept this argument. The question determined in *Dewar's* case [6] was in effect whether income existed which could

_____
[6] [1935] 2 K.B. 351, *supra*.

be brought into assessment. That question was answered in the negative because the interest, although admittedly exigible in law, was never paid or claimed and, therefore, had no existence. In the present case there was unquestionably income in existence, namely, the interest which accrued due on the trust investments and the accumulations during the period from April 5, 1938, and January 18, 1939. Consequently the question is not " Is there any income? " but " To whom did the income, which admittedly existed, belong? " In our judgment there can only be one answer to this question. It belongs to G. L. Hamilton-Russell. . . .

Note

See also *Spens* v. *I.R.C.* [1970] 1 W.L.R. 1173, and Chapter 15 generally.

A considerable limitation is placed upon the principle stated above in that, if there is actual " income " it is part of the total income of the person entitled to it, without the need for actual payment. Actual receipt is also unnecessary in the computation of profits from land (see esp. I.C.T.A. 1970, s. 87) and from a trade, etc. (*ante*, Chap. 9).

(ii) *Charges on Income*

EARL HOWE v. I.R.C.

Court of Appeal (*ante*, p. 112)

SWINFEN-EADY M.R.: . . . The point which has to be decided arises in this way: Earl Howe is tenant for life of certain settled estates, and in order to raise money has conveyed his life estate by way of mortgage, including in the security certain policies on his life, in respect of which he has covenanted to pay the assurance premiums.

In calculating Earl Howe's income for super-tax purposes, it is not disputed that he is entitled to deduct from his gross income the interest payable on his mortgages.[7] He claims, however, also to deduct the annual premiums payable in respect of his life policies; the Inland Revenue Commissioners deny that he has any right to make this deduction, and whether he is so entitled or not is the question to be decided.

. . . The contention on behalf of Earl Howe is that the annual premiums on the policies are " annual payments," and that they have to be made out of the profits brought into charge, and are charged thereon. And they are charged on his income in this manner, that if he fails to pay the premiums in accordance with his covenant, his mortgagees have power to pay the same and resort to the security for what they shall so pay. It cannot be disputed that these annual premiums are, in one sense, annual payments; but the question is, are they annual payments within the meaning of s. 164?[8] The Inland Revenue Commissioners contend that no annual payment is within the section unless the payment is one in respect of which the person paying can deduct from it the income tax he may have paid in respect of it, and so pass on the burden of the tax to the recipient of the income. Of course premiums on life insurance must be paid in full to the assurance company, and no deduction therefrom on account of income tax is permissible. On the one hand interest, from which tax has been deducted, will form part of the income of the payee, and will have to be treated by him as part of his income. Unless the payer could deduct the interest from his income the result would be that such income would be subjected to double taxation. On the other hand premiums of life assurance paid to an assurance

---

[7] For the deduction of interest, as a charge on income, see now the Finance Act 1972, s. 75.

[8] Income Tax Act 1842.

company are not subject to assessment as annual payments, although they doubt-less form items in an account upon which the gains and profits of the assurance company for the year are to be arrived at. . . .

Scrutton L.J.: . . . (*ante*, p. 112).

Note

See also *Re Hanbury, decd.* (1939) 38 T.C. 588n.; *ante*, p. 113.

I.R.C. v. FRERE

House of Lords [1965] A.C. 402; [1964] 3 W.L.R. 1193; 108 S.J. 938; [1964] 3 All E.R. 796; 42 T.C. 125

Viscount Radcliffe: . . . My Lords, Mr. Frere, the respondent, on two occasions borrowed large sums of money for short periods. On March 28, 1957, he borrowed £50,000 at interest on the terms that the loan should be repaid by January 31, 1958: it was repaid on December 3, 1957, together with £2,210 19s. 2d. by way of interest. On August 14, 1958, he borrowed £40,000 at interest for one month and repaid it on September 17 of the same year. The interest cost of the borrowing was £186 2s. 9d. The concern which made these loans to him was an unlimited company which, it is common ground, did not satisfy the description of a " banker," whatever that description may be.

The respondent's claim is that in computing his total income for assessment to surtax the moneys which he paid by way of interest on these loans ought to be deducted from the assessable figure. It is, again, common ground that the payments that he made were, in each case, " short interest."

. . . So I turn to my second difficulty about this supposed principle, which is to see what indications there are in the tax code that the payment of short interest is to be treated as a diminution of the payer's taxable income. One can start with some safe generalisations on this subject. Income that is assessed to tax is neither measured by expenditure nor is it the residual income that lies after expenditure of an income nature. It is not the savings of income. In principle it is gross income as reduced for the purposes of assessment by such deductions only as are actually specified in the tax code or are granted by way of reliefs, usually in the form of fixed sums or proportions. No doubt the assessment of profits under Schedule D has come to require a rather different approach, since in that case the basic figure for assessment is the balance between receipts and expenditure: but even there it is plain that the code is intended to keep a control over the forms of expenditure that can appear in the profit account. It follows from this general conception that in principle it is irrelevant to the determination of a person's taxable income that some part of it has been expended by him on what would normally be regarded as his own income account, in paying rent, wages, mortgage interest, rates, insurance, for example, or that the payments that he makes for such purposes will themselves constitute or contribute to assessable income in the recipient's hands. Under our system payments may run to and fro many times in the course of a single tax year, creating new taxable income at each separate point of receipt. The idea of double taxation does not even arise in these multiple assessments. The mere fact, then, that part of a taxpayer's income has been used to pay interest on a loan during a year, even assuming that you visualise " income " as a separate spending fund, would not in itself set up a reason for reducing the assessment of his taxable income. The payment of the interest, whether long or short, would be no more, for this purpose, than an " application " of his income.

On the other hand, it is notorious that, quite apart from fixed reliefs for such kinds of expenditure as support of dependants or life assurance premiums, the code does make provision for certain " charges " on income being treated for tax purposes as if the income of the payer was, to the extent of the charge, not his income but the income of the recipient. To take the crudest case, that of the income received by a trustee for his beneficiary, probably the holder of a life interest under a settlement. If you wanted to calculate the " total income " of those two persons for the purpose of working out their rights to tax relief, as individuals, you would not, nor does the tax code, stop at the bare fact that the income payments received by the trustee were actually charged to tax in his hands either by direct assessment or by the machinery of deduction. You would say that, when it came to arriving at a " total income " under the tax scheme, such payments must not be attributed to the trustee, through whose hands they passed, but must on the contrary be attributed to the beneficiary, whose hands they were from the beginning destined to reach. That is straightforward. But now take the next most straightforward case, that of the annuity which is by legal right charged upon property, income primarily, capital by way of resort. A man comes in to the right to that income subject to the charge of the annuity. Under the tax system, as in ordinary thinking, his own income is reduced by the amount of the charge. The gross income accruing to him is divided in ownership right, a part equal to the annuity figure belonging to the annuitant, the balance to him. The reality of this situation was recognised and allowed for by the tax system, because, while the payer of the annuity was assessed and charged on the gross income, he was from the earliest days allowed to deduct from his payments a proportionate part of the tax which he had borne or was to bear on the total. By this means his true taxable income was treated as being the residue left after the charge of the annuity, the burden of the tax being shifted from payer to recipient by the former's statutory right to recoup himself out of the payment due to the latter.

This recognition of a division of ownership between two or more persons entitled to rights in a single " fund " of income was not, however, confined to such cases as those where there was trust income or an annuity charge. There was also the case of " annual " or " yearly " interest—I do not distinguish between the two adjectives—payable under a mortgage, the characteristic feature of which seems to have been that, in setting up the mortgage situation, the borrower had in effect divided the gross income of his estate between himself and the mortgagee. Up to this point it could fairly be said that the division corresponded with and followed the lines of enforceable legal rights in an identifiable fund of property, the accruing income. But the tax system can be seen to go further than this, for it applied the same idea of division of proprietary right to situations in which legal distinctions draw no dividing line. Thus an annual payment secured by personal covenant only, involving no charge on any actual security, whether income or capital, was treated in the same way for tax purposes.[9] It had to be " annual," and it had also to be payable " out of profits or gains brought into charge " in order to rank as income of payee not of payer, because it was the division of taxable income with which the code was dealing; and it may well be asked what at this stage is the significance of the words " out of " as applied to a payment, the obligation for which was merely the personal one to find the money required out of whatever resources the payer might mobilise for the purpose. The answer was provided by the application of what is in truth an accountant's, not a lawyer's, conception, for it was accepted that, so far as the payer was found to have in the relevant year a taxable income larger than the gross amount required to make the pay-

[9] See now I.C.T.A. 1970, s. 434; *post*, Chap. 15.

ment, to that extent he was entitled to claim that he had made the payment
" out of profits or gains brought into charge " and to deduct and retain for his
own account tax at what in due course (after 1927) became the " standard
rate."

. . . It was also the basis of the court's decision in that case [10] that, in arriving
at the figure of total income, only those annual payments could be allowed as
deductions which were themselves payable under deduction and retention of
tax as between payer and payee. The decision itself is very well known, and I
must say that until this case I had never heard it questioned that the principle
the court had proceeded upon was the correct one. It is, after all, " yearly
interest of money annuity or other annual payment " that the income tax code
identified as forming the taxable income of the recipient and not of the payer,
and it seems to me correct, therefore, to assume that it is only payments so
identified that are to be taken as reducing the payer's " total income " under
the code.

. . . I have done what I can to attend to the argument which I understand the
respondent to propound as being the true and alternative principle, that all
payments are deductible in arriving at the payer's total income which represent
what is called " pure income " in the hands of the payee. The conception of
" pure income " as a significant category of income under the tax code is, I
think, a recent discovery which might have surprised, for instance, the makers
of the Income Tax Act 1842. All I can say is that, apart from the argument
founded upon the wording of Schedule (G) of that Act, to which I must come,
I cannot find any trace of an intention to treat part of a person's income as not
being taxable income merely because he uses it to make payments to another
person which are themselves taxable directly as part of the income of the
recipient. Nor can I see any principle which would support such a deduction,
once it is accepted that the making of a payment out of one person's income
does not in itself operate to frank that payment for purposes of tax when it
reaches the hands of the recipient. Conversely, the fact that a receipt will be
taxed as an element of the payee's income is not, without more, a ground for
holding that the taxable income of the payer is less by the amount of the payment. To think that, unless some such principle can be imported into the tax
system, there is an anomalous case of double taxation is, with great respect to
those who may have said otherwise, a begging of the question, for everything
depends upon just that question whether there is involved in the payment one
single income which is merely transferred or two separate elements of income
which have independent sources of origin. . . .

Note
    For the effect of deductible " charges on income " upon allowances and reliefs, see
Adams v. *Musker* (1930) 15 T.C. 413; *post*, p. 347, and the cases there noted.

4. Reliefs and Allowances

In determining an individual's liability to income tax, certain reliefs and
allowances may be deducted from total income. These reliefs and allowances are numerous [11] and may be claimed only by an " individual." [12]
Some of the more important reliefs are considered below.

[10] *Earl Howe* v. *I.R.C.* [1919] 2 K.B. 336; *ante*, pp. 112, 341.
[11] I.C.T.A. 1970, ss. 6–22.
[12] I.C.T.A. 1970, s. 5. They cannot be claimed by personal representatives, trustees or by a
    company.

(i) *Earned Income Relief* [13]

ROYAL COMMISSION ON THE TAXATION OF PROFITS AND INCOME

Second Report, 1953 Cmd. 9105

212. Earned income relief is a form of differentiation between two types of income. It is not based on the idea that income is not fully taxable because it is earned; it is based on the idea that, if a given amount is to be raised by taxation, the burden of that sum is more fairly distributed if a £ of earned income is treated as not being the taxable equivalent of a £ of investment income. Consequently, proposals to alter the tax structure by increasing the measure of earned income relief are either proposals for reducing the amount of tax to be raised without the benefit of the deduction being shared between both types of income or proposals for raising the same amount of tax in a greater proportion from investment income than hitherto. In either form they must be regarded as proposals for an increased differentiation in favour of earned income at the expense of investment income. According to figures supplied to us by the Board the chargeable earned income of individuals is £3,000m compared with a total of £850m for the chargeable investment income of individuals. It must follow, therefore, that any shift of burden from the one to the other will fall with much heavier impact on the smaller sector.

213. The differentiation in favour of earned income was originally based on the fact that it is " precarious." Whatever the exact idea that this phrase is intended to cover—and it has been the subject of somewhat conflicting explanations—it is at least true to say of earned income in general that it has less stability of source than investment income and its receipt does depend, as the other's does not, upon the receiver being available to give services in exchange for it. It does not accrue without the contribution of his own effort, and the prospects of its accrual are therefore affected by such circumstances as age, sickness or other disability. It seems probable that in course of time other ideas have attached themselves to and become associated with this conception of precariousness. It has been pointed out that there is an element of expense involved in obtaining remuneration from work that is not present in the obtaining of income from investment, and at the same time cannot be completely allowed for by deductions for expenses in tax assessment. It has been said, further, that the State has a direct interest in offering some incentive to taxpayers to stimulate personal effort, even though it may be well not to forget that the State may have a direct interest also in securing that disincentives are not placed in the way of investment.

214. We think that the idea of some differentiation based on these conceptions is a sound one.

DALE v. I.R.C.

House of Lords [1954] A.C. 11; [1953] 3 W.L.R. 448; 97 S.J. 538; [1953] 2 All E.R. 671; 34 T.C. 488

The appellant was a Trustee under a will. He performed certain special duties, including the running of a company and a research fund established by the testator. Under the terms of the will, he was to receive £1,000 a year,

[13] For earned income under the new structure, see *ante*, pp. 338–339. See also I.C.T.A. 1970, s. 530, for the definition of " earned income."

for so long as he continued to act as Trustee. *Held*, the income was earned income.

LORD NORMAND : . . . I think there is confusion here between the source of the payment, which is the testator's bounty as expressed in his will, and the quality of the payment as earned or not earned. There need be no incompatibility in saying that the income is the conditional gift of the testator but that it has to be earned by compliance with the testator's condition of serving as a trustee.

I would observe more generally that the question whether income is earned or not is a question which arises between the trustee and the Inland Revenue, and it has no relation either to the legal duty which a trustee owes to the trust and the beneficiaries, or to the legal conception that such a payment as that under consideration derives from a testator and can be regarded as a legacy. The source of the sum and its character as a receipt in the hands of the trustee are two separate and unconnected things.

FRY v. SHIELS' TRUSTEES

Court of Session (1915) 6 T.C. 583; 1915 S.C. 159

A business was carried on by Trustees under a will for the benefit of minor beneficiaries, who were absolutely entitled to the income. *Held*, it was not the earned income of the beneficiaries.

THE LORD PRESIDENT (STRATHCLYDE): I agree with your Lordships. Unquestionably, the profits of this business were, in the sense of the Statute, earned profits, but they were earned by individuals to whom they did not belong and they belonged to individuals who certainly did not earn them.

Note
See also *M'Dougall* v. *Smith* (1918) 7 T.C. 134.

WHITE v. FRANKLIN

Court of Appeal [1965] 1 W.L.R. 492; 109 S.J. 177; [1965] 1 All E.R. 692; 42 T.C. 283

The respondent was entitled under the terms of a settlement to the income from certain shares in a family company, " so long as he should be engaged in the management of the company." *Held*, the dividends were earned income.

HARMAN L.J. : . . . So here I think this payment, although not made by the employer, the company, is made in order to ensure that the taxpayer, whom his mother and brother considered to be the person best fitted for the purpose, should go on working for this company, and it is fair to say, therefore, that the payment arises out of the performance of his duties and is earned income in the sense that it is the product of the office of profit which he holds. It is not merely a limitation in a family settlement distributing income which arises from family property to persons with certain qualifications, although it can very plausibly be put in that guise. I think it is " because " he holds office, and not merely " during the time that he does," that is the paramount consideration in the settlors' minds and that when he receives the money he is entitled to say, " This is part of my remuneration for doing this particular job.". . .

Note
Dale v. *I.R.C.* [1954] A.C. 11; *ante*, p. 345, followed. See also *Recknell* v. *I.R.C.* (1952) 33 T.C. 201; *cf*. *Bucks* v. *Bowers* [1970] Ch. 431; F.A. 1971, s. 32 (4). The burden of proof apparently rests upon the taxpayer to show that income is earned, see *Hale* v. *Shea* [1965] 1 W.L.R. 290; *Thompson* v. *Bruce* (1927) 11 T.C. 607.

ADAMS v. MUSKER

King's Bench Division (1930) 15 T.C. 413

ROWLATT J.: In this case the Appellant had earned income of £1,000, and he had some independent income, otherwise taxable, and he had a sum which he had to pay annually which was treated as a charge upon both; whether it was applied in respect of a mortgage, I do not know, but it was treated as a charge upon both. It is conceded that he is to be treated as paying his charges first out of the other taxed income. When he has done that he still has to meet a sum of some £47, or £49, or something of that sort, out of his earned income of £1,000. The question is whether, in ascertaining the one-sixth [14] that he is entitled to deduct from his earned income for the purposes of the assessment to income tax, he is entitled to deduct one-sixth of the whole £1,000, or is only entitled to deduct one-sixth of £953 which is left after deducting the £47. It is not a question of the deduction being diminished by the £47; but the question is whether the sum, the proportion of which is to be taken for the deduction, is to be diminished by £47. It is true that in the operative section at the present time it appears to be clearly expressed that the deduction is to be from the amount of his earned income of a sum equal to one-sixth of the amount of that income, that is to say, he is to deduct one-sixth of £1,000, so far; but there is the section which is made to apply, section 17 of the Act of 1918,[15] which says that " A claimant shall not be entitled to allowance or deduction . . . in respect of any income the tax on which he is entitled to charge against any other person." " Allowance or deduction " have been inserted into that section which originally related to exemption or abatement. The earned income relief is an allowance, I think quite clearly in the nomenclature of the Act and this section 17 is in the same neighbourhood of the Act, if I may use that expression—in the same group—as the then operative sections as to earned income. This section 17 has a history; the germ was first found in section 163 of the Act of 1842 dealing with exemption where a person with an income under a certain sum was exempt. I think the words were that he shall be exempted from Income Tax except tax upon such income as he is to hand over to somebody else and deduct the Income Tax upon. That is, roughly speaking, the effect of it. So that there, and again later up to the Act of 1920 I think those were the words " exemption or abatement " and they applied to an exemption or abatement which took the form of releasing from income tax a certain number of pounds, and the scheme of it was if you are entitled to relief in respect of tax on a certain number of pounds then those pounds must not be pounds which you have to hand on to somebody else. That was the scheme of it. In 1920, and in the Act which is now in force a different scheme is introduced. Instead of saying that earned income shall be taxed at a lesser rate, it says that earned income shall be taxed at the same rate, but you are to take it as only being five-sixths of what it is, which is much the same thing as saying it is to be taxed at five-sixths of the normal rate. Then this rule is applied to that, and the only way you can apply it is by saying, in making the calculation you shall not bring into the calculation any income which has to

[14] Now two-ninths, I.C.T.A. 1970, s. 9.
[15] Now I.C.T.A. 1970, s. 25.

be handed on to somebody else; in other words, you must take the net. That is as I read it. I do not think there is any other way of making section 17 apply at all, except by reading it in that way. It is intended to apply, and always has been intended to apply in this way. I think it is quite clear. It seems to me that is the result of it, and the Commissioners were right in the view they took and, therefore, that the appeal must be dismissed with costs.

Note

Decision approved by the Court of Appeal in *Lewin* v. *Aller* [1954] 1 W.L.R. 1063. Charges on income may operate to reduce or remove other reliefs or allowances, *e.g.* the personal allowance: *O'Callaghan* v. *Newstead* (1940) 23 T.C. 535. A charge on income, paid from earned income, will normally be unearned income in the hands of the recipient: *Dealler* v. *Bruce* (1934) 19 T.C. 1; *Brister* v. *Brister* [1970] 1 W.L.R. 664.

(ii) *Relief for Children*

The relief [16] is in respect of children under the age of sixteen, or receiving full time instruction at an educational establishment. The relief is reduced, or lost altogether, where the child is entitled in his own right to income exceeding a certain amount.

HEASLIP v. HASEMER

King's Bench Division (1927) 13 T.C. 212; 138 L.T. 207; 44 T.L.R. 112; 72 S.J. 31

As to whether the Respondent was entitled to relief in respect of his daughter, a full time music student aged over sixteen.

Rowlatt J.: In this case I must take it as the fact—and I have no doubt that it is a fact—that this young lady was working as hard as she could at her music, and that her attendance at Mr. Crusha's, together with her assiduous practice at home, was all she could do towards fitting herself for a musical career. I think I can accept all that. But the question is whether the case is within the particular words of the Act of Parliament. It is not within the words of the Act of Parliament unless it can be said that she is receiving full time instruction at a university, college or other educational establishment—*i.e.* full time instruction at an educational establishment which is mentioned in connection with a university, college or school.

Now what the Commissioners have said is that " Mr. Crusha's establishment "—that means his house—" and his arrangements for giving instruction in musical subjects in conjunction with home practice and study supervised and directed by him," is a school or educational establishment, and that she received full time instruction at such school or educational establishment. I gather that what is meant is that, having regard to the fact that he tells pupils how to practise when they go away from his lesson, that makes his house, or his establishment, an educational establishment within the meaning of the Act. I gather that the Commissioners also find that she is receiving full time instruction, because while she is practising at home she is still constructively receiving instruction at Mr. Crusha's.

In my judgment it is perfectly clear that Mr. Crusha's is not an establishment which has any relation to full time. It is not an establishment at all, and it has no relation to full time. That a young lady is educating herself and is

[16] I.C.T.A. 1970, s. 10.

getting herself educated has no relation to full time. What she is doing is not receiving full time instruction at an establishment; she is taking her turn with other pupils for private lessons from a gentleman at his house. That is all, and nothing else. It is said it is a question of fact, but the Commissioners have stated facts which put the case absolutely outside the Act of Parliament.

Personally, I think it is hard on the Respondent that he has to pay income tax notwithstanding this expense, but I must allow the appeal.

YATES v. STARKEY

Court of Appeal [1951] Ch. 465; [1951] 1 T.L.R. 661; [1951] 1 All E.R. 732; 32 T.C. 38

Whether a child is " entitled in his own right " to income.

JENKINS L.J.: The question in this case is whether in the circumstances I am about to mention the taxpayer is entitled for the purposes of his assessment to income tax for the three years ended April 5, 1949, to children's allowances of £60 per annum for each child under section 21 of the Finance Act 1920,[17] as amended by later enactments, in respect of the three infant children of his marriage to his former wife, Barbara Mary Starkey.

The marriage was dissolved on the petition of the wife by a decree made absolute on December 10, 1945, the custody of the three children being given to her, and by an order in the divorce proceedings dated July 16, 1946, it was ordered (*inter alia*) that the taxpayer " do pay or cause to be paid to the said petitioner " (*i.e.* Mrs. Starkey) " as an interim provision until further order " as from the date of the decree absolute " the annual sum of £100 less tax in trust for each of the three children . . . all the said sums to be payable monthly; credit to be given for any sums paid since the said date, respondent to claim child allowances."

The taxpayer duly paid Mrs. Starkey the annual sum of £100, less tax, for each child as required by the order, and she as the children's guardian made and was allowed the appropriate repayment claims on their behalf, on the footing that the effect of the order was to make the annual sum payable in respect of each child thereunder the income of that child.

The taxpayer, on the other hand, claimed the statutory children's allowances of £60 for each of the three children, which he could only be entitled to do on the footing that the order did not have the effect of making the three annual sums of £100 payable thereunder income of the three children, inasmuch as under section 21, subsection 3, of the Finance Act 1920 (as amended), the allowance is inadmissible in respect of any child entitled in his or her own right to an income exceeding £60 a year.

The taxpayer's claim was supported before the General Commissioners and Vaisey J., on two grounds.[18]

. . . Secondly, and by way of alternative, it was contended that even if the order was effective to create a trust, the taxpayer was nevertheless entitled to claim the children's allowances, because on this footing: (i) the order was a " settlement " in relation to which the taxpayer was the " settlor " within the meaning of section 21 of the Finance Act 1936 [19]; (ii) accordingly, the income paid to or for the benefit of each of the three children of the settlor (*i.e.* the taxpayer) by virtue of the settlement (*i.e.* the £100 paid to Mrs. Starkey in trust for each of them in accordance with the order) must under the same section be

---

[17] Now I.C.T.A. 1970, s. 10.
[18] The first ground concerned the power of the divorce court to make the order.
[19] Now I.C.T.A. 1970, s. 437; see *post*, Chap. 15.

treated for all the purposes of the Income Tax Acts as the income of the settlor (*i.e.* the taxpayer) and not as the income of any other person; and (iii) it follows that for the purposes of the taxpayer's claim to children's allowances under those Acts the £100 payable in respect of each child must be treated as the taxpayer's income and not as the child's and the claim to such allowances admitted accordingly.

The General Commissioners rejected the first contention but accepted the second, and Vaisey J., on appeal by the Crown, came to the same conclusion on both points.[20] . . .

STEVENS v. TIRARD

Court of Appeal [1940] 1 K.B. 204; 109 L.J.K.B. 202; 161 L.T. 400; 56 T.L.R. 65; 83 S.J. 890; [1939] 4 All E.R. 186; 23 T.C. 326

In proceedings ancillary to divorce, a husband was ordered to pay to his former wife sums for the maintenance of their three children, the mother having been awarded custody. *Held*, the money formed part of the income of the mother and was not income to which the children were entitled in their own right. Consequently, the father was not prevented from claiming the relief.

CLAUSON L.J.: . . . I return now to the main point and, in my view, the only point in the case, that is, whether the effect of the Divorce Court order has been to create a title in the infant to the income of £90 there referred to. As a matter of construction of this order it appears to me abundantly clear that the scheme of the order is not at all to create an income to which the infant is in any way entitled. The scheme of the order is to increase the income of the mother so as to enable her to discharge the duty of maintenance laid upon her by the Court in view of her having the infant's custody. . . .

Note

   The mother would also have been entitled to claim the relief, but only one relief per child can be claimed. In the case of a double claim, see I.C.T.A. 1970, s. 11. Note also the remarks of Clauson L.J. [1940] 1 K.B. 204, 212, on the anomalous results where the payments, which a mother is obliged to spend on the children, nevertheless swells her income for surtax purposes: and see Potter and Monroe's *Tax Planning*, 6th ed., Chapter 2.

   For a child's entitlement to income, see also *Williams* v. *Doulton* (1948) 28 T.C. 522; *Miles* v. *Morrow* (1940) 23 T.C. 465; *Johnstone* v. *Chamberlain* (1933) 17 T.C. 706; and *Mapp* v. *Oram* [1970] A.C. 362; *ante*, p. 83.

(iii) *Life Insurance Relief*

Relief against income tax is given in respect of certain premiums paid under life insurance policies.[21] Certain other forms of saving are also encouraged by favourable tax treatment.[22]

REPORT OF THE ROYAL COMMISSION ON THE INCOME TAX

Colwyn Report, 1920 Cmd. 615

290. The principle of allowing life insurance premiums as a deduction from income for income tax purposes was restored, after a long interval of disuse,

---

[20] As did the Court of Appeal.
[21] I.C.T.A. 1970, ss. 19–21; Sched. 1.
[22] *e.g.* approved pension schemes, retirement annuities, etc.

in 1853. Mr. Gladstone, when opening his Budget for that year, defended the allowance as a mitigation of the taxation of savings. He stated that it was impossible to exempt savings from income tax altogether, but that to make an allowance for life insurance premiums would go some way in that direction, and would especially benefit those who derived their income from their own exertions. At that time, and for long afterwards, the privilege did not extend to premiums paid to foreign and colonial insurance companies, but later enactments have brought those premiums within the scope of the allowance. The deduction was, and still is, confined to insurances effected by the taxpayer on his own life or on the life of his wife.

291. The advantage given to insurers by this allowance has probably been a factor in the great increase and development of life insurance that has taken place since 1853, but, whether this be so or not, these developments both in volume and in variety of character were so great, and their influence on income tax was so important that it became necessary to review the position in 1915 and 1916.

. . . 296. Some witnesses advocated the total abolition of the special treatment accorded to life insurance on the ground that in granting to one particular mode of saving a valuable privilege that is not extended to other forms of thrift, the State acts unfairly towards those who for reasons of ill-health cannot, and to those who for other reasons do not, save in this particular fashion. Apart from the impracticability of extending the allowance to other forms of saving, sound reasons may, we think, be found for the action of the State in singling out this one form of thrift for preferential treatment. It is significant that this country is not alone in this matter; speaking generally, an allowance for life insurance premiums is a feature of the income tax systems of the Dominions and of foreign countries. The distinguishing feature of life insurance, which probably accounts for what would otherwise seem to be an unfair preference, is that by no other means can the less wealthy taxpayer, who has no accumulated capital in his earlier years of productive effort, secure a proper provision for his dependants. Viewing the matter in a broad and national way we consider that this reason is sufficient to justify the State in looking with favourable aspect upon life insurance and in treating income that is saved and applied in this manner with special indulgence.

Note
   The position was examined in the Report of the Committee on the Taxation Treatment of Provision for Retirement, 1953 Cmd. 9063, which concluded that the relief should continue, with certain modifications.

5. The Family Unit

Under the present system, the incomes of husband and wife are aggregated,[23] with additional relief in respect of the wife's earned income.[24] As from the year 1972–73, a couple may elect for the wife's earnings to be charged as if she were a single woman.[25]

   Prior to the year, 1972–73, the unearned income of an infant, if unmarried and not regularly working, was treated as the income of the infant's parent or parents.[26] The income of a child may also be aggregated with

---

[23] I.C.T.A. 1970, s. 37. See *e.g. Baker* v. *Archer-Shee* [1927] A.C. 844; *ante*, p. 284.
[24] *Ibid.* s. 8 (2). See *Thompson* v. *Bruce* (1927) 11 T.C. 607.
[25] F.A. 1971, s. 23; Sched. 4.
[26] I.C.T.A. 1970, ss. 43–48, repealed for the year 1972–73 and subsequent years by F.A. 1971, s. 16.

the income of the parent, being income under a settlement made by the parent.[27]

(A) Husband and Wife

LEITCH v. EMMOTT

Court of Appeal [1929] 2 K.B. 236; 98 L.J.K.B. 673; 141 L.T. 311; [1929] All E.R.Rep. 638; 14 T.C. 633

In the first year after her husband's death, a widow received income from stock, not taxed at source. *Held*, she was liable to tax under Case III of Schedule D computed on her income from the same source in the preceding year, notwithstanding that, in that year, the income was deemed to be the income of her deceased husband.

Lord Hanworth M.R.: . . . It has been for a long period of time, certainly from the date of the Income Tax Act 1842, provided that the income of a married woman living with her husband shall be deemed to be the profits of the husband. Section 45 of that Act provided " that any married woman acting as a sole trader by the custom of any city or place, or otherwise, or having or being entitled to any property or profits to her sole or separate use, shall be chargeable to such and the like duties, and in like manner, except as herein-after is mentioned, as if she were actually sole and unmarried: Provided always, that the profits of any married woman living with her husband shall be deemed the profits of the husband, and the same shall be charged in the name of the husband, and not in her name, or of her trustee."

. . . By the Finance Act 1914, section 9,[28] a scheme was provided making it possible for a husband to avoid being responsible for the tax on the profits of his wife. That section was passed in order to get rid of the inconvenience caused to husbands when they found it difficult to obtain from their wives the information required to fulfil section 45 of the Act of 1842—now rule 16 of the All Schedules Rules to the Income Tax Act 1918. Under this section a notice could be given by the husband requiring separate assessments on his income and that of his wife; but for all practical purposes the actual charge upon them remained as it would be, if the tax were all collected from the husband. The liability to tax and the amount of tax continued to be measured by the totality of their incomes, and they were unable to claim that a lower effective rate of tax should be imposed upon them because the income of each one separately came below a certain level. The system still remains that there must be the aggregation of their two incomes in order to see whether or not their total income is subject to tax and what is the effective rate at which it should be charged.

I turn to consider the point made on behalf of Mrs. Leitch that she is entitled to be treated as having received no profits in the year 1920 to 1921 because of the provision by which the profits for that year have for the purpose of collection been deemed the profits of her husband. We must, I think, take rule 16 as we find it and treat the proviso as a proviso. Rule 16 provides that a married woman shall be assessable and chargeable to tax. Bearing this in mind, the proviso will operate as a proviso and no more by allowing the husband to be the source through which collection shall be made. For that purpose and

[27] I.C.T.A. 1970, ss. 437–444; F.A. 1971, s. 16; *post*, Chap. 15.
[28] Now I.C.T.A. 1970, s. 38. This must not be confused with the election to have the wife's earnings taxed as though she were a single woman, F.A. 1971, s. 23.

in that sense the profits which are not his are to be deemed to be his and in no other sense. . . .

LAWRENCE L.J.: I agree. The case is one which deals with income tax falling under Case III of Schedule D. Under rule 1 applicable to that Case, the tax extends to the interest on the investments which belong to Mrs. Leitch for her separate use. Under rule 2 the tax is assessed on the full amount of that interest arising in the year preceding the year of assessment and has to be paid on that amount without any deduction. Now, throughout the year preceding the year of assessment Mrs. Leitch was a married woman living with her husband, and under rule 16 of the All Schedules Rules, although the interest on the investments in question was assessable and chargeable to tax as if she were sole and unmarried it was to be deemed the profits of the husband, and to be assessed and charged in his name and not in her name. Early in the year of assessment the husband died, and it is now contended that the effect of proviso 1 to rule 16 is that the interest on these investments became for all purposes the income of the husband and consequently that Mrs. Leitch must be treated as not having received any interest on her investments in the year preceding the year of assessment, with the result that her income for the year of assessment ought to be assessed at nothing.

In my opinion that contention is not well founded. Rule 16 provides, in the first instance, that a married woman entitled to any property to her separate use shall be assessable and chargeable to tax as if she were sole and unmarried. Then, turning back to rule 2 of the Rules applicable to Case III we find that the measure of that charge to tax is the amount of the income from her investments arising in the year preceding the year of assessment. It is clear to my mind, therefore, that the married woman is charged to tax in respect of her income for the year of assessment, to be measured by the income from the same investments received by her in the preceding year, thus showing that the income for the purpose of the charge and of the measure of the tax is treated as her income. The proviso does not alter the character of the income charged to tax or the measure of the tax, but merely provides, with the object of facilitating the collection of the tax, that the assessment and charge shall be made in the name of the husband and that for that purpose the wife's income shall be treated as the income of the husband. This provision does not, in my judgment, operate to convert the income of the wife into income of the husband further than is necessary for the purpose of collecting the tax; with the result that it affords no valid ground for the contention that there was no income arising from the wife's investments in the year preceding the year of assessment within the meaning of rule 2 of Case III.

For these reasons, I agree that the appeal ought to be allowed.

Note
See also *Re Cameron (deceased)* [1967] Ch. 1, where a repayment of tax assessed upon the deceased husband in respect of his wife's business profits was held to belong to the wife and not to the husband's estate.

REPORT OF THE ROYAL COMMISSION ON THE INCOME TAX

Colwyn Report, 1920 Cmd. 615

251. This position [29] does not satisfy the more extreme advocates of separate assessment; they say that husband and wife should be assessed as though they

[29] *i.e.* the option for separate assessment; I.C.T.A. 1970, s. 38.

were separate taxable units—without any regard to the amount of their combined incomes. This contention has been urged upon us by many witnesses, and it forms the burden of the many letters we have received on this subject— mainly written by persons who would themselves benefit by the change proposed. By those who take this view it is claimed that the right to a completely separate assessment is an essential part of separate citizenship, and that the principle of absolute equality in regard to civil obligations should override any principle of taxation. The statement was also made that the present method of assessment imposes a penalty on marriage.

252. On the other hand, it has been contended by several witnesses that this proposal for separate assessment of husband and wife is not reconcilable with a just view of the principle of ability to bear taxation, and that the common ménage which is our general mode of social life must be considered in any equitable system of taxation. From the point of view of ability to pay those who oppose separate treatment contend that it would be an anomaly if different sums of Income Tax were levied on two married couples enjoying equal incomes, merely because in one case the income belonged wholly to one spouse and in the other to both. In the case of a married man with £1,000 a year unearned income, the sacrifice involved by income tax, say £187 10s., may in most households be regarded as borne equally by each spouse, a sacrifice of £93 15s. each. If the husband and wife each have £500 a year there is no such difference in their taxable capacity as would justify a sacrifice of only £60 a year each, which is what would result from treating husband and wife as two separate units.

257. . . . . If separate assessment were granted the marriage allowance should logically be abolished, and the result would be a shifting of burdens from the rich to the poor, because in the vast majority of cases the wife has either no separate income at all or a separate income less than the amount of the present marriage allowance, and far less than the allowance we suggest should be made.

258. The question involved should not be regarded as a political question, but purely as one of finance and revenue, and we are satisfied that it must be decided, not on any theoretical grounds of equality of citizenship, but in accordance with the outstanding principle of " ability to pay," which we recognise as governing all questions of taxation. In the application of this principle we must regard the social conditions of the country in which the taxation is imposed. The great majority of married persons live together and use their several incomes for common purposes and this common ménage and joint dependency is recognised, to the benefit of the wife, for other purposes of taxation, e.g. Legacy and Succession Duties payable by a widow are less than those payable by a person unrelated to the deceased.[30]

259. The aggregation for Income Tax purposes of the income of husband and wife is not dependent upon any mediæval conception of the subordination of women: nor is it a question of sex disability, since either partner can claim separate assessment and separate collection. The incomes are aggregated because the law of taxable capacity is the supreme law in matters of taxation, and taxable capacity is in fact found to depend upon the amount of the income that accrues to the married pair, and not upon the way in which that income happens fortuitously to be owned by the members of the union. It is beyond question that in the immense majority of cases where the wife has separate means she contributes to the common purse, either by actual merger of her income with her husband's, or by bearing expenses which in less fortunate households fall upon the husband.

[30] For the purposes of Estate Duty, husband and wife are, in most respects, treated as entirely separate persons, but N.B. the surviving spouse exemption, post, p. 528.

260. We have given a great deal of time and attention to this subject and have considered with the utmost care all the arguments that have been put before us, and we have been forced to the conclusion that the grievance complained of is more vocal than real, in other words, that it is a grievance rather than a hardship. We therefore recommend that the aggregation of the incomes of wife and husband should continue to be the rule.

ROYAL COMMISSION ON THE TAXATION OF PROFITS AND INCOME

Second Report, 1953 Cmd. 9105

THE UNIT OF TAXATION

113. A system of graduation that is to take any account of personal circumstances must first decide what is to be the unit of taxation. That, in personal taxation, the unit will in some form be the individual is clear: but is it to be every individual separately, or is the married couple or the family the better unit? In this country a husband and wife living together have always been treated as one unit, though in recent years this principle has been much modified in its application to a wife's earnings. In the result the separate incomes of husband and wife are, subject to this exception, added together and income tax and surtax charged on the total as if it were the sole income of one person. Under a progressive system, which would normally extract more tax from one income than from two incomes half the size, this principle of aggregation weighs heavily upon those married couples in which each partner is the owner of a substantial income.

114. On the other hand the United Kingdom rule is by no means the general one. On the continent of Europe the unit of taxation is often the family. Thus in France not only are the incomes of husband and wife aggregated but the incomes of children are included in the income of the family unit. The aggregate income is then divided into a number of parts according to the number of persons in the family and tax is charged separately on each part. For this purpose a child counts as one-half. Thus, in effect, a married couple pays twice the tax paid by a single person with half their joint income, and a married couple with two children pays three times the tax payable by a single person with one-third of the joint family income. If this system, which is generally known as " the quotient system," were to be adopted as the rule in the United Kingdom, its immediate effect would be a marked improvement in the relative position of most married couples, especially those with children, in the upper income ranges.

115. While the rule of aggregating the incomes of husband and wife is found in Belgium, Holland, Denmark, Norway and Sweden as well as France, and in some other countries outside Europe, a completely separate assessment of incomes prevails in Canada [31] and Australia. If, however, a wife there has no income, or only a small one, the husband receives a special personal allowance, varying with the amount of the wife's means. In the United States yet another system is applied which, while nominally one of separate assessment, tends to produce some of the effects of aggregation under the quotient system. Prima facie, assessment of husband and wife is made separately, but they have a right to choose aggregation, in which event the tax charged is twice the tax on half the joint income. The resulting liability therefore can never be heavier

---

[31] But see the proposals of the Carter Commission for Canada, post, pp. 360–366.

than if the joint income was equally divided between them: whereas, if it is unequally divided, separate assessment at progressive rates may well produce the greater liability.

116. We though it well to investigate the outlines of these other systems. Our investigation has led us to the view that the unit of taxation itself is less important than the method of treating the unit in the scheme of graduation. But we received such a volume of representations from different quarters to the effect that aggregation of the incomes of husband and wife ought to be abolished and the income of each assessed as that of a separate individual that we find it necessary to express an opinion as to the principle upon which this rule rests.

117. We see in the existing rule nothing that embodies an outmoded or an unworthy conception of the relations of man and woman in marriage. It is true that aggregation has been a feature of the tax since it was first imposed in the year 1799: and that a married woman's legal control of her property was restricted then and thereafter in a way that it is not now. Nor was her personal status in the eye of the law as free as it is today. It does not follow that aggregation has ever had any real connection with her " servile " status in relation to her property. In fact, even in 1799, most women of substantial means were already protected in the control of property by the intervention of their separate trustees. It is more likely that aggregation was introduced upon no stronger theoretical ground than that it afforded a convenient means of collecting the tax, more especially as the husband was a necessary party to any suit against his wife at common law. It is worth while to point out that, so long as income tax remained a proportional tax, as it did, in substance, throughout the nineteenth century, the principle of aggregation raised no issue of major importance. In fact the historical argument seems to us neither a good argument for retaining the rule, if it is a bad rule, nor a good argument for abolishing the rule, if it is a good one.

118. It was said to us that aggregation is socially undesirable since it tends to discourage marriage and to induce a man and woman with separate incomes to live together without becoming husband and wife. We can give very little weight to this argument. First, it is not true as a general statement that aggregation operates as a tax on marriage. It is only true of a man and woman both of whom have incomes and then only if certain ranges of income are exceeded. . . . Secondly, we are sceptical of the suggestion that men and women are in fact dissuaded from marriage by any such nice calculation of the financial odds. In the nature of things it is impossible to establish or reject it by any concrete evidence, nor would there be any value in isolated instances of what might well be an altogether exceptional prudence. In the circumstances we think it sufficient to record our view that the reasons that impel men and women to prefer marriage to more casual associations are many and powerful and that the present treatment of the income of married couples for the purpose of tax is not more likely to lead people away from matrimony than to tempt them into it.

119. We have come to the conclusion that taxation of the combined incomes of husband and wife as one unit is to be preferred to their separate taxation as separate units because the aggregate income provides a unit of taxation that is fairer to those concerned. That is why we do not recommend a departure from the present system. The combined incomes of married persons are sometimes described as a joint purse. We do not think that so wide a generalisation can safely be made on such a question of social habit; but it does appear to us, on the other hand, that marriage creates a social unit which is not truly analogous with other associations involving some measure of joint living

expenses and that to tax the incomes of two married people living together as if each income were equivalent to the income of a single individual would give a less satisfactory distribution than that which results from the present rule. Such a method of taxation would mean that one married couple bore a greater or less burden of tax than another according to what must surely be an irrelevant distinction for this purpose, namely, the proportion in which the combined income was divided between the partners, for under a system of graduation, if each of two married couples has the same combined income but one owns its combined income in proportions more nearly equal than the other, that one would be likely to pay the less tax. There would be a natural tendency for husbands to try to arrange to transfer so much of their incomes to their wives as would produce an equal division. According to our information this was what happened in the U.S.A. before the option to choose aggregation was introduced into the tax code. If separate assessment of spouses as individuals was introduced into this country it would be necessary to contemplate either the very great loss of tax that could result (giving a potential loss of tax from abolishing aggregation of some £143m) or else the simultaneous introduction of special legislation, on the lines of that which already annuls for tax purposes a parent's transfer of income to an infant child. No doubt such legislation could be produced. But it is not at all clear to us that it would have any equity to support it, for it would mean an arbitrary insistence on maintaining the existing position as between different married couples at the date of the new system and would thus confer a permanent but unreasonable advantage on those whose combined incomes at that date happened to be more or less equally divided. Even if transfers of income to equalise holdings are not contemplated there would necessarily be a big loss of tax in abolishing aggregation.

120. Our recommendation is therefore in favour of maintaining the general rule of aggregation for the incomes of husband and wife. An income upon which two people have to live as married persons has not the same taxable capacity as the income of a single individual. But in our view the right way to allow for the difference is to make an appropriate allowance for the fact of marriage in the assessment of the unit rather than by treating the two incomes as if they were the incomes of single individuals. Given aggregation, the marriage allowance is due whatever the size of the wife's income because the allowance is made in the assessment of the unit which for this purpose is treated as the sole owner of the combined income.

121. We do not wish to recommend the adoption of either the quotient system or the American system to which we have alluded above. Each has its attractions but adoption of either would mean a shift in the distribution of the tax burden from married persons to single ones to an extent that seems to us excessive. The quotient system tends to favour the family, for we cannot persuade ourselves that a father, mother and two children living in a joint establishment on their combined income have no greater taxable capacity than three single individuals each living separately on a third of that income. Similarly, the U.S. system is based on an equation between the combined incomes of husband and wife and the separate incomes of two single individuals which does not strike us as sufficiently convincing.

. . . 132. In our opinion there is a valid difference between the taxable capacity of the married couple where the wife is at work and the married couple where the wife is at home. We adhere to the view that the fact of her employment throws a burden of expense on the married household that it would not otherwise bear. To recognise that this difference does exist for the purposes of taxation is not to ignore the fact that the wife or mother who stays at home to keep house or care for children makes a valuable, though unsalaried, contribution to society. Whether the measure of difference achieved by the reliefs as they now stand is excessive is another question to which we must attend. At a later stage we shall also take up the question of the present limit for earned income relief as it applies to the joint earnings of husband and wife and make a proposal for its alteration. In general, however, our conclusion is that the special treatment of wives' earnings is not so much a rejection of the principle of aggregation as a device for securing a measure of distinction between two different kinds of taxable unit.[32]

Note

The question of the most appropriate method of taxing married couples is discussed in a number of articles, in particular by H. G. S. Plunkett, " The Taxation of Married Women " [1957] B.T.R. 134, 248, 337; G. S. A. Wheatcroft, " Earned Income of a Married Woman " [1959] B.T.R. 309; G. C. Hockley, " Taxation and the Employment of Married Women " [1967] B.T.R. 171; G. P. Marshall and A. J. Walsh, " Marital Status and Variations in Income Tax Burdens " [1970] B.T.R. 236. For the Capital Gains Tax treatment of married couples, see *Wheatcroft on Capital Gains*, Chap. 4.

(B) PARENTS AND CHILDREN

ROYAL COMMISSION ON THE TAXATION OF PROFITS AND INCOME

Second Report, 1953 Cmd. 9105

122. It may be asked why the rule of aggregation, if correct in the case of husband and wife, is not correct also in the case of children still living as members of the family group. This would involve extending the conception of the taxable unit to include such a group and its combined income. To some extent our system already embodies this conception. A parent cannot, generally speaking, reduce his taxable income by transferring a part to an infant child or to trustees for the child: the income transferred is still reckoned as his.[33] In substance that income pays in the child's name expenses he would otherwise have to pay for it. The only exception to this is that a parent may transfer investments to trustees for his infant child provided that this settlement gives them the right to accumulate, and they do accumulate, the resulting income until the child comes of age. Again, the parent's right to the child allowance ($£85$) [34] is withdrawn if the child is the owner in its own right of an income exceeding that amount. But there is no general rule to the effect that the child's income is to be aggregated with that of the parent, and, although the number of infant children who enjoy substantial incomes of their own must be regarded as negligible, there is something to be said for a rule that would make it impossible for the tax bills of different families to differ according to the way in which the income of their members was distributed between them.

123. We found that we were not unanimous as to the answer to be given to this question. The majority of us did not accept the validity of the generalisation, on which all depends, that the income of an infant, which must be thought of as held and applied by trustees on its behalf, is never anything in substance but a part of the family income. Certainly its existence relieves the parent of some burden of expenditure, but it by no means follows that the relief to the parent is of the same magnitude as the expenditure made on behalf of the child.

[32] See now, F.A. 1971, s. 23.
[33] I.C.T.A. 1970, s. 437; *post*, Chap. 15.
[34] See now I.C.T.A. 1970, s. 10 (3) as amended by F.A. 1971, s. 15 (4).

It would be doubtful justice, therefore, to attribute the whole of the child's income to the parent and leave him merely to such relief as child allowance might afford him.

124. On the other hand, some of us thought that the essential fact was that parents and children forming part of a single family normally share the same standard of living, and considered that not to aggregate children's income with the income of their parents involved the privileged tax treatment of those particular families whose children happened to be possessed of property given to them by someone other than their parents. On this view of the matter the investment income of children ought to be aggregated with the income of their parents, subject to provisions for exempting small amounts of income accruing to a child from gifts or savings and for the separate treatment of earned income on the same general lines as those accorded to the earnings of a married woman.

125. We were not unanimous either as to the importance to be attached to the separate taxation of children's investment income from the point of view of tax avoidance. It is possible for a grandparent or other relative or friend to make settlements of property which have the effect of putting a child into the possession of substantial income during the life of its parents. But in the absence of evidence before the Commission as to the scale upon which any such settlements do in fact take place, the majority of us thought it improbable that it would be large enough to be of any importance. The minority, however, felt satisfied that the motive of tax avoidance frequently played a part in such settlements and that the rule of aggregation should be adopted as a method of correcting them.

126. Having recorded our divergent views on this question of the aggregation of children's income, we make no recommendation for a change in the existing law.

Reservation, by Mr. G. Woodcock, Mrs. V. Anstey, Mr. H. L. Bullock and Mr. N. Kaldor

23. The Commission has rightly, in our view, rejected the representations made to it to the effect that the existing system of aggregating the incomes of husband and wife (subject to the special treatment of the wife's earned income) should be abandoned. The fundamental reason for aggregation is that the family constitutes a common " spending unit." Members of a family share their resources on the basis of relative need rather than according to how income happens to be divided between them. Two identical families enjoying the same total income ought not, therefore, to be taxed any differently just because in the one case the income initially accrues to one of the members while in the other case it is divided among several.

24. This conception, in our view, logically implies that not only should the wife's income be aggregated with that of the husband but also that the children's income should be aggregated with that of their parents. Apart from earned income (which deserves the same treatment in the case of children as it receives in the case of the wife) children can possess substantial income of their own as a result of inheritance, or having property or income settled upon them by their parents, grandparents, or other persons. In the case of settlements of property or income by parents, the existing legislation already recognises that the child's income in such cases must continue to be treated as the parents' income (unless the income from settled property is itself accumulated in a trust until the child comes of age). This rule was introduced in recognition of the fact that the settlement of property or income by parents on children opens the door to widespread tax avoidance (particularly surtax avoidance) since the income thus transferred bears tax at a much lower rate than it would have borne in the hands of the parent.

25. If it is right to stop this method of tax avoidance in the case of settlements from parents to children we see no reason why the practice should continue to be permitted in the case of analogous settlements by grandparents, uncles or other persons. We see no justification why two families, in otherwise identical circumstances, should be called upon to pay differing amounts of tax just because in the one case the child possesses property transferred to it by a grandparent, while in the other case the grandparent's identical property was inherited by the parent.

Note
The approach advocated in the minority's Reservation was adopted in 1968 and is contained in I.C.T.A. 1970, ss. 43–48: see G. S. A. Wheatcroft, "Parents—take this as a Warning" [1968] B.T.R. 287. It has been repealed for the year 1972–73, and subsequent years, by F.A. 1971, s. 16.
For an overall review of the British tax treatment of families, see L. Lazar, "The basic law relating to Family Taxation" [1965] B.T.R. 298.

REPORT OF THE ROYAL COMMISSION ON TAXATION

Carter Commission, Canada, 1966

Volume 1: Objectives

Families and Individuals as Tax Units

The present system recognises only the individual and not the family as a unit for tax purposes. This has certain undesirable consequences. A couple with one income recipient often pays substantially more tax than another couple with the same aggregate income derived by both spouses. If a man with a substantial salary marries a woman with a substantial independent income, their aggregate tax is not changed by their marriage. Yet it is clear that their discretionary economic power is greater because of economies which can be realised by living together.

Because income splitting results in important and unwarranted tax savings, married business proprietors would find it advantageous to hire their wives at high salaries to perform nominal duties if this were not prohibited. The prohibition results in anomalies. If the proprietor's wife does in fact perform productive work for the business the proprietor and his wife would be better off, from a tax point of view, if the wife worked elsewhere and the proprietor hired another person to do the same work. The man who owns and manages an incorporated business can often circumvent the prohibitions by having " the corporation " hire his wife.

We therefore recommend in this *Report* that the income of families should be aggregated and taxed as a unit on a separate rate schedule. The rules against income splitting could largely be withdrawn because splitting would have no significance.

The most serious consequence of the failure to accept the family as a taxable unit arises when wealth is transferred from one spouse to another. Although in most families wealth accumulated by a couple is the result of their joint efforts and decisions, the passing of property from one spouse to another is a taxable event. Exemptions provide some relief, but we believe that the taxation of these intra-family transfers is wrong in principle. On the other hand, we have expressed our belief that all increases in the economic power of the taxpayer, regardless of their source, provide the same increase in tax-paying capacity. Thus, all gifts or bequests received from outside the family unit should be included in the comprehensive tax base.

We are of the opinion that the present system of gift and death taxes, both federal and provincial, is an anachronism. Through the use of personal corporations, trusts and exemptions, it is possible to avoid and postpone substantial gift and death taxes. These taxes almost certainly are not effective in breaking up pockets of wealth held by family dynasties, as is sometimes believed. They can, however, make it extremely difficult for a man to maintain his widow in the style she enjoyed when he was alive by substantially reducing the amount of property left for her support, even though he could not have accumulated the property without his wife's help.

We recommend an entirely different system. The present gift and death taxes should be withdrawn and transfers of wealth within family units should have no tax consequences. Transfers of wealth from one family unit to another tax unit should be taxed at full progressive rates to the recipient tax unit, subject to small annual exemptions and a $5,000 lifetime exemption. Transfers of wealth between husbands and wives and between parents and minor children would not therefore come within the purview of the tax system at all. However, when children leave home, all property taken from the family, with certain exemptions for administrative convenience, would be taxable to the child. Any subsequent transfers from the family to the grown-up son or daughter, or to anyone else for that matter, should be taxed to the recipient. The family would ordinarily cease to exist on the death of the last surviving spouse. Property passing to other individuals or families on the termination of the family unit would also be taxable to the recipients.

Specific Non-discretionary Expenditures

Through the progressive rate structure it is possible to reflect the reduced relative importance of non-discretionary expenses generally as income rises. There are, however, specific non-discretionary expenditures that should also be taken into account if equity is to be achieved.

We have already said that the system should recognise both families and unattached individuals as taxable units. This raises the question of the appropriate relationship between the taxes imposed on families and unattached individuals; on families with children relative to those with no children; and on families with one child relative to those with, say, ten children.

In our opinion a childless couple should pay lower taxes than an unattached individual with the same income. This difference would reflect the fact that two cannot live as cheaply as one. But when two people with incomes marry, and both continue to receive these incomes, their total tax should increase, because there are economies in living together. These tax differentials can be obtained by adopting two separate rate schedules: one to be applied to aggregate family income and another to be applied to the income of unattached individuals.

With separate rate schedules the present system of personal exemptions for the taxpayer and his or her spouse can be eliminated. The same result can be achieved in a simpler way by the use of a first income bracket taxed at a zero rate. This is what has been done in the proposed rate schedules. The significance of such a change is to bring closer together income and taxable income. Taken by itself it has no impact on the calculation of an individual's taxes.

The present system takes into account the non-discretionary expenses of raising children by providing parents with an exemption for each child. The size of the exemption is affected by the eligibility of the child for family allowances. This approach has two weaknesses. First, it does not recognise that the first child involves greater non-discretionary expenditures than subsequent children. The parents often must find different and more expensive accommodation, equipment must be bought and, most important of all, the mother must either stop working or hire someone to look after the child. Subsequent children involve additional costs, but they are not as great as for the first child. The second weakness is that the present exemptions for dependants provide a greater benefit to those with larger incomes.

These faults can be overcome by the use of tax credits for children, with a larger credit for the first child than for the others. This we have recommended.

Most medical expenses are clearly non-discretionary expenses. Taxes, therefore, should be lowered for those who have unusually heavy expenses of this type. The 3 per cent. of income floor should be retained as a rough-and-ready dividing line between the exceptional and the " ordinary " medical expense. Only out-of-pocket expenses in excess of this floor should be deducted and not, as at present, amounts reimbursed through insurance. The standard deduction for medical expenses should be withdrawn.

Working mothers with young children are faced with substantial non-discretionary expenses. A tax credit should be provided to taxpayers in this situation.

The present deductions for the costs of post-secondary education should be abandoned and a system of transferable credits adopted that would be of greater value to low income parents and students. Living costs of students taking such education should also be recognised.

Volume 3: Taxation of Income. (A) Individuals and Families

(D) *The Family Unit*

1. The present tax system treats the individual rather than the family as the basic unit for tax purposes. In our view this leads to inequities because we believe it is the ability to pay of the family, rather than of the individual members of the family, that should be taken into account in determining tax liabilities.

2. In our opinion a married couple should pay less tax than a single individual with the same aggregate income. However, we believe that at most income levels a married couple should pay higher taxes than two single individuals, each of whom has half the income of the couple, because of the economies that can be realised when two people live together. This result is not achieved with the present system.

3. The tax liabilities of married couples should be independent of the proportion of total income received by husband or wife. This result is not achieved under the present system, for the couple comprised of a husband and wife who have identical incomes pays a lower tax than a couple with the same income received by one of the spouses.

4. These problems could be eliminated by the aggregation of the income of husband and wife. By taxing the total income of the couple under a rate schedule that bears an appropriate relationship to the rate schedule applicable to individuals, a more equitable allocation of taxes between single individuals and couples could be achieved.

5. The aggregation of the income of husband and wife would have the important result that transactions between the two would have no tax consequences. In particular, *inter vivos* and testamentary transfers of property between spouses would not be subject to tax notwithstanding the general rule that gifts are included in the income of the donee tax unit.

6. Adopting the family as one of the basic units for tax purposes would have the advantage that the problems created by income splitting between husband

and wife under the present approach would be largely eliminated. The restrictive sections of the Act that are now necessary to prevent income splitting have been sharply criticised as discriminatory and inconsistent. These restrictions could be abolished.

7. There are both advantages and disadvantages to the aggregation of the income of dependent children with family income. Except under unusual circumstances, compulsory aggregation of the income of dependent children with that of their parents would be preferable from an equity point of view, and the administrative problems would probably be less with aggregation. We therefore recommend compulsory aggregation of the income of dependent children with family income, with modifications that would provide the flexibility necessary to accommodate the diverse relationships that prevail between parents and their children and the unique character of the income sometimes received by dependent children.

The Composition of the Family Unit

8. A husband and wife, if they are Canadian residents, should be treated as a tax unit (the " family unit ") for tax purposes. The family unit would commence at the beginning of the taxation year in which the marriage occurred.

9. Where there were resident dependent children, they should also form part of the family unit for tax purposes. With two exceptions, dependent children should be defined as unmarried children twenty-one years of age or less, or over twenty-one and infirm. Actual support should not be a test of dependency. Other close relatives dependent upon the family unit for support should not be included in the family unit for tax purposes. However, a tax credit should be available that would be related to expenditures made to support such dependents.

10. A family unit should also be formed at the commencement of the year in which any of the following events occurred: an unmarried woman has a child; an unmarried individual adopts one or more children; or a divorced or separated spouse retains custody of one or more dependent children. The unit would consist of the parent and the dependent child or children.

Options for Dependent Children

11. Two options should be available with respect to dependent status:

(a) An unmarried resident child twenty-one years of age or less, but over school-leaving age, who lived away from home and was employed or operated a business on a full-time basis, should be permitted to file as an individual, at the option of the child *or* of the child's parents.

(b) An unmarried resident child over twenty-one years of age but not over twenty-five who attended a recognised institution of post-secondary education on a full-time basis should be permitted, if acceptable to *both* the child and his or her parents, to remain a member of the family unit.

Family Rate Schedule

12. Normally, the income of the family unit would be aggregated on a joint return and this aggregate taxed on a " family unit rate schedule." Under that schedule family units would pay less tax than an individual with the same income.

13. Either spouse should be permitted to elect that they would not aggregate their incomes. In that event they would file separate returns and be taxed separately on the family unit rate schedule in a way that would usually involve somewhat higher taxes (in total) than if they had aggregated. A dependent child's income (in excess of the exemption referred to below) if any, would be aggregated with that of either parent.

Liability for Tax Payable by Family Unit

14. The spouses should be jointly and severally liable for the tax payable by the family unit unless they file separate returns. If there is only one parent, he or she would be liable for the tax. A dependent child with income should be liable for the tax allocable to that income.

Exempt Income for Dependent Children

15. Employment or business income up to $500 earned at arm's length by a child in a family unit should be exempt from tax and would therefore not be subject to aggregation. Only the dependent child's income in excess of that sum should be aggregated with the income of the family unit.

Individual Rate Schedule

16. A person who was not a member of a family unit should be treated as an " individual unit " and should be taxed on the " individual unit rate schedule."

Transfers of Property within Family Unit

17. With one exception, transfers of property, either *inter vivos* or on death, between members of a family unit should not involve a deemed disposition or the receipt of income. For example, a husband would be able to make *inter vivos* and testamentary gifts to his wife or dependent child free of any tax.

18. To prevent abuse through marriages undertaken solely for the purpose of reducing taxes on transfers of property, it should be provided that tax-free transfers would not be permitted until the marriage had lasted for five years or until there was a natural-born child of the marriage, whichever was earlier. One exception to this would be that tax-free transfers would be allowed during this period up to one half of the income after tax reported by the family unit.

Transfers of Property between Units

19. Gifts of assets from outside the family unit to a member of the family unit should be treated as income of the family unit, with the exception noted below.

20. The following special rules should apply to dependent children:

(a) A dependent child who received gifts or bequests from outside the family unit should be permitted to deposit such gifts or bequests, or the monetary value thereof, in an interest-bearing Income Adjustment Account. Such deposits would be deducted from family income for tax purposes. Withdrawals from these deposits would be taxable to the unit of which the donee is a member at the time of the withdrawal. Withdrawal would be compulsory when the child established a new tax unit.

(b) A dependent child with income earned at arm's length from employment or business in excess of the $500 annual allowance should be permitted to deposit the excess in an Income Adjustment Account on the same basis as gifts from outside the family unit.

(c) On marriage, on ceasing to be a resident, and on ceasing to qualify as a dependent child under the definitions given in 9 above:

    (i) there should be a deemed realisation of gains or losses to the original family unit, on the property the child takes to the new unit;

    (ii) the child should bring this property into the income of his or her new tax unit in its first taxation year at the fair market value, subject to a lifetime exemption of $5,000 and the applicable annual exemption for gifts; if the child has ceased to be resident the property would be subject to withholding tax as a gift.

(d) On the adoption of a dependent child who is an orphan by another family unit there should be no deemed realisation and the property of the child should not be included in the income of the new unit.

Termination of the Individual Tax Unit

21. The individual tax unit should terminate on death, on marriage or on giving up Canadian residence. Except on marriage there would be a deemed realisation of property gains to the terminating unit and the property passing to other resident units would be brought into the income of the recipient unit. On marriage there would be no deemed realisation and the property taken from the individual tax unit to the new family unit created by the marriage would not be brought into the income of the new unit. All deemed realisations of property would be at the fair market value.

Termination of the Family Tax Unit

22. The family tax unit should terminate if both spouses ceased to be resident and there were no resident dependent children. There would be a deemed realisation of property gains to the terminating unit. Property passing from the terminating unit to resident tax units would be brought into income by the latter. If a person becoming non-resident elects to continue to be taxed as a resident, he should be regarded as a resident for all purposes.

23. If one spouse became non-resident there should be a deemed realisation of gains on the property of that spouse. However, the family tax unit would not terminate if one spouse remained resident or if there were resident dependent children.

24. The family tax unit should terminate if the spouses were divorced or legally separated. However, there would be no deemed realisation of property gains to the family unit, and the property taken by any of the members of the family from the terminated unit would not be brought into the income of the new tax units they formed.

25. The family unit should terminate:

(a) On the death of the surviving spouse if there were no resident dependent children.

(b) On the remarriage of the surviving spouse.

(c) On the surviving spouse ceasing to be resident if there were no resident dependent children.

(d) On the loss of dependent status by all members of the family unit of
parents who have died or have ceased to be resident leaving dependent
children resident in Canada.

In the circumstances referred to in paragraphs (a), (c) and (d) there would be
a deemed realisation of all property gains to the family unit. In cases (a) and
(d) all property transferred from the terminated unit, after providing for its
tax liability, would be brought into the income of recipient tax units. In the
case of remarriage of a surviving spouse there would be no deemed realisation
and the property of the surviving spouse would not be included in the income
of the new unit. In the event of the marriage of a surviving spouse or of an
unmarried person who has a dependent child or dependent children, all members
of the tax unit would presumably become members of the new tax unit and
there would be no deemed realisation to the former unit or income to the new
unit.

Note
It appears unlikely that these proposals will be implemented in the near future; see the
Canadian Government White Paper, " Proposals for Tax Reform " (Ottawa, 1969), and G.
Bale, " The Individual and Tax Reform in Canada " (1971) 41 *Canadian Bar Review* 24.

CHAPTER 15

ESTATES, TRUSTS AND PARTNERSHIPS

INCOME tax is primarily and ultimately a tax upon the individual. It is only in the case of the individual that the concept of total income is relevant; only the individual is liable to surtax and only the individual is entitled to claim reliefs and allowances against income tax.[1] Nevertheless, the Income Tax laws recognise the existence of other taxable persons or bodies, which have income and are assessable thereon—in particular, the Administrators or Executors of an Estate, the Trustees of a Settlement, Partnerships and, for the purposes also of Corporation Tax, Companies.[2]

1. The Income of Estates and Trusts

It is an essential element of an estate or trust that ultimately there is a beneficiary entitled to the trust fund and to the income therefrom. However, income tax is an annual tax and it may well be that, in any year of assessment, no beneficiary can be said to be entitled to the income of the fund, as where income is accumulated under a discretion or power, or contingent upon a beneficiary attaining a vested interest. In such a case the income is the income of the trust, but not of any individual.

(A) TAXATION OF TRUST INCOME

As a rule, all income received by the Trustees (or by the Personal Representatives, in the case of a deceased's Estate) is assessed in their hands and bears income tax at the standard rate insofar as it has not already suffered such tax by deduction at source. Trustees are also assessable in respect of capital gains in relation to settled property.[3]

Trustees are not assessable to surtax, nor are they entitled to personal reliefs.[4]

WILLIAMS v. SINGER

House of Lords [1921] 1 A.C. 65; 89 L.J.K.B. 1151; 123 L.T. 632; 36 T.L.R. 661; 64 S.J. 569; 7 T.C. 387

Trustees resident in the United Kingdom held shares in a foreign company on behalf of a beneficiary resident and domiciled abroad. The dividends were

---

[1] A company may have "charges on income," deductible from profits in ascertaining liability to Corporation Tax.
[2] The position of companies will be considered in the following chapter.
[3] F.A. 1965, s. 25. As to a beneficiary who is absolutely entitled as against the Trustee, see *ibid.* s. 22 (5) and *Tomlinson* v. *Glyn's Executor and Trustee Co.* [1970] Ch. 112.
[4] *Fry* v. *Shiel's Trustees* (1914) 6 T.C. 583; *ante,* p. 346. A trustee may, of course, claim allowances in respect of his *own* income, which may be derived from the trust: *Dale* v. *I.R.C.* [1954] A.C. 11; *ante,* p. 345; see also *Brown* v. *I.R.C.* [1965] A.C. 244; J.G.M., " The Assessment of Trust Income on Trustees " [1964] B.T.R. 364.

paid direct to that beneficiary and were never received in this country. *Held*, the Trustees could not be assessed upon income which had not come into their hands.

VISCOUNT CAVE: My Lords, the question raised in these appeals is whether income from foreign investments which is received abroad by a person not domiciled in this country is chargeable with income tax under the Income Tax Acts by reason of the fact that the investments stand in the names of trustees who are domiciled here. As the point raised in both cases is the same, the appeals have been heard together.

In *Williams* v. *Singer* the respondents are the trustees of a settlement under which the Princesse de Polignac is the beneficial tenant for life in possession. The settlement is in English form, and the trustees are all domiciled and resident in the United Kingdom; but the Princess (who is a widow) is a French subject by marriage, and is domiciled and resident abroad. The settled fund, so far as it comes into question in these proceedings, consists of certain foreign investments of considerable value, and under orders signed by the trustees the whole income from these investments is paid to the account of the Princess at a bank in New York, no part thereof being remitted to this country.

. . . It is obvious that, having regard to the proviso to the above section, the Princesse de Polignac and Mrs. Munthe,[5] who are domiciled abroad, could not have been assessed to income tax in respect of the foreign income above referred to. But the revenue authorities contend that they are entitled to levy tax upon that income by means of assessments upon the trustees, who are domiciled in this country. If this contention is upheld, the trustees will of of course be entitled to retain the tax so paid out of the trust income payable to the beneficial life tenants, who will thus have to bear the burden of the tax from which the proviso appears to relieve them; but the appellants contend that this is the effect of the statutes. The question to be determined is whether they have that effect.

. . . Indeed, I understood Mr. Cunliffe to go so far as to say that, when funds are vested in trustees, the revenue authorities are entitled to look to those trustees for the tax, and are neither bound nor entitled to look beyond the legal ownership.

My Lords, I think it clear that such a proposition cannot be maintained. It is contrary to the express words of section 42 of the Income Tax Act 1842, which provides that no trustee who shall have authorised the receipt of the profits arising from trust property by the person entitled thereto, and who shall have made a return of the name and residence of such person in manner required by the Act, shall be required to do any other act for the purpose of assessing such person. And, apart from this provision, a decision that in the case of trust property the trustee alone is to be looked to would lead to strange results. If the legal ownership alone is to be considered, a beneficial owner in moderate circumstances may lose his right to exemption or abatement by reason of the fact that he has wealthy trustees, or a wealthy beneficiary may escape super-tax by appointing a number of trustees in less affluent circumstances. Indeed, if the Act is to be construed as counsel for the appellants suggests, a beneficiary domiciled in this country may altogether avoid the tax on his foreign income spent abroad by the simple expedient of appointing one or more foreign trustees. Accordingly I put this contention aside.

On the other hand, I do not think it would be correct to say that, whenever property is held in trust, the person liable to be taxed is the beneficiary and not

[5] The beneficiary in the other case considered, *Pool* v. *Royal Exchange Assurance*, where the facts were similar.

the trustee. Section 41 of the Income Tax Act 1842 [6] renders the trustee, guardian or other person who has the control of the property of an infant, married woman, or lunatic chargeable to income tax in the place of such infant, married woman, or lunatic; and the same section declares that any person not resident in Great Britain shall be chargeable in the name of his trustee or agent having the receipt of any profits or gains.

. . . The fact is that if the Income Tax Acts are examined, it will be found that the person charged with the tax is neither the trustee nor the beneficiary as such, but the person in actual receipt and control of the income which it is sought to reach. The object of the Acts is to secure for the State a proportion of the profits chargeable, and this end is attained (speaking generally) by the simple and effective expedient of taxing the profits where they are found. If the beneficiary receives them he is liable to be assessed upon them. If the trustee receives and controls them, he is primarily so liable. If they are under the control of a guardian or committee for a person not *sui juris* or of an agent or receiver for persons resident abroad, they are taxed in his hands. But in cases where a trustee or agent is made chargeable with the tax the statutes recognise the fact that he is a trustee or agent for others and he is taxed on behalf of and as representing his beneficiaries or principals.

. . . Applying the above conclusions to the present case, it follows in my opinion, first, that the respondent trustees, who have directed the trust income to be paid to the beneficial tenants for life and themselves receive no part of it, are not assessable to tax in respect of such income; . . .

Note
    See also *Kelly* v. *Rogers* [1935] 2 K.B. 446.

REID'S TRUSTEES v. I.R.C.

Court of Session (1929) 14 T.C. 512; 1929 S.C. 439

LORD PRESIDENT (CLYDE): . . . My own opinion—for what it is worth in view of the two cases above referred to—is that trustees are the proper persons to be assessed in all cases in which the income of the trust estate received by them, or to which they are entitled, is not tax-deducted at source; and that—in the case of income of the trust estate which is tax-deducted at source—they could not be heard to ask repayment of the tax on the plea that the income did not arise or accrue to them but to others, whether such others were income-beneficiaries or capital-beneficiaries. There is nothing inconsistent with the Income Tax Acts in recognising and respecting the distinction between property owned by a person as trustee and property owned by him in his own right. The result of the two cases, as regards Schedule D at least, is, I think, no more than this—that, while rule 1 of the miscellaneous rules applicable to that Schedule cannot now be regarded as making trustees, who receive or are entitled to income, assessable and liable *prima instantia* for the tax in all cases, it nevertheless has that effect in a great many.

The conclusion on the whole matter seems to be that trustees, albeit only the representatives of ulterior beneficial interests are assessable generally in respect of the trust income under rule 1 of the Miscellaneous Rules applicable to Schedule D; but that—just because they represent those beneficial interests— they may have a good answer to a particular assessment, as regards some share or part of the income assessed, on the ground that such share or part arises or accrues *beneficially* to a *cestui que trust* in whose hands it is not liable to

[6] See now T.M.A. 1970, s. 72.

income tax, *e.g.* a foreigner under Case V, rules 1 and 3. The fact that most trust income is subject to deduction of income tax at the source has probably obscured the specialty which attaches to the representative character of trustees as payers of income tax; but if the proposition now maintained for the trustees is a sound one it is incomprehensible that it should never have been advanced with regard to the very large sums of trust income which do not, and never can, reach the hands of an income-beneficiary. . . .

I.R.C. v. LONGFORD (COUNTESS)

House of Lords [1928] A.C. 252; 97 L.J.K.B. 438; 139 L.T. 121; 44 T.L.R. 410; 13 T.C. 616

An assessment to super-tax cannot be made upon Trustees in that capacity.

VISCOUNT SUMNER: . . . The imposition of personal liability for an additional duty of income tax, levied on the total income of the beneficiary, as ascertained by a complete enumeration of all sources subject only to certain authorised deductions, upon a trustee, who held a part only of the beneficiary's entire property and that part possibly only a small one or a part yielding no income, would be a travesty of rational taxation.

. . . In the case of income tax the extent of the liability, depending as it does on the various schedules and cases under which the particular part of the property is being assessed, is limited to the income of the property, which is under the trustee's control and is assessable within the particular assessment area. If the trustee returns that and pays on it, he is no further chargeable, although the infant may be beneficially interested in other taxable property, over which that trustee has no control at all. The manner in which he is made liable is by the method of local and separate assessments provided for income tax. Exemptions and deductions are the subject of a separate manner of reclaiming tax already paid, with which the trustee is not, as such, in any way concerned.

In the case of super-tax it is far otherwise. The person, who is chargeable, whether in a representative capacity for another person or on his own account, has to return the whole of the income, which is subject to super-tax, and he has to make the deductions, which the Act allows, if there are any, before his return, on which the tax is to be computed, is complete and ready for enforcement of the tax. In the case of a return by a person representing some one else, the super-tax, duly computed, is wholly and as a whole chargeable on him. For super-tax purposes there is no provision for making piecemeal assessments or for levying the tax in part on one person and in part on another. The person, who is made liable to charge at all, has to bear the entire burden of it. . . .

AIKIN v. MACDONALD'S TRUSTEES

Court of Exchequer (Scotland) (1894) 3 T.C. 306

Trustees in Scotland received remittances of income from trust properties abroad and distributed the net income, after deducting the expenses of management, among the beneficiaries. *Held*, the Trustees were assessable upon the full amount of income received by them, without deduction of expenses.

LORD PRESIDENT (ROBERTSON): My Lords, the Appellants are testamentary trustees, and in that capacity they are part proprietors of certain estates in

India. In the year ending April 5, 1894, there was remitted to the Appellants from India, as the proceeds of those properties, a sum of £1,684 2s. 2d., and that was a sum of money which came home net. That sum came into the hands of the Appellants free for them to spend or distribute according to the rights of their beneficiaries. They now propose to deduct certain expenses incurred in this country in connection with the management of the trust. Now my Lords, it is for them to point to the section of the statutes which entitles them to make such a deduction. I think they have entirely failed. It seems to me that all the authorised deductions and charges occur at an earlier stage than that at which these expenses have been incurred. When the net sum was placed in the hands of the trustees, it had passed through all the vicissitudes which entitled anyone to make deductions. It had come home, and was in their hands for them to apply to their uses. The fact that their uses are trust uses does not seem to me to make any difference in the present question, and the fact that this is a trust for the children of a person deceased again does not make any difference, as is shown by the fact that the trustees themselves are going to pay income tax upon this sum, and merely question the right of the government to refuse the deduction in question. It seems to me that the expenses which are authorised to be deducted are expenses excluded by the terms of the present claim, because the words of the present claim are quite explicit that these expenses have been incurred in this country in connection with the management of the trust, and they are not expenses at all specifically relating to the investment in question, except in this sense, that the income of the investment in question constitutes the bulk of the trust estate. I am of opinion that the determination of the Commissioners is wrong and should be reversed.

LORD McLAREN: . . . If we suppose the ordinary case of a commercial firm earning profits, and that one of the partners has died and left his share to be managed by trustees for the benefit of his family, the firm make a return to government of their net profits, and they are assessed upon those profits. Can it be for a moment maintained that after that return had been made, the family of the partner who has left his money to trustees are entitled to a further reduction in respect of the cost of administering this revenue through the trustees? It seems to me that in such a case the deduction would be no more claimable than in a case where an individual partner having money in many concerns chooses to employ a private secretary for the purpose of keeping an account of his income and his expenditure. The management of the trustees is really, I venture to think, of the nature of what is described in one of the rules as a private or domestic use, and so described for the purpose of making it clear that it is not to be allowed as a deduction. I think it is plain enough, reading these rules, that the only kind of deductions allowed is expenditure incurred in earning the profits, and that there is no deduction under any circumstances allowable for expenditure incurred in managing profits which have been already earned and reduced into money—pounds, shillings, and pence.

Note
 Where, however, a beneficiary is entitled to and assessed upon trust income, the income of the beneficiary is that part of the trust income to which he is entitled, which is arrived at *after* the deduction of prior charges, *including* management expenses: *Murray* v. *I.R.C.* (1926) 11 T.C. 133; *Macfarlane* v. *I.R.C.* (1929) 14 T.C. 532.

(B) TAXATION OF BENEFICIARIES

Income of the estate or trust is assessed to income tax in the hands of the personal representatives or trustees. Where, however, a beneficiary is entitled to that income, or a part of it, or receives income from the trust, such income forms a part of that beneficiary's total income for the year in question, and the beneficiary may be assessed to surtax or may be entitled to set personal reliefs against it and reclaim the income tax already deducted.[7]

(i) Income of the Beneficiary

If an item is to enter into the computation of a beneficiary's total income, there must be income [8] which the beneficiary has received or was entitled to receive.[9]

DRUMMOND v. COLLINS

House of Lords (ante, p. 286)

Income received by a person resident in the United Kingdom, who was an object of a foreign discretionary trust, formed part of his total income for income tax and surtax purposes.

EARL LOREBURN: . . . My Lords, in this case an American gentleman left by his will a large sum of money to trustees upon trusts which tied up his property with a view to its accumulation for a long time, and created a somewhat complicated series of interests. We have in my opinion no concern with the ultimate destination of these funds. We are concerned only with one provision. The will authorised and indeed required the trustees in America to exercise their discretion as to providing money for the maintenance of the testator's grandchildren, who are now minors. In pursuance of this authority the trustees exercised their discretion and remitted to the appellant, the mother of these children, certain sums of money for their maintenance, and the Court of Appeal by a majority has held that these sums are chargeable with income tax because the lady and the children reside in England, and the money was received in England.

. . . It is abundantly clear that the present case falls within the letter of the Act. These sums were derived from remittances from America payable in Great Britain or from money or value received in Great Britain and arising from property that has not been imported into Great Britain. They also come within the words of Schedule D as profits or gains accruing from property to a person residing in the United Kingdom.

It was argued, however, that these allowances sent from America are not "income" of the children, because they were voluntary payments by the trustees. I do not assent to the proposition that a voluntary payment can never be charged, but it is enough to say that these were not voluntary payments in any relevant sense. They were payments made in fulfilment of a testamentary disposition for the benefit of the children in the exercise of a discretion conferred by the will. They were the children's income in fact. . . .

---

[7] See *I.R.C.* v. *Hamilton-Russell's Executors* [1943] 1 All E.R. 474; *ante,* p. 340.

[8] *Dewar* v. *I.R.C.* [1935] 2 K.B. 351; *ante,* p. 340; and see *Woodhouse* v. *I.R.C.* (1936) 20 T.C. 673; *I.R.C.* v. *Henderson's Executors* (1931) 16 T.C. 282.

[9] For the entitlement of a beneficiary in respect of an estate during the course of administration, see I.C.T.A. 1970, ss. 426–433, and see G. Dworkin, " The Right of a Residuary Legatee in an Unadministered Estate " [1965] B.T.R. 60.

LORD PARKER OF WADDINGTON: . . . In my opinion it is enough for case 5 to apply that the person to be assessed has such an interest in the property as to entitle him to the profits or gains in question. The infants had in my opinion such an interest. Though they might be incapable because of their age of giving a receipt for the money, it is in my opinion nonetheless clear that the money in question was, as soon as the trustees had exercised their discretionary trust, held in trust for these infants as beneficiaries. . . .

LORD WRENBURY: . . . The gifts are each one of them in favour of the children, but the dates for payment to the children are fixed with reference to the exercise by the trustees of their discretion or the ages from time to time of the children. At the time with which your Lordships have to do there could be no payment except by exercise of the discretion vested in the trustees, but so soon as their discretion is exercised in favour of the child the resulting payment seems to me upon the language of the will to be a payment of income to which the child is entitled by virtue of the gift made by the testator. I cannot see any ground upon which such income is not subject to income tax.

My Lords, let me, however, assume that the above reasoning is not correct, and that the interest of the infants is contingent, that is to say, that the income is income of the child in one contingency and income of another (the person entitled under the gift over) in another contingency—that the money which is paid for the benefit of the child is not income of the child rendered payable by the action of the trustees, but is income which but for the action of the trustees would have been income of some one else (the person entitled under the gift over) which only comes to the child because the trustees under the provisions of the will divert it from that other person and make it available for the child. It remains, however, that in this case directly the trustees exercise their discretion in favour of the child the interest of the child ceases to be contingent and becomes vested. Whether the money is paid to the child or to the guardian of the child or to the schoolmaster or the tailor or other person who supplies the wants of the child it is paid to or to the use of the child and is income of the child. . . .

Note
See also *Lord Tollemache* v. *I.R.C.* (1926) 11 T.C. 277; *post*, p. 379; *Johnstone* v. *Chamberlain* (1933) 17 T.C. 706.

STANLEY v. I.R.C.

Court of Appeal [1944] K.B. 255; 113 L.J.K.B. 292; 170 L.T. 140; 60 T.L.R. 209; [1944] 1 All E.R. 230; 26 T.C. 12

The appellant was life-tenant of a trust fund, the income of which, apart from certain payments for the maintenance of the appellant, was accumulated during his minority. The Revenue claimed to assess the appellant to surtax on the accumulated income. *Held*, by virtue of section 31 (2) of the Trustee Act 1925, the income could not be said to be the income of the appellant during the years in question.

LORD GREENE M.R.: . . . Some highly technical arguments were addressed to us on the question what precise interest in surplus income an infant having a vested interest enjoys during his infancy in view of these provisions. This, no doubt, is a relevant question, but the fundamental question remains, namely, is that interest such as to make the surplus income income of the infant for the purposes of surtax? It was said on behalf of the Crown that the infant has a vested interest in the surplus income as it accrues and that there is nothing in the section that deprives him of that interest during infancy—all that the section does is to divest him of his title to the accumulations of surplus income if he dies before attaining his majority. In other words, it was said, he has a vested interest in the accumulations which is defeasible in the event of his dying under twenty-one and, therefore, the surplus income is, during minority, income of the infant and as such is assessable year by year. It is necessary at this point to call attention to a distinction which apparently was not appreciated by the Special Commissioners. The expression " defeasible interest in income " may be used in two senses. In the case of an adult he receives and enjoys the income until the defeasance takes place. Until that event occurs the income is his income and he is assessable accordingly, but the same expression (if it be the correct one to use in reference to surplus income in such a case as the present) means, in the case of an infant in the situation of the appellant, something quite different. The infant does not during infancy enjoy the surplus income. It is not his in any real sense. The title to it is held in suspense to await the event, and if he dies under twenty-one his interest in it (whether or not it be truly described as a vested interest) is destroyed. He is, in fact, for all practical purposes in precisely the same position as if his interest in surplus income were contingent. If he attains twenty-one he takes the accumulations, if he dies under twenty-one he does not. . . .

CORNWELL v. BARRY

Chancery Division (1955) 36 T.C. 268; [1955] T.R. 255

Property was settled upon discretionary trusts for the benefit of a number of possible objects, but during the relevant period there was in fact only one person within the discretion. Part of the trust income was applied by the appellant for the benefit of that object, the remainder being accumulated. On behalf of the beneficiary a repayment of the tax paid on the trust income was claimed. *Held*, the beneficiary was not entitled to the income of the fund, ᵗherefore it could not be regarded as his income for the purposes of relief.

HARMAN J.: . . . The question at issue can be stated tersely: Was the income of this fund in the years in question the infant's income? If it was, he is entitled, through his Trustee, to get the usual personal relief against the tax suffered. If, however, it could not be said to be his income, he is not a person who can get that relief.

The position is well illustrated, I think, by a case which was before the Court of Appeal, *Stanley* v. *Commissioners of Inland Revenue*.[10] In that case there was an infant who, under his father's will, took a vested interest in certain estates. On his father's death and subsequently during the rest of his minority, the Trustees accumulated surplus income not applied for his maintenance. When he attained twenty-one he became entitled to those accumulations, and the Crown then sought to charge him with surtax for the years of his infancy. But that claim was rejected by the Court of Appeal on the ground that the income was not the infant's income at the time that he should have been assessed, the reason being that under the Trustee Act 1925, if he had not attained twenty-one, the accumulations would never have been his but would have been added to the corpus of the fund which went over to the remainder-

[10] [1944] K.B. 255; *ante*, p. 373.

man. It was said, under those circumstances, that the income was not truly his income: true, it was vested, but liable to be divested, and a person holding an income on those comparatively precarious terms cannot be a person against whom the Crown can charge surtax, nor, by contrariety, can he be a person on whose behalf a claim for relief can be made.

It follows that the problem here is to decide whether this income, year by year, which was paid by the covenantor, became indefeasibly the income of the infant. He was, as I say, at all times the only object of the covenant. There was no other infant during the eight years of its duration, and it is said, there being no one else, the income was always all his notwithstanding that it was not applied for his benefit, and that if he had died during the duration of the covenant his estate would have become entitled to the accrued instalments up to the date of the death.

. . . Now, says Mr. Monroe, the trust applies " as and when moneys are received," and you should read it in this way: " The Trustee shall hold the moneys upon trust as and when received for all or any one or more of the children," and so on. I quite agree that that is a sensible way of reading it. It means that the trust applies to each half-yearly instalment of the covenanted sums as they reach the Trustee's hands, and that is the trust you would expect to find. So, directly he receives £75, that is, a half-yearly instalment, the Trustee holds it on trust. For whom? " . . . for all or any one or more of the children now living or born during the said period."

In other words, any child of the son either in existence when the deed is made or coming into existence during the eight years thereafter is an object of the trust. Mr. Monroe says that, so long as there is only one child who fulfils any of those qualifications, he is entitled to the whole income as and when received, and it is indefeasibly his. In my judgment, that would be an entirely mistaken view of this wording. The Trustee is to look not only at the child in existence but any child who may come into existence, and during the eight years he is not bound, as I see it, to make any application of the money at all. He would if he were a reasonable man, but he is not bound to. It is quite true that the trust is for the absolute use and benefit of these children, but it is in such shares and in such manner as the Trustee thinks fit. Consequently, he has the eight years in which to make up his mind. He may during that time divide it into shares or give it all to one or other of the objects of the trust, and even if at any time during the eight years there were no object of the trust, he would still, in my view, have to hold the money in case, before the end of the period, an object should come into being.

Consequently, though it may well be, and I think is, the fact that Michael being in existence had got a vested interest in this money, it was an interest which was liable to be divested if another object of the trust came into existence during the eight years. It is not until the end of this time that you could say: The class is closed; the object is achieved; and the money, if there be any unapplied, vests absolutely in any of the persons who were objects of the trust, and whether then dead or then living matters not. . . .

Note
But where a beneficiary *is* absolutely entitled, accumulated income forms part of his total income: *I.R.C.* v. *Hamilton-Russell's Executors* [1943] 1 All E.R. 474; *ante*, p. 340.

I.R.C. v. BLACKWELL

King's Bench Division [1924] 2 K.B. 351; 93 L.J.K.B. 1001; 40 T.L.R. 801; 10 T.C. 235;
affirmed by the Court of Appeal [1926] 1 K.B. 389; 95 L.J.K.B. 465; 134 L.T. 372; 42 T.L.R.
239; 70 S.J. 366; 10 T.C. 245

Income accumulated during the minority of an infant was not his income.
When the accumulations were subsequently paid to him, they came as capital
and he was not assessable to surtax in respect thereof.

ROWLATT J.: . . . In this case the testator by his will disposed of property in
two ways. There was a specific devise of certain real estate, as to which a
question arises whether the eldest son, who is the boy in respect of whose
resources this case arises, took a vested interest or only a contingent interest in
that property. As regards the rest and residue of the testator's property, both
real and personal, there is no doubt that all the children took a vested interest.

The first point which Mr. Latter makes is that it does not matter whether
the interest which the eldest son takes under the will is vested or contingent,
because, even assuming that this specific bequest is vested in the eldest son,
just as the shares in the residue are vested in all the children under the other
part of the will, still, inasmuch as there is a trust to accumulate a fund during
the infancy of the eldest son, subject to a power to the trustees to apply such sum
as they think proper for his maintenance, the part of the income which is
accumulated is not the income of the minor. It is a very important point, but I
have come to the conclusion that he is right. It is perfectly true to say, as Mr.
Harman did, that in a case of that kind the income must come to the infant
in the end if the interest which he takes is a vested interest: but in my judgment it will not come to him as income; it will come to him in the future in the
form of capital. The trustees are directed to accumulate the surplus income,
and they are bound to comply with that direction and to accumulate it. It is
income which is held in trust for him in the sense that he will ultimately
receive it, but it is not in trust for him in the sense that the trustees have to
pay the income to him year by year while he is an infant. All the minor can
get while he is an infant is such amount as the trustees allow for his maintenance. I think that view of the case is supported by what was said in *Inland
Revenue Commissioners* v. *Wemyss*.[11] In my judgment it is fallacious to look
into the future and say: This fund that is being accumulated is for his benefit
and he will get it all. What you have to do is to ask, whether the surplus
income that is accumulated is the annual profits and gains of the year of this
infant now; I do not think it is. I think this case is quite different from a case
where the infant has the right to the money now but where the money remains
in the hands of his trustees not because of any directions in the will which
directed it to be accumulated, but because he is an infant and cannot receive
the money and give a receipt for it, and it therefore remains in the hands of his
trustees, being invested but lying ready for him waiting for the time when the
infant can give a good receipt for it. I think that case is quite different. In
that case the income would be the income of the infant now, although he could
not touch it and could not give a receipt for it. But where the will expressly
provides that the surplus income shall be accumulated and only allows the
trustees to spend what they think proper on the minor's maintenance it seems
to me that it is not the income of the minor yet. . . .

(ii) *Capital or Income*

The preceding case illustrates that that which is income in the hands of the
Trustees may be received as capital by the beneficiary. Equally, payments

11 1924 S.C. 284; 8 T.C. 551.

from the capital fund may be received as income, and assessed as such, in the hands of the beneficiary.[12]

TRUSTEES OF THE WILL OF H. K. BRODIE (DECD.) v. I.R.C.

King's Bench Division (1933) 17 T.C. 432

FINLAY J.: . . . Mr. Brodie was a gentleman who was residing in Italy; he was domiciled there and he' died there in 1920, leaving a widow also domiciled in Italy; he left a will and in that will he bequeathed some shares in a company called Norton Megaw and Company, Limited, and the residue of his estate to trustees, upon trust, to pay the income of the said shares and of three-fourths of the residue of his estate to his widow during her life. It was provided that if, in any year, the amount of the income of the said three-fourths part of the residuary estate and of the said shares in Norton Megaw and Company, Limited, or the investments for the time being representing the proceeds, did not amount to £4,000, then the trustees of the will were directed to raise and pay to the testator's widow out of the capital such a sum as, added to such income, would amount to the total sum of £4,000 for that year. The intention, which was expressed in the will, was that the income payable to his widow during her life should be not less than £4,000 a year. That raises the point, and the main point which arises in the case, and the question is this: it is whether that £4,000 was in truth the income of the widow. The exact facts need not be gone into, but what happened was that, while a substantial income was derived from the shares and the other matters referred to in the will, that was not sufficient to bring the income up to the £4,000 and, accordingly, supplemental sums had to be paid and were, in fact, raised and paid out of capital in order that the income might be made up to £4,000. Now, the point is as to whether income tax is chargeable on that £4,000 and it appears to me to depend, and to depend entirely, upon what is the true nature of the payment which was made. Of course, if certain sums of capital were simply handed over by the trustees to the lady and received by the lady as capital, it is quite clear that income tax would not attach, but it is, to my mind, not less clear that, if the sums paid were paid to the lady and were received by the lady as income, then it is immaterial what they may have been in the hands of the trustees who paid them.

My attention was called to several cases, *Foley* v. *Fletcher* [13]; *Scoble and others* v. *Secretary of State for India* [14]; *Perrin* v. *Dickson*,[15] and *Michelham* v. *The Commissioners of Inland Revenue*.[16] The principle appears to me to be sufficiently clear and the whole difficulty arises, of course, in correctly applying it. When one gets cases like *Foley* v. *Fletcher* and *Scoble and others* v. *Secretary of State for India* and *Perrin's* case, and when one looks at them, it seems that the decision really turns upon this: was this in truth a sum received as income or was it in truth a payment or repayment of part of capital? In some cases the test may be as to whether there was or was not an antecedent debt. One has got, as the Master of the Rolls pointed out in one case, to look at each case. But, I think, the governing consideration is this; the question being, was the sum received as income, one has to consider what was the source from which it was received and what were the circumstances in which it was received. If the

---

[12] For the nature of a legatee's entitlement in respect of an estate, see *I.R.C.* v. *Hawley* [1928] 1 K.B. 578; *Re Morley's Estate* [1937] 1 Ch. 491.
[13] (1858) 3 H. & N. 769.
[14] [1903] A.C. 299; *ante*, p. 119.
[15] [1930] 1 K.B. 107.
[16] (1930) 15 T.C. 737.

capital belonged to the person receiving the sums—if he or she was beneficially entitled not only to the income but to the capital—then I should think that, when the payments were made, they ought to be regarded, and would be regarded, as payments out of capital, but where there is a right to the income, but the capital belongs to somebody else, then, if payments out of capital are made and made in such a form that they come into the hands of the beneficiaries as income, it seems to me that they are income and not the less income, because the source from which they came was—in the hands, not of the person receiving them, but in the hands of somebody else—capital. That is, I think, the principle which may be deduced from the cases, but, in truth, I am, I think, a good deal relieved on this matter by a passage in the decision of Mr. Justice Rowlatt in *Michelham's* case. I have had the advantage of hearing from counsel who were engaged in the case and the position appears, as I understand it, to be this. The point, undoubtedly, was raised in contentions before the Commissioners; I think that the point was, at all events, discussed before Mr. Justice Rowlatt. In the Court of Appeal, as I gather, it was not discussed, but Mr. Justice Rowlatt dealt, as I think, with the very exact point which I have to consider, and what he said was this: " I believe they have in part been paid out of capital, and that raises another question. If a person receives a payment which, so far as the payer is concerned, is paid out of capital, and the receiver receives it as income on his part, of course he has to pay income tax on it. How does the position stand as regards these payments? I myself cannot see any difference. I think it is near enough to what was said by Lord Tomlin in *Lady Miller's* case.[17] He said that where a liability was upon her and the money was paid in discharge of her liability, it was her income," and so forth. It seems to me that there Mr. Justice Rowlatt is laying down a principle which exactly covers the case which is before me. He is there, I think, deciding that, though the payer may pay out of capital which is his capital—he may, of course, hold it for other people, but that is immaterial—but which is not the capital of the beneficiary to whom he is paying it, where he is paying out of capital in that way, but the beneficiary is receiving the sum as income, then it is income and is liable to tax. When one looks at the terms of the will in the present case, they are exceedingly strong; I quite agree that what is said is not necessarily conclusive; one has to look at the reality of the thing, but, after all, there is a certain presumption that the intention will be expressed, and expressed in apt language in the document, and what is said there is this:

> " Provided that if, in any year, the amount of the income of the said three-fourth parts of my residuary estate and of my said shares in Norton Megaw and Company, Limited, or the investments for the time being representing the proceeds of the same, shall, in the aggregate, be less than £4,000, then I direct my trustees to raise and pay to my said wife out of the capital such a sum as will with the amount of such income make the total sum of £4,000 for that year, my intention being that the income payable to my wife during her life shall, in no case, be less than £4,000 a year."

It seems to me to be clear that the words mean, and the substance of the transaction was, that this lady was to have an income of £4,000 a year. If that is right, I think that, both upon principle and upon the authorities, and the whole line of authorities, she is liable to tax on the £4,000 which was her income. . . .

Note
    See also *Peirse-Duncombe's Trustees* v. *I.R.C.* (1940) 23 T.C. 199; *Jackson's Trustees* v. *I.R.C.* (1942) 25 T.C. 13.

[17] [1930] A.C. 222.

CUNARD'S TRUSTEES v. I.R.C.; McPHEETERS v. I.R.C.

Court of Appeal [1946] 1 All E.R. 159; 174 L.T. 133; 27 T.C. 122

LORD GREENE M.R.: . . . That the payments were " income " in Miss McPheeters' hands is, in my opinion, beyond dispute, and the fact that they were made out of capital is irrelevant. The payments were to be made " by way of addition to the income " in order to enable Miss McPheeters to live in the same degree of comfort as before. The testatrix was in fact providing for a defined standard of life for her sister, that provision being made in part out of income and in part (at the discretion of the trustees) out of capital. The purpose was an income purpose and nothing else. . . .

Note
See also *Williamson* v. *Ough* [1936] A.C. 384; *I.R.C.* v. *Castlemaine* (1943) 25 T.C. 408; *Milne's Executors* v. *I.R.C.* (1956) 37 T.C. 10; and *Lindus & Hortin* v. *I.R.C.* (1933) 17 T.C. 442.

In the case of a foreign trust, foreign law may be relevant in determining what is the interest of a beneficiary, but whether that interest is in capital or income is determined according to the law of this country: *Inchyra* v. *Jennings* [1966] Ch. 37; *Lawson* v. *Rolfe* [1970] Ch. 613; *ante*, p. 289.

(iii) *Benefits in Kind*

In some instances, the Trustees may apply trust income for the benefit of a beneficiary, rather than pay the income to the beneficiary in cash. In such a case, the beneficiary is assessable on the value of the benefit received.

LORD TOLLEMACHE v. I.R.C.

King's Bench Division (1926) 11 T.C. 277; 96 L.J.K.B. 766; 136 L.T. 444; 43 T.L.R. 58; [1926] All E.R.Rep. 568

Under the terms of a settlement the Trustees had a discretion to allow the appellant to occupy and enjoy certain property. *Held*, the appellant was assessable to super-tax on the annual value of the mansion occupied by him and on the amount of rates, etc. paid by the Trustees.

ROWLATT J.: In all these cases the question seems to me to be an extremely simple one. So simple does it seem that I am afraid I must have overlooked something. The position, as I understand it, in all these cases, is this: There is a house, and it is assessed under Schedule A, and that is all the income tax that that house bears. When you come to consider a question of rebate, or, in the case of a rich man, the case of super-tax, so that you have to find out what is the total income of the person who is living in the house, then comes the question: Are those annual profits and gains, which are represented by the annual value of the house, his income, so as to swell his total income from all sources, or are they the profits and gains of somebody else, so that they do not come into his total income at all, although he may have the saving to his private purse of having the house put at his disposal? That is all. The question is, who really has the profits? Of whose income are the profits and gains assessed under Schedule A a part? That is all. . . .

Note
See also *Donaldson's Executors* v. *I.R.C.* (1927) 13 T.C. 461; *I.R.C.* v. *Miller* [1930] A.C. 222; *cf. I.R.C.* v. *Wemyss* (1924) 8 T.C. 551. Note, too, how it was possible to distinguish *Tennant* v. *Smith* [1892] A.C. 150; *ante*, p. 255.

2. Income of the Settlor

The manner of taxing the income of trusts and of beneficiaries suggests two main methods of minimising the impact of taxation:

(i) by transferring income from a high-rate taxpayer to one who pays tax at a lower rate;

(ii) by ensuring that the income of the trust belongs to no individual, thereby avoiding surtax; e.g. by accumulating income, on which income tax alone is paid, and subsequently extracting it in the form of capital.[18]

Neither method of tax avoidance is necessarily undesirable (indeed, the voluntary transfer of income from the rich to the less rich may be socially desirable) but, were certain restrictions not imposed upon the use of trusts to reduce tax, avoidance would be both attractive and simple, by:

(i) splitting income among the members of the settlor's own family, for whom he already might be responsible, in particular the children of the settlor,[19] thereby reducing tax liability while retaining the same disposable wealth within the family unit; or

(ii) by disposing of income in other directions, or providing for its accumulation, while still retaining power to enjoy the income by parting with the income for a limited period only, by means of a power to revoke the settlement, by reserving a beneficial interest or by continuing to derive a benefit in some other manner.[20]

To prevent this type of avoidance, the Taxing Acts contain a number of provisions [21] whereby for income tax and/or surtax purposes the income under certain types of settlement is deemed to be the income of the settlor, thus nullifying any potential tax advantage. These provisions are widely drawn and are *not* mutually exclusive, so that a provision in a settlement may fall within the scope of more than one such provision.[22]

It should also be remembered that, in the case of an *ineffective* disposition, there will be a resulting trust in favour of the disponer, so that the income under the disposition will be his in any event.[23]

(i) Meaning of " Settlement " and " Settlor "

Part XVI of the Income and Corporation Taxes Act 1970, is headed " Settlements," but refers to both " dispositions " and " settlements," which are

---

[18] I.R.C. v. *Blackwell* [1924] 2 K.B. 351; *ante*, p. 376.

[19] There would be no point in transferring income to the settlor's wife, as husband and wife are assessed together: Chap. 14, *ante*.

[20] For a consideration of the principal methods of tax planning by means of settlements, see Potter and Monroe's *Tax Planning*, 6th ed., Chaps. 1, 3, 4, in which Estate Duty, Capital Gains Tax and Stamp Duty aspects are also dealt with.

[21] I.C.T.A. 1970, ss. 434–459.   [22] *Gillies* v. *I.R.C.* (1928) 14 T.C. 329.

[23] *Aked* v. *Shaw* (1947) 28 T.C. 286; *I.R.C.* v. *Allan* (1925) 9 T.C. 234; *Innes* v. *Harrison* [1954] 1 W.L.R. 668; *I.R.C.* v. *Broadway Cottages Trust* [1955] Ch. 20; *cf.* *McPhail* v. *Doulton* [1971] A.C. 424; *Re Baden's Deed Trusts (No. 2)* [1971] 3 W.L.R. 475. As to the partial failure of a trust, see *Vandervell* v. *I.R.C.* [1967] 2 A.C. 291; *post*, p. 394. These cases should be compared with those where, subsequent to an effective disposition, the disponer receives back the income in some other capacity: *Lee* v. *I.R.C.* (1943) 25 T.C. 485; *Russell* v. *I.R.C.* (1944) 26 T.C. 242; *cf.* *Waley Cohen* v. *I.R.C.* (1945) 26 T.C. 471.

defined widely [24] (as are the words " disponer " and " settlor ") in particular to include " arrangements."

THOMAS v. MARSHALL

House of Lords [1953] A.C. 543; [1953] 2 W.L.R. 944; 97 S.J. 316; [1953] 1 All E.R. 1102; 34 T.C. 199

LORD MORTON OF HENRYTON: . . . My Lords, the question which arises on this appeal is whether interest upon two Post Office Savings Bank accounts, one in the name of the appellant's son Michael, and the other in the name of the appellant's daughter Heather, and interest upon two holdings of £1,000 3 per cent. Defence Bonds in the names of Michael and Heather respectively, ought to be treated, for all the purposes of the Income Tax Acts, as the income of the appellant.

The relevant facts are fully set out in the case stated and may be summarised as follows:—On December 20, 1933, a Post Office Savings Bank account was opened by or on behalf of the appellant in the name of Michael (born September 8, 1933) with a deposit of £50, and on May 28, 1936, another Post Office Savings Bank account was opened by or on behalf of the appellant in the name of Heather (born February 1, 1936) with a deposit of £50. Thereafter the appellant paid further sums into the same bank for each of his children. Various sums were drawn from the accounts from time to time and were expended for the children's benefit. On December 31, 1948, Michael's account was in credit £844 9s. 0d. and Heather's account was in credit £844 8s. 3d. In the year 1945 the appellant bought £1,000 3 per cent. Defence Bonds for each of the two children. All the sums paid into the children's bank accounts, and the said Defence Bonds, were absolute and unconditional gifts made by the appellant to his children.

The Inspector of Taxes treated the interest upon the two Savings Bank accounts, exclusive of interest upon interest, and the interest upon the two holdings of Defence Bonds as being income of the settlor for the purposes of the Income Tax Acts. This he did in reliance upon the terms of section 21 of the Finance Act 1936.[25] That section provides as follows:

" (1) Where, by virtue or in consequence of any settlement to which this section applies and during the life of the settlor, any income is paid to or for the benefit of a child of the settlor in any year of assessment, the income shall, if at the commencement of that year the child was an infant and unmarried, be treated for all the purposes of the Income Tax Acts as the income of the settlor for that year and not as the income of any other person. . . . (9) In this section— . . . (b) the expression ' settlement ' includes any disposition, trust, covenant, agreement, arrangement or transfer of assets; (c) the expression ' settlor,' in relation to a settlement, includes any person by whom the settlement was made or entered into directly or indirectly. . . ." [26]

. . . Counsel for the appellant does not seek to draw any distinction between the interest on the bank account in Michael's name and the interest on the Defence Bonds bought in Michael's name, and it is common ground that if the gifts of money and Defence Bonds were " settlements " within the meaning of section 21 of the Finance Act 1936, the appellant was the settlor. It is also

---

[24] I.C.T.A. 1970, ss. 434 (2), 444 (2), 454 (3), 459.
[25] Now I.C.T.A. 1970, s. 437.
[26] See now I.C.T.A. 1970, s. 444 (2).

common ground that income was paid to Michael by virtue or in consequence of these gifts. Thus the only point for determination is—Were the absolute gifts in question " settlements " within the meaning of section 21 of the Finance Act 1936? This question has been answered in the affirmative successively by the Commissioners, by Donovan J. and by the Court of Appeal.

My Lords, I too would answer this question in the affirmative. It is true that an absolute gift of money or of an investment would not ordinarily be described as a " settlement," but it is expressly enacted that in section 21 the expression " settlement " includes, *inter alia*, " Any . . . transfer of assets." For my part, I see no escape from the conclusion that the appellant made a transfer of assets, in the ordinary meaning of that phrase, when he used his own money to make a payment into Michael's bank account and to purchase Defence Bonds in Michael's name. . . .

Note

　　Other examples of the extended meaning of " settlement," referred to elsewhere in the judgment, may be found in *Hood-Barrs* v. *I.R.C.* (1946) 27 T.C. 385 and in *Yates* v. *Starkey* [1951] Ch. 465; *ante*, p. 349. See also *I.R.C.* v. *Buchanan* [1958] 1 Ch. 289, where the surrender of a life interest under an existing settlement was itself held to be a " disposition " for these purposes.

CROSSLAND v. HAWKINS

Court of Appeal [1961] Ch. 537; [1961] 3 W.L.R. 202; 105 S.J. 424; [1961] 2 All E.R. 812;
39 T.C. 493

　　The respondent, a well-known film actor, claimed repayment of income tax on behalf of his three infant children by setting their personal and small incomes allowances against income paid for their benefit by Trustees under a settlement effected by the children's grandfather. The income of the settlement was derived from dividends paid to the Trustees in respect of shares held by them in a company which had been formed to employ and exploit the services of the respondent. The company received fees for the respondent's services, out of which he was paid a salary, the balance of the fees being available for payment of dividends to the trust. *Held*, there was an " arrangement " under which the respondent was the " settlor," as he indirectly provided the funds of the trust.

　　DONOVAN L.J.: . . . That prospect of dividend did not, however, mature for some time, during which the trustees got nothing on their shares, but at some time during the year 1956, the company received £25,000 for the lending or assigning of Hawkins' services to somebody, to act in a film called " Fortune is a Woman." Then, on October 18, 1956, the company declared a dividend of £500 free of tax which went to the trustees of the settlement. They, in turn, applied the bulk of this for the benefit of the taxpayer's three infant children as follows: Nicholas, £225; Andrew, £153; Caroline, £104.

　　In due course, repayment claims were submitted to the Inland Revenue by the taxpayer as the children's guardian, claiming back tax deducted at source from this dividend, to the extent that the children were entitled to small income relief and personal allowances. The inspector of taxes opposed the claim. The general commissioners on appeal by the taxpayer allowed it; and their decision has been upheld by the judge.

　　The Crown says that the income so received or enjoyed by the children under the deed of settlement is deemed to be the taxpayer's income by virtue of section

397 of the Income Tax Act 1952.[27] This reproduces section 21 of the Finance Act 1936, by which the growing habit of saving surtax by settling capital or income on one's children was checked. Subsections (1) and (2) of section 397 are as follows: [His Lordship read section 397 (1) and (2) and the relevant parts of section 403,[28] the definition section, and continued:] The true construction of the word "arrangement" in that definition is not in dispute. It will be found in the cases cited to us, which I will mention, but need not in the circumstances read. They are: *Copeman* v. *Coleman*[29]; *Inland Revenue Commissioners* v. *Prince-Smith*[30]; *Inland Revenue Commissioners* v. *Payne*[31]; and *Hood-Barrs* v. *Inland Revenue Commissioners*.[32] The argument for the Crown is first of all this: Here there is a settlement in the ordinary sense of the word, namely, the deed of settlement of March 3, 1955. Hawkins did provide money for the purpose of that settlement, the means of such provision being the service agreement producing money for the company, and the company in turn distributing part of the money to the trustees. Alternatively it is said that the formation of a company, the service agreement and the deed of settlement together form an arrangement within the terms of section 403, and so are a settlement for the purposes of section 397. For that settlement, likewise, Hawkins provided funds and is therefore a settlor.

It will be convenient to deal with this alternative argument, first, because it was the only argument advanced to the general commissioners, and, secondly, because Mr. Borneman agrees that if there is such an arrangement here, then the taxpayer was a settlor within the definition, and must fail in this appeal.

What he argues in opposition to the Crown's argument is this: To constitute an "arrangement" for this purpose, the whole of it must be in contemplation at the outset. Here it was not, and he prays in aid what the commissioners say in paragraph 7 of the case stated, after hearing all the evidence, namely—again I quote—that "there was no arrangement to which section 397 should apply." Therefore Hawkins did not provide funds for any such "arrangement," for when he agreed to sell his services to the company, the deed of settlement was not in being, nor, so far as the evidence goes—says Mr. Borneman—in contemplation.

After careful consideration, I am unable to accept these propositions. In the first place, I do not think that the language of section 397 requires that the whole of the eventual arrangement must be in contemplation from the very outset. Confining oneself for the moment to the facts of this case, and remembering that income tax is an annual tax, one finds the whole "arrangement" conceived and in being in the one income tax year, 1954–55. The company is formed, the service agreement executed, and the deed of settlement made, all in this one year. But even were it otherwise, I think there is sufficient unity about the whole matter to justify it being called an arrangement for this purpose, because, as I have said, the ultimate object is to secure for somebody money free from what would otherwise be the burden or the full burden of surtax. Merely because the final step to secure this objective is left unresolved at the outset, and decided on later, does not seem to me to rob the scheme of the necessary unity to justify it being called an "arrangement."

. . . An alternative way of looking at the matter would be this: Here the repayment claim is made in the year 1956–57. In that year the arrangement is complete, and that is enough. It would be irrelevant that it came into being by instalments in the year 1954–55.

. . . That is strictly enough to conclude the present case, for it is conceded that if there be an arrangement within the meaning of section 397, then Hawkins

---

[27] Now I.C.T.A. 1970, s. 437.   [28] Now I.C.T.A. 1970, s. 444.
[29] [1939] 2 K.B. 484.   [30] [1943] 1 All E.R. 434.
[31] (1940) 23 T.C. 610.   [32] (1946) 27 T.C. 385.

did indirectly provide funds for the purpose of the settlement constituted by such arrangement, and that accordingly the dividend must be regarded as his income and not that of his children. . . .

I.R.C. v. LEINER

Chancery Division (1964) 41 T.C. 589; [1964] T.R. 63; 43 A.T.C. 56

A company, Treforest, owed money to a Mrs. Leiner. By a series of trans-actions, the loan was repaid by the company, an equivalent sum was settled by Mrs. Leiner upon trusts under which the children of her son could take a benefit, the money was loaned by the Trustees to the son, at a proper rate of interest, who then loaned it to the company interest free. *Held*, the funds had in effect been provided under the "arrangement" by the son and he was the "settlor."

PLOWMAN J.: . . . In order to consider the validity of that argument it is, I think, instructive to compare the positions of Treforest and the respondent before the arrangement was entered into with their respective positions after it. Before the arrangement, Treforest owed Mrs. Leiner £34,000 and was paying no interest on it. After the arrangement it still owed £34,000 free of interest, though it owed the money to the respondent instead of to Mrs. Leiner. Its position financially was, therefore, exactly the same, and it is difficult to see how it can be said that it was the recipient of any bounty. As regards the respondent, before the arrangement he was neither a debtor nor a creditor; whereas after the arrangement he was a debtor to the trustees for £34,000 and a creditor of Treforest for a similar sum. In addition to that, he was liable to pay the trustees £2,040 a year. He was worse off to the extent of that £2,040 as a result of the arrangement. In my judgment one cannot dissociate the loan from the respondent to Treforest free of interest from the transactions which preceded it (compare *Commissioners of Inland Revenue* v. *Pay* [33]). The arrange-ment in my view must be looked at as a whole, and looked at in this way, I find it impossible to say that the respondent did not provide the trustees with an income of £2,040 a year in the sense in which the word "provided" is used in section 401 [34] of the Act; that is to say, as importing an element of bounty. The transaction, taken as a whole, was not, in my judgment, one which, from the point of view of the respondent, can be described as a commercial arrange-ment, because he was liable to pay £2,040 per annum without any compensating advantage to him. Since that sum has been applied for the benefit of a child of the respondent, in my judgment section 397 [35] applies and this appeal succeeds.

Note
    Cf. *Chamberlain* v. *I.R.C.* (1943) 25 T.C. 317; *Bulmer* v. *I.R.C.* [1967] Ch. 145. As to "arrangements" involving more than one disponer in the case of income settlements (*i.e.* covenants), see *I.R.C.* v. *Clarkson-Webb* [1933] 1 K.B. 507.

(ii) *Dispositions for Short Periods*

Where under a disposition income is payable to or applicable for the benefit of a person for a period which cannot exceed six years, such income is

[33] (1955) 36 T.C. 109.
[34] Now I.C.T.A. 1970, s. 441.
[35] Now I.C.T.A. 1970, s. 437.

deemed for all tax purposes to be that of the disponer, if living.[36] The product of this provision has been the familiar "seven-year covenant," [37] though the provision may apply to capital settlements as well as to income settlements.

I.R.C. v. TRUSTEES OF THE HOSTEL OF ST. LUKE, REGISTERED

Court of Appeal (1930) 15 T.C. 682; 144 L.T. 50; 46 T.L.R. 580

A covenant was made to pay yearly sums to Trustees during the term of seven years from April 6, 1926, the first annual payment to be made on December 31, 1926, and subsequent payments to be made on December 31 in each year. The covenant was dated February 3, 1927, and the first payment was made on the following day. *Held*, the income was payable for a period which could not exceed six years.

ROMER L.J.: I agree. With all respect to the learned Judge, I cannot find any justification in the section for giving the word "years" the meaning of income tax years. Giving to the words of the section their ordinary meaning as, in the absence of any context to the contrary we are bound to do, it seems to me that the period referred to is the actual period for which the income is payable under the disposition in question. That, of course, at once gives rise to the question as to whether the period is the period in respect of which the income is payable, or the period during which the payments of income have to be made under the disposition. To give an example, which was, I think, mentioned by Mr. Hills in the course of his argument, supposing a man covenants to pay an annual sum to a charity for the next twelve years and provides that the money shall be paid by twelve monthly instalments during the ensuing year from the date of the covenant, what is the period for which the income is payable? Is it the twelve years from the date of the disposition, or is it one year from the date of the disposition? In my opinion, it is in the case I have mentioned the latter period; the period for which, in the instance I have given, the income is payable is, in my opinion, one year from the date of the disposition. Applying that to the covenant in the present case, it will be observed that there are two periods mentioned in the document; the first period is one that begins on April 6, 1926, and ends seven years thereafter, if the covenantor shall so long live or, if he dies during that period, then until the date of his death. The other period is a period beginning on February 3, 1927, when the first payment would have to be made under the deed, and ending on December 31, 1932. The first period is a period which, as I read the document, really is mentioned for the purpose of fixing the liability of the covenantor, and the second period is the period over which, during which, that liability is being discharged. . . .

---

[36] I.C.T.A. 1970, s. 434. N.B. the position where the disponer is not resident in the United Kingdom: *Becker* v. *Wright* [1966] 1 W.L.R. 215; *ante*, p. 82; see also *Ormonde (Marchioness)* v. *Brown* (1932) 17 T.C. 333; *Astor* v. *Perry* [1935] A.C. 398; *ante*, p. 15.

[37] For the operation of income covenants, see the Final Report of the Royal Commission on the Taxation of Profits and Income, 1955 Cmd. 9474, paras. 144–150; *ante*, pp. 121–122; *Campbell* v. *I.R.C.* [1967] Ch. 651; *ante*, p. 123. For a tax saving to be effected it is necessary that the disponer be entitled to deduct the payments under the covenant from his total income as a charge on income; this he may do only if the payments are of an *income* nature: *I.R.C.* v. *Mallaby-Deeley* [1938] 4 All E.R. 818; *ante*, pp. 76, 118; *I.R.C.* v. *Ramsay* (1935) 20 T.C. 79; *cf.* *Vestey* v. *I.R.C.* [1962] Ch. 861, and the payments are "pure income profit" in the hands of the recipient: *I.R.C.* v. *National Book League* [1957] Ch. 488; *ante*, p. 114; *Campbell* v. *I.R.C.* In the case of settlements made on or after April 7, 1965, annual payments are not deductible for surtax purposes, unless made for certain specified purposes: I.C.T.A. 1970, s. 457.

Note
Cf. *I.R.C.* v. *Verdon-Roe* (1962) 40 T.C. 541 and *I.R.C.* v. *Hobhouse* [1956] 1 W.L.R. 1393.
As to the extension of an existing covenant, see *Taylor* v. *I.R.C.* (1946) 27 T.C. 93 and *I.R.C.* v. *Nicolson* [1953] 1 W.L.R. 809.

I.R.C. v. BLACK

King's Bench Division [1940] 4 All E.R. 445; 84 S.J. 597; 23 T.C. 715 (affirmed by the Court of Appeal, *ibid*. pp. 447, 720)

The respondents covenanted to pay annual sums to a company, payable for a seven year period or until a total amount of £100,000 had been paid. This amount was paid in a little over one year. *Held*, the respondents were entitled to deduct the amounts paid in computing their total income.

LAWRENCE J.: The question in these cases is whether the respondents are entitled to deduct for the purposes of surtax the sums paid by them to the Langford Property Co., Ltd., in the year ending April 5, 1937, under a deed dated December 16, 1936. The question arises upon the construction of the Finance Act 1922, s. 20 (1) (*b*).[38]
It was contended on behalf of the Crown that the sums paid could not be deducted because, when the appeal was heard in 1939, the respondents had paid the whole sum which they had covenanted to pay, and it was said, therefore, that the income was by virtue of a disposition payable for a period which could not exceed six years, since, in fact, it had been paid in two years.
In my opinion, this argument is unsound. The section does not say a period which in the events that happen does not exceed six years, but which by virtue of the disposition cannot exceed six years. It is obvious that sums of money might have to be paid by virtue of the deed in question during a period which exceeded six years, and, if the appeal had happened to be heard earlier, it would have been impossible to foretell whether payments were going to be payable for a period of over six years or not. In the next place, it was contended that, even if some sum may be deducted, that sum cannot exceed one-seventh of the £100,000, which was the maximum amount which the respondents might be called upon to pay, because in accordance with the decision in *Inland Revenue Commissioners* v. *Mallaby-Deeley*,[39] followed by *D'Ambrumenil* v. *Inland Revenue Commissioners*,[40] no higher amount than one-seventh could be deducted in any one year without lowering the figure paid in one of the other seven years below that figure, and then, so it was said, upon the authority of the above-cited cases, the income to be deducted must be the lowest amount paid in any year. In my opinion, this result does not follow from the cases cited, for in them the income paid by virtue of the disposition was a sum fixed by the disposition, whereas, in the present case, the disposition only fixes the formula upon which the payment is to be ascertained. In accordance with that formula, which can continue for more than six years, varying sums may be payable by virtue of the disposition, and these sums may, therefore, in my opinion, be deducted. . . .

(iii) *Revocability*

Income under a revocable settlement is deemed to be the income of the settlor for all purposes of the Income Tax Acts, where:

[38] See now I.C.T.A. 1970, s. 434.
[39] [1938] 3 All E.R. 463; *ante*, pp. 76, 118.
[40] [1940] 1 K.B. 850.

(a) being an income settlement, the settlor will cease to be liable to make annual payments on revocation (or on payment of a penalty), except where the power of revocation cannot be exercised within a period of six years from the time of the first such annual payment becoming payable [41]; and

(b) in the case of a capital settlement, where on revocation the settlor will or may become entitled to property or income under the settlement.[42]

References to the settlor include the settlor's spouse. The question of revocability has also to be considered in relation to accumulation settlements for the benefit of the settlor's child or children.[43]

JENKINS v. I.R.C.

Court of Appeal [1944] 2 All E.R. 491; 171 L.T. 355; 26 T.C. 265

On the meaning of " irrevocable."

LORD GREENE M.R.: . . . Now I turn to the case so far as it is affected by the Act of 1936. The Crown's appeal is based on the proposition that the settlement in this case was not, on April 22, 1936, an irrevocable settlement although in terms it is expressed so to be. Quite apart from the artificial and extended meaning of the word " irrevocable " which is to be found in subsection (8) of section 21 of the Act of 1936, it is argued, in the first place, that the settlement was not irrevocable in the ordinary sense of that word; and, putting it quite shortly, that argument was based on the proposition that the settlor could at any moment, if he so desired, destroy the whole of this edifice and get back into his own pocket whatever money there was lying about in the ruins, and it was said that the fact that he had power to do that made the settlement a revocable settlement. In my opinion that is placing much too wide a construction on the word " irrevocable " in subsection (10), taking it in its ordinary sense. The distinction between a revocable and an irrevocable settlement is the veriest A.B.C. in legal language; and nobody familiar with the language of lawyers, and in particular of those concerned with settlements, could have the slightest doubt, I should have thought, when finding the word " irrevocable " used in relation to a settlement, what that word was intended to mean. It seems to me quite illegitimate to take a word which has a technical and precise meaning in conveyancing and then to argue that it has some extended meaning. If the Legislature wished to give to the word " irrevocable " some unusual and extended meaning of this sort, I ask myself why in the world did it not do so. The Legislature is the master of the draftsmanship of these Acts, and if it intends to use a word which is to have the widest possible scope it is little short of carelessness or incompetence in drafting to select for that purpose a perfectly familiar word which to everyone has a quite limited scope. I cannot bring myself to give to the word " irrevocable " in subsection (10) the meaning which the Crown wishes to place upon it. . . .

Note
   Cf. I.R.C. v. *Jamieson* [1964] A.C. 1445; *I.R.C.* v. *Glenconner (Lord)* [1941] 2 K.B. 339.

[41] I.C.T.A. 1970, s. 445.
[42] *Ibid.* s. 446.
[43] *Ibid.* ss. 438 (2), 439.

I.R.C. v. WOLFSON

House of Lords (*ante*, p. 7)

LORD SIMONDS: . . . The respondent, Isaac Wolfson, was at all material times the holder of 700 ordinary shares of £1 each in a company called Leonard Gordon Estates, Ltd. which had been used by him and his brothers as a private investment holding company. The capital of the company was £1,000 and the remaining 300 shares were held as to 100 by his brother Charles Wolfson, as to 100 by his brother Samuel William Wolfson and as to the remaining 100 by the trustees (of whom the respondent was one) of a settlement known as Solomon Wolfson's settlement. Being minded to make provision for his sisters, on March 26, 1940, the respondent entered into a deed of covenant of that date to which he and his brothers, who were therein called "the settlors," were parties of the one part, and one Henry Arthur Chetham and the respondent as trustees, were parties of the other part. By this deed each settlor irrevocably covenanted with the trustees that he would, on April 1 in each year, during the period of seven years from April 1, 1940, or until his death (whichever period should be the shorter), pay to the trustees an annual sum calculated according to the provisions contained in clause 2 thereof, such annual sum to be held by the trustees on the trusts and subject to the powers therein declared and contained. The method of calculation was as follows:

> "Each annual sum hereinbefore covenanted to be paid by each settlor shall subject to the proviso hereinafter in this clause contained, be such an annual sum as after deduction of tax at the standard rate for the time being in force leaves a sum equal in amount to the net amount in the aggregate of all dividends received by him during the previous 12 months expiring on the said April 1 in each year upon the ordinary shares of Leonard Gordon Estates, Ltd. held by him as set out in Schedule 1 hereto."

There followed a proviso dealing with the event of the settlor selling or otherwise disposing for value of his shares but not with the event of his disposing of them gratuitously, and a further clause provided for the reinvestment of the proceeds of sale or disposal for value of such shares. The deed also contained trusts for the benefit of the settlors' sisters, who are therein described as the beneficiaries, or their children or next of kin.

Your Lordships will not be troubled with any details of figures in this case. It is sufficient to say that it is conceded for the purposes of this appeal that a net sum of £14,612 10s. 0d. was received by the trustees in discharge of the respondent's liability under the deed for the year ending April 5, 1940. The claim of the respondent was limited to the deduction from his income for Income Tax purposes of the gross sum representing this sum of £14,612 10s. 0d. and there is no question but that he is entitled to deduct such a sum unless the provisions of section 38 (1) (*a*) of the Finance Act 1938, are operative in regard to it. The Special Commissioners, conceiving that they were bound by the decision of Macnaghten, J., in *MacAndrew's* case,[44] held that the deduction was not permissible. But their decision was reversed by Atkinson, J., whose judgment was upheld by the Court of Appeal (Tucker and Somervell, L.JJ., Cohen, L.J., *dissentiente*).

Section 38 of the Finance Act 1938 is, so far as material, as follows [45]:—
. . . It is contended on behalf of the Crown that the sums received by the respondent during the relevant year of assessment and accounted for to the

---

[44] (1943) 25 T.C. 500.
[45] Lord Simonds then quoted the material parts of F.A. 1938, s. 38, now I.C.T.A. 1970, s. 445.

trustees of the deed must be treated as his income under section 38 (1) (a), because the terms of the deed were such that he (either by himself or with others or with the consent of others) had power to revoke or otherwise determine the settlement or a provision thereof and thereby would or might cease to be liable to make the annual payment payable under the deed. It is common ground that the " settlement " consists of the deed of March 26, 1940, alone. It is therefore the terms of that deed alone that have to be considered. In support of their contention it was said by learned counsel for the Crown that the settlor as the holder of seven-tenths of the shares of Leonard Gordon Estates, Ltd. (which I will call " the company ") was in a position to determine how much of the profits of the company should be distributed in any year by way of dividend. He might, if he thought fit, by the exercise of his majority vote prevent any dividend being declared during the whole period for which his covenant was operative. Thus, it was said, he could determine the settlement or a provision thereof. It was further urged that, as the holder of seven-tenths of the shares, he could, by procuring the co-operation or indeed the abstention of another shareholder holding a sufficient number of votes, secure the passing of a special resolution for winding-up the company. This too, it was said, was a power to determine the settlement or a provision thereof.

My Lords, the main part of the argument has revolved round the simple words: " If and so long as the terms of any settlement are such that." On the one hand, it is said that it is only in the terms of this settlement that one may look for the power which the subsection describes—that the words bear the same meaning as the words: " If and so long as the terms of the settlement provide." On the other hand, it is said that they have a meaning, which, to do justice to the argument of the learned Solicitor-General, I will state in his own words. This was his formula:

> " If the settlement is so framed that its immediate impact on the circumstances in relation to which it was executed produces the result that some persons, whether settlors or others, get the power, whether by the exercise of some independent right they already possess or however else, to revoke and thus finally cancel or otherwise bring to an end the continued happening of something for which the settlement provides."

My Lords, between these alternatives I must unhesitatingly adopt the former. I am not greatly influenced by the absurd results which flow from an adoption of the latter, though it would appear to cover every covenant that ever was entered into, since in this view the covenantee has power, by releasing the covenantor from his liability, to put an end to the settlement. I am chiefly influenced by the consideration that, if it had been intended that regard should be had to powers not to be found in the settlement and exercisable by persons not parties to or named in the settlement, nothing could have been easier than to say so. I agree with both Tucker and Somervell L.JJ., and Atkinson J., in thinking that the language of subsections (3) and (4) provide a valuable contrast to that employed in subsection (1). It was urged that the construction that I favour leaves an easy loophole through which the evasive taxpayer may find escape. That may be so, but I will repeat what has been said before. It is not the function of a court of law to give to words a strained and unnatural meaning because only thus will a taxing section apply to a transaction which, had the legislature thought of it, would have been covered by appropriate words. It is the duty of the court to give to the words of this subsection their reasonable meaning, and I must decline on any ground of policy to give to them a meaning which, with all respect to the dissentient Lord Justice, I regard as little short of extravagant. It cannot even be urged that, unless this meaning is given to the

subsection, it can have no operation. On the contrary, given its natural meaning it will bring within the area of taxation a number of cases in which by a
familiar device tax had formerly been avoided.

As I have already noted, in this case the " settlement " consists of the deed
of covenant alone. It is, therefore, unnecessary to consider the cases in which,
the settlement being held to consist of a number of documents and transactions,
it was found that the power to revoke or determine was among the terms of
the settlement. The question whether the court may look outside the terms of
the settlement did not arise. Of such cases *Inland Revenue Commissioners* v.
Payne,[46] is an example. I would expressly reserve the question how far such
decisions can be regarded as correct after the decision of this House in
Chamberlain v. *Inland Revenue Commissioners*.[47] Nor do I think it necessary
in this case to determine whether, if it could be regarded as a " term of the
settlement " that the settlor had power to dictate whether any and what
dividend should be declared, that would amount to a power to determine the
settlement, nor yet whether, if it is such a term that the settlor can with the
consent or co-operation of other shareholders wind-up the company, that would
be such a power. These are questions which may have to be determined in
other cases in which they are decisive. For the purposes of this appeal it is
sufficient to say, affirming the judgment of the Court of Appeal, that the terms
of the deed of March 26, 1940, are not such that the respondent has power to
revoke or otherwise determine the settlement or any provision thereof. I move,
accordingly, that the appeal be dismissed with costs.

Note
See also *Kenmare (Countess)* v. *I.R.C.* [1958] A.C. 267.

(iv) *Retention of an Interest*

If and so long as the settlor, or his spouse, has an interest in any income
arising under or property comprised in a settlement, any income so arising
during the life of the settlor, is, *to the extent to which it is not distributed*,
treated for all the purposes of the Income Tax Acts as the income of the
settlor.[48] The settlor is deemed to have an interest if any income or property under the settlement at any time is, or will or may become payable
to or applicable for the benefit of the settlor or his spouse in any circumstances whatsoever, apart from certain specified circumstances.

Further, in the case of income settlements made before April 7, 1965,
but on or after April 10, 1946, the income is to be treated as income of the
settlor for *surtax* purposes except in certain specified circumstances, one
of which exceptions is where the income is income from property of which
the settlor has divested himself absolutely by the settlement.[49] A settlor is
not deemed to have divested himself absolutely of any property if that
property or any income therefrom is, or will or may become, payable to
him or applicable for his benefit in any circumstances whatsoever, with
specified exceptions.[50]

---

[46] (1940) 23 T.C. 610. In *I.R.C.* v. *Payne*, the covenant was to pay for life, or until an
effective resolution for the winding-up of a company controlled by the settlor was passed.
This was held to amount to a power to revoke or otherwise determine the settlement.
Cf. I.R.C. v. *Rainsford Hannay* (1941) 24 T.C. 273.
[47] (1943) 25 T.C. 317.
[48] I.C.T.A. 1970, s. 447.
[49] *Ibid.* s. 458 (1).
[50] *Ibid.* s. 458 (2).

LORD VESTEY'S EXECUTORS v. I.R.C.

House of Lords (*ante*, p. 33)

Under the terms of a settlement premises owned by the settlor in France were leased to a company, the rent being payable to Trustees resident in France, to hold upon trust for such of the settlor's children as they should appoint, a power being reserved to the settlor to appoint an interest in the fund by will in favour of his widow. The settlor had a power to determine the lease, and power to direct investments.

LORD MORTON OF HENRYTON: . . . The claims of the Crown in the present case depend to a large extent upon three matters: (1) The power of the " authorised persons " to direct the investment by the Paris trustees of the sums received by them from Union [51]; (2) the contention of the Crown that all the properties comprised in the lease are " comprised in the settlement " within section 38 (2) (*b*) of the Act of 1938 [52]; (3) the power of appointment in favour of a widow contained in clause 11 of the deed of trust. For this reason, before considering in detail the relevant sections already quoted and their application to the income received by the Paris trustees, it is desirable to consider three questions of construction: (*a*) Is the right or power of the " authorised persons " under the trust deed to direct how the rent payable by Union shall be invested by the Paris trustees a power of the kind conveniently described as a fiduciary power, which must be exercised in the best interests of the beneficiaries under the trust deed, or is it a right or power which the authorised persons are entitled to exercise, if they so think fit, in any way which best serves their own interests? (*b*) Is the " settlement " which falls to be considered under section 38 (2) of the Act of 1938 the trust deed alone, or the trust deed together with the lease, and what is the " property comprised in the settlement " within the meaning of the same subsection? (*c*) Does the existence of the power of appointment in favour of the widow of Lord Vestey and Sir Edmund respectively have the effect of bringing any income within the ambit of either of the two sections in question? When these three questions have been answered, your Lordships will have gone a long way towards a solution of the numerous questions argued on these appeals.

. . . The result is that, in my view, on the true construction of the trust deed, the power of direction is a fiduciary power, and the authorised persons are not entitled to use it for the purpose of obtaining a benefit for themselves. They must exercise it bona fide in what they consider to be the best interests of the beneficiaries. This is not, to my mind, a case of latent ambiguity. I think that the Vesteys could have directed the trustees to lend trust moneys to Western, or even to themselves, but such a direction could only be justifiable if the loan were made at a commercial rate of interest and if the Vesteys honestly thought that it was in the best interests of the beneficiaries. If the trustees were to advance moneys to any company or to either of the Vesteys free of interest, they would commit a breach of trust, but there is no finding in any of the cases stated that this was ever done.

. . . It is contended on behalf of the Crown that as Union, on the one hand, and the Vesteys, on the other hand, had power to determine the lease, each of these parties had power to revoke or otherwise determine the settlement or a " provision " thereof, within section 38 (2) (*a*). Clearly they had no power to determine the settlement itself, for even if the lease was determined, the trusts

---

[51] The tenant company.
[52] See now I.C.T.A. 1970, s. 446. On this point *Chamberlain* v. *I.R.C.* (1943) 25 T.C. 317 was followed.

declared by the deed of trust concerning rents already accrued would continue undisturbed; and I gravely doubt whether the lease can be regarded as a " provision of the settlement." However, it is unnecessary to resolve this doubt, for even if the Crown can bring this case within sub-clause (*a*) of subsection (2) of section 38, it clearly does not come within sub-clause (*b*). Once it is ascertained that only the rent and property derived therefrom is " comprised in the settlement," it becomes clear that if the lease is determined neither Lord Vestey nor Sir Edmund nor the wife of either of them " will or may become beneficially entitled to the whole or any part of the property then comprised in the settlement " or of the income arising therefrom. The determination of the lease would make no difference at all to the position of any of these persons in regard to the property comprised in the settlement or the income thereof; it would merely have the effect that no further rent would reach the hands of the Paris trustees.

Question (*c*) should, in my opinion, be answered in the negative. . . . Could it be said, in any of the years of assessment, that any income comprised in the settlement might become payable to the wife (for instance) of William within the meaning of section 38 (4)? In my view, it could not. To my mind, if a payment is to come within the subsection it must be made to a lady who answers the description of a wife at the time of payment. No such payment could ever be made, because no payment could be made until after the death of William; the income then becomes payable, not to his wife, but to his widow. I do not propose to travel all through the language of section 38 of the Act of 1938 or of section 18 of the Act of 1936. I can find no passage in either section which is inconsistent with the view which I hold. Further, I think that the intention of each reference to a wife of the settlor is reasonably clear. It was thus stated by Lawrence J. (as he then was) in *Gaunt's* case [53] :

> " On the second point I am of opinion that the object of the section is to prevent the settlor from getting the benefit of the trust fund during his lifetime. It is not to prevent his wife enjoying the trust fund after his death, and I do not think the word ' wife ' is apt to describe the settlor's widow. The income must be capable of being paid to, or for the benefit of, the wife, which, in my opinion, means while she is his wife."

My Lords, I entirely agree with this passage. I think that the treatment of husband and wife by the legislature, for income tax purposes, rests on the view that any income enjoyed by one spouse is a benefit to the other spouse. It is not surprising, therefore, that in the sections now under consideration a benefit to the wife of the settlor is treated as being a benefit to the settlor; but it seems to me unlikely that this principle is being extended by these sections to the widow of the settlor. Further, if, for instance, section 38 (4) of the Act of 1938 is to be read as applying to the widow of the settlor, there would seem to be no reason why it should not have been extended to the children of the settlor. If it be said that the provision of a benefit for the widow of the settlor benefits the settlor himself, because he would naturally desire to make provision for his widow, exactly the same reasoning could be applied to the provision of a benefit for the settlor's children. Finally, although I do not myself think that there is a real ambiguity in the use of the word " wife " throughout these sections, if there is such an ambiguity it must be resolved in favour of the subject, according to principles which have been laid down many times. . . .

Note
   The case is, of course, authority also on the questions of revocability, and the meaning of " settlement," discussed above.

[53] [1941] 1 K.B. 706.

BOARD OF INLAND REVENUE PRACTICE

Letter from the Board published in the *Law Society's Gazette* in January 1959 (1959) 56 L.S.Gaz. 53

The Board of Inland Revenue have agreed to the publication of the letter set out below, which they recently sent to a firm of London solicitors regarding the Board's interpretation of those sections in Part XVIII of the Income Tax Act 1952,[54] and the Finance Act 1958,[54] which for tax purposes make the income arising under certain settlements the income of the settlor. In their letter to the Board, the solicitors had suggested that having regard to the Solicitor-General's remarks at the Committee Stage of the Finance Bill, the trustees of nearly all existing settlements not containing a clause prohibiting any benefit accruing to any wife of the settlor, might have to apply to the Court for variation of the settlements before April 5, 1959. They added that it seemed from what the Solicitor-General had said in the House of Commons that a settlement which permitted payment to a beneficiary who might ultimately marry the settlor would be caught by the legislation, unless the settlement were amended by April 5, 1959, so as to exclude the possibility of benefit in such circumstances. They also enquired whether the words " husband " and " wife " are regarded by the Board as including " widower " and " widow."

The following is the text of the Board of Inland Revenue's reply :—

" With reference to your letter of September 26, I am directed by the Board of Inland Revenue to say that they do not place the construction which you suggest on the Solicitor-General's observations in the House of Commons on the occasion to which you refer. The Board regard the decision in *C.I.R.* v. *Tennant* [55] as applying (*a*) where a settlor (as defined for the purposes of Part XVIII of the Income Tax Act 1952) is not at the material time a party to a subsisting marriage and the terms of the settlement (as so defined) are such that a benefit may be conferred on substantially any person who may become the wife or husband of the settlor in future, or (*b*) where, whether or not the settlor is married, the terms of the settlement (as so defined) are such as to indicate a specific intention that a future wife or husband of the settlor might be enabled to benefit.

" Within the foregoing limits the Board are of opinion that *Tennant's* case applies for the construction of the expression " the wife or husband of the settlor " wherever occurring in Part XVIII of the Income Tax Act 1952, and sections 20 to 22 of the Finance Act 1958, except in subsection (4) of section 21 and subsection (5) of section 22, where the context otherwise requires. It depends on the terms of the enactment concerned whether the extent to which the settlement income has been distributed affects the resulting liability.

" In reply to the question in the penultimate paragraph of your letter, I am to say that the Board agree that the expression ' the wife or husband of the settlor ' does not extend to a person who cannot take a relevant benefit during the settlor's lifetime.

" The Board would have no objection to your communicating this letter to The Law Society with a view to its publication in their Gazette if the Society think fit."

Note

See also *Blausten* v. *I.R.C.* [1972] Ch. 256.

[54] Now I.C.T.A. 1970, Pt. XVI.
[55] (1942) 24 T.C. 215.

VANDERVELL v. I.R.C.

House of Lords [1967] 2 A.C. 291; [1967] 2 W.L.R. 87; 110 S.J. 910; [1967] 1 All E.R. 1;
43 T.C. 519

LORD WILBERFORCE: . . . Mr. Vandervell's plans first began to take shape in the summer of 1958. Having formed the wish to give £150,000 to found a Chair at the Royal College of Surgeons and having consulted his experts, he had decided by September to make over to the college the 100,000 " A " shares in his manufacturing company, Vandervell Products Ltd. The advantage of so doing were threefold: first, Mr. Vandervell, as the controlling shareholder in the company, could vote the necessary £150,000, or whatever sum he ultimately decided to give by way of dividend on the " A " shares, as and when he pleased; secondly, the distribution of these dividends might help him to avoid a surtax assessment in respect of non-distributed profits of the company; thirdly, there might be a saving of estate duty.

The idea of the option came to Mr. Robins, Mr. Vandervell's personal friend and financial adviser, as second thoughts. He was concerned about a possible public flotation of the manufacturing company, and so as to avoid possible difficulties he thought " that it would not be desirable to give the shares outright to the college "—one may note at once some inherent hazards in the idea, or at least in the words in which he expressed it. So in November 1958, he put to the college (and they accepted) the proposal that the college should grant an option to resell the shares to a company called Vandervell Trustees Ltd. for £5,000. It was explained in a letter of November 19, 1958, that Mr. Vandervell had decided to make £150,000 available to the college and that £145,000 (gross) would be paid by way of dividend on the shares in Vandervell Products Ltd., the balance of £5,000 to be paid when the option should be exercised. The transaction was completed by transfer of the shares and the grant of the option on or about November 25, 1958.

The critical question is whether the grant of the option prevented Mr. Vandervell from having divested himself absolutely of the shares. Obviously this depends on ascertaining to whom the option beneficially belonged and this was the issue which was inquired into by the Special Commissioners, to which evidence was directed, and on which findings were made. The effect of this evidence and the special commissioners' conclusions upon it appear in the case stated and may be summarised as follows: The option was to be granted (and was granted) to Vandervell Trustees Ltd. " the only large shareholder apart from the appellant." This company is a private company, with a capital of £100 held by Mr. Robins, Mr. Jobson (Mr. Vandervell's solicitor) and Mr. Green (Mr. Robins' partner) which three gentlemen were also the directors of the company having taken office at Mr. Vandervell's request. The trustee company has power by its memorandum to carry on a wide range of business activity but its principal object is to act as trustee. At all material times it had only three activities: (i) as trustee of a settlement of December 30, 1949, of which Mr. Vandervell's children were the main beneficiaries, in which capacity it held 2,053,308 " B " shares in the manufacturing company; (ii) as trustee of a savings fund set up by the manufacturing company; (iii) as grantee of the option.

The deed by which the option was granted merely states that it was granted by the college to the trustee company. In what capacity did the trustee company receive it? It has never been suggested that it received the option as trustee of the savings fund, because no part of that fund could, under the rules, be invested in shares of the manufacturing company. So there are left three alternatives:

   (i) that the option was held on the trusts of the 1949 settlement;

   (ii) that the option was held on trusts not at the time determined, but to be decided on at a later date;

   (iii) that the option was held by the trustee company free from any trust and (at most) subject to an understanding that it or the shares when it was exercised would be disposed of in a suitable manner.

. . . If, then, as I think, both the first two alternatives fail, there remains only the third, which, to my mind, corresponds exactly with Mr. Robins' intentions, namely, that the option was held by the trustee company on trusts which were undefined, or in the air.

As to the consequences, there has been some difference and possibly lack of clarity below. The Special Commissioners held that the initially undefined trusts could be defined later in a way which might benefit the appellant, and they found the benefit to the appellant in this circumstance. The Court of Appeal, starting from the fact that the trustee company took the option as a volunteer, thought that this was a case where the presumption of a resulting trust arose and was not displaced. For my part, I prefer a slightly different and simpler approach. The transaction has been investigated on the evidence of the settlor and his agent and the facts have been found. There is no need, or room, as I see it, to invoke a presumption. The conclusion, on the facts found, is simply that the option was vested in the trustee company as a trustee on trusts, not defined at the time, possibly to be defined later. But the equitable, or beneficial interest, cannot remain in the air: the consequence in law must be that it remains in the settlor. There is no need to consider some of the more refined intellectualities of the doctrine of the resulting trust, nor to speculate whether, in possible circumstances, the shares might be applicable for Mr. Vandervell's benefit: he had, as the direct result of the option and of the failure to place the beneficial interest in it securely away from him, not divested himself absolutely of the shares which it controlled.[56]. . .

LORD UPJOHN: . . . But the doctrine of resulting trust plays another very important part in our law and, in my opinion, is decisive of this case.

If A intends to give away all his beneficial interest in a piece of property and thinks he has done so but, by some mistake or accident or failure to comply with the requirements of the law, he has failed to do so, either wholly or partially, there will, by operation of law, be a resulting trust for him of the beneficial interest of which he had failed effectually to dispose. If the beneficial interest was in A and he fails to give it away effectively to another or others or on charitable trusts it must remain in him. Early references to Equity, like Nature, abhorring a vacuum, are delightful but unnecessary. Let me give an example close to this case.

A the beneficial owner informs his trustee that he wants forthwith to get rid of his interest in the property and instructs him to hold the property forthwith upon such trusts as he will hereafter direct; that beneficial interest, notwithstanding the expressed intention and belief of A that he has thereby parted with his whole beneficial interest in the property, will inevitably remain in him for he has not given the property away effectively to or for the benefit of others. As Plowman J. said [57]: "As I see it, a man does not cease to own property simply by saying 'I don't want it.' If he tries to give it away the question must always be, has he succeeded in doing so or not?"

---

[56] Consequently the settlement fell within the provisions of Income Tax Act 1952, s. 415 (2), now I.C.T.A. 1970, s. 458. The same principle would apply when considering s. 447.

[57] [1966] Ch. 261, 275.

. . . I agree with the conclusions of the Court of Appeal and Plowman J. that the intention was that the trustee company should hold on such trusts as might thereafter be declared by the trustee company or the appellant and so in the event for the appellant.

That is sufficient to dispose of the appeal, but one question was debated in the Court of Appeal, though not before your Lordships, and that is whether the option was held by the trustee company upon such trusts as the trustee company in its discretion should declare or as the appellant should declare. Once it is established that the trustee company held solely as trustee that, as the Court of Appeal held, matters not. The appellant could at any time revoke that discretion if he had vested it in the trustee company.

Then, for the reasons I have given earlier, it follows that until these trusts should be declared there was a resulting trust for the appellant. This is fatal to his case, and I would dismiss the appeal.

Note

Cf. where there is a total failure of the trusts and a resulting trust to settlor: *Aked* v. *Shaw* (1947) 28 T.C. 286; *I.R.C.* v. *Broadway Cottages Trust* [1955] Ch. 20.

I.R.C. v. WACHTEL

Chancery Division [1971] Ch. 573; [1970] 3 W.L.R. 857; 114 S.J. 705; [1971] 1 All E.R. 271; 46 T.C. 543

GOFF J.: This is an appeal from a decision of the Special Commissioners discharging assessments on the taxpayer, Mr. Wachtel, for the years 1960–61 to 1963–64. The Inland Revenue Commissioners appeal and claim to support the assessments under section 405 [58] of the Income Tax Act 1952 or alternatively, as to part only, under section 408.[59]

The facts are fully set out in the case stated, and may be summarised as follows. On April 4, 1960, the taxpayer made a settlement in the ordinary sense of the word of £1,000 for the benefit of his children. On April 5, 1960, the trustees contracted to purchase the whole of the issued shares in an investment company, Ebor Investments Ltd., for a price which, after certain agreed adjustments had been made, was fixed at £7,690 14s. 2d. Paragraph 5 (3) of the case states:

> " As the trustees had no money with which to pay for the said shares apart from the £1,000 settled upon them by the deed of settlement of April 4, 1960 (. . .) an arrangement was made with the District Bank Ltd. (hereinafter called ' the Bank ') under which the Bank would open a current account in the names of the trustees and would advance to them an amount sufficient to enable them to pay for the said shares, on the basis that the [taxpayer] would guarantee the trustees' overdraft and would place on deposit with the Bank an amount sufficient to cover the said overdraft. Copies are annexed . . . forming part of this Case, of a guarantee in favour of the Bank signed by the [taxpayer] on March 22, 1960, and of an authority to the Bank signed by the [taxpayer] on the same day authorising the Bank to hold a security for the said guarantee and to apply in or towards satisfaction of such guarantee any sum or sums of money at any time standing to his credit with the Bank."

It will be observed that the guarantee was prior in date to the trust deed, and reference to an exhibit shows that it was expressly made—

[58] Now I.C.T.A. 1970, s. 447.
[59] *Ibid.* s. 451.

"In consideration of your having at my request agreed to open or continue a banking account with or otherwise to grant banking facilities to The Trustees of Saul Wachtel's Settlement."

Paragraph 5 (4) of the case, so far as material, states:

"It was agreed between the [taxpayer] and the Bank that the rate of interest to be charged by the Bank on the amount from time to time of the trustees' overdraft would be limited to 1% and that no interest would be payable by the Bank on the amount deposited with the Bank by the [taxpayer] in support of his guarantee of the said overdraft. . . . In arriving at this agreement the Bank stipulated that the income of the trust should be applied to reduce its indebtedness to the Bank and that the [taxpayer's] deposit could be reduced accordingly."

The trustees' current account with the bank was opened on April 5, 1960, with a debit of £7,500, which was used to implement the share purchase agreement, and on the same day the £1,000 was paid in, leaving an overdraft balance of £6,500. On April 22, 1960, a further sum of £190 14s. 2d. was placed in the deposit account, and on April 25, 1960, a like sum was drawn by the trustees on overdraft to complete the purchase. Thereafter, as appears from the case stated and the exhibits, the trustees duly paid the dividends on the shares into the bank in reduction of their overdraft, and a like amount was then withdrawn by the taxpayer from the deposit account; and when interest was debited to the trustees on their overdraft the taxpayer added the same amount to the deposit account, so the two accounts were maintained in complete balance.

On March 28, 1961, a company called Saul Wachtel Ltd. was incorporated, and it took over the taxpayer's business, but that had no connection with the settlement. At all material times, the taxpayer and his wife were the beneficial owners of all the issued shares in this company and directors, and he was a creditor on loan account. In June 1962, however, the company took over the taxpayer's position with regard to the bank deposit and guarantee. A new guarantee was signed by him on behalf of the company on June 22. On June 29, the company opened a new deposit account with the sum then required to balance the trustees' overdraft subject to a minor discrepancy of pence which was afterwards corrected; and on July 6, 1962, the taxpayer withdrew his own deposit. A substituted authority to hold the company's deposit account as security was signed by the taxpayer, but for some reason or other not until February 1, 1963; but nothing turns on that.

Paragraph 5 (8) of the case states that it was the taxpayer's intention that Saul Wachtel Ltd. should step into his shoes as guarantor to the bank of the trustees' overdraft. The practice of the payment in of the dividends by the trustees in reduction of their overdraft and of the withdrawal (now of course by the company) of equivalent amounts, and the payment in by the company of amounts to offset the interest debits, continued as before, at all events until after the latest material date in this case. It is claimed by the Crown that the substitution of the company made no difference so far as their claim under section 405 is concerned, but it is conceded that if they have to rely on section 408 they cannot support assessments in respect of any period after June 1962.[60]

The Special Commissioners held that the deed of settlement of April 4, 1960, and the arrangements between the taxpayer and the bank and between the company and the bank together were an arrangement and, therefore, a settlement within the definition in section 411 (2) of the Income Tax Act,[61] and

---

[60] Sums not having been paid *to* the settlor, see *Potts' Executors* v. *I.R.C.* [1951] A.C. 443, *post*, p. 399.   [61] Now I.C.T.A. 1970, s. 454.

that the taxpayer was the settlor in relation to that settlement, and that in their opinion the sums placed in the taxpayer's deposit account and subsequently in the company's account fell within the description of funds provided directly or indirectly by the taxpayer for the purpose of the settlement. In the argument before me, the Crown have not contended that the deposit accounts were funds so provided.

The Special Commissioners thought the present case distinguishable from *Jenkins* v. *Inland Revenue Commissioners*,[62] because there was in the present case no specific power to apply income under the settlement to repay borrowed moneys. They held, therefore, that the taxpayer did not have an interest in any income arising under or property comprised in the settlement, and that accordingly section 405 did not apply. In relation to section 408, it appears from the Special Commissioners' decision that it was agreed that Ebor Investments Ltd. was at the material time a body corporate connected with the settlement within the meaning of section 411 (4). The contrary was conceded before me, though it is immaterial. As to section 408, the Special Commissioners said this:

> " We think that the *De Vigier* case [63] is distinguishable from the case before us. Section 408 is a penal section, which must be strictly construed, and we cannot find that either the trustees or a body corporate connected with the settlement paid any capital sum directly or indirectly to the settlor or his wife. We therefore hold that section 408 does not apply."

The Special Commissioners, in their decision, made reference to other cases cited before them, but I think that I have sufficiently summarised their decision.

I turn now to consider section 405, and I have to determine whether there was a settlement within the wide definition contained in section 411 (2); whether the taxpayer was a settlor within the same definition, and, if so, whether of the whole fund or only that part representing the £1,000 which he undoubtedly provided; and whether he had an interest in undistributed income by virtue of section 405 (2).

. . . Then comes the question [64] whether, by virtue of section 405 (2), the settlor had an interest in the income. The point here is whether the payments by the trustees to the bank were payments indirectly for the benefit of the settlor, or perhaps more accurately whether, because of those payments having to be made, the income was indirectly applicable for his benefit. I bear in mind that this is a taxing statute which must be construed strictly, although Mr. Lomas [counsel for the taxpayer] conceded that the width of section 405 did not impose on me any more stringent a standard than that, and that I must look at what was in fact done and not at the substance of the transaction or whether it produces the same result as would have obtained if it had been done differently. So regarded, however, apart from authority it seems to me that the payments were for his benefit, since they entitled him to withdraw an equivalent amount of his frozen capital. It is not like the commercial transactions envisaged in the cases; for example, the purchase of his house or a loan at a commercial rate of interest, where he derives an incidental benefit.

When I turn to authority, I derive great assistance from *Jenkins* v. *Inland Revenue Commissioners*,[62] to which I have already referred. There, money was paid to the settlor to discharge an interest-free loan, and it was conceded that that was a payment for his benefit. Lord Greene accepted that without question.

---

[62] [1944] 2 All E.R. 491; 26 T.C. 265; *ante*, p. 387.
[63] [1964] 1 W.L.R. 1073; [1964] 2 All E.R. 907; 42 T.C. 24; *post*, p. 404.
[64] Having given a positive answer to the other questions.

There is also a dictum of Pennycuick J. in *Muir* v. *Inland Revenue Commissioners* [65] as follows which is important:

"On this point I find myself unable to agree with the Special Commissioners. Section 405 is in very wide terms, but it must, I think, be confined to cases where income or property ' will or may become payable to or applicable for the benefit of the settlor ' either under the trusts of the settlement itself or under some collateral arrangement having legal force"

—and that, incidentally, is also important—"for example, the repayment of an interest-free loan, such as was considered by the Court of Appeal in *Jenkins* v. *Inland Revenue Commissioners*."

I respectfully agree, and it seems to me that the release of an interest-free deposit is in pari materia.

As I have said, the Special Commissioners distinguished that case because of the express power to apply income in one of three ways, including paying off the loan, but in the present case they found that the bank stipulated that income of the trust fund should be applied to reduce the trustees' indebtedness to the bank and that the taxpayer's deposit could be reduced accordingly. There was therefore an express requirement in the arrangement constituting the settlement, or at least by a legally enforceable collateral agreement, that payment should be made. This distinction, therefore, seems only to make the present an a fortiori case.

. . . There remains the subsidiary question whether the position was altered when the company took over the taxpayer's position *vis-à-vis* the bank and deposited its own money, but in my judgment it was not. Mr. Lomas argued at first that one could not pierce the company veil, but he was driven to concede, and in my judgment rightly, that a discretion in the settlement to pay income to a company in which the settlor and his wife owned all the shares would be within the section so that the veil can be pierced. Then it follows, if I am right that the release of the settlor's frozen funds was a payment indirectly for his benefit, the release of the frozen funds of a company in which he and his wife were the sole shareholders would be no less so. . . .

Note
For a consideration of this case and of the relationship between sections 447 and 451, see R. Burgess, " The Settlor and Section 447 " [1971] B.T.R. 278.

(v) *Sums Paid to the Settlor*

If the Trustees of a settlement pay to the settlor, or to his spouse, any capital sums, then, to the extent to which such sums are paid from available undistributed income of the fund, they are treated for all the purposes of the Income Tax Acts as the income of the settlor.[66] The provision further extends to payments to the settlor by a " body corporate connected with the settlement."

POTTS' EXECUTORS v. I.R.C.

House of Lords (*ante*, pp. 8, 23)

A company, the shares of which were held by Trustees of a settlement, made payments on behalf of the settlor, including payments of certain subscriptions

[65] [1966] 1 W.L.R. 251, 267; [1966] 1 All E.R. 295, 305.
[66] I.C.T.A. 1970, s. 451.

and of his income tax and surtax liabilities. *Held*, the company was a " body corporate connected with the settlement " but the payments were not made " to " the settlor and the section (now s. 451) did not apply.

LORD SIMONDS: . . . My Lords, I have come to a different conclusion. Reading the definition into the subsection I must be satisfied that according to the fair meaning of the words these sums were sums paid by way of loan to the settlor directly or indirectly by the company. I do not think it matters whether the words " directly or indirectly " qualify the payment or the receipt. I will assume they qualify both or either. The question is still whether the conditions of the composite phrase are fulfilled—were the sums paid to the settlor by way of loan? I do not doubt that in certain contexts money paid at A's request to B may be properly described as " paid to A."

. . . But this is not the way in which a taxing statute is to be read. I am not, in the construction of such a statute, entitled to say that, because the legal or business result is the same whether on the one hand I borrow money from the company and with it make certain payments, or on the other hand the company at my request makes certain payments on my implied promise to repay, therefore it is immaterial what words are in the statute if that result is attained.

. . . That question remains as I have stated it, and my answer is that according to the ordinary fair meaning of the words the company did not pay any sums to the settlor by way of loan. It would in fact be as inapt to say that the company paid him sums by way of loan when he was in debit on the account as to say that he paid the company sums by way of loan when he was in credit. Some stress was laid on the distinction in the old forms of pleading between the plea for money lent to the defendant and the plea of money paid at the request of the defendant to a third party. I am not inclined to give much weight to this consideration but it does indicate that there is at least a formal difference between the two transactions.

So far, my Lords, I have not specifically dealt with the word " indirectly." It is sufficient to say that it cannot so enlarge the meaning of the words " paid to the settlor " as to include payment to some other person than the settlor for his own use and benefit. I do not feel called on to determine positively what transactions it might be apt to cover. It may be that it is not apt to cover any that are not already covered by the normal meaning of the words " paid to the settlor." [67] . . .

LORD OAKSEY: My Lords, I agree that this appeal should be allowed. The object of the Act, in my opinion, was to tax a settlor who obtained payment of capital sums from the trustees of his settlement or from companies connected with the settlement for which he had not given full consideration in money or money's worth; it cannot have been the object of the Act to tax him in respect of payments for which he had given full consideration. In these circumstances it appears to me that if the words of the Act are fairly susceptible of a meaning which attains this object they should be given that meaning rather than a meaning which goes beyond the object of the Act and leads to admitted injustice.

The first question is whether the sums in question are capital sums within the meaning of section 40, subsection 5 (*a*).[68] It was contended for the Crown that the sums paid by the company were sums paid by way of loan. In my opinion in the particular circumstances of this case the payments were not

[67] The passage quoted *ante*, at p. 8, immediately follows this part of Lord Simonds' judgment.
[68] Of the Finance Act 1938, now I.C.T.A. 1970, s. 451.

made by way of loan. They were made in accordance with the practice which had long existed by which the governing director of the company in which he had held all the shares directed or requested the company to make payments on his behalf as a matter of ordinary convenience. The company had never carried on a business of bankers or moneylenders and it is not in my opinion a fair use of language to describe payments made for the governing director in such circumstances as loans. According to the respondents' argument whenever the governing director's account became in debit there was a loan by the company to him and whenever it was credited with any sum thereafter until the account balanced there were repayments of loans.

The second question is whether even if the payments were made by way of loan they were paid directly or indirectly to the settlor. None of them was in fact paid to the settlor and from some of them the settlor derived no financial benefit since some of them were contributions to charities. Having regard to the object of the statute I think the words " paid directly or indirectly to the settlor " should be held to mean paid into the settlor's hands or into the hands of someone accountable to him.

For my own part, I should also be prepared to decide the case upon the ground that the true construction of subsection 5 (a) (i) is that it refers only to sums paid by way of loan which are not paid for full consideration in money or money's worth and that in the present case the accommodation offered to the appellant was given for full consideration in money or money's worth.[69]

BATES v. I.R.C.

House of Lords (ante, p. 15)

LORD REID: My Lords, this is an appeal against additional assessments to surtax in the years 1953–54, 1954–55 and 1955–56 laid under Part XVIII of the Income Tax Act 1952, and in particular under section 408 thereof.[70] The appellant was a director and shareholder of a company, T. Ambler & Sons, to which the provisions of Chapter III of Part IX applied.[71] In 1948 he made an irrevocable settlement in favour of his children in which accumulation of the trust income was directed, and he conveyed to the trustees of the settlement some of his shares in that company. It was his practice to have a current account with that company. From time to time sums accruing to him were paid in and sums owing by him were paid by the company and debited to this account. There was generally a considerable balance owing by him but at the end of each financial year of the company he paid to them enough to meet this balance, thereby creating a large overdraft from his bank, and at the beginning of the next year the company paid out enough to cover that overdraft from his bank. In April of 1950, 1951 and 1953 this was done by the company paying a sum direct to the bank but in 1952 and 1954 it was done by the company drawing cheques in favour of the appellant which he paid into his account with the bank. We are particularly concerned with a payment of £9,100 made by the company to the appellant on April 5, 1954. I have no doubt that this was a sum paid by way of loan within the meaning of section 408 (7).

---

[69] The opinion expressed by Lord Oaksey (that the section does not apply to loans made for full consideration) does not appear to be justified on the wording of the statutory provision, and a contrary view was taken in *Bates* v. *I.R.C.* [1968] A.C. 483, *infra*, and *I.R.C.* v. *De Vigier* (1964) 42 T.C. 25; *post*, p. 404. A loan not made for full consideration might also amount to a " benefit " to the settlor, within I.C.T.A. 1970, s. 447; this question is discussed by R. Burgess, " The Settlor and Section 447 " [1971] B.T.R. 278.

[70] Now I.C.T.A. 1970, s. 451.

[71] *i.e.* a close company. See I.C.T.A. 1970, s. 454 (5).

The case against the appellant is that section 408 requires that the sum of £9,100 shall be treated as the income of the appellant to the extent therein provided. The section requires that any loan to the settlor by " any body corporate connected with the settlement " shall be treated as having been paid by the trustees of the settlement, and the definition in section 411 (4) [71] of " body corporate connected with the settlement " is so wide that in my opinion it must be held to include this company although there was in fact no connection whatever between the company and the settlement beyond the fact that the settlement trustees held some shares of the company, and the appellant had no intention of gaining any tax advantage and in fact gained none by taking this loan from the company.

This startling proposition makes it necessary to examine these statutory provisions with some care.[72]

. . . These provisions were first enacted in 1938. The mischief against which they were directed appears to have been that some taxpayers, intending to avoid paying surtax, transferred to trustees of settlements shares in companies controlled by them : then they borrowed money from the trustees, who used the dividends in these shares to make the loans. In that way the settlors got possession of the income from the shares which they had settled in the form of capital payments which did not attract surtax. And if the trustees were complacent the settlors might never repay these " loans."

The reason why some companies were brought in appears to have been that some settlors had devised rather more elaborate schemes. A settlor might form a company, controlled by him, to which he transferred assets yielding income. He would then put the whole, or the greater part, of the shares of that company in the settlement, and then he would cause that company to lend to him the whole or a part of its income, thereby diminishing the dividends which would otherwise have gone to the settlement trustees. He would not repay these loans during his lifetime and in that way he would receive and enjoy the income of the assets which he had transferred to the company without being liable to pay surtax in respect of it.

Of course it was necessary to stop that kind of tax evasion,[73] and of course it was necessary to try to anticipate and forestall more complicated variations of this plan. But this was an early example of legislation directed against tax evasion, and experience has shown that in at least one respect it is too narrow— see Potts' Executors v. Inland Revenue Commissioners [74] to which I shall return—and in other respects it is too wide. Its provisions suffer from two glaring defects. In the first place they impose heavy liabilities in respect of many kinds of ordinary and innocent transactions which no laymen and indeed few lawyers not familiar with this section would ever imagine could be caught in this way—in short they are a trap. And, secondly, they are framed in such a way that their plain meaning in many cases leads to a result which Russell L.J.[75] has rightly called monstrous.

Normally when we construe a statute we are attempting to discover the intention of Parliament from the words used in the Act; but here it is obvious, and indeed admitted, that Parliament could never have intended some of the results which are inescapable if certain of the provisions of the section are not to be disregarded. But we cannot apply a statutory provision in one way in cases where it creates injustice and in a different way in cases where it serves to defeat attempts to evade tax.

---

[72] The provisions of Income Tax Act 1952, ss. 408, 411 (4), follow in the judgment.
[73] On a number of occasions, Lord Reid uses the word " evasion " where, it is submitted, he should have said " avoidance," there being nothing unlawful in the practices described : see Chap. 2, and I.R.C. v. De Vigier (1964) 42 T.C. 24, post, p. 404.
[74] [1951] A.C. 443; ante, pp. 8, 23, 399.   [75] [1965] 1 W.L.R. 1133, 1153–1154.

The first and main question in this case involves the construction of section 411 (4). I have tried to explain why it was necessary to bring in companies controlled by settlors and used in aiding schemes for tax evasion, and this subsection is intended to do that. The fact that it is so widely drawn as to be a trap for the innocent does not in my judgment entitle a court to attribute to any of its provisions a strained or unnatural meaning so as to make it impotent in those cases where tax evasion is attempted.

. . . The next point is the extent to which the loan is to be regarded as the settlor's income in any year. . . . The draftsman has chosen such a complicated method that he has obviously failed to realise the absurd results to which it leads in all but the simplest cases and I think in almost every case where the trust income has to be accumulated; so the Inland Revenue have taken it on themselves to disregard the statute and substitute a method which they think fair and, if I understood counsel rightly, in accord with the spirit of the Act. . . . But the fact that the respondents have chosen to assess for a smaller sum than the terms of the section would appear to justify does not entitle us to hold that the assessment is bad.

. . . Before I conclude I must again draw attention to the very unsatisfactory state in which the law has been allowed to remain since the decision by this House in 1950 of *Potts'* case.[74] In that case the question was whether sums paid by a company connected with the settlement to creditors of the settlor to discharge his debts fell within the scope of this section. It was argued by the present respondents that a decision against them " would make it so easy to circumvent the Act as to render it useless for its object."

. . . But when the case was decided against the present respondents nothing was done to amend the section. In the present case it appears that in five different years payments were made by the company for the purpose of discharging the appellant's debt to his bank. In three cases these payments were made direct to the bank, and *Potts'* case shows that they were not caught by section 408. But it so happened that in the other two years the payments were made by cheques drawn in favour of the appellant and not in favour of the bank. It is this fortuitous circumstance alone that has brought the appellant within the scope of section 408 and imposed on him tax liability for several thousands of pounds. This case may well afford ammunition to that body of opinion which holds that redrafting of the Income Tax Act ought to be taken out of the hands of those at present responsible. . . .

LORD UPJOHN: . . . My Lords, I only desire to refer briefly to a more general aspect of this matter. First, the monstrous result of this series of sections, which has been so clearly set out by Lord Reid in his speech; putting it very shortly, if a large capital sum was paid and that had to be spread over income of the settlement for, say, five years, it would follow that the income available in the settlement in the first year would be taken into account five times and would be taxed five times over; income available in the second year taxed four times over and so on. Such a result cannot of course have been intended: but that seems to be the perfectly plain result of the provisions of section 408 (2). It is regrettable, especially having regard to the decision in *Potts' Executors*,[74] now sixteen years ago, that it has not been thought fit to amend this section. Instead the Commissioners of Inland Revenue, realising the monstrous result of giving effect to the true construction of the section, have in fact worked out what they consider to be an equitable way of operating it which seems to them to result in a fair system of taxation. I am quite unable to understand upon which principle they can properly do so and, like Lord Reid, I hope this matter may receive some consideration in the proper place. . . .

Note

For further comment on this provision, see J. Silberrad, " Misdrafting of Section 451 of the Income and Corporation Taxes Act, 1970 " [1970] B.T.R. 380; J. F. Avery-Jones, " Section 408 must go " [1967] B.T.R. 81; J.G.M., " Section 408 Again " [1967] B.T.R. 282 (considering *McCrone* v. *I.R.C.* (1967) 44 T.C. 142); and S.T.C., " No Misfire " [1965] B.T.R. 330.

DE VIGIER v. I.R.C.

House of Lords [1964] 1 W.L.R. 1073; 108 S.J. 617; [1964] 2 All E.R. 907; *sub nom.*
I.R.C. v. *de Vigier*, 42 T.C. 24

Sums were advanced by the settlor's wife to the Trustees of the settlement to enable them to acquire further shares in a company. The loan was repaid to her. *Held*, the repayment was a capital sum within section 408 (now s. 451).

LORD REID: My Lords, I agree with your Lordships that there is no escape from the conclusion that this appeal must fail. There is no suggestion that either the appellant or his wife was trying to evade tax, and the transaction which has attracted tax liability was one which would never suggest that possibility to anyone unless he was familiar with income tax law. But the Revenue do not and probably should not have any discretion to remit tax legally due on the ground that the innocent taxpayer has fallen into a trap.

I realise that if legislation is to be effective to forestall attempts at evasion it must often be drafted in terms so wide that it can apply to a variety of quite innocent transactions. So one can only say that it is very unwise for any one unfamiliar with income tax law to depart from the beaten paths of trust administration in any case where the settlement involves or provides for accumulation of income, without first obtaining an opinion from counsel experienced in income tax matters.

3. Partnerships

(A) ASSESSMENT OF PARTNERSHIPS

Although at law a partnership has no separate existence apart from its constituent members, income tax in respect of the profits of a firm is computed and assessed in the partnership name.[76] A joint return of partnership income must be made by the " precedent partner "[77]; the income of the partnership is computed in accordance with the ordinary rules applicable to individuals and must then be allocated among the partners.

REPORT OF THE COMMITTEE ON THE TAXATION OF TRADING PROFITS

1951 Cmd. 8189

25. *Partnerships.* Some of the worst evils of the existing system arise in the case of partnerships. The existing law contains special provisions about partnerships. Where the constitution of a partnership changes through the taking in of a new member, or the retirement or death of an existing member,

[76] I.C.T.A. 1970, s. 152.
[77] T.M.A. 1970, s. 9.

the partners are given an option. If they make a claim to that effect the assessments for all relevant years are made on the footing that, at the date of the change, the old business ceased and a new business commenced and the cessation and commencement provisions are applied. If, however, the partners do not exercise this option within a stated period, the assessments continue to be made on the normal preceding year basis. The option has to be exercised by all the partners who were carrying on business both before and after the change; if a partner has died his personal representatives must be a party to the claim. This position gives rise to two difficulties.

26. In the first place the exercise of the option may be beneficial to some partners and injurious to others, according to their individual circumstances. In such a case the partners who gain by the exercise of the option may have to indemnify their partners before they can persuade them to join in a claim. Even where there is good will between the partners this is obviously a difficult situation : if there is not, some partners may be seriously penalised.

27. Secondly, the provisions afford considerable scope for tax avoidance in cases where the profits of a partnership fluctuate. This position arises out of the decision of the courts in the case of *Osler* v. *Hall & Co.*[78] That case was concerned with a partnership the constitution of which changed twice in a comparatively short space of time. The option referred to above was exercised on the occasion of the second change but not on the occasion of the first change. The result of the court's decision in this case is that a partnership, by making changes in its constitution at suitable times, can avoid paying tax on part of the profits of an unusually profitable period. It is easy for a partnership to effect a nominal change in its constitution by making one of its employees a partner with a very small share of profits in addition to his salary, and a short time later either making him revert to the position of an employee or introducing a second new partner on similar terms.

28. A further anomaly of the present law relating to the assessment of partnerships is that the allocation of shares of the partnership assessment to individual partners for purposes of personal allowances and surtax is based on the division adopted by the partners for the year of assessment and not that for the year the profits of which are the subject of the assessment. The anomaly can best be illustrated by an example. Suppose that A and B share profits equally up to April 5, 1953, and thereafter A takes three-quarters and B one-quarter. Suppose that the profits made by the partnership for the accounts year ending March 31, 1953 are £5,000 and for the accounts year ending March 31, 1954 are £2,000. An assessment will be made on the partnership for the year 1953–54 on £5,000. The allocation of this assessment between A and B for purposes of personal allowances and surtax will be based on their allocation for the year of assessment, and accordingly £3,750 will be treated as A's income and £1,250 as B's income. A will be penalised because, although he was only entitled to half of the profit of £5,000 he will be treated as having received three-quarters of it; B will correspondingly gain because, although he was entitled to half of the profit of £5,000, he will be charged only on one-quarter of it.

. . . 69. It will also be useful at this stage to set out what seemed to us to be the main requirements of any satisfactory scheme dealing with the assessment of partnerships. These are as follows : —

> (*a*) Notwithstanding any change either in the constitution of a partnership, or in the basis of allocation of profits between the partners, no partner should be treated for tax purposes as entitled to an amount of profit substantially different from that to which he is in fact entitled.

[78] [1933] 1 K.B. 720.

(*b*) The scheme must provide a satisfactory basis of allocation for tax purposes not only of profits assessed on the preceding year basis, *e.g.* under Cases I and II, but also on any income chargeable on the current year basis, *e.g.* dividends taxed at the source, and business premises charged under Schedule A. While the number of partnerships receiving taxed dividends [79] may not be large, there are many which own their business premises.

(*c*) On a change in the constitution of a partnership the continuing partners should not in equity be deprived of the right to carry forward losses or capital allowances for which relief has not been given owing to insufficiency of profits.

(*d*) The scheme must limit as far as possible the opportunities for avoidance. (As already explained in paragraph 27, the existing law does enable a partnership to avoid paying tax on, at any rate, part of the profits of an unusually profitable period.)

70. Some of the main difficulties of the present system spring from the fact that the profits assessed for a particular year are for tax purposes allocated between the partners in accordance with the partners' allocation in force for the year of assessment, even though the assessment will normally be based on the profits of the preceding accounts year, when a different allocation may have been in force. It may be thought that the difficulties would be solved by providing that the allocation for tax purposes should follow the basis adopted by the partnership itself in relation to the profits on which the assessment is based. It would, however, be quite impossible to adopt this idea unless the rule prescribing the tax treatment of changes in the constitution of partnerships were also radically amended. At present, a partnership remains chargeable on the preceding year basis, notwithstanding that a new partner has joined the firm or an old one has left it on resignation or death, unless all those who were partners both before and after the change elect that the cessation and commencement provisions should apply. If this rule were retained, but the basis of allocation of profits for tax purposes among the partners were altered, extremely anomalous results would follow. Thus, if a new partner joined the firm at, say, the beginning of an income tax year, no part of the assessment for that year would be allocated to him; though there might be no break in his business activities (indeed he might well have been an employee of the partnership up to the the time when he became a partner) he would in effect get a year's tax holiday. Conversely, if a partner left the firm at, say, the end of an income tax year, and took employment or set up business elsewhere, he would, for the following year, have allocated to him a share of profits even though he was not a member of the partnership for that year. As he would also be chargeable for that year on the emoluments of any new employment, or, if he had set up a new business, on the profits of that business, two years' income would be telescoped into a single year of assessment. Only one year's personal allowances would, however, be available against the two years' income; moreover, he might be liable to surtax at a far higher rate than the income of either year justified; indeed, he might be liable to a substantial amount of surtax notwithstanding that in no year did his actual income exceed £2,000. A further anomaly would be that on the death of a partner surtax might be due from his estate for the year after his death.

71. It is clear therefore that, apart from any other objections there might be to the proposal, it would be impracticable to allocate partnership income by reference to the shares of the partners in the basis year unless the cessa-

---

[79] N.B. *Bucks* v. *Bowers* (1970) 46 T.C. 267; F.A. 1971, s. 32 (4).

tion and commencement provisions were applied on all changes in the constitution of a partnership. We gave serious consideration to the possibility of treating all changes in partnership as cessations, but we came to the conclusion that the idea must be rejected. Its effect would be that, on the occasion of every change, the assessments for some three or four years would be, or might be, on the current year basis. As the profits of the accounting period of a business cannot be ascertained until some considerable time after the end of that period, the result would be that there would be very considerable delay in clearing up the liability of the partners for the years affected. Remembering that the majority of partnerships are in business in a small way, and that changes in their constitution arise most frequently from the introduction of a member of the same family or one who has been hitherto an employee in the business, we came to the conclusion that the complications which would be caused by the compulsory application of the cessation provisions in all cases would be highly unpopular, and that we could not recommend such a provision.

72. It is not necessary for us to go through the various other suggestions that we considered; we have probably said enough to show that there is no easy and obvious solution of the difficulties involved. After much consideration we evolved a scheme which, though perhaps not logically perfect, seemed to us to remove the major anomalies and to be free from serious objection. This scheme, which we accordingly recommend, is as follows: —

(*a*) The present basis of allocation (namely, by reference to the partners' allocation in the year of assessment) to be preserved.

(*b*) On a change in the constitution of a partnership the cessation and commencement provisions to be applied unless all those who were members of the partnership both before and after the change elect that the assessments should continue to be made on the normal preceding year basis. (Where the change arises by reason of the death of a partner, the surviving partners should be entitled to exercise the option without being required to secure the agreement of the deceased's personal representatives.)

(*c*) Whether or not the cessation provisions apply on a change in partnership, the continuing partners should be entitled to carry forward their share of any loss or capital allowances for which relief has not already been given.

(*d*) Where there is a change in the basis of allocation of profits among the partners the cessation provisions should apply if, and only if, there is a formal dissolution in writing of the partnership followed by the creation of a new partnership, and notice in writing is given to the Inland Revenue within a specified period.

(*e*) Any additional liability arising from the application of the cessation provisions, either on the coming to an end of the business, or under sub-paragraphs (*b*) or (*d*) above, should be enforceable on the persons who were members of the partnership during the relevant years, notwithstanding that in these years there may have been another change in partnership in relation to which the cessation provisions did not fall to be applied.

Note

For the present treatment of partnerships, in particular on change of partners, see I.C.T.A. 1970, ss. 152, 154. See also *Commissioners for General Purposes of Income Tax for the City of London* v. *Gibbs* [1942] A.C. 402.

Other aspects of assessment of partnership income are mentioned in *I.R.C.* v. *Lebus' Executors* (1946) 27 T.C. 136; *post*, p. 411.

HARRISON v. WILLIS BROS.

Court of Appeal [1966] Ch. 619; [1966] 2 W.L.R. 183; 109 S.J. 875; [1965] 3 All E.R. 753;
43 T.C. 61

LORD DENNING M.R.: This case raises the question: How should a partnership be taxed after one partner dies? Many years ago two brothers, W. H. Willis and H. H. Willis, carried on business in partnership under the name of Willis Bros. They were dairymen at the Manor Park Dairy, 2, Ascot Road, Aylesbury. They were assessed for tax under Schedule D in the partnership name for all the years from 1941–42 to 1948–49, inclusive. Their profits were assessed at figures ranging from £480 to £858. In the year 1950 the brothers dissolved the partnership. W. H. Willis went out and thereafter H. H. Willis carried on the business alone. A few years later the Crown took the view that, during the partnership, the brothers had returned the profits at too low a figure: and in 1955 the Crown made an additional assessment in the partnership name for the year 1948–49: thus rendering the two brothers (who were both alive) liable. This was within the six years permissible. On December 17, 1957, H. H. Willis died. His executors took out probate of his will, and presumably sold the business. By the year 1962 the Crown took the view that, during the partnership, the brothers had consistently returned the profits at too low a figure. In consequence, on March 29, 1962, the Crown made additional assessments [80] for all the years from 1941–42 to 1947–48 in figures ranging from £62 to £838. These additional assessments described the " person assessed " as " Willis Bros. (W. H. Willis and executors of H. H. Willis, deceased) " and the " place of assessment " as " Manor Park Dairy, 2, Ascot Road, Aylesbury." I regard these assessments as made in the partnership name Willis Bros. but with a notification in brackets that the Crown would seek to make W. H. Willis liable and also the executors of H. H. Willis. The surviving brother, W. H. Willis, did not appeal, but the executor of the dead brother, H. H. Willis, did appeal. That executor died before the hearing but the executor's widow obtained probate of his will and carried on the appeal.

. . . The executors of H. H. Willis, deceased, defend themselves by saying that they are protected by the limitation of time contained in the statutes, because section 47 (2) of the Act of 1952,[81] and section 53 of the Act of 1960,[82] make it clear, even in the case of fraud, wilful default, or neglect, when a person has died, an assessment on his personal representatives must be made within three years after the year of assessment in which he died. It cannot be made against the executor of the deceased partner. Nor also, they add, can it be made against the surviving partner.

The Crown, in reply, admit that if H. H. Willis was an individual trader, they could not proceed against his executors more than three years after the year in which he died: but they say it is different with a partnership. There is no limit of time, they say, to assessments against a partnership in respect of tax accruing while the partnership was in existence. They can go against both the survivor and the executor with no limit of time.

In order to determine the dispute, we must decide what is the nature of the liability of a partnership to tax. Is it the liability of the firm itself, or of the partners? If it is the liability of the partners, is their liability joint, or several, or joint and several? This question depends on the true interpretation

---

[80] An additional assessment must normally be made within six years after the year of assessment to which it relates—T.M.A. 1970, s. 34—but the Crown claimed to be entitled to go further back because there had been fraud or neglect on the part of the partnership: see T.M.A. 1970, ss. 36, 37, 41.

[81] Now T.M.A. 1970, s. 40 (1).

[82] *Ibid.* s. 40 (2).

of the statutes. The liability of any one of us to pay tax is a statutory liability. It does not arise out of contract, nor out of tort, but out of the statute. The Revenue makes an assessment on the person chargeable. The tax becomes payable when the assessment becomes final, either because no appeal is made against it or when it is resolved in the Revenue's favour on appeal. The liability attaches when the assessment becomes final and not before—see *B.P. Refinery (Kent) Ltd.* v. *Lower Medway Internal Drainage Board, per* Donovan J.[83]

It has been suggested that for taxing purposes " a partnership firm is treated as an entity distinct from the persons who constitute the firm "—see *Income Tax Commissioners for the City of London* v. *Gibbs, per* Lord Macmillan.[84] But I do not think this is correct. The statutes from 1842 to 1960 make it plain that the liability of partners to pay tax is the *joint* liability of *all* the partners, and not the *several* liability of each. It is not " joint and several." It is a *joint* liability only. The partnership firm is not an entity for taxing purposes or any other purposes. Its name is simply a convenient way of describing the persons who constitute the firm. My reasons are these: section 144 of the Income Tax Act 1952 [85] (which repeats provisions which go back to the first Act in 1842) says that

> " Where a trade or profession is carried on by two or more persons jointly, the tax in respect thereof shall be computed and stated jointly and in one sum, and shall be separate and distinct from any other tax chargeable on those persons or any of them, and a joint assessment shall be made in the partnership name."

The provision for a *joint assessment* shows that it is a joint liability imposed on all those who were partners during the year of assessment, that is, during the year when the profits were made which are being taxed. (If there was a change in partners in the course of a year, the situation is met by section 145, but that does not arise here.) The provision that the assessment is to be made " in the partnership name " is machinery by which those persons are designated who were partners during the year when the profits were made. They are still to be designated by that name, even after the partnership is dissolved. This use of the partnership name is a familiar piece of machinery. We all know that in an action at law, when two or more persons are liable as partners in respect of a cause of action, they can be sued in the name of the firm of which they were partners at the time when the cause of action accrued, even though it has since been dissolved—see R.S.C., Ord. 81. So also in taxing matters, when a joint assessment is made on partners in respect of a year when they were partners, the assessment can be made, and indeed *must* be made, in the partnership name of the firm, even though it has since been dissolved. So long as they are all alive, they are all chargeable for the tax in the years that they traded in partnership. The assessment must be made in the partnership name. But in point of law an assessment is made on those persons jointly and the tax is charged on and payable by them. This is clearly accepted as the law of England by section 63 (3) of the Finance Act 1960.[86]

What is the position when one of the persons (who were jointly chargeable) dies? The answer is, I think, that the survivors become chargeable.

. . . In any such case, of course, when a surviving partner is made liable, he may be able to obtain a contribution from the estate of the deceased partner. But that is no concern of the Revenue. The Revenue must make the assessment in the partnership name and impose liability on the survivor, as I have said, and not on the executor of the deceased partner. . . .

83 [1957] 1 Q.B. 84, 98.   84 [1942] A.C. 402, 419.
85 Now I.C.T.A. 1970, s. 152.
86 Now T.M.A. 1970, s. 118 (3).

(B) The Existence and Constitution of a Partnership

In order that an assessment may be made in respect of partnership profits it is necessary to determine (i) whether in fact a partnership exists or not, and (ii) who are the members of that partnership.

DICKENSON v. GROSS

King's Bench Division (1927) 11 T.C. 614; 137 L.T. 351

The appellant entered into a Deed of Partnership with his three sons, providing for the lease of farming land by the appellant to the partnership, the preparation of annual accounts and the division of profits. None of these things was ever done.

Rowlatt J.: I need not trouble you, Mr. Solicitor. I have not any difficulty about this case.

The partnership deed here, of course, was a deed perfectly good according to its tenor; and if it had been what really governed the relations of the parties it would have effected the object of those who entered into it or purported to enter into it, because it would have produced another legal position to which a tax attached differently from the legal position which existed before. As I pointed out in the case Mr. Bremner cited to me—and as has been often pointed out before—people can arrange their affairs, if they do really arrange them, so as to produce a state of facts in which the taxation is different, and it is no answer—it is perfectly immaterial—to say that they have done it for that purpose.[87] But in this case the facts show that in very many ways the deed was simply set on one side and disregarded, and when you find the deed is disregarded, and also that it was entered into for the purpose of obtaining relief from taxation one is apt, perhaps naturally and quite properly upon the question of fact, to pay a little more attention to those circumstances and those points in which it was disregarded. Now Mr. Bremner, I think, has very truly said that if these young men had come forward and pointed to this deed and said: " Here, Father, you have signed this deed; kindly carry it out," he would have been in a very great difficulty, as King Lear was, in getting out of it, and they probably would have held him to it; and if they had held him to it the Commissioners would have had no justification for finding as they have. But they did not. On the contrary they let the deed slide and proceeded in the ordinary patriarchal way which everybody who is the least familiar with the habits of the countryside, as I have no doubt these three Commissioners were, knows very well.

Now what the Commissioners have done is that they have found that there was no partnership in fact.[88] Mr. Bremner says that looks as if they were splitting some hair and saying there was no partnership in fact, although there was a partnership in law. I do not think that is the way to look at the finding at all. A partnership, of course, is a legal position and a legal result, but like

---

[87] See *Ayrshire Pullman Motor Services* v. *I.R.C.* (1929) 14 T.C. 754; *ante*, p. 33.

[88] *Cf. Fenston* v. *Johnstone* (1940) 23 T.C. 29, where a partnership was held to exist *in fact* despite an express provision in the agreement between the persons concerned that their relationship should not constitute a partnership. Similar questions also arise in determining *when* a partnership comes into existence or ceases: *Waddington* v. *O'Callaghan* (1931) 16 T.C. 187; *J. & R. O'Kane & Co.* v. *I.R.C.* (1922) 12 T.C. 303; *Hillerns & Fowler* v. *Murray* (1932) 17 T.C. 77.

every other legal position it depends on facts, and what the Commissioners are saying here is: " The facts are not those from which a legal partnership results, because although there was the deed they are not acting on it; it is not governing their transactions; they are not paying the slightest attention to it. They are going on just as before." They have not used the word " fictitious," and they have not used the word " sham," but I think they have put it even more clearly. They say: " The facts here were not a partnership although there was a bit of paper in the drawer, which if the facts had been according to it, would have shown there was a partnership."

Then Mr. Bremner says there is some *dolus* lurking in the phrase that " for income tax purposes there was no partnership," as if meaning to say: " You may say there is a partnership, but for income tax purposes it will not do, because it is meant to evade income tax." I do not think it means that at all. That is not what they are saying at all. What they are saying is this: " There is not any partnership in fact, and there cannot be any partnership for the special purposes of income tax when there is no real partnership." That is what they are saying. Many people think there can be. They think by putting a bit of paper in the drawer they can make an income tax partnership, and they go on treating the undertaking as though it were still the sole uncontrolled property of the one person, the father, instead of a partnership. I do not think there is any doubt. I do not think the Commissioners could have found otherwise, if I may say so, but I think they clearly have found in a way which makes the position quite right, and the appeal must be dismissed with costs.

I.R.C. v. LEBUS' EXECUTORS

Court of Appeal [1946] 1 All E.R. 476; 174 L.T. 358; 27 T.C. 136

The widow of a deceased partner was entitled under his will to receive a share of the partnership profits for the rest of her life. The share due remained largely unpaid. The Revenue attempted to assess her on the share. *Held*, she was not a partner and the share did not form part of her income unless and until paid to the executors for her benefit.

LORD GREENE M.R.: . . . The argument proceeds somewhat in this way. It is said that, where partners carry on business and make profits, they are assessable to income tax in respect of those profits, whether they take them out of the business and divide them or whether they do not. For example, a partnership has had a very profitable year. The whole of its property may be so locked up in its assets that it is quite impossible in that year to get any money out to pay to the partners their shares or the whole of their shares of the profits. That is a thing which commonly happens. But, in assessing a partnership in respect of the profits of its business, what you do is to take the account as between the Revenue and the partners and say: " In this year the partners have made so much profit; it belongs to those partners, and the fact that they cannot pay themselves out in cash has nothing in the world to do with it, for the very simple reason that the partners own the entirety of the assets, and they have themselves realised these profits in the sense that the profits have resulted in an accretion to the value of their assets which belong to the partners. For income tax purposes it is their profit on taking the proper income tax account." In the case of partners that is perfectly clear. The fact that the profits are not released and paid over in cash to the partners has nothing to do with it from the income tax point of view. From the income tax point of view, they have made profits and are taxable.[89]

Now, says the Crown: "That is really what is happening here. The three partners have made profits and they are taxable even though they did not draw those profits out of the business." Similarly, the Crown says: "Mrs. Lebus has made some profits and it makes no difference whether she draws the profits out of the business or does not." But there is all the difference in the world between the two cases, because Mrs. Lebus is not a partner,[90] and the assets of the partnership do not belong to her. It is, therefore, impossible to say as against her what can be said as against the partners—that she has in the accretion to the value of the partnership assets realised a profit in the income tax sense. She has not realised a profit unless and until the profit is paid to her.[91] It is a complete confusion, with great respect to the argument, to put her in the same position as if she had been a partner.

The Crown endeavoured to get out of the difficulty by saying that in some sense—I hope I am not putting it inaccurately—the partners carried on the business as trustees for her. It is said they are trustees for her of one-quarter share of the profits of the business. What does that mean? If it means that she is beneficially interested in the business and its assets, that is one thing; but, with all respect, it is quite untrue. She is not. If, on the other hand, all it means is that she is entitled to call for one-quarter share of the profits and receive it, it means something totally different. If it means only the latter, then I cannot myself see how she can be said to have received any income, unless and until she has received her share of the profits. The Crown puts her, in substance, in exactly the same position as if she had been a partner for these purposes. The argument failed to realise why it is that a partner who has not received his share of profits nevertheless is liable to taxation in respect of those profits. It is because he is a joint owner of the business and its assets. As soon as the accounts show a profit the partnership has made a profit for income tax purposes. On the other hand, a person who is only entitled to payment by the partners of a share of the profits has no proprietary interest in anything whatsoever unless and until it is paid over. . . .

Note
    As to the constitution of a partnership, reference should also be made to *Pickford* v. *Quirke* (1927) 13 T.C. 251; *ante*, p. 149.

---

[89] See also *I.R.C.* v. *Blott* [1920] 1 K.B. 114, 131, *per* Rowlatt J. Similarly, if partnership profits are described as " salary," " commission " or " interest on capital," this does not affect their nature as profits: *Lewis* v. *I.R.C.* [1933] 2 K.B. 557.
[90] See the Partnership Act 1890, s. 2.
[91] Following *Dewar* v. *I.R.C.* [1931] A.C. 566; *ante*, p. 340.

CHAPTER 16

COMPANIES

UNDER the system of corporate taxation which has existed in this country since 1965, a company resident in the United Kingdom is liable to Corporation Tax on all its profits wherever arising.[1] " Profits " means income and chargeable gains.[2] The income of a company is computed in accordance with income tax principles[3] and determined by reference to accounting periods. Thus, income from different sources is computed in accordance with the rules applicable to the appropriate Schedule; likewise, chargeable gains are computed in accordance with Capital Gains Tax principles. In addition to items which may be deducted in computing profits,[4] a company may have deductible charges on income,[5] and other allowable reliefs or deductions.[6] Dividends and other distributions are not deductible in computing income; they are properly regarded as an application of profits.[7] However, a company acts as a collector of taxes on behalf of the revenue, by deducting income tax under Schedule F upon dividends and distributions paid by it, accounting to the revenue for the tax so deducted.[8]

1. Theories of Corporate Taxation

The treatment of a company as a taxable entity presents a number of problems. The company possesses a separate legal identity apart from its shareholders, who, rather in the position of beneficiaries under an accumulation or discretionary trust, are not entitled to the income of the company unless a divided is declared or other distribution made.

They may nevertheless enjoy the benefit of undistributed profits on a return of capital (*e.g.* on winding-up) or by reflection in the value of their shares. On the other hand, in view of the progressive nature of income tax, and the distinction between capital and income, it is difficult to ignore the intermediate nature of a company as a means whereby the profits of a business are held and channelled to the real owners of the business.

Possible approaches to corporate taxation appear to be[9]:

---

[1] I.C.T.A. 1970, ss. 238, 243.
[2] *Ibid.* s. 238 (4).
[3] *Ibid.* s. 250.
[4] *e.g.* the salaries of employees and directors, if wholly and exclusively expended for the purposes of trade: *Copeman* v. *Flood* [1941] 1 K.B. 202; *ante*, p. 190.
[5] I.C.T.A. 1970, s. 248. In particular, such interest payments as a company is allowed to deduct, and other annual payments; N.B. *Ball* v. *National and Grindlays Bank* [1971] 3 All E.R. 485.
[6] *e.g.* in respect of losses, capital allowances or franked investment income.
[7] See *Mersey Docks and Harbour Board* v. *Lucas* (1883) 8 App.Cas. 891; *ante*, p. 133.
[8] I.C.T.A. 1970, s. 232.
[9] Commencing with respect to profits earned after March 31, 1973, a new system of corporate taxation will apply: Finance Act 1972, ss. 84–111.

   (i) the treatment of a company as a taxable person wholly distinct from its shareholders—the so-called " classical " method.[10] The company is taxed on all its income; so much of its income as is distributed is regarded as the income of the recipient and taxed as such (the effect often criticised as " double taxation ");

  (ii) a system of complete " fiscal transparency," regarding the company as a mere intermediary recipient of income on behalf of its members and apportioning that income among them whether or not it is actually paid to them [11];

 (iii) an intermediate system, which distinguishes between retained and distributed profits, either by applying different rates or by treating the payment of tax by the company in respect of distributed profits as, in part or in whole, a pre-payment of income tax on account of the recipient.[12]

FINAL REPORT OF THE ROYAL COMMISSION ON THE TAXATION OF PROFITS AND INCOME

1955 Cmd. 9474

44. The subject of corporate taxation itself invites certain preliminary observations of a general character. For we have to begin with the fact that the part of the country's commercial and industrial enterprise which is carried on by limited liability companies or other incorporated organisations is taxed differently from the part which is in the hands of individual proprietors, whether single persons or partnership firms. It is important to distinguish and account for this difference of treatment. No doubt the most conspicuous feature of distinction is the levying of a profits tax which is not charged upon the business profits of individuals but is charged upon the business profits of corporations, though subject to certain exemptions which we shall refer to later.

45. At the outset, we think it is well to enquire what is the justification for holding a company liable to pay income tax on its profits at all. A detached observer, coming fresh to the United Kingdom tax system and noting that that system had been so shaped as to impose a highly progressive levy on the incomes of individuals, might well suppose that the factor of crucial importance in determining the appropriate treatment of a given fund of income was ownership by an individual possessing total resources of a particular amount and with his own peculiar personal circumstances. If he were to think of a company as being in substance nothing but an aggregate of a number of shareholders banded together for the achievement of some common purpose under limited liability, his first expectation might well be that the profits earned by a company became significant for the purposes of the tax system when they fell into the personal incomes of the several shareholders by way of dividend,

---

[10] The method at present in use in this country and in the United States of America. For a study of the various methods, see J. Chown, *The Reform of Corporation Tax* (London, 1971), in which the proposals for reform and harmonisation in the European Economic Community are also considered. For further consideration of the " classical " method, see R. W. Parsons, " An Australian View of Corporation Tax " [1967] B.T.R. 14. The method is advocated in the *Memorandum of Dissent*, 1955 Cmd. 9474, *post*, p. 418.

[11] As suggested by the Carter Commission in Canada, *post*, p. 423. The position of the shareholder would thus be analogous to that of a beneficiary under a trust with a vested interest, *ante*, pp. 372–379.

[12] As in the case of the pre-1965 system in this country and the new system, coming into force in 1973.

and not before. On such an approach, the income tax would take account of dividends distributed in the form of personal income but would ignore company profits as such. This is not, however, the plan that has been adopted.

46. On the other hand, the observer would learn that the general law of the land clothes a company with a personality of its own and regards it as an entity distinct from the shareholders who are its members. On the assumption that the company's separate legal personality was a more important consideration than the fact that its income was no more than the income from the joint stock of certain individuals, the observer might, as an alternative to his first conjecture, expect to find that the company bore income tax on its profits and that its shareholders bore income tax on their dividends as a separate matter. This result, which has been criticised as being in effect double taxation of the same subject, has been avoided by treating the joint stock company as if it were a kind of large partnership, so that the payment of income tax by the company upon its income and profits is taken as discharging the shareholders from any liability to pay that tax upon dividends they receive out of its income and profits.[13]

49. Under the existing system, then, the undistributed profits and the distributed profits alike are made to serve in turn as a base for part of the taxation burden imposed upon companies. The special stress which the existing profits tax scheme lays upon distributed profits as an object of taxation is discussed in Chapter 20 below; but before we reach that branch of our subject it is convenient to examine further the general case for the taxation of corporate profits according to a separate code.

50. The arrangement which assesses corporate bodies to income tax upon their gross profits before payment of any dividend but requires those who draw dividends therefrom to submit to a proportionate deduction in respect of the income tax chargeable on the corporation is as old as Addington's Income Tax Act of 1803. Corporate taxation, then, began as part of a tax system which contained only income tax and virtually no progression. In that setting it was a form of taxation at source, the idea being that the income was taxed as soon as it reached the hands of the corporation and the corporation recovered the tax for itself when distributing the income among the members. On that view it was only natural not to assess the dividend over again in the hands of the shareholder. This arrangement took care of the case of undistributed profits, so long as income tax was virtually a proportional tax and the profits distributed were not markedly less than the profits made. But once large retentions become a permanent feature and the income tax becomes progressive, there is no theoretical justice in taxing undistributed profits at the standard rate. Given progressive rates for an individual's total income, from the lowest reduced rates to the highest surtax rates, personal allowances and exempted or partially exempted taxpayers, the taxation of undistributed profits at the standard rate cannot be fairly explained as taxation of the members' shares in the undistributed pool of income. Since there is a very wide range of total incomes for which the rate chargeable upon an extra pound added to the taxpayer's income would be the standard rate, it is sometimes asserted that the average marginal rate of tax for all the members of a large public company must often differ very little from the standard rate. But there is no means of determining how much validity to attribute to so very general an assertion.

51. If the income tax that falls upon undistributed profits can no longer be explained as a rough and ready way of taxing individuals upon their respective

---

[13] This describes the income tax and profits tax system in force prior to 1965. As to the treatment of companies as partnerships, see further pp. 429–431.

shares in those profits, some other approach is needed for an answer to the question how a company's profits should be taxed. As was pointed out in paragraph 45 above, a simple course would be not to tax them at all except as distributions to shareholders, thus leaving the progressive system of taxing personal incomes to occupy the whole field. But this extreme course would lead to certain marked inequities. The individual proprietor of a business is liable to be assessed on the whole of the profits earned by him irrespective of how much of them he may retain for the purpose of strengthening and expanding his undertaking. This treatment would be in sharp contrast to the untaxed growth in wealth that would occur if a corporate undertaking was permitted to enjoy exemption in respect of undistributed profits. Moreover, this untaxed growth would be accompanied by an increase in the capital value of the company's shares and would contribute a striking instance of capital sums being built up out of untaxed income. Clearly, the idea of outright exemption must be rejected. On the other hand, it does not seem to us to dispose of the matter to say that a company is a legal person capable of owning property and that the tax system has always taxed the corporate income of such a body. For the fact remains that the company's profits are derived from the employment of the wealth of individual shareholders, and the real problem is to relate the taxation of the company's profits at the undistributed stage to the general scheme of progressive taxation of personal incomes, bearing in mind that distributions when they take place in dividend form fall under the progressive system. A tax on corporate income that is not ultimately adjusted in account with each shareholder according to his share of that income means that income accruing on joint stock is taxed by a standard peculiar to itself and at a rate for each shareholder that may be heavier or may be less heavy than his true marginal rate. Profits tax introduced a new complication into the system of corporate taxation from this point of view.

52. We considered whether this measure of disadvantage could be accounted for by treating the company's total tax burden as including the equivalent of a " franchise " tax—that is to say, an annual levy by the State in return for the grant of the benefits of incorporation and limited liability.[14] We do not accept this as an adequate explanation. It is doubtful whether a levy based upon profits would be a natural way of expressing the idea; but in any event the scale of taxation represented by (i) income tax on retained profits, and (ii) profits tax on total profits—which together make up the corporate taxation not passed on to shareholders—is so high that it is out of all relation to the State's equivalent for the direct benefits of legal incorporation.

53. Profits tax itself has been defended as a super-tax on company profits designed as a rough counterpart to surtax on personal incomes. There is a risk of some confusion if the matter is stated in those terms. The situation is that the equity shareholders first have to suffer the diminution of their share in the company's profits through the payment of profits tax and thereafter must bear income tax and, if appropriate, surtax on what is made available for distribution out of the diminished balance of their share. As the same element of profit has been successively exposed both to profits tax and to surtax, it is difficult to see how, in the case of distributed profits the former tax can aptly be described as a counterpart to the latter. But the analysis is incomplete unless account is taken of those profits that are retained to strengthen the position of the company and, it may be, to finance some expansion of its undertaking. The individual proprietor of a business who

---

[14] For further consideration of this view, see the Report of the Committee of Inquiry on Small Firms, 1971 Cmnd. 4811; para. 13.58, *post*, p. 431.

retains part of his profits in the business must, if his total income requires it, bear not only income tax but also surtax upon the amount so set aside, for it is not treated any differently from the sums that he withdraws for personal spending or for investment outside his business. In other words, his saving through the medium of his business must be effected out of income that has borne the full burden of personal taxation. Generally speaking, the saving of other taxpayers out of other sources of income must likewise be found out of income after taxation. A company, on the other hand, can set aside out of profits, without any question of surtax arising, whatever amounts are necessary or advisable for the maintenance and development of its business. It operates therefore as a medium through which the whole body of its equity shareholders are enabled to achieve a measure of saving out of profits in respect of which no one of them has been required to pay surtax.

54. This indirect benefit of incorporation cannot fairly be ignored in framing the tax system applicable to corporate profits. It is a fiscal matter and bears upon the proper distribution of the burden of tax upon different kinds of income. The difficulty remains, however, that the saving achieved is achieved on behalf of the shareholders as a whole; the money is in most cases outside the control of any one individual shareholder and it is certainly not directly at his disposal as free personal income. It is true that a regular course of investing retained profits must have an influence on the market or realisable value of shares in a company: but experience indicates that the connection is too uncertain to justify the idea that the shareholder's liability to dispose of part of his holding gives him the power year by year to enjoy in his own hands a spendable income in any real sense equivalent to his aliquot share of the undistributed profits. Finally it is only surtax that is escaped by corporate saving: and many shareholders would not be surtax-payers even if profits were fully distributed.

55. Nor does this analysis give a clear indication whether it is (*i*) the undistributed profits themselves, (*ii*) the distributed profits, or (*iii*) the total profits, that afford the aptest measure for apportioning among companies a tax burden that is intended to take account of the benefit gained by their respective shareholders, namely, the achievement of savings that are not subject to the full impact of personal taxation. All three have some claims to serve as a base, but all three have unsatisfactory features. The undistributed profits are, of course, the very source of the advantage to the shareholder that is in view; yet, as we remarked in the preceding paragraph, their influence on the value of the shares is unpredictable. It is the distributed profits that tend most directly to influence the market value of a share; yet the higher the proportion of distributed profit to total profit, the smaller is the benefit which the shareholders of the company are deriving from the facility which incorporation affords for surtax-free saving. Lastly, the total profits and the company's capacity to go on earning them are the ultimate source of the wealth that accrues to the equity shareholders; yet the market makes little difference in valuation for differences in the earnings cover of dividends if plainly adequate.

56. In the circumstances, it does not seem possible to find a satisfactory basis of taxation for corporate profits by any line of reasoning that would treat companies as if they were the same sort of taxpayers as individuals. Moreover, the taxation of personal income that takes the form of dividends cannot rightly be determined without regard to the character of the source of profit from which they are derived. If the problem is to be judged according to purely fiscal principles we conclude that the governing considerations are these : —

(1) Undistributed corporate profits should not escape taxation.

(2) It would be wrong to tax those profits without recognising that they represent, though in a special form, income belonging ultimately to individuals.

(3) Because of its special form, that income is *sui generis*.

(4) The special features which distinguish it are that generally speaking an individual shareholder has no direct ownership of, or control over, his " share " in those profits or the assets by which they are represented.

(5) Income represented by a right of this kind has a lower taxable capacity than ordinary income by any method of comparison that treats each as part of the total income of some individual.

57. If we are right in thinking that these are the governing conditions it follows that none of them offers any really satisfactory principle for determining a relationship between the burden of corporate taxation and the burden of personal taxation. Indeed no comparison of the respective burdens can attain precision in the face of a highly progressive system of personal taxation imposing widely differing rates of tax upon the marginal income of many millions of individuals. The standard rate is now little more than one step on the ladder that stretches from the lowest reduced rate to the highest combined rate of income and surtax. In the result any corporate taxation that is not merely a method of taxation at the source has to be measured according to its effect upon the undistributed profits upon which its burden will fall; and in the absence of any clear guidance from principles of fiscal equity we must expect that the rate will be determined primarily by the current need for revenue and by the economic objects that it may be hoped to achieve by changes in the impact of taxation—*e.g.*, by reference to the current policy of favouring company investment at the expense of personal income or personal income at the expense of company investment, as the case may be.

544.[15] It seems to us a wrong principle to subject the shareholder (whether by deduction at source or otherwise) to income tax liability on his receipt from the company in any way that altogether ignores the fact that the profits from which the dividend is drawn have paid corporation tax in the company's hands. We accept the criticism that it is double taxation to treat a company dividend as being a wholly new source of income. Even in some countries where the double taxation of dividend income has long been a familiar and accepted feature of the tax system we understand that steps have recently been taken, or are proposed, for the purpose of allowing some tax credit to a shareholder for the corporation tax payment by the company from which he draws his dividend.

Memorandum of Dissent, by Mr. G. Woodcock, Mr. H. L. Bullock and Mr. N. Kaldor

90. In the view of the Majority it would constitute " double taxation " if the shareholder were subjected to income tax on his dividends without allowance for the fact that " the profits from which the dividend is drawn have paid corporation tax in the company's hands." [16] It seems to us that this view rests on a misconception. Once we recognise that the profits tax paid by companies is a different tax from the income tax paid by individuals, and therefore the one can be levied at rates which are quite independent of the other, the principles of equity no more require us to offset the payment of the profits tax against the individual's liability to income tax than to call for such a tax credit in connection with the many other taxes (such as local rates, the petrol duty or the stamp duty) the incidence of which directly or indirectly falls on the individual income tax payer.

[15] This paragraph comes from the chapter dealing with possible alternatives to profits tax.
[16] Para. 544, *supra*.

91. Nor does it follow that the individual shareholder would be in a better position if such offsetting arrangements were made than if they were not made. The Majority argument assumes in effect that the Government would levy the corporation profits tax at the same rate (whatever that rate is) irrespective of whether the tax is credited against the shareholder's income tax or not. But since the net revenue from the tax would be very different in the two cases, no such supposition would be justified. From the shareholder's point of view, on the other hand, what matters is the amount by which his profits are reduced through corporate taxation, not the precise form in which they are reduced. Since not only the rates of profit taxation but the nominal dividends declared by the companies can be expected to be adjusted to the difference in the mode of charging, it is not clear why the shareholder is put under any disadvantage under the one system as against the other. We greatly regret therefore that the Majority felt themselves unable to recommend a scheme which would have brought about a considerable improvement in both the equity and the administrative simplicity of the tax system.

A Corporation Profits Tax

92. We therefore recommend that company profits should be made subject only to one tax, the Corporation Profits Tax, which should be drawn up on principles appropriate to company taxation and levied at rates that are independent of personal income tax. No income tax should be levied on companies as such, but companies should be asked to act as agents to the Revenue and deduct income tax at the ruling standard rate on all interest and dividends paid out.

93. Assuming that companies are only charged with a Corporation Profits Tax the primary questions to be considered are (i) the manner in which the tax should be levied—i.e. whether it is to be levied at a proportional rate or a progressive rate, and whether there should be a differentiation according as the profits are distributed or retained; (ii) what should be the total amount of taxation levied on companies having regard to the amount of taxation borne by individuals, the needs of revenue and the ultimate incidence of the taxes charged on companies.

94. With regard to the first question we do not believe that either considerations of equity or of economic expediency would justify taxation at a progressive rate. The considerations which require a rich individual to be taxed at a higher rate than an individual of more moderate means do not apply to comparisons between large and small corporations. Considerations of economic efficiency on the other hand undoubtedly favour the levying of tax at a rate or schedule of rates which is independent of the total profits earned by the corporation. This still leaves the question open, however, whether the tax should be at the uniform rate on the whole of profits, or whether the part of the profits that is distributed should pay tax at a higher rate or at a lower rate than the part which is undistributed. The existing profits tax (charged in addition to income tax) levies a tax of 22½ per cent. on distributed profits and 2½ per cent. on undistributed profits. The Majority of the Commission felt that if this matter were considered on equity considerations alone the differentiation ought to be the other way round, the tax being confined to that part of the profits which is retained.

95. It seems to us that whilst equity considerations are undoubtedly relevant to the issue, it is impossible to arrive at an ideal method of taxation of companies by applying the same principles to the consideration of this problem as

are appropriate in the case of personal taxation. Whilst it is true that the ultimate burden of the taxes levied on corporations falls on individuals (in much the same way as in the case of any other tax) it cannot be assumed without qualification that a tax levied on a corporation is merely an indirect way of levying a tax on a definite body of individuals, who are the owners of the corporation at any one time.

Reservation, by Mr. W. F. Crick

2. My colleagues acknowledge, as I do, a significant difference between the nature of the " income " of individuals and that of corporate bodies. It is when we come to inquire: " How different, and how far should the difference be recognised in the tax system? " that we part company. For me, the distinguishing quality of true money income is that it is at the free disposal of the individual to whose benefit it accrues. So far as corporate profits are distributed as dividends they assume this quality by being transmuted into personal incomes, and to that extent they become subject to the progressive tax scale laid down for personal incomes. So far as they are not thus distributed they retain their own distinctive quality, as a corpus of funds quite separate and apart from the current flow of personal incomes. It is indeed only in a remote and formal sense—at least in all but the closest of " close corporations " [17]—that they can be regarded as comprising personal property or possessions of the individual shareholders, who in fact have little or no command over their retention or distribution.

3. For tax purposes, personal incomes are accepted as the prime measure of capacity to pay—a measure that is modified in its application by a number of adjustments and refinements as set out in our Second Report. There is—and seemingly can be—no tenable corresponding concept, of relative capacity to pay, that is valid for the undistributed profits of companies. The detailed adaptability of the personal income tax system to the individual case, according to the governing principle of capacity to pay, underlines the essential difference between personal incomes, each under the control of an individual, and corporate profits, as earnings of an impersonal venture which may or may not be turned into personal incomes.

4. It follows, in my view, that we are looking at things the wrong way round when we treat a corporate body—as we now do—as an entity having an income of its own and paying income tax thereon (at standard rate, since the system of allowances and graduation can have no applicability in this field), some part of which it is authorised to recover from its shareholders. Its proper status, as is recognised in the deduction of tax from some forms of debt interest, is rather that of agent for the Revenue in the collection of tax due (subject to subsequent adjustment according to the position of each separate recipient) from the individuals who derive a benefit, in the form of true income, from a distribution of the profits by way of dividend. The contrast of status is crucial, for it emphasises the inherent distinction, already noted, between personal incomes and corporate profits. And this distinction ought, in my judgment, to be given formal recognition in the tax system.

GREEN PAPER—REFORM OF CORPORATION TAX

1971 Cmnd. 4630

1. In his Budget statement on March 30, 1971 the Chancellor of the Exchequer announced the Government's intention to reform the structure of corporation

---

[17] The treatment of " close corporations " is considered, *post*, p. 426.

tax so as to remove the present discrimination against distributed profits. Of the various possible systems of company tax which would achieve this end, the Government consider that the one which would be most appropriate on domestic grounds would be the system usually referred to as the " two-rate system." Subject to suitable safeguards, however, the Government are perfectly prepared to consider the possibility of adopting what is commonly called the " imputation system " of corporation tax. The Government have examined, but would not favour, a third system of tax involving a return in substance to the profits tax and income tax arrangements which applied in this country until 1965. A decision on the system to be adopted will be taken in the light of the comments and discussion which this paper seeks to encourage and of developments in company taxation within the European Economic Community.

ALTERNATIVE SYSTEMS OF COMPANY TAXATION

The " two-rate System "

2. Under a two-rate system distributed profits would be liable to corporation tax at a lower rate than undistributed profits. In addition, distributed profits would be paid under deduction of income tax and this tax would, as at present, be paid over to the Inland Revenue and would be an advance payment of the shareholder's own eventual tax liability.

The " Imputation System "

3. Under the imputation system all profits, whether distributed or not, would be liable to corporation tax at the same rate, but part of the tax on the distributed profits would be available to be set as a credit against the shareholder's own tax liability and could in appropriate circumstances be repaid to him. To fit such a system into the tax structure as it exists in this country, it would be necessary, as a safeguard, for income tax to be deducted from dividends as it is at present and paid to the Inland Revenue. In the case of a company all of whose profits were liable to United Kingdom corporation tax, the tax deducted from dividends and paid to the Inland Revenue would merely represent an advance payment of the company's eventual corporation tax liability. In the case of a United Kingdom company which paid dividends out of profits which had not borne United Kingdom corporation tax, it would ensure that the Exchequer was not put in the position of having to repay to shareholders tax which it had never received from the company.

The " Pre-1965-type System "

4. This system, in substance though not in form, involves a return to the arrangements in operation before 1965. Company profits, whether distributed or not, would be subject to corporation tax as at present at a single rate. In addition, dividends would as now be subject to deduction of income tax at the standard rate; the difference would be that companies would be allowed to retain this income tax instead of paying it over to the Inland Revenue as they do now.

5. There is an important difference between this third system and the imputation system which it otherwise resembles. The difference is in the treatment of dividends paid out of profits which—for example, because of relief for foreign tax—have not borne the full rate of corporation tax at home. In those circumstances the imputation system would in effect impose a supplementary charge on the company in the manner described in paragraph 3 above. By

contrast a pre-1965 kind of system would deal with this problem by restricting the amount of the repayment to shareholders, such as pension funds, charities and elderly people living on small investment incomes, who would otherwise be able to reclaim the income tax on their dividends.

6. The third system would thus involve a return to the net United Kingdom rate arrangements which were in force in this country before 1965. The Government see serious difficulties in such arrangements. First, they are complicated both for the company and for the shareholder and involve a considerable administrative burden. Second, they are uneven in their incidence, and prejudice mainly exempt shareholders, like pension funds or charities, or those living on small investment incomes. Any return to a net United Kingdom rate system would mean that shareholders of these kinds would have a strong incentive to move their investments into companies trading wholly in this country whose dividends were unaffected by any restriction for foreign tax. The pattern of investment could thus be distorted and in the short term there might well be a considerable upheaval in the stock market—perhaps with hardship to some small shareholders—as exempt funds and other shareholders affected by the change took steps to rearrange their portfolios.

THE CHOICE

7. The Chancellor has therefore indicated that, in the Government's view, the real choice for a reformed company tax lies between a two-rate system and an imputation system—that is, between the first and second systems described in paragraphs 2 and 3 above. In many respects these two systems, though different in form, are in substance alike. For example, a two-rate system, in its simplest form, would be one in which the rates of tax were such that the rate of tax on distributed profits plus the rate of income tax deducted from dividends would be equal to the rate of corporation tax on undistributed profits. Similarly, assuming the same yield of corporation tax, the tax rate on all profits under an imputation system would be equal to the higher (undistributed) rate under a two-rate system. Under either system, therefore, the company would pay tax (whether corporation tax alone or corporation tax plus income tax on distributions) at effectively the same rate on the whole of its profits. Similarly, under either system the shareholder would receive a dividend effectively net of income tax, which in appropriate cases could be reclaimed.

8. Again, it is sometimes suggested that an imputation system with its high corporation tax rate on all profits, whether distributed or not, is more favourable to income from foreign investment because it sets a higher ceiling on the credit which may be given for foreign tax. This is not in fact the case. Under either system the measure of relief for foreign tax could be the same.

9. There is however one substantial difference between the two systems. The two-rate system maintains a firm line of demarcation between the corporation tax liability of the company and the income tax liability of the shareholder in a way that the imputation system does not, for under the imputation system what is at one stage part of the company's corporation tax bill becomes in effect a payment on account of the shareholder's income tax. The Government regard this demarcation as an advantage and as likely to lead to greater simplicity in the administration of the tax. However, this does not of course affect the reality of the matter: both the two-rate and the imputation systems substantially avoid the double taxation of distributed profits—the feature of the existing system which has tended to divorce the interests of the company and the shareholder.

Note
    The question was referred to the Select Committee on Corporation Tax, whose report
(1971 H.C. 622) favoured the "imputation" method, largely because it facilitates the renego-
tiating of double-taxation agreements and because it is the method most likely to be adopted
in the European Economic Community. See J. Chown, "The Reform of Corporation Tax:
Some International Factors" [1971] B.T.R. 215; A. R. Prest, "The Select Committee on
Corporation Tax" [1972] B.T.R. 15.
    The recommendation was implemented by the Finance Act 1972, Pt. V (ss. 84–111),
described by J. Chown and P. Rowland, "The Finance Bill—The Reform of Corporation Tax"
[1972] B.T.R. 133.

REPORT OF THE ROYAL COMMISSION ON TAXATION

Carter Commission, Canada, 1966

VOLUME I: INTRODUCTION

Integration of Personal and Corporation Income Taxes

It is frequently argued that shareholders should not be given credit for underlying corporation taxes because corporations pass such taxes on, typically by
charging higher prices for what they sell, sometimes by paying less for what
they buy. We accept that this is often true, but do not think it is a valid
objection to the full credit to shareholders.

Corporation taxes are "passed on" in two ways: through immediate
increases in prices or reductions in costs that quickly restore the after-tax rate
of return to corporate assets; through gradual increases in product prices
(relative to what they otherwise would be) resulting from reduced capital
spending and hence output. In the former case the corporation tax is a crude
and inequitable tax on wealth, because the tax is borne by those who happen to
hold the "wrong" shares at the time the tax is imposed. These shareholders
bear the tax because it is capitalised in lower share prices.

Consumers are worse off in either case. Either their real purchasing power
is reduced because prices are higher or wages are lower or there are fewer
goods and services available.

The important issue is, of course, what would happen if full credit was
allowed for corporation taxes now. Here again there are two possibilities. The
tax reduction on corporate source income could be quickly passed on to consumers through lower prices or passed on to workers through higher wages.
The tax reduction could be capitalised in higher share prices. Only when the
corporation was completely insulated from the competition provided by the
entry of new firms attracted by the higher after-tax rate of return to shareholders
would the full amount of the tax reduction likely be capitalised in the price
of the shares. Few corporations have such a monopoly position. Probably the
rise in share prices would be relatively small. If the tax reduction was not
shifted quickly through lower prices, the higher after-tax rate of return to
shareholders would stimulate capital spending, increased output and lower
product prices and hence push down after-tax rates of return toward earlier
levels. This process of adjustment would take a substantial period of time.

Consumers would benefit from the corporation tax credit if the tax reduction was passed on in lower prices or brought about increased output or both.
Consumers generally would not benefit from the corporation tax credit if the
tax reduction was simply reflected in higher share prices without any increase
in capital expenditures and output.

We are confident that the instances of full capitalisation of the tax reduction
without favourable price and output effects would be the exception rather than
the rule. To deny the tax reduction because the shareholders of a few corporations would obtain windfall share gains would be to cut off our collective noses

to spite our collective faces. We would be denying ourselves greater output from the economy generally to ensure that the few did not get what they did not deserve. There are other methods for dealing with corporations that have massive and persistent monopoly power. To design a tax system to suit the exceptional case would be to lose all perspective.

Another advantage of the integration of corporation and shareholder taxes and the full taxation of property gains would be the prevention of tax avoidance. Under this system profits of all kinds and from all sources would be taxable in the same manner. Accordingly, there would be relatively little incentive to arrange transactions in such a way as to change the form of payment. The basic inconsistencies in our law which have resulted in widespread " surplus-stripping " and other abuses would be eliminated. This result is, in our view, further evidence of the fundamental soundness of the system we propose.

VOLUME III : TAXATION OF INCOME. CHAPTER 7

The Income of Organisations as a Tax Base

Intermediaries such as corporations and trusts should not be regarded as entities with tax-paying capacity. It should be recognised that the taxes they pay are borne by people, and accordingly there should be integration of the taxes on resident individuals and families with the taxes imposed on intermediaries. This can be achieved by providing a refundable tax credit to resident shareholders for the income taxes collected from organisations.

VOLUME IV : TAXATION OF INCOME (PART B). CHAPTER 19

1. Taxes can be collected from organisations such as corporations but the burden is ultimately on people—customers, employees, suppliers or shareholders— whose power to consume is reduced by the tax on the organisation. Corporations have the rights and obligations of persons under the law; management often makes corporate decisions without consulting the shareholders. These are valid but irrelevant propositions in considering who bears the corporation tax.

2. Equity and neutrality could best be achieved under a tax system where there were no taxes on organisations, and all individuals and families selling and holding interests in organisations were taxed on the realised and accrued net gains derived from these sales and holdings. The net gains from selling and holding interests in organisations would be treated in the same way as other kinds of net gains, and the net gains, from selling and holding interests in all kinds of organisations would be taxed identically.

3. Unfortunately this ideal system cannot be recommended for two reasons:

(a) At the present time, valuation problems preclude the annual taxation of accrued net gains. In the absence of accrual taxation, and if there was no tax on the income of corporations, some individuals could postpone their personal income taxes on the income they wished to save.

(b) If the Canadian corporate source income of non-residents were taxed at lower rates than are now in effect, it would reduce the net benefit Canada derives from foreign direct investment in Canada. Because of existing tax treaties and the retaliation that would follow if these treaties were ignored, it would not be feasible to tax this income at the present level except by a corporation income tax like the tax now imposed at a rate of approximately 50 per cent.

4. Retaining the corporation income tax at a rate of approximately 50 per cent., but providing full integration of this tax with the personal income tax

of residents, would solve the deferment problem, would maintain the net benefit from foreign direct investment in Canada and would achieve the greatest possible equity and neutrality.[18]

The Proposed Integration System

5. The basic features of the full integration system we recommend are as follows:

(a) The income of corporations should be subject to tax at a flat rate of 50 per cent.

(b) The income of individuals and families should be subject to progressive rates of tax with a top marginal rate of 50 per cent.

(c) The corporation should be allowed to allocate after-tax corporate income to shareholders without having to pay cash dividends.

(d) The tax base of the resident shareholder should include the corporate income paid or allocated to him, grossed-up for the corporation tax paid.

(e) The resident shareholder should receive credit against his personal tax liability for the full amount of the corporation tax on after-tax corporate income paid or allocated to him, with a refund of the corporation tax if the credit exceeded the liability.

(f) Realised gains and losses on corporate shares should be included in income and taxed at full progressive rates.

(g) The cost basis of shares should be increased when the corporation allocated retained corporate earnings to shareholders and thereby created " allocated surplus," so that share gains resulting from the retention of earnings that had been taxed to the shareholder would not be taxed again to the shareholder when realised.

(h) When dividends were paid out of allocated surplus they should not be included in the shareholder's income but should be deducted from his cost basis for the shares, because such dividends would represent a realisation of funds already included in income and previously added to the cost basis of the shares.

(i) A corporation with a small number of shareholders which met specified conditions should be entitled to elect to be taxed as a partnership in order to avoid the payment by the corporation of tax at 50 per cent. and the claiming by the shareholders of refunds equal to the difference between that tax and tax calculated at their personal rates.

2. Related Companies

Although every company is a separate legal person, relationships between two or more companies, as successors in a trade or by virtue of common control (as parent and subsidiary or as members of a group or consortium) may be important. The relationship is especially relevant in the case of the payment of dividends or other distributions by one company to an associated company[19] and the availability of relief for the loss of one company against the profits of an associated company.[20]

---

18 In particular, the proposed system would be neutral as between retained and distributed profits.

19 Reliefs are available in respect of " group income," I.C.T.A. 1970, ss. 256–257; F.A. 1972, s. 91.

20 " Group relief " enables the loss of one member of a group to be set against the profits of another, I.C.T.A. 1970, ss. 258–264. As to the treatment of losses of a predecessor company in the hands of the successor company, see I.C.T.A. 1970, ss. 252–253 and 483; see also *Pritchard* v. *M.H. Builders (Wilmslow) Ltd.* [1969] 1 W.L.R. 409.

REPORT OF THE COMMITTEE ON THE TAXATION OF TRADING PROFITS

1951 Cmd. 8189

289. We received a number of representations about the treatment of parent and subsidiary companies. It was suggested that some provisions should be introduced under which groups of companies could elect to be treated for Income Tax purposes as single assessable units, . . .

. . . 290. Objections of principle can be raised against the proposal to amalgamate, for income tax purposes, the results of trading by two or more separate legal entities, but we do not think that on balance any such objections should prevail. The question is therefore whether the proposal is practicable. . . .

297. . . . It is sometimes contended that if a group does not like the taxation consequences of division into separate legal entities, the remedy lies in its own hands, because it can transact business by means of separate branches of a single company instead of separate companies; . . . There may, however, be very weighty commercial reasons for carrying on business in the way they do, particularly where trading operations are carried on in some countries outside the United Kingdom, so that the customs and other requirements of that country have to be considered. In any event we do not think that taxation law should lag behind the general law in recognising that no true profit can arise to a group from the sale of goods until they have been sold to a purchaser outside the group.

3. Close Companies

It has long been recognised that " closely-held " corporations, *i.e.* those where " control " rests in the hands of relatively few shareholders, present particular problems. A number of provisions have in consequence been enacted in respect of " close companies," [21] aimed mainly at the prevention of tax avoidance, either by extracting profits in some (prima facie) non-taxable form,[22] by attempting to deduct as expenditure of the company or as charges on its income what is in reality an application of its profits,[23] or by avoiding surtax by an excessive retention of profits.[24]

(i) *Shortfall*

Under the current method of taxing companies, the distributed profits of a company bear Corporation Tax and, in the hands of the recipient, income tax and (where applicable) surtax: retained profits bear only Corporation Tax. However, if the distributions made by a close company fall short of the " required standard," the company is assessed to income tax upon the shortfall as if it had been distributed.[25] Further, the amount of the short-

---

[21] As defined by I.C.T.A. 1970, s. 282. See further, ss. 302, 303 as to " control," etc., and N.B. *J. Bibby & Sons Ltd.* v. *I.R.C.* (1945) 29 T.C. 167; *Willingdale* v. *Islington Green Investment Co.* [1972] 1 All E.R. 199.

[22] Such as a loan or payment for restrictive covenant, see I.C.T.A. 1970, ss. 286–288.

[23] By making annual payments or certain payments of interest, or paying excessive rents or royalties or expenses to a participator, see I.C.T.A. 1970, ss. 284–285.

[24] The fact that a company is " closely-held " is also relevant for Estate Duty purposes, see *post*, p. 517. A close company may also be a " body corporate connected with the settlement " for the purposes of I.C.T.A. 1970, s. 451, see *Potts' Executors* v. *I.R.C.* [1951] A.C. 443; *ante*, p. 399; *I.R.C.* v. *Bates* [1968] A.C. 483; *ante*, p. 401.

[25] I.C.T.A. 1970, ss. 289–295.

fall is apportioned among the " participators " who would have been entitled to receive it had it been distributed, and they are assessable to surtax upon the amounts so apportioned. When the new " imputation " method of taxing companies comes into force, in relation to accounting periods ending after April 5, 1973, retained profits will no longer receive favoured treatment and the concept of shortfall will cease to be of importance. Rules relating to apportionment, on the other hand, will continue to be necessary.[26]

THOMAS FATTORINI (LANCASHIRE) LTD. v. I.R.C.

House of Lords [1942] A.C. 643; 111 L.J.K.B. 546; 167 L.T. 45; [1942] 1 All E.R. 619; 24 T.C. 328

An investment company borrowed money from a bank, agreeing with the bank not to pay any dividends to its shareholders until the loan was repaid. A surtax direction (the then equivalent of a shortfall assessment and surtax apportionment) was made on the ground that the company had not distributed a reasonable part of its income. *Held*, the direction should be discharged.

VISCOUNT SIMON L.C.: My Lords, counsel for the appellant company, in his excellent argument, placed before the House the statutory history of successive efforts made by the legislature to prevent the avoidance of super-tax, or of its successor surtax, by using the cloak afforded by company law. Since the tax is charged only in respect of the income of an individual, its incidence might be avoided by transferring to a company controlled by such an individual, in return for shares, the source of such income and by securing that, instead of any dividends being declared, the profits made by the company should be accumulated and ultimately distributed in a capital form as the results of voluntary liquidation or by creating bonus shares: *Inland Revenue Commissioners* v. *Blott* [27]; or otherwise. Accordingly, by section 21 of the Finance Act 1922, it was enacted [28] : . . .

LORD ATKIN: . . . It seems clear that the discussion must proceed *ab initio* on the footing that the action of the directors must be judged by considering what their conduct would reasonably be if no question of surtax influenced their decision. Withholding of distribution for the purpose of " avoidance of the payment of surtax " by shareholders would, if found, obviously negative the reasonableness of any part so withheld. The other general point to be observed is that, as it seems to me, what has to be found is that the company acted unreasonably in withholding some part of its income from distribution. It is not enough to show that a part could reasonably be distributed, if at the same time it could be said, as it well might, that it was equally reasonable to withhold distribution. The section is highly penal, and I feel no doubt that the onus is originally and remains on the revenue to show that the company acted unreasonably in withholding part of its income from distribution. What is reasonable has consistently been held to depend on the actual conditions known at the time for decision. In the application of this section it is what *these* directors recommend and *these* shareholders decide in *those* conditions of *that* company. There is no abstract conception of reasonableness, and the conclusion is not to be reached on a priori reasoning. Assuming that the directors are business men, have they acted unreasonably in the circumstances in withholding a distribution?

---

[26] The new system of taxing close companies is contained in Finance Act 1972, ss. 94, 95; Scheds. 16, 17. [27] [1921] 2 A.C. 171.

[28] The Lord Chancellor then proceeded to quote that section, the forerunner of the present provisions.

. . . I come to the clear conclusion that there was no evidence that the company failed to distribute a reasonable part of its income.

. . . If the arrangement with the bank was, in fact, made as part of a plan for avoiding surtax there might very well be evidence of a failure to distribute a reasonable part of the income, but, in the absence of any evidence or finding to that effect and in view of the respondents' disclaimer of any attack on that agreement, it must be taken to represent a genuine business arrangement and is a circumstance of the highest importance in estimating the reasonableness of the company's action. . . .

Note

Note now, in determining the " distributable income " of a close company, the distinction drawn between trading and estate income on the one hand and investment income on the other: I.C.T.A. 1970, s. 290. As to the requirements of a company's business, see s. 293 and D. C. Milne and G. B. Bunker, " A Practical Approach to Shortfall " [1971] B.T.R. 20.

REPORT OF THE COMMITTEE OF INQUIRY ON SMALL FIRMS

1971 Cmnd. 4811, para. 13.56

. . . we do not believe that any harm would be done to the national interest if all control over the distribution of trading incomes were to be relinquished. With the existence of capital gains taxation we think it unlikely that significant abuses would occur if close companies were permitted to retain the whole of their trading income. It is therefore our view that shortfall assessment on the trading income of close companies should be abolished, and that no parallel provisions should be included in the forthcoming revision of corporation tax. However well drafted, such provisions would inevitably give rise to the kind of misunderstanding which has bedevilled the administration of the present rules, and their cost, in terms of administration and disaffection, would in our view outweigh any harm they might avert. *We hope the Government will bear this view in mind in their consultations on this subject.* We recognise that if close trading companies were to be given this significant advantage it would be necessary to draft a watertight definition, for we accept that there is no case for such a concession to investment companies, where the real mischief of the " incorporated money-box " arises. . . .

GREEN PAPER—REFORM OF CORPORATION TAX

1971 Cmnd. 4630

CLOSE COMPANIES

26. Under the system described above [29] the burden of tax on profits (including the income tax deducted from dividends) would be the same whether the profits were distributed or not. This would have important implications for the present rules governing the taxation of close companies. At present, if a close company withholds money from distribution, it thereby saves both the income tax on a dividend and any additional surtax [30] which the shareholder might have had to pay if he had received a dividend. Under a two-rate system only the shareholder's surtax would be at issue and the problem of close companies

[29] The two-rate system (see *ante*, p. 421). The same would broadly be true for the Imputation system.

[30] The Green Paper points out that the expression " surtax " will not be in use after 1973–74, and the word should be understood in the context of the proposed reformed system of personal taxation, see *ante*, p. 338.

would be a matter of ensuring that distributions were not kept down below a reasonable level in order to limit the surtax liability of the shareholders; and in this respect it would be a return to a position not unlike the position before 1965.

27. The Government intend to secure a major simplification of the rules applying to close companies. The proposals announced in the Budget Speech, which will make a major reduction in the number of companies coming under review, are a first step in this direction. For companies remaining within the scope of the legislation it is envisaged that it would be necessary to use the legislation only for the purposes of preventing surtax avoidance (as was the case before 1965); but it is not the intention to restore the power to deem the company to have made, for surtax purposes, a 100 per cent. distribution. Instead, in the cases where it is clear that the retention of profits would put significant amounts of surtax at stake, companies would be required to make reasonable distributions—the maximum level of such distributions certainly being no higher than the law now requires. Even this maximum level of distribution would not apply to trading or estate companies which could show that, having regard to their requirements for finance for development or other suitable purposes, a lower level of distribution would be reasonable. The Government intend to consult with representative organisations with a view to evolving a new code of practice which, while protecting the essential interests of the Revenue, will impose the minimum administrative burden on close companies.

Note
   Special reliefs for small companies, to apply when the "imputation" method comes into force, are contained in the Finance Act 1972, s. 95. Most small companies will pay corporation tax at a lower rate.

(ii) *Small Businesses—the Choice of Business Medium*

The method of taxing close companies has advantages and disadvantages for the proprietors of the business and these may influence the choice of business medium, in particular the decision whether or not to incorporate.[31] Suggestions have been made that a small company should be entitled to elect to be assessed as though it were a partnership.[32]

FINAL REPORT OF THE ROYAL COMMISSION ON THE TAXATION OF PROFITS AND INCOME

1955 Cmd. 9474

559. Secondly, it is suggested that a great majority of the smaller companies, what we describe as "close" corporations, are more nearly akin to the individual trader or partnership than to the public company. The individual or partner without other income does not pay surtax on profits under £2,000 and it is argued that here is therefore good ground for exempting their corporate counterparts from profits tax below that figure. We were not persuaded by

---

31 See especially "Talbot on Corporation Tax" (Pt. I of the *British Tax Encyclopaedia*), Chap. 24; M. Grundy, *Tax and the Family Business* (4th ed.), Chap. 5; P. Bird, "The Finance Act 1967 and the Incorporation of Small Businesses" [1968] B.T.R. 346; "The Incorporation of Small Businesses: effects of the Finance Act 1965" [1965] B.T.R. 393; D. A. Chaffey, "Tax-Saving Remuneration to Directors" [1963] B.T.R. 156.
32 As permitted in the United States of America, see H. R. Kent, "United States Income Tax Relief for Small Businesses" [1959] B.T.R. 33.

this argument. The individual or the partnership assumes corporate status voluntarily, presumably because there are practical advantages in doing so, and as we have said elsewhere, it is over-simplifying the picture to equate profits tax and surtax. Further, it must be remembered that under the existing law the provisions governing the remuneration of directors of director-controlled companies mean that the law puts no obstacle (within generous limits) in the way of directors of small concerns taking their profits out of their companies in the form of remuneration.[33]

REPORT OF THE ROYAL COMMISSION ON TAXATION

Carter Commission, Canada, 1966

VOLUME IV: TAXATION OF INCOME (PART B). CHAPTER 19

26. A corporation with a relatively small income and with a small number of shareholders should be entitled to be taxed as a partnership if it complied with certain conditions. This would avoid the necessity for payment of the corporation tax and the claiming of refunds. Each shareholder would include in his tax base his portion of the corporation's income. If the corporation had a loss, each shareholder could claim his portion of the loss as a deduction from other income, but the corporation could not then carry the loss back or forward.

REPORT OF THE COMMITTEE OF INQUIRY ON SMALL FIRMS

1971 Cmnd. 4811

13.57   A further consequence of the introduction of corporation tax, uncon-nected with shortfall, is the inequality of treatment as between different forms of business organisation to which it gave rise. We have suggested that the great majority of small unincorporated businesses pay income tax on their profits at rates substantially below the fixed rate of corporation tax. In other circum-stances an individual or partnership may be heavily disadvantaged by compari-son with an incorporated business. The tax system thus has an important bearing on the choice of status in the carrying on of a business. We think this unfortunate: there are many reasons for the choice of business status, but the tax consequences should not be among them. Some of the major differences in treatment, apart from the difference in rates already referred to, are the following:

(i) An individual or partnership cannot retain profits in a business or pro-fessional partnership without paying surtax on total profits—an incorpora-ted business can.

(ii) An individual trader can set losses in his business against other personal income, but the same man carrying on a trade as a one-man company cannot do so.

(iii) The individual trader or partner has relatively beneficial treatment in the early years of his business or partnership if he is well advised as to the date to which he should draw his accounts, but this is not available to the same business carried on through a company.

---

[33] At various times restrictions have been placed upon the amount of directors' remuneration which a close company is entitled to deduct in computing its profits. At present, there are no limits other than that the payments must be a proper expenditure of the trade, see *Copeman* v. *Flood* [1941] 1 K.B. 202; *ante*, p. 190.

13.58 One effect of the differential between corporation tax and the lower rates of income tax is to deter some small businessmen from incorporation, and thus from enjoying the security of limited liability. This is undesirable, not because incorporation is always advantageous, but because when it is advantageous a firm should not be deterred from it by marginal tax considerations. The Inland Revenue have pointed out to us that this problem has largely disappeared as a result of the 1969 Finance Act, which permitted close companies, if they wished to avoid the liability to corporation tax, to take out all profits in the form of directors' remuneration, and face assessment to income tax on that basis. We accept that this disposes of the problem for a profitable company where there is identity of interest between shareholders and directors, but where this is not so, it is not to be expected that outside shareholders would be prepared to countenance such a solution, and present law does not provide a method by which relief for losses incurred by a company can be offset against other personal income. We have been impressed by the advantages of a different and more radical proposal, which is that close companies should be allowed to opt to be taxed as though they were partnerships, the shareholders being taxed on their earnings from the company as though they were partners in an unincorporated business. In the United States this option is granted under sub-chapter S of the Internal Revenue Code to " Small Business Corporations," which are specially defined for the purpose of this sub-chapter. We feel that this possible disadvantage of incorporation in the United Kingdom should be removed, and to do so by this means would help to attract private capital into the small business sector, since outside shareholders would be enabled to offset their " share " of the trading losses of the company against tax on their other income. The view of the Inland Revenue, with whom we discussed this proposal, was that if there were any disadvantage in being taxed as a company, this should be weighed against the undoubted advantages of limited liability, and accepted if the balance of advantage worked out that way, but we feel that this is to elevate a purely incidental differential into a point of principle. We do not believe that a point of principle arises here, unless it is held that a price should be paid for limited liability in the shape of a higher tax bill. We therefore recommend that close companies should be allowed to elect, by unanimous decision of the shareholders, to be taxed as partnerships. Once exercised, this election should be irrevocable for a period of, say, five years; it would not be acceptable that businesses should assume and discard corporate status from year to year as their profits rose and declined.

Note
The possibility of a " partnership option " is also considered in the Report of the Select Committee on Corporation Tax, 1971 H.C. 622, para. 41. For an analysis of the Bolton Report, see M. A. Pickering, " Tax and the Small Firm " [1972] B.T.R. 163.

CHAPTER 17

DOMICILE AND RESIDENCE

THE general scheme of the tax system is to tax all income arising in the United Kingdom, no matter to whom it belongs, and to tax all residents in the United Kingdom, no matter where their income arises.[1] The residence of the taxpayer is consequently of paramount importance. In some instances, the taxpayer is only liable if he is not only resident but "ordinarily" resident,[2] or, in other instances, domiciled in the United Kingdom. Citizenship, or nationality, may also be relevant in certain circumstances.[3]

FINAL REPORT OF THE ROYAL COMMISSION ON THE TAXATION OF PROFITS AND INCOME

1955 Cmd. 9474

RESIDENCE, ORDINARY RESIDENCE, DOMICILE

The Three Conceptions

279. There are three conceptions which have an effective bearing upon the taxability of a person's overseas income—residence, ordinary residence, domicile. Each presupposes a certain relation to be subsisting between the person concerned and the United Kingdom or another country in the year in which the question of taxing his income arises, and since each requires a different set of facts to support it any one relation can subsist without the other. Thus, a man can be resident in the United Kingdom without being either ordinarily resident or domiciled there: or ordinarily resident there while being domiciled in another country.

Residence

280. The most important of the three conceptions is that of residence. For upon the test whether a man is resident in a particular year will depend the question whether he is to be taxed in respect of every part of his income wherever arising or only in respect of that part of it which arises in the United Kingdom. Secondly, personal allowances and reliefs are not available in full to an "individual who is not resident in the United Kingdom."[4] Thirdly, the question of residence is material for some more limited purposes, such as the establishment of title to certain of the double taxation reliefs.

---

[1] First Report of the Royal Commission on the Taxation of Profits and Income, 1953 Cmd. 8761, para. 8; *ante*, p. 277. See also the O.E.C.D. Model Double Taxation Agreement, paras. 4, 5; *ante*, p. 298.
[2] But liability to Capital Gains Tax depends upon the taxpayer being resident *or* ordinarily resident in the United Kingdom, F.A. 1965, s. 20 (1).
[3] *e.g.* I.C.T.A. 1970, ss. 27 (2), 49, 122 (2). N.B. *I.R.C.* v. *Watts* (1958) 38 T.C. 146.
[4] I.C.T.A. 1970, s. 27 (1), but see s. 27 (2).

Ordinary Residence

281. There is a statutory rule to the effect that if a British subject is ordinarily resident in the United Kingdom he remains chargeable to tax as a resident when he leaves the country " for the purpose only of occasional residence abroad." [5] On the other hand, the benefit of the remittance basis for overseas income is extended to British subjects or citizens of the Irish Republic who can show that, though resident in the United Kingdom, they are not ordinarily resident there.[6] As we explained in our First Report the remittance basis involves that the measure of the income which is taxed is not the income itself but that portion of it, if less than the whole, which is remitted to the United Kingdom. Moreover, the interest on certain British Government securities is exempt from tax while they are in the beneficial ownership of a person not ordinarily resident in the United Kingdom.[6]

Domicile

282. Persons who, though resident in the United Kingdom, are not domiciled there also get the benefit of the remittance basis for their overseas income.[7]

Note
  Domicile and ordinary residence may also be relevant for Estate Duty purposes, Finance (No. 2) Act 1931, s. 22; Finance Act 1949, s. 28 (2); Finance Act 1951, s. 34.

1. Residence of Individuals

The residence of an individual is primarily a question of fact.[8] As well as determining *whether* or not a person is resident it may also be necessary to determine *when* that person becomes, or ceases to be, resident.[9]

FINAL REPORT OF THE ROYAL COMMISSION ON THE TAXATION OF PROFITS AND INCOME

1955 Cmd. 9474

RESIDENCE AND ORDINARY RESIDENCE

289. Neither of these conceptions is defined by statute, but " ordinary residence " has been treated in legal decisions as the equivalent of " habitual residence." The two conceptions interact upon each other, sometimes being indistinguishable and sometimes in conflict. Thus, the great majority of persons living in the United Kingdom are both resident and ordinarily resident. On the other hand, a person who comes here from overseas may well be resident without being or having yet become ordinarily resident: so may a person who comes back after an extended period of absence.

290. Subject to the statutory rules which we have already set out, prescribing that six months' physical presence in the country makes residence, while temporary presence or absence has no effect, the established practice of the

---

[5] *Ibid*. s. 49.   [6] *Ibid*. s. 99.
[7] *Ibid*. s. 122 (2). See Chap. 12, pp. 290–295.
[8] See *ante*, Chap. 3. And see *Levene* v. *I.R.C.* [1928] A.C. 217; *ante*, pp. 33, 49; *post*, pp. 438, 444; *I.R.C.* v. *Lysaght* [1928] A.C. 234; *ante*, p. 50; *post*, pp. 441, 443.
[9] *Back* v. *Whitlock* [1932] 1 K.B. 747; *Carter* v. *Sharon* (1936) 20 T.C. 229. See J. D. Wells, " On Becoming Non-Resident " [1970] B.T.R. 304.

Revenue seems to be capable of being reduced to the following working principles:

(1) It is necessary to approach questions involving the residence of a man who has previously been ordinarily resident in the United Kingdom but has then gone abroad in a different way from questions involving the residence of a man who begins his connection as a visitor.

(2) A visitor who does not maintain a place of abode here and does not make habitual visits to the country is not resident unless he is present for more than six months in all during the tax year.[10]

(3) A visitor who maintains a place of abode here is resident for any year in which he pays a visit, however short, to the United Kingdom.[11]

(4) A visitor who habitually visits the country for substantial periods becomes a resident, even if he does not maintain a place of abode or spend in the United Kingdom six months in all in the tax year. For this purpose visits are treated as " habitual " if they have occurred in four more or less consecutive years, and " substantial " if they have averaged three months a year.[12]

(5) A man who has been regularly resident in the United Kingdom and has then gone abroad may or may not be treated as a visitor if he comes back again at any time. That depends primarily on the question whether the circumstances in which he went abroad indicate a clear break with the United Kingdom as his place of ordinary residence.[13]

(6) Many of the cases just mentioned occur when men who have taken up employment overseas return to this country, either on leave or in connection with the duties of their employment.[14]

291. These working principles are not statutory. It is claimed that they are proper deductions from the few statutory rules that do exist and from decided cases. We cannot give any positive confirmation of this claim, and we think that appeal Commissioners at any rate might be in much the same difficulty. In any event the position of the ordinary taxpayer can hardly be an easy one. We quote the view of the Codification Committee on this point.[15]

" We are fully conscious of the complexities which surround this question and of the advantages which, from the point of view of a taxing authority, lie in the absence of a statutory definition. We are, however, of the opinion that the present state of affairs, under which an enquirer can only be told that the question whether he is resident or not is a question of fact for the Commissioners, but that by the study of the effect of a large body of case law he may be able to make an intelligent forecast of their decision, is intolerable and should not be allowed to continue."

292. We agree with the Committee's general view that this state of affairs is unsatisfactory, particularly for the visitor. But we do not accept their diagnosis in all respects. It is true that a visitor who wishes to arrive at an

---

10 If there are recurring visits, the purpose, *e.g.* business, may be relevant, see *I.R.C.* v. *Combe* (1932) 17 T.C. 405.

11 *Cooper* v. *Cadwallader* (1904) 5 T.C. 101; *Loewenstein* v. *de Salis* (1926) 10 T.C. 424; but see *Withers* v. *Wynyard* (1938) 21 T.C. 724.

12 *Levene* v. *I.R.C.* [1928] A.C. 217; *post,* pp. 438, 444; *I.R.C.* v. *Lysaght* [1928] A.C. 234; *post,* pp. 441, 443; *Lord Inchiquin* v. *I.R.C.* (1948) 31 T.C. 125, where the availability of double-taxation relief turned on the question of residence.

13 See, for example, *I.R.C.* v. *Combe* (1932) 17 T.C. 405.

14 See now I.C.T.A. 1970, s. 50.

15 1936 Cmd. 5131, para. 59. See also the remarks of Viscount Sumner in *Levene* v. *I.R.C.* [1928] A.C. 217, 227; *ante,* p. 49.

independent assessment of his position will be met with the difficulties that they indicate: but on the other hand he will be able to obtain without difficulty a printed leaflet which sets out at any rate the main lines of the Revenue Department's established practice.[16] Nor do we think that the present general uncertainty is maintained in any way for the convenience of the taxing authority. On the contrary fixed rules would simplify the work of administration even if they worked unreasonably in some instances. But it is one of the arguments against the existing system that it does lead to the devotion of a great deal of time and skill to considering and adjudicating upon individual cases, whereas the establishment of certain fixed rules would make this unnecessary without giving any individual a serious cause of complaint. Indeed we think that the visitor or potential visitor would normally prefer certainty to the assurance that there will be the fullest consideration of his personal circumstances.

Note

The Commission concluded that further statutory provisions were desirable. With the exception of the provisions introduced in 1956 relating to persons working abroad (now I.C.T.A. 1970, s. 50) this has not been implemented.

Re YOUNG

Court of Exchequer (Scotland) (1875) 1 T.C. 57

THE LORD PRESIDENT: . . . The class to whom this appellant belongs is a very extensive class, and the question raised here is one of very great importance. He is the master of a trading vessel, a trading vessel belonging to this country and hailing from the port of Glasgow; and when he is not at sea the appellant resides in Glasgow, and when he is at sea is represented in that residence in Glasgow by his wife and family. Now, that he has, in the ordinary and plain meaning of the words, a residence in Glasgow is, in these circumstances, I think, clear beyond all doubt, and it is equally clear upon the facts stated that he has no residence anywhere else, unless a ship can be called a residence, which I rather think it never has.[17] A residence, according to the ordinary meaning of the word, must be a residence on shore, a dwelling in a house. A residence is a dwelling-place on land, and the only dwelling-place on land which this appellant has is in Glasgow, where, as I said before, he dwells when at home, and where his wife and children dwell when he is at sea.

. . . In the present case we have it stated that the absence of the appellant from the United Kingdom is, in one year as compared with another, longer or shorter on account of the briskness or dulness of trade, and therefore, it is a mere accident that calls on a captain to be absent from his residence in any one part of the year. All these, I think, are within the meaning of this statute temporary absences, because I do not think a temporary absence necessarily means something shorter than the presence of the party in this country. Temporary absence may be for a very long time, and I think it may be temporary because it may be in prosecution of some special purpose. . . .

LORD ARDMILLAN: . . . In the next place he has done nothing to change his residence. He had no other residence in any part of the world except on the

---

[16] " Visitors from other countries: Liability to U.K. Income Tax." Leaflet issued by the Inland Revenue.

[17] But see *Bayard Brown* v. *Burt* (1911) 5 T.C. 667. The yacht, though flying the American flag, had not left its mooring in the River Colne for some 20 years.

deck of the ship and in Glasgow, and in Glasgow he leaves in his house his wife and family. Now, I do not think we can recognise in a question of this kind that he lives so entirely on the sea as to have no residence on the land. A man living on the sea and having a house on shore, and if he is a married man his house is on shore, is shown by the case which I quoted in the course of the discussion to reside on the shore, although he might be at sea for a time. But, taking the first part of the statute only to be the subject, and that the party is not a resident elsewhere, the choice is betwixt his having no residence,[18] and that residence which he has engaged for his wife and family, which I believe is his true residence, and I think, therefore, that the appellant is liable to assessment.

ROGERS v. INLAND REVENUE

Court of Exchequer (Scotland) (1879) 1 T.C. 225

THE LORD PRESIDENT: I have no doubt about this case at all. It is ruled by the case of *Young*. Every sailor has a residence on land, . . . and the question is, Where is this man's residence? The answer undoubtedly is that his residence is in Great Britain. He has no other residence, and a man must have a residence somewhere. The circumstance that Captain Rogers has been absent from the country during the whole year to which the assessment applies does not seem to me to be a speciality of the least consequence. That is a mere accident. He is not a bit the less a resident in Great Britain because the exigencies of his business have happened to carry him away for a somewhat longer time than usual during this particular voyage.

Note
     This appears to be the only reported case of a person being held resident although not being physically present in the country throughout a complete year of assessment, *cf. Turnbull* v. *Foster* (1904) 6 T.C. 206, *infra*

TURNBULL v. FOSTER

Court of Exchequer (Scotland) (1904) 6 T.C. 206

LORD MONCRIEFF: . . . My Lords, I am of the same opinion. During the year of assessment, that is to say ending April 5, 1903, this gentleman was not residing in this country at all. I don't think that that fact taken by itself would be by any means conclusive, because if he had been travelling, or had been a mariner and had been absent the whole of the year, I don't think that would have prevented him from having a residence in this country. But, then, in addition to that, we find that his business is in Madras, and that I rather take to be his usual place of residence. It is quite true that between the years 1899 and 1901 he occasionally visited this country for longer or shorter periods. That was for the purpose of seeing his wife and children, and I presume residing here, because they were unable to stand the climate of India. Looking to the whole of the facts taken together, I think the fair inference is that his residence in the sense of the statute was not in this country.

---

[18] There seems to be nothing to prevent a person having no residence at all, as may have been the case in *I.R.C.* v. *Zorab* (1926) 11 T.C. 289; *cf.* Rogers v. *Inland Revenue* (1879) 1 T.C. 225, *infra*.

LLOYD v. SULLEY

Court of Exchequer (Scotland) (1884) 2 T.C. 37

The appellant had a business in Italy, where he lived for most of the year. He also owned a home in Scotland where he spent several months during the year in question.

THE LORD PRESIDENT: This gentleman, Mr. Lloyd, is charged with income tax for the year 1883–84, the current year, and during that year he has resided in Scotland at Minard Castle, from July 6 to October 31, 1883. . . . Now, the only question which can be raised upon that is whether Mr. Lloyd was, for the year 1883–84, to which alone this case applies, residing in the United Kingdom. There is no mention in this taxing clause of the character of the residence as being ordinary residence, or temporary residence, or residence for any particular part of the year or proportion of it; " residing in the United Kingdom " are the only words we have to guide us. Now, if a man could only be a resident in one place in any particular year there might be a great difficulty, but surely there is nothing more familiar to one's mind than that a man has during a particular year or during a course of years, residences in different places existing at the same time. A man cannot have two domiciles at the same time, but he certainly can have two residences. He can have a residence in the country, and a residence in town; he can have a residence in Scotland and another in England, or he may have three or more residences. We know some persons in exalted stations who have so many residences that they find them a very great encumbrance. And yet these are all residences in the proper sense of the term, that is to say, they are places to which it is quite easy for the person to resort as his dwelling place whenever he thinks fit, and to set himself down there with his family and establishment. That is a place of residence, and if he occupies that place of residence for a portion of a year he is then within the meaning of the Clause as I read it, residing there in the course of that year.

A great deal of argument has been founded upon the 39th section of the previous statute of 5th and 6th Vict. which no doubt is still in operation; and it is necessary to advert to that for a single moment in order to clear away any embarrassment or misunderstanding which may have arisen about it. There are two parts of that section : One regards the effect of what is called an ordinary residence from which the person who possesses it is absent; and the other regards a certain exemption, as I shall venture to call it notwithstanding the doubt thrown upon the expression, in regard to certain persons who come to this country for a temporary purpose, but which second portion of the section is admittedly not applicable to the present case because it does not apply to the income tax laid on upon profits accruing from trade or professions. Now, as regards the first part of section 39 it is enacted—

> " that any subject of Her Majesty whose ordinary residence shall have been in Great Britain, and who shall have departed from Great Britain and gone into any parts beyond the seas for the purpose only of occasional residence at the time of the execution of this Act, shall be deemed, notwithstanding such temporary absence, a person chargeable to the duties granted by this Act, as a person actually residing in Great Britain."

Now, that is a very important provision as extending the meaning of the words in the taxing clause, " residing in the United Kingdom." It extends it to a person who is not for a time actually residing in the United Kingdom, but who has constructively his residence there because his ordinary place of abode and his home is there, although he is absent for a time from it, however long continued that absence may be. That disposes of the first part of section 39. Now, with regard to the second part, it provides that any person who shall actually be in Great Britain for some temporary purpose only, and not with the view of establishing a residence, and who shall not have remained there for a period on the whole amounting to six months within the year of taxation, shall be exempt from a certain portion of the income tax. I have said it does not apply to the present case, but an argument has been founded upon it for the purpose of showing that coming to Great Britain for a temporary purpose is not considered by the statute to be residing in Great Britain. Now, I consider that is a fallacy. The meaning of it is this, if a foreigner comes here for merely temporary purposes connected with business or pleasure, or something else, and does not remain for a period altogether within the year of six months, he shall not be liable for a certain portion of taxation imposed by Schedule D. He would have been liable but for this exemption; he would have been a person *de facto* residing in Great Britain. But it is thought that it would be rather hard to charge him when it is merely a visit here for a temporary purpose, and therefore this exemption is introduced. But that so far from derogating from the force of the words by which the tax is laid on in Schedule D, only confirms the view which I have taken of the true force of these words, because it shows that residence for a temporary purpose would have subjected to the tax if it had not been for this clause of exemption. Therefore, I am very clear on the whole matter that this charge has been properly sustained, and that the appeal should be dismissed.

LEVENE v. I.R.C.

House of Lords (*ante*, pp. 33, 49; *post*, p. 444)

VISCOUNT CAVE L.C.: . . . From March 1918, until January 1925, the appellant had no fixed place of abode, but stayed in hotels, whether in this country or abroad. In the course of the years 1922, 1923 and 1924, he made endeavours to find a suitable flat in Monaco, but the negotiations came to nothing since none of the premises inspected were suitable, until in January 1925, the appellant took a lease of a flat in Park Palace, Monte Carlo, for nine years, for which he paid a premium of 130,000 francs, and he lived there with his wife until he came to England for the purposes of the appeal to the Commissioners. Both he and his wife have indifferent health, and have been advised to live in the South of France and avoid the United Kingdom in the winter months. One of the reasons for their visits to England was to obtain medical advice. They also came to visit their relatives in England, and (on one occasion) to make arrangements for the care of a brother of the appellant who is mentally afflicted. Other reasons for his coming to England annually were to take part in certain Jewish religious observances, to visit the graves of his parents, who are buried in Southampton, and to deal with his income tax affairs.

After setting out the above facts and the contentions of the parties, the Commissioners gave their decision in the following terms:—

"The appellant is a British subject and until March 1918, he was a householder in London. He then surrendered the lease of his house and sold his furniture, and from March 1918, until January 1925, he did not occupy any fixed place of residence, but lived in hotels, whether in this country or abroad.

He was admittedly resident and ordinarily resident in the United Kingdom until December 1919. He then went abroad, and in each subsequent year he has spent between seven and eight months abroad and between four and five months in the United Kingdom.

We are satisfied upon the evidence that when he left the United Kingdom in December 1919, he had formed the intention, which he has consistently carried out ever since, of living abroad for the greater part of the year, but of returning to this country each year and remaining here for considerable periods but not for a period equal in the whole to six months in any year.

The questions for decision are whether he was entitled to exemption from income tax on War Loan interest under section 46 of the Income Tax Act 1918,[19] as a person not ordinarily resident in the United Kingdom, and on interest on securities of British Possessions under rule 2 (d) of the General Rules applicable to Schedule C as a person not resident in the United Kingdom, and the years under review are 1921–22, 1922–23, 1923–24 and 1924–25.

These are in our opinion questions of degree, and taking into consideration all the facts put before us in regard to the appellant's past and present habits of life, the regularity and length of his visits here, his ties with this country, and his freedom from attachments abroad, we have come to the conclusion that at least until January 1925, when the appellant took a lease of a flat in Monte Carlo, he continued to be resident in the United Kingdom. The claims for the years in question therefore fail."

It is obvious that the conclusions of the Commissioners above quoted are so worded as not to be mere inferences in law from the facts found in the earlier part of the Case, but to be themselves substantive findings of fact; and accordingly under the well established rule those findings cannot be disturbed by the courts unless there was no evidence to support them. But before dealing with that question I think it desirable to say something about a matter which was much discussed during the argument—namely, the meaning of the word " reside " and the expression " ordinarily reside " as used in the Income Tax Act.

My Lords, the word " reside " is a familiar English word and is defined in the Oxford English Dictionary as meaning " to dwell permanently or for a considerable time, to have one's settled or usual abode, to live in or at a particular place." No doubt this definition must for present purposes be taken subject to any modification which may result from the terms of the Income Tax Act and Schedules; but, subject to that observation, it may be accepted as an accurate indication of the meaning of the word " reside." In most cases there is no difficulty in determining where a man has his settled or usual abode, and if that is ascertained he is not the less resident there because from time to time he leaves it for the purpose of business or pleasure. Thus, a master mariner who had his home at Glasgow where his wife and family lived, and to which he returned during the intervals between his sea voyages, was held to reside there, although he actually spent the greater part of the year at sea: Re Young[20]; Rogers v. Inland Revenue.[21] Similarly a person who has his home abroad and visits the United Kingdom from time to time for temporary purposes without setting up an establishment in this country is not considered to be resident here—although if he is the owner of foreign possessions or securities falling within Case IV or V of Schedule D, then if he has actually been in the United Kingdom for a period equal in the whole to six months in any year of assessment he may be charged with

[19] Now I.C.T.A. 1970, s. 99.
[20] (1875) 1 T.C. 57; ante, p. 435.
[21] (1879) 1 T.C. 225; ante, p. 436.

tax under rule 2 of the Miscellaneous Rules applicable to Schedule D. But a man may reside in more than one place. Just as a man may have two homes—one in London and the other in the country—so he may have a home abroad and a home in the United Kingdom, and in that case he is held to reside in both places and to be chargeable with tax in this country. Thus, in *Cooper* v. *Cadwalader*,[22] an American resident in New York who had taken a house in Scotland which was at any time available for his occupation, was held to be resident there, although in fact he had only occupied the house for two months during the year; and to the same effect is the case of *Loewenstein* v. *de Salis*.[23] The above cases are comparatively simple, but more difficult questions arise when the person sought to be charged has no home or establishment in any country but lives his life in hotels or at the houses of his friends. If such a man spends the whole of the year in hotels in the United Kingdom, then he is held to reside in this country; for it is not necessary for that purpose that he should continue to live in one place in this country but only that he should reside in the United Kingdom. But probably the most difficult case is that of a wanderer who, having no home in any country, spends a part only of his time in hotels in the United Kingdom and the remaining and greater part of his time in hotels abroad. In such cases the question is one of fact and of degree, and must be determined on all the circumstances of the case: *Reid* v. *Inland Revenue Commissioners*.[24] If, for instance, such a man is a foreigner who has never resided in this country, there may be great difficulty in holding that he is resident here. But if he is a British subject the Commissioners are entitled to take into account all the facts of the case, including facts such as those which are referred to in the final paragraph above quoted from the case stated in this instance. Further, the case may be different, and in such a case regard must be had to rule 3 of the General Rules applicable to all the Schedules of the Income Tax Act, which provides that every British subject whose ordinary residence has been in the United Kingdom shall be assessed and charged to tax notwithstanding that at the time the assessment or charge is made he may have left the United Kingdom, if he has so left the United Kingdom for the purpose only of occasional residence abroad.

Turning to the facts of this case, I think it clear that the appellant falls within the category last described. He is a British subject and formerly resided in England. Early in the year 1918 he formed the project of living abroad and thereupon broke up his establishment in this country; but in fact he continued to reside here in hotels until the end of the year 1919. He then went abroad from time to time, but continued to live in hotels either here or in France and he did not actually find a home abroad until the month of January 1925, when he took a lease of a flat at Monte Carlo. The result is that during the period from the end of 1919 until January 1925, he went much abroad, partly for the sake of his own and his wife's health, partly no doubt to search for a house or flat, and partly (as may be inferred from the finding of the Commissioners) in the hope of escaping liability to the English income tax; but none of these purposes was more than a temporary purpose, and he regularly returned to England for the greater part of the summer months though for less than one half of each year. On these facts I think that it was plainly open to the Commissioners to find that during the years in question he was resident in the United Kingdom, and I think it probable that rule 3 above quoted applied to him.

---

[22] (1904) 5 T.C. 101.
[23] (1926) 10 T.C. 424.
[24] (1926) 10 T.C. 673; *post*, p. 442.

It remains to be considered whether during the period in question the appellant " ordinarily resided " in the United Kingdom for the purposes of section 46 [19] of the Act, and I think that there was material upon which the Commissioners could answer this question in the affirmative. The suggestion that in order to determine whether a man ordinarily resides in this country you must count the days which he spends here and those which he spends elsewhere, and that it is only if in any year the former are more numerous than the latter that he can be held to be ordinarily resident here, appears to me to be without substance. The expression " ordinary residence " is found in the Income Tax Act of 1806 and occurs again and again in the later Income Tax Acts, where it is contrasted with usual or occasional or temporary residence; and I think that it connotes residence in a place with some degree of continuity and apart from accidental or temporary absences. So understood the expression differs little in meaning from the word " residence " as used in the Acts; and I find it difficult to imagine a case in which a man while not resident here is yet ordinarily resident here. Upon this point also, as upon the other, I think that the finding of the Commissioners cannot be disturbed.

For these reasons I am of opinion that this appeal fails.

I.R.C. v. LYSAGHT

House of Lords (*ante*, p. 50; *post*, p. 443)

In 1919, the respondent went to live permanently in Ireland. He retained a position of advisory director to a family company and visited England regularly to attend board meetings, usually staying in hotels.

Viscount Sumner : . . . No doubt, on the authority of the merchant seamen's cases, Mallow was Mr. Lysaght's home and he resided there. There were his family seat and his demesne lands, his wife and family, his farming and his sport, and, though some people may be able to make themselves at home from home anywhere, I do not suppose that the Spa Hotel, Bath, however excellent, was much of a home to Mr. Lysaght. This, however, is not conclusive. Who in New York would have said of Mr. Cadwalader [25] " his home's in the Highlands; his home is not here "? After all, many nomads are homeless folk, though they may reside continually, here or there, within the limits of the United Kingdom. Property obviously is no conclusive test. Whether Mr. Lysaght resides in his own or in a hired house in Ireland cannot have much to do with it, nor is a person precluded from being resident, because he puts up at hotels, and not always the same hotel, and never for long together. . . .

Lord Warrington of Clyffe : . . . I have reluctantly come to the conclusion that it is now settled by authority that the question of residence or ordinary residence is one of degree, that there is no technical or special meaning attached to either expression for the purposes of the Income Tax Act, and accordingly a decision of the Commissioners on the question is a finding of fact and cannot be reviewed unless it is made out to be based on some error in law, including the absence of evidence on which such a decision could properly be founded. . .

[25] *Cooper* v. *Cadwallader* (1904) 5 T.C. 101.

2. Ordinary Residence

The relevance of " ordinary residence," as opposed to mere " residence," has already been referred to.[26]   The distinction between the concepts is by no means clear; in the words of the Royal Commission, they " interact upon each other, sometimes being indistinguishable and sometimes in conflict." [27]

REID v. I.R.C.

Court of Session (1926) 10 T.C. 673; 1926 S.C. 589

THE LORD PRESIDENT (CLYDE): . . . What is meant by saying that a person is " resident " in the United Kingdom?—and when is a person properly said to be " ordinarily resident " there?   It is obvious that the more general and wide the scope of expressions used in a statute, the more difficult it may become to convict those whose duty it is to interpret it of an error or mis-direction in applying it to a given state of facts.   It may be possible in such cases to predicate of a particular state of facts that they lie outside the scope of the expressions used, although it may be really an impossible task to define that scope positively and with exact accuracy.   The expression " resident in the United Kingdom " and the qualification of that expression implied in the word " ordinarily " so resident are just about as wide and general and difficult to define with positive precision as any that could have been used. The result is to make the question of law become (as it were) so attenuated, and the field occupied by the questions of fact become so enlarged, as to make it difficult to say that a decision arrived at by the Commissioners with respect to a particular state of facts held proved by them, is wrong.

. . . Take the case of a homeless tramp, who shelters tonight under a bridge, tomorrow in the greenwood and as the unwelcome occupant of a farm out-house the night after.   He wanders in this way all over the United Kingdom. But will anyone say he does not *live* in the United Kingdom?—and will anyone regard it as a misuse of language to say he *resides* in the United Kingdom?   In this case there may be no relations with family or friends, no business ties, and none of the ordinary circumstances which create a link between the life of a British subject and the United Kingdom; but, even so, I do not think it could be disputed that he *resides* in the United Kingdom. There are other and very different kinds of tramps, who—being possessed of ample means, and having the ordinary ties of birth, family, and affairs with the United Kingdom or some part of it—yet prefer to enjoy those means without undertaking the domestic responsibility of a home, and who move about from one house of public entertainment to another—in London today, in the provinces tomorrow, and in the Highlands the day after.   They, too, are homeless wanderers in the United Kingdom.   But surely it is true to say that they *live* in the United Kingdom, and *reside* there?   The section of the Act of Parliament with which we are dealing speaks of persons " residing," not at a particular locality, but in a region so extensive as the United Kingdom.

Now, the appellant—a lady of independent means—has, partly on account of considerations of health, been for many years past in the habit of going abroad for the larger portion of the year, and spending only the summer months (say three and a half months) in the United Kingdom.   In 1916,

[26] Final Report of the Royal Commission on the Taxation of Profits and Income, 1955 Cmd. 9474, para. 281; *ante*, p. 433.
[27] *Ibid*. para. 289; *ante*, p. 433.

owing to the death of a sister, she and her only surviving sister gave up their house in Scotland, and sold their furniture. The surviving sister went to London, and the appellant also removed there, living in various London hotels until July 1919. Since about that time—the war being ended and travelling abroad having become possible—she has reverted to her former mode of life, and has moved about between various places on the Continent of Europe for about eight and a half months of each year, returning to this country for the remaining three and a half months. This applies to each of the two tax years to which the present appeal relates. The appellant is a British subject, her family ties are with this country; her business matters (including her banking) are conducted here; the address by which she can be found at any time is in this country; and her personal belongings not required when she is travelling are kept in store in London.

It was contended on her behalf that, even if these facts are consistent with her being held to " reside " in the United Kingdom, they are inconsistent with the view that she " ordinarily " so resides. And, here again, the argument was that the meaning of the word " ordinarily " is governed—wholly or mainly—by the test of time or duration. I think it is a test, and an important one; but I think it is only one among many. From the point of view of time, " ordinarily " would stand in contrast to " casually." But the appellant is not a " casual " visitor to her home country; on the contrary she regularly returns to it, and " resides " in it for a part—albeit the smaller part—of every year. I hesitate to give the word " ordinarily " any more precise interpretation than " in the customary course of events," and anyhow I cannot think that the element of time so predominates in its meaning that, unless the appellant " resided " in the United Kingdom for at least six months and a day, she could not be said " ordinarily " to reside there in the year in question. A more plausible way of presenting the same argument was used by the appellant's counsel, who maintained that the appellant " ordinarily resided " on the Continent rather than in this country, inasmuch as she spent nearly three times as much of her life abroad as here. I am not sure that there is anything impossible in a person " ordinarily residing " in two places, although no doubt he cannot physically be present in more than one place at the same time. Would it be clearly wrong to say of His Gracious Majesty that he " ordinarily resides " at Windsor Castle and at Buckingham Palace? I observe that the third paragraph of Rule 4 of the Miscellaneous Rules applicable to Schedule D of the Income Tax Act 1918, speaks of a person " who has two or more places of ordinary residence," not, observe, ordinary *places of residence,* but places of *ordinary residence.* However this may be, and keeping in mind the qualities as well as the durability of the relation between a person and the place (here the United Kingdom) in which he " resides," I find myself unable to affirm that the Commissioners were mistaken in law in regarding the circumstances of the appellant's life in the two tax years ended April 5, 1921, as putting her within the category of a person " ordinarily resident " in the United Kingdom.

I.R.C. v. LYSAGHT

House of Lords (*ante*, pp. 50, 441)

VISCOUNT SUMNER : . . . My Lords, the word " ordinarily " may be taken first. The Act on the one hand does not say " usually " or " most of the time " or " exclusively " or " principally " nor does it say on the other hand " occasionally " or " exceptionally " or " now and then," though in various sections it applies to the word "resident," with a full sense of choice, adverbs like "temporarily" and "actually." I think the converse to "ordinarily" is "extraordinarily" and that part of the regular order of a man's life, adopted voluntarily and for settled purposes, is not "extraordinary." Having regard to the times and duration, the objects and the obligations of Mr. Lysaght's visits to England, there was in my opinion evidence to support, and no rule of law to prevent, a finding, that he was ordinarily resident, if he was resident in the United Kingdom at all. . . .

LEVENE v. I.R.C.

King's Bench Division (1927) 13 T.C. 486
Court of Appeal [1927] 1 K.B. 780; 13 T.C. 495
House of Lords (*ante*, pp. 33, 49, 438)

ROWLATT J.: . . . Now it seems to me what the phrase " ordinary residence " means is this; I think that " ordinary " does not mean preponderating, I think it means ordinary in the sense that it is habitual in the ordinary course of a man's life, and I think a man is ordinarily resident in the United Kingdom when the ordinary course of his life is such that it discloses a residence in the United Kingdom, and it might disclose a residence elsewhere at the same time. Therefore, I think, as has been thought in Scotland, that a man can have two ordinary residences not because he commonly is to be found at those places, but because the ordinary course of his life is such that he acquires the attribute of residence at those two places. . . .

LORD HANWORTH M.R.: . . . I find it difficult to attach any distinction of meaning to the word " ordinarily " as affecting the term " resident," unless it be to prevent facts which would amount to residence being so estimated, on the ground that they arose from some fortuitous cause, such as illness of the so-called resident or of some other person, which demanded his continuance at a place for a special purpose otherwise than in accordance with his own usual arrangement and shaping of his movements.[28] . . .

LORD WARRINGTON OF CLYFFE : . . . I do not attempt to give any definition of the word " resident." In my opinion it has no technical or special meaning for the purposes of the Income Tax Act. " Ordinarily resident " also seems to me to have no such technical or special meaning. In particular it is in my opinion impossible to restrict its connotation to its duration. A member of this House may well be said to be ordinarily resident in London during the parliamentary session and in the country during the recess. If it has any definite meaning I should say it means according to the way in which a man's life is usually ordered. . . .

MIESEGAES v. I.R.C.

Court of Appeal (1957) 37 T.C. 493; [1957] T.R. 231; 36 A.T.C. 201

PEARCE L.J.: . . . The case stated shows that the appellant was born on April 12, 1933, in Amsterdam, of Dutch parents. His nationality is Dutch and his domicile has never been English. His parents were divorced before 1939, and he was at all material times in the custody of his father. In 1939 he came with his father as a refugee to England. In March 1946, the father went to live

---

[28] *Cf. Re Mackenzie* [1941] Ch. 69; *post*, p. 445.

in Switzerland for health reasons, intending to make his home there permanently. There, after some months in a sanitorium, he moved to an hotel, and started to build himself a house. Before it was completed he died in Switzerland on July 10, 1948. When the father went to live in Switzerland the appellant was nearly 13 years old. He was attending a preparatory school in England. There he stayed until 1947, when he went to Harrow. He spent his school holidays with his father in Switzerland until his father's death, and thenceforth partly with his former governess in England but mostly abroad. He remained at Harrow until July 1951. On August 17, 1951, he went abroad, and continued his education at a Swiss university. Thereafter he has not lived in England. During the material years, therefore, it was only as a schoolboy at Harrow that he lived in England.

Mr. Foster's main argument is this. Such residence (assuming, but not admitting, that it can properly be called residence at all) cannot constitute ordinary residence. It has not the quality of ordinary residence. It is not voluntary residence; and it is institutional.[29] If one asked a schoolboy, Mr. Foster argues, where he lived, he would never say that he lived at his public school. Although a person may admittedly have more than one ordinary residence, his school would never be one of them. In order to succeed in this appeal, he must establish that such residence by a boy at a public school cannot constitute an ordinary residence.

. . . Education is a large, necessary and normal ingredient in the lives of adolescent members of the community, just as work or business is in the lives of its adult members. During the years of youth education plays a definite and dominating part in a boy's ordinary life. In this case the school terms at Harrow dictated the main residential pattern of the boy's life. Education is too extensive and universal a phase to justify such descriptions as " unusual " or " extraordinary." It would be as erroneous to endow educational residence with some esoteric quality that must, as a matter of law, remove it from the category of residence, or ordinary residence, as it would be to do so in the case of business residence.[30]

. . . On those facts and the other facts in the case stated the Commissioners clearly had material on which they could find that the appellant was ordinarily resident in England during his years at Harrow. It is impossible for us to interfere with that finding. . . .

Re MACKENZIE

Chancery Division [1941] Ch. 69; 110 L.J.Ch. 28; 164 L.T. 375; 57 T.L.R. 107; 84 S.J. 670; [1940] 4 All E.R. 310

The case concerned liability to estate duty in respect of $3\frac{1}{2}$ per cent. war stock (see Finance (No. 2) Act 1931, s. 22). The deceased was born in Australia, came to visit England with her mother in 1885, four months later she became of unsound mind and remained in England, without recovering, until her death fifty-four years later. It was argued that the Government stock was exempt from duty as she was not ordinarily resident here.

MORTON J.: . . . At first sight it might seem strange if the court were to hold that a lady who spent the last fifty-four years of her life continuously in this country was not ordinarily resident in the United Kingdom, but Mr. Spens and Mr. Jopling, for the applicant, suggest that she could not be said

29 Cf. Re Mackenzie [1941] Ch. 69, infra.
30 As to the relevance of " business residence," see I.R.C. v. Lysaght [1928] A.C. 234; ante, pp. 441, 443.

to be ordinarily resident in September 1885, when she was certified as of unsound mind, and that during the whole of the rest of her life she was under constraint, unable to exercise any will of her own. They submit that this period, the last fifty-four years of her life, cannot be taken into account at all as making her ordinarily resident in this country. They put the case of a prisoner of war who has come to this country and has been detained here, it might be for years. They say that he would not be ordinarily resident because the element of constraint is present. They also put the case of a foreigner with a home abroad, who comes to this country on a visit and commits some offence against the laws of the country, and is imprisoned for a considerable time, and ultimately dies in this country. They say he would not be held to be ordinarily resident, and they say that the same reasoning ought to apply to the case of this lady.[31]

. . . Taking into account the whole of the circumstances of this case, I think I must arrive at the conclusion that the lady was ordinarily resident in England. I do not understand Viscount Sumner, in the passage which I have quoted, as saying that a period of residence in this country which is involuntary must be wholly disregarded for the purpose of ascertaining whether a person is ordinarily resident here or not. In my view it must not be left out of account that the intestate, having come to this country voluntarily at the age of twenty-eight, never left it. Whether I could have held that she was ordinarily resident in this country immediately before she was taken to a sanatorium I am not sure.

. . . With regard to the cases put by Mr. Spens and Mr. Jopling of the prisoner of war, or the prisoner incarcerated for some offence, such cases must be dealt with on their particular facts if and when they arise, but I can well imagine, taking the case of a prisoner of war, that, if a man had a permanent residence in Germany and came over here in an aeroplane to attack this country, and if he was captured and kept here for a considerable period, it might well be held that his ordinary residence was his home in Germany. However, as I have said, I do not propose to express any view upon hypothetical cases. Taking the case which is before me, I have arrived at the conclusion that the Crown's contention succeeds.

3. Domicile and Residence of Corporations

A company is an artificial person. Nevertheless, its domicile, nationality or residence may have to be determined for tax purposes.[32] The domicile and nationality of a company is now of limited importance.[33] The term " ordinarily " apparently adds nothing to the word " residence " so far as a company is concerned.[34]

The residence of a company is determined according to where its central management and control actually abides; a company may, like an individual, be resident in two or more countries at the same time; a company

---

[31] Reliance was placed upon the word " voluntarily " in the judgment of Viscount Sumner in *I.R.C.* v. *Lysaght* [1928] A.C. 234, 243; *ante*, p. 443.

[32] Thus Corporation Tax is charged on the profits of company resident in the United Kingdom: I.C.T.A. 1970, s. 238 (2); such a company may not cease to be so resident without Treasury consent: *ibid.* s. 482. See G. R. Bretten, " Companies: Residence and Taxation " (1967) 31 *Conveyancer* (N.S.) 194.

[33] The remittance basis not being applicable to companies: I.C.T.A. 1970, ss. 129 (4), 247 (1); but N.B. s. 478 and see *Gasque* v. *I.R.C.* [1940] 2 K.B. 80.

[34] *Union Corporation Ltd.* v. *I.R.C.* [1953] A.C 482.

is not necessarily resident in the country in which it is incorporated and has its registered office.

Whether a company is resident in the United Kingdom and whether it is carrying on a trade here are two distinct questions.[35]

EGYPTIAN DELTA LAND AND INVESTMENT CO. LTD. v. TODD

House of Lords [1929] A.C. 1; 98 L.J.K.B. 1; 140 L.T. 50; 44 T.L.R. 747; 72 S.J. 545; sub nom. Todd v. Egyptian Delta Land and Investment Co. Ltd., 14 T.C. 138

Incorporation in the United Kingdom does not of itself constitute a company resident in the United Kingdom.

VISCOUNT SUMNER: . . . Throughout the Income Tax Acts " resident," with its various qualifications " actually," " ordinarily," " occasionally," " temporarily," and so forth, is used in a sense in every way appropriate to natural persons, but only artificially applicable to incorporated persons, and never really appropriate.

. . . At first, perhaps, the courts might have said that, as a corporation could not " reside " anywhere in any true sense, they must leave it to the Legislature to enact residence in an artificial sense, but they felt bound to make the Acts work as they found them and arrived at a compromise, under which certain propositions, I think, are now well settled. The word " resident," it is laid down, has to be applied to artificial persons by analogy from natural persons. With these, residence depends on personal facts. . . . Accordingly, under the decisions, as well as in principle, " resident " is a term exceedingly unsuited to describe a statutory " person," which can never be non-resident, because by the law of its being, it is a fixture. The analogy that is really possible between a natural person and a company is that of carrying on business at a place, great or small, and in my opinion, for the purpose of income tax, both on the words of the Acts and on the cases, the residence of a foreign company is preponderantly, if not exclusively, determined by this kind of fact.

DE BEERS CONSOLIDATED MINES LTD. v. HOWE

House of Lords [1906] A.C. 455; 75 L.J.K.B. 858; 95 L.T. 221; 22 T.L.R. 756; 50 S.J. 666; 13 Mans. 394; 5 T.C. 198

LORD LOREBURN L.C.: . . . Now, it is easy to ascertain where an individual resides, but when the inquiry relates to a company, which in a natural sense does not reside anywhere, some artificial test must be applied.

Mr. Cohen propounded a test which had the merits of simplicity and certitude. He maintained that a company resides where it is registered, and nowhere else. If that be so, the appellant company must succeed, for it is registered in South Africa.

I cannot adopt Mr. Cohen's contention. In applying the conception of residence to a company, we ought, I think, to proceed as nearly as we can upon the analogy of an individual. A company cannot eat or sleep, but it can keep house and do business. We ought, therefore, to see where it really keeps house and does business. An individual may be of foreign nationality, and yet reside in the United Kingdom. So may a company. Otherwise it

---

[35] See ante, Chap. 12. Similarly in the case of a partnership, cf. Colquhoun v. Brooks (1889) 14 App.Cas. 493; ante, p. 277; Ogilvie v. Kitton (1908) 5 T.C. 338; ante, p. 279.

might have its chief seat of management and its centre of trading in England under the protection of English law, and yet escape the appropriate taxation by the simple expedient of being registered abroad and distributing its dividends abroad. The decision of Kelly C.B. and Huddleston B. in the *Calcutta Jute Mills* v. *Nicholson* [36] and the *Cesena Sulphur Co.* v. *Nicholson*,[36] now thirty years ago, involved the principle that a company resides for purposes of income tax where its real business is carried on. Those decisions have been acted upon ever since. I regard that as the true rule, and the real business is carried on where the central management and control actually abides.

It remains to be considered whether the present case falls within that rule. This is a pure question of fact to be determined, not according to the construction of this or that regulation or bye-law, but upon a scrutiny of the course of business and trading.

. . . The Commissioners, after sifting the evidence, arrived at the two following conclusions, *viz.*:—(1) That the trade or business of the appellant company constituted one trade or business, and was carried on and exercised by the appellant company within the United Kingdom at their London office. (2) That the head and seat and directing power of the affairs of the appellant company were at the office in London, from whence the chief operations of the company, both in the United Kingdom and elsewhere, were, in fact controlled, managed, and directed.

These conclusions of fact cannot be impugned, and it follows that this company was resident within the United Kingdom for purposes of income-tax, and must be assessed on that footing. I think, therefore, that this appeal fails. . . .

SWEDISH CENTRAL RAILWAY CO. LTD. v. THOMPSON

House of Lords [1925] A.C. 495; 94 L.J.K.B. 527; 133 L.T. 97; 41 T.L.R. 385; [1924] All E.R.Rep. 710; 9 T.C. 370

The appellant company was incorporated and registered in England, but controlled and managed in Sweden. It was assessed under Case V of Schedule D on the income from its foreign possession, namely the trade carried on in Sweden. *Held*, the company was resident in the United Kingdom and properly assessed.

VISCOUNT CAVE L.C.: . . . My Lords, in my opinion a registered company can have more than one residence for the purposes of the Income Tax Acts. It has often been pointed out that a company cannot in the ordinary sense " reside " anywhere, and that in applying the conception of residence to a company it is necessary (as Lord Loreburn said in the *De Beers* [37] case) to proceed as nearly as possible upon the analogy of an individual.

. . . The effect of this decision is that, when the central management and control of a company abides in a particular place, the company is held for purposes of income tax to have a residence in that place: but it does not follow that it cannot have a residence elsewhere. An individual may clearly have more than one residence: see *Cooper* v. *Cadwalader* [38]: and on principle there appears to be no reason why a company should not be in the same position. The central management and control of a company may be divided, and it may " keep house and do business " in more than one place; and if so, it may have more than one residence.

[36] (1876) 1 T.C. 83.
[37] [1906] A.C. 455; *ante*, p. 447.   [38] (1904) 5 T.C. 101.

. . . In the present case it was found by the Commissioners that, while the business of the company was controlled and managed from the head office at Stockholm, so that the company would in the contemplation of English law have a residence in Sweden, the company was resident in the United Kingdom for the purposes of the Income Tax Acts; and it was hardly disputed that, assuming that a company can have two residences, there was sufficient material upon which that finding could be based. I am not at present prepared to say that registration in the United Kingdom would itself be sufficient proof of residence here; that point does not arise in this case, and I express no opinion upon it. But, however that may be, I am satisfied that the fact of registration together with the other circumstances which were found by the Commissioners to exist, were sufficient to enable them to arrive at their finding. . . .

Note

As explained in *Egyptian Delta Land and Investment Co. Ltd.* v. *Todd* [1929] A.C. 1; *ante*, p. 447, this case merely established that a company *can* have two residences. It is established in the *De Beers* case, and in *Goerz & Co.* v. *Bell* [1904] 2 K.B. 136, that a company registered abroad can nevertheless be resident in this country. In the present case, the court appears to have assumed that a company will be resident where it is incorporated, whether or not it is also resident elsewhere: see also *Egyptian Hotels Ltd.* v. *Mitchell* [1914] 3 K.B. 118 (*ante*, p. 280) especially Buckley L.J. at p. 132: "This company is incorporated in the United Kingdom; it is therefore resident here." As explained in the *Egyptian Delta* case, this is not necessarily so. However, although central control and management will normally be exercised in one place only, it will not always be so, and a company may have dual residence, see *Union Corporation Ltd.* v. *I.R.C.* [1953] A.C. 482, and N.B. *New Zealand Shipping Co. Ltd.* v. *Thew* (1922) 8 T.C. 208.

UNIT CONSTRUCTION CO. LTD. v. BULLOCK

House of Lords [1960] A.C. 351; [1959] 3 W.L.R. 1022; 103 S.J. 1027; [1959] 3 All E.R. 831; 38 T.C. 712

The appellant company made subvention payments to subsidiary companies registered in Kenya, the payments being deductible in computing its profits provided the recipient companies were resident in the United Kingdom. The memorandum and articles of association of the recipient companies provided for management to be exercised in Kenya, but in fact it was exercised from London. *Held*, the companies were resident in the United Kingdom.

VISCOUNT SIMONDS: . . . For it has been trite law for two generations or more that a limited company " resides for purposes of income tax where its real business is carried on," and that its " real business is carried on where the central management and control actually abides." . . . The familiar words that I have cited come from Lord Loreburn's speech in *De Beers Consolidated Mines Ltd.* v. *Howe.*[39] At that time the possibility of an artificial person such as a limited company residing in two countries at one and the same time had not been fully examined. Twenty years later, in *Swedish Central Railway Co. Ltd.* v. *Thompson,*[40] Rowlatt J. saw no difficulty in such a concept and, indeed, found it easier for a corporation to have two residences than for a natural person and, though in the same case in the Court of Appeal Atkin L.J. (as he then was) said that he felt constrained by authority to come to a different conclusion, and in the House of Lords Lord Atkinson in a powerful dissenting speech took the same view, it must now be regarded as clear law that an artificial person may, like a natural person, have more than one residence. The relevance of this consideration is that at an early stage in the proceedings

[39] [1906] A.C. 455, 458; *ante*, p. 447.
[40] (1923) 9 T.C. 342, 352; see *ante*, p. 448.

(before the special commissioners, I think) it was admitted on behalf of the appellant company that the African subsidiaries were resident in Africa. I do not know what considerations led to this admission being made, but it appears to me to have no weight, if it is conceded as a matter of law that a company may have two residences. It is not necessary for me (and I count it my good fortune) on this occasion at any rate to determine in what sense a company may be said to reside not only in that country in which, and in which alone, the central management of its business is exercised, but in another country also. I share to the full the difficulty entertained and expressed by Dixon J. in *Koitaki Para Rubber Estates Ltd.* v. *Federal Commissioner of Taxation*,[41] to which reference was made in the judgment of the Court of Appeal. I leave to others the reconciliation of the *Swedish Central Railway Co.* case,[40] to which I have referred, and *Egyptian Delta Land and Investment Co. Ltd.* v. *Todd*.[42]

. . . The business is not the less managed in London because it ought to be managed in Kenya. Its residence is determined by the solid facts, not by the terms of its constitution, however imperative. If, indeed, I must disregard the facts as they are, because they are irregular, I find a company without any central management at all. For, though I may disregard existing facts, I cannot invent facts which do not exist and say that the company's business is managed in Kenya. Yet it is the place of central management, which, however much or little weight ought to be given to other factors, essentially determines its residence. I come, therefore, to the conclusion, though truly no precedent can be found for such a case, that it is the actual place of management, not that place in which it ought to be managed, which fixes the residence of a company. If it were not so, the result to the Revenue would be serious enough. In how many cases would a limited company register in a foreign country, prescribe by its articles that its business should be carried on by its directors meeting in that country, and then claim that its residence was in that country though every act of importance was directed from the United Kingdom? . . .

---

41 (1940) 64 C.L.R. 15.
42 [1929] A.C. 1; *ante*, p. 447.

Part Four

ESTATE DUTY

CHAPTER 18

INTRODUCTION: THE CHARGE TO DUTY

(A) INTRODUCTION

THE present system of estate duty was introduced by the Finance Act 1894.[1] Like other branches of revenue law, estate duty is the creature of Statute and the legal issues raised are primarily questions of statutory interpretation. The general principles of interpretation of taxing statutes apply,[2] though there has perhaps been a tendency in estate duty cases to attach relatively more importance to the substance of a transaction and less to the pure form.[3]

For some time law relating to estate duty, and indeed the entire system of taxing wealth, gifts and inheritances, has been widely thought to be in need of reform.[4] It has been criticised as complicated, uncertain and too onerous yet too easily avoided. The reform of the system is currently under review.[5]

EARL COWLEY v. I.R.C.

House of Lords [1899] A.C. 198; 68 L.J.Q.B. 435; 80 L.T. 361; 63 J.P. 436; 47 W.R. 525; 15 T.L.R. 270; 43 S.J. 348

LORD MACNAGHTEN: My Lords, the principle on which the Finance Act 1894 was founded is that whenever property changes hands on death the State is entitled to step in and take toll of the property as it passes without regard to its destination or to the degree of relationship, if any, that may have subsisted between the deceased and the person or persons succeeding. . . .

Note
The case concerned the passing of settled property, subject to a mortgage, on the death of the life tenant. Only the equity of redemption was held to pass. It was important mainly for certain remarks on the relationship between sections 1 and 2 of the Finance Act 1894, now resolved by the Finance Act 1969.

[1] The enactment of that statute and the discussions of the fundamental issues involved are described by C. T. Sandford, " Estate Duty versus Inheritance Taxation 1894 " [1968] B.T.R. 10, and in the same author's book, *Taxing Personal Wealth* (London, 1971). These issues have again become of current interest.
[2] Chap. 1, *ante*; see, for example, *Re Earl Fitzwilliam's Agreement* [1950] Ch. 448 at pp. 461–462, *per* Danckwerts J. and the Canadian cases of *Re Taylor*, *Re Hume* (1958) 13 D.L.R. (2d) 470; *post*, pp. 470, 492.
[3] *e.g.* in *Att.-Gen.* v. *Gretton and Shrimpton* [1945] 1 All E.R. 628; *Munro* v. *Commissioner of Stamp Duties* [1934] A.C. 61 at p. 68, *per* Lord Tomlin, *post*, p. 486; *Att.-Gen.* v. *Earl of Sandwich* [1922] 2 K.B. 500 at p. 519, *per* Scrutton L.J.
[4] Criticisms and proposals have been made in many works. Readers are referred in particular to C. T. Sandford, *Realistic Tax Reform* (London, 1971), *Taxing Personal Wealth* (London, 1971), " Taxing Inheritance and Capital Gains " (I. E. A. Hobart Paper No. 32); A. B. Atkinson, " The Reform of Wealth Taxes in Britain " (1971) 42 *Political Quarterly* 45; G. S. A. Wheatcroft, " Proposals for a System of Estate and Gift Taxation " [1965] B.T.R. 199, 283, and " Estate and Gift Taxation—A Comparative Study " (London, 1965) and [1964] B.T.R. 345.
[5] Green Paper, " Taxation of Capital on Death : A possible Inheritance Tax in place of Estate Duty," 1972 Cmnd. 4930; *post*, p. 454.

I.R.C. v. HOLMDEN

House of Lords [1968] A.C. 685; [1968] 2 W.L.R. 300; (1967) 112 S.J. 31; [1968] 1 All E.R. 148; *sub nom. Holmsden's Settlement, Re* [1967] T.R. 323

LORD REID: My Lords, it has long been notorious that the estate duty legislation can cause great injustice or hardship in many cases. . . .

Re KILPATRICK'S POLICIES TRUSTS

Court of Appeal [1966] Ch. 730; [1966] 2 W.L.R. 1346; 110 S.J. 232; [1966] 2 All E.R. 149

DIPLOCK L.J.: . . . As in nearly all appeals about estate duty, I reach my decision without confidence. Were I a betting man I should lay the odds on its being right at 6 to 4 (*i.e.* 3 to 2) on—or against. If ever a branch of law called for reform in 1966, it is the law relating to estate duty. It ought to be certain: it ought to be sensible—it is neither. One cannot read even the scores of cases which have been cited in the present case without realising that it has got into a mess from which I see no hope of the court's rescuing it without drastic legislative assistance.

GREEN PAPER—" TAXATION OF CAPITAL ON DEATH : A POSSIBLE INHERITANCE TAX IN PLACE OF ESTATE DUTY "

1972 Cmnd. 4930

1. Since its introduction in 1894, the estate duty has been the principal duty charged on capital on the occasion of death and it has been the sole duty charged since 1949. As the Chancellor of the Exchequer announced in his Budget statement,[6] the Government believe that the time has come for a thorough-going review which should extend to possible alternative forms of death duty. A detailed examination of these alternatives must be carried out before there can be any question of changing and the Government do not intend to reach a decision on such an important matter without a full public discussion of the possibilities. It is the aim of this paper to encourage such discussion and if, in the light of it, the Government decide that the time is ripe for a change they will, in deciding the form of the new tax, wish to take account of views expressed on the suggestions made in this paper. The main alternative to an estate duty of the type that now exists in this country is an inheritance tax.

2. The essential feature of an estate duty as we now have it is that the tax is graduated by reference to the total value of the property passing on a death, so that for an estate of any given size the same tax is payable whether the whole estate passes to one person or is dispersed among a number of beneficiaries. An inheritance tax, on the other hand, would take no account of the total value of an estate but would be charged on the amounts received by individual beneficiaries. In its simplest form the rate of inheritance tax would be determined for each beneficiary by the total amount of the inheritance he had received on the death in question.

. . . 3. An inheritance tax might also take account of other circumstances. The burden could for example be varied according to the relationship between the beneficiary and the deceased.

. . . 4. Another possibility would be to fix the rate of tax payable by aggregating all bequests received by the beneficiary during a prescribed period of time.

[6] On March 21, 1972.

. . . 12. The rates of estate duty have been increased on many occasions since 1894. They were increased in 1946 to a scale with a maximum rate of 75 per cent., and in 1949, at the time of abolition of the legacy and succession duties, to a scale with a maximum rate of 80 per cent. Between 1946 and 1969, however, there were a series of adjustments to the rates on smaller estates, increasing the threshold below which no duty is payable; in 1946 this was £100: by 1963 it had risen to £5,000. The introduction of the new type of scale in 1969 was accompanied by further relief for the smaller estates (the exemption limit was raised to £10,000) but the new scales were constructed so as to impose much the same burden of tax as before on other estates. In 1971 the exemption limit was raised from £10,000 to £12,500.

13. Although in money terms the rates of tax on many estates are much the same as in 1949, the effective burden on estates has been greatly exacerbated by the effects of inflation. A present day estate has a much higher value in money terms than its 1949 equivalent in real terms and under a scheme of graduated rates therefore suffers much more tax. This burden which has thus automatically grown with inflation will now be substantially eased under the proposals announced in the Budget speech, under which, in addition to the relief for surviving spouses, the exemption limit is to be raised to £15,000 and rates are to be reduced generally.

Outline of the Present Estate Duty

14. The present estate duty is a tax on the capital value of property which "passes" on a death. This means, broadly, property in which the deceased had a beneficial interest at his death or within the previous seven years. All property situated in Great Britain is within the scope of the duty, regardless of the domicile of the deceased [7]; property outside Great Britain is liable to duty if the deceased died domiciled here, or if the title regulating its disposition is governed by the law of any part of Great Britain. [8]

Criticisms of the Estate Duty

. . . 23. Estate duty has come under increasing criticism in recent years partly because of the growing burden which it represents by reason of the effect of inflation on property values, and partly because of its nature as a tax upon the estates of those who die rather than upon the receipts of those who benefit. Taking the latter first, several points of criticism can be identified. First, although its imposition reduces the amount available to individual beneficiaries, the duty payable is not related to the size of the legacies that they receive nor to their taxable capacity. Second, the tax does not lend itself to variation of the burden by reference to the relationship of the deceased to the beneficiary or by reference to some other special circumstance such as the charitable status of the beneficiary. Third, the tax charged on the value of property passing on death does not take account of expenses incurred in the administration of an estate, a significant part of which can, in some circumstances, arise from the determination of liability to the duty itself. [9]

[7] Apart from certain United Kingdom Government securities—Finance (No. 2) Act 1931, s. 22; 1951, s. 34—and property exempt by virtue of a double taxation convention.

[8] F.A. 1949, s. 28 (2); F.A. 1962, s. 28 (1). The location of property is consequently of great importance, see *New York Life Insurance Co.* v. *Public Trustee* [1924] 2 Ch. 101; *English, Scottish and Australian Bank* v. *I.R.C.* [1932] A.C. 238; *Re Kettle's Gift* [1968] 1 W.L.R. 1459.

[9] *Cf.* the position with regard to Capital Gains Tax: *I.R.C.* v. *Richards' Executors* [1971] 1 W.L.R. 571.

24. Other criticisms of the estate duty commonly made spring not from the essential nature of the tax, as do those in the preceding paragraphs, but from the rules associated with its administration. Thus the requirement that duty must be paid before probate is granted is frequently the subject of complaint. So, too, is the rule that all property subject to the duty should be valued at the date of the death. This can cause hardship if the value of the property falls before it can be sold, *e.g.* to meet the duties.

25. The other main area of complaint is that the duty constitutes an excessive burden on property because of the prevailing rates and the level of the starting point of the charge. The burden can be held to discourage the creation and preservation of wealth while, on the other hand, the duty does nothing to encourage the wider distribution of wealth because it is assessed on the total property passing on death. The recently published Report of the Committee of Enquiry on Small Firms [10] under the chairmanship of Mr. J. E. Bolton drew special attention to the possible adverse effects of the burden of duty on small firms (despite the 45 per cent. relief for business assets). In general, they felt that the increasing incidence of estate duty has increased the difficulty of passing on the ownership of a business from one generation to another and so weakened an important motivating force of entrepreneurial effort. In particular, they were concerned with the possibility that small businesses might have to be broken up or starved of working capital by the need to provide funds to pay duty on the death of a proprietor.

26. Estate duty has also been criticised on the grounds that it is not sufficiently comprehensive and is subject to the risk of avoidance. It is possible to distinguish two strands in this line of criticism. The first relates to artificial devices by which a person can reduce the charge on property of which he had effective enjoyment at the time of his death. The second relates primarily to the reduction by gifts *inter vivos* in the value of the property left to be caught by the tax. These issues raise the question of how far anti-avoidance legislation should be taken. There is already a considerable body of such law, much of it passed in recent years, and in relation to gifts *inter vivos* the ambit of charge has been progressively widened. Indeed, the seven-year period for such gifts is itself criticised as being too severe.

Advantages of the Estate Duty

27. Despite the strength of some of these criticisms, the estate duty still has a number of real advantages to which the Government must give due weight in considering whether to change to a new system. Compared with a tax which had to take account of the circumstances of individual beneficiaries, the estate duty is comparatively simple, both for the Inland Revenue and for executors. It is easily collectible and certain as soon as the value of the total property passing on death has been ascertained. It is also less affected than alternative taxes by the intricacies of wills and settlements.

PART II: POSSIBILITY OF CHANGE

Death Duties in other Countries

28. The EEC countries, together with Norway and Denmark, have inheritance taxes; Italy has an estate duty as well. The general picture is that the inheritance tax is imposed on all the property belonging to a person who dies resident in the country concerned wherever it is situated and also on property

---

[10] Report of the Committee of Enquiry on Small Firms, 1971 Cmnd. 4811.

situated within the country belonging to non-residents. The taxes are charged at graduated rates and these countries have different scales according to class of beneficiary; there are, for example, three classes in Norway, four in France, and five in Germany and Denmark. Gifts are subject to tax in all these countries—Norway, France and Germany apply one tax to both inheritances and gifts; others have a separate gift tax. The general principle is that for the purpose of graduation bequests or gifts passing to a beneficiary from any one testator or donor are treated separately from bequests or gifts passing to him from another testator or donor. The tax on close relatives is comparatively light but higher on bequests to strangers. For example, the maximum rate on bequests and gifts to surviving spouses and direct descendants in France is 20 per cent. and in Germany 15 per cent.; in Germany the top rate, and in France the flat rate, on bequests to strangers is 60 per cent. Some countries, Germany and the Netherlands for instance, have a wealth tax as well.

29. There is at present no requirement to harmonise our death duties with those charged in the other countries of the EEC. But in evaluating the case for a change there is the consideration that as the years go by it will become increasingly difficult to subject a man who dies in the United Kingdom to a significantly different death duty regime from a man who dies in another EEC country.

30. Most of the English speaking countries charge an estate duty on the same lines as the United Kingdom duty.

31. In considering experience in other countries it should be borne in mind that there may be important differences in law, in particular in the law of inheritance, trusts and settlements, and this is important in relation to comparisons between varying systems of death duties.

Improvements in the Estate Duty

. . . 33. If the Government decide to retain the estate duty system they will wish to consider, in the light of the public discussion stimulated by this Green Paper, how it might be improved.

Relief for Specified Beneficiaries

34. The criticism that the burden of the tax takes no account of the size of legacies or the circumstances of the individual beneficiaries is fundamental; any arrangements which meet this criticism would mean the introduction of another type of death duty. The criticism that the duty at present takes no account of the status of the beneficiary or of relationships to the deceased can to some extent be met by the sort of reliefs proposed in the Chancellor's Budget speech for surviving spouses and charities, but these arrangements are not ideal because the benefit does not necessarily go direct to the surviving spouse or the charity. In many, perhaps most, cases the property leaving the deceased person is not the same as the property taken by the beneficiaries; for example when property is sold, debts paid and money invested during the course of administering an estate, or when the beneficiary takes only a life interest. While the property dutiable is ascertained at the moment of death the incidence of the duty may not be ascertainable until the estate has been administered. Moreover, the duty on the deceased's own personal estate is a testamentary expense, which means that legacies are not usually charged with any part of the duty. There can thus be no certainty that the reliefs will necessarily benefit those they are intended to. These difficulties could be substantially lessened by a change in the general law in relation to the incidence of estate duty, but such a change would add to the difficulties of administering an estate.

Relief for Aministration Expenses

35. Relief for expenses incurred in the administration of an estate would run counter to the principle that estate duty is charged on the property passing on death. Such relief would introduce a further complication in that in all cases there would have to be corrective assessments after the expenses had been ascertained, and the adjustment of the duty would have to be the last stage in the completion of the administration of the estate.

Date of Valuation [11]

36. Amendment of the rule governing the date of valuation would be possible, but the uniform imposition of some later date would be arbitrary and in some cases would increase the duty payable. It has been suggested that the estate should be valued, at the option of the persons accountable for duty, either at the death or at some convenient later date (*e.g.* the date of the grant of probate). This would be complicated since it would involve comparative valuations and make it necessary to provide for changes in the constitution of the estate after the death. Many more corrective assessments than at present would be required.

37. Another suggestion which has been made is that if property realised by the executors fetches less than its value at the date of death, the lower figure should be substituted for estate duty purposes. This too would involve many more corrective assessments and would require complicated provisions governing the treatment of shares in unquoted companies.

Domicile and Residence

38. Whether the estate duty is retained or whether it is replaced by a different form of death duty the question of *domicile* needs consideration. At present duty is chargeable on the world property of a person who dies domiciled within Great Britain. Domicile depends, in broad terms, on where a person intends to reside permanently. A man who has spent the whole of his life in this country may move abroad shortly before his death and his executors may then maintain that he had acquired a new domicile in the overseas country. On the other hand it may be maintained that a person who came to settle in this country some years before his death always meant to go back to his country of origin and was therefore domiciled there. An improvement on the present position may be to make the charge depend on a person's ordinary residence within a given period of his death.

Surviving Spouses and Settled Property

39. The present estate duty provides a special relief where a surviving spouse takes on the other's death a limited interest in settled property.[12] The settled property is liable to estate duty on the death of the first spouse but not when it passes on the death of the survivor. This is a relic of the time when settled property generally could pass free of duty and, in the context of the present estate duty law, may be thought anomalous in that the benefit of the relief goes, not to the surviving spouse, for whom relief may be most needed, but to the person who inherits on his or her death (who may be a complete stranger). It is for consideration whether this relief should be replaced by one which ensured that the full benefit went to the widow or widower.

[11] Problems of valuation are considered, *post*, Chap. 20.
[12] *Post*, pp. 528-531.

Possible New Forms of Death Duty

40. Death duties can take a variety of forms. The charge can either be proportional, *i.e.* at a flat percentage rate, as in the case of the old legacy and succession duties, or, as in the case of the present estate duty, it can be graduated, *i.e.* the rate increases on increasing amounts. The duties can be based on the total property passing or on the property received by individual beneficiaries. They can, like the old legacy and succession duties, take account of the relationship between the deceased and the beneficiaries, or they can be imposed regardless of this relationship. They can embody, as with the British system before 1949, some combination of these different features.

41. The reliefs for surviving spouses, charities, and certain bodies, announced in the Chancellor's Budget speech will introduce into the estate duty for the first time the principle of differentiation according to the consanguinity or special status of beneficiaries (although as pointed out in paragraph 34 no such arrangements under the existing system of estate duty can be ideal). The primary purposes of a change to a different scheme of death duties would thus be either to relate the burden to the amount received by, or other financial circumstances of, the beneficiaries or to permit improved arrangements for differentiation by reference to consanguinity or to the charitable or special status of a beneficiary, or to achieve a combination of these.

42. There is something to be said for a much smaller estate duty (say half of the present charge) supplemented by a duty graduated according to the circumstances of the beneficiaries. This indeed is what the Colwyn Committee had in mind.[13] The objection to this, however, is the administrative consideration that there would be two duties to be paid and collected instead of one and from this point of view it would be a retrograde step. In view of this the only practical alternative to the present system would be the introduction in its place of an inheritance tax.

PART III: AN INHERITANCE TAX

Basic Principles

43. The essential difference between an inheritance tax and an estate duty is that, whereas an estate duty is charged by reference to the value of the property left by the deceased, an inheritance tax is concerned with what the beneficiaries get. It would therefore be charged on the total amount which each beneficiary received on a death by way of inheritances (which might include, as well as absolute bequests, one or more interests in settled property and gifts from the deceased within a prescribed period before death). The tax so charged would be borne by a beneficiary out of his receipts (or by trustees on his behalf) and would be graduated, like the estate duty. But the graduation would take into account, instead of the total value of the property left by the deceased, either the size of a beneficiary's inheritances on any one occasion, or the amount of his inheritances over a specified period, or perhaps other circumstances of the beneficiary. These might include the beneficiary's relationship to the deceased, so that differentiation for consanguinity could readily be extended beyond surviving spouses to take account of varying degrees of consanguinity.

[13] Report of the Committee on National Debt and Taxation, 1927 Cmd. 2800.

General Considerations

Scope of Charge

45. At present the estate duty is levied on all property, wherever situated, passing on the death of a person domiciled within Great Britain and on all property situated in Great Britain passing on the death of a person domiciled abroad. The domicile or residence of the beneficiary is irrelevant. It can be argued that a tax intended to be borne by individual beneficiaries ought to take account of their residence or domiciliary status, so that one would charge a beneficiary resident in Great Britain on a bequest of foreign property from a foreign testator; as a corollary, there would be an argument for relieving bequests of foreign property to foreign residents from a testator in Great Britain. It would, however, not be easy for the Death Duty Office to ensure the discovery and enforce the collection of the tax on all bequests of foreign property made by foreign testators to beneficiaries in Great Britain. The right answer therefore might be that the charge should fall, like the estate duty, on all property passing on the death of a person domiciled within Great Britain and on property situated in Great Britain passing on the death of a person domiciled abroad (subject to the considerations regarding ordinary residence mentioned in paragraph 38). This is the general pattern of the inheritance taxes in European countries.

Administration

46. If an inheritance tax were introduced, its efficient administration would demand the following features:

(*a*) Executors, administrators and trustees should be primarily liable for payment of the tax to the Revenue, as in the case of the estate duty. Liability would ultimately fall on the individual beneficiary but a system of deduction of duty at source would seem appropriate.

(*b*) A statutory obligation should be imposed upon executors, administrators and trustees to furnish full information necessary to enable the Death Duty Office to assess and collect the tax.

(*c*) The tax should be applied to gifts made within a given period of death, as is the case with the present estate duty.

47. It might be necessary to require a provisional payment on account of inheritance tax before a grant of probate was obtained, corresponding to the present provisions for the advance payment of estate duty. This requirement would be designed to obviate risks of serious delay in the ultimate discharge of liabilities with a correspondingly increased burden on the Revenue in enforcing collection. Moreover, if no tax were payable until the beneficiaries received their bequests there might be loss of almost a year's revenue in the period of the change-over to an inheritance tax from an estate duty.

48. Despite the presence of provisions of this kind, assessment and collection of an inheritance tax would lead to a greater administrative burden than the assessment and collection of the present estate duty. It is impossible to quantify the increase in work this would involve, as this would depend on the precise nature of the tax adopted. Any inheritance tax would involve an increase in the staff of the Estate Duty Office which now numbers about 1,000. The simplest variant would probably mean an increase of not less than 200. The Government will also wish to take into account the likely effect of a change on the work involved for executors and their agents.

Legal Avoidance

49. A change to an inheritance tax would provide an occasion on which the existing complicated legislation designed to prevent the legal avoidance of estate duty could be reviewed to see if any simplification would be made possible by the change. Nevertheless it would be essential under an inheritance tax to deal with events taking place after the death as well as those taking place before. A particular possibility is that property could be left to beneficiaries with a low rate of inheritance tax under arrangements which meant that it would shortly pass, wholly or in part, to persons whose rates would have been high. Trusts with short-term limited interests would particularly lend themselves to arrangements of this nature and it might be necessary to provide that if an interest under a trust set up by a will terminated within, say, five years, inheritance tax should be payable as if the remainderman had received the capital sum as a direct bequest on the death (with credit for any tax actually paid on the property passing to the trust). Whether or not corresponding provisions would have to be introduced in respect of absolute bequests and gifts which could have been made out of the bequests would in part depend on the extent of the reliefs provided, in whatever scheme was finally selected, for specified classes of beneficiary.

Revenue Yield

50. Whatever form an inheritance tax took, the adoption of the estate duty scale would lead to a reduction in the yield, because in most cases an estate would be divided up into several separate inheritances to which the scale would be applied instead of to the whole estate.

If on the other hand the scale of rates was increased to produce the same yield as the estate duty the effect in many instances would be to increase the burden on the beneficiary.

It would be for the Chancellor of the day to decide the level of yield and the rates which would be required. The point should be made that if a reduction in yield were thought acceptable this could also be achieved by retaining the estate duty but with reduced rates. . . .

Transitional Problems

51. The change in the incidence of the duty following the introduction of an inheritance tax could radically alter the relative benefits of different beneficiaries under the terms of any given will and it would therefore be necessary to give people the opportunity of considering and altering their wills. . . .

52. The change could also have considerable repercussions on settled property. Settlements can be broken or varied by the agreement of all the beneficiaries if they are living and *sui juris*, or, otherwise, with the consent of the court under the Variation of Trusts Act 1958 or the Trusts (Scotland) Act 1961. On the introduction of an inheritance tax the courts might be flooded with applications and be unable to deal with the applications within reasonable time. In that event, special legislation to deal with the difficulties might be required.

Differentiation for Consanguinity

53. The case for extended differentiation according to consanguinity is, in brief, that for a stranger a legacy is an out-and-out windfall on which he can reasonably be expected to pay tax at a higher rate than that charged on a legacy to a widow or other near member of the family who has a greater claim on the property of the deceased and is inherently more likely to be financially dependent

on him. The problem to which this gives rise is that it draws distinctions, which many would regard as artificial, between different categories of persons and that these distinctions may not reflect differences in taxable capacity. For example, a niece might have been financially dependent on the deceased to a far greater extent than his son.

54. A simple method of differentiation would be by way of a system of "consanguinity allowances"—*e.g.* strangers and remote relatives might be exempt from duty on the first £15,000 of an inheritance, close relatives (other than spouses) on the first £20,000, and spouses on the first £30,000. A more complex method would be to introduce different scales. There could, for example, be three scales as with the former legacy and succession duties, *i.e.* one scale for spouses and children, a second scale for brothers, sisters, nephews and nieces and a third scale for remoter relatives and strangers. It would also be possible to have more than three scales (or more than three "allowances"). There might, for example, be one scale for spouses, a second scale for children, a third scale for brothers, sisters, nephews and nieces, a fourth scale for remoter relatives and a fifth scale for complete strangers. As an alternative to an "allowance" system, another simple form of differentiation would be to have one "standard" set of exemption limits and rates but to provide that, for specified degrees of consanguinity, the charge should be only a fraction of the tax due under the standard scale, *e.g.* spouses and children might be charged to one-half of the standard tax, brothers etc. to three-quarters. The objection to this simplification would be lack of flexibility, because it would not be possible to vary the proportionate benefits as between small and large estates.

55. Alternatively it would be for consideration whether husbands and wives might be treated as one so that there would be no question of charging property passing between them but any inheritance of one spouse would be combined with inheritances of the other for the purpose of determining the rate of duty. This step could be associated with either a single scale for all other cases or a number of scales.

Method of Graduation

56. If it were decided to introduce extended differentiation for consanguinity, this could, whatever form it took, be combined with one or other of a number of possible varieties of inheritance tax. Any one of these could equally be introduced without differentiation for consanguinity (although it is assumed that at least the estate duty relief for surviving spouses announced in the Chancellor's Budget speech would continue to be reflected).

The differences between the possibilities turn primarily on the method of graduation to be adopted, and if an inheritance tax were to be introduced this would be one of the most important questions for decision.

57. The fundamental question in relation to graduation is whether the principle should be to relate the tax charge to inheritances on any one death or whether to adopt some wider test of a beneficiary's capacity to pay. The simplest principle would be to aggregate all inheritances (including gifts *inter vivos* within the relevant period) which any one beneficiary receives on any one death and to ignore any other circumstances of the beneficiary. This would correspond with the general treatment of inheritances in European countries and, simplicity apart, would recognise that receipt of a substantial inheritance tends to be an isolated occurrence in an individual's experience. It would also accord with the general principle that a death duty sets out to tax capital on the occasion of its passing on death. This method is subsequently referred to as Variant I.

58. On the other hand it can be argued that the tax should take into account wider considerations than the amount which a beneficiary has received on any one occasion. Thus the approach described in paragraph 57 would mean that on a bequest of £20,000 the same rates would be charged on a poor man, who might have received no other significant inheritances during his lifetime, and a rich man who had recently inherited a very large sum indeed.

59. One way sometimes suggested of adjusting the tax burden to the beneficiary's capacity to pay would be to graduate the inheritance tax by reference to the beneficiary's total wealth. Adoption of this principle would, however, mean that on the occasion of every death it would be necessary to obtain returns of the total wealth of each beneficiary. These would have to be verified and valuations made of many types of property. Apart from other considerations, the resulting administrative burden would be quite impossible.[14]

60. An alternative principle would be to relate the tax to the totality of bequests which a beneficiary had received during his lifetime. Theoretically there is something to be said for this approach but administratively it would represent a most formidable task because it would involve keeping a record over a lifetime for every person who might at some time receive an inheritance above any *de minimis* limit that might be prescribed. Moreover it might be objected that a taxpayer receiving an inheritance in his middle or late years could have his tax bill settled by reference to events of long ago which might have no bearing on his present taxable capacity.

61. There would thus be strong objections to aggregation over a lifetime. But the simplest form of inheritance tax (Variant I) would have the unsatisfactory consequence that the tax burden could be artificially reduced if the members of a family in one generation agreed among themselves that each would divide his estate among the members of the family in the next generation. Each member of the next generation would thus get a number of modest inheritances (taxed at a low rate) from his father and his uncles instead of one large inheritance from his father (taxable at a higher rate). This possibility could be prevented by aggregating inheritances over a specified period of years. Such a scheme, which would be more realistic than aggregation over a lifetime, would also have the advantage that, to produce any given yield from the tax, a lower set of rates would be needed than for Variant I. What the period for aggregation should be would be a matter of judgment; it might be as long as ten years but could well be less. The examples below assume a period of ten years solely for the purpose of illustration. This scheme would call for some *de minimis* exemption of small inheritances in order to simplify administration. This method is subsequently referred to as Variant II.

62. The purpose of aggregation over a period would be to determine the appropriate rate (or rates) of tax on successive inheritances; there would be no question of revising, on the occasion of a later inheritance, the tax charge on an earlier one. A suitable method of achieving this purpose would proceed by the following stages:

(1) The most recent inheritance would be aggregated with those received earlier within the preceding ten years.

(2) The total of the earlier inheritances would be treated as the bottom slice of the aggregate.

(3) The tax due on the most recent inheritance would be calculated on the balance as the top slice of the aggregate.

[14] One possible solution would be to treat "accretions" (*e.g.* gifts and inheritances), or a proportion thereof, as the *income* of the recipient in the year received, as suggested by the Carter Commission in Canada.

63. Any scheme based on the aggregation of previous inheritances introduces transitional problems in relation to inheritances received during the period in which estate duty was in force. In accordance with the logic of a tax which sets out to measure the beneficiary's capacity to pay by reference to the totality of inheritances over a period, any such inheritances should be brought into aggregation. It might be said that this involved a measure of double taxation, since the inheritances would usually have come out of funds which had borne the estate duty. But aggregation of earlier inheritances merely serves to determine the rate of tax payable on later inheritances; it does not involve levying further tax on the earlier. Even with the aggregation of inheritances received before the change-over, the full yield of the new tax could hardly be realised in the first few years because, if only for practical reasons, the inheritances net of estate duty would be all that could be taken into account, whereas, when the new tax was in full operation, the gross inheritances would be aggregated.

(B) The Charge to Duty

Estate duty is a charge on the principal value of property which " passes " on death. It is imposed by section 1 of the Finance Act 1894. Section 2 of that Act (as amended) states the heads of charge upon property " deemed " to pass,[15] and numerous other provisions contained in the Estate Duty Statutes bring specific items of " property " within one or other of those heads of charge.

The relationship between sections 1 and 2, which previously had given rise to controversy and difficulty,[16] was resolved by the Finance Act 1969, s. 30.

In determining liability to estate duty it is necessary to consider (i) what property is deemed to pass on death, (ii) the valuation of such property, (iii) the deductions which are permitted from the estate, (iv) the rules for the aggregation of the property passing into one or more estates and the rate or rates of duty applicable, (v) the person or persons accountable for the duty and the incidence of the duty, (vi) the collection and administration of estate duty. There is also the question of exemptions and reliefs, which may apply at various of these stages, e.g. to exempt certain property from the charge, to reduce the dutiable value, to exempt from aggregation or to relieve a person accountable.

1. Property of which the Deceased was Competent to Dispose

The first head of charge, under section 2 (1) (a) of the Finance Act 1894, relates to property of which the deceased was at the time of his death " competent to dispose." [17] Such property includes (i) property in the absolute

---

15 The other " charging " provisions are F.A. 1940, s. 46, and F.A. 1966, s. 41 (2) (b).

16 See Public Trustee v. I.R.C. (Re Arnholz) [1960] A.C. 398; Re Weir's Settlement [1971] Ch. 145; Sanderson v. I.R.C. [1956] A.C. 491. The effect of the 1969 revision is considered by J. Silberrad, " The Estate Duty Provisions of the Finance Act 1969 " [1969] B.T.R. 210.

17 Competence to dispose is also important in relation to the surviving spouse exemption under F.A. 1894, s. 5 (2), post, p. 528, the reverter to disponer exemption under F.A. 1896, s. 15, post, p. 531, and in relation to accountability, F.A. 1894, s. 8 (3). See, especially, I.R.C. v. Priestley [1901] A.C. 208; post, p. 528; Re Parsons [1943] Ch. 12; post, p. 530.

ownership of the deceased at the time of his death, including an interest in expectancy,[18] the undivided share of a tenant in common and the severable share of a beneficial joint tenant,[19] and property which the deceased was entitled to recover from another; (ii) property subject to a general power of appointment, or a special power if the deceased could have appointed himself or was entitled in default; (iii) property coming into existence after the death of the deceased but payable to the deceased's personal representatives, including benefits payable as of right under a life assurance policy, pension or superannuation scheme and damages paid under the Law Reform (Miscellaneous Provisions) Act 1934.

Re PENROSE

Chancery Division [1933] Ch. 793; 102 L.J.Ch. 321; 149 L.T. 325; 49 T.L.R. 285; [1933] All E.R.Rep. 796

By a will the deceased was given a power to appoint a fund among the issue of his father and was consequently able to appoint to himself. *Held*, he was competent to dispose of the fund.

LUXMOORE J.: . . . Three questions arise. The first, as I understand the argument, is purely one of law. Could the husband, as donee of the power and being within the class of objects, exercise it in his own favour to the exclusion of all other objects? If the answer is in the negative, the other questions are immaterial. If, on the other hand, it is in the affirmative, the second question arises—namely: Is the husband, on the true construction of the will, an object of the power? If the answer is in the negative, again no further question arises, but if it is in the affirmative a further question has to be answered: Was the husband, on the true construction of the relevant sections of the Finance Act, competent to dispose of the testatrix's residuary estate or any part of it?

It is argued that the power in the present case is a limited power and does not authorise the donee to appoint or dispose of the property subject to it as he thinks fit. It is said that if he appoints to himself he only acquires the property but does not dispose of it, and that his power to dispose of it as he thinks fit does not arise under the power but after he has exercised it in his own favour. In my judgment this is too narrow a construction to place on the words of the definition. A donee of a power who can freely appoint the whole of the fund to himself and so acquire the right to dispose of the fund in accordance with his own volition, is, in my judgment, competent to dispose of that fund as he thinks fit, and it can make no difference that this can only be done by two steps instead of by one—namely, by an appointment to himself, followed by a subsequent gift or disposition, instead of by a direct appointment to the object or objects of his bounty. If under a power the donee can make the whole of the property subject to it his own, he can by exercising the power in his own favour place himself in the position to dispose of it as he thinks fit. The power to dispose is a necessary incident of the power to acquire the property in question. In my judgment, the word " power " in the phrase " a power to appoint or dispose of as he thinks fit," is not used in the definition section in

---

[18] Special rules relate to the valuation of an interest in expectancy—F.A. 1894, s. 7 (6)—and to the purchase of such an interest: F.A. 1969, s. 38.

[19] F.A. 1969, s. 36 (7).

the strict legal sense attaching to it when used with reference to a power of appointment, but in the sense of capacity; and I think this is made clear by the use of the words "or dispose of" in addition to the words "to appoint," because otherwise the words "or dispose of" would be mere surplusage.

In the result I hold that, on the true construction of the relevant sections of the Finance Act 1894, the testatrix's husband was after her death competent to dispose of the residuary estate, and consequently on his death estate duty became payable in respect of such part of the residuary estate as then remained subject to the trusts of the testatrix's will.

COMMISSIONER OF ESTATE AND SUCCESSION DUTIES (BARBADOS) v. BOWRING

Privy Council [1962] A.C. 171; [1960] 3 W.L.R. 741; 104 S.J. 868; [1960] 3 All E.R. 188; [1960] T.R. 253

LORD COHEN : . . . As their Lordships have already indicated . . . they are satisfied that upon the true construction of section 3 (a) of the Barbados Estate and Succession Duties Act 1941, a person cannot be said to have a general power making him competent to dispose of property within the meaning of that paragraph if the consent of the trustees is required to the exercise of that power, and that provision is so framed that the court will not control the trustees in the exercise of the power, if they act honestly and do not act from an improper motive. The Act is a taxing Act, and their Lordships would not be justified in giving to the words used an extension of meaning which, in their Lordships' view, they would not naturally bear.

Note
The case was concerned with the accountability for duty of the deceased's executors.

ATTORNEY-GENERAL v. QUIXLEY

Court of Appeal (1929) 98 L.J.K.B. 652; 141 L.T. 288; 93 J.P. 227; 45 T.L.R. 455; 27 L.G.R. 693; [1929] All E.R.Rep. 696

The deceased at her death was in the service of a public school trust. A death gratuity was payable to her sister, as personal representative, under a superannuation scheme. *Held*, the gratuity was property of which the deceased was competent to dispose.

LORD HANWORTH M.R.: . . . Counsel was, I think rightly, compelled to admit that she could dispose of a sum ultimately to be received, or could dispose of this interest by her will, although he said she could not raise any money upon it in the sense that there could not be an assignment of it while she was alive. But it would appear to me that to suggest that the deceased lady had no power to dispose of this sum by will would be to take away half the merit of the gratuity upon her decease. If and when it is received it must be subject to her will, and her absolute right to receive some sum is of benefit and of comfort to her, because she is, by means of that knowledge and that competence to dispose of it, able to make some provision for those who are the objects, and rightly the objects, of her disposing power. It appears to me, therefore, that in view of the right which this lady had, she had this power to dispose of the sum by will, and thus, when one looks at the Act of 1894, section 1, the charging section, and section 2, which I have referred to as a section which sweeps into the charge under section 1 property which is to be deemed for the purpose of section 1 to be property passing on the death, and when one looks at the still wider interpretation under section 22, sub-section 2 (a), it is clear that this sum that is ultimately received, £429 17s. 6d., does fall within the charge imposed by section 1 of the Finance Act 1894.

. . . *Id certum est quod certum reddi potest* is the old maxim, and, just as in the illustration which I ventured to put, of the case where a man is possessed of freehold property which is, unfortunately, devastated by fire just before his death, but, being fully assured, enables his executors to receive under a contract of fire insurance a sum which is to be estimated by an award made as a condition precedent to their liability, so also here the mere ascertainment of the amount at a later date does not alter the nature of the right which the lady had, or prevent that right from being within the term " property," and, as such, chargeable to estate duty. . . .

Note
    The charge applies only to benefits receivable as of right. Benefits payable by reason of the exercise of a discretionary power by the trustees of a pension fund escape duty, see *e.g.* *Re Leek, deceased* [1969] 1 Ch. 563.

2. Settled Property

The law of estate duty in relation to settled property was completely recast by the Finance Act 1969 and an entirely new section 2 (1) (*b*) of the Finance Act 1894 was enacted, relating to " property comprised in a settlement " at the date of the deceased's death, or at certain specified times prior thereto, and in which the deceased had had an interest or from which the deceased had received a benefit. Decisions under the old law remain important, if at all, chiefly in relation to the law of property, in so far as they determine the nature of a person's " interest " in settled property [20]; the new provisions have not yet been considered by the courts.[21]

---

[20] *e.g. Gartside* v. *I.R.C.* [1968] A.C. 553; *Sainsbury* v. *I.R.C.* [1970] Ch. 712; and *Re Gulbenkian's Settlements (No. 2)* [1970] Ch. 408, concerning the interest of an object under a discretionary trust.

[21] For descriptions and commentary upon the " new " section 2 (1) (*b*) see, in particular, Potter & Monroe's *Tax Planning* (6th ed.), Chaps. 3, 4, 8; J. Mowbray, *Estate Duty on Settled Property* (London, 1970); H. Cohen, " Discretionary Trusts and Estate Duty " (1971) 35 *Conveyancer* (N.S.) 82; G. S. A. Wheatcroft, " Some Estate Duty Problems in relation to Accumulating and Discretionary Trusts " [1969] B.T.R. 283; P. A. Lovell, " Discretionary Trusts and Estate Duty—The Dutiable Slice " [1970] B.T.R. 220; and D. Goldberg, " The Curious Case of the Finance Act 1969 and Sub-Trusts " [1971] B.T.R. 117.

Chapter 19

CONTINUATION: THE CHARGE TO DUTY

3. Gifts

I<small>F</small> the charge to estate duty were restricted to property owned by the deceased at his death, or property of which he was competent to dispose, and to property comprised in a settlement in which he had had some interest, the avoidance of estate duty would be an extremely simple matter. A person would simply give away property in anticipation of his death. Consequently, the need has long been recognised to extend the charge to property given away within a certain period of death; the prescribed period has from time to time been extended, from the original three months to the present seven years. Section 2 (1) (*c*) of the Finance Act 1894 charges to duty any *donatio mortis causa* or gift whenever made by the deceased unless made more than seven years before death (one year for public and charitable gifts [1]) and from which the donor was entirely excluded of any benefit by way of contract or otherwise.[2] Such a gift may qualify for certain reliefs [3]; certain other transactions are treated as gifts.[4]

In considering whether or not a transaction falls within the scope of the charge it is necessary to determine (i) its nature, i.e. whether it is a " gift " or some other transaction, (ii) whether it took effect as a gift and, if so, when, (iii) whether possession was assumed by the donee to the entire exclusion of the donor of any benefit, and (iv) the precise subject-matter of the gift.

(A) WHAT CONSTITUTES A GIFT?

A gift may take the form of a transfer of money or property, or of an interest in property to or for the benefit of one or more persons, or it may take the form of a release, surrender or disclaimer of a right or interest. A " gift " involves an element of bounty and must be distinguished from a sale or exchange. However, it may be difficult to distinguish between, on the one hand, a gift with the reservation of a benefit to the donor or a gift with a collateral benefit to the donor [5] and, on the other hand, a sale or exchange of property. Likewise, what is apparently a sale or exchange may

---

[1] Special reliefs for gifts and bequests made to charities are contained in F.A. 1972, s. 121.

[2] Customs and Inland Revenue Act 1881, s. 38 (2), as amended.

[3] *e.g.* small gifts relief, F. (1909–10) A. 1910, s. 59 (2), F.A. 1949, s. 33; gifts in consideration of marriage, F.A. 1963, s. 53, F.A. 1968, s. 36; *post*, p. 533; gifts forming part of the normal expenditure of the deceased, F.A. 1968, s. 37, and " tapering " relief, in respect of gifts made more than four but less than seven years before death, F.A. 1960, s. 64 (1), F.A. 1968, s. 35 (2).

[4] *e.g.* payments of certain debts, F.A. 1939, s. 31 (2); certain dispositions in favour of relatives, F.A. 1940, s. 44; the creation of a burden or the release of rights, F.A. 1940, s. 45; and the payment of premiums on certain life policies, F.A. 1959, s. 34.

[5] *Post*, pp. 477–493.

nevertheless contain an element of bounty as, for example, in the case of sale for partial consideration [6] or an exchange where the properties exchanged are of different values.[7]

Re STRATTON'S DISCLAIMER

Court of Appeal [1958] Ch. 42; [1957] 3 W.L.R. 199; 101 S.J. 533; [1957] 2 All E.R. 594; [1957] T.R. 161

Some time after the death of her husband, a widow disclaimed all her interest in certain properties to which she was entitled under his will, the property in consequence passing to her sons as residuary legatees.

JENKINS L.J.: . . . Mrs. Stratton died on June 27, 1953, a date well within five years of the disclaimer. Clearly if she had accepted the gifts made to her by the will and had then within five years of her death transferred the assets comprised in them to her three sons by way of gift, estate duty would have been exigible on her death in respect of such gift by virtue of section 2 (1) (c) of the Finance Act 1894, the provisions incorporated therein of section 38 of the Customs and Inland Revenue Act 1881, and section 11 of the Customs and Inland Revenue Act 1889, and the extensions of the liability to duty first to gifts made within three years of the death by the Finance (1909–10) Act 1910, and then to gifts made within five years of the death by the Finance Act 1946. But instead of proceeding by way of acceptance and transfer, Mrs. Stratton (as one would expect in the circumstances) preferred to achieve substantially the same result by the simpler and cheaper method of a disclaimer, which did not transfer her interest to the three sons by way of gift but destroyed her interest with the legal consequence that the disclaimed assets fell into residue for their benefit.

The question in the case is whether section 45 (2) of the Finance Act 1940, has the effect of extending the liability to duty on gifts *inter vivos* imposed by section 2 (1) (c) of the Finance Act 1894 (as amended) to the comparable benefit conferred on a residuary legatee or devisee by means of a disclaimer, whereby the subject-matter of the gift disclaimed is caused to sink into the residue to which he is entitled.

. . . It will be seen that to found liability under subsection (2) of the section there must be (i) a debt or other right, and (ii) an extinguishment of that debt or other right, (a) at the expense of the deceased, and (b) for the benefit of some other person. Where these elements are present the enactment imputes to the deceased for estate duty purposes a disposition in favour of the person for whose benefit the debt or right was extinguished of property consisting of the benefit conferred by such extinguishment. This produces the result that the benefit conferred by a transaction falling within the ambit of subsection (2) of section 45 of the Act of 1940 is to be treated as " property . . . taken under a disposition made by ' the deceased' purporting to operate as an immediate gift *inter vivos* " within the meaning of section 2 (1) (c) of the 1894 Act, and the provisions incorporated therein of section 38 (2) (a) of the Customs and

---

[6] Although the courts will not be concerned with the adequacy or otherwise of the consideration in an " arm's length " transaction where there is a bona fide sale or exchange, special provisions apply in the case of dispositions to relatives: F.A. 1940, s. 44, F.A. 1950, s. 46. See *Re Harmsworth, deceased* [1967] Ch. 826; *post*, p. 524. *Re Leven and Melville, deceased* [1954] 1 W.L.R. 1228. In particular, this is so where the consideration for the transfer is an annuity, but see *Re Earl Fitzwilliam's Agreement* [1950] Ch. 448; *post*, p. 470.

[7] As in *Letts* v. *I.R.C.* [1957] 1 W.L.R. 201.

Inland Revenue Act 1881, and is therefore to be deemed under section 2 (1) (c) of the 1894 Act to pass, and, accordingly, attract estate duty, on the death of the deceased within the statutory period (now five years) of the making of such disposition.

The application of section 45 (2) of the 1940 Act to the transaction now in question thus demands an affirmative answer to each of the following questions:

(1) Did Mrs. Stratton have a " right " in respect of the policies and freehold property bequeathed and devised to her during the period between the death of the testator and the execution of the deed of disclaimer?

(2) If so, did the disclaimer bring about an " extinguishment " of that right?

(3) If so, was such extinguishment effected " at the expense of " Mrs. Stratton?

(4) If so, was the right extinguished " for " the " benefit " of the three sons? . . .

Note
His Lordship concluded that each question should be answered in the affirmative. Another example of a gift by way of a disclaimer is to be found in *Re Parsons* [1943] 1 Ch. 12; *post*, p. 530; *cf. Re Hall* [1942] Ch. 140.

Re EARL FITZWILLIAM'S AGREEMENT

Chancery Division [1950] Ch. 448; 66 T.L.R. (Pt. 1) 174; 94 S.J. 49; [1950] 1 All E.R. 191

The deceased had transferred shares and life policies to the Trustees of a settlement, effected on the occasion of the marriage of his son, in consideration for an annuity payable to himself. The property transferred was valued at £375,000 and the settlor received an annuity of £50,000 a year. He died nine years later. *Held*, the transaction was not a gift at all but a bona fide transaction for full value and estate duty was not payable on the settled property.

DANCKWERTS J.: Duty is claimed in the present case under section 2, subsection 1 (c), of the Finance Act 1894. The words " voluntarily " or " voluntary " do not appear in the provision, but the words " gift " and " donee " and " donor " appear in it; and, as it was originally enacted, there seems to be no reason to attribute to this statutory provision any intention to include transactions for value. But the contention of the Commissioners of Inland Revenue is that by reason of the removal of the words " voluntary " " voluntarily " and " volunteer " by section 2, subsection 1 (c) of the Finance Act 1894, from the former provisions of the Customs and Inland Revenue Acts 1881 and 1889, transactions for value, even though sales for full monetary consideration, are now included in those provisions as re-enacted by the Finance Act 1894.

If it was the intention of the legislature to make such a striking change as to include sales for full monetary value in the former provisions relating to gifts, it certainly seems that an odd method of carrying out such a change was adopted. So long as the provisions were dealing with gifts and purely voluntary transactions, the words " gift," " donor " and " donee " were the natural words to use and were entirely logical. It seems to me that it would have been perfectly simple (if it had been desired to include sales) to have substituted the word " assurance " for " gift " and " grantor " and " grantee " or " transferor " and " transferee " for the words " donor " and " donee." . . .

Note
The relationship to the " bona fide purchase " exemption in F.A. 1894, s. 3, was considered. In the opinion of Danckwerts J., that provision has no application to situations falling within s. 2 (1) (c); *cf. Re Bateman* [1925] 2 K.B. 429; *post*, p. 527; and *Att.-Gen.* v. *Johnson*, *infra*.

Although the disposition by the deceased was in favour of relatives, and the consideration received was an annuity, the transaction was held not to be within F.A. 1940, s. 44. See now, however, F.A. 1950, s. 46, and *Re Harmsworth, deceased* [1967] Ch. 826; *post*, p. 524.

ATTORNEY-GENERAL v. JOHNSON

Court of Appeal [1903] 1 K.B. 617; 72 L.J.K.B. 323; 88 L.T. 445; 67 J.P. 113; 51 W.R. 487; 19 T.L.R. 324; 47 S.J. 367

The deceased made a payment of £500 to a charitable society in return for an agreement to pay an annuity to himself, and to his wife if she survived him, of £25 a year. The commercial value of such an annuity at that time was £210.

VAUGHAN WILLIAMS L.J.: . . . Having regard to the terms of section 11 of the Customs and Inland Revenue Act 1889, which speaks of a benefit to the donor by contract, and to the language of the Finance Act 1894, section 2, subsection 1 (c), which incorporates the provisions of section 11 of the Customs and Inland Revenue Act 1889, as if the words " voluntary " and " voluntarily " and " volunteer " were omitted, and to the decisions in *Crossman* v. *Reg.*[8] and *Attorney-General* v. *Worrall*,[9] we come to the conclusion that the Legislature intends that property shall be treated as taken under a " gift," although such gift may have been made under a contract by which the donor takes a benefit.

If, then, the substance of the transaction between Mr. Burton and the Missionary Society be looked at, it seems to us that it was intended not to be a matter of pure business, but one of bounty on the part of Mr. Burton. The facts that the payment was made " in lieu of a legacy," and that the amount paid largely exceeded the market value of the annuities agreed to be paid to Mr. and Mrs. Burton are sufficient to establish this. Consequently, the transaction must, in our opinion, be held to be a gift within the meaning of section 2, subsection 1 (c), of the Finance Act 1894. In truth this was not seriously disputed by the learned counsel for the Missionary Society, who urged that the gift ought not to be treated as consisting of £500, but of that amount less the deduction of £210. This contention was based partly on the language of the Customs and Inland Revenue Act 1898, s. 11, subs. 1, and partly on the terms of section 3 of the Finance Act 1894.

As to the first of these grounds, it is to be observed that by the terms of the Finance Act 1894, property passing on the death of the deceased is to be deemed to include the property in question as being property which would be required " on the death of the deceased " to be included in an account. The point of time to which regard must be paid is that of the death of the deceased—in this case Mr. Burton. If at that moment the £500 had remained in the hands of the society undiminished, then (subject to any question arising as to the effect of the annuity which was to be paid to Mrs. Burton) it would seem that the whole sum must be taken to have passed and to be subject to estate duty. This is in accordance with the decisions in *Attorney-General* v. *Worrall*, where no deduction was allowed in respect of the yearly sum of £735 covenanted to be paid by the donee to the donor during his life, and *Attorney-General* v. *Grey (Earl)*,[10] where no deduction was made in respect of an annual rent charge reserved to the donor during his life.

What the society actually did with the £500 does not appear; but it is contended that they ought not to be treated as having the whole of that sum in their hands at Mr. Burton's death, because no investment of that sum, proper

8 (1886) 18 Q.B.D. 256.
9 [1895] 1 Q.B. 99.
10 [1900] A.C. 124; *post*, p. 477.

to be made by trustees, would at the present time yield £25 (that is, 5 per cent. on £500) per annum; and consequently that, for the purpose of paying the annuity, the capital originally placed in their hands must be treated as having been encroached upon to a certain extent. We do not think that this contention ought to prevail, for, if one looks at the real substance of the transaction and its object, it is difficult to avoid the conclusion that it was intended to be a testamentary gift of £500.

Suppose the transaction in this case had been that, in consideration or upon the condition of the society paying to the donor the interest on £500 for his life, he would make a present gift of £500. It seems to us that such a case would clearly have fallen within the operation of section 11 of the Act of 1889. Now what is the difference between that case and the present? It seems to me that, instead of the consideration being the interest on £500, it is an arbitrary annuity of £25 for the lives of the donor and his wife, and it is said that interest at this rate could not be obtained on an investment of trust money which we assume to be true. This difference does not in our judgment convert the transaction into a purchase of an annuity. A consideration is given whether the promise is to pay interest at the rate obtainable on trust investments, or to grant an annuity exceeding that rate and in either case the substances of the transaction is a testamentary gift. The donor gives the £500, less the profits to be made thereout, until his death and that of his wife. The fact that, by the condition of the gift which the transferee accepts, the rate of profit is fixed above the rate of interest which might be reasonably expected upon a trust investment does not seem to us to divest the transaction of its character as a gift, nor does the fact that the gift is subject to a life interest at the fixed rate in favour of the wife. The corpus of the gift is in no way encroached upon. It seems to us that to hold the contrary would be to disregard the decision in *Attorney-General* v. *Worrall*, for we do not think that consistently with that case one can take into account the quantum of the profit of the subject-matter of the gift which are retained by the donor. The profit retained in respect of the £500 presently paid may of course be so large that one cannot regard the £500 as a gift, and must regard that which is retained or reserved as an annuity for two lives purchased at the price of £500. But then there would be no gift, and only a sale, and the section would have no application. But that does not seem to be the case here . . . really the only question, as pointed out by Phillimore J., is—whether the transaction in this case amounts to the purchase of an annuity, and is therefore exempt from estate duty under the provisions of section 3, subsection 1, of the Finance Act 1894, or to the grant of an annuity " for partial consideration in money or money's worth paid to the vendor or grantor for his own use or benefit," so that the value of the consideration ought to be allowed as a deduction from the value of the property for the purpose of estate duty under subsection 2 of section 3. Phillimore J. has held that the whole £500 is, in the first instance, taxable—a conclusion in which we agree—but has further held that in this case £210, the value of an annuity of £25 a year for two lives, ought to be deducted from the £500, and that therefore only £290 remains to be taxed. This is a conclusion in which we cannot agree, because, in our judgment, this is not a case of a bona fide purchase of an annuity at all. It is a case of a testamentary gift effected by the machinery of a present donation, subject to a reservation of something intended to be the equivalent of a life interest in the subject-matter of the donation. . . .

(B) When is a Gift Effective?

It is necessary to determine whether a purported gift took effect at all and, because of the seven year period, if it did so the date on which it took effect. The probable consequence of an ineffective gift is that the subject matter remains the property of the would-be donor and of which he is competent to dispose.[11]

Re OWEN (DECD.)

Chancery Division [1949] 1 All E.R. 901; [1949] W.N. 201; [1949] L.J.R. 1128; 93 S.J. 287

Gifts were made by the deceased by cheques which were drawn by him more than three years before his death but were presented for payment within the three years.

ROMER J.: . . . The proper interpretation of the facts is that until the donees had received their cheques and paid them into their own banking accounts, and the cheques were cleared and the money came into the donees' banking accounts, no property was transferred at all, nor was any effectual gift achieved. . . . I am satisfied that the three gifts referred to in the summons were made within three years of the testator's death on June 1, 1944, because they were made on the occasion on which each of the cheques was cleared into the donee's own account.

Re ROSE

Court of Appeal [1952] Ch. 499; [1952] 1 T.L.R. 1577; [1952] 1 All E.R. 1217; [1952] T.R. 175

JENKINS L.J.: . . . I agree. The combined effect of section 38 (2) (*a*) of the Customs and Inland Revenue Act 1881, section 11 (1) of the Customs and Inland Revenue Act 1889, and section 2 (1) (*c*) of the Finance Act 1894, together with subsequent legislation affecting the period of time before the death of a deceased within which transactions inter vivos are to be taxable, is that any disposition made by a deceased person purporting to operate as an immediate gift inter vivos not made at least the prescribed minimum period before the death attracts duty. Furthermore, any gift, whenever made, of which bona fide possession and enjoyment is not assumed forthwith on the gift and thenceforth retained to the entire exclusion of the donor, or of any benefit to him, by contract or otherwise, likewise attracts duty, unless there has been complete exclusion of the donor and of any benefit to him for at least the prescribed minimum period prior to the death.

As the law stood at the date of the death, on February 16, 1947, of the deceased, with whom this case is concerned, the relevant minimum period before the death had in general been increased to five years; but by virtue of certain transitional provisions contained in the Finance Act 1949, applicable to his case, a transaction of either of the kinds I have mentioned would escape duty, provided that any such gift or disposition made by him was made before April 10, 1943, and provided, further, that as regards any gift or disposition made by him before that date bona fide possession and enjoyment had been assumed by the donee to the entire exclusion of the deceased and any benefit to him, by contract or otherwise, from before the same date, April 10, 1943.

The question in this case, therefore, is whether the transfers of shares, admittedly effected, so far as the deceased was concerned, on March 30, 1943,

---

[11] As, for example, in *Re Wale (deceased)* [1956] 1 W.L.R. 1346; *Re Cole, a bankrupt* [1964] Ch. 175; and *Re Fry* [1940] Ch. 312. The same principles apply, *e.g.* to a settlement void for uncertainty, as argued in *Re Leek (deceased)* [1969] 1 Ch. 563; *cf.* the position for income tax purposes, *ante*, p. 380.

and therefore before the critical date, were caught by the provisions to which I have referred so as to attract duty. There is no doubt, as my Lord has said, that on March 30, 1943, the deceased did execute, under seal, instruments of transfer purporting in each case to transfer 10,000 shares in the company, the instruments of transfer complying strictly with the clause in the company's articles, which states the manner in which shares are to be transferred. Furthermore, before April 10, 1943, those transfers, and the relative share certificates, were duly delivered to the respective transferees or their agent. So far, all seems plain; but as the property transferred consisted of shares in a company, a further event was necessary in order to perfect the legal title of the transferees, and that further event was the entry of the names of the transferees in the company's register of members as holders of the shares transferred.

[His Lordship quoted the relevant provisions of the articles of association of the Leweston Estates Co. and continued:] On the deceased executing the transfers and handing them over, together with the relative share certificates, to the transferees or their agent, the matter, then, stood thus: The deceased had done all in his power to divest himself of and to transfer to the transferees the whole of his right, title and interest, legal and equitable, in the shares in question. He had, moreover, complied strictly with the procedure prescribed by the company's articles. Nevertheless, he had not transferred the full legal title, nor could he do so by the unaided operation of any instrument of his; for under its articles the company was only bound to recognise, and in fact would only recognise, the registered holder of a share, and none other, as the absolute owner of the share. The deceased had thus done all he could, in appropriate form, to transfer the whole of his interest, but so far as the legal title was concerned, it was not in his power himself to effect the actual transfer of that, inasmuch as it could only be conferred on the transferees in its perfect form by registration of the transfers. But he had, in my judgment, transferred to the transferees the right to be placed on the register in his stead as the owners of the shares, subject to the directors' power to refuse registration.

That being the nature of the transactions, two questions arise: *First*, when was the disposition or gift made; *secondly*, if it was made before April 10, 1943, did the transferees forthwith (or at least before the last-mentioned date) assume possession or enjoyment under the gift and thenceforth retain the same to the entire exclusion of the deceased, or any benefit to him, by contract or otherwise? As to the first question, with respect to those who have contended otherwise, it seems to me plain enough that this gift or disposition must have been made on the date when the deceased executed instruments of transfer and delivered them, with the certificates, to the transferees. After all, any transaction of gift imports a donor and a donee—a disposition by the donor and receipt of the subject-matter of the disposition by the donee. In this case the only gift or disposition by the deceased, the only act of bounty on his part as regards either parcel of shares, took place before April 10, 1943. This claim for duty could not have been made at all except on the footing that the transferees derived their beneficial title to these shares from a disposition or gift made by the deceased. To say that the gift was made on the date subsequent to April 10, 1943, when the company's directors in fact registered the transfers, and was therefore dutiable, seems to me a quite untenable proposition; for the registration of the transfers was an act over the doing or refusing of which the deceased had no relevant control, and was moreover an act the doing of which he could not, consistently with his own deeds, oppose. In my view, the directors of the company, when they registered the transfers, registered them because, by virtue of the transfers, the transferees had become owners of the shares, and as such had become entitled to get in the legal estate by being put on the register in respect of the shares.

The second question—that is to say: Did the disposition or the gift operate to the entire exclusion of the transferor, and so forth—can be expressed alternatively by the question: Was this an incomplete gift which was only completed by the registration? That, I think, is the real basis of the Crown's contention. The Crown claims that this was an incomplete gift, because until the moment of registration of the transfers the company could not be compelled to recognise any other person than the deceased as the holder of the shares, and until that happened the gift was incomplete.

It seems to me that the formulation, in terms of an incomplete gift, of the character and effect of the disposition constituted by the execution of the transfers and delivery of them to the transferees with the certificates involves considerable difficulty. I can understand that in given circumstances a gift might, rightly or wrongly, be claimed to be incomplete because it could be recalled by the donor. If here it could be said that the deceased, had he changed his mind at any moment before registration, could by the taking of appropriate proceedings, recall the transfers and recover the certificates and restrain the directors of the company from registering the transfers, then I would understand the proposition that the gift was incomplete, inasmuch as the property had never passed irrevocably to the donees. But that argument is disclaimed by the Crown, for reasons which I can well understand. It seems to me impossible to suppose that any such action could have been brought by the deceased in this case with any prospect of success. That contention having been disclaimed, it is said, on the part of the Crown, that nevertheless the gift is incomplete because, although the deceased could not recall it, he remained the owner of the shares until the transferees were registered in respect of them. That proposition seems to me to disregard entirely the form of the transfers. And, indeed, Mr. Pennycuick, for the Crown, in the end said that the effect of the transfers was no more than some sort of conditional authority or promise that, if the directors of the company chose to register the transfers, then, but not otherwise, the transferees should become the owners of the shares. That is a proposition which I cannot accept, and it seems to me to read into the transfers—which are simple and straightforward documents, apt, as I think, to effect an immediate out-and-out transfer and nothing else—conditions of which the language of the documents themselves contains no trace whatever, for the purpose of bringing these transactions within the charge for duty. Accordingly, I adhere to the view I have already expressed, that these transfers were nothing more nor less than transfers of the whole of the deceased's title, both legal and equitable, in the shares, and all the advantages attached to the shares, as from the date on which he executed and delivered the transfers—subject, of course, as regards the legal title, to the provisions of the articles of association of the company as to registration, and to the directors' discretionary power to refuse registration.

If that was the effect of the transfers, what was the position between the delivery of the transfers and the actual registration of the transferees as the holders of the shares? Mr. Pennycuick has referred us to the well-known case of *Milroy* v. *Lord*,[12] which has been his sheet-anchor. He says that on this authority we must be forced to the conclusion that, pending registration, the transfers had no effect at all, and he arrives at that conclusion in this way: He says that these transfers, while purporting to be transfers of the property in the shares and not declarations of trust, did not transfer the property in the shares, because registration was necessary in order to get in the legal title. He says, further, that being transfers purporting to be transfers of the property in the shares and failing of their effect as such for want of registration, they could, pending registration, have no operation at all because in the case of *Milroy* v.

[12] (1862) 4 De G.F. & J. 264.

Lord it was held that a defective voluntary disposition purporting to operate as a transfer or assignment of the property in question would not be given effect to in equity as a declaration of trust. I agree with my Lord that the case of *Milroy* v. *Lord* by no means covers the question with which we have to deal in the present case. If the deceased had in truth transferred the whole of his interest in these shares so far as he could transfer the same, including such right as he could pass to his transferee to be placed on the register in respect of the shares, the question arises, what beneficial interest had he then left? The answer can only be, in my view, that he had no beneficial interest left whatever: his only remaining interest consisted in the fact that his name still stood on the register as holder of the shares; but having parted in fact with the whole of his beneficial interest, he could not, in my view, assert any beneficial title by virtue of his position as registered holder. In other words, in my view the effect of these transactions, having regard to the form and the operation of the transfers, the nature of the property transferred, and the necessity for registration in order to perfect the legal title, coupled with the discretionary power on the part of the directors to withhold registration, must be that, pending registration, the deceased was in the position of a trustee of the legal title in the shares for the transferees. Thus in the hypothetical case put by the Crown of a dividend being declared and paid (as it would have been paid in accordance with the company's articles) to the deceased as registered holder, he would have been accountable for that dividend to the transferees, on the ground that by virtue of the transfers as between himself and the transferees the owners of the shares were the transferees, to the exclusion of himself.

In my view, in order to arrive at a right conclusion in this case, it is necessary to keep clear and distinct the position as between transferor and transferee and the position as between transferee and the company. It is, no doubt, true that the rights conferred by shares are all rights against the company, and it is no doubt true that, in the case of a company with ordinary regulations, no person can exercise his rights as a shareholder *vis-à-vis* the company or be recognised by the company as a member unless and until he is placed on the register of members. But in my view it is a fallacy to adduce from that the conclusion that there can be no complete gift of shares as between transferor and transferee unless and until the transferee is placed on the register. In my view, a transfer under seal in the form appropriate under the company's regulations, coupled with delivery of the transfer and certificate to the transferee, does suffice, as between transferor and transferee, to constitute the transferee the beneficial owner of the shares, and the circumstance that the transferee must do a further act in the form of applying for and obtaining registration in order to get in and perfect his legal title, having been equipped by the transferor with all that is necessary to enable him to do so, does not prevent the transfer from operating, in accordance with its terms as between the transferor and transferee, and making the transferee the beneficial owner. After all, where duty is concerned, the only relevant type of ownership is beneficial ownership, and the situation of the legal estate does not affect the question.

For these reasons, as well as those given by My Lord, I am of opinion that the learned judge came to a right conclusion in this case, and that the shares comprised in these transfers did not attract duty on the death of the deceased.

Note

On the effectiveness of an allotment of new shares, see *Letts* v. *I.R.C.* [1957] 1 W.L.R. 201.

(C) Exclusion of Donor

A gift will be dutiable whenever made unless bona fide possession and enjoyment of the gifted property was assumed by the donee immediately upon the gift and thenceforth retained, to the entire exclusion of the donor, or of any benefit to him by contract or otherwise. A distinction must be drawn between cases where the donor continues to " enjoy " the property given,[13] or when he receives a collateral benefit [14] and those where the donor retains no interest and receives no benefit from the property which was the subject matter of the gift although that property was " carved out " of some larger property, the remainder of which is retained by the donor.[15]

ATTORNEY-GENERAL v. EARL GREY

Queen's Bench Division [1898] 1 Q.B. 318; affirmed in the House of Lords [1900] A.C. 124; 69 L.J.Q.B. 308; 82 L.T. 62; 48 W.R. 383; 16 T.L.R. 202

In 1885 the deceased settlor gave estates to his nephew subject to the reservation of an annual rentcharge in his own favour, the value of which was considerably less than the income from the estates. The deceased also reserved a power of revocation.

CHANNELL J.: I am of the same opinion. On the question whether this was property passing under a settlement " whereby an interest in such property for life " was reserved to the settlor within the meaning of section 38, subsection 2 (c), of the Act of 1881, it was argued for the defendant that, as the interest reserved was limited to £4,000 a year, the property was only taxable to that extent. But it is to be observed that the words are " an interest in such property." Any interest however small will do, provided it issues out of such property—that is, out of the property sought to be taxed. I agree that if several parcels of land be given by one and the same deed of gift, and an interest be reserved to the donor out of one of those parcels only, estate duty would not be payable upon the whole subject-matter of the gift, but only out of that specific portion in which the interest is expressed to be reserved. But that is not the case here. The rent-charge of £4,000 is expressed to be issuing out of the whole of the hereditaments passing under the deed. Further, I think that there was a power of revocation reserved as to the entirety of the property. Although the power of revocation was conditional upon certain events happening, it was not the less a right in the settlor to restore to himself the absolute interest in the property within the meaning of the Act. On both these grounds I think that the property was chargeable to estate duty to the full principal value.

EARL OF HALSBURY L.C. [in the House of Lords] : My Lords, there are some cases so extremely plain that it is difficult to give any better exposition of the question than that which the statute itself provides. In the present case I did

---

13 But see *Att.-Gen.* v. *Seccombe* [1911] 2 K.B. 688; *post*, p. 490; and *Re Taylor* (1958) 13 D.L.R. (2d) 470; *post*, p. 492.
14 As in *Att.-Gen.* v. *Johnson* [1903] 1 K.B. 617; *ante*, p. 471; and *Att.-Gen.* v. *Worrall* [1895] 1 Q.B. 99. See also F.A. 1959, s. 35.
15 Questions concerning the entire exclusion of the deceased also fall to be considered in relation to the charge in respect of settled property under F.A. 1894, s. 2 (1) (b), as amended by F.A. 1969, and in relation to F.A. 1940, s. 46, see *St. Aubyn* v. *Att.-Gen.* [1952] A.C. 15; *post*, p. 479.

not at first quite understand the argument presented to your Lordships, and I am not absolutely certain that I have got much further now; but at all events, forming my own judgment upon the statute, nothing appears to me much more plain than this, that what the Act of Parliament intended to prevent was that what has been described as a gift inter vivos should nevertheless reserve to the settlor some benefit, or some part of that which purported to be given inter vivos. In this case can anybody doubt that something has been reserved to the settlor? The settlement itself has reserved £4,000 a year, and has reserved a right also on the part of the settlor that all his debts up to the period of his death should be paid, and the payment secured by the estate. It seems to me that it is burning daylight to say that is not within the express language of the statute, and I am really wholly unable to understand why these words are not as plain in the statute itself as any explanatory exposition could make them. That, my Lords, is really all I have to say upon the subject. It seems to me it is a particularly plain case, and I move your Lordships that this appeal be dismissed with costs.

COMMISSIONER FOR STAMP DUTIES OF NEW SOUTH WALES v. PERPETUAL TRUSTEE CO. LTD.

Privy Council [1943] A.C. 425; [1943] 1 All E.R. 525; 112 L.J.P.C. 55; 168 L.T. 414

The deceased settlor had transferred shares of which he was the owner to Trustees (of whom he was one) in trust for his son.

LORD RUSSELL OF KILLOWEN: . . . For the reasons hereinafter appearing their Lordships are in agreement with the decision of the High Court in this case. In their opinion the property comprised in the gift was the equitable interest in the eight hundred and fifty shares, which was given by the settlor to his son. The disposition of that interest was effected by the creation of a trust, *i.e.* by transferring the legal ownership of the shares to trustees, and declaring such trusts in favour of the son as were co-extensive with the gift which the settlor desired to give. The donee was the recipient of the gift; whether the son alone was the donee (as their Lordships think) or whether the son and the body of trustees together constituted the donee, seems immaterial. The trustees alone were not the donee. They were in no sense the object of the settlor's bounty. Did the donee assume bona fide possession and enjoyment immediately upon the gift? The linking of possession with enjoyment as a composite object which has to be assumed by the donee indicates that the possession and enjoyment contemplated is beneficial possession and enjoyment by the object of the donor's bounty. This question therefore must be answered in the affirmative, because the son was (through the medium of the trustees) immediately put in such bona fide beneficial possession and enjoyment of the property comprised in the gift as the nature of the gift and the circumstances permitted. Did he assume it and thenceforth retain it to the entire exclusion of the donor? The answer, their Lordships think, must be in the affirmative, and for two reasons: namely, (1) the settlor had no enjoyment and possession such as is contemplated by the section; and (2) such possession and enjoyment as he had from the fact that the legal ownership of the shares vested in him and his co-trustees as joint tenants, was had by him solely on behalf of the donee. In his capacity as donor he was entirely excluded from possession and enjoyment of what he had given to his son. Did the donee retain possession and enjoyment to the entire exclusion of any benefit to the settlor of whatsoever kind or in any way whatsoever? Clearly, yes. In the interval between the gift and his death, the settlor received no benefit of any kind or in any way from the shares, nor did he receive any benefit whatsoever which was in any way attributable to the gift. . . .

Note
There may, however, be other disadvantages where a donor (especially of shares) retains property as trustee: see *Barclays Bank Ltd.* v. *I.R.C.* [1961] A.C. 509; *post*, p. 517.
This case is considered further in *Oakes* v. *Commissioner of Stamp Duties of New South Wales* [1954] A.C. 425; *post*, p. 480.

ST. AUBYN v. ATTORNEY-GENERAL (No. 2)

House of Lords [1952] A.C. 15; [1951] 2 All E.R. 473; 30 A.T.C. 193

LORD SIMONDS: . . . I apply the provisions of this section to the facts that I have stated. On March 27, 1927, Lord St. Levan had an interest in possession limited to cease on his death in the settled property which on that date had assumed the form of (1) 50,000 ordinary shares of the company and (2) the sum of £750,000 payable in the instalments that I have mentioned and (3) the sum of £100,000 paid or immediately payable by the company. But he had also jointly with Mr. Ponsonby an overriding general power of appointment which could be exercised so as to vest all or any part of the settled property in him absolutely. They so exercised it as to vest in him the properties I have numbered (2) and (3), and, when they had done so, he surrendered his life interest in the ordinary shares. It is agreed that bona fide possession and enjoyment of the shares was assumed immediately thereafter by the persons becoming entitled upon the determination of Lord St. Levan's interest. But was it—and this is the only question—" thenceforth retained to the entire exclusion of [Lord St. Levan] and of any benefit to him by contract or otherwise? "

My Lords, I cannot think that any doubt could be entertained upon this matter but for the use which the Crown seeks to make of certain decisions, particularly *Attorney-General* v. *Worrall* [16] and *Grey* v. *Attorney-General*,[17] to which I will refer later. If A, being the owner in fee of an estate in Yorkshire and an estate in Wiltshire, gives outright to B his estate in Yorkshire, it is an irrelevant circumstance that he retains his estate in Wiltshire: equally it is irrelevant, if, being the tenant for life of the two estates, he surrenders his interest in one and retains it in the other: and equally so, if, his interest being not in two geographically separate estates but in land and capital moneys subject to the same settlement, he surrenders his interest in the one form of property and retains it in the other. But let it be supposed that he is neither the owner in fee, nor the tenant for life and nothing more, but that he is tenant for life with an overriding general power of appointment, by virtue of which he can dispose of all or any part of the settled property at his absolute discretion. I cannot doubt that, if he chooses so to exercise the power as to make some part of the settled property his own, it is wholly irrelevant that by a contemporaneous or later transaction he surrenders his life interest in other parts of it. It is true that he has disposed of his life interest in one part of the property and is true that he has enlarged his life interest in the other part of it into an absolute interest, but these two truths do not add up to the proposition that the property in which he has surrendered his interest is not retained by the trustees to the entire exclusion of him and of any benefit to him by contract or otherwise.

. . . It appears to me, my Lords, that this is nothing but the logical application to a more complex situation of the proposition which I venture to think was self evident, *viz.* that the life tenant of two separate pieces of property can surrender his life interest in one and retain it in the other without duty becoming exigible in respect of the former. The question is what he

[16] [1895] 1 Q.B. 99.
[17] [1900] A.C. 124; *ante*, p. 477.

has given: it may be a life interest in part of the settled property; it may be a part of the income of settled funds and that part may be a fixed sum which is payable in priority or the residue after the prior payment of a fixed sum thereout. I venture to think that much of the argument that was addressed to the House in this case and much of the confusion that has arisen in the past on this admittedly difficult branch of the law have been due to the failure to bear in mind that that of which enjoyment is to be assumed and retained and from which there is to be exclusion of the donor and any benefit to him by contract or otherwise is that which is truly given, a proposition which is obvious enough in the case of two separate estates but more difficult to follow and apply where trusts are declared of a single property which are not completely exhaustive in favour of a donee. It should at least be clear from the judgment of Lord Russell of Killowen that by retaining something which he has never given a donor does not bring himself within the mischief of the section. I venture to repeat in other words what I have already said when dealing with section 43 alone, for its underlying principle is not altered by an alliance with section 56. In the simplest analysis, if A gives to B all his estates in Wiltshire except Blackacre, he does not except Blackacre out of what he has given: he just does not give Blackacre. And if it can be regarded as a " benefit " to him that he does not give but keeps Blackacre, it is a benefit which is in no relevant sense (to use the language of Lord Tomlin) " referable " or (to use that of Lord Russell of Killowen) " attributable " to the gift that he made of the rest of the Wiltshire estate. Applying this principle to the artificial situation created by the statutory hypothesis, I see no reason for saying that that which Lord St. Levan gave was not retained by the donee to the entire exclusion of him and of any benefit to him by contract or otherwise. To avoid misunderstanding I must add that different considerations arise where the donor obtains some benefit which is " referable " to the gift or " attributable " to it. Thus, if in the present case there had been a bargain by which in consideration of the surrender of his life interest in part of the settled property Lord St. Levan had been enabled to enlarge his life interest in another part of it, it might be that following *Worrall's* case I should be bound to hold that he had not been excluded from the surrendered part. But as I have already pointed out, here was no bargain of any kind. What Lord St. Levan chose to give he gave, and what to keep he kept. He made no bargain and he was entirely excluded from, and obtained no benefit referable to, that which he gave. . . .

Note
  This case was concerned with the charge in connection with the extinguishment of a life interest under F.A. 1940, s. 43 (and of s. 56 of that Act, relating to " associated operations " concerning certain companies); the charge is substantially replaced by the new F.A. 1894, s. 2 (1) (*b*) (i) (ii). Although dismissing the claim to duty in respect of the extinguished life interest, the court held that there was a charge to duty under F.A. 1940, s. 46, in so far as the deceased had transferred property to a company from which he had subsequently received benefits: see *post*, pp. 489, 499.

OAKES v. COMMISSIONER OF STAMP DUTIES OF NEW SOUTH WALES

Privy Council [1954] A.C. 57; [1953] 3 W.L.R. 1127; 97 S.J. 874; [1953] 2 All E.R. 1563; [1953] T.R. 453

The deceased, the owner of certain grazing property, executed a deed poll by which he declared that he held the property on trust for himself and and for his four children as tenants-in-common in equal shares. The deed gave him wide powers of management and entitled him to remuneration for work done in managing the property, on which he continued to reside. He managed the property until his death, receiving remuneration and dividing the profits into five shares. The children's shares he applied for their maintenance and education during their respective minorities. Duty was claimed on his death under section 102 (2) (d) of the New South Wales Stamp Duties Act 1920–1940.

LORD REID: The appellant admits that the value of one-fifth share of the whole trust property was properly included in the final balance of the deceased's estate, but contends that the value of four-fifths of that property, being the value of the shares of the four children, ought to be excluded from the final balance as being property comprised in a gift made by the deceased of which bona fide possession and enjoyment was immediately assumed by the children and thenceforth retained by them to the entire exclusion of the deceased or of any benefit to him. The respondent contends that there was not entire exclusion from the children's shares of the deceased or of benefit to him, and the respondent founds on several advantages to the deceased as being benefits within the meaning of the above section. He founds on the application of the children's income from the trust for the maintenance and education of the children as being of advantage to the deceased in that he was thereby relieved, at least in part, from the obligation to maintain his children. Then he founds on the deceased having had power to take, and having taken, remuneration as trustee in accordance with the provisions of the trust deed. He also founds on the provisions of clauses 4 (h) and (k) as conferring benefits on the deceased.[18] And finally he founds on the deceased having resided with his family on the trust property as a further benefit. The case stated makes no reference to this residence, but it appears that this matter was raised in argument in the Supreme Court and it was admitted before their Lordships that the deceased had resided on the property in his capacity as trustee and manager. It appears to their Lordships that it may well be that the property could not have been properly managed unless the manager resided there and that there is nothing to show whether this residence was in itself an advantage to the deceased; moreover, it is not clear whether this residence went beyond the rights of the deceased as co-owner of the property. Their Lordships are therefore not prepared to regard this residence as being in itself a benefit to the deceased in any relevant sense.

In all but one respect section 102 (2) (d) corresponds with section 11 (1) of the United Kingdom Customs and Inland Revenue Act 1889, and section 43 (2) (a) of the United Kingdom Finance Act 1940.[19] The only substantial difference between them is that section 102 brings in " any benefit to him of whatsoever kind or in any way whatsoever whether enforceable at law or in equity or not "; whereas section 11 and section 43 only bring in " any benefit to him by contract or otherwise." But that difference was not founded on in argument and is not material in this case. These sections have given rise to much litigation and British authorities have frequently been cited in Australian cases and vice versa. In St. Aubyn v. Attorney-General [20] the earlier cases, including the Australian cases, were fully considered. In their Lordships' judgment it is now clear that it is not sufficient to bring a case within the scope of these sections to take the situation as a whole and find that the settlor has continued to enjoy substantial advantages which have some relation to the settled property; it is necessary to consider the nature

---

[18] See the last paragraph of the judgment.
[19] See now F.A. 1894, s. 2 (1) (b) (ii), as amended by F.A. 1969.
[20] [1952] A.C. 15; ante, p. 479.

and source of each of these advantages and determine whether or not it is a benefit of such a kind as to come within the scope of the section.

Their Lordships will first consider whether the use of the income which accrued to the settlor's children from the settled estate was such as to bring the case within the section. If property comprised in a gift is to be excluded from the estate of the deceased donor the statute requires that bona fide possession and enjoyment of the property shall have been assumed and retained by the donee to the entire exclusion of the donor. If property is held in trust for the donee, then the trustee's possession is the donee's possession for this purpose, and it matters not that the trustee is the donor himself. The donor is entirely excluded if he only holds the property in a fiduciary capacity and deals with it in accordance with his fiduciary duty. But the statute requires not only exclusion of the donor but also exclusion of any benefit to him, and it was on that matter that the argument turned. It appears from the case that after the children came to age they received payment of their shares of the income; it is not said that that involved any benefit to the deceased. But before they came of age their shares of income were used to pay for their maintenance and education, and it was said that this afforded some relief to the deceased, who would otherwise have had to pay out of his own money. Two arguments were submitted. In the first place it was said that spending the children's money in this way was improper or at least disadvantageous to them, and that this combination of advantage to the donor with disadvantage to the donee brought the case within the statute. Their Lordships do not find any sufficient basis in fact for this argument. There is nothing in the case from which it can be inferred that the deceased acted at all improperly in this matter. At least after 1925 this money could properly be spent on the children's maintenance under statutory powers if that was in the best interests of the children. In the absence of anything to indicate the contrary it must be taken that the deceased acted properly in so applying his children's income, that this was in the best interest of the children, and therefore the children must be held to have had full benefit and enjoyment of their money. The case might have been very different if it had appeared that the deceased had so spent his children's shares of the income from the trust not entirely in their interests but wholly or partly for his own benefit in order to relieve himself from the expense of maintaining his children.

. . . Then it was said that even if the income which accrued to the children was properly spent for their maintenance and they are to be held to have had full benefit and enjoyment of it, yet there was also a benefit to the deceased because if it had not been available he would have had to spend more of his own money. The findings in the case are not very specific, but their Lordships will assume that there was some advantage to the deceased; but that advantage was not at the expense of the children and did not impair or diminish the value of the gift to them or their enjoyment of it. It is possible for a donee, in the full and unrestrained enjoyment of his gift to use or spend it in a way that happens to produce some advantage to the donor without there being any loss or disadvantage to the donee. But, in their Lordships' judgment, any such advantage is not a benefit within the meaning of the section. The point is not strictly covered by authority, but the contrary view would be difficult to reconcile with what was said in the House of Lords in *St. Aubyn's* case.[21]

---

[21] *Cf.* the views of Viscount Simonds in *Chick* v. *Commissioner of Stamp Duties* [1958] A.C. 435; *post*, p. 486; and of Spence J. in *Re Taylor, Re Hume* (1958) 13 D.L.R. (2d) 470; *post*, p. 492.

. . . On the view of the facts of the case which their Lordships have felt bound to adopt, this alleged benefit neither encumbered the enjoyment of the gift nor arose by way of reservation out of that which was given, and their Lordships can find no good reason for holding that it brings this case within the statute.

For similar reasons their Lordships are not able to accept the ground of judgment of the Supreme Court of New South Wales to the effect that the linking together of the one-fifth beneficial interests of the donor and the donees resulted in a benefit or advantage to each share, and that this advantage to the donor brought the case within the section. Even if this linkage was of advantage to the deceased (of which there is no evidence) that advantage did not in any way impair the enjoyment of the gift by the donees or trench upon their rights.

The next advantage to the deceased was of quite a different character. The deceased, under the power which he reserved to himself under clause (4) (j) of the deed of trust, took considerable sums as remuneration for his services in managing the trust property. Their Lordships will assume that those sums were reasonable and no more than would have been appropriate remuneration for any other manager. But receiving those sums was clearly an advantage or benefit to the deceased, and the question is whether it was a benefit of such a kind as to come within the section. If a donor reserves to himself a beneficial interest in property and only gives to the donees such beneficial interests as remain after his own reserved interest has been satisfied, it is now well established that such reservation of a beneficial interest does not involve any benefit to the donor within the meaning of the section.[22]

. . . It follows that if the right to take remuneration could be regarded as a beneficial interest in the property reserved by the deceased when making the deed of trust, then his remuneration would not be a benefit within the scope of the section. But their Lordships cannot regard a right to take remuneration for managing property as a beneficial interest in the property. A trustee is not permitted to take remuneration for services performed by him unless he is authorised to do so: in this case the trustee was authorised to do so because the deceased provided in the deed of trust that he as trustee or the trustee for the time being should be entitled to remuneration as if he were not a trustee. If the deceased had resigned office and another trustee had taken his place it could hardly have been contended that this provision gave to the new trustee a beneficial interest in the trust property, and in their Lordships' judgment the deceased did not reserve to himself a beneficial interest in the property by inserting this provision in the deed of trust. Indeed, the terms of the deed of trust make it clear that the whole beneficial interest in the property passed to the deceased and his children in equal shares, so that the subject-matter of the gift to each child was one-fifth of the whole beneficial interest in the property. Clause 2 declared that the capital and interest of the trust fund should be held upon trust for the deceased and his first named children as tenants in common in equal shares, and neither the right of the trustee to take remuneration, nor any other right, power or discretion conferred on the trustee affected the position of the deceased or his children as tenants in common of the whole beneficial interest in the trust property. Any remuneration taken by the deceased or any other trustee must come out of the trust property and must therefore diminish the amount available for division among the tenants in common for their enjoyment.

---

[22] See *Commissioner for Stamp Duties of New South Wales* v. *Perpetual Trustee Co. Ltd.* [1943] A.C. 425; *ante*, p. 478; *St. Aubyn* v. *Att.-Gen.* [1952] A.C. 15; *ante*, p. 479; both relied upon by Lord Reid.

But the appellant argued that the children had had all the possession and enjoyment to which they were entitled under the deed of trust: they could only possess through the trustee and subject to his rights and powers, and therefore the exercise of his rights by the trustee could not trench on or impair that possession. The appellant founded on another passage in the judgment of Lord Russell in the *Perpetual Trustee Co.* case,[23] when he referred to the donee being " put in such bona fide beneficial possession and enjoyment of the property comprised in the gift as the nature of the gift and the circumstances permitted." It was said that in the present case the nature of the gift to the children and the circumstances never permitted the children to have any greater possession or enjoyment than in fact they had. But to understand what Lord Russell meant by those words it is necessary to quote the preceding passage:

" In their opinion the property comprised in the gift was the equitable interest in the eight hundred and fifty shares, which was given by the settlor to his son. The disposition of that interest was effected by the creation of a trust, *i.e.* by transferring the legal ownership of the shares to trustees, and declaring such trusts in favour of the son as were co-extensive with the gift which the settlor desired to give. The donee was the recipient of the gift; whether the son alone was the donee (as their Lordships think) or whether the son and the body of trustees together constituted the donee, seems immaterial. The trustees alone were not the donee. They were in no sense the object of the settlor's bounty. Did the donee assume bona fide possession and enjoyment immediately upon the gift? The linking of possession with enjoyment as a composite object which has to be assumed by the donee indicates that the possession and enjoyment contemplated is beneficial possession and enjoyment by the object of the donor's bounty. This question, therefore, must be answered in the affirmative, because the son was (through the medium of the trustees) immediately put in such bona fide beneficial possession and enjoyment of the property comprised in the gift as the nature of the gift and the circumstances permitted."

Lord Russell was there explaining in general terms how the section is to be interpreted when the subject-matter of the gift is an equitable interest. He was not dealing with a case like the present, when the donor received money which, if he had not taken it, would have gone to the donee under the terms of the gift. In the *Perpetual Trustee Co.* case the settlor derived no actual benefit from the shares or their dividends. He might have exercised voting powers in respect of the shares, but did not do so; and he was one of several trustees and they might have used trust money for the maintenance of the son, but did not do so. With the exception of some insurance premiums the whole income was accumulated and the trust fund was paid to the son on his majority. Their Lordships do not read the words on which the appellant founds as modifying or intended to modify the later passage in Lord Russell's judgment which has been quoted above and in which he only refers to reservation by the donor of a beneficial interest in the property.

But, even if there is no authority to support it, the appellant's case requires further examination. The argument is clearly and forcibly stated in the dissenting judgment of Kitto J. in the High Court of Australia where he said [24]:

" If the property comprised in the gift had consisted of four one-fifths of the fee simple of the trust property (whether legal and equitable or

[23] [1943] A.C. 425; *ante*, p. 478.
[24] (1952) 85 C.L.R. 421.

only equitable), and the donees, pursuant to a collateral agreement or otherwise, had allowed the deceased to have the benefits which in fact he enjoyed, the case would have fallen clearly enough within section 102 (2) (*d*). But it seems to me that, in order to hold that four-fifths of the fee simple was the property comprised in the gift, one would have to construe the deed, not as a whole, but as if it were divided into two sections, effecting two quite distinct transactions; the first transaction being a disposition in equity of aliquot parts of the fee simple, and the second transaction consisting of a set of provisions operating to exact from the disponees a power for the disponor to derogate from the possession and enjoyment which an undivided share of an equitable fee simple enables the owner of it to have and to keep to himself. I cannot construe the deed in that way. It was a deed poll, and the benefits which the deceased derived in accordance with its provisions were benefits which the donees neither permitted him to derive nor had any power to deny him. They were in this position of impotence, not by their own choice, but because the deceased, in exercise of his right to give exactly what interests he liked and withhold exactly what he liked, had chosen to give them interests so hedged about as not to enable them to exclude him from those benefits. It was for him, when framing his deed, to delimit the interests he was parting with; and he did delimit them, not by any one part of the deed considered by itself, but by the entirety of its provisions. The donees had no voice in deciding to what extent their interests should be subject to rights, powers or privileges retained by the deceased. They got interests which were limited *ab initio*, by the terms of their creation; and the limits were such that the interests were inherently insusceptible of being so possessed and enjoyed as to preclude the deceased from deriving those benefits which in fact he derived."

It is true that the deceased did not exact from his children his power to take benefits and that the benefits which he took were benefits which they neither permitted him to derive nor had any power to deny him. But in their Lordships' judgment the question is not whether the donees permitted the donor to take benefits. It is whether the donor took benefit out of that which was given. If a benefit arises by way of reservation out of interests which were given then no doubt the donees' interests are inherently insusceptible of being so possessed and enjoyed as to preclude the donor from taking that benefit, but the section applies because there is not entire exclusion of the donor or of benefit to him from the interests comprised in the gift. The contrast is between reserving a beneficial interest and only giving such interests as remain on the one hand, and on the other hand reserving power to take benefit out of, or at the expense of, interests which are given, and for reasons already stated their Lordships are of opinion that the present case is within the latter class.

Two other powers reserved by the deceased were also founded on as benefits—power to appropriate and partition the trust property under clause 4 (*h*), and power to purchase it under clause 4 (*k*). It may be that the deceased could legitimately have used those powers to his own advantage, but in fact he made no use of them at all. So, at most, there were here potential benefits. As their Lordships have already decided that taking remuneration was a benefit within the scope of the section, they find it unnecessary to deal with these other matters. . . .

MUNRO v. COMMISSIONER OF STAMP DUTIES

Privy Council [1934] A.C. 61; 103 L.J.P.C. 18; 150 L.T. 145; [1933] All E.R.Rep. 185

In 1909 the deceased agreed with his children that his business as a grazier should be carried on by them as partners under a partnership at will, whereby he was to be sole manager and each partner was to receive a specified share. Ten years later he transferred a part of the grazing land to each child by way of gift, the property being taken subject to the partnership agreement.

LORD TOMLIN: . . . It is unnecessary to determine the precise nature of the right of the partnership at the time of the transfers. It was either a tenancy during the term of the partnership or a licence coupled with an interest. In either view what was comprised in the gift was, in the case of each of the gifts to the children and the trustees, the property shorn of the right which belonged to the partnership, and upon this footing it is in their Lordships' opinion plain that the donee in each case assumed bona fide possession and enjoyment of the gift immediately upon the gift and thenceforward retained it to the exclusion of the donor. Further, the benefit which the donor had as a member of the partnership in the right to which the gift was subject was not in their Lordships' opinion a benefit referable in any way to the gift. It was referable to the agreement of 1909 and nothing else, and was not therefore such a benefit as is contemplated by section 102, subsection 2 (d).[25]

. . . In their Lordships' opinion it is the substance of the transactions which must be ascertained and if when so ascertained the substance does not fall within the words of the statute it cannot be brought within them merely because the forms employed did not give true effect to the substance. It is not always sufficiently appreciated that it is for the taxing authority to bring each case within the taxing Act, and that the subject ought not to be taxed upon refinements or otherwise than by clear words. . . .

CHICK v. COMMISSIONER OF STAMP DUTIES

Privy Council [1958] A.C. 435; [1958] 3 W.L.R. 93; 102 S.J. 488; [1958] 2 All E.R. 623

In 1934 the deceased gave certain grazing lands to his son, without any reservation or condition. Some time later they entered into a partnership agreement whereby the lands belonging to each were to be used by the partnership.

VISCOUNT SIMONDS: It is not in dispute that the donee assumed bona fide possession and enjoyment of the property immediately upon the gift to the entire exclusion of the deceased or of any such benefit to him as is mentioned in the subsection. The question is whether he also thenceforth retained it and this depends on the impact of the subsection on the facts. Their Lordships have no doubt that the Supreme Court were right in upholding the contention of the respondent.

The respondent took his stand upon the plain words of the section. How, he asked, could it be said that the deceased was entirely excluded from the property, the subject of the gift, or from the possession and enjoyment thereof, when for some seventeen years before his death he had been a member of a partnership, whose right it was to agist their stock upon it, and himself,

25 Of the Stamp Duties Act (N.S.W.) 1920–1931.

moreover, was the manager of the partnership business with the power to make final and conclusive decisions upon all matters relating to it.

. . . It is, however, right to refer to some of the contentions which were advanced on behalf of the appellants. In the first place, it is not disputed that the property was given outright by the deceased to his son. As was said by Dixon C.J. in *Commissioner of Stamp Duties* v. *Owens* [26]: " If ever there was a gift of an estate in fee simple, carrying the fullest right known to the law of exclusive possession and enjoyment, surely this was such a gift." It follows that the decision of this Board in *Munro* v. *Commissioner of Stamp Duties*,[27] on which the appellants relied, has no application to the present case. It must often be a matter of fine distinction what is the subject-matter of a gift. If, as in *Munro's* case, the gift is of a property shorn of certain of the rights which appertain to complete ownership, the donor cannot, merely because he remains in possession and enjoyment of those rights, be said within the meaning of the section not to be excluded from possession and enjoyment of that which he has given. This view of the section, which was reaffirmed in *St. Aubyn* v. *Attorney-General* [28] upon a consideration of a similar section in a British statute, need not be further elaborated. But the question may arise and, having arisen, may lead to a difference of opinion as to what is the subject-matter of the gift. It was, as it appears to their Lordships, for this reason that in *Owens'* case Williams and Taylor JJ. dissented from the majority of the court. In the present case there is no room for any such difference.

Then it was contended that the subsection had no operation because the partnership agreement was an independent commercial transaction for full consideration later than and in no way related to the gift,[29] and was a mode of enjoyment by the donee of his property and an exercise by him of the possession of it. (These are the words of the appellants' second formal reason.) In this reason there are several elements. The partnership agreement was " later " than the gift. This point was not pressed by counsel for the appellants. If possession and enjoyment are " thenceforth " to be retained by the donee, it is clearly irrelevant that there is an interval between the dates when the donor is excluded and ceases to be excluded. Nor is there wanting ample authority which shows that this is an irrelevant consideration. A recent example is *Commissioner of Stamp Duties of New South Wales* v. *Permanent Trustee Co. of New South Wales (Davies'* case).[30] Next, it was an " independent commercial transaction for full consideration." It is to be assumed that it was an " independent " transaction: there was no evidence to the contrary. But the subsection says nothing about independent transactions. The sole question is one of fact—was the donor excluded? If he was not excluded, it is not relevant to ask why he was not excluded. Equally with regard to the transaction being " commercial " and " for full consideration." Their Lordships see no reason why a gloss should be put upon the plain words of the subsection by excluding from its operation such transactions.

. . . Then it is said that the transaction was " in no way related to the gift and was a mode of enjoyment by the donee of his property." . . . the words " was a mode of enjoyment by the donee of his property " may be linked with the appellants' contention that the subsection was not applicable because (again to cite the formal reason) " neither the partnership agreement nor the use of the property pursuant thereto impaired or detracted from bona fide

[26] (1953) 88 C.L.R. 67, 88.
[27] [1934] A.C. 61; *ante*, p. 486.
[28] [1952] A.C. 15; *ante*, p. 479.
[29] But see now F.A. 1959, s. 35 (2).
[30] [1956] A.C. 512, *post*, p. 488.

possession and enjoyment by the donee of the property given." This contention, in their Lordships' opinion, involves a misconception, for which the subsection provides no justification. It may be that the donee can make no better use of the property given to him than, for instance, by leasing it back to the donor. The question still is whether as a fact the donor has been excluded. This appears to be the contention raised in another form that a commercial transaction is not within the subsection. The answer is that the possession and enjoyment by the donee of the property given to him in the manner most advantageous to himself are by no means incompatible with the donor not being excluded from it. It was, however, natural that the appellants should refer to and rely on the case of *Oakes* v. *Commissioner of Stamp Duties of New South Wales*.[31]

. . . But it was the cited passage on which the appellants relied.[32] Applying it to the facts of this case they said that the partnership agreement and all that was done under it by the deceased may have been beneficial to him, but the benefit or advantage derived by him did not impair or diminish the value of the gift of the property to the donee. On the contrary, it was the method most advantageous to the donee of dealing with the property. It was therefore not a benefit to the donor which brought the subsection into operation. Their Lordships cannot accept this view. It is in flat contradiction to the law cogently stated by Isaacs J. in *Lang* v. *Webb*[33] at an earlier stage in this opinion which has been consistently followed. Where the question is whether the donor has been entirely excluded from the subject-matter of the gift, that is the single fact to be determined. If he has not been so excluded, the eye need look no further to see whether his non-exclusion has been advantageous or otherwise to the donee. It must be observed that in *Oakes'* case the Board appears to have been dealing with the second limb of the subsection, the question being whether the donor was entirely excluded from any benefit to him of whatsoever kind or in any way whatsoever. It is possible that in the consideration of this very difficult part of the subsection it may be pertinent in some cases to inquire whether the benefit derived by the donor is one that impairs or detracts from the donee's enjoyment of the gift. Their Lordships, with great respect, think that this is a matter which may require further examination, but, as they have already said, they are clearly of opinion that it is not a relevant consideration where the question arises under the first limb of the subsection and is whether the donor has been entirely excluded from the subject-matter of the gift, and they repeat that in the present case that question can only be answered in the negative. . . .

Note

The effect of this decision has largely been reversed by F.A. 1959, s. 35 (2), which was enacted as a result, and provides that subsequent possession or enjoyment of the gifted property by the donor is to be disregarded if for full considerattion in money or money's worth.

COMMISSIONER OF STAMP DUTIES OF NEW SOUTH WALES v. PERMANENT TRUSTEE COMPANY OF NEW SOUTH WALES

Privy Council [1956] A.C. 512; [1956] 3 W.L.R. 152; 100 S.J. 431; [1956] 2 All E.R. 512; [1956] T.R. 209

In 1924 the deceased transferred to the respondent company certain shares and other property upon trust for his daughter. Many years later the daughter

31 [1954] A.C. 57; *ante*, p. 480.
32 [1954] A.C. 57 at pp. 73–74, quoted *ante*, p. 482.
33 (1912) 13 C.L.R. 503, 517.

authorised her father to draw on her account with the respondent company; he did so on occasions, using the money withdrawn for his own purposes.

VISCOUNT SIMONDS: . . . it appears to their Lordships that the inference is not only open but inevitable that from 1939 onward the testator was (to use the words of the Chief Justice) " master of the income as it was paid over by the trustee." He was, too, in a position to ensure that it was so paid over. His dual authority from his daughter, which enabled him on the one hand to direct the trustee how her money should be disposed of and on the other to deal with it when it reached the bank, placed him in a position of unchallengeable control, unless and until it was revoked. And it was not revoked. In these circumstances the conclusion is irresistible that the daughter, who at material times was the sole beneficiary under the settlement, did not retain bona fide possession and enjoyment of the trust property to the entire exclusion of her father or of any benefit to him. Here it does not seem that any nice question arises whether it was from the subject-matter of the gift that the donor (the testator) was excluded or, alternatively, from any benefit, nor whether it is necessary that the benefit taken by the donor should impair the possession and enjoyment by the donee of the subject-matter of the gift. For here the design and the result of the arrangement were that the daughter's possession and enjoyment were reduced and impaired precisely by the measure of the testator's use and enjoyment of her income.

It was argued for the respondent that this was not the way in which the whole transaction should be regarded. It was said that when the testator, armed with the authority given by the daughter's letter of December 1, 1938, directed the trustee to pay the trust income to her bank account, he acted in a fiduciary capacity, and that when he drew upon that account for his own purposes, he was not using the trust income but was borrowing from her money which had lost its identity. She chose, it was said, to lend it to him: she might equally well have lent it to a stranger. In the joint judgment of Kitto and Taylor JJ. (in which Webb J. concurred) this is the decisive point. It would, they say, be difficult to resist this conclusion (i.e. a conclusion favourable to the appellant) if the testator, when he took moneys out of his daughter's bank account, had taken them free from any obligation of repayment. In that case, though the same relationship of creditor and debtor had been established between the bank and the daughter, the trust income presumably retained its identity so far at least that for the purpose of the section it could not be said that the donee had retained exclusive possession and enjoyment of the subject-matter of the gift. But this does not appear to their Lordships to be a valid distinction. The transaction must be viewed as a whole and, since an integral part of it was that the testator before the account was opened was authorised to draw on it for his own purposes, it is irrelevant whether, when he did draw on it, he was or was not under any obligation to repay. Gift or loan, he for his own advantage used her money, paying no interest for it, and by so much reduced her enjoyment of what was her trust income and nothing else. The obligation to repay affected the quantum of the benefit obtained by him: it did no more. . . .

Note

For a similar view that a loan amounts to a " benefit," see *St. Aubyn v. Att.-Gen.* [1952] A.C. 15; *ante*, p. 479, *per* Lord Radcliffe (at p. 57): " A man receives for his own benefit moneys paid to him on an advance by way of loan, not the less because the transaction involves an obligation to repay an equivalent amount at a future date with interest in the meantime." A comparison with the Income Tax concept of exclusion of settlor is also instructive, see *ante*, Chap. 15.

ATTORNEY-GENERAL v. SECCOMBE

King's Bench Division [1911] 2 K.B. 688; 80 L.J.K.B. 913; 105 L.T. 18

HAMILTON J.: By the deed of gift of May 26, 1897, John Hocken Seccombe the elder in consideration of natural love and affection gave his farmhouse and farm lands of Tregawne and other tenements and all his other lands, houses, and premises of whatever tenure of which he was seised or to which he was entitled to the defendant, his great-nephew, in fee simple; and it was further declared that all the live and dead stock, furniture, plate, goods, and chattels in and upon the said farms and tenements were the sole property of the defendant, and by way of confirmation John Hocken Seccombe the elder assigned them to the defendant. The deed was executed upon the advice of a solicitor in order to confirm a gift to the like effect which had been made in the preceding year, when the defendant came of age. At the time of the execution of the deed the donor was eighty-two years of age, and was becoming incapacitated for active work. He had for some time past taken little active part in the management of the farm outside at any rate the farmhouse and stock yard, the active management having been in the hands of the defendant. The intention that the whole farm should belong to the defendant when he came of age had been expressed to him more than once by the donor, and the condition of things at the farm continued with little outward change until the donor died in 1906. From the time the defendant came of age the donor ceased to take any part in the management of the farm. He no longer signed cheques on the banking account; he no longer received the annuity of £15, which was charged upon another property belonging to the defendant; and, so far as domestic details are concerned, he no longer sat at the head of the dinner table, but at the side.

The Crown claims estate duty upon the death of the donor in respect of the property comprised in the deed of 1897, by virtue of section 2, subsection 1 (c), of the Finance Act 1894, which incorporates section 38 of the Customs and Inland Revenue Act 1881, as amended by section 11 of the Customs and Inland Revenue Act 1889, as being "property taken under any gift, whenever made, of which property bona fide possession and enjoyment shall not have been assumed by the donee immediately upon the gift, and thenceforward retained to the entire exclusion of the donor or of any benefit to him by contract or otherwise." No point is made upon the words "assumed by the donee immediately upon the gift," and although the defendant merely continued living in much the same way after as before the gift, it seems to me that those words are satisfied, and that if bona fide possession and enjoyment were assumed by him at all, they were assumed by him immediately upon the gift and thenceforth retained.

This is an arrangement by which an aged donor, out of love and affection, purports to give his property to a great-nephew, who stands in a filial relation to him, while at the same time no apparent change is made. It may be that from such circumstances unexplained an inference might be drawn which would entitled the Crown to estate duty. But the inference would be that the transaction was not bona fide, and that possession and enjoyment so assumed were not bona fide assumed—in other words, that the arrangement was a sham. No such case, however, is made here. The Crown does not suggest that the transaction was not bona fide, and that the deed of gift was a sham and not a real deed. I am satisfied upon the facts that there was entire good faith throughout, and that the transaction was carried through without any idea of escaping revenue duties.

. . . The intention of the Legislature was to exclude from liability to estate duty a certain category of gifts, and there is a danger of entirely nullifying this provision if the section is construed so that any enjoyment, however slight, by the donor subsequently to the gift will bring the property within the charging words and attach the duty to the whole corpus of the property which passes. I think that grammatically the words must be construed thus: " Property taken under any gift, whenever made, of which property bona fide possession and enjoyment shall not have been assumed by the donee immediately upon the gift, and of which property bona fide possession and enjoyment shall not have been thenceforward retained by the donee to the entire exclusion of the donor from such possession and enjoyment, or of any benefit to him by contract or otherwise." The word " exclusion " refers, in my opinion, to the bona fide possession and enjoyment of the property just as the word " assumed " does. It is clear that the clause is not limited to a reservation out of the property passing under the gift. That point seems to me to be concluded against the defendant by the decision in *Attorney-General* v. *Worrall*,[34] which was recognised in *Attorney-General* v. *Johnson*.[35]

It is said on behalf of the Crown that, though the donor may not have reserved to himself any right to possession or enjoyment of the property or any part thereof, there is not an " entire exclusion " of him within the meaning of the clause if he has in fact access to the place, that is, if he has in fact a considerable degree of presence in the place which is the subject-matter of the gift, and enjoys an advantage, whether sentimental or otherwise, by being there.

. . . In the present case I am satisfied that there was no contract that in consideration of the gift the donor should be permitted to reside and be maintained by the donee, in part or in whole, in the house; nor was there any understanding to that effect in the sense of an arrangement, or as it is called an honourable understanding, which is not legally enforceable. I have no doubt that neither the donor nor the donee contemplated for one moment that the former would under any circumstances be turned out of the house; but there was no discussion upon the point, and the donor before he executed the deed was fully aware of the fact that after executing the deed he would be at the defendant's mercy, and was fully content to rely upon the filial affection which the defendant bore towards his great-uncle and benefactor. Upon this affection, and not upon any contract or honourable understanding, the donor was content to rely for the advantage which he in fact enjoyed of being allowed to reside in his old house until his death. The transaction was free from any element of harshness or overreaching. The solicitor, who drew the deed and who was an old friend and adviser of the family, told the donor that if he signed the deed the defendant could turn him out of doors; to which the donor replied that he had no fear of that, as the defendant loved him too well. I am satisfied therefore that the donor was entirely excluded from any possession and enjoyment of the property except such as is involved in his being allowed to sit in his old chair and sleep in his old bed, and to walk round the garden.

The only remaining question is as to the meaning of the latter words of the section, " or of any benefit to him by contract or otherwise." The word " benefit " is not, in my opinion, confined to a benefit conferred by the deed of gift or to a benefit issuing out of the property thereby conveyed. A benefit issuing out of some other property or a benefit given by some separate and independent contract will come within the section. But the burden

34 [1895] 1 Q.B. 99.
35 [1903] 1 K.B. 617; *ante*, p. 471.

of proof is upon the Crown. It is for the Crown to bring the subject within the charge, and therefore it was rightly assumed in paragraph 4 of the information that it lay upon the Crown to establish that there was not an entire exclusion of the donor or of any benefit to him by contract or otherwise. The section does not impose an obligation to pay the duty, leaving the defendant to bring himself within the exception. The Crown must show, in order to make out its right to the tax, that the property was taken under a gift, and that bona fide possession and enjoyment of it had not been assumed by the donee immediately upon the gift and thenceforward retained to the entire exclusion of the donor or of any benefit to him by contract or otherwise. It is contended on behalf of the Crown that the words " by contract or otherwise " mean by a contract which is enforceable or by any other arrangement whether enforceable or not. It is said that there cannot be anything *ejusdem generis* with a contract, and therefore the words " or otherwise " must be given full effect to and the clause must be read as meaning any benefit, sentimental or pecuniary, which is in fact enjoyed, whether it be conferred by contract or not. . . . There is no reason why the rule of *ejusdem generis* construction should not apply to these words. The enactment might have stopped at the words " or of any benefit to him," or it might have said " of any benefit to him of whatsoever kind." It has not done so. The words " by contract or otherwise " indicate a genus of which contract is one species, and all other species are intended to be swept in. I do not see the difficulty of saying that there is a genus of which contract is a species. There are two points to notice about the word " contract " as used in this connection. In the first place it points to a legal obligation; and in the next place it points to a contract between the same persons as were parties to the gift. Hence I think that the words " by contract or otherwise " are aimed at any contract between the parties to the deed of gift or any contract with third parties having the effect of conferring a benefit on the donor, and also any transaction enforceable at law or in equity which, though not in the form of a contract, may confer a benefit, such as a lien. It is therefore not necessary to give any unusual or exceptional construction to the words. In construing a taxing Act the presumption is that the Legislature has granted precisely that tax to the Crown which it has described, and no more; and there is no presumption in favour of extending the scope of the Act. I must therefore follow the usual rule of construction, and in doing so proper operation can be given to the words. There was in this case no benefit to the donor by contract or by any other enforceable arrangement. That is sufficient to dispose of the case.[36] . . .

Re TAYLOR, Re HUME

Ontario High Court (1958) 13 D.L.R. (2d) 470

The deceased had transferred the matrimonial home to his wife, continuing to live there after the transfer.

SPENCE J.: . . . I think, similarly here, the residence of the deceased in both these appeals is not shown to be and was not anything other than a husband residing with his wife in her residence. As Judson J. put it in *Re Hommel*,[37] it was not due to any benefit conferred upon him by his wife, but to the marriage relationship—to the fact that the husband and wife are

---

[36] The donor was further held to have paid for his board and lodging out of the annuity of £15 a year which had been retained by the donee.   [37] (1953) 1 D.L.R. (2d) 536.

entitled to each other's society. I am therefore of the opinion that the Judicial Committee in the *Oakes* v. *Com'r of Stamp Duties*[38] case, came to exactly the same decision as Judson J. in the *Hommel* case, for the same reason, *i.e.* that the word "benefit" even if it be a voluntary benefit, does not refer to a benefit arising altogether apart from and not in any way connected with the gift, but from a relationship quite apart from the gift.

. . . I adopt the words of Lord Reid at page 75 and, on the view of the facts of this case, which I adopt, "this alleged benefit neither encumbered the enjoyment of the gift nor arose by way of reservation out of that which was given" and I can find no good reason for holding that it brings these cases within the statute.

. . . I am reinforced in my view by the consideration of the type of tranaction involved. No more natural gift *inter vivos* can be imagined than the gift by a husband to his wife of the residential property in which they then resided and in which they continued to reside until the death of the husband. As Judson J. pointed out in *Re Hommel, supra,* that to hold that this situation gave rise to a disposition which was taxable "would mean that a wife could never get this exemption unless she and her husband parted company when the gift was made." It should also be noted that in each case the wife could have sold the property one day after it was conveyed to her and could in fact have reinvested the proceeds in another home in which she and her husband resided until his death, and no question of liability for taxation would have arisen.

Note
Note esp. the treatment of property transferred into the joint names of husband and wife and the practice of the Estate Duty Office: see B. Pinson, *Revenue Law* (6th ed.), 25-07.

(D) Subject-Matter of the Gift

The need to establish the precise subject-matter of a gift or other transaction can be seen when considering the problems discussed above, *i.e.* the nature of a transaction and whether it constitutes a gift at all,[39] and whether or not a donor has been excluded from the gifted property.[40] Further, the dutiable value of all property, including gifts, deemed to pass on death is to be ascertained as at the date of death.[41] Elaborate provisions are contained in section 38 of the Finance Act 1957 for identifying the property deemed to pass by virtue of section 2 (1) (*c*), in particular where the gifted property no longer exists at the date of death, or has been sold or exchanged for other property.[42] But before these provisions can be applied it is necessary to establish what property was originally given.

LORD STRATHCONA v. LORD ADVOCATE

Court of Session 1929 S.C. 800; 1929 S.L.T. 629

The Lord President (Clyde): . . . As I understand section 2 (1) (*c*), that which is to be deemed to be included in the property passing on the death of the deceased is the identical subject of the former gift, just as it was at the

---

[38] [1954] A.C. 57; *ante*, pp. 480, 483.
[39] *e.g.* in *Att.-Gen.* v. *Johnson* [1903] 1 K.B. 617; *ante*, p. 471.
[40] *e.g. St. Aubyn* v. *Att.-Gen.* [1952] A.C. 15; *ante*, p. 479; and *Munro* v. *Commissioner of Stamp Duties* [1934] A.C. 61; *ante*, p. 486.
[41] F.A. 1894, s. 7 (5); see *post*, Chap. 20.
[42] For description and discussion of these provisions, see G. S. A. Wheatcroft, "Feather-Bedding Death, or Second Thoughts on Section 38" [1958] B.T.R. 375; [1959] B.T.R. 244; J. G. Monroe, "The Subject Matter of a Gift Inter Vivos" [1962] B.T.R. 139.

date of the gift—and nothing other, nor more, nor less. It is therefore that subject—as it was when taken by the donee—which must, in my view, be deemed (contrary of course both to fact and to possibility) to be included in the property which actually passes on the donor's death. And it is that same identical subject—just such as it was when originally taken by the donee— whose value must, under the directions of section 7 (5), " be estimated to be the price which, in the opinion of the Commissioners, such property would fetch if sold in the open market at the time of the death of the deceased."

It might well have been thought both reasonable and natural to fix the value of a gift as at the date when the gift was made; for the only reason for assimilating *inter vivos* gifts to the passing of property on death (weak as it is) is that— if made shortly before death—they may be supposed to have been made in contemplation of death and possibly to be intended to avoid the incidence of death duties. But *dis aliter visum*. And of the many cases which were referred to in argument—as presenting difficulty in applying the directions of section 7 (5)— there was not one (if the view of the statutes which I have ventured to express is sound) of which it could be said that the difficulty was serious. The case was instanced of the gift, three years ago, of a valuable young horse of high racing pedigree and good prospects, which the donee, or some of those deriving title from him, train for the turf. Between the date of the gift and the date of the donor's death the horse was supposed to cover itself with glory, but to die of a broken neck before the latter date. The problem of valuation would, as it appears to me, be the very simple one of estimating the price of just such a valuable young horse as formed the subject of the gift three years ago, if it were bought and sold in the market at the date of the donor's death. The level of price for such a young horse might have risen or fallen between the date of the gift and the date of the donor's death; but, while such variations in price must of course affect the valuation, I see no ground or warrant for following the fortunes of the horse during that period—whether the horse has come through it alive or not—or for allowing either its history or its fate during that period to affect the estimation as at the date of the donor's death of the value of the original subject of gift. The same principle would apply to the gift of a house which was altered, or taken down to admit of the substitution of some other structure, by the donee or some other person through whose hands it passed, during the same period. And again the same principle would apply to the gift of a business which, before the donor's death, had been amalgamated with some other concern; and to the gift of shares in a company whose capital had, prior to the same event, undergone reconstruction, no matter how drastic. No doubt all these valuations would be hypothetical; but in a statute which abounds in hypotheses there is nothing startling in that.

Fortunately, the decision of the present case is not necessarily embarrassed by any difference of opinion which may exist with regard to the topics just discussed. For the subject of the gift consisted of blocks of certain well-known stocks, and it is not in question that those stocks are still in the market, although the original blocks are no longer in the hands of the donees.

Note
These remarks must be read subject to F.A. 1957, s. 38.

SNEDDON v. LORD ADVOCATE

House of Lords [1954] A.C. 257; [1954] 2 W.L.R. 211; 98 S.J. 105; [1954] 1 All E.R. 255; [1954] T.R. 15

A gift of cash was made to Trustees and invested by them in shares.

LORD MORTON OF HENRYTON: . . . No one doubts that the truster made a disposition which comes within the section and that estate duty is payable upon certain property which is deemed to pass upon his death, but the question is: What is the property which is deemed to pass; is it the £5,000 or is it the trust fund constituted by the deed of trust, in its state of invesment at the death of the truster, *i.e.* the Creamola shares. It is common ground that £9,250 was the value of the Creamola shares at the truster's death. Thus no question as to value or as to the proper method of valuation arises in the present case.

What, then, is the property which is deemed to pass? The statute says it is the " property taken " under the disposition made by the truster. My Lords, I feel no doubt that the property taken under that disposition was the sum of £5,000. That was the only property which passed from the truster, and it was the only property taken by the trustees from the truster under his disposition.

. . . It is perhaps surprising that gifts *inter vivos* should be valued as at the death of the donor and not as at the date of the gift. The latter value represents that which was withdrawn from the donor's estate, and the statute is directed to preventing the avoidance of tax by such withdrawals. Further, if the latter value were taken for the purposes of estate duty, the donee would know that he would be charged with tax on that value, and no more, if the donor died within five years, and he could make provision for that event. . . .

Note
Both the above cases preceded F.A. 1957, s. 38; they do illustrate the type of problems which the section attempts to resolve. See also *Re Payne* [1940] Ch. 576; *Iveagh* v. *I.R.C.* [1954] Ch. 364; *Att.-Gen.* v. *Oldham* [1940] 2 K.B. 485.

RALLI BROS. TRUSTEE CO. LTD. v. I.R.C.

Chancery Division [1968] Ch. 215; [1967] 3 W.L.R. 1274; 111 S.J. 833; [1967] 3 All E.R. 811; [1967] T.R. 279

In 1961, the deceased instructed the secretary of the plaintiff company, who managed her business affairs, that she wished to effect assurance policies on her life for the benefit of certain members of her family, by way of gifts to them. She desired the plaintiff company to be Trustees of the policies. Money was paid by the deceased to the insurance company and the policies were issued to the plaintiffs. *Held*, the subject matter of the gifts was the policies.

GOFF J.: . . . In my judgment, therefore, that case [43] still leaves open the questions I have to determine; namely, what was the disposition, and what did the trustees take under it?

Mr. Bagnall propounds four classes of case. The first is where he supposes that A contracts to buy Blackacre from B and then directs a conveyance to C. That, he says—and I agree—would be a gift of Blackacre, not the purchase money. Secondly, he says—and I agree—that if there be no contract but A hands B, say, £10,000 in notes and says, " Transfer Blackacre to C," which B does, then that again is a gift of Blackacre; and he says that A disposed of it by directing B to transfer to C, and he got the power by handing over the notes.

[43] *Sneddon* v. *Lord Advocate* [1954] A.C. 257; *ante*, p. 494.

He contrasts with these two the third and fourth classes. The third is where C contracts to buy Blackacre from B and A pays the price. That, he says, discharges C's liability, and is a gift of the money. So it is. Fourthly, he submits that if C says to A, " I would like to buy Blackacre, but I cannot afford it," or A says to C, " I would like to give you Blackacre," but A gives no directions to B, the owner of Blackacre, C does all the negotiations, but A provides the £10,000, that is a gift of £10,000 because A never obtained any legal power to dispose of anything save £10,000. But in my view that depends on how A provides the money. If he pays it direct to B, it seems to me indistinguishable from the second class.

He also gave an example of the fourth class with respect to a chattel. A girl and her fiancé go to a shop together, and the girl chooses a mink coat, does all the negotiation and is about to write a cheque when her fiancé says he will pay, and writes a cheque which he gives to the shopkeeper. That, he says, is a gift of the money. I am not at all satisfied that it is. In any case, I cannot see that it governs this case, where the project was initiated by the deceased and the donees did not by any means do all the negotiating.

I should note one more submission by Mr. Bagnall, that before you can have a gift of something the donor has not got you must have a nexus known to the law between the donor and the person out of whose ownership the property is to be taken. I do not think that is a necessary condition.

. . . Looking at it from the other angle—what was the disposition, and what did the trustees take under it?—surely the disposition was the settlement of October 12, 1961, and the payment of the premium and the price of the annuity.

Even if the covenant was unenforceable, which I think it was (because, in the case where an action for damages lay, the daughter was a contracting party), still it cannot in my opinion be disregarded as it was in fact performed and the payment was made to carry it into effect. Moreover, it declared the trusts on which the policy was to be held.

What did the trustee company take under it? Surely the policy and nothing else. The trustee company never received any money. In my judgment, the cheque was delivered by Mr. Turvey to the insurance company as agent for the deceased, and not the trustee company. The money was raised by Ralli Bros. Ltd. out of the deceased's securities pursuant to her authority in that behalf, and they debited her account. Therefore, in my view, Mr. Turvey, who was at the material time employed by them, must be taken to have handled and delivered the cheque as their servant, they being her agent, or alternatively, as directly her agent under his original authority.

Even if I am wrong about this and Mr. Turvey received the cheque as agent for the trustee company, it was made payable to the insurance company, so that the trustee company never received any money and were a mere conduit pipe. It was not a case of a payment to the trustee company albeit for a specific purpose. There was no payment to them at all. It is, I think, significant that in the somewhat complicated book-keeping entries the trustee company was wholly omitted.

For these reasons, and on the facts of the case, I am definitely of opinion that the payment of the £100,000 was a gift, not of that sum but of the policy and of all moneys payable thereunder, and accordingly I answer question 1 in sense (b).

Note

This question, as it relates to insurance policies, is of especial importance where a policy was effected before March 20, 1968, it being possible for such a policy to be exempt from aggregation with the remainder of the deceased's estate as property in which the deceased never had an interest: F.A. 1894, s. 4; F.A. 1969, s. 40 (2) (c). And see *Haldane's Trustees* v. *Lord Advocate*, 1954 S.C. 156.

On the question of enforceability, see *Beswick* v. *Beswick* [1968] A.C. 58, in which earlier cases on insurance policies are considered, and J. G. Monroe, " The Jus Quaesitum Tertio " [1966] B.T.R. 303; *cf. Re Miller's Agreement* [1947] Ch. 615. The case should be contrasted with that of *Potter* v. *Lord Advocate*, *infra*, see J. G. Monroe, " The Subject Matter of a Gift Inter Vivos " [1967] B.T.R. 421.

POTTER v. LORD ADVOCATE

Court of Session 1958 S.C. 213; 1958 S.L.T. 198; [1958] T.R. 55

A father gave to his son a cheque to pay for shares in a company. The cheque was drawn in favour of the company. *Held*, the gift was a gift of money.

LORD PATRICK : . . . The argument is that, if a donor hands a sum of money to a donee for the limited purpose of the donee discharging a liability the donee is about to incur by the purchase of shares, what is taken by the donee under the donor's disposition is the shares, not the money. It would follow, if that is sound, that when a donor hands a sum of money to a donee for the limited purpose of the donee discharging a debt the donee has already incurred, what is taken by the donee under the donor's disposition is the discharge of the debt. All this is quite unsound if the view I have already expressed is correct that what we are concerned with under this section is solely property belonging to the deceased which he has given away, and which is deemed to be part of his estate passing on his death as if he had never parted with it.

There is no hardship in this. A donor may wish to be certain what sum will fall to be aggregated with the estate he leaves at his death, if he should fail to survive for five years. In that case he gives the money to the donee to purchase the shares. On the other hand, the donor may be willing to take the chance of the market rising or falling. In that case he purchases the shares and transfers them to the donee.

COMMISSIONER OF STAMP DUTIES v. GALE

High Court of Australia (1958) 101 C.L.R. 96

The donor had arranged to purchase his sister-in-law's undivided half share in land. Subsequent thereto the share was sold to his intended spouse at his request for the same price, the donor providing the money. *Held*, the gift was one of money.

DIXON C.J. : . . . There is much in the speeches of their Lordships who formed the majority in *Sneddon* v. *Lord Advocate* [44] that supports the view that in legislation such as that under consideration you look for what has been alienated by the deceased. The legislature there considered was cast in a different form and moreover was referential but plainly enough Lord Morton regarded the form of the property as it passed from the donor as a test and so did Lord MacDermott and Lord Reid citing from *Attorney-General* v. *De Préville*.[45]

In the end one may say that for present purposes it comes down to the question what did the deceased alienate?

[44] [1954] A.C. 257; *ante*, p. 494.
[45] [1900] 1 Q.B. 223.

MENZIES J.: . . . The present case is a case where the donee herself agreed to purchase the half interest in " Bibaringa," albeit at the instance of the donor and relying upon him to find the purchase money, and the donor paid the vendor the purchase money owing to her by the donee. What passed from the donor was money; each payment was made to the vendor in satisfaction *pro tanto* of the liability of the donee; in consequence of such payments the vendor in accordance with the contract of sale transferred the property to the donee. I agree with the Full Court that in these circumstances the gift was a gift of money and I consider that the gift was made at the time of the payments of the money. This is a case where the donor paid all the purchase money owing by the donee but it would, in my opinion, make no difference to the character of the gift if the donee had herself paid part of the purchase price. If that had been the case it would have been difficult to treat the gift as a gift of a half interest in " Bibaringa." Furthermore, I think that some assistance can be derived from taking a case where a donor makes a series of payments in satisfaction of the liability of a donee for the purchase price of property, some of which are made within and some of which are made outside the period of three years before the death of the donor. If, on the one hand, the payments constitute the gift, then those within the period would be brought to duty by section 102 (2) (*b*) [46] but those ouside the period would not for the simple reason that they were not gifts made by the deceased within three years before his death. On the other hand, the unreality of treating the gift as a gift of the property purchased is, in such a case, revealed by asking whether such a gift was made within or without the three year period.

Note

As pointed out by J. G. Monroe, " A Gift of What? Again " [1959] B.T.R. 147, the transaction could as easily have been carried out in another way with the opposite result, as suggested in the passage quoted from *Potter* v. *Lord Advocate*, *ante*, p. 497.

4. Other Charging Provisions

Further charges to duty are imposed under heads (*e*), (*f*) and (*g*) of section 2 (1) of the Finance Act 1894, as amended by the Finance Act 1969, and under section 46 of the Finance Act 1940.

The interest of a deceased partner in the assets of partnership will normally be charged under section 2 (1) (*a*), as property of which the deceased was competent to dispose at the time of death. Where the deceased is not so competent, *e.g.* by reason of a prior agreement that his share shall pass to the surviving partners, section 2 (1) (*e*) applies, " without prejudice to section 3." The application of that section to partnership property is considered in *Attorney-General* v. *Boden*.[47]

Where a deceased is not competent to dispose of property by reason of an option granted in respect of that property and exercisable on or by reference to his death, duty may be chargeable under section 2 (1) (*f*).[48]

[46] Of the Stamp Duties Act (New South Wales) 1920–49.

[47] [1912] 1 K.B. 539; *post*, p. 522.

[48] And see F.A. 1969, s. 37 (5). Note also *Perpetual Executors and Trustees Association of Australia Ltd.* v. *Commissioner of Taxes of the Commonwealth of Australia* [1954] A.C. 114.

Certain interests in property in Scotland, corresponding to settled property in England, are charged under section 2 (1) (g).

The charge imposed by section 46 of the Finance Act 1940 applies where property has been transferred to a controlled company by the deceased, who has received " benefits " from the company before his death.[49]

---

[49] As in *St. Aubyn* v. *Att.-Gen.* [1952] A.C. 15; *ante*, p. 479. Further provisions relating to " controlled " companies, in particular to the special rules for the valuation of shares in such companies, are considered in Chap. 20, *post*, pp. 517–519. See also G. A. Rink, " Estate Duty on Companies " [1956] B.T.R. 237.

CHAPTER 20

VALUATION

ESTATE Duty is levied upon " the principal value . . . of all property, real or personal, settled or not settled, which passes on the death of such person " (dying after the commencement of the appropriate part of the Finance Act 1894).[1] Section 7 of the same Act provides how property is to be valued for estate duty purposes; in particular:

> " The principal value of any property shall be estimated to be the price which, in the opinion of the Commissioners, such property would fetch if sold in the open market at the time of the death of the deceased." [2]

1. Market Value

The basic rule is that stated above. Valuation is a task for an expert and will normally be carried out by a surveyor, accountant or actuary, depending upon the nature of the property to be valued. Special problems arise, in particular, in cases where:

(i) there is a large estate, consisting of a number of units;

(ii) there exists a " special purchaser," or some other special circumstance likely to affect the normal working of the particular market; or

(iii) there are restrictions upon the free alienation of the property.[3]

The meaning of " open market " must also be considered.[4]

EARL OF ELLESMERE v. I.R.C.

King's Bench Division [1918] 2 K.B. 735; 88 L.J.K.B. 337; 119 L.T. 568; 34 T.L.R. 560

SANKEY J.: . . . Upon the death of the late Earl his successor resolved to sell the estate and for that purpose consulted an eminent firm of auctioneers, with the result that he determined to sell it in one lot. It was well advertised, and various offers for its purchase were received. Eventually an offer was made to buy the whole estate for £68,000, which offer, on the advice of the auctioneers,

---

[1] F.A. 1894, s. 1.

[2] *Ibid.* s. 7 (5). Further provisions relating to the valuation of property are contained in Finance (1909–10) Act 1910, s. 60, and in F.A. 1965, s. 26, as amended by F.A. 1971, Sched. 12, para. 15, governing the relationship between estate duty valuation and valuation for Capital Gains Tax purposes on death. Under the provisions of F.A. 1957, s. 38, property the subject of a gift *inter vivos* may fall to be valued at a time other than the date of death.

[3] These and other problems are considered by G. H. Newsom, " The Assessment of Estate Duty " [1956] B.T.R. 58, 114.

[4] See, especially, *Buccleuch* v. *I.R.C.* [1967] 1 A.C. 506; *post*, p. 501; *I.R.C.* v. *Clay* [1914] 3 K.B. 466; *post*, p. 507; *Lynall* v. *I.R.C.* [1972] A.C. 680; *post*, p. 512.

was accepted. Subsequently the purchaser resold the farms to the tenants, and put up the other portions of the estate for sale by auction in lots. The bulk of the lots was resold for about £65,000, the residue being still in the purchaser's hands at the time of the appeal to the referee. The Commissioners of Inland Revenue fixed the market price of the estate at £77,000, and the Earl appealed to a referee, contending that the market price was the sum for which it had actually been sold. The Commissioners on the other hand contended that, having regard to the varied character of the property and the fact that it did not all lie together, the price realised by a sale in one lot could not represent the true value. The referee upheld the contention of the Commissioners, though he reduced their figure to £75,618, and he ordered the appellant to pay the Commissioners' costs of the appeal. From that decision the present appeal is brought. It is said that the referee misdirected himself upon the question of the value, and also that he had no jurisdiction to make a successful appellant pay costs.

Now the Act of 1894 says that the value of the property shall be estimated to be the price which it would fetch if sold in the open market. That, in my opinion, does not necessarily mean the price which it would fetch if sold to a single purchaser. There may be many cases where a sale to a single purchaser cannot realise " the price which it would fetch if sold in the open market." Take the case of an owner having property including a colliery and a draper's shop. It is conceivable that if the colliery and the draper's shop were sold separately the best possible price might be obtained for each. On the other hand a purchaser who was anxious to buy the draper's shop might not wish to be encumbered with a colliery, and vice versa, and consequently if the owner insisted upon selling the whole property to one purchaser he would not obtain the market price which the Act contemplates. So, too, with regard to property of the same character situate in different areas. It may well be that if in such case the vendor insists upon the different parts being all sold to the same person he will not get as good a price as if he allowed different persons to buy the portions situate in the different districts. No doubt a sale in one lot of a varied property such as that in the present case may be highly convenient to the vendor. He may want to get the money quickly; he may not care to risk an auction. He may be going abroad, or may be called up to serve in the Army, and it may be of great importance to him to sell at once. But it does not at all follow that the price which he obtains under such circumstances is " the price which it would fetch if sold in the open market." What is meant by those words is the best possible price that is obtainable, and what that is is largely, if not entirely, a question of fact. I can readily conceive cases in which a sale of the whole property in one lot would realise the true market price, but I can equally imagine cases in which it would not. Here the referee held that because the property was of a miscellaneous character and not lying in a ring fence the price paid by the single purchaser was not the true value. I think he was entitled so to hold, and that the contention as to misdirection fails. . . .

Note
The report of this judgment appearing in 119 L.T. 568 is longer and contains important observations. These are considered in the judgment of Lord Reid in *Buccleuch* v. *I.R.C.*, *infra*.

DUKE OF BUCCLEUCH v. I.R.C.

House of Lords [1967] 1 A.C. 506; [1967] 2 W.L.R. 207; 111 S.J. 18; [1967] 1 All E.R. 129

Lord Reid: My Lords, the appellants are trustees of a settlement made by the 10th Duke of Devonshire in 1946. The Duke died on November 26, 1950, within five years of making the settlement and estate duty is admittedly payable on the whole of the settled property. This case is concerned with shares of the Chatsworth Estates Company and admittedly they must be valued with reference to the company's assets. These included 119,000 acres of land in England.

In 1961 the respondents determined the value of this land to be £3,176,646. The appellant appealed to the Lands Tribunal, maintaining that the valuation ought to be £2,743,760. The tribunal upheld the determination of the respondents and stated a case for the decision of the Court of Appeal, the question of law being: " Whether upon the findings of fact we came to a correct decision in law." On July 23, 1965, the Court of Appeal by a majority dismissed the appeal.

It is not very easy to determine what were the findings of fact of the tribunal or to state precisely the question of law which must now be decided. I think it best first to state the relevant law as I understand it and then to attempt to discover whether and if so where the tribunal misdirected themselves.

Section 7 of the Finance Act 1894 provides that in determining the value of " an estate " certain deductions are to be made. Estate there means the whole estate. Then section 7 (5) provides:

" (5) The principal value of any property shall be estimated to be the price which, in the opinion of the commissioners, such property would fetch if sold in the open market at the time of the death of the deceased; "

In my view " any property " does not refer to the whole estate of the deceased. His estate generally consists of a wide variety of different kinds of property—land, chattels, and incorporeal rights—and it would clearly be impossible to value it as a whole. The context shows that " any property " must mean any part of the estate which it is proper to treat as a unit for valuation purposes. This case turns on the determination of what are the correct principles to apply in subdividing an estate into units for valuation purposes, and it shows how greatly the total value of the estate may differ according to how it has been subdivided. The statute is silent as to the proper methods of division.

Subsection (5) only applies after the division has been made but I think that it throws some light on this matter. It requires an estimate of the price which a particular unit would fetch if sold in a certain way, so one must envisage a hypothetical sale of the actual unit. And that sale must be supposed to have taken place " in the open market " and " at the time of the death." The section must mean the price which the property *would have fetched* if sold at the time of the death. I agree with the argument of the respondents that " at the time of death " points to a definite time—the day on which the death occurred: it does not mean within a reasonable time after the death. No doubt the words " at the time of " are capable of such a meaning but I see nothing to recommend this meaning in this context. The value of some kinds of property fluctuates from day to day and there at least a particular day must be taken.

There was some argument about the meaning of " in the open market." Originally no doubt when one wanted to sell a particular item of property one took it to a market where buyers of that kind of property congregated. Then the owner received offers and accepted what he thought was the best offer he was likely to get. And for some kinds of property that is still done. But this phrase must also be applied to other kinds of property where that is impossible. In my view the phrase requires that the seller must take—or here be supposed to have taken—such steps as are reasonable to attract as much competition as possible for the particular piece of property which is to be sold. Sometimes this will be by sale by auction, sometimes otherwise. I suppose that the biggest open market is the Stock Exchange where there is no auction. And there may be two kinds of market commonly used by owners wishing to sell a particular kind of property. For example, it is common knowledge that many owners of houses first publish the fact that they wish to sell and then await offers: they only put the property up for auction as a last resort. I see no reason for holding that in proper cases the former method could not be regarded as sale in the open market.

But here what must be envisaged is sale in the open market on a particular day. So there is no room for supposing that the owner would do as many prudent owners do—withdraw the property if he does not get a sufficient offer and wait until a time when he can get a better offer. The commissioners must estimate what the property would probably have fetched on that particular day if it had then been exposed for sale, no doubt after such advance publicity as would have been reasonable.

I am confirmed in my opinion by the fact that the Act permits no deduction from the price fetched of the expenses involved in the sale (except in the case of property abroad under subsection (3)). It is notorious that the rough and ready provisions of many sections of this Act can lead to great injustice with estate duty at its present level.[5] But one must construe the Act keeping in mind that the maximum rate of duty which it provided was 8 per cent. Parliament—or the Liberal Government of the time—seems to have thought that it was best to keep the scheme simple and to omit things which justice would seem to require if the practical difference with a low rate of duty would in most cases be negligible or would at worst be small. I find it impossible to suppose that they can have contemplated that the kinds of hypothetical sale which they envisaged would involve heavy expenses. In applying the provisions of any Act one must always try to find a construction which is not unreasonable.

With these matters in view I turn to consider the main question of law in this case—how the whole estate of the deceased should be divided into units for separate valuation. Generally the estate will consist of what one may call natural units—units or parcels of property which can be easily identified without there being any substantial difficulty or expense in carving them out of the whole estate. In my opinion it is implicit in the scheme of the Act that section 7 (5) should be applied to each of such units, and there is no justification for requiring elaborate subdivision of natural units on the ground that if that had been done before the hypothetical sale the total price for the natural unit would have been increased. We must take the estate as it was when the deceased died; often the price which a piece of property would fetch would be considerably enhanced by small expense in minor repair or cleaning which would make the property more attractive to the eye of the buyer. But admittedly that cannot be supposed to have been done. And I see no more justification for requiring the supposition that natural units have been subdivided. This subsection applies to all kinds of property. A library was instanced by Winn L.J. Generally there would be little difficulty, delay or expense in getting someone knowledgeable to pick out valuable books for separate valuation and I would therefore regard such books as natural units. But suppose that the deceased had bought a miscellaneous and mixed lot of surplus stores intending to sort out and arrange them in saleable lots. That might involve a great deal of work, time and expense and I see no justification for requiring the supposition that that had been done and then valuing the saleable lots that would have emerged.

It is sometimes said that the estate must be supposed to have been realised in such a way that the best possible prices were obtained for its parts. But that cannot be a universal rule. Suppose that the owner of a wholesale business dies possessed of a large quantity of hardware or clothing or whatever he deals

---

[5] See also the remarks of Lord Wilberforce and the Green Paper, " Taxation of Capital on Death," 1972 Cmnd. 4930, paras. 23, 35–37; *ante*, pp. 455, 458.

in. It would have been possible by extensive advertising to obtain offers for
small lots at something near retail prices. So it would have been possible to
realise the stock at much more than wholesale prices. It would not have been
reasonable and it would not have been economic, but it would have been
possible. Counsel for the respondents did not contend that that would be a
proper method of valuation. But that necessarily amounts to an admission
that there is no universal rule that the best possible prices at the date of death
must be taken.

I have said that this Act applies rough and ready methods. It is vain to
apply theoretical logic. The question of what units to value is a practical
question to be solved by common sense. So if the commissioners apply the
right criteria there is no appeal. But in this case it is difficult to discover
whether the commissioners or the tribunal have applied the right criteria.

The matter has been made more difficult by misconceptions about what
seems to be the only authority, *Ellesmere (Earl of)* v. *Inland Revenue Commissioners*.[6] We were invited to consider the report in the *Law Times* series.
But I find that there is a notable discrepancy between the two reports, which
I feel sure that counsel would have drawn to our attention had they been aware
of it. I find that in the Court of Appeal Lord Denning M.R.[7] adopted and
gave great weight to a passage from the judgment of Sankey J. as reported in
the *Law Times* which is absent from the report in the Law Reports. I do not
know what the practice was in 1918, but I suspect that the judgment in the
Law Reports may have been revised by the learned judge and that the judgment in the *Law Times* was not. The report in the Law Reports appears over
the initials of the senior King's Bench reporter named in the title page of the
volume and I cannot believe that an experienced reporter would have cut out
this passage without the authority of the judge himself. I think that it goes
too far and on second thoughts Sankey J. may well have thought the same.

. . . I see nothing wrong with the decision, and, subject to what I have said
about the best possible price, I would quarrel with nothing in the passage which
I have quoted from the Law Reports. But in the *Law Times*[8] there is inter-
polated in that passage the passage, quoted by Lord Denning, that the property
must be sold " in such a manner and subject to such conditions as might reasonably be calculated to obtain for the vendor the best price for the property "
and this has been taken to justify elaborate and expensive subdivision of natural
units if that course would increase the gross price. If Sankey J. did delete
this passage when he revised his judgment I think he was wise. But it was
strongly founded on by the respondents in argument and it may well have
misled the tribunal. They quote it in full in their interim decision.

The property assessed includes ten estates in England and the respondents
did not determine their valuation until eleven years after the Duke's death.
They proceeded on the basis that these ten estates had to be notionally divided
into some 3,500 units and that each of these units had to be valued separately.
All that we learn from the tribunal about the way in which the estates were
so divided is contained in a sentence in a letter from the respondents and in a
short paragraph in the interim decision. The letter states that the valuation
had been made on the basis of such lotting of the whole property as was
calculated to produce the best price. Before the tribunal the Hardwick estate
(some 20,000 acres) alone was investigated, it being taken as typical. With regard
to it the tribunal say:

"For the purposes of arriving at the valuation, the estate had been
divided into some 532 separate units, each unit representing a lot which,

6 [1918] 2 K.B. 735; *ante*, p. 500.   7 [1966] 1 Q.B. 851, 871.
8 119 L.T. 568, 573.

in the Revenue's view, would have commanded the best market price if sold on the date of the Duke's death."

If the dubious passage in the judgment of Sankey J. were right if given the meaning for which the respondents contend there would be no need to say more. And it must be said in fairness to the tribunal that the argument as then presented for the appellant did not raise the method of lotting. So we do not know whether or not substantially all the units which were valued separately were what I have called natural units nor do we know how much time, work or expense was involved in the lotting or would have been involved if the owner of these estates had decided to sell them in these units. What we do know is that the tribunal quote and apparently accept evidence of one of the appellants' witnesses " that it would have been impossible to sell all the individual units within a reasonable time of the date of death, and [he] took the view it would take at least seven years." The respondents' witness said that it would be impossible to sell all the units within a year, but he did not say how long he thought it would take. The argument for the appellants before the tribunal and their first argument before your Lordships was that this by itself was enough to show that the respondents' method must be wrong. For reasons which I shall state in a moment I cannot accept that argument. Before I could reach any decision in favour of the appellants I should at least have to know how far this delay of seven years would have been caused by initial difficulties of lotting and drawing up conditions of sale for these numerous lots, how far it would have been caused by the lack of sufficient professional men with the necessary skill, and how far it would have been caused by a desire not to flood the market.

The ten estates to be valued were each managed as a separate unit at the time of the Duke's death and the appellants maintain that each should now be valued as a single unit subject to the excision and separate valuation of a number of outlying parts which were easily severable. The tribunal have found that, if that is the proper method of dividing the property for valuation, the total value of these estates would be some £433,000 lower than the respondents' valuation based on separate valuation of smaller units. The reason for this large difference is that only speculators or property developers or investors would be interested in buying entire estates. A buyer who intended to resell the estate in small lots would have to incur the trouble and expense involved in dividing up the estate, he would have to lie out of his money for a long time, and he would expect to make a reasonable profit. He might therefore only pay for the estate some 80 per cent. of the total amount which he would expect to realise from re-selling it in small lots.

The appellants say that the true value of these estates at the date of death must be the amount which would be realised within a reasonable time. If the respondents' values could only be realised over a period of seven years and after incurring much expense which is not a permissible deduction, then the basis of their valuation must be wrong.

But we cannot approach the problem in that general way, however just and attractive it may seem. And if we could look at the problem broadly there is another side to it. If the deceased only owned two or three farms then it could not be disputed that the proper method of valuation would be to suppose each farm to have been sold as a separate unit; so what justification can there be for valuing a particular farm in one way if the deceased had owned few others but in another way if he had owned a great many. I do not think that we can decide the question on general arguments of this kind. We must go back to section 7 (5).

If I am right in thinking that section 7 (5) is dealing one by one with the units into which the estate has already been divided then the hypothetical sale which it envisages must be a supposed sale of one unit in the conditions which in fact existed at the date of the death. To add one unit to those which in fact were then for sale would not have disturbed the market. But if we had to suppose that a large number of the units owned by the deceased had been put on the market simultaneously, the conditions which in fact existed would have been materially altered and prices would have dropped. This is expressly dealt with by section 60 (2) of the Finance (1909–10) Act 1910, but I doubt whether this subsection did more than express what was already implicit in the Act of 1894.

It must follow that the fact that it would have taken a long time to sell separately the units of a large estate is irrelevant in so far as that delay would have been caused by the need to avoid flooding the market. And in so far as delay would have been caused by there not being enough qualified professional men to make the necessary preparations for a very large number of separate sales within a short period, that factor must, I think, be equally irrelevant. So in my view we come back to the question with which I have already dealt— whether the estates were so easily separable into large numbers of units that these units can be regarded as what I have called natural units.

This matter was never separately investigated by the tribunal because the appellants did not raise it as a separate point. I think that the problem could be approached in this way. Suppose that each of these 532 units had been separately owned. Then if the owner of one of them had died it would have cost his executors an appreciable percentage of its value to sell it—say on the average X per cent. But that would not have been a permissible deduction. So if the owner of 532 units dies his executors cannot reject in so far as the cost of realisation amounts to X per cent. of the total value of the units. But in so far as it exceeds that amount they have a legitimate grievance. As the Act deals with such problems in a rough and ready way, they would have to tolerate a moderate excess. But if there were a great excess caused by initial difficulty and cost in dividing the estate into lots, that would be evidence—it might be strong evidence—that these units were not truly natural units.

In a case such as the present I would not regard it as fatal to the appellants' case that this point was taken before the tribunal: I would be prepared to consider whether justice required a remit for further findings. But in this case it seems to me obvious from the facts already in the case that the factor which I have tried to describe could not have accounted for the greater part of the difference between the valuations of the appellants and the respondents. So I do not think that this is a case in which the exceptional course of making such a remit would be justified. I must therefore move that the appeal be dismissed.

LORD MORRIS OF BORTH-Y-GEST: . . . The stipulation that an estimate must be made of the value which a property would fetch if sold in the open market does not, in my view, require an assumption that the highest possible price will be realised. It involves that an estimate should be made of the price which would be realised under the reasonable competitive conditions of an open market on a particular date. . . .

LORD WILBERFORCE: . . . There remains one other matter as to which I feel much difficulty. The appellants claim, in general terms, that, even if the Revenue's basis of valuation is correct, a deduction should be allowed for the extra expense of realisation in individual lots. The Revenue dispute this, contending that expenses of sale are in law not deductible. The wording of the Finance Act 1894, s. 7 (5), adequate perhaps when it was passed, but with the great increase of rates of duty now severe and even unjust, requires the gross open market price, *i.e.* what the purchaser pays, and not what the vendor ultimately receives, to be taken as the valuation figures. . . .

Note
For comments on this case, see M. Flesch, " Do Fence Me In " [1966] B.T.R. 60; " Only Natural " [1967] B.T.R. 218; G. R. Bretten, " Estate Duty: the Principal Value Concept " (1970) 34 *Conveyancer* (N.S.) 111.

I.R.C. v. CLAY

Court of Appeal [1914] 3 K.B. 466; 83 L.J.K.B. 1425; 111 L.T. 484; 30 T.L.R. 573; 58 S.J. 610; [1914–15] All E.R.Rep. 882

A house, which fell to be valued for the purposes of estate duty and which would normally not have been worth more than £750, adjoined a nurses' home, the Trustees of which desired to extend the home and were prepared to pay £1,000 for the house. *Held*, the value for estate duty was £1,000.

COZENS-HARDY M.R.: . . . I can see no ground for excluding from consideration the fact that the property is so situate that to one or more persons it presents greater attractions than to anybody else. The house or the land may immediately adjoin one or more landowners likely to offer more than the property would be worth to anybody else. This is a fact which cannot be disregarded. . . .

SWINFEN-EADY L.J.: . . . The Solicitor-General contended that as the section said " if sold at the time in the open market," the price which only one particular buyer was prepared to pay must be excluded from all consideration; it might possibly be a fancy price which had no relation to market price; that a reference to open market showed that the statute referred to a current market price of land, a price which one or more valuers might determine to be the market value of the land.

In my opinion this contention is unsound. A value, ascertained by reference to the amount obtainable in an open market, shows an intention to include every possible purchaser. The market is to be the open market, as distinguished from an offer to a limited class only, such as the members of the family. The market is not necessarily an auction sale. The section means such amount as the land might be expected to realise if offered under conditions enabling every person desirous of purchasing to come in and make an offer, and if proper steps were taken to advertise the property and let all likely purchasers know that the land is in the market for sale. It scarcely needed evidence to inform us—it is common knowledge—that when the fact becomes known that one probable buyer desires to obtain any property, that raises the general price or value of the thing in the market. Not only is the probable buyer a competitor in the market, but other persons, such as property brokers, compete in the market for what they know another person wants, with a view to a resale to him at an enhanced price, so as to realise a profit. A vendor desiring to realise any land would ordinarily give full publicity to all facts within his knowledge likely to enhance the price. The local conditions and requirements, the advantages of the situation of the property for any particular purpose, and the names of the persons who are probable buyers, would ordinarily be matters of local knowledge to the property brokers and agents and speculators. In order to arrive at the amount which land might be "expected to realise," all these matters ought to be taken into consideration. . . .

Note
As to "local knowledge," *cf. Lynall* v. *I.R.C.* [1972] A.C. 680; *post*, p. 512, and the remarks of Lord Pearson (at p. 774). In that case, the special factor enhancing the value of the property was not (as in *Clay's* case) local knowledge, but highly confidential information. See also *Crabtree* v. *Hinchcliffe* [1972] A.C. 707.

The existence of a " special purchaser " is also considered, and the decision in *I.R.C.* v. *Clay* approved in *Glass* v. *I.R.C.*, 1915 S.C. 449; *Raja Vyricherla Narayana Gajapatiraju* v. *Revenue Divisional Officer, Vizagapatam* [1939] A.C. 302.

I.R.C. v. CROSSMAN

House of Lords [1937] A.C. 26; 105 L.J.K.B. 450; 154 L.T. 570; 80 S.J. 485; [1936] 1 All E.R. 762

Shares fell to be valued on the death of a member of a private company. The Articles of Association of the company imposed restrictions upon the alienation of shares, giving existing directors and members certain rights of pre-emption. *Held*, the value of the shares for the purposes of estate duty was the price which the shares would obtain if sold on the open market, it being assumed that the hypothetical purchaser should be entitled to be registered as the holder of the shares and to hold them subject to those same provisions in the Articles, including the restrictions upon alienation, as had the deceased.

VISCOUNT HAILSHAM L.C.: . . . Since the articles forbid a sale in the open market until the rights of pre-emption have been exhausted, all that the executors could sell in the open market at the time of the death was the right to receive the restricted price fixed by article 34, subclause 14*a*, from any shareholder exercising his right of pre-emption. Obviously the value of this could not exceed the sum which such a shareholder would have to pay and accordingly the Court of Appeal have held that that sum, *i.e.* the restricted price, is the value in the open market.

My Lords, it seems to me that this construction involves treating the provisions of section 7, subsection 5, as if their true effect were to make the existence of an open market a condition of liability instead of merely to prescribe the open market price as the measure of value. The right to receive the price fixed by the articles in the event of a sale to existing shareholders under subclause 14*a* is only one of the elements which went to make up the value of the shares. In addition to that right, the ownership of the share gave a number of other valuable rights to the holder, including the right to receive the dividends which the Company was declaring, the right to transmit the share in accordance with article 34, subclauses 1, 2 and 3, and the right to have the shares of other holders who wished to realise offered on the terms of article 34, subclause 14*a*. All these various rights and privileges go to make up a share and form ingredients in its value. They are just as much part of the share as the restriction upon the sale. The construction placed upon the statute by the Court of Appeal seems to me to ignore all these elements in the value of the share and to treat as its value what, in truth, is only the value of one of the factors which go to make up that share. But the purpose of section 7, subsection 5, is not to define the property in respect of which estate duty is to be levied, but merely to afford a method of ascertaining its value. If the view entertained by the Court of Appeal were correct, it would follow that any property which could not be sold in the open market would escape estate duty altogether. That seems to me quite an unnecessary and unnatural construction to place upon the language of the statute. In the words of Lord Buckmaster in *Poplar Assessment Committee* v. *Roberts* [9] " so to interpret the statute would be to deal with something which was nothing but a measure of value in such a manner as completely to destroy the very object for which that measure was set up." On the other hand, I can see no difficulty in treating the subsection as meaning that the Commissioners of Inland Revenue are to assume that the property which is to be valued is being sold in the open market and to fix its value for estate duty purposes upon that hypothesis. A somewhat similar problem is familiar in rating cases. . . .

LORD ROCHE: . . . Upon an actual sale there must be an actual passing of property. Upon a notional sale there must be a notional or assumed passing of property. In so far as the passing or transfer of property is thus notional or hypothetical, no restriction upon actual passing or transfer comes into question, and the article as to the prescribed price which is to rule under certain circumstances, though it is no doubt a constituent part of the bundle of rights which constitutes a share, does not, as I think, govern such a notional transfer so as to make the notional purchaser no more than a person who acquires an obligation to offer the shares to others at the prescribed price. . . .

LORD RUSSELL OF KILLOWEN (dissenting): . . . It may be that owing to provisions in the articles of association the subject matter of the sale cannot be effectively vested in the purchaser because the directors refuse to and cannot be compelled to register the purchaser as shareholder. The purchaser could then secure the benefit of the sale by the registered shareholder becoming a trustee for him of the rights with an indemnity in respect of the obligations. In the case of the sale of such a share the risk of a refusal to register might well be reflected in a smaller price being obtainable than would have been obtained had there been no such risk. The share was property with that risk as one of its incidents.

But a further restriction may exist, as in the present case. The articles may stipulate that a shareholder must first give existing shareholders the chance of buying his shares at a price fixed and not competitive. In such a case a sale to an outsider of the shareholder's interest in the Company must and can only be made subject to that obligation, which is one of the incidents which attach to and are part of the subject matter of the sale; and the sale to the outsider must necessarily include as an incident of the subject matter of the sale, the right to receive the fixed price if the right of pre-emption is exercised by the other shareholders. The consequence is that by reason of the nature and incidents of the subject matter of the sale, neither Sir William Paulin nor his executors, at the time of the death, could have sold these shares in the open market to any one otherwise than subject to the right of pre-emption at the fixed price. The result of the existence of this right of pre-emption must inevitably be that no one at an actual sale in the open market would be prepared to offer more than the fixed price if even that. . . .

Note

In *Re Aschrott* [1927] 1 Ch. 313, the fact that the deceased as an enemy alien was disqualified from transferring shares in English companies did not prevent the shares being valued on the " open market " basis. Nor did it render the deceased not " competent to dispose " of them.

The Articles of Association of private companies invariably impose restrictions upon the free transfer of shares : this is necessarily a factor to be taken into account in placing a value

[9] [1922] 2 A.C. 93, 103.

upon such shares: see *Holt* v. *I.R.C.* [1953] 1 W.L.R. 1488, *infra*; *Lynall* v. *I.R.C.* [1972] A.C. 680; *post*, p. 512.

2. Particular Types of Property

Certain types of property pose their own special problems of valuation. For example, special rules govern the valuation procedure, and appeals therefrom, applicable to land.[10]

As may be seen from *I.R.C.* v. *Crossman, supra,* the valuation of shares gives rise to special problems. In the case of shares quoted on a recognised Stock Exchange there will normally be no difficulty, the Stock Exchange itself being an open market,[11] and the value will normally be taken on the basis of the price quoted in the official list for the date of death or the nearest business day to the date of death.[12] Unquoted shares are more likely to give rise to difficulties.[13] In certain circumstances, special rules apply to the valuation of shares in a "controlled company," these being valued on the basis of the underlying assets of the company.[14] Special rules also apply to interests in expectancy.

(i) *Valuation of Shares*

By their nature, shares in a private company are not readily disposed of in the "open market." In attempting to estimate the price which might be realised in the event of a hypothetical sale, many factors fall to be considered, in particular the past dividend record of the company, its financial and trading stability and prospects, the policy of the directors and the degree to which a new shareholder might be able to influence that policy, the size of the shareholding which is notionally to be sold,[15] and the amount of information available to a prospective purchaser.

Re HOLT, HOLT v. I.R.C.

Chancery Division [1953] 1 W.L.R. 1488; 97 S.J. 876; [1953] T.R. 373; *sub nom. Holt* v. *I.R.C.* [1953] 2 All E.R. 1499; [1953] 2 Lloyd's Rep. 506

Shares in a private company fell to be valued on the death of a shareholder. The Articles of Association contained restrictions on alienation and gave the Directors a first option and power to refuse to register transfers. The Company carried on a hazardous trade in West Africa, had a widely fluctuating profit

---

10 F.A. 1911, s. 18; Lands Tribunal Act 1949, s. 3 (4) (ii). See C. W. N. Miles, " Valuation of Agricultural Assets for Capital Gains Tax and Estate Duty " [1971] B.T.R. 32.
11 See the remarks of Lord Reid in *Buccleuch* v. *I.R.C.* [1967] 1 A.C. 506, 524; *ante*, p. 502.
12 Special circumstances might exist to render the quoted price an inaccurate reflection of the true value: see *Crabtree* v. *Hinchcliffe* [1972] A.C. 707, a case concerning the value of quoted shares for Capital Gains Tax purposes and the interpretation of F.A. 1965, s. 44 (1) (3).
13 See, especially, W. B. S. Walker, " Valuation of Minority Shareholdings in Private Companies for Estate Duty Purposes " [1958] B.T.R. 16; T. A. Hamilton-Baynes, " Capital Gains Tax and the Private Company " [1967] B.T.R. 103.
14 F.A. 1940, s. 55.
15 Thus a controlling interest is generally thought to be worth more than the sum of the value of the shares when owned by minority shareholders: see E. W. C. Lewis, " The Work of the Estate Duty Office " (1960) 57 *Law Society's Gazette* 370.

record, paid only small dividends and needed to replace several substantial capital assets.

The Crown initially claimed £3 per share, subsequently determined the value at £1 14s. and now contended that the value was £1 5s. The Petitioners initially contended that each share was worth 11s. 3d., and later 17s. 2d. *Held*, each share should be valued at 19s.

DANCKWERTS J.: . . . By the terms of section 7, I have to imagine the price which the property would fetch if sold in the open market. This does not mean that a sale by auction (which would be improbable in the case of shares in a company) is to be assumed, but simply that a market is to be assumed from which no buyer is excluded: see *Inland Revenue Commissioners* v. *Clay, per Swinfen Eady L.J.* ([1914] 3 K.B. 475).[16] At the same time, the court must assume a prudent buyer who would make full inquiries and have access to accounts and other information which would be likely to be available to him: see *Findlay's Trustees* v. *Inland Revenue Commissioners*.[17]

. . . One question of some importance dealt with by Mr. Holt [18] was how far a prospective purchaser would have been able to obtain information as to the company's position and prospects by inquiry from the directors. Mr. Holt said that all the information which he had given in evidence would not have been given directly to a buyer of a small quantity of shares, but that it would have been made available, in confidence, to a reputable firm of accountants, acting on behalf of a buyer and approved by the board of directors, with the result, as I understood the position, that the information so revealed would not be passed on to the buyer, but his accountant would be in a position to advise him as to the prudence of the purchase and the price which could reasonably be offered for the shares.

. . . As I have already indicated, the problem to be decided is purely hypothetical because, in a company in which the family are determined to retain control, it is obvious that a member or person selected by the directors would be found to enforce a transfer at " the fair value " under article 25 of the company's articles of association. I am bound to assume, however, that this provision in the articles was not being enforced, and that the shares were thrown open for purchase by anyone who was willing to buy them.

It is plain that the shares do not give a purchaser the opportunity to control the company, or to influence the policy of the directors to any great extent, as the shares available only represent 43,698 shares out of 697,680 ordinary shares which had been issued. Any purchaser would, therefore, be dependent on the policy of the directors, so long as they should have the support of the general body of the shareholders. I think the kind of investor who would purchase shares in a private company of this kind, in circumstances which must preclude him from disposing of his shares freely whenever he should wish (because he will, when registered as a shareholder, be subject to the provisions of the articles restricting transfer) would be different from any common kind of purchaser of shares on the Stock Exchange, and would be rather the exceptional kind of investor who had some special reason for putting his money into shares of this kind. He would, in my view, be the kind of investor who would not rush hurriedly into the transaction, but would consider carefully the prudence of the course, and would seek to get the fullest possible information about the past

[16] *Ante*, p. 507.
[17] (1937) 22 A.T.C. 437.
[18] The chairman of the company, who gave evidence. One amusing feature of cases such as this is the manner in which directors giving evidence tend to paint a uniformly depressing picture of the stability and prospects of their companies!

history of the company, the particular trade in which it was engaged and the future prospects of the company. . . .

LYNALL v. I.R.C.

House of Lords [1972] A.C. 680; [1971] 3 W.L.R. 759; 115 S.J. 872; [1971] 3 All E.R. 914; *sub nom. Lynall, Re* [1971] T.R. 309

LORD REID: My Lords, Mrs. Lynall died on May 21, 1962. At her death she owned 67,886 shares in Linread, a private company whose articles contained restrictions on the rights of shareholders to sell their shares. The question at issue in this case is the proper value of these shares for estate duty purposes. At first the executors suggested £2 per share. The Revenue claimed on the basis of a value of £4 per share which figure on obtaining further information they increased to £5 10s. Plowman J.[19] fixed a value of £3 10s. On appeal the Court of Appeal[20] increased this to £4 10s. Now the appellants claim that the value should be fixed at £1 or alternatively £3 10s. per share.

Linread began on a very modest scale in 1925. It prospered greatly but remained a family concern. At Mrs. Lynall's death there were only five shareholders. She held 28 per cent. of the capital: her husband held 32 per cent.: each of their two sons held 20 per cent. and the manager only held 200 shares. All five were directors. Both she and her husband were elderly and it had been realised that there would be financial difficulties if they died without steps being taken to avoid that. So in 1959 Messrs. Thomson McLintock were asked to carry out a survey with a view to a public issue. They recommended that course and in March 1962, a report was obtained from Messrs. Cazenoves as to the best method of flotation. No decision about this had been taken by Linread before Mrs. Lynall's death but the company was then ripe for " going public."

The shares must be valued as provided by section 7 (5) of the Finance Act 1894:

" (5) The principal value of any property shall be estimated to be the price which, in the opinion of the commissioners, such property would fetch if sold in the open market at the time of the death of the deceased. . . ."

But neither Mrs. Lynall nor her executors were entitled to sell these shares in the open market. Linread's articles of association provided:

" 8. The directors may in their absolute and uncontrolled discretion refuse to register any proposed transfer of shares and regulation 24 of Part I of Table ' A ' shall be modified accordingly and no preference or ordinary share in the company shall be transferable until it shall (by letter addressed and delivered to the secretary of the company) have been first offered to Ezra Herbert Lynall so long as he shall remain a director of the company and after he shall have ceased to be a director of the company to the members of the company at its fair value. The fair value of such share shall be fixed by the company in general meeting from time to time and where not so fixed shall be deemed to be the par value. The directors may from time to time direct in what manner any such option to purchase shares shall be dealt with by the secretary when communicated to him."

No fair value had been fixed by the company. So the position at Mrs. Lynall's death was that the shares were not transferable until they had been first

[19] [1969] 1 Ch. 421.
[20] [1970] Ch. 138.

offered to her husband at £1 per share and even if he did not want them they were only transferable to a purchaser accepted by the directors.

A similar situation occurred in *Inland Revenue Commissioners* v. *Crossman*.[21] The appellants asked us to reconsider that decision. I have done so and I agree with the decision of the majority in this House. They followed the Irish case of *Attorney-General* v. *Jameson*.[22] The most succinct statement of the ground of decision is that of Holmes L.J.[22]:

> "Turning to the 7th section of the Act, I find therein the very test of value which I should have applied in its absence. 'The principal value shall be estimated to be the price which, in the opinion of the commissioners, such property would fetch if sold in the open market at the time of the death of the deceased.' The Attorney-General and the defendants agree in saying that in this case there cannot be an actual sale in open market. Therefore, argues the former, we must assume that there is no restriction of any kind on the disposition of the shares and estimate that [sic] would be given therefor by a purchaser, who upon registration would have complete control over them. My objection to this mode of ascertaining the value is that the property bought in the imaginary sale would be a different property from that which Henry Jameson held at the time of his death. The defendants, on the other hand, contend that the only sale possible is a sale at which the highest price would be £100 per share, and that this ought to be the estimated value. My objection is that this estimate is not based on a sale in open market as required by the Act. Being unable to accept either solution, I go back to my own, which is in strict accordance with the language of the section. I assume that there is such a sale of the shares as is contemplated by article 11, the effect of which would be to place the purchaser in the same position as that occupied by Henry Jameson. An expert would have no difficulty in estimating their value on this basis. It would be less than the Crown claims, and more than the defendants offer; but I believe that it would be arrived at in accordance not only with the language of the Act, but with the methods usually employed in valuing property."

The appellants urged your Lordships to accept the view of the minority in *Crossman's* case. They appear to assume that there could be a sale by a shareholder of shares subject to a right of pre-emption. In my view it is legally impossible for the shareholder to sell such shares in the open market or otherwise without first obtaining from the holder of the right of pre-emption an agreement not to exercise that right. I agree with Lord Roche that sale means a transaction which passes the property in the thing sold. All that the shareholder could offer would be an undertaking that if the right of pre-emption was exercised he would assign to the " purchaser " his right to receive the pre-emption price and that if the right of pre-emption was not exercised he would transfer the shares to the purchaser so that if the directors registered the transfer the property in the shares would pass but if they did not he would hold the shares in trust for the purchaser. In my view that would not be a sale. I support the view of the majority on the ground that section 7 (5) is merely machinery for estimating value, that it will not work if section 7 (5) is read literally, that it must be made to work, and that the only way of doing that is the way adopted in *Crossman's* case.

If *Crossman's* case stands then the first submission of the appellants fails. The parties admit that then the choice is between the valuation of £3 10s. and £4 10s. per share.

21 [1937] A.C. 26; *ante*, p. 508.
22 [1905] 2 I.R. 218, 239.

We must decide what the highest bidder would have offered in the hypothetical sale in the open market, which the Act requires us to imagine took place at the time of Mrs. Lynall's death. The sum which any bidder will offer must depend on what he knows (or thinks he knows) about the property for which he bids. The decision of this case turns on the question what knowledge the hypothetical bidders must be supposed to have had about the affairs of Linread. One solution would be that they must be supposed to have been omniscient. But we have to consider what would in fact have happened if this imaginary sale had taken place, or at least—if we are looking for a general rule—what would happen in the event of a sale of this kind taking place. One thing which would not happen would be that the bidders would be omniscient. They would derive their knowledge from facts made available to them by the shareholder exposing the shares for sale. We must suppose that, being a willing seller and an honest man, he would give as much information as he was entitled to give. If he was not a director he would give the information which he could get as a shareholder. If he was a director and had confidential information, he could not disclose that information without the consent of the board of directors.

In the present case if we are to suppose that the bidder only had information which he could obtain himself or which could be given without the consent of the board then admittedly £3 10s. is the correct estimate of what the highest bid would have been. But the Revenue maintains and the Court of Appeal would seem to have held that it must be supposed that the board would have authorised the hypothetical seller to communicate highly confidential information to all who might come forward as bidders.

Bidders would know that both Mrs. Lynall and her husband were elderly and that they held most of the shares. Their general experience would tell them that in such circumstances it is common for a private company to make a public issue and remove restrictions on the transfer of its shares. The successful bidder would have to lock up a sum of £200,000 or more until there was a free market in the shares. If there was a prospect of an early public issue he would be prepared to pay considerably more than if it were uncertain whether or when the company would " go public."

I have said that the board had reports which made it very probable that a public issue would be made in the near future. If bidders must be supposed to have known about these reports then it is agreed that there would have been a bid of £4 10s. per share.

The case for the Revenue is based on evidence as to how large blocks of shares in private companies are in fact sold. There is no announcement that the shares are for sale and no invitation for competitive bids. The seller engages an expert who selects the person or group whom he thinks most likely to be prepared to pay a good price and to be acceptable to the directors. If that prospective purchaser is interested he engages accountants of high repute and the directors agree to co-operate by making available to the accountants on a basis of strict confidentiality all relevant information about the company's affairs. Then the accountants acting in an arbitral capacity fix what they think is a fair price. Then the sale is made at that price. Obviously the working of this scheme depends on all concerned having complete confidence in each other, and I do not doubt that in this way the seller gets a better price than he could otherwise obtain.

In my view this evidence is irrelevant because this kind of sale is not a sale in the open market. It is a sale by private treaty made without competition to a selected purchaser at a price fixed by an expert valuer. The Act of 1894 could have provided—but it did not—that the value should be the highest price that could reasonably have been expected to be realised on a sale of the property at the time of the death. If that had been the test then the respondents would succeed, subject to one matter which I need not stop to consider. But the framers of the Act limited the inquiry to one type of sale—sale in the open market—and we are not entitled to rewrite the Act. It is quite easily workable as it stands.

No doubt sale in the open market may take many forms. But it appears to me that the idea behind this provision is the classical theory that the best way to determine the value in exchange of any property is to let the price be determined by economic forces—by throwing the sale open to competition when the highest price will be the highest that anyone offers. That implies that there has been adequate publicity or advertisement before the sale, and the nature of the property must determine what is adequate publicity. Goods may be exposed for sale in a market place or place to which buyers resort. Property may be put up to auction. Competitive tenders may be invited. On the Stock Exchange a sale to a jobber may seem to be a private sale but the price has been determined, at least within narrow limits, by the actions of the investing public. In a particular case it may not always be easy to say whether there has been a sale in the open market. But in my judgment the method on which the respondents rely cannot by any criterion be held to be selling in the open market.

If the hypothetical sale on the open market requires us to suppose that competition has been invited then we would have to suppose that steps had been taken before the sale to enable a variety of persons, institutions or financial groups to consider what offers they would be prepared to make. It would not be a true sale in the open market if the seller were to discriminate between genuine potential buyers and give to some of them information which he withheld from others, because one from whom he withheld information might be the one who, if he had had the information, would have made the highest offer.

The respondents' figure of £4 10s. per share can only be justified if it must be supposed that these reports would have been made known to all genuine potential buyers, or at least to accountants nominated by them. That could only have been done with the consent of Linread's board of directors. They were under no legal obligation to make any confidential information available. Circumstances vary so much that I have some difficulty in seeing how we could lay down any general rule that directors must be supposed to have done something which they were not obliged to do. The farthest we could possibly go would be to hold that directors must be deemed to have done what all reasonable directors would do. Then it might be reasonable to say that they would disclose information provided that its disclosure could not possibly prejudice the interests of the company. But that would not be sufficient to enable the respondents to succeed.

Not all financiers who might wish to bid in such a sale, and not even all the accountants whom they might nominate, are equally trustworthy. A premature leakage of such information as these reports disclose might be very damaging to the interests of the company, and the evidence in this case shows that in practice great care is taken to see that disclosure is only made to those of the highest repute. I could not hold it right to suppose that all reasonable directors would agree to disclose information such as these reports so widely as would be necessary if it had to be made available to all who must be regarded as genuine potential bidders or to their nominees. So in my opinion the respondents fail to justify their valuation of £4 10s. I would therefore allow this appeal.

LORD MORRIS OF BORTH-Y-GEST: . . . The somewhat limited issue as between the two figures of £3 10s. or £4 10s. mainly depends upon the question whether knowledge of the category B documents and of the information which they contain would be " open market " knowledge. The conclusion of the learned judge was that as such information was not published information and as (on Mr. Alan Lynall's evidence which the learned judge accepted) it would not in fact have been elicited on inquiry it ought not to enter into the calculation of price and value. The differing view of the Court of Appeal was based on the evidence, above referred to, of the practice of boards of directors to answer reasonable questions in confidence to the advisers of an interested potential pur- chaser. If this is the practice and even if the sought-for information may be given " in confidence " to an interested potential purchaser himself, I cannot think that this equates with open market conditions. It was said that it should be assumed that a purchaser would make reasonable inquiries from all available sources and that it must further be assumed that he would receive true and factual answers. If, however, the category B documents and the information contained in them were confidential to the board, as they were, the information could not be made generally available so that it became open market know- ledge. On this somewhat limited issue I therefore prefer the figure of £3 10s. and I would restore the decision of the learned judge.

On the wider issues I doubt whether it is possible to define with precision the extent or the limits of the information on the basis of which a hypothetical purchaser of shares on a sale in the open market might purchase. There may be cases where prudent and careful potential purchasers of a large block of shares will be unwilling to purchase unless they have the inducement of being given confidential information which is not generally known. If in practice some large deals take place on the basis that some information is given which must be kept secret, then any such practice is the practice not of an open market but of a special market operating in a special way. . . .

Note
    Cf. the evidence given by Mr. Holt in *Holt* v. *I.R.C.* [1953] 1 W.L.R. 1488, 1494; *ante*, p. 511; and see *Crabtree* v. *Hinchcliffe* [1972] A.C. 707.

ATTORNEY-GENERAL OF CEYLON v. MACKIE

Privy Council [1952] 2 All E.R. 775; [1952] T.R. 431; 31 A.T.C. 435

Shares fell to be valued, on the basis of the price they would fetch if sold on the open market at the date of death, under the Ceylon Estate Duty Ordinance 1938, s. 20 (1). The past history of the company showed wide fluctuations and the business had now become disrupted. *Held,* the valuation should be arrived at by reference to the balance sheet valuation of the company's business as a going concern.

LORD REID: . . . Evidence was given in the District Court as to the value of the shares. The leading witness for the respondents was Mr. Lander, a chartered accountant, who had experience of rubber companies. The gist of his evidence was that a buyer would first ask what was the last dividend and when was it paid, but, as no dividend had been paid for many years, it was impossible to value the shares on a yield basis. He then pointed out that in 1940 the future was unpredictable and it was difficult to find anyone who was willing to invest large sums of money on speculation. He valued the shares on a balance sheet basis because, in his view, no one would have paid more than that at the time. When asked in cross-examination whether a buyer would not have taken into account the probability that the high profits of 1940 would last for some time, he said that the buyer " would have needed to know precisely what was going to happen in the world which was devastated by a war the length of which could not be guessed by the man in the street. In other words, if a purchaser could have guessed that there was going to be a long war, no government interference, no form of increased taxation, and that he was not going to have competition from others, he might take that view. He would be a brave man. It would possibly be a gamble." . . .

(ii) *Shares in Controlled Companies*

In certain instances, reference to the value of the company's assets may provide the best basis for valuation of its shares.[23] On the death of a person who, at any time during the seven years preceding his death, had had control of a " controlled company," [24] valuation on an assets basis is the prescribed method.[25] " Control " is widely defined.

BARCLAYS BANK LTD. v. I.R.C.

House of Lords [1961] A.C. 509; [1960] 3 W.L.R. 280; 104 S.J. 563; [1960] 2 All E.R. 817; [1960] T.R. 185

Lord Reid: . . . I think that it is quite clear that the purpose of that Act is to prevent a person from diminishing the value of his property for estate duty by erecting a screen between himself and his assets in the form of a company of which he retains control but the constitution of which contains convenient restrictions so that, if there are say 1,000 shares, each share valued in the ordinary way is worth less than 1/1,000 part of the value of the net assets of the company. There are so many possible variants of such a scheme that the provisions of the Act had to be elaborate, and it may be that the statutory provisions sometimes go beyond what is necessary to counteract schemes of this kind. But if the meaning of any particular provisions is in doubt, I would incline to that meaning which can reasonably be related to the apparent purpose of the Act. . . .

Viscount Simonds: My Lords, this appeal once more demands your Lordships' consideration of section 55 and section 58 of the Finance Act 1940, and it is not surprising that it raises questions which to me at least appear to be of outstanding difficulty.

At the date of his death on December 15, 1955, Tom Shipside, whom I will call " the testator," was the registered holder of 1,100 fully paid ordinary shares of £1 each of T. Shipside Ltd. Of these shares he was the beneficial owner. At all times the issued ordinary share capital was 8,350 £1 shares. On December 1, 1936, the testator settled 3,650 of these shares upon trust for the benefit of his wife and children, himself taking no beneficial interest. The original trustees were the testator and two other persons, but upon the retirement of one of them the testator, in exercise of a power reserved to him by the settlement, appointed two more persons to be trustees. Thus at his death there

---

[23] See *Att.-Gen. of Ceylon* v. *Mackie, supra.*
[24] As defined by F.A. 1940, s. 58 (1); F.A. 1965, s. 88 (5). *Cf.* the provisions relating to " close companies " for income tax and corporation tax purposes, *ante*, Chap. 16.
[25] By F.A. 1940, s. 55.

were four trustees registered as the holders of the 3,650 shares, and as his name appeared first in the register he was under the articles of association of the company entitled to vote in respect of them. He was therefore entitled to vote in respect altogether of shares amounting to more than half the issued share capital of the company.

The question then arose whether the 1,100 shares which passed on his death should be valued for estate duty in accordance with section 7 (5) of the Finance Act 1894, that is, by reference to their market value, or with section 55 (2) of the Finance Act 1940, that is, by reference to the estimated value of the assets of the company. Upon a summons issued for the determination of this question Danckwerts J. decided in favour of the former method, the Court of Appeal of the latter.

... The first question—much discussed, though the answer to it may not be decisive—is whether section 55 (3) is an exhaustive definition of the words occurring in section 55 (1), " control of the company," or is an expansive provision, extending the scope of those words beyond their natural meaning.

... In the present case I agree with Romer L.J. in thinking that the so-called " deeming " provision of subsection (3) is expansive of subsection (1) and that, if a case falls naturally within subsection (1), it is unnecessary to look beyond it.

... As I have said, I doubt whether the answer that is given to this primary question is conclusive of the problem raised in this appeal, but it leads me to examine it upon the footing that I must ask whether the testator, being under the constitution of the company entitled to vote in respect of both the 1,100 and the 3,650 shares, " had the control of the company " within the natural meaning of those words. My Lords, in *B. W. Noble Ltd.* v. *Inland Revenue Commissioners*, the words " controlling interest in the company " occurring in the Finance Act 1920 were said by Rowlatt J.[26] to mean the interest of one " whose shareholding in the company is such that he is the shareholder who is more powerful than all the other shareholders put together in general meeting," in other words, one who can, by his votes, control the company in general meeting. His opinion was approved in later cases in this House, see *British American Tobacco Co. Ltd.* v. *Inland Revenue Commissioners*[27] and *Inland Revenue Commissioners* v. *F. A. Clarke & Son Ltd.*[28] I see no difference between the natural meaning of the two phrases " having a controlling interest in the company " and " having control of the company," though it might be desirable, and in the case of the latter phrase was found to be so, to give an extended meaning to the words. If so, I think that your Lordships should accept the guidance given by this House in *Inland Revenue Commissioners* v. *J. Bibby & Sons Ltd.*[29] That case determined that control must be ascertained by reference to the company's constitution and that it is irrelevant that a shareholder who has the apparent control may himself be amenable to some external control.

... I come to the conclusion, without recourse to the expansive provision of subsection (3), that the testator had control of T. Shipside Ltd. If I found it necessary to look at the later subsection I could not come to a different conclusion. For, unless subsection (3) is to be interpreted as excluding from the category of persons having control a person who obviously has control by virtue of shares standing in his own name, the same result must follow. It is not the necessary or natural consequence of an extended meaning being given to a phrase that it should lose its natural one. . . .

26 (1926) 12 T.C. 911, 926.
27 [1943] A.C. 335.
28 (1942) 29 T.C. 49; *sub nom. British American Tobacco Co. Ltd.* v. *I.R.C.* [1943] A.C. 335.
29 [1945] 1 All E.R. 667.

Note

The principles according to which assets of a company should be valued are considered at length by Ungoed-Thomas J. in *Jones (M.)* v. *Jones (R. R.)* [1971] 1 W.L.R. 840; see also *Re Duffy* [1949] Ch. 28; *Re Sutherland (deceased)* [1963] A.C. 235.

(iii) *Interests in Expectancy*

Where an interest in expectancy passes on the death of the person possessed of such interest it is prima facie dutiable under section 2 (1) (*a*) of the 1894 Act on its value ascertained at that date (by actuarial methods).[30] The person accountable for the duty may, however, elect to defer payment of duty until such time as the interest falls into possession, duty then being payable on the value at the date when the interest " falls in." [31]

FRY v. I.R.C.

Court of Appeal [1959] Ch. 86; [1958] 3 W.L.R. 381; 102 S.J. 617; [1958] 3 All E.R. 90

ROMER L.J.: This appeal raises a somewhat difficult question as to the construction of section 7 (6) of the Finance Act 1894, which deals with the payment of estate duty on interests in expectancy.

. . . The question, then, which falls for decision can be posed as follows. A testator settles a fund on trust for A for life with remainder to B absolutely. B predeceases A and his executors exercise the option conferred by section 7 (6) of the Finance Act 1894 to defer payment of duty on the reversionary interest until the interest falls into possession. A subsequently purchases the interest from B's executors. What duty (if any) falls to be paid by B's executors in consequence of the purchase, when is it payable, and how should it be assessed?

It would seem that there are four possible answers to this question. The official view (which was upheld by the judge's declaration) is that no duty is payable by B's executors until the death of A and that then duty will become payable on the value of the fund as then existing. The alternative official view is that duty becomes payable upon the execution of the sale agreement and that such duty is assessable upon the value of the fund (and not merely on the value of the reversion) at the date of the agreement. The plaintiff contends that duty becomes payable upon the execution of the sale agreement but that such duty is only assessable upon the then value of the reversionary interest. The plaintiff alternatively contends that no duty is payable or ever will become payable at all.

. . . The question, then, before us is free from authority and falls to be determined on the meaning and effect of the language of section 7 (6) of the Act. The subsection is not drafted with strict accuracy on any view of the matter. It speaks of an interest in expectancy falling into possession, whereas such an interest always is in possession from the date when the instrument which creates it takes effect. What does, or may, fall into possession is the property in respect of which the interest in expectancy has been created; and it was presumably in that sense that the legislature referred to the interest itself falling into possession. Apart altogether from this inaccuracy of language the provisions of the subsection are by no means easy to apply to cases where a life tenant sells or voluntarily surrenders his life interest to the remainderman or where, as here, the life tenant purchases the interest of a deceased reversioner;

---

[30] See *I.R.C.* v. *Priestley* [1901] A.C. 208; *post*, p. 528.
[31] F.A. 1894, s. 7 (6); *Re Eyre* [1907] 1 K.B. 331; N.B. Finance (No. 2) Act 1940, s. 17.

and it is, we think, a fair assumption that in fact the draftsman of the subsection had no such possibilities in mind.

. . . It seems to us that on the language of section 7 (6) neither the view of the Inland Revenue Commissioners nor that of the plaintiff can be said to be obviously wrong. The court, then, when faced with two possible constructions of legislative language, is entitled to look at the results of adopting each of the alternatives respectively in its quest for the true intention of Parliament. " In general," said Lord Reid in *Coutts & Co.* v. *Inland Revenue Commissioners*,[32] " if it is alleged that a statutory provision brings about a result which is so startling, one looks for some other possible meaning of the statute which will avoid such a result, because there is some presumption that Parliament does not intend its legislation to produce highly inequitable results."

. . . On that view of the matter the subordinate contention of the plaintiff that no duty is payable at all does not succeed; and beyond observing that it would be somewhat startling if payment of duty could be avoided altogether by the simple expedient of a life tenant purchasing a deceased reversioner's interest in expectancy from executors who had exercised the option conferred by section 7 (6), we need say no more about it.

On the footing, then, that Conrad Fry's interest in expectancy fell into possession when Mrs. Cooke-Hurle agreed to buy it, the next question that arises is as to the assessment of the duty which became payable by his executor, the plaintiff. The Crown contends that duty became payable upon the value of the whole fund. The plaintiff submits that, for purposes of duty, the interest should be taken at its then value as a reversion and that duty is only exigible in respect of that value. It was decided in *Re Eyre*,[33] and is now the established practice, that where under section 7 (6) of the Act an executor of a deceased reversioner has exercised the option thereby given and deferred the payment in respect of the interest in expectancy until that interest has fallen into possession, the amount on which the duty is payable is the value of the interest when it has fallen into possession, and not merely its value on the death of the deceased. The Crown says that the plaintiff cannot have it both ways and that if he succeeds in establishing that Conrad Fry's interest in expectancy fell into possession when Mrs. Cooke-Hurle agreed to buy it then he must take the consequences and one of such consequences is that the principle of *Re Eyre* applies. Mr. Wilberforce submitted that as the parties chose to accelerate the falling into possession of Conrad Fry's interest they must abide by the results and the executor must pay duty on the footing that the whole fund did in fact fall into possession in the hands of Mrs. Cooke-Hurle, as Conrad Fry's assign; and that the assumption that her life interest still continued to exist cannot co-exist with the assumption that the reversionary interest had fallen into her possession. Mr. Stamp, in supporting Mr. Wilberforce's submission, submitted that a vested reversionary interest ripens sooner or later into the right to possession of the property in which the interest has been created, and the reversioner's executor is entitled to postpone payment of duty until he (or his assign) has acquired such possession; that it is irrelevant how possession is acquired or if it is acquired prematurely, for example by surrender of the life tenant's interest; and that in the present case Mrs. Cooke-Hurle, as assign of the reversioner, did get possession of the property, albeit prematurely. The plaintiff, on the other hand, contends that what has to be valued, and that which attracts liability to duty, is the interest in expectancy at the moment of time when it fell into possession. At the life tenant's death, it is said, the value of the reversion is the value of the property itself, for no prior interest stands in its

32 [1953] A.C. 267, 281.
33 [1907] 1 K.B. 331.

way; but that in the present case there were two interests which coalesced in Mrs. Cooke-Hurle's hands, namely, her life interest and the reversionary interest which she bought, and that the value of the property is not solely represented by the interest in expectancy but is the sum of that interest and the life interest. It was submitted that Mrs. Cooke-Hurle has not given up her life interest; that merger is a question of intention and the amount of duty payable could not depend on whether Mrs. Cooke-Hurle did or did not make a declaration against merger when she bought the reversionary interest.

The case for the Crown on this point is certainly not without attraction and makes a logical appeal. Nevertheless, it could lead to unexpected consequences, some of which were pointed out by Mr. Pennycuick. He suggested by way of illustration the case of a young tenant for life of a fund worth £100,000, buying for £10,000 the interest of a deceased reversioner, whose executors had exercised the option conferred by section 7 (6). In such a case the executors, though receiving only £10,000, would be liable to duty on the full value of the fund, namely, £100,000. Mr. Wilberforce's answer to this was that the executors need not enter into such a transaction and must accept the consequences if they do. This is true; but they might find it necessary to sell the reversion and obviously the highest bidder for it would be the life tenant, for he is the only person on whose death no duty would become payable in respect of it. We cannot think that in Mr. Pennycuick's illustration the Crown's claim would be in accord with the intention of section 7 (6) of the Act. It seems to us that such a claim would be wholly inequitable and we would again refer to Lord Reid's observations in *Coutts & Co.* v. *Inland Revenue Commissioners*, already cited. In our opinion that which became subject to duty was that which Mrs. Cooke-Hurle bought, namely, the interest in expectancy; and it would be quite wrong to say that for the purposes of valuing that interest Mrs. Cooke-Hurle's pre-existing right to enjoy the income of the fund for the rest of her life should be disregarded. That which has to be valued, in our judgment, was that which she did not possess before and not the aggregate of that and her own life interest. . . .

CHAPTER 21

EXEMPTIONS AND RELIEFS

A CONSIDERABLE number of exemptions and reliefs apply in a variety of manners to reduce the amount of estate duty which might otherwise be payable. The effect may be to avoid a charge to duty altogether or in part, to reduce the dutiable value of property passing, to relieve certain property from aggregation with the remainder of the property passing, to reduce the rate of duty appropriate to a particular item, or to relieve a person who might otherwise be accountable for duty.

The exemption or relief may apply (a) to certain types of property,[1] (b) to certain transactions,[2] (c) to certain persons or bodies,[3] or (d) to deaths in certain circumstances.[4]

1. Bona Fide Purchase

By virtue of the Finance Act 1894, s. 3, estate duty is not payable in respect of property passing on the death of a deceased by reason only of a bona fide purchase from the person under whose disposition the property passes, where such purchase was made for full consideration in money or money's worth paid to the vendor or grantor for his own use or benefit. Thus, the sole reason for the passing must be the purchase. The consideration must be full consideration in money or money's worth.[5] In the case of a bona fide sale for partial consideration, the value of the consideration is allowed as a deduction from the value of the property.[6]

ATTORNEY-GENERAL v. BODEN

King's Bench Division [1912] 1 K.B. 539; 81 L.J.K.B. 704; 105 L.T. 247

The deceased, H. B., carried on a business in partnership with his two sons, manufacturing lace net. Under the terms of the deed of partnership, the sons

---

[1] *e.g.* to agricultural property, F.A. 1925, s. 23; to industrial hereditaments, F.A. 1954, s. 28; to timber, F.A. 1912, s. 9; or to objects of national, scientific, historic or artistic interest, F.A. 1969, s. 39.

[2] *e.g.* to certain small gifts, Finance (1909–10) Act 1910, s. 59 (2), and F.A. 1949, s. 33; or to gifts forming part of the normal expenditure of the deceased, F.A. 1968, s. 37.

[3] *e.g.* the recipients of otherwise dutiable property, such as charities or surviving spouses, F.A. 1972, s. 121, or the National Trust and certain other public bodies, F.A. 1931, s. 40, and F.A. 1951, s. 33.

[4] *e.g.* deaths on active service, F.A. 1952, s. 71; or deaths in quick succession, F.A. 1958, s. 30.

[5] The consideration may take the form of a family arrangement or the exchange of property: *Lethbridge* v. *Att.-Gen.* [1907] A.C. 19; for work or services: *Att.-Gen.* v. *Boden* [1912] 1 K.B. 539, *infra*; for the surrender of a right or compromise of an action: *Att.-Gen.* v. *Kitchin* [1941] 2 All E.R. 735; or, subject to the provisions of F.A. 1940, s. 55, in return for an annuity: *Att.-Gen.* v. *Sandwich (Earl)* [1922] 2 K.B. 500; *cf. Re Harmsworth, deceased* [1967] Ch. 826; *post*, p. 524. The exemption has no application where property which would otherwise have been dutiable is exchanged for other property: *Att.-Gen.* v. *Smith-Marriott* [1899] 2 Q.B. 595; *Lord Advocate* v. *Lyell*, 1918 S.C. 125; *Att.-Gen.* v. *Gretton and Shrimpton* [1945] 1 All E.R. 628.

[6] F.A. 1894, s. 3 (2); *Re Bateman* [1925] 2 K.B. 429; *post*, p. 527; *cf. Att.-Gen.* v. *Johnson* [1903] 1 K.B. 617; *ante*, p. 471.

were bound to devote so much time and attention to the business as the proper conduct of its affairs required; their father was not so bound. It was further provided that, in the event of the father's death, his share of the assets of the firm was to be sold to the sons, but that his share of the goodwill should pass to them in equal shares without payment. *Held*, the share of goodwill passed by reason only of a bona fide purchase for full consideration in money's worth.

HAMILTON J.: . . . That brings me to the third and last point. The defendants contended, under section 3 of the Act, that the property within the meaning of section 2, which passed on the death of the deceased, passed only by reason of a bona fide purchase by the defendants from their father for full consideration in money or money's worth. Whether the consideration for this property was full or not is a question of fact. . . . Furthermore, the question whether full consideration was given or not may no doubt be solved by putting a value on the property which passed on the one side, and weighing against it the money value of the obligations assumed on the other; but that is not the only method of solving the question. Another method is by looking at the nature of the transaction and considering whether what is given is a fair equivalent for what is received; and that is the way in which the question should be approached in this case.

. . . I am satisfied that the purchase contained in the partnership articles of 1907 was perfectly bona fide. The real character of this transaction, rather than its good faith, has been impugned. Henry Boden having declared that on his death his share in the business was to be sold to his sons, but that they were not to pay anything for goodwill, it is said that as to the goodwill, this transaction was not a sale but a gift. I do not agree. . . . Mr. Danckwerts argued that on proof of intention to give, or of the fact of giving, full consideration, the matter was concluded, as it was not the design of the Legislature to reopen in the light of after events dealings which the parties at the time regarded as purely commercial. That contention is not wholly sound. The fact that the parties to the transaction, knowing more of the business than anybody else, always believed and believe now that they respectively gave and received full consideration is strong evidence that they did so in fact. But the Act does not say that estate duty shall not be payable by reason only of a bona fide purchase " intended " or " believed to be for full consideration paid by the vendor "; it says simply " for full consideration paid by the vendor." It was agreed on both sides that, for the purpose of measuring whether full consideration was paid or not, one must look at the state of affairs at the time of the contract. The mutual promises themselves, not their result or realisation, form the subject-matter of the inquiry.

. . . Looking at the substance of this transaction as well as at the form I think that it was a sale and purchase to take effect upon the death of the senior partner. The contract was one and indivisible; its terms are not to be examined each by itself alone, but the combined effect of all must be regarded. Looked at as a whole and also in each of its stipulations, it may fairly be considered as merely a partnership deed regulating the contractual relations between the parties and not as in part a settlement making provision for children. The blood-relationship may be eliminated from the case. If Henry Boden had died or had been paid out and Walter Boden had been party to the deed of 1907 instead, it would in my opinion have been a very reasonable and natural bargain for him to have made. As the matter stood Henry Boden might have lived for twenty years after the execution of the deed; during that time he would not be bound to give more time or attention to the business than he chose, whereas both his sons, one at Chard and one at Derby, were bound to give all the time and attention to it that the proper conduct of the business required, and in addition they were not to carry on or engage in any other business whatsoever. The shares in the profits were just and fair shares, taking into account the burdens which Henry Boden took upon himself with regard to the employees Richardson and Nelson. . . . Having regard to the facts, first, that the partnership was to last as long as Henry Boden lived, whether he was compos mentis or not—if any two of the partners should so long live, and for the further period of two years after his death if the two sons survived him; secondly, that he was to have his capital employed as long as he lived in this lucrative business, where the profits were earned by the efforts of his two sons, he not being bound to give any more attention to the business than he chose, while he had the absolute control and right of final decision in case there was any difference of opinion among the partners as to its management; and thirdly, that the goodwill, of which they thought little, was to pass with the rest of the corpus of his interest to them on payment of a price which was liberal to himself, I think that Henry Boden and his sons were justified in believing, as I am satisfied they did believe, that full consideration was being given, in the shape of their covenants to serve and their other covenants, for any property which accrued to them on his death otherwise than by payment in cash. In my opinion therefore the defendants have made out their defence under section 3 of the Act. The property in question passed by reason only of this purchase which was a bona fide purchase for full consideration in money or money's worth, money for the tangible assets and money's worth for the goodwill, paid to the vendor for his own use or benefit and in fact enjoyed by him in his lifetime. . . .

Re HARMSWORTH (DECD.)

Court of Appeal [1967] Ch. 826; [1967] 3 W.L.R. 152; 111 S.J. 236; [1967] 2 All E.R. 249; [1967] T.R. 87

LORD DENNING M.R.: Sir Leicester Harmsworth was a man of means. His wife, Lady Harmsworth, had considerable investments of her own. A year or two before his death he made a will in which he made some specific bequests, but he left his residuary estate to his five children and their families. One of the specific bequests was this: he left his wife an annuity of £5,000 a year for her life. But he imposed a condition on this bequest. In order to get the annuity, she had to tie up one-half of her own investments. This has been called the " moiety fund." She was to receive the income from this moiety fund during her life, but she was to leave the capital of the fund by her will to her husband's residuary legatees, i.e. to their five children and their families.

The bequest was in these terms:

" I bequeath to my wife during her widowhood a conditional annuity of £5,000 and I direct that the same shall be paid upon the following terms: The bequest shall be conditional upon my said wife within a period of three months of my death agreeing to hold one moiety of the real property and income-producing investments to which she may be entitled at the time of my death, upon trust to retain the same and the income thereof for her use during her life and subject thereto to devise and bequeath the said moiety to the trustees of her will to be held by such trustees upon the same trusts as those of my residuary estate."

Sir Leicester Harmsworth died on January 19, 1937. Within the three months Lady Harmsworth accepted the condition. On April 7, 1937, her solicitors wrote to the executors of Sir Leicester's will and to the trustees of the will and their solicitors saying that she accepted the conditional annuity of £5,000 on the terms laid down in his will.

Lady Harmsworth lived on for nearly 27 years. She died on December 1, 1963. All that time she received the annuity of £5,000 from her husband's estate. She also did her part. She set aside one-half of her investments. That half was valued in 1937 at £44,310 2s. 11d. It was kept as a separate fund. She received the income from it during her life: and by her will she left it, as she was bound to do, to her husband's residuary legatees, i.e. to their five children and their families.

At her death in 1963 the moiety fund had increased in value to £186,030 19s. The Revenue claimed estate duty on it on the ground that the moiety fund passed on her death. Prima facie the moiety fund did pass under section 2 (1) (b) of the Finance Act 1894. The moiety fund was property which the deceased, Lady Harmsworth, had a life interest ceasing on her death. The whole benefit accrued to the residuary legatees. So, prima facie, estate duty was payable on the whole. The duty came to £102,316 17s. 8d. Her personal representatives paid it. But they now say that no estate duty was payable on it and claim that it should be returned. They base their case on section 3 of the Finance Act 1894, which says:

"Estate duty shall not be payable in respect of property passing on the death of the deceased by reason only of a bona fide purchase from the person under whose disposition the property passes . . . where such purchase was made . . . for full consideration in money or money's worth paid to the vendor . . . for his own use or benefit."

In order to understand this section, I will take two illustrations: The first is where a young man agrees to pay an old man an annuity for life on the terms that the old man will leave the young man his house in his will. In that case, on the old man's death, estate duty would, prima facie, be payable on the house under section 2 (1) (a): but under section 3 it is not payable because the young man had purchased the house for its full value by paying the annuity. It would be unjust that he should have to pay estate duty on a house for which he had already given full value: see Attorney-General v. Dobree,[7] per Darling J.

The other instance is the converse case: when a man buys a life interest in a house for full value on the terms that it is to revert to the seller after his death, that would, prima facie, be caught by section 2 (1) (b): but it is exempt by section 3 as the purchase was for full value: cf. Attorney-General v. Sandwich (Earl of).[8]

In the present case " the property passing on the death of the deceased " was the moiety fund. It passed on the death of Lady Harmsworth from her to her husband's residuary legatees. Under whose " disposition " did that property pass? At first sight one might think it passed under the disposition which Lady Harmsworth made by her will in 1963. But that is not correct. She had bound herself as long ago as 1937 to dispose of the moiety fund to her husband's residuary legatees. As soon as she agreed on April 7, 1937, to the condition attached to the bequest, she became under a trust to hold the moiety fund as trustee for herself for life with an obligation to leave it to the residuary legatees after her death. The " disposition " was her acceptance on April 7, 1937, of the bequest. By that acceptance she disposed of her reversionary interest in return for an annuity. The annuity was " full consideration in money or money's worth." That is admitted. The only question is: Was there a " purchase " from her?

. . . It is obvious that " purchase " is not used in section 3 in any technical sense, because it covers the case where the consideration is not in money but in money's worth. I think that in this section " bona fide purchase for money or

7 [1900] 1 Q.B. 442, 450; post, p. 526.
8 [1922] 2 K.B. 500.

money's worth " means a " bona fide acquisition in return for a fair equivalent in money or money's worth." So interpreted, the reversionary interest in the moiety fund here was acquired by reason of a bona fide *purchase* by Sir Leicester (through his executors) from Lady Harmsworth. It was acquired in return for the annuity. The property in it passed on her death by reason *only* of that purchase, seeing that but for that purchase it would probably not have passed at all, because if she had not sold the moiety fund in return for the annuity, she might have disposed of the moiety fund elsewhere long before her death.

If the matter had stopped there, there would have been no estate duty payable on the moiety fund. But now comes the second point. Lady Harmsworth made this disposition in favour of her relatives as well as his (being their own five children and their families). Dispositions in favour of relatives are caught by special statutory provisions.

By section 44 of the Finance Act 1940, as originally enacted in 1940 (omitting immaterial words):

" Where a [deceased] person has made a disposition in favour of a relative of his, the creation in favour of the deceased of an annuity shall not be treated for the purposes of section 3 of the Finance Act 1894 as consideration for the disposition made by the deceased."

If that section had remained unamended, it would have fitted this case exactly. Lady Harmsworth made the disposition of the moiety fund in favour of her relatives. She received the annuity in exchange for it. That is not to be treated as consideration for the purpose of section 3. So section 3 would be of no avail. Estate duty would be payable.

But section 44 was amended by section 46 of the Finance Act 1950. This amendment was provoked by the decision of Danckwerts J. in *Re Fitzwilliam's (Earl) Agreement*; *Peacock* v. *Inland Revenue Commissioners*.[9] ... section (1A) shows that the annuity is not to be regarded as consideration; and section 1 shows that the disposition by Lady Harmsworth is to be treated for the purposes of section 2 (1) (*c*) of the Act of 1894 as a " gift."

... Applying [the words of section 11 of the Customs and Inland Revenue Act 1889], the " property " was the reversionary interest in the moiety fund. The " gift " was the disposition on April 7, 1937. The " donor " was Lady Harmsworth. The " donees " were the executors and trustees of Sir Leicester's will on behalf of the residuary legatees. The property is, therefore, under section 2 (1) (*c*) liable to estate duty unless the donees immediately on April 7, 1937, assumed bona fide possession and enjoyment of the reversionary interest and thenceforward retained it to the entire exclusion of Lady Harmsworth or of any benefit to her by contract or otherwise.

Now it is plain that the donees did not assume possession or enjoyment on April 7, 1937. No one did. For the simple reason that it was a reversionary interest, which did not become an interest in possession until Lady Harmsworth died.[10] ...

ATTORNEY-GENERAL v. DOBREE

Queen's Bench Division [1900] 1 Q.B. 442; 69 L.J.Q.B. 223; 81 L.T. 607; 64 J.P. 24; 48 W.R. 413; 16 T.L.R. 80; 44 S.J. 103

Shortly before his marriage the deceased effected a policy of insurance on his life, expressed to be payable to his intended wife. The policy was assigned to

---

[9] [1950] Ch. 448; *ante*, p. 470.
[10] Additionally, Lady Harmsworth was not excluded from benefit.

Trustees of a settlement made in consideration of the marriage. *Held*, the policy was not exempted by virtue of the Finance Act 1894, s. 3. ....

DARLING J.: ... I do not think that provision applies. It seems to me to be aimed at something entirely different from what has happened here. I think it is aimed at the kind of case where a person has bought something and paid for it a price—" a consideration in money or money's worth "—but is not to get the benefit of his purchase until the death of his vendor. It is clear, then, that he gets no immediate benefit at all; he has bought and paid for something the delivery of which to him is postponed. In such a case the Legislature has recognised that it would be unjust to make him pay duty upon the death of his vendor when he has paid the full value of the interest to the vendor—it may be years and years ago. I do not think that section 3 was intended to include such a transaction as the one before us. ....

Re BARONESS BATEMAN

King's Bench Division [1925] 2 K.B. 429; 95 L.J.K.B. 199; 134 L.T. 153

In consideration of the sum of £5,100 paid to her by her son, the deceased conveyed certain furniture upon trust for herself for life with remainder to the son absolutely. On her death some years later the furniture was worth £45,000. *Held*, the transaction was a bona fide purchase by the son for partial consideration. A proportion of the property passing was accordingly exempt from duty.

ROWLATT J.: ... In the present case the mother was in want of money, and she obtained it by a simple sale of her furniture subject to her life interest. The sum paid, whether it was the full amount which would have been obtained for it or not, was certainly not so inadequate as to be an unreality. I think therefore that this was a bona fide sale and purchase by the son, and that no succession duty is payable.

The next question is whether the matter comes within the Finance Act, s. 3, subs. (2). In *Re Lombard*[11] it was held that " partial " consideration as used in these subsections does not necessarily mean " consideration " in money, but applies to cases in which the consideration varies in kind and includes such considerations as marriage. It seems to me that having regard to *Brown* v. *Attorney-General*[12] and other cases to which I have been referred it is difficult to follow *Lombard's* case. I cannot treat a marriage settlement as consideration for purchase within the meaning of the Finance Act, s. 3.[13] " Partial " consideration is opposed to " full " consideration in money or money's worth, which means that the full fair price has been paid and that nothing is left over for gift or natural love and affection or any other consideration. In other words it is the full and fair value as between buyer and seller, while partial consideration means something less than that. ... The object of section 3, subsection (2), is to see how much of this property is passing by way of bounty and how much by way of purchase. That can only be done by ascertaining what proportion of the property was the subject of purchase and what proportion is represented by gift. Under that interpretation the words " the value of the consideration " mean " the value which corresponds to the consideration," that is to say, the value in the article partially bought which was bought by the consideration. In

11 [1904] 2 I.R. 621.
12 (1898) 79 L.T. 572.
13 See *Att.-Gen.* v. *Dobree* [1900] 1 Q.B. 442; *ante,* p. 526.

other words, this proportion can be allowed as a deduction from the value of the property. . . .

Note

The consideration paid by the son was held to represent four-fifths of the value of the property at the time of the purchase.

2. Settled Property

Certain provisions apply specifically to settled property.[14] Of particular importance are the exemptions in favour of a surviving spouse and on the reverter of settled property to the disponer.

(i) *The Surviving Spouse Exemption*

If estate duty has already been paid in respect of any settled property since the date of the settlement upon the death of one person, duty is not payable in respect of the death during the continuance of the settlement of any former spouse of that person, unless the latter person was at death or at any time during the continuance of the settlement competent to dispose of the settled property.[15]

Duty must have been payable on the first death. Where part only of the settled property was dutiable on the first death, that part only is exempt from duty on the death of the surviving spouse.[16]

I.R.C. v. PRIESTLEY

House of Lords [1901] A.C. 208; 70 L.J.P.C. 41; 84 L.T. 700; 49 W.R. 657; 17 T.L.R. 507

LORD MACNAGHTEN : . . . On the marriage of Mr. and Mrs. Studdert a deed was executed for the purpose of regulating the enjoyment and disposition of certain funds which formed part of the lady's fortune. The deed was a " settlement "; the funds became " settled properly " within the definition of those expressions in the Act. The settled property was limited to the husband for life with remainder to the wife for life, and subject thereto, in the events which happened, the property was at the absolute disposal of the wife. The wife died in the lifetime of her husband. . . . But under section 2 (a), taken in conjunction with section 1, estate duty became leviable in respect of the settled property as being property of which, at the time of her death, Mrs. Studdert was competent to dispose. And so the Commissioners claimed estate duty in respect of the settled property on Mrs. Studdert's death, as they were entitled and bound to do. It was then in the option of the persons accountable for the duty either to defer payment until the interest in expectancy at the time of Mrs. Studdert's death fell into possession, or to pay at once under discount. The latter alternative was the one adopted. The principal value of the settled

---

[14] *e.g.* F.A. 1894, s. 16 (3), as to exemption of certain estates from aggregation with settled property.

[15] F.A. 1894, s. 5 (2), as limited by Finance (1909–10) Act 1910, s. 55, F.A. 1914, s. 14, and F.A. 1954, s. 32. See also F.A. 1969, Sched. 17, Pt. II, para. 6. On the question of competence to dispose, see also *ante*, pp. 464–467.

[16] *I.R.C.* v. *Coutts & Co.* [1964] A.C. 1393; *post*, p. 529; and see F.A. 1969, Sched. 17, Pt. II, para. 6.

property was estimated (as the Act directs) at the price which, in the opinion of the Commissioners, the property would have fetched if sold in the open market at the time of the death of Mrs. Studdert. The Commissioners seem to have arrived at their estimate in the ordinary way in which buyers of such property in the market make their calculations, by taking the market value of the securities forming the settled property as at the time of Mrs. Studdert's death, and then making an abatement or allowance in respect of Mr. Studdert's life interest, reckoning the probability of life according to the accepted tables of mortality.

... Shortly after his wife's death Mr. Studdert died. And the Commissioners now claim estate duty once more in respect of the principal value of the settled property. Are they entitled to payment of duty over again? In my opinion, most clearly and certainly not. Since the date of the settlement, estate duty has been paid in respect of the settled property, and therefore, under the express provisions of section 5, subsection (2), estate duty is not payable again on Mr. Studdert's death. He was not at the time of his death, nor had he been at any time during the continuance of the settlement, competent to dispose of the settled property. So the one and only event which could have entitled the Commissioners to estate duty on Mr. Studdert's death has not occurred.

The only difficulty about the case, in my opinion, has arisen from the circumstance that for some reason which at present I do not understand, and for which I have not at present been able to discover any authority in the Act, the respondents offered to pay, and the Commissioners seem to be prepared to accept, a sum as and by way of estate duty on the amount which the Commissioners in their own minds allowed as a deduction from the full value of the settled property at Mrs. Studdert's death, in respect of her husband's life interest. . . .

Note
The last paragraph of the judgment refers to the fact that, as on Mrs. Studdert's death duty was paid not on the entire settled property but only on the then value of her interest in expectancy, duty was charged on the portion which had not previously borne duty when her husband died, see *I.R.C.* v. *Coutts & Co.*, *infra*.

I.R.C. v. COUTTS & CO.

House of Lords [1964] A.C. 1393; [1963] 2 W.L.R. 1407; [1963] 2 All E.R. 722; [1963] T.R. 173; *sub nom. Coutts & Co.* v. *I.R.C.*, 107 S.J. 592

In 1914 a settlement was made on a husband and wife, providing for a yearly rentcharge in favour of the wife and, subject thereto, for the husband for life, the wife for life, with remainder to the children, etc. The husband died in 1916 and estate duty was paid on the whole of the settled fund less the " slice " referable to the wife's rentcharge. The wife subsequently remarried, resettled her interest in the settled property and died many years later. *Held*, on her death duty was payable only on so much of the settled property as represented her yearly rentcharge, the remainder being exempted by virtue of Finance Act 1894, s. 5 (2).

LORD REID: . . . The appellants say that the exemption can only have been intended to apply to devolutions under the settlement itself and cannot have been intended to apply when an interest in the settled property passes under a disposition by the owner of that interest. I have been unable to discover any particular reason for that limitation of the scope of the subsection. If it applies at all when only an interest in the settled property passes and the settled property itself does not pass, then I think it must apply generally. So the question must be whether it ever applies when only an interest passes and the settled property itself does not pass. If the estate duty has been paid in respect of the whole property and there is to be any subsequent exemption at all it would seem quite irrational that the exemption should apply to the larger claim for duty when the whole property passes but not to the smaller claim when something less than the whole property passes.

. . . Section 5 (2) cannot apply unless estate duty " has already been paid in respect of " the settled property. In *Priestley's* case [17] the whole interest in the settled property did not pass on the wife's death. Her interest was an indefeasible interest but nevertheless an interest in expectancy because her husband's life-interest was unaffected by her death and did not pass on her death. And the duty paid on her death was not calculated on the principal value of the settled property but on the principal value less the value of the surviving husband's life-interest. So the decision necessarily involved a decision in law that a payment of duty in respect of something less than the whole interest in the settled property and based on something less than the principal value of the property can nevertheless be a payment of duty in respect of the settled property within the meaning of section 5 (2).

. . . The only distinction that I can see between *Priestley's* case and the present case is this. In *Priestley's* case payment of duty in respect of less than the whole interest in the settled property was effective to exempt from a later claim for duty in respect of passing of the whole property. In this case the question is whether payment of duty in respect of the whole of the settled property on Captain Stanhope's death is effective to exempt from a later claim in respect of the passing of less than the whole—a defeasible interest. If payment on the passing of less than the whole exempts from a later claim on the passing of the whole, I can see no possible ground on which it could be held that payment in respect of the whole does not exempt from a later claim in respect of the passing of less than the whole. . . .

Note
   See now F.A. 1969, Sched. 17, Pt. II, para. 6. And see *In re Hall* [1942] Ch. 140.

Re PARSONS

Court of Appeal [1943] Ch. 12; 112 L.J.Ch. 65; 167 L.T. 384; 59 T.L.R. 19; 86 S.J. 359;
[1942] 2 All E.R. 496

   Under his wife's will a widower received a legacy of certain stock, together with a life interest in the residue. Shortly after her death he formally disclaimed the legacy by a deed of disclaimer. On his subsequent death, duty was held to be payable in respect of the stock as he had been, between the date of his wife's death and that of the disclaimer, competent to dispose of the legacy.

   LORD GREENE M.R.: Two arguments have been advanced by Mr. Nesbitt on behalf of the trustees of the will. The first turns entirely on the words " competent to dispose " in section 5, subsection (2), of the Finance Act 1894. It is said that the competence of the husband in relation to the £10,000 consols ceased on the disclaimer. No criticism can be made of that. It is also conceded that between the dates of the death of the testatrix and disclaimer some interval of time passed during which the husband had not yet decided to disclaim, and

[17] [1901] A.C. 208; *ante*, p. 528.

that during that period he was competent to acquire the right to dispose of the consols, but it is said that he never in fact acquired the right because he disclaimed the legacy. The argument then proceeds on the basis that on the true construction of the subsection a legatee who is competent to acquire the right to his legacy, that is, who is competent to take it if he decides not to disclaim, is not competent to dispose of the subject-matter of the legacy within the meaning of the subsection.

In my opinion, that argument cannot prevail. The phrase " competent to dispose " is not a phrase of art, and, taken by itself and quite apart from the definition clause in the Act, it conveys to my mind the ability to dispose, including, of course, the ability to make a thing your own. From the moment of the testatrix's death the husband was able to make the legacy his own. In fact, if he had died without doing anything, his executors would have been entitled to the legacy merely because he had not disclaimed it. During the period between the death of the testatrix and the disclaimer he was unquestionably " competent to dispose " within the meaning of those words in the subsection, which, I think, are wide and, in a sense, popular in meaning.

... In my opinion, the judgment of the learned judge on that argument was right, but there was a second argument which is not dealt with by the learned judge, although it was mentioned before him. It was that a competence to dispose of the property must be shown to have existed during the continuance of a settlement which comprised the property in question. It was argued that it was only by virtue of the disclaimer that the consols became settled property, and, therefore, that the husband was not competent to dispose of that settled property during the continuance of the settlement, it being one and the same act which brought the property into the settlement and terminated the husband's competence to dispose of it. In my judgment, that argument also fails. The settlement was the will and the property comprised in it was the residue of the testatrix, whatever that might turn out to be. Looking at the situation at the moment after death, it was obviously impossible to say what would be included in the residue. It was impossible at that date to say specifically that this sum of consols would ultimately be included in the residue after the estate was clear and the legatee had made up his mind. Nevertheless, it seems to me that the residue, whatever it might turn out to be, was settled by the will, and the date of that settlement was the day of the death of the testatrix. . . .

(ii) The " Reverter to Disponer " Exemption

Where, by a disposition of any property, an interest is conferred on any person other than the disponer for the life of such person or determinable on his death, and such person enters into possession of the interest and thenceforward retains possession thereof to the entire exclusion of the disponer or of any benefit to him by contract or otherwise, and the only benefit which the disponer retains in the property is subject to that interest and no other interest is created by the disposition, the interest is deemed not to pass on the death of such person if it reverts to the disponer during his lifetime.[18]

ATTORNEY-GENERAL v. PENRHYN

Queen's Bench Division (1900) 83 L.T. 103; 64 J.P. 552; 16 T.L.R. 464; 44 S.J. 574

By a settlement made on the occasion of her marriage, the settlor conveyed property to trustees upon trust to pay her an annuity of £100 and subject thereto

18 F.A. 1896, s. 15; F.A. 1969, Sched. 17, Pt. III, para. 5.

for her husband for life, remainder to the survivor of them for life, and then for their children, with an ultimate remainder to the settlor. The husband died during the lifetime of the settlor. *Held*, the " reverter to disponer " exemption did not apply.

GRANTHAM J.: . . . I cannot help saying in the first place that it does seem to me as if the case that we have to determine must have been one—or ought to have been one—that the framers of this Act of 1896 had in view when this exception was passed, but I have a difficulty in saying that it is one that was exempted by the particular section of the Act of Parliament.

. . . and the case that was suggested (I think by the Attorney-General) was that of a person who for the benefit of an old servant (or for the benefit of any-one else) gave a life interest in some property, with the natural intention that that life interest should be for the benefit simply of the life of the person for whom it is given, and with the direct intention that on that person's death the property should fall into the residue of his estate, just as it was before. It would have been very hard indeed that upon the death of the tenant for life, the person who out of his generosity had provided for the comfort of the old servant should have to pay duty on that reverting to him; and that seems to me to have been the only object the Legislature had in view in framing this section. It may be said that it is very hard that they did not increase the extent of the exception, and I think that perhaps it is so; but what we have to determine is whether they did in fact extend it. . . . But interpreting the section by the natural meaning of the words used it does seem to me that in this case—where she reserves to herself as a first charge on this estate £100 a year—(supposing that the husband's property is not sufficient to provide it) it cannot be said that " the only benefit which the disponer retains in the said property is subject to such life interest," because that £100 a year was not subject to such life interest; it was a first charge; therefore, I think it is not within the exception. Of course a great deal has been said already by Mr. Haldane against that; but on the whole, I think that as this £100 a year was a first charge, it cannot be said that the only benefit was subject to the life interest, because that £100 a year which was to come to her was not subject to it at all, but was to be paid to her before the husband could have anything. Now then, there is one more difficulty, that is, where it is said by those who appear on behalf of the trustees, that no other interest is created by the said disposition, because on the death of Mr. Vaughan there were no children. . . . By that deed there was another interest created besides Mr. Vaughan's life interest—namely, there was an interest for Mrs. Vaughan's life on that £100 a year. But not only was that interest created by the deed, but the purport of the deed was that the children of the marriage were to be affected by that deed. She divested herself of all interest after the death of her husband except her life interest, and then the property was to be divided into certain shares amongst the children. It is quite true that she also provided that if there were no children the property then was to go according to her will or whatever may be the language used by the settlement—I forget the exact expression—but I think it was to be subject to her will or her disposition. But how can it be said that at the time the settlement was made there was no interest created when the most important interests were interests that were provided for the children attaining twenty-one or on marrying? For those reasons it seems to me that we are not at liberty to go outside the special wording of this section, which was a section passed expressly to relieve people under certain conditions. We have no right to bring other people within these conditions who are clearly not within them. . . .

Note
The fact that the settlor and her husband had no children did not prevent it being held that some other interest (in the children's favour) had been created by the disposition.

3. Gifts

A number of exemptions and reliefs apply to gifts.[19] An important exemption, though its scope has been restricted in recent years, is that in favour of gifts made in consideration of marriage.[20]

I.R.C. v. RENNELL

House of Lords [1964] A.C. 173; [1963] 2 W.L.R. 745; 107 S.J. 232; [1963] 1 All E.R. 803; [1963] T.R. 73

VISCOUNT RADCLIFFE (dissenting): . . . I turn now to the facts of this case. Mr. Augustine Courtauld (whom I will refer to as "the deceased") died on March 3, 1959. Less than three years before his death, on March 20, 1956, he had made a settlement under which he transferred investments of very considerable value to the respondents, who were to hold them on the trusts declared by the settlement. The occasion of the making of the settlement was the forthcoming marriage between his daughter Perina and a Mr. Fordham, which marriage took place on April 14, 1956. Both parties to the marriage were parties to the settlement and the deed recited in the form usual in a marriage settlement that a marriage was intended shortly to be solemnised between them and that " upon the treaty for the said intended marriage it was agreed that " Mr. Fordham should settle certain personal estate belonging to him, the settlement to be effected by a separate deed of even date, and that the deceased should make such a settlement as was thereinafter contained.

The terms of the settlement that followed are, however, less easily described as those usual to the conventional marriage settlement. To state them briefly, since nothing turns upon the details, there was created a class of beneficiaries defined as including Mrs. Fordham, her issue and all other issue of the deceased, children or more remote, present or future (he had five other children), Mr. Fordham and every other person, now alive or coming into existence in the future, who should at any time have intermarried with any of the issue before mentioned. For this class of beneficiaries the trustees were directed to hold the capital and income of the trust fund upon trust at their absolute discretion to make such appointments, revocable or irrevocable, for the benefit of any one or more exclusively of the others or other as they should decide: and, subject to and in default of such appointments, the income of the trust fund was to be distributed among the beneficiaries or any one or more of them exclusively of the others or other as the trustees in their discretion should decide, and so that no payment or application made by them was to confer any right to any future income. These trusts were to come to an end, subject to any outright appointments made by the trustees, at the close of a period limited by various contingencies, of which the arrival of January 1, 2006, is the simplest to mention, and at the end of that period the trust fund, subject as above, was to belong to the issue then living of the deceased, to be divided per stirpes. I ought to mention

---

[19] *e.g.* small gifts, Finance (1909–10) Act 1910, s. 59 (2); F.A. 1949, s. 33; gifts forming part of the normal expenditure of the deceased, F.A. 1968, s. 37; gifts to certain public bodies, F.A. 1931, s. 40; F.A. 1951, s. 33. Relief also applies in the case of gifts made more than four years but less than seven years before the death of the deceased, F.A. 1960, s. 64; F.A. 1968, s. 35.

[20] Finance (1909–10) Act 1910, s. 59 (2); F.A. 1963, s. 53 (1); F.A. 1968, s. 36.

that, subject to all the foregoing trusts and powers, there was an ultimate trust for Mrs. Fordham and her personal representatives.

There is no difficulty in stating what the deceased had achieved by this disposition. He had transferred a considerable fortune from his own resources to the ownership of the trustees selected by him to be held and applied by them for the benefit of his family in general, a phrase that includes all his children, all their descendants and their future husbands and wives; and the allocation of it between those persons or lines of descent was entirely at the mercy of the trustees, present or future. The occasion of his doing so was the marriage of his eldest daughter, Mrs. Fordham, and by what he had done he had certainly made available a fund which could be used to support or provide for her and her family. But that is all: he had secured nothing for her or her family. He had made a family settlement; but I think that it would be a misuse of any conventional words known to lawyers to say that the terms of the trust that he had created amounted to those of a marriage settlement.

I do not myself think that the question whether this divesting of assets was a gift made in consideration of marriage depends upon what was contemplated or intended by the settlor at the time of the divesting. In my opinion, if settlement rather than outright donation is involved, the answer is provided by the test whether the terms of the settlement amount to a secured provision for the marriage and any resulting family. To try each case by a post-obit inquiry into the supposed contemplations or intentions of the deceased is to apply a criterion that is at once improbable and unsatisfactory. But since Buckley J. at any rate seems to have guided himself to some extent by what he supposed the deceased to have contemplated, and since the argument for the respondents in this House was based on the proposition that every gift must be treated as made in consideration of marriage if it was (1) made on the occasion of marriage, (2) contingent on the marriage taking effect and (3) made by the donor for the purpose of or with a view to encouraging or facilitating the marriage, I will note briefly what the evidence reveals as to the intentions or contemplations of the deceased.

His daughter's engagement to Mr. Fordham preceded in date any proposal of his to make provision for her. On October 14, 1955, he wrote to his solicitor, Sir Leslie Farrer, " It seems that Perina has got engaged to be married. Ought I to do anything about it? Marriage settlement or anything? " On November 29, he had a meeting with Sir Leslie and Lord Rennell, at which, as Sir Leslie states in his affidavit, the deceased formed or expressed the wish to " make provision for Mr. and Mrs. Fordham and their issue as well as for his other descendants and their spouses, and to do so in consideration of the intended marriage, so as if possible to avert any risk of estate duty in respect of the settled funds." No stipulations as to the intended provision were made by the deceased's daughter or by Mr. Fordham or his family. There was no bargaining or any thought of it. The scheme adopted, by which I mean no more than the form and terms of the settlement to be made, originated with Sir Leslie and he gave the deceased to understand that if he did decide to make a settlement in this form, " it would or could possibly result in the avoidance of substantial estate duty on the whole fund." As the deceased wrote to Sir Leslie on the next day (November 30) " I think your scheme seems excellent and I should like to go ahead with it."

There is nothing whatsoever in this arrangement that invites criticism. It was straightforward and above-board and there is nothing colourable about it, as was at one time suggested. If Sir Leslie was right in what he thought would or could be the legal consequence of the proposed settlement, there would be a big saving of estate duty in the event of the deceased dying within the statutory period and he would have passed over part of his fortune to the possible benefit of numerous members of his family, quite apart from the Fordham branch, irrespective of the occasion or contingency of their marriage. But the question for a court of law is simply that of deciding whether a gift provided in the form of a settlement of this kind does properly come within the terms of the legal exemption as being " made in consideration of marriage " and I cannot for my part see how the answer to this question is assisted by investigating the hopes or expectations of the deceased man.

What, then, is the meaning of the phrase " gift which is made in consideration of marriage " as used in the Finance (1909–1910) Act 1910?

. . . I do not think, therefore, that a gift can be accepted as having been made in consideration of marriage merely because the making of it was part of the property arrangements occasioned by a marriage and, if you please, the marriage took place with the knowledge of the parties that these arrangements had been or were going to be carried out. In my view, the words themselves require that the recipient, by which I mean the beneficiary, of the gift should be one or more of those persons who are, to use the old phrase, " within the marriage consideration."

. . . My understanding of the matter is, therefore, that a gift made in consideration of marriage is a transfer made on the occasion of marriage, contingently on the marriage taking place, and containing such limitations, if made by way of settlement, as amount to the customary provision for the spouses and the issue of the marriage. No doubt a settlement that contained ultimate trusts for other persons to take effect subject to the interests of the family, if they failed, would be within the category: so, I should suppose, would be one in which a man bringing property into settlement reserves a limited power to withdraw a proportion of it to provide for issue of a later marriage. But I do not think that the words are satisfied unless the terms of the settlement are such that they unequivocally secure provision for the spouses and their issue and by so doing declare that the marriage is the consideration upon which the transfer is to be rested.

Tried in this way the settlement made by the deceased does not seem to me to satisfy the description.

. . . I must, however, make plain that I do not regard this as an interpretation which either limits or narrows the meaning of the words " gifts made in consideration of marriage." These are words of description not of definition. There is no more reason why the description should be said to include the idea that the gift must be made " for the purpose of or with a view to encouraging or facilitating the marriage," a condition which, I gather, commends itself to the majority of your Lordships, than that it should include the idea that the gift should unequivocally secure provision for the spouses and their issue. It is merely that, as I think, the latter description accords better with the words used by the legislature as understood by lawyers. . . .

LORD JENKINS: . . . I would, however, record my general agreement with the views of Buckley J. as expressed in the following passages from his judgment:

" A gift can, in my judgment, be made in consideration of marriage that is made to someone who is not a party to the marriage or issue of the marriage. I put to counsel in the course of the argument the example of a supposed case in which the father of a girl says to his prospective son-in-law ' If you marry my daughter, I will make some provision for your parents,' which it seems to me might well be quite a realistic example to suppose. It might be quite sensible for the prospective father-in-law to relieve his prospective son-in-law of the burden (to some extent) of maintaining his parents. Such a gift would, in my judgment, be a gift made in consideration of marriage notwithstanding that the persons who would benefit from the gift would not be parties to the marriage or issue of the marriage. . . . There seem to me in this case to be really only two alternatives open to me: either to reach the conclusion that this settlement was genuinely executed in consideration of the marriage or that the marriage consideration which purports to support it is wholly colourable. There might, I think, in other cases be a third choice open, coming to the conclusion that the document really contains more than one transaction and that the transactions can be severed and that the marriage consideration ought properly to be related to only one or some of the severed transactions. But having regard to the way in which these trusts are framed and to the fact that the interests of the beneficiaries who are parties to the marriage or issue of the marriage and those who are strangers to the marriage are inextricably interwoven and could not be given effect to without regard to each other, it seems to me to be quite impossible to sever any part of this trust from another and say: 'The marriage consideration relates to that part but not to the other.' Therefore, unless I reach the conclusion (as I am invited to by Mr. Salt) that this settlement is really not made in consideration of the marriage at all, I think the conclusion one must reach is that it is made in consideration of the marriage notwithstanding that many of the beneficiaries are strangers to the marriage.

Now, the matters which seem to me to point to the view that this settlement is one which ought properly to be described as having been made in consideration of the marriage are these: first, that in terms it is so expressed; secondly, that it was made as part of a bargain under which Mr. Fordham himself executed a settlement on himself, his wife and his family; thirdly, that the settlement was one which I am satisfied the settlor contemplated would confer substantial benefits on Mr. and Mrs. Fordham; fourthly, that the trusts are trusts of a kind which could not come into force unless the marriage was solemnised. Those considerations all lead me to the conclusion that had this particular marriage not taken place this particular settlement would never have been made and that the settlement was made in pursuance of an arrangement between Mr. Courtauld and his daughter and prospective son-in-law that he would make such a settlement in consideration of their marrying one another.

That view leads me to the conclusion that the consideration is not a colourable consideration and that the settlement is one that is genuinely made in consideration of the marriage notwithstanding the fact that the trusts are such as to enable benefits to be given to large numbers of persons who are strangers to the marriage and that the extent of the benefits that would be taken by those beneficiaries who are not strangers to the marriage could not be quantified in any way at the time when the settlement was executed." . . .

LORD GUEST: . . . The argument for the Revenue necessarily in my view involves that the words " gifts made in consideration of marriage " were to be read as " gifts made on the occasion of marriage to parties within the marriage consideration." I reject the argument by the Attorney-General that these words are a necessary implication from the words of the Statute. The expression " parties within the marriage consideration " was well known in the law before the Finance Act 1910 was passed and if Parliament had intended to limit the exemption to such gifts nothing could have been simpler than to say so. I can find no ambiguity in the words of section 59 (2). They are plain and clear and must in my view be interpreted in the way which ordinary words of the English language are used. . . . A gift made in consideration of marriage is a gift under which the consideration which moved the settlor was marriage. Reinforcement is obtained for this view when the words of section 38 (2) of the Customs and Inland Revenue Act 1881, " any property . . . taken under . . . a disposition purporting to operate as an immediate gift inter vivos " are contrasted with the words in section 59 (2) of the Finance (1909–10) Act 1910 " gifts made in consideration of marriage." This indicates in my view that the motive of the donor or the purpose of the gift is the determining factor. The section contains no restriction on the class of beneficiaries to whom the gift is made. I am, therefore, content to take Sir Andrew Clark's three requisites for a gift to be made in consideration of marriage. First, it must be made on the occasion of the marriage, secondly, it must be conditioned only to take effect on the marriage taking place, and thirdly, it must be made by a person for the purpose of or with a view to encouraging or facilitating the marriage.

. . . If the test is whether the gift was made in consideration of marriage, this is a question of fact which depends for its solution upon the terms of the settlement under consideration in the light of the surrounding circumstances. Both Buckley J. and the Court of Appeal unanimously have found as a fact that the settlement in question was made in consideration of marriage and for my part I have heard nothing in the arguments which persuades me that they were wrong in so holding. . . .

Note
  This case must now be considered in the light of F.A. 1963, s. 53 (1), whereby, for deaths after July 31, 1963, and in regard to any disposition not made before April 4, 1963, a disposition is not to be treated as a gift made in consideration of marriage for the purposes of the exemption, if, in the case of an outright gift, it is made to a person other than a party to the marriage or, in the case of any other disposition, the persons who are or may become entitled to any benefit under the disposition include any person other than the parties to the marriage, issue of the marriage or spouse of any such issue. The 1968 Act imposes further restrictions upon the amount of the gift which qualifies for the exemption. The *Rennell* case remains important, however, in determining whether or not a particular gift has been made " in consideration of marriage " at all, see Re Park (deceased) (No. 2), *infra*.

Re PARK (DECD.) (No. 2)

Court of Appeal [1972] Ch. 385; [1972] 2 W.L.R. 276; 116 S.J. 124; [1972] 1 All E.R. 394

A gift was made by the deceased to his grandson on the occasion of and in consideration of his intended marriage. The grandson subsequently resettled the bulk of the property on trust for the benefit of other descendants of the deceased.

RUSSELL L. J.: . . . There are some matters that are perfectly plain. First : when the gift took effect it did so absolutely in favour of the grandson, and the settled property became his absolute property with no qualifications known to the law. Second : it was a gift contingent upon the marriage of the grandson and Miss Stockwell taking place. Third : it was a gift to take immediate effect upon the celebration of that marriage. Fourth : it was a gift to one of the parties to that marriage and to nobody else.

We ask ourselves how can such a gift be other than a gift made in consideration of marriage when it has those four qualities?

. . . It was argued for the Crown that the *Rennell* case [21] totally jettisoned the conception of persons ordinarily regarded by the law as within the marriage consideration as relevant to this exemption : and that consequently the circum-

[21] [1964] A.C. 173; *ante*, p. 533.

stances in all cases must be fully investigated in order to probe the motive or main purpose of the donor or settlor. We do not accept this. We have listed the four significant facts of this settlement or gift. In our judgment, the fourth of these, granted the others, must speak for itself to define the gift as one made in consideration of marriage. The Crown instanced an employer who selected an employee on the verge of marriage, and who, contingent and effective upon that marriage, settled a substantial sum upon him absolutely, after making it plain to the employee that he was expected after marriage to transfer the money or property to children of the employer. But if in such case there was nothing in law or equity binding the employee to do this, we do not see why this should not be within the terms of the exemption, any more than in the instant case.

We must stress that the property after the marriage was absolutely the property of the grandson. Had he died a week after the marriage, estate duty would have been exigible thereon on his death. It is true that later he settled some £55,000 worth of the funds on descendants of the settlor (other than, for obvious reasons, himself and his wife). But he would only have done this, we have no doubt, after legal advice that in law this would be a voluntary gesture on his part, and that it was against his interest and that of his wife and future children (by the marriage on the occasion of which he received the £80,000) that he should do it. We say all this in order to stress the obvious: that the settlor intended this to be, and it was, in law and equity absolutely the grandson's property, provided that, and when, he married Miss Stockwell; and that is true whatever may have been the hopes of the settlor that, by voluntary action of the grandson, other members of the settlor's family would share in a fund free of estate duty. The settlor no doubt considered, when he made this gift, that the risk was small that his grandson would not act in a gentlemanly fashion: but that is no way to impose a trust. . . .

. . . In short, therefore, in our judgment all reference in the *Rennell* case to the purpose or motive of the donor or settlor is wholly irrelevant to a case where the sole absolute beneficiary is a spouse of the marriage in question. . . .

INDEX

ACCOUNTANCY,
  evidence, 18, 80, 101–103, 154
  principles, 152–155, 170, 191–202, 206–207
ACCOUNTING PERIODS, 154, 191, 202–209
ACCUMULATION SETTLEMENTS, 340, 367, 373–376, 380, 387
ADMINISTRATION,
  expenses of, 455, 458, 503
  income arising during, 346, 367, 372
ADVENTURE IN THE NATURE OF TRADE. See TRADE.
AGGREGATION,
  estate duty, 463, 464, 496
  income of husband and wife, 351–358, 363
AGRICULTURAL PROPERTY,
  estate duty on, 522
  See also FARMING.
ALLOWANCES,
  capital. See CAPITAL ALLOWANCES.
  personal. See RELIEFS.
ANNUAL,
  meaning of, 152, 153, 219, 220
ANNUAL PAYMENTS,
  assessable under Case III, 110–127
  charge on income, as, 111, 121, 123, 341–344, 347
  deduction of tax from, 23, 24, 76, 87, 113, 119–127, 294, 369, 382, 413
  distinguished from instalments of capital, 22, 76, 77, 117–121
  distinguished from receipts of trade, 111–117, 122, 134
  pure income profit, 111–117, 123–125, 385
ANNUITY,
  assessable under Case III, 22, 110, 117, 119
  consideration for disposition, as, 469–471, 524–526
  purchased life, 117, 120, 121
APPEALS,
  from Commissioners, 46–61, 108, 109, 115, 116, 128, 144, 145, 181, 188, 221, 223, 240, 396, 410, 411, 438, 439, 445
ASSESSMENT,
  basis of, 85, 161, 166, 167, 203, 205, 212–214, 339
  direct, 110
  past years, 408, 409
  See also PARTNERSHIPS; PERSONAL REPRESENTATIVES; TRUSTEES.
ASSETS VALUATION, 510, 517–519
AVOIDANCE. See TAX AVOIDANCE.

BACK DUTY,
  recovery of, 13, 14, 408, 409

BALANCING ALLOWANCES AND CHARGES, 6, 215–219
BASIC RATE, 338, 339
BENEFICIARIES,
  income from settlements, 110, 286, 289, 292, 340, 346, 364–379
BENEFITS,
  in kind, 253–267, 379
  reservation of, 390–404, 468, 473, 477–493, 531, 532
BOARD OF INLAND REVENUE,
  practice of, 103, 201, 393, 403, 435
BONA FIDE PURCHASE,
  exemption for, 470–472, 522–528
BUSINESS. See TRADE.

CAPITAL,
  circulating and fixed, 66, 67, 81, 158, 159
  distinguished from income, 65–70, 75–81, 99–103, 117–121, 159–161, 169–180, 214–217, 220–228, 287–290, 306–311, 376–379
  instalments of, 76, 77, 117–121
CAPITAL ALLOWANCES, 6, 7, 214–219
CAPITAL GAINS, 76, 140, 302, 306–311, 367
  inflation, effect of, 314, 320, 321, 330–332, 455
  short term, 140, 309–313, 326, 327
CAPITAL GAINS TAX, 35–39, 98, 140, 142, 190, 215, 428, 432, 500
  economic effects of, 315, 318, 319
  justification for, 311–329
  losses, treatment of, 309–314, 327, 328
CASE STATED. See APPEALS.
CASES OF SCHEDULES, 89, 95
CASH BASIS, 161, 166, 167
CESSATION. See TRADE.
CHARGES ON INCOME, 111, 121, 123, 339, 341–344, 413, 426
CHARITIES,
  gifts to, 114, 123–125, 169, 186, 459, 468, 471, 522
  income of, 20, 114, 123–125
  trading by, 132, 134
CHILD,
  income of, 83, 253, 349–351, 358, 372–376
  relief for, 83, 348–350, 358, 361
  settlement on, 110, 286, 352, 358–360, 380–384, 387
CLOSE COMPANIES, 29, 396–404, 420, 426–431, 517
  distributions of, 426, 427
  shortfall, 426–429
  surtax apportionment, 426, 427
  See also CONTROLLED COMPANIES.

COMMISSIONERS. *See* APPEALS.

COMPANIES,
associated with settlement, 396–404, 426
distinct from shareholders, 413–415, 418–420, 423–425
dividends and distributions, 287, 288, 300, 316, 323, 346, 413, 414, 421, 425–428
incorporation, tax upon, 416, 417, 431
option to be taxed as partnership, 415, 425, 429–431
related, 300, 425, 426, 449
residence of, 446–450
See also CLOSE COMPANIES; CONTROLLED COMPANIES; CORPORATION TAX.

COMPENSATION,
cancellation of contract, 156–159
loss of office, 85, 172, 173, 177, 206, 247
nationalisation, 6, 19, 110
sterilisation of asset, 156–161

CONTROLLED COMPANIES,
benefits from, 479, 480, 499
meaning of " control," 30, 518
valuation of shares, 510, 517–519

COPYRIGHT. *See* ROYALTIES.

CORPORATION TAX, 204, 335, 367, 413, 420–423, 446
reform of, 413, 414, 420–423
theories of corporate taxation, 413–425
two-rate and imputation methods, 421–423, 427, 428

COVENANTS,
" seven year," 7, 23, 29, 76, 82, 114–118, 121–125, 374, 375, 384–390

DEBTS,
bad, 168
creation or extinguishment, 468

DEDUCTION OF TAX, 23, 24, 76, 87, 113, 119–127, 294, 369, 382, 413

DEPRECIATION, 214–216

DIRECTORS,
remuneration of, 172–177, 183, 190, 230, 261–267, 303, 426, 430

DISCLAIMER, 468–470, 530

DISCOUNTS, 85, 110

DISCRETIONARY TRUSTS,
estate duty, 467, 533
income of, 110, 286, 367, 372–375

DISPOSITIONS. *See* GIFTS.

DISTRIBUTIONS. *See* CLOSE COMPANIES; COMPANIES.

DIVIDENDS. *See* CLOSE COMPANIES; COMPANIES.

DIVIDEND-STRIPPING, 47, 93, 129, 135–140

DOMICILE,
estate duty, 455, 458
income tax, 37, 293–297, 432, 433

DONATIONES MORTIS CAUSA, 468

DOUBLE TAXATION RELIEF, 10, 13, 295–305, 423, 432, 434

EEC,
harmonisation of taxes in, 414, 423, 457

EARNED INCOME, 335, 338, 339, 345–348, 351

EARNINGS BASIS, 166, 167

EMOLUMENTS OF EMPLOYMENT, 229–276, 302, 303
benefits in kind, 249, 253–267
deduction of expenses, 94, 261, 262, 267–276
directors, etc., 183, 190, 191, 230, 240, 261–267, 303, 430
expense allowance, 235, 248, 250–253, 261, 262
free accommodation, 3, 248, 254–256, 260–266, 379
gifts, 24, 235, 237–248
share options, 257, 258, 260
source of payment, 234, 235, 244
terminal payments, 85, 172–177, 180, 206, 235, 237, 246–248

EMPLOYMENT,
distinguished from profession, 93–95, 229–234

ENTERTAINMENT EXPENSES, 186, 187

ESTATE DUTY,
accountable persons, 460, 464, 466
aggregation, 463, 464, 496
agricultural property, 522
charging provisions, 453, 464, 498
competence to dispose, 464–467, 473, 509, 528–531
controlled companies, 479, 480, 499, 510, 517–519
exemptions, 455, 464, 522–538
bona fide purchase, 470–472, 522–528
reverter to disponer, 531–533
surviving spouse, 354, 455, 458, 459, 522, 528–531
gifts *inter vivos*, 456, 460, 468–498
charities and public bodies, 468, 522, 533
distinguished from sale or exchange, 468–472, 522–527
effectively constituted, 468–476, 497
exclusion of donor, 468, 473–476, 477–493, 531, 532
marriage, in consideration of, 468, 533–538
normal expenditure, 522, 533
relatives, dispositions to, 468, 470, 524–526
small, 522, 533
subject-matter of, 471, 479, 480, 493–498
survival of donor, 456, 460, 468, 469, 472–426, 497, 533
industrial hereditaments, 522
interests in expectancy, 465, 510, 519–521, 528–530
joint property, 465
life assurance policies, 468, 495, 496
options, property subject to, 498
partnership property, 498, 522, 523
principal value, meaning of, 464, 500
property situated abroad, 455
quick succession relief, 522
reform of, 361, 453, 454–464
residence and domicile, 433, 445, 455, 458
settled property, 453, 458, 467, 528–533
timber, 522
valuation, 456, 458, 464, 493, 495, 500–521
works of art, 522

EVASION. *See* TAX AVOIDANCE.

EXCESS PROFITS DUTY, 31, 131, 143, 146, 154, 159, 178, 205

EXECUTORS. *See* PERSONAL REPRESENTATIVES.

EXPENSES. *See* EMOLUMENTS OF EMPLOYMENT; TRADE.

EXTRA-STATUTORY CONCESSIONS, 103, 169

FACT AND LAW,
the distinction, 46–61, 78, 79, 116, 128, 129, 150, 181, 206, 229, 410, 411, 441

FAMILY,
estate duty treatment of, 459, 461, 462
parent and child, 83, 253, 348–351, 358–366, 380
tax unit, as, 337, 351–366, 461, 462
See also HUSBAND AND WIFE.

FARMING,
income from, 92, 93, 161

FOREIGN INCOME, 76, 83, 95, 277–305, 372, 373
anti-avoidance provisions, 30, 33
double taxation, relief from, 10, 13, 295–305, 423, 432, 434
possessions, from, 76, 277, 278, 283–287, 367
remittance of, 83, 85, 277, 278, 283, 285, 290–295, 433, 446
securities, from, 10, 95, 277, 283–286
trade, profession, from, 128, 230, 277–283, 447
See also DOMICILE; RESIDENCE.

FOREIGN TAX,
payment of, 184, 295–305

FORM AND SUBSTANCE, 9, 21–25, 77, 119, 120, 124, 248–250, 410, 411, 453, 486, 523

FURNISHED LETTINGS, 96, 220

GAMBLING, 65, 76, 130–132, 223

GIFTS,
effective constitution of, 293, 380, 394–396, 468, 469, 472–476, 497
income, as, 65, 76, 110, 122, 228, 237–244, 360, 364, 373, 463
See also EMOLUMENTS OF EMPLOYMENT; ESTATE DUTY.

GOLDEN HANDSHAKES, 85, 180, 237, 246–248

GOODWILL, 175–177, 216, 523

GOVERNMENT SECURITIES, 93, 110, 433, 445

HARMONISATION OF TAX LAWS, 414, 457

HIGHER RATE, 338, 339

HOBBY FARMING, 130, 140, 161

HUSBAND AND WIFE, 349, 350, 387, 391–393, 399, 404, 458, 459
aggregation of income, 351–358, 363
estate duty, 354, 455, 492, 493, 522, 528–531, 533–538
maintenance payments, 126, 350
separate assessment, 352, 354
wife's earnings, 351, 352, 355

ILLEGALITY, 129, 130

IMPUTATION METHOD, 421–423, 427

INCOME,
defined, 65–75
sources of, 65–67, 74, 85, 87, 110, 128, 235, 244, 277, 283, 307, 413
tax base, as, 70–75, 306–311, 360
taxable, 65, 74, 81–84
total, 112, 339–344, 372, 386
transfers of, 28, 29, 121–125, 380

INCOME TAX ACTS. *See* STATUTORY INTERPRETATION.

INDUSTRIAL HEREDITAMENTS, 522

INFANTS. *See* CHILD.

INHERITANCE TAX, 453–457, 459–464

INITIAL ALLOWANCES. *See* CAPITAL ALLOWANCES

INSURANCE,
cost of, 104, 105
mutual, 11, 134, 135
See also LIFE ASSURANCE.

INTEREST,
assessable under Case III, 87, 110
charge on income, as, 413
deduction of tax from, 121, 126, 342–344, 347

INTEREST IN EXPECTANCY, 465, 510, 519–521, 528–530

INVESTMENT,
allowances, 217
incentives, 214, 215, 318, 339, 350
income, 288, 335, 338, 339, 351

JOINT PROPERTY, 465

LAND,
artificial transactions in, 97
dealing in, 57–61, 96, 147–150
income from, 90–93, 96–105, 220, 298
valuation of, 46, 500–510

LEASES,
premiums, 73, 76, 97–99, 169
rents, 23, 96–99

LIFE ASSURANCE POLICIES,
gifts of, 10, 11, 468, 495, 496
premiums, 112, 253, 341
reliefs for, 112, 343, 350, 351

LOANS,
close companies, by, 400, 401, 426
settlor, to, 396–404, 489

LOSSES,
capital, 309–311, 313, 327, 328
disallowance of, 130, 132, 140
relief, 128, 154, 209–214, 425

MACHINERY, 215–218

MAINTENANCE,
payments of, 126, 350
property, expenditure on, 99–104

MANAGEMENT,
expenses of, 90, 103–105, 371

MARKET VALUE,
    disposal at, 136, 161–167
    estate duty, 500–510
    stock-in-trade, 191–199
MARRIAGE,
    gifts in consideration of, 468, 533–538
MARRIED WOMAN. *See* HUSBAND AND WIFE.
MINES AND MINERALS,
    income from, 4, 48, 80–81, 97, 159, 160, 212
MUTUAL TRADE, 11, 12, 134, 135

NATIONALITY, 432, 433, 446
NATIONALISATION,
    compensation for, 6, 19, 110
NON-PROFIT-MAKING ORGANISATIONS, 132–134

OFFICE,
    meaning of, 229–234
OPTIONS,
    estate duty on, 498

PARTNERSHIPS,
    assessment of, 33, 207–209, 211, 234, 335, 367, 404–409
    change of partners, 207, 404–407
    deceased partner, 150, 151, 404, 408, 409
    estate duty, 498, 522, 523
    existence of, 33, 149, 410–412
PATENT RIGHTS,
    sale of, 77–79, 219
PENALTIES, 13, 14
PENSION SCHEMES, 253, 350
PERQUISITES. *See* EMOLUMENTS OF EMPLOYMENT.
PERSONAL ALLOWANCES. *See* RELIEFS.
PERSONAL REPRESENTATIVES,
    accountability of, 335, 344, 408, 409, 460, 466
    trading by, 150, 151, 346
PERSONAL TAXATION,
    reform of, 338, 339
PLANT, 216–218
POST-CESSATION RECEIPTS, 85–87, 167, 219
POWER OF APPOINTMENT, 391, 465, 466
PREMIUMS,
    lease, 73, 76, 97–99, 169
    life assurance, 112, 253, 341
PROFESSION,
    adventure in the nature of, 224–228
    definition, 50, 129, 131
    distinguished from employment, 93–95, 229–234
    income of, 128, 166, 167, 302
PROFITS,
    annual, 152, 219, 220
    computation of, 152–218, 449
    See also LOSSES; TRADE.
PROFITS TAX, 414, 416–419

PROGRESSIVE TAXATION, 72–74, 122, 314, 325, 335–338, 355, 413–415
PURCHASED LIFE ANNUITY, 117, 120, 121
PURE INCOME PROFIT, 111–117, 123–125, 385

QUICK SUCCESSION RELIEF, 522

RELIEFS,
    child, 83, 348–350, 358, 361
    earned income, 335, 338, 339, 345–348, 351
    life assurance, 112, 343, 350, 351
    personal, 335, 338, 339, 344–351, 367, 372, 382, 432
REMITTANCE BASIS, 85, 278, 283, 290–295, 433, 446
RENTS,
    computation, 96–99
    deductions from, 90, 99–105
REPAIRS,
    business expenditure, as, 168, 169, 178–180
    distinguished from renovation, 99–103, 158, 178–180
RESIDENCE,
    companies, 277, 278, 297, 298, 446–450
    estate duty, 433, 445, 458
    individuals, 49–50, 145, 297, 298, 432–446
    ordinary, 432–434, 437, 441–446
    temporary absence abroad, 433–436
    trustees, 35–39, 367, 391
RESTRICTIVE COVENANT,
    payment for, 173–177, 246–248, 426
REVERTER TO DISPONER, 531–533
REVOCATION,
    power of, 7, 380, 386–392, 477
ROYALTIES,
    copyright, 225, 301
    patent, 77–79, 117, 301

SALE AND LEASE BACK, 23
SCHEDULES,
    cases of, 89, 95
    relationship between, 72, 85–97, 111, 219
    Schedule A, 87, 90, 96–105, 210, 277, 379
    Schedule B, 92, 93, 105–109, 277
    Schedule C, 93, 110, 277, 439
    Schedule D,
        Cases I and II, 77, 81, 87, 90–96, 105–109, 114, 122, 128–214, 221, 233, 269–271, 274, 277, 279, 406
        Case III, 85, 87, 110–127, 352
        Cases IV and V, 10, 17, 83, 95, 232, 277–295, 370, 373, 439, 448
        Case VI, 74, 76, 85, 96, 105, 111, 211, 219–228, 314
        Case VII, 311
        Case VIII, 92
    Schedule E, 94, 210, 229–277
    Schedule F, 413
SCOTLAND,
    estate duty on property in, 499
    interpretation of tax Acts in, 54, 55, 214

SECURITIES,
  foreign, 10, 95, 277, 283–286
  transactions in, 40–42, 136–140

SERVICES,
  performance of, 220, 224–229, 302

SETTLEMENTS,
  accumulations, 340, 367, 373–376, 380, 387
  administration, expenses of, 370, 371
  "arrangements," 381–384, 397
  benefits under, 379
  body corporate connected with, 396–404, 426
  capital and income, 376–379
  child of settlor, 349, 351, 358–360, 380–384, 387, 396
  covenants, 7, 23, 29, 76, 82, 114–118, 121–118, 121–125, 374, 375, 384–390
  discretionary, 110, 286, 367, 372–375, 467, 533
  estate duty, 453, 458, 467, 528–533
  foreign, 110, 284, 286, 289, 292, 293, 367, 368, 372, 373, 379
  income of beneficiary, 110, 286, 289, 292, 340, 346, 369–379
  income of settlor, 82, 123, 349, 380–404
  income of trustees, 345, 346
  meaning of, 349, 380–384, 391, 392, 397
  revocable, 7, 219, 380, 386–390, 391, 392
  settlor,
    payments to, 23, 396–404
    reservation of interest by, 390–399

SHARES,
  bonus issues, 68, 287–289, 316
  options, 257, 258, 394
  valuation of, 329–332, 508–519
  See also SECURITIES.

SMALL FIRMS, 428–431, 456

SMALL GIFTS, 522, 533

SMALL MAINTENANCE PAYMENTS, 216

STAMP DUTY, 23

STATUTORY INTERPRETATION,
  principles of, 3–25, 43, 77, 82, 84, 265, 266, 332, 385, 387, 389, 392, 400–403, 453, 486, 492, 518, 523, 536

STOCK-IN-TRADE,
  valuation of, 154, 191–202

SURTAX, 29, 30, 122, 203, 326, 335, 338, 339, 340, 350, 367, 370, 373, 379, 380, 385, 390, 402, 426–429

SURVIVING SPOUSE, 354, 365, 366, 455, 458, 459, 522, 528–531

TAX ADVANTAGE, 40, 41, 135, 402

TAX AVOIDANCE,
  distinguished from evasion, 8, 26, 27, 402, 404
  judicial attitudes towards, 28, 32–34, 136, 404, 534
  judicial participation in, 34–39
  legislation, 29–32, 39–45, 65, 97, 219, 426, 461
  motive, relevance of, 25, 26, 35, 42–45, 136–140, 428, 490, 538

TIMBER,
  estate duty on, 522
  See also WOODLANDS.

TIPS, 242

TOTAL INCOME,
  computation of, 112, 339–344, 372, 386

TRADE,
  adventure in the nature of, 47, 48, 51–61, 129, 141–148, 222
  artificial transactions, 22, 136
  badges of, 54, 133, 140–151
  basis of assessment, 161, 202–205, 212–214
  capital and revenue distinguished, 67, 79–81, 155–161, 169–180, 214–217
  cessation, 86, 151, 203, 204, 207
  commencement, 203–209, 213
  defined, 56, 128–130
  dividend-stripping, 129, 135–140
  entertainment, provision of, 186, 187
  expenditure, deduction of, 48, 67, 79–81, 94, 99–103, 112, 126, 163, 165, 168–191, 269–271, 274
  finding of fact, 51–61, 128, 129, 145, 150, 180, 181, 191, 196
  hobby trading, 130, 140, 161
  illegality, 129, 130
  isolated transactions, 51–61, 76, 130, 140, 145, 146, 153, 219–224, 306
  land, as subject-matter of, 57–61, 147–150
  losses of, 128, 132, 140, 154, 209–214
  mutual, 11–13, 134, 135
  notional receipts of, 136, 161–167
  personal representatives, by, 150, 151, 346
  post-cessation receipts, 85, 87, 219
  profit motive, 132–134, 139, 140, 142, 144
  profits, computation of, 152–218, 449
  receipts of, 154–167, 299
  trustees, by, 346, 370, 371

TRANSFER OF ASSETS ABROAD, 30, 33, 219

TRANSFERS OF INCOME, 28, 29, 121–125, 380

TRAVELLING EXPENSES, 251–253, 267, 268, 272–275

TRUSTEES,
  accountability of, 335, 367–371
  remuneration of, 345, 346, 481, 485
  residence of, 35–39, 367, 391
  trading by, 346, 370, 371
  See also PERSONAL REPRESENTATIVES; SETTLEMENTS.

TRUSTS. See SETTLEMENTS.

UNEARNED INCOME, 288, 335, 338, 339, 351

UNIFIED SYSTEM OF TAXATION, 338, 339

VALUATION,
  benefits in kind, 258–260
  change in method, 199, 201–204
  estate duty, 46, 456, 458, 494, 495, 500–521
  land, 46, 500–508, 510
  shares, 329–332, 508–519
  stock-in-trade, 154, 191–202
  work-in-progress, 199–201

VARIATION OF TRUSTS, 35–39
VOCATION, 128, 129, 131, 132

WASTING ASSETS, 67, 215
WEAR AND TEAR, 214–217
WIFE. *See* HUSBAND AND WIFE.
WOODLANDS,
   occupation of, 91, 105–109
      See also TIMBER.

WORK-IN-PROGRESS,
   valuation of, 199–201
WORKS OF ART, 522

YEAR,
   accounting, 154, 202–209, 212–214
   assessment, of, 85, 202, 203, 205, 212–214,
   339